To my father

CONTENTS

~~~~~~

ABBREVIATIONS

~~~~~~

C.C.	*Constitution; or Cork Advertiser.*
C.E.	*Cork Examiner.*
H.C.	House of commons.
N.L.I.	National Library of Ireland.
n.p.	no place of publication.
P.R.O.	Public Record Office of England.
P.R.O.I.	Public Record Office of Ireland.
S.P.O., C.S.O.	State Paper Office of Ireland (Dublin Castle), Chief Secretary's Office.
W.C.E.	*West Cork Eagle and County Advertiser.*

Note: For other abbreviations used in footnotes, see 'Rules for contributors to *Irish Historical Studies*', second edition, by T. W. Moody, in *Irish Historical Studies*, supplement I (Jan. 1968).

ACKNOWLEDGMENTS

~~~~~~

IT IS BEYOND my ability either to recall all of my obligations or to acknowledge properly those which I do remember. My ardent wish would be to do both. Among the many individuals who generously assisted me in locating manuscripts and other documents in private keeping, I am particularly grateful to Sir John Ainsworth, Mr C. J. F. MacCarthy, Mr Michael Mulcahy, Professor David O'Mahony, the late Eoin O'Mahony, Mr Seamus Ó Coigligh, and Dom Mark Tierney, O.S.B. For countless favours in this respect as well as many others, I gladly record my deep indebtedness to my friend Pádraig Ó Maidín, Cork County Librarian.

For their generosity in allowing me to consult records in private ownership and possession, or to quote from documents in copyright, I wish to thank Charles M. Barry and Son, P. W. Bass and Company, Mr R. P. Beamish, Sir Richard La Touche Colthurst, the late Henry L. Conner and his executors, Mr John F. Conolly, the Secretary of the Cork Archives Council, Viscountess Doneraile, Sir Terence E. P. Falkiner, Mr Thomas H. M. Gollock, Mrs Beatrice Grosvenor, Miss Phyllis Hodder, Mr H. H. D. Holroyd-Smyth, the Director of the Irish Folklore Commission, Commander M. C. M. Jephson, the late Brigadier M. D. Jephson, C.B.E., the Directors of Lismore Estates Ltd, Miss Cynthia Longfield, the Earl of Midleton, the Directors of Midleton Estates Ltd, Mr J. W. Moher, Moore, Keily, and Lloyd, the Director and Trustees of the National Library, Dublin, Mr W. P. Worth Newenham, W. E. O'Brien and Company, The O'Donovan, the Rev. Thomas A. O'Regan, Lord Ormathwaite, Mr Michael Powell, the Deputy Keeper of the Public Record Office, Dublin, Mrs C. E. M. Shelswell-White, the late Benjamin Shorten, and Warrens, Solicitors, of London. Without their co-operation and willingness to suffer inconvenience, this book would not have been written. Extracts from two letters in the Cowdray Archives appear by courtesy of the Right Hon. the Viscount Cowdray, with acknowledgments to the County Archivist of West Sussex. I am also grateful to the Cork University Press for permission to reprint a table from Raymond D. Crotty's *Irish agricultural production: its volume and structure* (1966).

For their expert advice and efficient service, I am heavily indebted to the staffs of the Boston College Library, the British Museum Newspaper Library, the Baker Library of Columbia University, the Cork City Library, the Cork County Library, the Cork Public Museum, the Guildford Museum and Muniment Room, the Kress, Law School, and Widener Libraries of Harvard University, the House of Lords Record Office, the Irish Folklore Commission, the Kinsale Regional Museum, the Customs House Library, London, the National Library of Ireland, the National Registry of Archives, the Public Record Office, Dublin, the Public Record Office, London, the Royal Irish Academy, the State Paper Office, Dublin Castle, the Tipperary County Library, the Library of Trinity College, Dublin, the Fletcher Library of the University of Tennessee at Chattanooga, the Memorial Library of the University of Wisconsin, Madison, and the West Sussex County Record Office.

I have benefited at various stages of my work from conversations or correspondence with Professor Galen Broeker, Professor Thomas N. Brown, Professor K. H. Connell, Dr Kevin Danaher, Professor J. H. Delargy, the late E. R. R. Green, Professor Emmet Larkin, Mr Frank Mawson, Professor Kevin B. Nowlan, Professor John O'Donovan, Dr Liam O'Sullivan, Mr Seán Ó Súilleabháin, Dr Barbara L. Solow, Professor F. M. L. Thompson, the late Maureen Wall, and Dr Thomas Wall.

I am especially grateful to my mentors at Harvard University, the late David Owen and Professors H. J. Hanham and David S. Landes, under whom this work was begun as a doctoral dissertation. By their steady encouragement, painstaking guidance, and well directed criticism, they showed me what could be done and, more importantly, how to do it well.

I have profited greatly from the judicious comments and telling criticisms of Professors L. M. Cullen, Oliver MacDonagh, T. W. Moody, and James A. Ward, who carefully read parts or the whole of this work in typescript. Having saved me from numerous errors of commission and omission, they bear no responsibility for the inaccuracies that remain.

For extraordinary acts of friendship, never to be forgotten, I am deeply grateful to Mr and Mrs James E. Murphy and to Dr and Mrs Timothy O'Neill.

For a generous grant in aid of my research, I wish to thank the

Acknowledgments

American-Irish Foundation of Boston, Massachusetts.

I am also indebted to the editors of *Studia Hibernica* and the *Irish Archives Bulletin* for permission to reprint parts of two articles of mine that appeared in those publications.

My heaviest obligations are to my wife Joan, whose research assistance, secretarial help, and infinite patience have yet to receive their due reward; and to my father, an historian whose inspiration, encouragement, and peerless editing of all my wayward prose have contributed more to this work than I will ever fully appreciate. So large has been the overdraft on my father's skill, energy, and purse that, in hopes of reducing it a little, I wish to dedicate this book to him.

JAMES S. DONNELLY, JR.

The University of Wisconsin, Madison

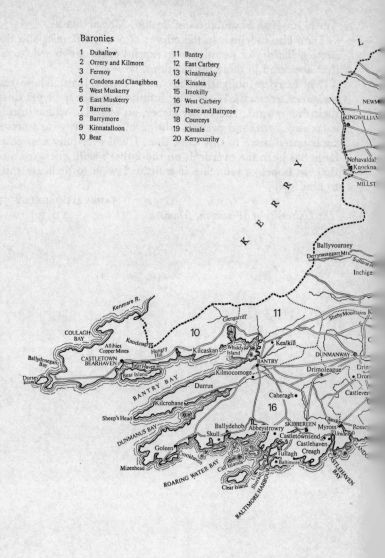

Baronies

1. Duhallow
2. Orrery and Kilmore
3. Fermoy
4. Condons and Clangibbon
5. West Muskerry
6. East Muskerry
7. Barretts
8. Barrymore
9. Kinnatalloon
10. Bear

11. Bantry
12. East Carbery
13. Kinalmeaky
14. Kinalea
15. Imokilly
16. West Carbery
17. Ibane and Barryroe
18. Courceys
19. Kinsale
20. Kerrycurrihy

MAP I Cork

ERICK

•Shandrum   CHARLEVILLE
•Tullylease   •Dromina   :Ballyhay
Liscarroll   •Churchtown

2   DONERAILE   3   Farahy   MITCHELSTOWN
Shanballymore   KILDORRERY   4
KANTURK   Buttevant   Wallstown   Glanworth
Castlemagner   Ballywater
CASTLETOWNROCHE   KILWORTH
MALLOW   Carrigacunna   •Rahan
•Drominagh   Blackwater R.   Funcheon R.

TIPPERARY

WATERFORD

•Rathcool   Nagles Mountains   FERMOY
Boggeragh Mountains   Castlelyons
6   •Mourneabbey   RATHCORMACK   Mogeely
Donaghmore   •Garryadeen   Watergrasshill   Gortroe   9
Whitechurch   Dunbulloge   Clonmult
7   Carrignavar   8   Templenacarriga   Dungourney
Lisgoold   Killeagh   Ardagh
Blarney   NORTH   Ballyedmond   YOUGHAL
Magourney   LIBERTIES   Carrigtohill
CROOM   Inishcarra   Ardrum   Cork   MIDLETON   Clonpriest
Coachford   Carrigrohane   Blackrock   CASTLEMARTYR
BALLINCOLLIG   Douglas   Little I.   CLOYNE   15
Movidy   SOUTH   Passage   Great Island   Ballymacooda
Five Mile   COVE   Aghada   Shanagarry   Ballycottin
13   Bridge   Carrigaline   Rostellan   Whitegate   Ballycottin Bay
BANDON   14   20   Crosshaven   Inch
Ballinadee   INISHANNON   Fountainstown   Trabolgan
19   Nohaval   CORK HARBOUR
Kilbrittain   KINSALE   Kilmonoge
Timoleague   18   Oysterhaven
Old Head
of Kinsale   KINSALE HARBOUR
CLONAKILTY BAY   COURTMACSHERRY BAY

St GEORGE'S CHANNEL

0   5   10   20
IRISH MILES
0   5   10   20
ENGLISH MILES

xiii

1 Bandon
2 Bantry
3 Cork
4 Dunmanway
5 Fermoy
6 Kanturk
7 Kinsale
8 Macroom
9 Mallow
10 Midleton
11 Skibbereen

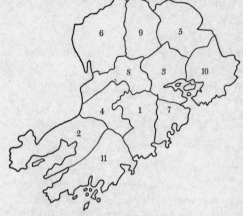

(a) Cork poor-law unions, pre-1850

1 Bandon
2 Bantry
3 Castletown
4 Clonakilty
5 Cork
6 Dunmanway
7 Fermoy
8 Kanturk
9 Kinsale
10 Macroom
11 Mallow
12 Midleton
13 Milford
14 Millstreet
15 Mitchelstown
16 Skibbereen
17 Skull
18 Youghal

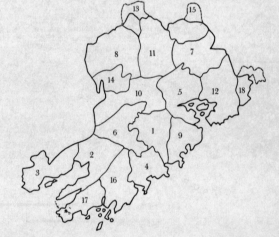

(b) Cork poor-law unions, post-1850

MAP 2

Source: *First report of the commissioners appointed to inquire into the number and boundaries of the poor law unions and electoral divisions in Ireland, with appendix and plans* [1015], H.C. 1849, xxiii, 369.

INTRODUCTION

~~~~~~

NINETEENTH-CENTURY IRISH history has largely been the preserve of students of politics and government, and, more narrowly, of those fascinated by the leading political personalities and their movements or parties. This trend in modern Irish historical scholarship has produced several biographical works of outstanding merit on prominent political figures and equally stimulating analytical studies of nearly all the great political movements—catholic emancipation, repeal, Young Ireland, the Tenant League, Fenianism, and home rule. Rarely, however, as Nicholas Mansergh points out, has the question been asked, what was the relation of these personalities and movements to the social and economic conditions of their times?

Is it not deserving of consideration whether Parnell—to take the classic example—was in part at least the product of a particular environment and, if so, why? Could he have emerged as a leader twenty or thirty years earlier, in the fifties or the sixties? . . . Had the tenant farmers accumulated enough capital, and in consequence did they possess the necessary minimal independence, in those earlier years, to make the politico-social struggle of the eighties under Parnell's and Davitt's leadership possible? Did Parnell attain his position because of or in spite of emigration? Could he have maintained the struggle without American funds? Would those funds have been forthcoming twenty years earlier, before the Irish emigrants were established in the United States? Even the asking of such questions suggests the lacunae in historical knowledge which overmuch dependence on political narrative may leave.[1]

The 'vast expanses of virtually unworked territory' in the field of Irish economic history have now been widely recognized, as has the need for local studies, although the ground that must be recovered is indeed great.[2]

[1] Mansergh, *Ir. question*, p. 291.
[2] T. W. Moody, 'A new history of Ireland' in *I.H.S.*, xvi, no. 63 (Mar. 1969), pp. 244–5.

This study seeks to cover a portion of that ground by focusing on two central and interrelated themes of nineteenth-century Irish history—the rural economy and the land question—from the perspective of the country's southernmost county, Cork. The choice of Cork was determined by several considerations. As the largest and most populous of the thirty-two counties, covering some 1,850,000 acres, or almost 10 per cent of the country's total area, and containing 850,000 inhabitants in 1841, or slightly more than 10 per cent of its population, Cork accounted for substantial fractions of both the land and the people of nineteenth-century Ireland.[3] Moreover, neither the quality of the land nor the manner of life of the people was uniform throughout the county. Just as the east and west of Ireland manifested substantial differences with respect to population density, soil fertility, and patterns of landholding and land use, so too did East and West Cork.[4] The county has therefore some claim to be regarded as a microcosm of the entire country. To have chosen one of the naturally impoverished counties of Connaught or one of the Leinster counties richly endowed by nature would have entailed the loss of this microcosmic quality.

Although this work is concerned almost exclusively with rural life and takes cognizance of urban developments only in a few cases where they impinged directly on the rural economy, the presence of an urban metropolis further enhanced County Cork's attractiveness as an area of investigation. With nearly 81,000 inhabitants in 1841, Cork city on the River Lee was not only Ireland's second largest town but also the great agricultural mart for the six counties of Munster province. Drawing on the large produce of a wide hinterland, its grain warehouses and livestock yards, its provision stores and bacon-curing factories, its distilleries and breweries, and above all its world-famous butter market made Cork city the third largest Irish port in trade volume after Dublin and Belfast.[5] The city's two outstanding newspapers, the catholic and nationalist *Cork Examiner*, and the protestant and conservative *Cork Constitution*, provided a wealth of information relating to the economic and social circumstances of their rural constituency.

If there are sound reasons for selecting County Cork as the area of inquiry, the choice of the rural economy and the land question as the central themes was virtually predetermined by socio-economic realities. 'The catholic of Ireland', wrote the French

[3] *Census Ire., 1841* [504], H.C. 1843, xxiv, 1, pp. 169, 190.
[4] T. W. Freeman, *Pre-famine Ireland: a study in historical geography* (Manchester, 1957), pp. 203, 226, 229, 236.
[5] Ibid., pp. 203, 225, 227.

traveller Gustave de Beaumont in 1839, 'finds only one profession within his reach, the culture of the soil; and when he has not the capital necessary to become a farmer, he digs the ground as a day labourer. . . . He who has not a spot of ground to cultivate, dies of famine.' [6] And Karl Marx observed in 1870 that 'the *land question* has hitherto been the *exclusive* form of the social question in Ireland, because it is a question of existence, *of life and death*, for the immense majority of the Irish people'. [7] Outside the northeast, there was very little factory industry, although much domestic spinning and weaving of wool and linen. The classification of the Irish population by occupations in 1841 showed that 66 per cent of all families depended upon farming for their livelihood. [8] In County Cork in the same year, slightly more than 70 per cent of all families—almost 98,000 out of a total of 133,000 families—were employed in agriculture. [9]

Despite their supreme importance, the rural economy and the land question have claimed relatively little scholarly attention. The half-century leading up to the great famine is much better known and understood in this respect than the second half of the century, thanks largely to the work of Kenneth H. Connell and a few other researchers. Both in his pioneering study, *The population of Ireland, 1750–1845* (Oxford, 1950), and in subsequent articles, Connell has deftly explored the concatenation of factors—the expansion of tillage, the fragmentation of holdings, the spread of the potato, and the earliness of marriage—which he believes were responsible for the great population explosion that led ultimately to the famine catastrophe. In so doing, he has corrected several errors of interpretation in the old but still useful survey by George O'Brien, *The economic history of Ireland from the union to the famine* (London, 1921). Connell's views on the importance of early marriages and the spread of a potato diet as well as on the unimportance of inoculation against smallpox have been challenged, however, and these questions still remain open to debate. Irish economic underdevelopment attracted wide attention among contemporary British and foreign economists. Their perceptions of the outstanding problems have been analysed comprehensively in R. D. Collison Black's *Economic thought and the Irish question, 1817–1870* (Cambridge, 1960), which

[6] G. de Beaumont, *Ireland: social, political, and religious*, ed. W. C. Taylor (London, 1839), i, 262.
[7] K. Marx to S. Meyer and A. Vogt, 9 Apr. 1870, quoted in Mansergh, *Ir. question*, p. 100.
[8] Freeman, *Pre-famine Ireland*, p. 75.
[9] *Census Ire., 1841*, p. 191. Cork city is not included in these figures.

shows the influence of these theoreticians over the Irish policies of British governments as well as the counterinfluence of Irish realities upon the theoreticians.

Certain subjects discussed in the present study of County Cork have received excellent treatment from a national perspective. The second chapter has been greatly influenced in organization and argumentation by Mrs Cecil Woodham-Smith's *The great hunger: Ireland, 1845–1849* (New York, 1962) and even more by the scholarly contributions to *The great famine: studies in Irish history, 1845–52*, edited by R. Dudley Edwards and T. Desmond Williams (Dublin, 1956). The discussion of agriculture throughout this work is heavily indebted, despite disagreement at a number of points, to John O'Donovan's *The economic history of live stock in Ireland* (Cork, 1940) as well as to Raymond D. Crotty's more recent *Irish agricultural production: its volume and structure* (Cork, 1966). While Crotty's work is too theoretical in approach and weak and confusing on the eighteenth- and early nineteenth-century background, his illuminating observations on rents, land tenure, and agricultural investment, as well as his painstaking compilation of the first price series for the principal farm products before 1840, have proved extremely helpful. Equally instructive is Crotty's account of post-famine structural changes in agriculture, although in treating the years from 1850 to 1900 as a single unit, he blurs the important distinction that should be made between agricultural conditions before and after 1876. The exploration of this vital distinction is one of the outstanding merits of Barbara L. Solow's *The land question and the Irish economy, 1870–1903* (Cambridge, Mass., 1971). Mrs Solow has clearly demonstrated the substantial improvements made in Irish agriculture between the famine and the late 1870s. Moreover, she has argued quite convincingly that the land-tenure system during those years was not a significant obstacle to agricultural progress. Her study is a much needed corrective to the misleading treatment of the economic background of the land war found in nearly all previous works concerned with that great socio-political upheaval.

Hopefully, the present work will also help to clarify the fundamental changes which took place in both the rural economy and the land question during the nineteenth century. This study begins by showing why rural society became engulfed after 1815 in a crisis of appalling dimensions. Special emphasis is given at the very outset to the middleman system of estate management because of its crucial role in fostering fragmentation of holdings and population growth that in the case of the agricultural labourers and cottiers outstripped

4

the land's capacity to produce anything more than a bare subsistence diet of potatoes. Also explored is the extent to which this system, along with the severe deflation that followed the close of the Napoleonic wars, reduced the incomes of landowners and retarded the proper development of their estates. Agriculture, burdened with the serious difficulties imposed by population pressure, fragmented holdings, depressed prices, and dwindling overseas markets, is nevertheless shown to have responded strongly to these challenges through greatly expanded output in the tillage sector and through significant advances in farming techniques. Whether producers responded quickly enough to changing prices and market conditions that favoured a greater emphasis on livestock for export to Britain from the 1830s cannot yet be resolved conclusively, but this question is important and receives consideration. One possible solution to many of these pressing difficulties lay in a thorough revamping of estate administration. The fall in landowners' revenues after 1815 provided the incentive for this, and the decay of the middleman system in the 1830s and early 1840s furnished the opportunity. The widespread movement for the reform of estate administration before 1845 is examined, along with the considerable obstacles to change imposed by popular resistance, unexpired old leases, the deep indebtedness of many landowners, and the heavy weight of past neglect.

The great famine, with its horrifying toll of starvation, disease, death, and emigration, provided its own drastic answers to the problems of Irish agrarian society and left enduring marks on the rural economy and the land question. Chapter II shows that commercial farming in County Cork, oriented towards dairying and dry cattle, was strengthened by this human disaster, while subsistence agriculture was largely destroyed. Because of the inadequacy of relief measures and the inefficacy of food riots and food stealing, labourers and cottiers perished by the thousand. How landowners met or failed to meet the enormous difficulties of collecting rent and paying increased charges for poor rates and employment is discussed in some detail. Also examined are the ways in which they seized what seemed to them a great opportunity to pursue the reform of estate administration by ousting bankrupt middlemen, clearing their estates of paupers, weeding out broken tenants, and enlarging the holdings of those who remained. The geographical and social incidence of mortality and emigration is closely analysed in order to determine how drastically the famine altered the class structure and distribution of the population.

In their optimistic analysis of the rural economy and the land question in the years between the great famine and the agricultural crisis of the late 1870s, Chapters III and IV confirm and extend recent challenges to the long accepted pessimistic interpretation. The third chapter shows that with the exception of the early 1860s, these years witnessed almost unparalleled prosperity for Cork farmers. Rising population and the benefits of the industrial revolution pushed the British demand for imported food steadily upward. With the shortage or absence of foreign supplies of meat and butter, the prices of Irish agricultural exports to Britain soared. The fourth chapter seeks to demonstrate that while estate management in Cork was deficient in some respects, most notably in the character of land agency, rack rents were far from being characteristic between 1850 and 1880. Indeed, increases in rent lagged far behind the price rise, as most Cork landowners displayed surprising moderation in their financial demands. Another objective of Chapter IV is to show that in so far as insecurity of tenure was an economic problem in Cork, it was largely the product of extraordinary pre-famine circumstances, that it had abated substantially by 1870, and that it was further modified by the land legislation of that year. By 1880, in fact, a solid majority of Cork tenants were leaseholders. And Cork landlords generally recognized the tenant's possessory interest in his holding, at least *de facto*, although, as is explained, they usually imposed restrictions upon the sale of that interest to an incoming tenant. The sale of goodwill and tenure arrangements in Cork were both affected by Gladstone's land act of 1870. While generally accepting Mrs Solow's new interpretation of the results of this legislation, the present study argues that Gladstone's ill-conceived measure helped to generate grievances that did not exist before.

The conventional view of the land war as the product of an intolerable, rapacious land system which finally cracked under the weight of a severe agricultural crisis in the late 1870s is rejected in this study of County Cork. Chapter V lays the basis for an alternative interpretation which largely attributes the land war to a 'revolution of rising expectations', or, in other words, to the conviction of tenant farmers that their impressive material gains in the preceding quarter-century could and must be preserved by a determined stand against the customary rents. The postponement of marriage, emigration, and agricultural prosperity are shown drastically to have changed the quality and style of rural life for the better. In order to demonstrate this far-reaching improvement in living standards, attention is focused upon capital accumulation in the form of bank savings and livestock as well as upon such important criteria as housing, diet, and education. The struggle of the agricultural labourers, whose progress

6

lagged behind that of tenant farmers, to achieve a fairer share of this increased prosperity is given special consideration.

The final two chapters of this work provide an extensive treatment of the land war in County Cork. Throughout, an attempt is made to take full advantage of the work of political historians by interweaving the political narrative with the story of a great national social movement which hastened the passing of the landlord from the Irish landscape. The immediate economic background is reconstructed at length and with extreme care because of its complex role in shaping the course and determining the tempo of events. On the whole, the character of economic causation presented in these chapters is quite different from that suggested by political historians. While the agricultural crisis of 1877–9 is given due prominence, the accepted view of the agrarian struggle as a revolt of semi-starved peasants is rejected. The improvement in economic conditions that began in mid-1880 is shown to have created a favourable atmosphere for a great assault against landlordism in which the techniques of agitation ranged from rent strikes and boycotting to violent 'moonlighting' and agrarian outrage, sometimes verging upon anarchy. While the 1881 land act, the suppression of the Land League, and the 'Kilmainham treaty' are shown to have helped to cause the simmering of agrarian strife from 1882, unaccustomed emphasis is also placed upon economic factors leading to this result. The local administration of the land legislation is examined to demonstrate its limited impact on rents and estate revenues in County Cork. But the influence of the first phase of the agitation in destroying the former credit standing of landlords and in depressing the market value of their estates is underscored.

The second phase of the land war (1884–92), like the first, is shown to have been rooted in economic difficulties, but the precise problems were different in kind or degree from those experienced earlier. Attention is called to major droughts in 1884 and 1887 as well as to the causes of the sharp downturn in agricultural prices, which previous writers on this period have often either overlooked completely or explained inaccurately. Chapter VII also assesses the influence of the extra-legal National League courts and of greatly extended boycotting in restraining the violence that had marked the land war's initial phase. In concept as well as in practice, the National League's 'Plan of Campaign' is shown to have been patterned upon earlier rent strikes, although these were notably less successful than the nationally organized resistance that began in October 1886. The operation of the Plan of Campaign in County Cork, and the countermeasures taken by the conservative government and by the landlords' Cork Defence Union are analysed at length. In particular, the fascinating story of the protracted, bitter struggle on the Ponsonby estate is recounted in detail, as this property was the premier showcase in Ireland for Arthur Balfour's efforts to destroy the Plan through landlord victories on 'test estates'. In the winding down of the land war, an assessment is made of the local effects of the government's stern law enforcement and remedial land legislation, but equally strong emphasis is placed upon economic fluctuations. The notorious O'Shea divorce case of November 1890, with its disastrous political repercussions on Irish politics, is viewed as delivering the *coup de grâce* to a languishing agitation and preventing its revival. In the conclusion, an attempt is made to summarize the significance of the land war in the complex history of the nineteenth-century Irish land question.

In doing the research for this study, I have made extensive use of census data and agricultural returns, which are the most important of a whole series of statistical collections made by the highly efficient English administrative bureaucracy in Ireland. Much invaluable information has also been gathered from parliamentary inquiries, reports, and returns, beginning with the famous poor-law inquiry of 1835–6 and the Devon commission's voluminous investigation of the land question from 1843 to 1845. By far the most important sources for this study, however, were local newspapers and estate records—letter books, valuations, rentals, leases, etc. Unfortunately, as a result of human carelessness and Ireland's turbulent history, only a relatively small quantity of estate records has survived, especially for the pre-famine period. Moreover, the surviving material is often very fragmentary for individual estates. Nevertheless, after exhaustive searches in public and private archives in England and Ireland as well as in attics, cellars, stables, and barns throughout County Cork, enough has been discovered to furnish a solid basis upon which to reconstruct the framework of estate administration and to measure its impact on the rural economy and the land question. These records often suggest a course of events and causation that conflict with contemporary polemical assertions and with the views later adopted by historians of the period.

I

THE RURAL ECONOMY, 1815–45

~~~~~~

ESTATE ADMINISTRATION, LAND TENURE, AND LABOUR

THE CENTRAL PURPOSE of this chapter is to explore certain aspects
of the economy of County Cork between 1815 and 1845, beginning
with the system of estate administration and land tenure. An understanding of this system and the alterations it underwent is essential
for an accurate assessment of the various other forces determining
economic and social change in this period. Pre-famine Cork may
have had only about 1,000 landed proprietors, or head landlords. [1]
But because of the prevalence of the middleman system, there were
several times as many intermediate landlords as there were head
landlords. During the eighteenth century, the most common method
of managing large estates in Ireland was to split them into considerable tracts of from 100 to 1,000 acres or more, and then to give them
to middlemen on long leases. The 'lower and middling sort' of
protestant gentlemen made an easy but not untroubled living by
taking, redividing, and subletting such land, usually to the tenants
who actually occupied it, but sometimes to other intermediate

---

[1] The category of landed proprietor was unfortunately omitted from the
classification of occupations given in the 1841 census, and the break-up and
sale of many large estates under the incumbered estates act of 1849 greatly
increased the number of landowners during the next twenty-five years.
According to an official return of 1876, there were 1,763 owners of 100 acres
or more in County Cork; the total number of persons owning property of
one acre or more outside the towns of the county was 2,381 (*Copy of a return
of the names of proprietors and the area and valuation of all properties in the several
counties in Ireland, held in fee or perpetuity, or on long leases at chief rents* . . . ,
H.C. 1876 (412), lxxx, 395, p. 73).

landlords. Middlemen held by leases for various terms. Some leases were for a term of ninety-nine years or for even longer terms of years amounting to a perpetuity, but ordinarily they were for either two or three lives of young persons named in the lease, sometimes with a concurrent term of thirty-one or sixty-one years, and at other times with a reversionary term of twenty-one or thirty-one years that became operative after all the lives had 'dropped', or died.[2] Until 1778 catholics were prohibited from taking leases either for any term of years exceeding thirty-one or for lives, under a penal law of 1704. Saville's relief act of 1778, however, allowed them to take leases for any fixed term of years not exceeding 999 or for any number of lives up to five.[3] After the passage of this measure, many wealthy catholic farmers and merchants exercised their restored rights by becoming middlemen in increasing numbers for about a generation.[4]

The reason most frequently advanced by contemporaries for this curious system of estate management was that the occupying tenants generally lacked the means of making the needed but expensive permanent improvements. The likelihood was much greater, it was alleged, that middlemen of substance would carry them out. In a country largely without resident, improving landowners, the next best thing was resident, improving intermediate landlords. As the argument was crudely put to Arthur Young during his tour of Ireland in the late 1770s, the middleman would 'at least improve a spot around his own residence, whereas the mere cottar can do nothing'.[5] Young, who could find nothing good to say about the system, objected that middlemen very frequently were neither resident nor the progressive promoters of improvement that their defenders claimed. London, Bath, Dublin, and the country towns of Ireland, said Young, were full of non-resident middlemen. Indeed, he found that 'these men very generally were the masters of packs of wretched hounds, with which they wasted their time and money, and

---

[2] J. Barry, 'The duke of Devonshire's Irish estates, 1794–1797: Reports by Henry Bowman, agent, with a brief description of the Lismore Castle MSS in the National Library' in *Anal. Hib.*, no. 22 (1960), pp. 275–6.

[3] Formerly, catholics had been debarred not only from purchasing land but even from inheriting it by primogeniture. The relief act, however, permitted them to inherit and bequeath land on the same terms as protestants (17 & 18 Geo. 3, c. 49; Beckett, *Mod. Ire.* (New York, 1966), p. 214).

[4] Even before 1778, while they were still restricted to short leases for terms not exceeding thirty-one years, catholics seem to have often become middlemen. For examples of this, see *Kenmare MSS*, pp. 184–5, 211–15 229–30, 254–62.

[5] A. Young, *Arthur Young's tour in Ireland (1776–1779)*, ed. A. W. Hutton (London and New York, 1892), ii, 25.

it is a notorious fact that they are the hardest drinkers in Ireland'. [6] Characteristics that appeared damning to Young, however, were not necessarily deprecated by late eighteenth-century Irish landowners, who valued middlemen for relieving them of the always troublesome collection of rent from a horde of seemingly rude and often poverty-stricken tenants.

The middleman system underwent an important change beginning in the 1790s. The simple picture of intermediate landlords who were either protestant gentry or wealthy catholic farmers and merchants became much more complex. In 1793 the parliamentary franchise was widened to include in the county electorate catholic leaseholders for lives as well as catholic forty-shilling freeholders. [7] The extension of the vote to catholic leaseholders for lives had considerable economic significance. Not all landowners, of course, had delegated the management of their estates to middlemen; some preferred to deal directly with the ordinary occupying tenants. These landowners, generally desiring local political influence, were encouraged by the legislation of 1793 to grant leases to their tenants under which the latter could qualify for the vote. This was in fact done to such an extent that most occupying tenants in County Cork who held their farms directly from the proprietor rather than from some middleman seem by the early 1800s to have been leaseholders, not yearly tenants. [8] Invariably, at least one franchise-qualifying life was inserted in the stated term of the lease. Despite the fact that by the early 1800s the general trend in cases of new lettings was towards short leases either for one life or for a term of twenty-one or thirty-one years, whichever lasted longer, [9] the Rev. Horatio Townsend observed that in the baronies of East and West Carbery 'the usual leases are for three lives, those of thirty-one years being discontinued since the extension of the elective franchise'. [10] The possession of a lease gave many occupying tenants the opportunity to join the ranks of the middlemen.

Head landlords expected that middlemen who leased large tracts

[6] Ibid., ii, 26.
[7] Beckett, *Mod. Ire.*, p. 250.
[8] In his discussion of the forms of tenure in different parts of Cork, Townsend mentions yearly tenants or tenants at will only once: some landholders in the baronies of Barrymore and Kinnatalloon depended upon 'the will of the landlord' (H. Townsend, *Statistical survey of the county of Cork, with observations on the means of improvement; drawn up for the consideration and by the direction of the Dublin Society* (Dublin, 1810), p. 584; hereafter cited as Townsend).
[9] Ibid., pp. 253, 468, 617.
[10] Ibid., p. 321.

of land from them would subsequently relet this land to the occupying tenantry, and therefore rarely inserted a covenant against subletting in their leases. [11] Nor did those proprietors who increasingly let their estates directly to the occupiers on long or short leases often insist upon such a covenant before 1815. Consequently, no legal obstacle existed to prevent these occupiers from becoming small middlemen in their own right by yielding either to the pressure of the population explosion on land resources during the Napoleonic wars, or to the need which they felt to augment their incomes during the long period of deflation following the wartime boom. Both the non-resident middleman of gentle birth and the occupying farmer with a lease tended to practise subletting because in the short run at least they succeeded in augmenting their incomes. The landowner who recognized that in the long run much of the security for the payment of the head rent was being seriously jeopardized by this injurious practice was very often powerless to correct the situation.

Probably a clear majority of Cork landowners found themselves at the mercy of long leaseholders up to the 1820s and 1830s, to a greater or lesser extent. As much as 65 per cent of the earl of Bandon's rent roll of £23,000 in 1821 was drawn from lessees for two, three, or four lives, 22 per cent from those with still longer terms, and only 13 per cent from those with shorter terms or from yearly tenants. [12] A similar pattern was evident on Viscount Midleton's estates. No less than 83 per cent of Midleton's rental of £15,000 in 1828 was paid by lessees for three lives, 9 per cent by those with equivalent or yet longer terms, and a mere 8 per cent by those with shorter leases or yearly tenures. [13] The earl of Kenmare's agent Christopher Gallwey informed the Devon commission that up to 1835 'all his lordship's estates in the barony of Bantry were held by middlemen at a very low rent, and yielding to them a very large beneficial interest'. [14] The earl of Egmont's agent Edward Tierney remarked in June 1835 that 'almost the entire of the estate is underlet, a great part on old leases for lives that soon may be expected to fall in'. [15] Lord Audley's whole estate had been let to a single

[11] Guildford Muniment Room, Surrey, Midleton papers: T. Foley to H. Marshall (extract and copy), 30 July 1842.

[12] Doherty papers, Cork Archives Council: Rent roll of the earl of Bandon's estates, Nov. 1821.

[13] Guildford Muniment Room, Midleton papers: Rent roll of Viscount Midleton's estates, 1828, with schedule of tenancies. The above percentages exclude most of the income from town property.

[14] *Devon comm. evidence*, pt iii [657], H.C. 1845, xxi, 1, p. 735.

[15] Barry papers, Printed copy of documents of respondents presented to the English court of chancery, *Egmont v. Darell* (1861): E. Tierney to

middleman on a ninety-nine-year lease in 1755, and the lease was not scheduled to expire until 1854.[16]

Careless, inefficient estate administration in general and the middleman system in particular furnished a hospitable framework within which the forces of the population explosion and the expansion of tillage farming brought about a striking and extremely dangerous increase in small holdings. Existing holdings were divided to provide the tenant's children with settlements when they married, or were sublet to augment the intermediate landlord's income from the rents of poor cottiers. New holdings were created through the reclamation and colonization of waste land. Viscount Midleton's estates, where the middleman system was entrenched until the 1830s, provide an extreme example of the encouragement which that system gave to subdivision and subletting. As the valuer Charles Bailey critically observed in his report of April 1840,

many of the townlands are incumbered by an over population created by the improvident subdivisions and sublettings, and in several cases the pernicious system has been carried to such an extent as to create mouths sufficient to swallow up the whole of the produce, leaving nothing for rent.[17]

The holdings of middlemen swarmed with poor cottiers and cabin dwellers. The Rev. William Greene, himself a subtenant of thirty-seven acres, had 'allowed 45 cottages and cabins to be erected on the side of Ballynacurragh road, for which he receives the annual rent of £147 13s. 6d.'.[18] Joseph Haynes, who paid an annual rent of £73 for forty-six acres, had permitted sixty-four persons 'to build cabins on this holding and to occupy them, paying from 20s. to 25s. each as ground rent'.[19] On the sixty-six-acre farm of the Leahys, no less than ninety-eight cabins had been thrown up on the sides of a road. 'It is difficult to suggest what should be done with these cabins', Bailey commented; 'they are a nuisance to the property and a nursery for increasing the population.'[20] The thirty acres held by James Baggs under an old lease at a rent of less than £9 per

[16] W. N. Hancock, *On the causes of distress at Skull and Skibbereen during the famine in Ireland: a paper read before the statistical section of the British Association, at Edinburgh, August 2nd, 1850* (Dublin, 1850), p. 5.

[17] P.R.O.I., ref. no. 978, Midleton papers: Charles Bailey's summary report on the valuation of the Midleton estates, 6 Apr. 1840.

[18] Ibid.: Valuation of Viscount Midleton's estates, 1840, p. 16.

[19] Ibid., p. 52.

[20] Ibid., pp. 56–7.

W. Woodgate, 29 June 1835, pp. 204–6; hereafter cited as *Egmont v. Darell, documents of respondents* (in the possession of Charles M. Barry and Son, Solicitors, Cashel, Co. Tipperary).

annum had been entirely sublet at £4 an acre, and on a portion of the holding thirty-seven cabins had been built. [21] John Scanlan, who paid an annual rent of £85 for forty-six acres, had underlet almost all of it to five other tenants for £146, and also collected £30 from ten cabin holders. [22] Much larger farms had also been minutely subdivided. A number of joint tenants of the lands known as Ballyannan had sublet to many others, 'making together 63 occupiers on 292½ acres'. [23] A tenant named Wigmore had divided a large tract of 400 acres between his two sons, Thomas and William; Thomas Wigmore's portion had been further divided among eight tenants and his brother William's among seven. The Wigmores paid a combined rent of only £69 under an old lease for three lives, but collected £321 from the fifteen undertenants. [24]

The encouragement which the system of long leases gave to the population explosion was painfully evident on other estates. A 750-acre tract on the Rathcool property of Sir George Colthurst, which had originally been let to a middleman on a lease for three lives sometime before 1770 and then sublet to two other tenants, came out of lease in late 1845. Colthurst's agent, Peter Fitzgerald, found that 'instead of two tenants and their families, with the proportionate number of labourers, there were on these lands over 300 inhabitants'. [25] Fitzgerald, who owned practically all of Valentia Island off the southwestern coast of Kerry, also suffered from the mistaken predilection of one of his ancestors for the middleman system. He explained the circumstances to Lord Cloncurry in December 1847:

My estate was let in 1795 . . . on thirteen leases of 3 lives, to 13 substantial middlemen—those tenures average four to five hundred acres each. The [middlemen] tenants, after building houses and performing nominally a few other covenants, violated their engagements of improvement and became nearly altogether absentees, sub-dividing and sub-letting their lands, the fruit of which has been the augmentation [of the population] from something like 400 to above 3,000 persons. Of the leases originally granted, but three have fallen in after a lapse of 52 years. [26]

Table 1—based on the 1841 census—shows that almost 65 per cent of all Cork holdings of one acre or more did not exceed fifteen acres. [27]

[21] Ibid., p. 74.
[22] Ibid., p. 75.
[23] Ibid., pp. 33–4.
[24] Ibid., pp. 282–3.
[25] *C.C.*, 30 Apr. 1846.
[26] P. Fitzgerald to Lord Cloncurry, 8 Dec. 1847, quoted in *C.E.*, 22 Dec. 1847.
[27] *Census Ire., 1841*, pp. 454–7.

TABLE I Number and percentage of holdings of over one acre according to farm size, 1841

size of holdings (acres)	Cork (no.)	(%)	Ireland (no.)	(%)
1–5	13,683	30·0	310,436	44·9
5–15	15,790	34·7	252,799	36·6
15–30	10,362	22·8	79,342	11·5
over 30	5,691	12·5	48,625	7·0
total no. of holdings	45,526		691,202	

Contemporaries noted, however, that there was a very wide discrepancy between the size of holdings indicated in the census and that shown by a similar return made by the poor-law commissioners to the Devon commission a few years later. Many regarded the poor-law return as being nearer to the truth, because it was calculated as a basis for taxation and was subject to periodic revision.[28] As Table 2 illustrates, the poor-law return gave a version of farm size radically different from that of the census, even though the categories were altered slightly.[29]

TABLE 2 Number and percentage of persons with holdings of over one acre according to farm size, 1844

size of holdings (acres)	Cork (no.)	(%)	Ireland (no.)	(%)
1–5	7,468	14·5	181,950	22·7
5–10	7,659	14·9	187,909	23·5
10–20	11,075	21·5	187,582	23·5
20–50	14,842	28·9	141,819	17·7
over 50	9,021	17·6	70,441	8·8
unclassified joint tenancies	1,340	2·6	30,433	3·8
total no. of persons	51,405		800,134	

The discrepancy between the poor-law return and the census is greatest with respect to holdings of from one to five acres. Both in County Cork and in Ireland as a whole, the poor-law return revealed only about half as large a percentage of holdings in this category as the census had indicated. Recently, P. M. Austin Bourke

[28] *Devon comm. digest*, i, 393–6.
[29] *Devon comm. evidence*, pt iv [672], H.C. 1845, xxii, 1, pp. 280–3.

has argued that in the census, farm size was predominantly expressed in terms of the larger Irish acre (1·62 statute acres) and that waste land was ignored in computing the size of each holding, thus creating the greatly exaggerated and traditionally accepted picture of the smallness of holdings before the famine.[30] On the basis of Bourke's thorough analysis of the available evidence, it may safely be concluded that the census figures do indeed grossly overstate the fragmentation of holdings and that the poor-law return gives a close approximation to the facts of farm size in the early 1840s. From both returns it is clear that the dangerous subdivision of holdings did not proceed so far in County Cork as it did in Ireland generally or in the counties along the western seaboard in particular. This divergence is partly attributable to the dominant role of dairying, which tended to obstruct the progress of subdivision, within the agricultural economy of Cork. A slower rate of population growth in Cork than in the country as a whole may also have been an important contributing factor. Even so, some Cork estates, such as Viscount Midleton's, suffered as much from the evil of subdivision as the most badly fragmented properties of Galway and Mayo, and relatively few landowners could boast of having eliminated or even greatly mitigated the abuse before the 1830s.

The tiny plots of agricultural labourers constituted the last stage of subdivision. The 1841 census recorded over 145,000 labourers and farm servants in County Cork as compared with less than 41,000 farmers.[31] The relationship between the farmer and his hired, or bound, labourer was based essentially on the exchange of land for work. Thus the 'cash nexus' detested by Carlyle was generally inoperative. Describing the typical arrangement in Cork, a witness from the parish of Dromdaleague remarked before the poor-inquiry commission in 1835:

The agreement between the landlord and cottier tenant is generally of this kind: the farmer agrees to employ such a man as a regular labourer. He then sets him a house, engaging to give him every year a certain portion of ground, from half [an acre] to an acre, on which to put his manure for a potato garden; he generally also allows him to keep a couple of sheep on the farm, at 2s. a quarter each for their grazing; sets him a portion of bog for turf, and tillage for flax. For all these the tenant has to pay by his labour. . . .[32]

[30] P. M. A. Bourke, 'The extent of the potato crop in Ireland at the time of the famine' in *Stat. Soc. Ire. Jn.*, xx, pt iii (1959), pp. 20–6; *idem*, 'The agricultural statistics of the 1841 census of Ireland: a critical review' in *Econ. Hist. Rev.*, ser. 2, xviii, no. 2 (Aug. 1965), pp. 377–81.

[31] *Census Ire., 1841*, pp. 172–88.

[32] *Poor inquiry (Ireland): Appendix (E) containing baronial examinations*

In many parts of the county, however, the labourer struck two separate bargains, the first of which was for the cabin, a kitchen garden used to grow cabbages, the liberty to cut turf and collect dung on the farmer's lands, and the run of a pig.[33] The charges for the cabin and these customary privileges generally ranged from £1 10s. to £2 per annum, although prices as high as £3 were not unknown.[34] The labourer made a second, distinct agreement for his potato ground, and this was of course his most pressing concern. The rents of potato gardens varied from about £2 or £3 per acre when the labourer himself manured the land and cultivated it with the spade to £4 or £6 when the farmer prepared the ground for the crop.[35] In return for his cabin, privileges, and potato garden, the labourer was obligated to work for the farmer whenever he was called. On those days he worked, the labourer was credited with having earned 6d. to 8d., or only 4d. to 6d. if he was 'dieted' by the farmer.[36] Accounts were kept usually in writing, but frequently on tally sticks, and in neither case very carefully, with the inevitable result that many wage disputes were adjudicated at quarter sessions. At year's end, when the farmer compared wages credited against charges debited, the labourer sometimes found himself with a small favourable balance, but it rarely amounted to more than a few pounds.[37]

Distrust and acrimony very often poisoned the relations between farmers and their bound labourers. This is scarcely surprising in view of the grossly exorbitant rents farmers charged for cabins and potato gardens. Labourers' cottages were generally miserable excuses for dwellings; they were poorly thatched and sometimes even lacked doors and windows. The initial outlay for these cabins was so small that many farmers recovered the expense of throwing

[33] *Poor inquiry, supplement to appendix E*, pp. 173, 179, 187.

[34] Ibid., pp. 163–209, answers to question 14.

[35] Ibid., pp. 173, 179, 198–9; *Devon comm. evidence*, pt iii, p. 96; *Devon comm. digest*, i, 485.

[36] *Poor inquiry (Ireland): Appendix (D) containing baronial examinations relative to earnings of labourers, cottier tenants, employment of women and children, expenditure; and supplement containing answers to questions 1 to 12 circulated by the commissioners* [36], H.C. 1836, xxx, 1, answers to question 4 (hereafter cited as *Poor inquiry, supplement to appendix D*), pp. 163–209.

[37] *Copies of papers relating to experimental improvements in progress on the crown lands at King William's Town, in the barony of Duhallow, in the county of Cork . . .*, H.C. 1834 (173), li, 69, pp. 62–3.

---

relative to food, cottages and cabins, clothing and furniture, pawnbroking and savings banks, drinking; and supplement containing answers to questions 13 to 22 circulated by the commissioners [37], H.C. 1836, xxxii, 1, p. 179 (hereafter cited as *Poor inquiry, supplement to appendix E*). See also *Devon comm. digest*, i, 484, 487.

them up in only two years. Double or even triple the rent that farmers paid for the same land was exacted for labourers' potato gardens. The earl of Carbery stated to the poor-inquiry commission that 'the cottier tenant frequently suffers hardship from the farmer not fulfilling his engagements, not keeping the house well thatched, or giving the quantity of land promised for potato culture, or the full portion of work'. [38] The earl of Bantry's agent, the Rev. Somers Payne, remarked before the Devon commission, 'I have been a long time in the commission of the peace, nearly thirty years, and I never sat a court day without witnessing some act of oppression on the part of the farmer on his labourer'. The farmers' worst offence was that of 'leaving the houses uncovered', said Payne; 'I have known a [labouring] man's potatoes left without dung for weeks and even months'. [39] In the complaint book for the Ballineen petty-sessions district, covering the period from 1825 to 1840, disputes between farmers and their hired labourers recur with startling frequency, much more often in fact than disputes between farmers and their landlords. Labourers were constantly hauling farmers before petty sessions to have them answer charges of withholding wages, refusing to draw out manure or plough potato ground, failing to re-thatch cabins, or illegally taking possession of potato gardens, dung, sheep, or pigs. [40]

Even though their relations with their employers were often acrimonious, bound labourers at least enjoyed much greater security and much steadier employment than unbound agricultural workers. The great and constantly growing mass of casually employed labourers was being crushed under the weight of the increase in its own numbers and represented the most critical aspect of the population problem after 1815. Cork had been a principal centre for the provisioning of the British military effort during the Napoleonic wars as well as an important centre of army and navy recruitment. At the end of the wars, the labouring population in Cork as elsewhere in Ireland was swelled 'by the return of the thousands of men who

[38] *Poor inquiry, supplement to appendix E*, p. 192.
[39] *Devon comm. digest*, i, 486.
[40] Of course, not all labourers were without fault. From some labourers, farmers could obtain neither work nor rent nor possession of their cabins. Before petty sessions, farmers charged labourers with overholding possession of their cabins, 'making off with the surface of a kitchen garden', and unlawfully rescuing dung, sheep, or pigs distrained for non-payment of rent (Conner papers: Ballineen petty-sessions complaint book, 1825–40; in the possession of the executors of the late Henry L. Conner, Manch House, Ballineen, Co. Cork).

had joined the British army'. [41] Moreover, the decline of small-scale factory and domestic industry, particularly the weaving of coarse linens and cottons in the towns of West Cork during the late 1820s and the 1830s, must have added several thousand displaced hand-loom weavers to the already overcrowded agricultural labour market. [42] In Bandon alone, the number of weavers was reduced from about 2,000 in 1825 to only a few score by the early 1840s. [43]

At the same time that the supply of rural labour was mushrooming after 1815, the demand for it was shrinking. As farms became smaller through subdivision, the dependence on family as opposed to hired labour grew. To weather the long deflation that followed the wartime boom, farmers were forced to cut their labour costs. There was little regular employment in the parishes of Drinagh and Kilcrohane near Bantry in 1835, because 'the chief work of farmers is done by themselves and their servants, and in the spring and harvest the neighbours assist each other, giving an interchange of work'. [44] A protestant clergyman from the parish of Drinagh stated to the poor-inquiry commission that constant employment scarcely existed, 'except for well grown boys, who hire by the quarter with farmers, living with the family and doing, in fact, the work of a man at very low wages'. [45] The decline in wheat growing and the expansion of sheep farming beginning in the 1830s were also detrimental to the labourer's already tenuous position. [46] Technical improvements to be discussed below, such as the spread of better ploughs, the drilling of potatoes, and the use of the scythe instead of the sickle in harvesting grain, further curtailed the demand for labour.[47]

Labourers employed by the day endured a precarious existence. Whereas bound labourers generally received half an acre to an acre of potato ground in return for giving their labour whenever it was required, casually employed labourers had no choice except to hire land on which to grow their food. This practice was known as 'taking land in conacre', or simply as 'taking potato garden'. Such land, when manured and cultivated by the labourer, was sometimes let gratuitously or at only a nominal rent. It was said in 1835 that in the mountain district near Rosscarbery, 'land is sometimes let for a potato crop without any rent or consideration, save only that it

[41] K. Danaher, *Irish country people* (Cork, 1966), p. 109.

[42] *Poor inquiry, supplement to appendix E*, pp. 168, 172–3, 181, 200.

[43] Freeman, *Pre-famine Ireland*, pp. 87–8. See also W. A. Spillar, *A short topographical and statistical account of the Bandon union, with some observations on the trade, agriculture, manufactures, and tideways of the district* (Bandon, 1844), pp. 36–7; hereafter cited as *Bandon union*.

[44] *Poor inquiry, supplement to appendix D*, p. 164.   [45] Ibid., p. 175.

[46] See below, pp. 34, 43–4.   [47] See below, pp. 31, 37–9.

should be manured, the landlord finding his remuneration in the subsequent corn crop'. [48] Near the town of Kinsale at the same time, it was customary for the poor to

collect dung, which the farmer draws out on his ground without any charge for rent or draught; the person who finds the dung provides seed potatoes and attendant labour, and thus the farmer gets his ground prepared for subsequent crops at no expense but drawing out the dung. [49]

Unless there were exceptional facilities for gathering manure or fertilizer in a particular district, however, farmers commonly refused to let unprepared land in conacre, because the poor labourer tended to manure inadequately and to leave the land too exhausted to produce good corn crops. Thus, even though labourers would generally have preferred cheap, worn-out pasture or unmanured land, they were increasingly forced to take valuable ley ground or manured land much less suited to their requirements and to pay dearly for it. [50]

Conacre rents varied according to the quality of the land and the cost incurred by the farmer or landlord in preparing it for a crop. The protestant clergyman, the Rev. Thomas Gollock, who farmed a demesne at Forest near Macroom and who had to have lime drawn from a distance, let potato gardens at £8 8s. per acre in 1840. [51] Only £6 was charged for prepared ground in the parishes of Nohaval and Kilmonoge, not far from Kinsale and Oysterhaven, where fertilizing kelp and sand were raised from the bay. [52] Even unmanured potato gardens brought 35s. to 50s. in four parishes near Cork city, however, and prepared land was let at an average of £7 per acre. [53] In one sense, conacre rents in the vicinity of towns should have been moderated by the accessibility of town dung; but the availability of cheap manure was more than counterbalanced by excessive competition for the limited amount of land. Foreign travellers in Ireland and English observers were frequently amazed at the price of conacre land, which occasionally commanded as much as £10 or £12 per acre near very populous towns. [54] They

---

[48] *Poor inquiry: Appendix (F) containing baronial examinations relative to con-acre, quarter or score ground, small tenantry, consolidation of farms and dislodged tenantry, emigration, landlord and tenant, nature and state of agriculture, taxation, roads, observations on the nature and state of agriculture; and supplement* [38], H.C. 1836, xxxiii, 1, p. 177. (hereafter cited as *Poor inquiry, supplement to appendix F*)

[49] Ibid., p. 199. See also ibid., pp. 186, 188.

[50] *Devon comm. digest,* i, 522.

[51] Gollock papers: Demesne account book, 1838–43, 1 May 1840, p. 164 (in the possession of Mr Thomas H. M. Gollock, Monkstown, Co. Cork).

[52] *Poor inquiry, supplement to appendix F,* p. 199.

[53] Ibid., p. 107.   [54] *Devon comm. digest,* i, 521–2.

quickly became convinced that when such high rents were exacted, the crop could not possibly repay the conacre men. Undoubtedly, population pressure had driven rents to almost 50 per cent, and sometimes more, of the market value of a potato crop taken from prepared ground by the 1840s. Still, the market value of six tons of potatoes (the normal produce of an acre) was nearly £15 at the average price of about 2s. 6d. per cwt prevailing in 1830 and 1840.[55] The sad truth was, however, that in their effort to grow what was mainly their food and not a cash crop, the conacre men were forced to take a desperate gamble. R. N. Salaman has recorded no less than fourteen partial or complete failures of the potato crop in Ireland between 1816 and 1842.[56] Because of these repeated failures and the virtual impossibility of collecting conacre rents after such an event, farmers often demanded payment of the whole or a substantial part of the rent before the crop was harvested.[57] This demand may have considerably reduced the amount of land that labourers could afford to hire.[58]

Pitifully small wages were another facet of the unbound labourer's marginal existence. The wages of unbound labourers in County Cork ranged from 4d. to 8d. per day in ordinary times, with an increase to 10d. or 1s. 2d. at the harvest and during potato planting and digging.[59] Women were employed at 3d. or 4d. per day in digging or picking stones from pasture and meadow land, and in weeding potato plots; at busy times they occasionally earned 5d. or 6d. in planting or gathering potatoes and in binding corn.[60] The demesne-farming gentry usually paid their daily labourers in cash; they also gave steadier employment and somewhat higher wages than ordinary farmers. Farmers seldom provided steady work and rarely paid wages entirely in money; at least in part, they paid wages in conacre land or provisions and generally dieted their daily labourers, with a corresponding reduction in the rate of wages.[61] There was some geographical variation in the cost of labour. The

---

[55] *Irish Farmers' Gazette*, 1 Nov. 1879. See also *Poor inquiry, supplement to appendix F*, p. 192; *C.E.*, 16 Jan. 1846.

[56] R. N. Salaman, *The history and social influence of the potato* (Cambridge, 1949), pp. 603–8.

[57] *Devon comm. evidence*, pt iii, p. 101; *Devon comm. digest*, i, 521, 523.

[58] Of the thirteen labourers to whom the Rev. Thomas Gollock let land in 1840, only four could afford to hire as much as an acre or more, and the average letting was only about half an acre. Gollock required full payment in advance (Gollock papers: Demesne account book, 1838–43, 1 May 1840, p. 164).

[59] *Poor inquiry, supplement to appendix D*, pp. 163–209, answers to question 4.

[60] Ibid., pp. 163–209, answers to question 6.

[61] Ibid., pp. 166, 173, 199.

Mallow poor-law guardians noted the following rates in their locality in 1845:

Males 8*d*., females from 4 to 6 without diet; during harvest and potato planting . . . , males from 10*d*. to 12*d*. and occasionally more, females' wages at some times higher, but not in proportion. In some districts men can now be got for 4*d*. wages, near the town always higher.[62]

In the Kanturk district, however, workers received 5*d*. to 6*d*. per day with diet, even 'in the most hurried season of the year, and that for the best class of labourers'.[63] And in the parish of Inishannon, daily wages were only 4*d*. with diet, and from 6*d*. to 7*d*. without diet.[64]

Not only were their wages miserably small, but daily labourers rarely enjoyed regular employment. It is difficult to interpret many of the replies contained in the *Poor inquiry* to the question of how many labourers in particular parishes were in 'constant' or merely 'occasional' employment. It appears, however, that at least one-third, and perhaps as many as one-half, of all agricultural workers in Cork were employed only 'occasionally'.[65] They could find scarcely any work during midwinter, from the beginning of December to the end of February, or during midsummer, from the middle of June to the middle of August.[66] Staggering underemployment existed in the southwestern part of the county, where the population was extremely dense, especially along the seacoast. In the parishes of Rosscarbery and Kilkerranmore, not more than 100 labourers out of nearly 1,100 had constant work; in the parish of Creagh (including the town of Skibbereen), only fifty-five out of 341 labourers were permanently employed; and in the parish of Skull, only 100 or 200 labourers out of perhaps 2,000 had regular work.[67] The problem was much less acute in the northern and eastern parts of the county. One-half of the labourers in the parish of Fermoy, two-thirds of those in Castlemagner, and seven-eighths of those in Rathcormack and Gortroe were permanently employed.[68] Large numbers of casual labourers were concentrated in the narrow lanes and on the outskirts of towns throughout Cork. As many as 311 out of 908 families

---

[62] Archives Council, Cork: Minute book, Mallow board of guardians, 1844–6, 26 Dec. 1845, p. 337. (All minute books of boards of guardians cited in this work are in the custody of the Cork Archives Council.)

[63] *Devon comm. evidence*, pt iii, p. 103.

[64] *Poor inquiry, supplement to appendix D*, p. 198.

[65] Ibid., pp. 163–209, answers to question 1.

[66] Ibid., pp. 163–209, answers to question 5.

[67] Ibid., pp. 177, 181–2.

[68] Ibid., pp. 170, 183–4.

of labourers living in the lanes of Youghal in late 1845 were headed by a man who worked less than six months of the year. [69] T. C. Foster, a correspondent for *The Times*, reported in November 1845 that 120 families out of a total of 600 to 700 in Bantry were without a livelihood. 'I am assured that about 50 families live entirely by begging', observed Foster; 'the rest get a job to do when they can, and live by a bit of garden and a pig, and by raising coral-sand and sea-weed out of the bay, which they sell.' [70]

In spite of serious underemployment, abysmally low wages, and high conacre rents, there was wide disagreement over the change in the economic position of the labouring population since 1815. Most of the upper-class respondents to the poor-inquiry commission claimed that the labourers' condition had improved or at least remained stationary during the twenty years since the peace. Many of these respondents believed that they had seen an improvement in the clothing, housing, and diet of the poor. They attributed this to the removal of the tithe burden from labourers' potato gardens and to an increase in real wages. Money wages, they said, had remained about the same or fallen less than the price of clothing or provisions. [71] Their reasoning, however, is unconvincing. Far more persuasive are the arguments of Cork parish priests. The Rev. M. Sheehan, P. P., Killeagh, was certain that the labourers' condition had deteriorated,

owing to the fall of wages, which during the war were 10*d.* per day; and also owing to the fall of the price of pork, the pig being the chief means by which the labourers provide clothing and other necessaries; [and] to the increase of population. [72]

The Rev. John Ryan, P. P., Drimoleague, also pointed to a deterioration. Before 1815, he noted,

the labourers received a higher rate of wages, and the farmers were enabled to give them more constant employment; whilst the potato gardens, ... then attended to by their wives and children, are now attended to by themselves, for the want of general employment. [73]

It is difficult to imagine how the housing and diet of the labouring population could have been worse before 1815 than it was during the 1830s and early 1840s. Both in the towns and villages and in the country, the labourers and their invariably large families were

[69] *C.E.*, 13 Feb. 1846.

[70] T. C. Foster, *Letters on the condition of the people of Ireland* (2nd ed., London, 1847), p. 402. See also Freeman, *Pre-famine Ireland*, pp. 24–5.

[71] *Poor inquiry, supplement to appendix E*, pp. 163–209, answers to question 18.

[72] Ibid., p. 194. See also ibid., p. 204.

[73] Ibid., p. 179. See also ibid., p. 181.

squeezed into one-room cabins without windows. There were nearly 16,000 such wretched habitations in Cork in 1841, accounting for almost 50 per cent of the occupied dwellings in the county at that time. All along the coast, from Bantry Bay almost to Cork harbour, the density of the labouring population was painfully apparent from the high proportion of these one-room cabins. They represented more than 80 per cent of the total habitations in the baronies of Bere and Courceys. [74] Foster described the hovels on the outskirts of Bantry as consisting

usually of a single room, a hole for a window with a board in it, the door generally off the hinges, a wicker-basket with a hole in the bottom or an old butter-tub stuck at one corner of the thatch for a chimney, the pig, as a matter of course, inside the cottage, and an extensive manufacture of manure . . . [taking place] on the floor. [75]

The cabins were as bad in the country as they were in the towns. Those in the parish of Drinagh were 'the worst that can well be conceived'. A handy labourer usually built the walls and roof with

rough field stones and clay mortar; a few rough sticks, procured generally out of the bogs, which serve to support a bad covering of straw; sometimes interlined with heath for want of a sufficiency of straw, and seldom renewed while it is possible to inhabit it. [76]

The cabins in the parishes of Castlehaven and Myross were 'very wretched', said the Rev. James Mulcahy; 'humanity would assign better accommodation to the beasts of the field'. [77] Often neither airtight nor waterproof, these cabins cost next to nothing to build, and their impermanence was shown by the ease and speed with which they were demolished during and after the famine. Not surprisingly, the cabins were meagrely furnished: a large, black iron pot used to boil the 'praties', an uncovered box for meal, a board attached to the wall serving as a table, a few fir stumps serving as stools, and perhaps a dresser. The bedsteads and bedding were woefully insufficient. [78] Bedsteads were not uncommon, but for many labourers some straw placed on the floor had to suffice. The Rev. Charles O'Donovan remarked to the poor-inquiry commission:

When called upon to administer the last consolations of religion, it has often been my lot to see the poor labourers of these parishes [Kilmeen and Castleventry] in the agonies of death, with no bed but the wisp of straw, no

---

[74] *Census Ire., 1841*, pp. 172–88.
[75] Foster, *Condition of the people*, p. 402.
[76] *Poor inquiry, supplement to appendix E*, p. 175.
[77] Ibid., p. 179.
[78] Ibid., pp. 163–209, answers to question 15.

pillow but a piece of fir raised in some neighbouring bog, and no other bed-clothes than the tattered rags in which they were accustomed to labour in the fields. [79]

If their housing was generally miserable and unhealthy, the same could not be said about the labourers' staple foods, potatoes and milk, at least not when they had them in sufficient quantity and quality. Unfortunately, this was becoming less and less the case after 1815. It was generally agreed that with the exception of the summer and autumn months, labouring families drank little milk by the 1830s. [80] They could no longer afford to pay £5 per year for the grass and hay of a cow, although a group of labourers occasionally joined in purchasing part interest in a cow and its feed. [81] When they were dieted by farmers, the most that labourers could expect to receive was four or five pounds of potatoes and one quart of sour milk twice a day. [82] 'Their ordinary diet, when employed by farmers, is potatoes and salt fish, occasionally a little milk . . . .' [83] But milk was definitely a luxury. During four or five months of the year, labouring families ate dry potatoes with either 'meal and water, salt and water, salt herring, or something as a relish, which they call kitchen; in some instances potatoes and salt only, but this is rare'. [84] Meat and bread were almost never eaten, except on a few feast days, a chance Sunday, or at a wedding or christening. [85]

Even the quality of the potato used by most labourers had deteriorated. Two old varieties, the minion and the apple, made excellent table potatoes, and the apple was especially valued for its keeping qualities. But Townsend had observed that in the barony of Duhallow the apple was being superseded by the more prolific variety known as the cup. [86] By the 1840s the cup seems to have been replaced in most parts of Cork by the coarse, watery, yet even more prolific white potato, or 'lumper', commonly described as 'the people's food' or 'the poor man's crop'. Lumpers did not keep well and always went bad in early August, leaving the poor without their staple food until a new crop was ready for digging in early October. [87] Many labourers, unable to obtain sufficient land, found

[79] Ibid., p. 179.
[80] *Poor inquiry, supplement to appendix D*, pp. 163–209, answers to question 3.
[81] Gollock papers: Demesne account book, 1824–6, 24 Dec. 1824, p. 71; 16 Apr. 1826, p. 191.
[82] *Poor inquiry, supplement to appendix D*, pp. 173, 185.
[83] Ibid., p. 181.   [84] Ibid., p. 184.
[85] Ibid., p. 166; *Devon comm. digest*, i, 489.   [86] Townsend, p. 407.
[87] *C.E.*, 20 Oct. 1845; *C.C.*, 17 Mar. 1846, 31 Aug. 1848; E. R. R. Green, 'Agriculture' in Edwards & Williams, *Great famine* (New York, 1957), p. 96.

their supply of potatoes exhausted at the beginning of June or even earlier in some cases. [88] During these 'hungry months', labouring families often survived on a variety of cabbage, nettles, seaweed, and fish. Some subsisted on an occasional meal of potatoes from more fortunate friends, but 'they would not allow this to be considered begging; they do not allow a man to be put down as an actual beggar until he shall carry a bag on his back and beg for potatoes'. [89] Others sold their pigs and sheep, pawned their clothes (if they had clothes fit to be pawned), and bought potatoes or obtained meal on usurious terms. Surely, many half starved. [90]

AGRICULTURAL PRODUCTION

The middleman system of estate management, by strongly encouraging the reckless subletting and subdivision of farms, stimulated the rapid growth of population that was primarily responsible for the impoverishment of agricultural labourers after 1815. At the same time, however, subdivision and population growth helped to bring about a great expansion of both the land area under cultivation and agricultural output during and after the Napoleonic wars. K. H. Connell has carefully studied the reclamation of waste land in Ireland between 1780 and 1845. He concludes that 'during the French wars and in the following thirty years, while there was probably no county which did not experience a fair amount of reclamation, in many there may well have been an astonishing amount'. [91] Cork seems to fall into the latter category.

A small part of the work of reclamation in County Cork was performed by landowners like Charles Colthurst, who brought into cultivation some 160 acres of bog near Ballyvourney during the early 1840s. [92] Most of the reclamation, however, was done by poor cottiers primarily for potato growing. Landlords frequently encouraged them by charging insignificant rents. The earl of Mountcashel gave a large tract of mountain land to 'poor people, who have built houses upon it'; he rented the land 'so exceedingly cheap that they contrived by degrees to bring in one acre in one year, and another in another'. [93] When a large holding on an estate near Macroom came out of lease in 1835, the agent James Carnegie

---

[88] *Poor inquiry, supplement to appendix D*, pp. 173, 179.
[89] Ibid., p. 183.
[90] Ibid., pp. 164, 172, 179, 182.
[91] K. H. Connell, 'The colonization of waste land in Ireland, 1780–1845' in *Econ. Hist. Rev.*, ser. 2, iii, no. 1 (1950), p. 45.
[92] *Devon comm. digest*, i, 616–19.
[93] Quoted in Connell, 'Colonization of waste land', p. 51.

'removed the under-tenants to the mountains and gave them from twenty to fifty acres each, rent free for seven years'. [94] The valuer Charles Bailey reported in 1840 that the subtenants of a middleman on Viscount Midleton's estate had enclosed a considerable portion of mountain, claiming that the middleman had 'permitted them to do so, and that the rents for the same are included in the sums paid for their other holdings'. [95] On another part of Midleton's estate, seven tenants holding altogether fifty-seven acres had 'enclosed and cultivated many acres of the south mountain, without paying any rent for the same'. [96]

Even though statistical proof is lacking, other evidence points to a substantial amount of reclamation in many parts of Cork. 'Great quantities of land have been brought into cultivation since 1812' in the parish of Clondrohid near Macroom, stated a report in the late 1830s. [97] A large portion of the parish of Kilmocomoge (including the town of Bantry) was also said to have been brought into a profitable state since 1815. [98] In the parish of Ardfield near Clonakilty, there were reportedly 800 acres 'wholly in the occupation of poor people who have enclosed it'. [99] In the parish of Creagh (including the town of Skibbereen) in the late 1830s, there were 'few fields where the rock does not appear, but there is scarcely an acre which does not afford some pasture or tillage, which is carried even to the top of the hills'. [100] In the parish of Dunbulloge at the same time, the reclaimable mountain was 'constantly being brought into cultivation or planted'. [101] Charles Bailey observed in 1840 that much of the mountainous tract known as Walshtown More on Viscount Midleton's estate 'has been reclaimed within the last three years . . . , but there are about 180 acres [out of 302] still unreclaimed'. [102] He also stated that the middleman's tenants on the holding known as Coome Fitzgerald had 'enclosed from the north and south mountains immense tracts of land'. [103]

The construction of new roads on a large scale in Cork after 1815 fostered reclamation, which heavily depended upon the accessibility

[94] *Devon comm. digest*, i, 463.
[95] P.R.O.I., ref. no. 978, Midleton papers: Valuation of Viscount Midleton's estates, 1840, p. 403.
[96] Ibid., p. 406.
[97] Lewis, *Topog. dict. Ire.*, i, 355.
[98] Ibid., i, 164.
[99] Ibid., i, 50.
[100] Ibid., i, 432.
[101] Ibid., i, 567.
[102] P.R.O.I., ref. no. 978, Midleton papers: Valuation of Viscount Midleton's estate, 1840, p. 302.
[103] Ibid., p. 382.

of cheap fertilizers. These new roads made it feasible to work formerly dormant limestone quarries and to transport kelp, shell gravel, and coral sand far into the interior. The government, in a largely successful effort to promote the maintenance of public order, carried out by far the most significant road building in northwest Cork and northeast Kerry following serious uprisings there during the famine of 1821–2. The principal branches of the network connected Listowel and Newmarket (thirty-two miles), Newmarket and Charleville (fourteen miles), and Castleisland and Killarney with Mallow (forty-two miles). [104] 'Since the construction of the new government roads, lime has been extensively used as manure, and the state of agriculture greatly improved', it was said of the Kanturk district in the late 1830s. [105] The many new roads built under grand-jury presentments also stimulated agricultural development. In the parish of Kilmeen near Clonakilty, 'about half of the land has been brought into tillage . . . since new roads were opened in 1820'. [106] In the parish of Drinagh near Dunmanway, 'great improvements have been recently made in agriculture by the opening of new lines of road'. [107] Enormous quantities of kelp and coral sand were dredged by lightermen from the bays at Youghal, Crosshaven, Kinsale, Clonakilty, and Bantry, and then conveyed, very often along these new roads, as much as fifteen or twenty miles into the interior. [108] The Red Strand at Clonakilty bustled with activity in the late 1830s: 'More than 1,000 horses and carts may be reckoned at the strand in one day. This sand is esteemed the best on the southern coast, except the Bantry sand.' [109]

Cheap fertilizers, new roads, and waste-land reclamation lay behind the rapid growth of potato production in the half-century before the famine. Potatoes were already grown so widely throughout Cork in Townsend's time that after feeding their families and livestock, farmers and labourers in many districts had some available for export. [110] In the next thirty-five years, population growth raised output even further, and by 1845 the land area devoted to this vital subsistence crop in Cork is estimated to have

---

[104] *A copy of any reports on the experimental improvements on the crown estate of King William's Town in the county of Cork, submitted to her majesty's commissioners of woods and forests since the 8th day of August 1844 . . .*, H.C.1851 (637), 1, 437, p. 3.

[105] Lewis, *Topog. dict. Ire.*, i, 509.

[106] Ibid., ii, 177.

[107] Ibid., i, 497.

[108] Ibid., i, 162, 182, 590; ii, 26.

[109] Ibid., ii, 489.

[110] Townsend, pp. 230–2.

reached no less than 394,000 acres. P. M. Austin Bourke's map of potato-crop densities shows that 287 acres of potatoes were planted in that year for every 1,000 acres of crops and pasture, thereby giving Cork a higher density than any other county in Ireland.[111] Cork's pre-eminence in potato cultivation is partly due to the early introduction of this crop in that part of the country. The old tradition that Sir Walter Raleigh introduced the potato into Ireland from South America at his Myrtle Grove seat near Youghal is probably spurious.[112] Quite apart from the Raleigh tradition, however, the growing of potatoes in the Youghal district from the seventeenth century is well attested.[113] Cork was also favoured geologically for potato cultivation. Most of the county's soil consists of old red sandstone, 'flanked by accumulations of local detritus, which yields sandy loams well suited for tillage and dairying',[114] but not herbage luxuriant enough to fatten cattle or sheep. Cork's long coastline afforded potato growers unusually good facilities for heavily fertilizing their crops with kelp and sea sand, and this factor was largely responsible for the prominence of Skibbereen, Kinsale, and Carrigaline as potato-growing districts. In the tillage rotations of farmers, the potato became the universally accepted restorative crop rather than turnips or mangels, even though for restorative purposes there is little to choose between them. Aside from its superior advantages as human food, the potato was preferred, partly because until the 1830s there was almost no market for fat sheep fed on turnips.[115] Dairy farmers were prejudiced against turnips, because butter made from the milk of cows fed on them had a turnip taste, while their pigs throve on dairy refuse and potatoes. All of these factors help to account for the fact that nearly 30 per cent of the cultivated land in the county was devoted to this one crop on the eve of the famine.[116]

[111] Bourke, 'Extent of the potato crop', p. 7.

[112] Lewis, *Topog. dict. Ire.*, ii, 728; W. H. McNeill, 'The introduction of the potato into Ireland' in *Jn. Mod. Hist.*, xxi, no. 3 (Sept. 1949), pp. 218–22.

[113] W. D. Davidson, 'The history of the potato and its progress in Ireland' in *Dept. Agric. Jn.*, xxxiv (1937), p. 290.

[114] J. R. Kilrose, 'The soils of Ireland' in W. P. Coyne (ed.), *Ireland, industrial and agricultural* (Dublin, 1902), p. 32.

[115] Crotty, *Irish agricultural production*, p. 27.

[116] Cullen suggests that heavy dependence upon the potato for human food occurred earlier in the southwest of Ireland than elsewhere, because the expansion of dairying up to the 1770s drove the cottiers to smaller plots and less fertile soil. This development presumably laid a solid foundation for the simultaneous advance of potato cultivation and population soon after 1780, when the shift to tillage farming began (L. M. Cullen, 'Irish history without the potato' in *Past and Present*, no. 40 (July 1968), p. 77).

The methods of potato cultivation, like so much else in Irish agriculture, were rather primitive in 1815, but improvements took place in the next thirty years. In Townsend's time the practice of paring and burning, or 'graffing', the land in preparation for sowing potatoes was still in general use. [117] Under this system, the skin was scraped off the bawn (i.e., old pasture) or stubble field with a special instrument called a graffane, which was similar to the English breast plough. [118] The sods were collected in heaps, allowed to dry thoroughly, and then mixed with turf and burned; the ashes were spread over the field and turned under with the spade or the common wooden plough. [119] Graffing was unobjectionable when used to reclaim waste land, and even a critical observer of farming methods like Townsend was forced to admit that the practice had resulted in widespread improvement in the barony of Kinalea: 'Large tracts of land, covered with heath and furze, have been brought into tillage, and produce good crops of hay, besides corn and potatoes'. [120] In fact, agricultural experts considered the burning of bog and coarse mountain land not only necessary but beneficial as well. They regarded it as pernicious, however, on light and shallow soils where sand or limestone was near the surface, and most of the cultivated land of Cork falls into this category. [121] Partly for this reason, and partly because graffing was so frequently associated with the minimal use of other fertilizers besides ashes and with an exhausting sequence of crops, landlords and agents increasingly prohibited or severely penalized this practice. [122] Greater landlord watchfulness, the growing access to lime, kelp, and sea sand through the cutting of new roads after 1815, and the increasing attention paid to the use of farmyard and town manure greatly diminished the practice of burning by 1845, although it had by no means disappeared entirely. [123]

Once the ground had been prepared, the potatoes were sown in ridges, or 'lazy beds' (so called because the sod beneath the ridge was not dug or ploughed). Earth from the trenches that separated the ridges was used to build up the beds. This technique of planting

[117] Townsend, p. 197.
[118] *Munster Farmers' Magazine*, no. 20 (Jan. 1817), pp. 266–7.
[119] Irish Folklore Commission, Dublin: MS 107, pp. 468–9.
[120] Townsend, pp. 544–5.
[121] *Devon comm. digest*, i, 67.
[122] Conner papers: Lease to John Good, 6 Sept. 1825; Guildford Muniment Room, Midleton papers: T. Foley to H. Marshall (extract and copy), 18 July 1844.
[123] W. B. Jones, *The life's work in Ireland of a landlord who tried to do his duty* (London, 1880), p. 99.

in ridges probably preceded the introduction of the potato into Ireland. It appears to have originated in the effort to solve the farming problems arising from the wet climate and poor natural drainage of the country. The trenches were usually about two feet deep and followed the slope of the land, thus allowing the water to drain off.[124] A tremendous amount of labour with the spade was required for the cultivation of lazy beds, but, unfortunately, an almost equally great oversupply of labour existed in pre-famine Ireland. The growing adoption after 1840, however, of the Deanston system of permanent field drainage with pipes and the increasing use of better ploughs tended to make the lazy-bed system obsolete.[125] Among large farmers at least, the system was being abandoned before the famine. 'They had now drilled potatoes instead of the old lazy beds, which were exploded, and large tracts of drills might be seen daily' in the Midleton district, it was said in February 1846.[126] Many farmers in the district between Bandon and Dunmanway were also sowing their potatoes in drills. Approving the new practice at a meeting of the Ballineen farming society, largely composed of his own tenants, the earl of Bandon remarked in November 1845 that only 'some of them, still wedded to their prejudices, seemed to prefer the doctrines of the old school'.[127]

Just as potato production expanded and the methods of potato cultivation improved between 1815 and 1845, so too the output of cereals greatly increased and the methods of growing them became much more efficient. There is an instructive parallel between Irish and English agricultural developments in the patterns of response to the depression that replaced the wartime boom in cereal prices after 1815. English economic historians have recently begun to confront the paradox that cereal output continued to increase during the deflation of 1815–36, 'a phase formerly depicted as a universally crushing depression for farmers'.[128] Irish cereal production also took great strides after, as well as during, the Napoleonic wars. The unresolved question of whether cereal production or the area under crops reached a peak and then began to contract several years before the famine has sometimes been allowed to obscure the

[124] E. E. Evans, *Irish folk ways* (London, 1957), p. 143.
[125] *Devon comm. digest*, i, 81, 84–5.
[126] *C.C.*, 21 Feb. 1846.
[127] Quoted in T. Shea, 'The minute book of the Ballineen Agricultural Society, 1845–47: a famine document' in *Cork Hist. Soc. Jn.*, ser. 2, li, no. 173 (Jan.–June 1946), p. 53.
[128] E. L. Jones, *The development of English agriculture, 1815–1873* (London, 1968), p. 9.

enormous increase in grain exports between 1815 and 1845.[129] As Table 3 demonstrates, total grain exports rose from an average of less than 126,000 tons a year between 1813 and 1817 to an average of over 450,000 tons a year between 1835 and 1839, or by more than three and one-half times.[130]

TABLE 3   Irish exports of corn, meal, and flour to Great Britain, 1813–44 (in long tons)

years (average)	oats	barley	wheat	oatmeal	wheat meal & flour	total
1813–17	71,855	14,867	28,906	10,173*		125,801
1824–8	264,950	16,633	106,037	—	—	—
1830–4	226,871	32,618	115,090	30,088	41,980	446,647
1835–9	266,914	29,752	58,134	45,098	50,163	450,061
1840–4	247,393	16,915	36,075	67,725	25,452	393,560

*This figure includes both oatmeal and wheat meal and flour.

Even though Table 3 shows that exports reached a peak in the late 1830s and then declined, other considerations must be taken into account before the conclusion is drawn that these export figures reflect a fall in either cereal acreage or production before the famine. The declining trend of exports in the early 1840s resulted largely from the need to divert grain normally exported to home consumption following the general potato failure of 1839 and the partial failures of 1840 and 1841. These same three years also witnessed extremely poor corn harvests in Ireland, since heavy rains seriously damaged the crops.[131] Although there was national thanksgiving for an abundant harvest in the autumn of 1842, the early part of that year had seen great distress in many counties and

[129] Connell and Crotty lean towards opposite views on this question (Connell, *Population*, pp. 113–20; Crotty, *Irish agricultural production*, pp. 42, 50n., 53).

[130] P.R.O., Customs 5: Ledgers of imports, England, 'Corn exported from Ireland to Great Britain', 1830–44, nos 19–33 (special abstract on last pages of each ledger); Crotty, *Irish agricultural production*, Table 65 A, p. 276. It is debatable whether this enormous increase in grain exports can be taken to indicate a corresponding expansion of cereal acreage and production. One response to falling farm incomes after 1815 was the substitution of the potato for oatmeal in the diet of the farming classes. This substitution undoubtedly made more grain available for export. But this writer inclines to the view that the expansion of the cereal acreage was responsible for by far the greater part of the increase in grain exports.

[131] *Census Ire.*, *1851*, pt v, vol. i [2087–I], H.C. 1856, xxix, 261, pp. 344, 363.

food riots in Cork, Clare, Mayo, and Galway.[132] Table 4 simply rearranges the data for the figures given in Table 3 in order to show the average exports of the three best consecutive years in the 1830s and 1840s respectively, as well as the low average exports of 1839–42. Although grain exports reached their maximum of almost 529,000 tons in 1838, they still amounted to nearly 516,000 tons in 1845, when they were greater than in any other year of the century, with the single exception of 1838 itself. The 1845 figure would undoubtedly have been higher but for the fact that the partial potato failures of 1844 and 1845 again diverted some grain from export to home consumption. It therefore appears extremely doubtful that either cereal acreage or production contracted much before the famine, if indeed they decreased at all.

TABLE 4 Irish exports of corn, meal, and flour to Great Britain, 1836–45 (in long tons)

years (average)	oats	barley	wheat	oatmeal	wheat meal & flour	total
1836–8	290,193	35,063	60,306	50,446	55,541	491,549
1839–42	236,303	14,172	26,702	60,399	18,649	356,225
1843–5	263,990	19,613	63,789	65,280	50,587	463,259

The principal cereal crop in Cork as in most of Ireland was oats, followed closely by wheat; barley was extremely important in certain parts of the county. When the first official agricultural statistics were collected in 1847, there were about 127,000 acres under oats, 114,000 acres under wheat, and 44,000 acres under barley in Cork.[133] The main wheat-growing areas were located in the eastern part of the county (i.e., east of a line drawn from Charleville to Cork city) and along the seacoast about as far as Rosscarbery in the southwest. Oats were sown chiefly in the western part of the county, especially in the interior and the more hilly or mountainous districts. Barley was grown extensively in almost all the coastal districts.[134] Because of the strong demand for barley from local distilleries and breweries, very little of this crop was exported. Wheat and oats, on the other hand, were almost entirely exported, the wheat usually after being first ground into flour by the millers.[135]

[132] Ibid., pp. 360, 363.
[133] *Returns of agricultural produce in Ireland in the year 1847*, pt i: *Crops* [923], H.C. 1847–8, lvii, 1, p. viii.
[134] Townsend, pp. 232–3, 312–13, 397, 463–5, 611, 663.
[135] For the composition of cereal exports from the port of Cork between 1840 and 1843, see Spillar, *Bandon union*, pp. 36–7.

The enormous wartime prices for wheat and the expansion of wheat growing had led to the establishment of a large number of flour mills in Cork before 1815, and more than eighty of them were still functioning in 1835.[136] Many of these were small country mills, sometimes owned by landlords and used by the tenants of their estates. Almost all the larger country mills were water-powered rather than steam-driven and usually had a milling capacity of 10,000 to 12,000 bags or sacks of flour per annum.[137] The mills in Cork city operated on a much larger scale, particularly the Lee mills and those of Beamish and Crawford.[138] When violent price fluctuations in the 1820s and abnormally low prices in the early 1830s finally persuaded farmers to reduce their wheat production after 1833, the milling industry fell upon hard times.[139] Most of the country mills in Cork were working at much less than full capacity by the early 1840s, and many of the less efficient ones were being squeezed out of business. The Anderson mills on the Awbeg at Buttevant, with a capacity of 20,000 barrels per annum, were lying idle.[140] And Spillar observed that of the twenty-two mills within the poor-law union of Bandon, 'six are completely idle, and several others are only half at work, in consequence of the progressive decline in business, and the great uncertainty of any remuneration to the Irish miller since the late introduction of Canadian flour into this country'.[141]

For entirely different reasons, the brewing and distilling industries were also plagued by difficulties in the 1840s. Both appear to have prospered after 1800, and by 1835 there were no less than twenty-eight breweries, thirty-three separate malting houses, and twelve distilleries in County Cork.[142] The decided preference, said to be

[136] *Second report of the commissioners appointed to consider and recommend a general system of railways for Ireland* [145], H.C. 1837–8, xxxv, 449, appendix B, p. 97 (hereafter cited as *Second report of the railway commission*).

[137] Such were the Castlelyons mills on the Bride, the Maryville mills on the Funcheon near Kilworth, the Barry mills on the Dalua near Kanturk, the Brady and Molloy mills on the Blackwater at Mallow, and the Milltown mills on the Owennacurra at Midleton (Lewis, *Topog. dict. Ire.*, i, 301; ii, 33, 220, 340, 369).

[138] H. D. Inglis, *Ireland in 1834: a journey throughout Ireland during the spring, summer, and autumn of 1834* (4th ed., London, 1836), p. 108.

[139] Irish exports of wheat, wheat meal, and flour reached a maximum in 1833 and then gradually declined.

[140] Lewis, *Topog. dict. Ire.*, i, 235.

[141] Spillar, *Bandon union*, pp. 36–7. When Spillar wrote, the importation of Canadian flour almost duty-free had just been allowed, and although little arrived before the famine, this breach of the corn laws cast a gloom over the Irish milling industry.

[142] *Second report of the railway commission*, appendix B, p. 97.

34

almost universal even as early as 1800, for malt liquors over spirits and the strength of the legal spirits industry help to explain the remarkable absence of illicit distillation throughout the county.[143] Most of the distilleries, and by far the largest of them, were found in Cork city. But the town of Bandon in the heart of the West Cork barley district possessed two large concerns, as did the town of Midleton in the centre of the East Cork barley district.[144] The breweries followed almost the same pattern of centralization. Towering above all the others stood the Cork city concern of Beamish and Crawford,[145] the leading brewery in Ireland until 1833, when it was surpassed in porter and ale production by the now world-famous Dublin firm of Messrs Guinness and Company.[146] Bandon had no less than five porter and ale breweries and Midleton four, but most of the other large towns in Cork had at least one.[147] In the late 1830s and the 1840s, however, the stirring national crusade of the Capuchin friar and 'apostle of temperance', Fr Theobald Mathew, severely damaged the prosperity of the drink industry and the income of barley growers, especially in Cork, where the total abstinence movement was centred.[148] Brewing was less hard hit than distilling, but during the decade following the start of the temperance campaign in 1838, the number of bushels of malt upon which the required duty was paid fell from over 2 million to only about 1·5 million, or by about 25 per cent.[149] Domestic consumption of grain spirits in Ireland declined from nearly 12·3 million gallons in 1838 to only about 6 million gallons in 1847, or by more than 50 per cent.[150]

---

[143] *Poor inquiry, supplement to appendix E*, pp. 163–209, answers to question 22; K. H. Connell, *Irish peasant society: four historical essays* (Oxford, 1968), pp. 31, 34–5.

[144] Allman's and Fitzgerald's in Bandon, and Murphy's and Hacket's in Midleton (Lewis, *Topog. dict. Ire.*, i, 179; ii, 368).

[145] Henry Inglis, who visited Cork city in 1834, wrote that 'of the concerns of Beamish and Crawford, in breweries and flour mills, some idea may be formed from the circumstance . . . that one-eighth of the whole rate of the city of Cork is paid by that firm' (Inglis, *Ire. in 1834*, p. 108).

[146] Lynch & Vaizey, *Guinness's brewery*, p. 89.

[147] Lewis, *Topog. dict. Ire.*, i, 186, 623; ii, 33, 370, 558, 727.

[148] P. Rogers, *Father Theobald Mathew: apostle of temperance* (Dublin, 1943), *passim*.

[149] T. C. Macardle and W. Callan, 'The brewing industry in Ireland' in Coyne, *Ire.*, p. 456.

[150] *Report from select committee on the spirit trade (Ireland), with minutes of evidence*, H.C. 1842 (338), xiv, 423, p. 63; *An account of the quantity of spirits distilled in Ireland, the quantity of spirits on which duty was paid for home consumption in Ireland, and the quantity of spirits imported from Ireland into England, on which duty was paid, in each year from 1841 to 1850 inclusive*, H.C. 1851 (368), liii, 455.

The methods used by Cork farmers to grow their corn crops in 1815 were extremely inefficient. Relatively few farmers possessed harrows, rollers, or good ploughs. The common wooden plough generally used in Townsend's time was a heavy, unwieldy implement that barely scratched the surface of the land.[151] One man had to drive four to six horses, while another held the plough in the ground by pressing down on the beam, and a third man had to follow in the wake of the plough to turn back the furrows.[152] Spade cultivation was of course very widespread. Furthermore, farmers were 'totally ignorant' of how to drain land properly and 'but little acquainted' with the practice of irrigation. 'At least one third of every farm is unproductive every year', said W. R. Townsend of Inishcarra with some exaggeration in 1816.[153] The land was trenched for corn in the same way that it was for potatoes; the seed was sown broadcast and then covered with earth from the trenches. Careful, deep trenching provided a perfect, though only temporary, system of drainage, and compensated, if only in part, for shallow ploughing or none at all.[154]

Crop rotation was poorly understood and even less practised. The valuer William Nicholls complained in 1827 that the earl of Egmont's tenants near Kanturk habitually left their land 'in a state of tillage until it is completely exhausted and will no longer produce a crop, before it is given any rest in a state of pasture, for which all the lands, with very trifling exceptions, are well calculated'.[155] William Bence Jones tersely described the sequence of crops in vogue before the famine among the tenants on his estate near Clonakilty as 'potatoes followed by wheat, and then oats, oats, oats, whilst the land would grow any'. 'No grass seeds', said Jones, 'were sown when the land was left to "rest", as it was called.'[156] Farmers also frequently neglected to lime their lands, partly because of the absence of good roads. William Nicholls pointed out that the earl of Egmont's Churchtown estate abounded with fine limestone but added regretfully that 'a naturally rich soil is, throughout the property, . . . brought to a state of extreme poverty for want of its application.' 'In short', said Nicholls, 'in Ireland, farming is not at

---

[151] The Scottish swing plough was then confined to the neighbourhood of Cork city and to a few other places (Townsend, p. 191).

[152] Green, 'Agriculture', p. 100. The only merit of the common wooden plough was that it cost as little as 10s. or 15s.

[153] *Munster Farmers' Magazine*, no. 18 (July 1816), pp. 99–106.

[154] *Devon comm. digest*, i, 84–5.

[155] Barry papers, *Egmont v. Darell, documents of respondents*: William Nicholls's general report on the Kanturk estate, 20 Oct. 1827, p. 82.

[156] Jones, *Life's work*, p. 99.

all understood, and the better the land, the worse it is managed.'[157]

Far-reaching improvements, however, took place in farming practices between 1815 and 1845. Surely, one of the most important changes was the replacement of the old Irish wooden plough by the iron swing plough from Scotland, which economized on the labour of men and horses, broke up the subsoil, and made possible the drilling of crops. Although they achieved little in other respects, the farming societies sponsored by the gentry at least served to spread the use of better ploughs. The Cork landlord Thomas Herrick admitted before the Devon commission that the farming society in his district was mainly confined to the landlords and had otherwise made scant impact on the working farmers. But he insisted that 'it brought iron ploughs and Scotch [*sic*] ploughs into the country very generally'.[158] Only five improved ploughs, all belonging to the principal landowners of the locality, had been entered in competition at the first ploughing match held by the agricultural society in the remote district of Skibbereen in the 1830s. But there were twenty-eight Scottish iron ploughs, only two of which belonged to gentlemen, submitted for the annual trial in 1846.[159] Improved farming implements had in fact become widespread by the 1840s. In the Timoleague district, many farmers had 'adopted the use of the Scotch [*sic*] plough and other improved agricultural implements'.[160] Spillar contrasted the 'mere scratching of the surface of the land by an ill constructed plough, in the use of which all the help upon the farm was sure to be employed' in 1815, with the 'keen, deep ploughing with first rate implements, well tackled horses, guided only by one man' in almost universal use in the Bandon district by the early 1840s.[161]

Although the sickle remained the usual implement for cutting down the corn, the long-handled scythe, which brought it down more rapidly and efficiently if fields had been cleared of rocks and boulders, was quickly coming into use during the 1840s.[162] Reaping and threshing machinery, however, remained practically unknown

---

[157] Barry papers, *Egmont v. Darell, documents of respondents:* William Nicholls's general report on the Churchtown estate, 20 Oct. 1827, pp. 83–4.

[158] *Devon comm. digest,* i, 17.

[159] *C.C.,* 14 Mar. 1846.

[160] Lewis, *Topog. dict. Ire.,* ii, 625. See also ibid., i, 356; ii, 617.

[161] Spillar, *Bandon union,* p. 28. The common wooden plough and spade cultivation had by no means been completely superseded before 1845.

[162] The Midleton poor-law guardians noted in August 1848 'the recent tho' very general substitution of the scythe for the sickle' (Minute book, Midleton board of guardians, Mar.–Dec. 1848, 19 Aug. 1848, p. 133). See also Evans, *Irish folk ways,* p. 157.

in Cork until after 1850. The threshing machines on the market before then, costing £30 to £35, were clearly beyond the reach of all except the wealthiest farmers.[163] Corn was still threshed with a flail, usually on the public roads because of the absence of proper buildings. This was often a serious handicap under normal Irish autumn weather conditions. The agent Thomas Foley pointed out to Viscount Midleton's English solicitor in January 1845 that Midleton's tenants generally lacked barns and were obliged to thresh their corn in the open air; 'from the extreme wetness of the climate, they are often for weeks together unable to send a barrel of corn to market'. 'During all the time that you had lately fine frosty weather in England', chided Foley, 'we were deluged with rain & all farm work was at a stand.'[164]

Another important improvement was the gradual abandonment of the soil-exhausting practice of taking more than two corn, or white, crops in succession after a highly manured crop of potatoes. (Despite the strictures of would-be agricultural improvers, however, potatoes invariably remained the first rotational crop before 1845.)[165] Some landlords and agents were attempting to break the custom of sowing even two white crops in a row, but their efforts were rarely successful.[166] The chief agent of the duke of Devonshire's estates, F. E. Currey, stated before the Devon commission:

Our covenants are not sufficiently stringent for good farming, for one of them is that they shall not take more than two corn crops in succession, and they ought not to take that, but it is of no use to insert covenants that could not be enforced.[167]

Even the poorest farmers, however, were sowing some artificial grasses with the second white crop or after it;[168] in doing so, they were often following the advice of a concerned land agent or the local agricultural society. The Bandon and Midleton farming societies were given credit for the better rotations in their areas. Spillar observed of the Bandon district in the early 1840s that twenty-five years earlier it would have been necessary to

travel out of these baronies to see a field of turnips or even drilled potatoes, whilst now in our own locality there are amongst the working farmers many

---

[163] Green, 'Agriculture', p. 100. The national exhibition of 1852 in Cork was said to have led to the introduction of mechanical reapers (*C.C.*, 6 Sept. 1860).

[164] Guildford Muniment Room, Midleton papers: T. Foley to H. Marshall (extract and copy), 21 Jan. 1845.

[165] Shea, 'Minute book, Ballineen Agricultural Society', p. 54.

[166] *Devon comm. evidence*, pt iii, p. 73.

[167] *Devon comm. digest*, i, 278.   [168] Ibid., i, 71.

fields of both, and among the higher classes we see cultivated ... acres of mangel wurzel, carrots, and beans. [169]

In the Midleton district in the early 1830s, 'they had not their green crops, and good ploughing was little valued', but by 1845 'green crops, turnips, and good ploughing were to be seen everywhere. ... The land was better laid down than formerly.' [170]

While tillage farmers adopted improved methods and expanded output, graziers and dairy farmers followed suit. Cattle exports (beef and live cattle combined) declined in Ireland after 1815 and remained stagnant at least until the 1830s. But the exports of butter, sheep, and pigs (pork, bacon and hams, and live pigs combined) all increased substantially between 1815 and 1835, as shown in Table 5. [171]

TABLE 5   Irish exports of cattle, butter, pigs, and sheep, 1811–35

years (average)	total cattle (no.)	butter (cwt)	pigs (no.)	sheep (no.)
1811–15	110,775	438,197	610,787	17,301
1816–20	87,983	455,810	529,864	26,595
1821–5	84,490	478,538	640,568	49,890
1835 (1 yr)	120,510	527,009	873,352	125,452

Live-cattle exports almost doubled during this period, but beef exports fell by nearly two-thirds, thus holding total cattle exports and presumably dry-cattle production not much above their peak of 1811–15. Crotty has argued that the growing export of butter does not reflect a rise in the number of milch cattle, because domestic *per capita* consumption of milk and butter fell, as Irish living standards deteriorated after 1815. More butter from the same number of cows was simply released for export. [172] This fall in *per capita* consumption, however, was probably more than counterbalanced by a rise in

169 Spillar, *Bandon union*, p. 30.
170 *C.C.*, 21 Feb. 1846.
171 O'Donovan, *Econ. hist.*, pp. 159, 193, 196, 212. The three forms of pig exports have been made equivalent: 1 half-barrel of pork and 1 cwt of bacon and hams have each been taken to equal one pig. The exports of pork and beef in 1835 were not distinguished from one another; since the combined exports of pork and beef fell by about 40 per cent between the early 1820s and 1835, the exports of each in the latter year have been taken as 60 per cent of the exports of each between 1821 and 1825 (Crotty, *Irish agricultural production*, pp. 277n., 280).
172 Crotty, *Irish agricultural production*, p. 47.

total consumption, as population continued to grow.[173] If this view is correct, then rising butter exports do indicate that the number of cows had increased substantially by 1835. Population growth and the rapidly changing class structure of the rural population, in which cottiers and landless labourers were increasingly dominant after 1800, largely explain the extraordinary rise in pig production as reflected by exports. The 350 per cent increase in total pig exports, from a yearly average of only 251,000 between 1801 and 1805 to more than 873,000 in 1835, firmly fixed the almost automatic connection between the Irishman and his pig in the eyes of the outside world.[174] Sheep, neglected by Irish farmers since 1780, became a significant part of the rural economy again between 1815 and 1845. The continued expansion of the area under crops until the famine seems to indicate that farmers grazed more sheep and dairy cattle by increasing their stocking ratios within a fairly stable area of pasture.

Despite the great expansion of tillage after 1780 and the large increase in cereal production, dairying and the provision trade remained by far the most important income-earning sector of Cork agriculture. In 1835 butter accounted for perhaps half of the estimated £2 million worth of Cork exports of provisions, and the latter were more than five times as valuable as the exports of cereals.[175] Probably about 45 per cent of the cultivated land in County Cork was devoted to grassland and meadow in the early 1840s (600,000 acres out of 1,300,000 acres), whereas only about half as much land was sown to corn, with potatoes accounting for the remaining cultivated land.[176] The overwhelming majority of the 178,000 cattle on Cork farms in 1841 were milch cattle rather than dry cattle,[177] for the exports of both live cattle and beef from the port of Cork at this time were extremely small. If the export trade in live cattle was not large, neither was it expanding rapidly. Whereas some 4,200 cattle had been shipped from Cork in 1835, cattle exports averaged only about 4,400 during the three years

[173] J. Lyons, 'The history of our dairying industry' in *Agricultural Ireland*, xvi, no. 7 (July 1959), pp. 190–3.

[174] O'Donovan, *Econ. hist.*, pp. 159, 193.

[175] *Second report of the railway commission*, appendix B, p. 75.

[176] *Census Ire., 1841*, p. 452; *Returns of agricultural produce in Ireland in the year 1847*, pt i: *Crops*, p. viii; Bourke, 'Extent of the potato crop', p. 7.

[177] The figure of 178,000 cattle is an estimate correcting the number of 150,588 given in the 1841 census, which excluded 'calves of the current year' (*Census Ire., 1841*, p. 455; Bourke, 'Agricultural statistics', pp. 381–2). The census made no distinction between cows and dry cattle.

ending 1 August 1843.[178] Townsend had observed in 1810 that most Cork dairy farmers bred only a few calves, and that even the very largest of them rarely bred more than from six to ten.[179] Except in the vicinity of Cork city and a few other large towns,[180] calves were not fed for veal, since there was little domestic market for it. Most of the calves born every year before 1845 were slaughtered as soon as they were dropped.

If the live cattle trade of Cork was stable in the late 1830s and early 1840s, so too was the great export trade in butter centred on the famous market in Cork city. The receipts of the Cork butter market, the largest of its kind in the British Isles, had steadily increased during the first two decades after Waterloo, rising from an average of 253,000 firkins a year between 1815 and 1820 to one of 300,000 firkins a year between 1830 and 1835; but then receipts stabilized in the last decade before the famine.[181] Butter production took place on a small scale. Although dairy herds of twenty to forty cows could be found in certain districts, especially in the baronies of Barrymore, Kinnatalloon, and parts of Imokilly, the average herd was very much smaller.[182] Excluding the holders of five acres or less, most of whom had but one cow, the average dairy herd in Cork in 1841 consisted of less than five cows per farm.[183] While most farmers managed their own dairies, some large farmers as well as some landlords rented cows and the land necessary for feeding them to persons known as dairymen at a fixed price per cow for the year. Payment was made either in money or butter, or by some combination of these two. Townsend observed in 1810 that dairymen in the baronies of Muskerry and Barretts hired cows at the rate of one hundredweight of butter and 1 guinea each.[184] At the time of high butter prices during the French wars, dairymen in the

---

[178] *Second report of the railway commission*, appendix B, p. 75; Spillar, *Bandon union*, pp. 36–7.

[179] Townsend, p. 581.   [180] Ibid., p. 614.

[181] Public Museum, Cork, Cork Butter Market (hereafter C.B.M.) MSS, C. 38: Account of the total annual quantity of butter in casks, firkins, and kegs passed through the weigh-house, 1770–1869. The official figures of market receipts from 1830 have been raised by 18 per cent in order to take into account the change in the size of the firkin; before 1830 the firkin held only about 56 lb. of butter, whereas from that year it held about 66 lb. of butter (ibid., G. 131, Correspondence record book, 1827–48: secretary of the Committee of Merchants to Viscount Bernard, 6 Oct. 1842, pp. 230–1).

[182] Townsend, pp. 579, 614.

[183] *Census Ire., 1841*, pp. 454–5. All references in the text to the number of livestock on holdings of different sizes, as given in the 1841 census, must be understood in the light of P. M. Austin Bourke's critique of these statistics ('Agricultural statistics', pp. 377–9, 381).   [184] Townsend, p. 664.

baronies of Kinalea and Kerrycurrihy paid up to 10 guineas per cow. [185] By the 1830s, however, rents had fallen considerably and varied from £4 to £8, depending on the quality of cows and pasture and on the proximity to Cork city. [186]

There was much experimentation with the breeding of dairy cattle between 1815 and 1845. In Townsend's time half-bred Holderness cows were said to be the most prized milkers, often equalling the yields of the native Kerries, the best of which gave twenty to twenty-four quarts per day. The Devon breed had been tried and found wanting; its yield was generally only about twelve quarts per day, although its milk was rich in butterfat. [187] Gentlemen farmers often favoured Durham bulls in their attempts to improve the breeding of dairy stock after 1815, but working farmers generally preferred Ayrshires, which required much less winterfeed. [188] This was the great advantage of the native breed. Experiments conducted in 1841 on the crown estate at Kingwilliamstown demonstrated that while Kerries gave only about five-sixths as much milk and four-fifths as much butter as Ayrshires, the former required only about two-thirds as much winterfeed as the latter. [189] Cows were increasingly valued, however, for the butcher at the end of their days as well as for the pail during their prime. In the former respect, the small, light Kerries were at a decided disadvantage when matched with the Scottish cattle and the recently introduced but rapidly spreading shorthorns. [190] At least in certain districts, much was done to improve the breeding of dairy stock between 1815 and 1845. Spillar remarked in 1844 that it was no longer a rare occurrence in the poor-law union of Bandon 'to see fine stocks of cattle obtained by crosses of the Durham, Ayrshire, or Dutch bulls, whilst it is an allowed fact that these crosses are found to be excellent milkers and kind to the butchers'. [191]

In a dairy county like Cork, pig breeding was certain to be important, as it was an excellent means of utilizing the waste products of the dairy. The largest export of live pigs in 1835 was from Drogheda with about 94,000, followed by Cork with 75,000

---

[185] Ibid., p. 546.

[186] *Poor inquiry, supplement to appendix D*, pp. 177, 194, 200, 204.

[187] Townsend, pp. 579–80.

[188] *C.E.*, 3 Nov. 1845.   [189] Ibid., 10 Jan. 1842.

[190] Few of the Kerries were purebred; most had been crossed with the longhorns. Except in a few pedigree herds, there were no shorhorns in Ireland in 1827, but in the following fifteen years 'the shorthorns became Ireland's premier breed'. On the whole subject of cattle breeding, see O'Donovan, *Econ. hist.*, pp. 169–82.

[191] Spillar, *Bandon union*, p. 31.

and Waterford with 74,000.[192] But the total export of pigs both live and dead from Cork was probably greater than that from any other Irish port. During the year ending 1 August 1843, not only were 74,000 live pigs shipped but also 24,500 bales of bacon, equivalent to about 49,000 more pigs, and a small though undetermined quantity of pork.[193] The German traveller J. G. Kohl marvelled at the bacon-curing and -packing stores of Cork city, where the hams were 'ranged in long rows, like the folios and octavos of a library'. Well might he have wondered 'with what thoughts and feelings poor hungry Paddy studies these vast libraries of bacon!' 'It is dreadful', said Kohl, 'that the poor Irish should have to furnish other countries with such vast quantities of that which they themselves are starving for want of.'[194] The importance of the pig to the labourers and cottiers is shown by the fact that nearly one-third of the 177,500 pigs in Cork in 1841 were kept on holdings of less than one acre.[195]

Unlike cattle and sheep, Irish pigs were rarely sent to Britain as stores; they were almost always finished in Ireland at about two years old, when they weighed approximately two hundredweight.[196] The breeding sows generally belonged to the larger dairy farmers, who sold off many of their bonhams at ten weeks old to labourers and cottiers. The bonhams were then kept until ready for the Cork city bacon curers at about six months old or until fully finished.[197] The old native pigs reached a great size, had 'long legs, flat sides, large ears, narrow backs, and in general every defect of shape that could well be imagined'.[198] The increasing use of Hampshire and Berkshire boars, however, brought about some improvement in Cork by the early 1840s, especially with respect to earlier maturity,[199] and by the 1850s pigs were usually ready for slaughter at about fifteen months instead of the two years needed at the beginning of the century.[200]

Of all the livestock pursuits, that of sheep rearing was expanding most rapidly in Cork during the 1830s and 1840s. Whereas only 7,500 sheep had been exported in 1835, that number more than

---

[192] *Second report of the railway commission*, appendix B, pp. 75, 87.

[193] Spillar, *Bandon union*, pp. 36-7.

[194] J. G. Kohl, *Ireland: Dublin, the Shannon, Limerick, Cork, and the Kilkenny races, the round towers, the lakes of Killarney, the county of Wicklow, O'Connell and the Repeal Association, Belfast, and the Giant's Causeway* (London, 1844), p. 45.

[195] *Census Ire., 1841*, pp. 454-5. See above, p. 41, n. 183.

[196] O'Donovan, *Econ. hist.*, p. 191.

[197] A. W. Shaw, 'The Irish bacon-curing industry' in Coyne, *Ire.*, pp. 244, 252.

[198] Quoted in O'Donovan, *Econ. hist.*, p. 191.

[199] Spillar, *Bandon union*, p. 31.

[200] Shaw, 'Bacon-curing industry', p. 243.

doubled to an average of 16,000 during the three years ending
1 August 1843.[201] There were actually more sheep in Cork in 1841
than in Galway, where sheep rearing had been developed most
intensively. For best results, large farms were needed; one-fifth of
the 253,000 sheep were kept on holdings not exceeding one acre, but
there were nearly twice as many on farms of thirty acres or more.[202]
The expansion of sheep rearing at this time stimulated the cultivation
of turnips, against which Cork farmers had long had a strong
prejudice. When urged to grow turnips, farmers objected that they
were always stolen, 'a fact not to be disputed', said Charles Bailey in
1840; 'but this proves their worth, and if they were more plentifully
grown, that objection would vanish, as in the case of potatoes, tho'
perhaps turnips will never be considered so sacred a production as
the baneful population-increasing-potatoe'.[203] The chairman of the
farming society in the poor-law union of Midleton, Garrett Barry,
pointed out in early 1846, however, that the cultivation of turnips
had become much more general in the last ten years, and that
'farmers who never expected that they should grow them, now
fatten' their cattle and sheep with them.[204]

The improvement in the breeding of sheep after 1815 was
certainly more far-reaching than the better breeding of either cattle
or pigs. In Townsend's time even sheep in the prosperous and
fertile barony of Imokilly were generally of the 'small mountain
breed' and required perpetual fetters. But Townsend also observed
that the gentry had introduced Leicesters and occasionally South
Downs.[205] Throughout those parts of Ireland where sheep rearing
became important after 1815, the Leicester ram was crossed with the
Roscommon ewe. Although the first result of the Leicester cross was
a marked decrease in the size of the progeny, this was 'more than
counterbalanced by the enhanced quality, better general conforma-
tion, and more early maturing properties which the combination of
blood produced'.[206] In fact, the Leicester cross effected a minor
revolution, for it reduced the time required to bring sheep to
maturity from often nearly four years at the beginning of the century
to only two years by the early 1830s.[207]

[201] *Second report of the railway commission*, appendix B, p. 75; Spillar,
Bandon union, pp. 36–7.
[202] *Census Ire., 1841*, pp. 454–5. See above, p. 41, n. 183.
[203] P.R.O.I., ref. no. 978, Midleton papers: Charles Bailey's summary
report on the valuation of the Midleton estates, 6 Apr. 1840.
[204] *C.C.*, 21 Feb. 1846.
[205] Townsend, pp. 312, 517–18, 614.
[206] 'Sheep-breeding in Ireland' in Coyne, *Ire.*, p. 365.
[207] O'Donovan, *Econ. hist.*, p. 199.

PRICES, MARKETS, AND RENTS

The soaring prices and windfall profits of the Napoleonic wars ended with the arrival of peace in 1815, and a long, painful period of deflation followed. The deflation lasted until about 1836 and caused Irish farmers severe difficulty and loss, especially at the outset. The products of the provision trade were most affected by the price fall of 1816–20, and when corn prices declined drastically between 1818 and 1822, farmers everywhere raised a cry for permanent reductions in rent.[208] Although corn prices tended to fluctuate violently, the slump was fairly uniform for all products except beef. By the early 1830s prices had fallen as much as 30 to 40 per cent below wartime levels. A limited recovery occurred in the late 1830s, stronger in the case of butter and weaker in the case of beef, but other products remained about 25 per cent lower in price than they had been between 1812 and 1815, as Table 6 shows.[209]

TABLE 6   Index numbers of Dublin market agricultural prices, 1812–40

(base 1812–15 = 100)

years (average)	wheat	oats	barley	butter	bacon	beef	mutton
1812–15	100	100	100	100	100	100	100
1816–20	91	89	90	81	80	81	83
1821–5	66	68	66	77	64	60	72
1826–30	75	80	83	62	74	58	67
1831–5	60	62	63	68	65	51	64
1836–40	79	76	75	86	77	64	73

The withdrawal of the large wartime victualling contracts after 1815 was the major cause of the sharp fall in the prices of Irish provisions. The price of Irish mess beef in London dropped from 173*s.* per hundredweight in 1813 to 114*s.* per hundredweight in 1838, and Irish butter from 130*s.* per hundredweight in 1814 to 66*s.* per hundredweight in 1838.[210] The provision merchants of Cork had enjoyed unprecedented prosperity during the French wars,

---

[208] Farmers' difficulties were increased by the complete failure of the potato crop in the south and west of Ireland in 1821. Serious uprisings occurred in many districts during the famine of 1821–2, perhaps most notably in County Cork (*Papers presented by his majesty's command, relative to the disturbed state of Ireland*, H.C. 1822 (2), xiv, 741, pp. 3–5, 8–16).

[209] Crotty, *Irish agricultural production*, table 68 C, p. 284.

[210] O'Donovan, *Econ. hist.*, p. 153.

since their city had received the largest share of the British government's victualling contracts. Cork was still by far the most important centre of the Irish provision trade in 1835. The estimated value of its exports of provisions was more than twice that of its nearest rival, Belfast.[211] Salted beef and pork, however, now accounted for a much smaller share of its trade. The combined exports of these commodities had declined from almost 8,400 tons in 1807 to only 4,800 tons during the year ending 1 August 1841.[212] The loss of the West Indian and Newfoundland markets for Irish salted beef and pork in the late 1820s and early 1830s contributed to the decline. The United States quickly captured the lucrative nearby trade once Britain had removed its high tariffs.[213] Only the remaining government contracts kept this part of Cork's provision trade alive by the 1830s.[214]

Dwindling markets also confronted the butter merchants. A large share of Cork's butter exports was still destined for colonial markets rather than for Britain during this period. As many as 77,000 out of 209,000 firkins exported from Cork in 1825 were sent to Portugal (for re-export to Brazil) and to the British West Indies; many of the 49,000 firkins shipped to Liverpool also had colonial destinations. Lisbon was in fact the most important single market for Cork butter during the 1820s and 1830s, importing 50,000 to 60,000 firkins annually.[215] In 1842, however, Peel's government equalized the duties on French and Portuguese wines, and Portugal, which had formerly enjoyed a competitive advantage over France in the English wine market, promptly retaliated by placing prohibitive duties on all imports of provisions from the United Kingdom. The duties on butter of 40 to 45 per cent *ad valorem* hit Cork hardest. Cork butter exports to Lisbon reportedly plunged from 80,000 firkins in the early 1840s to only 16,000 firkins by 1852.[216] Although some of the slack was taken up by increased exports to Britain, the recovery of Cork butter prices in the late 1830s was not maintained in the following decade.[217]

Ireland had become a granary for Britain when the French succeeded in curbing British grain imports from Europe during the

---

[211] *Second report of the railway commission*, appendix B, pp. 73, 75.

[212] O'Donovan, *Econ. hist.*, p. 155; Spillar, *Bandon union*, pp. 36–7.

[213] O'Donovan, *Econ. hist.*, p. 285.

[214] Inglis, *Ire. in 1834*, p. 107.

[215] More than 209,000 firkins were exported in 1825, but the destination of exports was indicated only for that number (*Report from the select committee on the butter trade of Ireland*, H.C. 1826 (406), v, 135, p. 90).

[216] *C.E.*, 13 Oct. 1852.

[217] O'Donovan, *Econ. hist.*, p. 444.

wars, especially at the height of Napoleon's power between 1807 and 1813.[218] But the restoration of Britain's grain trade with Europe after 1813 and increased cereal production in both Britain and Ireland caused prices to fall, even though the corn laws protected farmers from the full effects of foreign competition. Through a system of heavy duties, the corn laws insured that alternative foreign supplies were kept out during years of abundant harvests and brought in during years of scarcity only when the prices of home supplies reached remunerative levels, under both the fixed scale of duties of 1815 and the sliding scales of 1822 and 1828.[219] Irish cereal producers had as much interest in the maintenance of a protected home market as their British counterparts. Their difficulties up to the late 1830s were largely due to the wild fluctuations of home supplies, for the demand was constantly growing. Between 1815 and 1836 the total population of England and Wales increased from about 11 million to almost 15 million. This growing population 'was fed from home supplies, with no sustained help from imports and clearly without the per capita consumption of foodstuffs falling much, if indeed it fell at all'.[220] Cereal producers suffered, however, when bumper harvests alternating with dreary ones produced violent price fluctuations which the corn-law restrictions exacerbated.[221] Even before the corn laws were repealed in 1846, breaches were made in the protective wall by a reduction of the duties on foreign corn in 1842 and by a grant of favoured status to Canadian wheat and flour in 1843.[222]

Changing price and market conditions might have been expected to reorient Irish agriculture away from corn growing and towards the production of store cattle and sheep much more quickly than they did eventually. Several factors favoured such a reorientation before the late 1830s. The cereal grower's variable costs of production and his difficulties in covering fixed costs were certainly greater at the outset of the deflation than those of the livestock producer.[223] This was especially true between 1815 and 1824, when tilled land alone was burdened with the payment of tithes (one of the heaviest variable costs), amounting to as much as 10s. per Irish acre for

[218] W. H. B. Court, *A concise economic history of Britain from 1750 to recent times* (Cambridge, 1964), p. 141.

[219] Lord Ernle, *English farming, past and present*, with introductions by G. E. Fussell and O. R. McGregor (6th ed., London and Chicago, 1961), pp. 270–4.

[220] Jones, *English agriculture*, p. 13.

[221] Lord Ernle, *English farming*, p. 271.

[222] Ibid., p. 495.

[223] Crotty, *Irish agricultural production*, pp. 35–6.

wheat and potatoes and to 7s. or 8s. for oats.[224] The expansion of pasture farming was also favoured by the introduction of the steamship in the cross-channel livestock trade in 1825 and by the availability of rail transport to British inland centres beginning in the 1830s. Steam and rail largely diminished the former deterioration in the weight of livestock during shipment.[225] The returns to farmers at least were certainly greater in shipping live cattle and sheep to Britain without any processing costs than in selling them to Irish provision merchants whose foreign markets were contracting.[226] There is some evidence that the prices of store stock, particularly sheep, were much more buoyant by the 1830s than is suggested by beef and mutton prices, which were those paid by the declining provision trade.[227] If store-stock prices were actually more buoyant, it was probably due to slowly rising British living standards, which in the long run were by far the most important factor in the reorientation of Irish agriculture. Citing these factors as evidence of a dramatic change in market conditions by the 1820s, Crotty has argued that while the expansion of grassland and the contraction of tillage were economically desirable, 'the population position made such a change not merely difficult but impossible'.[228] Broadly, this analysis is very plausible. The altered market conditions, however, probably did not take effect until the 1830s. And the obstacles to the readjustment of agriculture should also include the tremendous possibilities for labour economies latent within pre-famine tillage farming as well as the demonstrated capacity greatly to expand cereal output in response to the deflation.

The collapse of cereal prices between 1818 and 1822 and the drastic decline in the prices of Irish provisions called for the reduction of wartime rents. Those landed proprietors who let their estates mainly or exclusively to the occupying tenants rather than to middlemen were hit hard by the fall in their rental incomes after 1815. The earl of Mountcashel, a hopelessly indebted aristocrat as a result of lavish living and an untrustworthy agent's embezzlement, claimed in April 1846 that rents increased during the Napoleonic wars had to be reduced by 50 per cent soon after the peace.[229] Despite excessive competition for farms caused by the population explosion,[230] rents did fall after 1815, though scarcely to the extent

[224] A. Macintyre, *The liberator: Daniel O'Connell and the Irish party, 1830–1847* (London, 1965), pp. 170–1.

[225] O'Donovan, *Econ. hist.*, p. 213.

[226] Crotty, *Irish agricultural production*, p. 36.

[227] Ibid., pp. 287–93.   [228] Ibid., p. 37.

[229] *C.C.*, 16 Apr. 1846.

[230] P.R.O.I., ref. no. 978, Midleton papers: Charles Bailey's summary

suggested by Mountcashel. (The rents of cottiers undoubtedly rose, but such tenants actually paid a small percentage of total rents.)[231] In 1819 the rental of Sir John Anderson's 2,600-acre estate, located in the rich grazing district of Buttevant, had to be pared nearly 40 per cent below the level of 1812.[232] The rental of George Hodder's Fountainstown estate was placed at £1,100 in 1822, and in a revealing note it was flatly stated, 'This is considered the present value of [the] land, the rents being reduced more than z from what they were set [at] 20 years ago'.[233] These rent reductions by Anderson and Hodder are probably extreme examples of the general trend. More typical no doubt was the duke of Devonshire's temporary abatement of 25 per cent first given in 1822 'upon all lands in the occupation of tenants holding them' and continued until 1842.[234] Middlemen enjoying large profit rents were carefully excluded from the abatement made on the Devonshire estates.

Little positive evidence exists to show that intermediate gentry-landlords were forced by the depression to grant similar concessions to their tenants. The general unwillingness of head landlords to abate the rents of middlemen made it at least unlikely that middlemen, in a spasm of generosity, would substantially lower the rents of cottiers and small farmers. On the other hand, there is considerable negative evidence suggesting either that profit rents shrank between 1815 and 1845 because of reductions, or that if war rents were maintained, heavy default ensued, bringing about smaller profit rents *de facto* and often insolvency.[235] On the earl of Bandon's estates, several gentlemen, who held large tracts which they had partly sublet at a profit, fell hopelessly into arrears between 1815 and 1845 and had to surrender their leases for three lives long before

[231] Crotty, *Irish agricultural production*, pp. 51–3.

[232] Doneraile papers: Rental and valuation of Sir John Anderson's Buttevant estate, 1825, sent to William Hill, Viscount Doneraile's agent, 25 Mar. 1826.

[233] Hodder papers: Draft settlement of the Hodder family estates, 1822 (in the possession of Miss Phyllis Hodder, Fountainstown House, Fountainstown, Co. Cork).

[234] Lismore papers, N.L.I., MS 6929: Rent receipts and disbursements, 1818–90; *Devon comm. evidence*, pt iii, pp. 183–4.

[235] For an illuminating example of an intermediate landlord caught between a pressing head landlord and defaulting undertenants, see F. S. L. Lyons, 'Vicissitudes of a middleman in County Leitrim, 1810–27' in *I. H. S.*, ix, no. 35 (Mar. 1955), pp. 300–18.

report on the valuation of the Midleton estates, 6 Apr. 1840; Lismore papers, N.L.I., MS 7183, Letter book, 1842–50: F. E. Currey to B. Currey, 17 Oct. 1844, pp. 95–7.

these might have been expected to expire.[236] To his delight, Sir John Benn-Walsh discovered in the early 1820s that the middleman of Derrindaff was an 'embarrassed, insolvent man, [who] had mortgaged & encumbered the estate so deeply & to so many parties that . . . no single individual was in a position to pay up the arrear, & that they would never combine to do so'. When the agent served a warrant for the recovery of the arrears, the middleman failed to redeem and was dispossessed.[237] Few middlemen on the earl of Egmont's estates were prospering in the early 1830s. When an attempt was being made to sell these estates in 1832, it was thought at first that some of the middlemen would wish to become owners in fee. After testing the waters, however, William Nicholls was forced to abandon this plan: 'My idea that some of the lessees would become purchasers I have given up; they have not the means'.[238] Charles Bailey strongly recommended in 1840 that Viscount Midleton rid himself of the middlemen Thomas and George Courtney, who held 440 acres under an old lease for lives at £138 per annum, subletting most of the land to fourteen other tenants at £230 per annum. Said Bailey acidly:

The Messrs Courtney are fox-hunting squires. . . . The payment of rent should not be enforced until Christmas next, and then an ejectment should be brought to destroy the lease. The lessees could not redeem without paying *all* the arrears [£650] which they have so unjustly withheld.[239]

R. H. Popham, a large middleman on the duke of Devonshire's Bandon estate, finally had to be evicted from his holdings in 1843, after six years' rent had accumulated on one farm and as much as ten years' rent on another. The resident agent Alexander Swanston noted that 'the total loss to the duke of Devonshire was nearly £600'.[240]

Even when gentry-middlemen paid their rents punctually between 1815 and 1845, this system of intermediate lettings involved the proprietors in an enormous loss of income. The earl of Shelburne,

[236] Doherty papers: Schedule of leases on the earl of Bandon's estates, 1864; see under Branagh, Ballymountain, Currowrane, Castletown, Gurtnaskarty, Raharoon, Shanaway, and West Toames.

[237] Ormathwaite papers: Journal of Sir John Benn-Walsh, 12 Sept. 1855, p. 158 (in the possession of Lord Ormathwaite, Penybont Hall, Llandrindod Wells, Radnorshire, Wales).

[238] Barry papers, *Egmont v. Darell, documents of respondents:* W. Nicholls to Currie and Co., 29 June 1832, pp. 90-1.

[239] P.R.O.I., ref. no. 978, Midleton papers: Valuation of Viscount Midleton's estates, 1840, pp. 246-7.

[240] Lismore papers, N.L.I., MS 7127: Bandon memorandum book, 1839-43, p. 109.

the owner of vast estates in Kerry, had remarked as early as 1791 that one of the cardinal lessons he had learned from thirty years' experience of managing property in Ireland was to grant no long tenures to middlemen. He wrote:

There are not only all the reasons against it in Ireland that have been already stated against it in England, but this strong additional one, that in Ireland nothing has taken its value, and everything is necessarily in a more progressive [i.e., appreciating] state than in England. [241]

The windfall profits enjoyed by leaseholders during the French wars must have been unrelieved agony to those proprietors whose rent rolls were largely frozen by long leases. Although they often had to reduce the rents charged by middlemen from ephemeral wartime levels, landowners still eagerly awaited the expiration of old leases to middlemen after 1815, because land values were much greater than at the time when most of these leases had first been granted. Sir John Benn-Walsh avidly discussed with his bailiff in the early 1820s 'which of my farms was nearest to me, by which he [i.e., the bailiff] meant which would soonest revert to me by the determination of the middleman's interest'. [242] Rents amounting to only £1,239 were reserved in the four leases dating back to the 1760s and held by the middlemen who were in possession of the entire Cork estate in the early 1820s. Benn-Walsh calculated, however, that the land was worth at least double that figure in 1829. [243] Other Cork landowners plagued by middlemen were making similar discoveries. William Nicholls noted in 1827 that the reserved rents on the earl of Egmont's estates at Kanturk and Churchtown amounted to only £7,757. If the lands could all have been newly let at current prices, Nicholls calculated that their annual value would have risen to as much as £12,759, and the prices Nicholls adopted to make his valuation were, as he said, 'fair average' ones. [244] Charles Bailey strongly advised Viscount Midleton in 1840 to grant 'no more life leases or renewals of leases for lives on the demesne lands', which

---

[241] Marquis of Lansdowne, *Glanerought and the Petty-Fitzmaurices* (London and New York, 1937), p. 108.

[242] Ormathwaite papers: Journal of Sir John Benn-Walsh, 12 Sept. 1855, p. 157.

[243] As a result of the termination of middlemen's leases, and of improvements Benn-Walsh subsequently made or encouraged his tenants to make, the rental of his estates in both Cork and Kerry rose from £3,439 in 1829 to £5,317 by 1847, an increase of 35 per cent (ibid.: Account of the property and income of Sir John Benn-Walsh, 1829–66).

[244] Barry papers, *Egmont v. Darell, documents of respondents*: General reports of William Nicholls on the Kanturk and Churchtown estates, 20 Oct. 1827, pp. 80, 85.

included all the agricultural property. Although the rental of the demesne lands was then only £16,358, Bailey estimated that their annual value, if new lettings at current prices could have been made in all cases, would have nearly doubled to £28,966. He saw good reason to hope, however, that the situation would soon improve:

Many of the farms and houses . . . are held by tenants for one, two, or three lives at rents, in most cases, grossly inadequate to the real value, but the advanced ages of many of the lives will admit of the fair presumption that such holdings will soon become extinct, when by ordinary care in the consolidation of many of the small ones, the subdividing of others, and the selection of good tenants, rents approximating the real value may be realized. [245]

THE REFORM OF ESTATE ADMINISTRATION

Falling rents and the middleman system's postponement of larger rent rolls were the proximate causes of the much more vigorous management of Irish estates that became clearly visible in the 1830s and early 1840s. In order to increase their rents, or at least to make the payment of them more certain and secure, landowners began to show a strong desire to eliminate middlemen, consolidate small and scattered farms, stop subdivision and subletting, and execute badly needed permanent improvements. The two decades before the famine were marked by the expiration of a great number of old leases held by middlemen, even though many were still outstanding in 1845. Sir John Benn-Walsh purchased the interest in the mid-1820s of one middleman who had held almost half his 2,200-acre Cork estate but did not recover the remainder until after the famine. [246] Benn-Walsh was more fortunate, however, with his 9,900-acre Kerry property. Here middlemen had also been long entrenched under leases for three lives granted by his great-uncle during the last third of the eighteenth century. Most of the land was recovered before the famine, but the last middleman was not eliminated until 1851. [247] The commissioners of woods and forests immediately assumed the direct management of the 5,000-acre crown estate near Kingwilliamstown when the middleman's ninety-nine-year lease

---

[245] P.R.O.I., ref. no. 978, Midleton papers: Charles Bailey's summary report on the valuation of the Midleton estates, 6 Apr. 1840.

[246] Ormathwaite papers: Account of the property and income of Sir John Benn-Walsh, 1829–66; ibid.: Journal of Sir John Benn-Walsh, 17 Aug. 1850, pp. 164–6.

[247] Ibid.: Journal of Sir John Benn-Walsh, 6 and 7 Oct. 1848, pp. 76–7; Journal, 23 Aug. 1851, pp. 132–6; Journal, 12 Sept. 1855, p. 158.

expired about 1830.[248] James Carnegie reported that on one of the Cork estates he managed, a 3,000-acre tract 'which was held by a middleman, and by him under-let to a number of miserable tenants, came into the hands of the head landlord [in 1835] by the expiration of the lease'.[249] Middlemen holding 7,350 acres on the earl of Kenmare's Bantry estate saw their leases run out between 1835 and 1844.[250] The agent Thomas Foley reported that there were only about twenty middlemen remaining on Viscount Midleton's estates by 1844, even though the majority of Midleton's immediate tenants had been middlemen as recently as the late 1820s.[251]

With few exceptions, landowners refused to renew the leases of middlemen after 1815.[252] Christopher Gallwey remarked before the Devon commission in 1844 that several years earlier

Lord Kenmare laid down, as rules for my future guidance, 'that whenever a middleman's lease fell in, I should re-let the lands to such of the resident tenantry, of good character and industrious habits, as I found upon the land. That in future there should be no tenant between himself and the actual occupier of the soil.'[253]

'There are many middlemen through the country,' said Daniel Leahy, the agent of both the earl of Cork and Orrery and the earl of Shannon, 'but it is generally the wish of proprietors now to let to the occupier as far as it can be carried out.'[254] Such a policy had been widely implemented, with the result that the majority of Cork tenants probably held directly from the landowner on the eve of the famine. There were said in 1844 to be 'not many' middlemen left on the Colthurst estates, only 'some' with very old leases on the Aldworth property near Newmarket, and 'none' on the estates of the earl of Cork or Lord Lisle.[255]

Once middlemen had been eradicated, landed proprietors and their agents were confronted with the problem of the cottiers and smallholders. In order to improve the methods of cultivation, to expand pasture farming, and to secure adequate rents, the removal of the excess population from the land seemed imperative. Of course,

[248] *Copies of papers relating to experimental improvements in progress on the crown lands at King William's Town, in the barony of Duhallow, in the county of Cork . . .*, p. 60.
[249] *Devon comm. digest*, i, 463.
[250] *Devon comm. evidence*, pt iii, pp. 736–8.
[251] Ibid., pt iii, p. 197.
[252] Some Cork landowners had refused to renew such leases before 1815. For evidence of this, see Young, *Tour in Ire.*, i, 459, 462–3.
[253] *Devon comm. evidence*, pt iii, p. 736.
[254] Ibid., pt iii, p. 11.
[255] Ibid., pt iii, pp. 71, 90. See also ibid., pt iii, pp. 46, 52, 172.

such a socially disruptive goal could hardly be aired publicly, but there is no doubt that suitable strategy and tactics were being formulated. Charles Bailey's report on Viscount Midleton's estate in 1840 bristled with potentially explosive recommendations. Whenever fitting opportunities presented themselves, Bailey advised making single farms of separate holdings then in the possession of nineteen subtenants in one case, sixty-three occupiers in another, and eleven undertenants in a third.[256] He thus dismissed summarily a 560-acre holding occupied by seventeen tenants: 'The whole should be laid down to pasture and kept as sheep walks. All the tenants are under notice to quit in consequence of their bad management and non-payment of rent.'[257] Bailey could scarcely have been more emphatic about one large townland of 430 acres, held jointly by nine tenants who farmed their lands scandalously and owed staggering arrears of rent: 'The arrear due the late viscount in respect of these lands was £5,447 9s. 0d.!! and to the present viscount £1,037 17s. 1d.!!! All the miserable cabins should be destroyed, and the townland divided into two farms.'[258]

A large gap existed, however, between the penchant for consolidation and its achievement before the famine. The cold fear of provoking agrarian outrage restrained many landowners altogether and narrowly restricted the operations of others. Ordinarily, agrarian disturbances were rare in Cork, especially in contrast to the recurrent violence in neighbouring Tipperary. No less than 254 agrarian outrages were reportedly perpetrated in Tipperary during 1844 (slightly more than one-fourth of the total committed in that year throughout Ireland), as compared with only thirty-two in far more populous Cork.[259] The startling difference between the two counties was largely the consequence of the much greater difficulties faced by labourers and cottiers in obtaining adequate potato gardens and conacre at reasonable rents in the grazing county of Tipperary.[260] In Cork, however, the unpopular act of taking a holding from which the previous tenant had been evicted frequently invited violent reprisal. Charles McCarthy, a farmer near Bantry, stated before the Devon commission that the 'houghing', or maiming, of cattle and the burning of dwelling houses or out-offices had often occurred in his district, always as a result of 'having the old occupying tenants turned out'.[261]

[256] P.R.O.I., ref. no. 978, Midleton papers: Valuation of Viscount Midleton's estates, 1840, pp. 31–4, 50.
[257] Ibid., pp. 158–9.   [258] Ibid., p. 135.
[259] *Devon comm. digest*, i, 327.
[260] Ibid., i, 336.   [261] Ibid., i, 342.

One alternative available to landowners anxious to consolidate but fearful of outrage was assisted emigration. Charles Bailey told Viscount Midleton in 1840 that since the introduction of the poor law in 1838, the old urgent question, '*Where am I to go?*' eternally asked by evicted Irish tenants could now be answered as it was in England, '*Go to the union if you have no other resource for a maintenance*'. Bailey recognized, however, that with 'an overpopulation and no means of sufficient and profitable employment at the union house, a burthen is at once created in another altho' less objectionable shape', namely, poor rates. He therefore suggested that assisted emigration was 'the most reasonable mode of lessening the redundant population, by which alone the small holdings may be consolidated and made to form properly sized farms to command respectable and safe tenants'. He had learned, he said, that adults could be sent over to Canada for £3 per head, and children for as little as £1 or £2 (both these estimates were unrealistically low), and concluded by suggesting that £2,000 thus spent 'would be money judiciously and profitably laid out'. [262] Consolidation according to this plan was carried out systematically on the Midleton estates during the early 1840s. [263] It could not be done fast enough, however, to suit Lord Midleton's London solicitor, who charged in July 1842 that the new agent Thomas Foley was insufficiently aware of the injury that the head landlord suffered 'in having his property left covered with cottier tenants who, notwithstanding they are an absolute nuisance, are ever ready to claim compensation for fancied improvements'. [264] Foley replied indignantly:

You do me wrong in supposing that I am not impressed with the injury the landlord sustains 'in having his land covered with cottier tenants'. I am as fully aware of it as anyone can be & the number which I have removed during the last 3 years affords strong evidence on the subject. Indeed, I omit no opportunity of getting rid of them, but my long experience in the management of property in this country points out the necessity of doing so in the manner least objectionable to the habits & prejudices of the people. [265]

Despite the fact that Lord Midleton incurred 'a very great expense in sending to America all such as were disposed to emigrate', Foley's clearances aroused public indignation but apparently no

[262] P.R.O.I., ref. no. 978, Midleton papers: Charles Bailey's summary report on the valuation of the Midleton estates, 6 Apr. 1840.

[263] Guildford Muniment Room, Midleton papers: T. Foley to H. Marshall (extract and copy), 29 Sept. 1840; Marshall to Foley (extract and copy), 8 July 1842.

[264] Ibid.: Marshall to Foley (extract and copy), 23 July 1842.

[265] Ibid.: Foley to Marshall (extract and copy), 30 July 1842.

violent disturbances.[266] The earl of Kingston also consolidated many holdings on his Cork estate through assisted emigration, allegedly 'with great prudence and consideration for those involved'. About 200 families were reportedly sent to Upper Canada in the 'first emigration' before 1835 at the appreciable expense of £20 to £50 per family.[267]

Other consolidating landowners, however, discovered that their tenants were extremely reluctant to accept a prepaid passage to North America. Richard Longfield was accused in September 1844 of turning ninety-six people out of their holdings on his estate near Kanturk. According to Longfield, only forty-six people had left so far, and only two tenants had taken his offer of assisted emigration; the remaining evicted tenants had been forgiven one gale of rent and allowed to retain their holdings free of rent for six months to enable them to settle somewhere else.[268] H. R. Jackson, who reportedly ejected thirteen tenants from his property near Midleton about the same time, was also willing to assist them to emigrate to Canada. But the tenants allegedly said that 'if they were forgiven the half-year's rent then due, they would prefer staying at home'. Jackson consented to this and also permitted them to 'remain on their land for the following six months, without charge or cost, to enable them to try for some other places'.[269]

The fragmentation of holdings was much less acute on the duke of Devonshire's Cork and Waterford estates than on many other properties, thanks to careful management at least since the 1790s. Nevertheless, some consolidation was carried out when old leases expired. The agent of the duke's Bandon estate noted in 1843 that because the holding of the former middleman William Popham was 'in a very divided state . . . when the lease expired, it was necessary to remove these [six] tenants, to whom their lots were let for one year, the rent of which has been forgiven them, together with what rent they owed Mr Popham'.[270] The duke's chief agent F. E. Currey admitted before the Devon commission that it was a regular practice to expel the weakest tenants and annex their holdings to those of the strongest whenever land came out of lease in an overcrowded condition. Currey cited one case in which only two tenants out of

[266] Ibid.: 'Instances showing the position in which the head landlords of Ireland stand in reference to middlemen & sub-occupying tenants', by Henry Marshall, undated, *c.* 1842.

[267] *Poor inquiry, supplement to appendix F,* p. 183.

[268] *C.E.*, 2 Oct. 1844.

[269] Ibid. But see also ibid., 23 Sept., 4 Oct. 1844.

[270] Lismore papers, N.L.I., MS 7127: Bandon memorandum book, 1839–43, p. 110.

eleven were compelled to surrender their holdings; a second in which three out of fourteen had to leave; and a third in which as many as eight out of twenty-one were removed. This last case, he said, involved the highest proportion of undertenants ever dispossessed during the consolidation of a former middleman's holding.[271] The unfortunate smallholders were induced to depart peacefully by the cancellation of arrears and by the enjoyment of the last year's tenure of house and land free of rent, with liberty to carry away the timber and thatch of their cabins at the end. Physical eviction was rarely necessary, since failure quietly to surrender possession entailed the loss of even these meagre benefits.[272] Similar precautions were adopted on other properties. When the lease of 600 acres on Lady Boyle's estate near Kanturk terminated in 1844, the agent Daniel Leahy promptly reorganized the land into compact farms of thirty to forty acres. These he assigned to fifteen or twenty of the most respectable and industrious occupying tenants. Some of the other tenants became labourers on the enlarged farms, but most of them simply received small sums of money and the materials of their houses as an inducement to go away. The account of their dispossession, in which 'all the poor people' concerned were described as 'satisfied and pleased' with Leahy's arrangements, is highly improbable in view of the cottier's fanatical attachment to the smallest bit of ground. But what little was done for them was probably sufficient to weaken their natural urge to resist.[273]

Strangers to an estate were rarely accepted as new tenants for evicted farms, because such action would have substantially increased the possibility of an outrage. It was considered much more prudent to confine new arrangements to existing tenants. William Bence Jones boasted of the clever way in which he kept public opinion on his side when he evicted six or eight tenants from his estate near Clonakilty shortly before the famine:

Every good tenant soon found out that a broken tenant being put out might mean a substantial gain to himself, one very dear to his heart; he got the field close to his own house that he had coveted all his life, his very Naboth's vineyard....[274]

Christopher Gallwey, the earl of Kenmare's agent, stated before the Devon commission that he invariably relet consolidated holdings 'to those tenants who are willing to offer the rent I fix upon it...,

[271] *Devon comm. evidence*, pt iii, p. 186.
[272] Ibid., pt iii, p. 185.
[273] *C.E.*, 25 Feb. 1845.
[274] Jones, *Life's work*, p. 102.

provided they had previously been living upon the land'.[275] It was reported in October 1844 that 230 persons had been evicted from Kenmare's Bantry estate and that seventy others were under notice to quit. This report was not denied; it was simply emphasized that occupying tenants were always preferred to strangers when old leases expired.[276]

Some consolidating landowners overrode popular resentment against their clearances by retaining the land in their own possession for a number of years until the storm subsided. Pierce Nagle evicted some 280 persons from his estate near Mallow between 1827 and 1843, leaving him by the latter date with approximately 1,000 plantation acres in his own hands and only about 300 in those of tenants.[277] St John Jeffreys began to amalgamate holdings on his Blarney estate in the early 1830s in order to drain permanently the lands taken up, and by 1844 he seems to have had about 1,000 acres in his possession.[278] When the middleman's lease of a 96-acre holding on the Foott estate at Carrigacunna expired in November 1843, the land was occupied by six families of farmers and twenty-six families of cottiers and labourers. Foott graciously allowed one of the farmers, who had served as his steward for the past forty years, to retain his own small lot. But he placed all the other families, including 167 persons altogether, under notice to quit, granting them the 'great boon' of carrying away the timber and thatch if they would tumble their wretched cabins themselves.[279] Foott intended to retain possession of at least half the land recovered.[280]

During consolidation, landowners and agents occasionally found it expedient to remove the smallest tenants to other and usually poorer land. G. Standish Barry asserted in 1835 that he had enlarged the farms on his property near Midleton 'to a great extent, but by degrees'. He had 'provided the former tenants and occupiers of small houses with land and sites to build upon, in part of this parish [Lisgoold] or on my property in adjoining ones'.[281] When a large tract on an estate near Macroom came out of lease in 1823, it was covered with 'a number of miserable cottiers' who 'dragged the life and soul out of the ground'. The agent James Carnegie removed the cottiers somewhere else, giving each of them a house and five or six acres of land at a nominal rent during their own lives and reletting

[275] *Devon comm. evidence*, pt iii, p. 739.
[276] *C.E.*, 25 Oct. 1844.
[277] *Devon comm. evidence*, pt iii, pp. 131–3.
[278] Ibid., pt iii, p. 3.
[279] *C.E.*, 9 Feb. 1844.
[280] *Devon comm. evidence*, pt iii, pp. 132–3.
[281] *Poor inquiry, supplement to appendix F*, p. 170.

the land recovered in larger units to solvent tenants.[282] Under similar circumstances in 1835, Carnegie again removed the smallest occupiers, this time to holdings of twenty to fifty acres requiring reclamation on the mountains nearby. He freely admitted the great difficulties that he had initially faced in persuading these tenants to accept their reduced status. In fact, he was providing out of his own pocket the money that enabled them to drain and reclaim their holdings.[283]

Consolidation was useless unless subletting and subdivision could be halted. When landowners were or became the masters of their own estates after 1815, they and their agents increasingly opposed these twin evils. Lord Arden induced the tenants on his 5,000-acre estate between Mallow and Kanturk to surrender their leases, which were wide open to abuse, by reducing their rents to as little as 5s. 9d. per acre, even though the land was probably worth three times as much in the mid-1820s. A 'particular requirement' of this exceptionally low rent was that the tenants never sublet or subdivide.[284] Soon after becoming agent of the 23,000-acre Colthurst estates in 1842, Peter Fitzgerald carefully instructed his bailiffs to make certain that there were no additional houses built on any farm. He also sent every tenant a plainly worded letter in which, among other things, they were strictly warned against subdivision.[285] Other Cork landowners were grappling with this problem in the early 1840s. Subletting was an issue in the evictions on the Jackson estate mentioned earlier. Jackson discovered that a number of unauthorized persons

were brought to live on the lands, contrary to his agreement with the tenants . . . , and to such tenants and to all those they brought on the lands, he gave notice that they would not be allowed to remain any longer . . . after the expiration of their term.[286]

Two brothers on Sir William Wrixon Becher's estate near Skibbereen had received unequal portions of their father's farm. After they had quarrelled bitterly over the division for some years past, Becher's bailiff suddenly evicted one of the brothers in January 1843, unroofing his house in the process. Allegedly as a result, the evicted tenant's wife was delivered shortly afterwards of a stillborn child and became deranged.[287]

[282] *Devon comm. digest*, i, 463.
[283] Ibid., i, 463–4.
[284] *Devon comm. evidence*, pt iii, pp. 142–4.
[285] Ibid., pt iii, pp. 73–4.
[286] *C.E.*, 2 Oct. 1844. See also ibid., 4 Oct. 1844.
[287] Ibid., 18 Jan. 1843.

The tenant in question and his brother [Becher publicly explained] have long been at variance, which was one reason for my having recourse to the ejectment; if anything wrong has been done . . . , it is likely to be the act of the brother than of any person employed by me. [288]

A few years later Becher was attacked by a local parish priest for threatening to evict another tenant who had brought a son-in-law to live with her upon her daughter's marriage. 'I am already well acquainted', replied Becher in February 1846, 'with the widow Cadogan's case, who was to be dispossessed of her farm if she persevered in subdividing or subletting it contrary to agreement.' [289]

The duke of Devonshire's agents worked diligently to prevent subdivision and subletting. One tenant on the duke's Bandon estate who sought a building allowance, but who had sublet part of his farm, was told pointedly in January 1839 that the matter simply could not be considered until he had all the land in his own hands. [290] In July 1840 Alexander Swanston sternly warned another tenant who had split his farm with his son upon the latter's marriage that 'unless the family come to some arrangement . . . by which the ground shall be entirely surrendered to one or the other, a notice to quit will be served before Sept. 29th'. [291] In one instance two brothers who had each received a portion of their uncle's farm, the lease of which was about to expire, were bluntly informed in July 1841 that only one of them could possibly be accepted as tenant for the whole farm once the lease fell in. [292] In another case where a father had bequeathed his holding to two sons jointly, Swanston advised the younger son that he would permit him to 'continue in the house with his brother for the present, but as he can never have any claim to the ground, he should look out for some place for himself, which they both promise shall be done'. [293] The duke's chief agent was equally vigilant on the Kinnatalloon property. Two brothers who had each been given a portion of their father's holding upon their marriage quickly learned that 'this was not allowed, and that if one of them did not leave, the property would be taken up'. [294] After much wrangling between the two brothers, one finally did

[288] Ibid., 23 Jan. 1843.
[289] Sir W. W. Becher to Rev. J. B. Noonan, 10 Feb. 1846, quoted ibid., 23 Feb. 1846.
[290] Lismore papers, N.L.I., MS 7127: Bandon memorandum book, 1839–43, p. 8.
[291] Ibid., p. 41.
[292] Ibid., p. 44.
[293] Ibid., p. 45.
[294] Ibid., MS 7122: Particulars of lettings, 1839–47, p. 10.

leave, receiving £30 from the other.[295] The agent was forced to evict another tenant in 1841 when he persisted in dividing his farm with his sons.[296]

Not all Cork landowners, however, were brave enough to defy the local outcries that often followed the rigid enforcement of a policy against subdivision and subletting. Richard White, the owner of a large estate near Bantry, had inserted stringent clauses against these abuses in some of his leases since 1832 but had not enforced them. 'In fact,' said White, 'I think it is a dangerous thing in Ireland to do it.'[297] William Collis complained that while he and other landowners well understood the evil of subdivision, they could not prevent it 'except by the most rigid and unpopular means'; the odium 'that is attached to a landlord, under any circumstances, for dispossessing a tenant' restrained them from taking effective action.[298] Most new leases granted since the 1820s contained covenants strictly forbidding both subdivision and subletting upon pain of forfeiture or payment of a penal rent.[299] Moreover, the subletting act of 1826 had the effect of inserting in every lease made subsequently a non-alienation clause as stringent as the legal mind could devise, even though the lessors may not actually have included such a clause.[300] Some landowners, however, found it too bothersome and expensive to enforce their legal rights. Thomas Ware claimed in 1844 that because 'the remedy afforded by law is so difficult of attaining', landlords were 'generally obliged to yield' to alienation.[301] Prosperous tenants could afford to contest the question in the courts, where the juries were notoriously partial to their cause. Thomas Foley remarked in July 1844 that it had been found 'useless to adopt English forms in granting leases to Irish tenantry from the reluctance or rather refusal of Irish juries to find for the plaintiff in penal actions for breaches of covenant'.[302] Only a small minority

[295] Ibid., p. 35. See also ibid., p. 40.
[296] Ibid., p. 41. See also *Devon comm. digest*, i, 441.
[297] White also stated, however, that 'subletting upon my estate is carried out to a very slight extent compared to others' (*Devon comm. digest*, i, 424).
[298] Ibid., i, 434.
[299] Doneraile papers: Lease to John Sullivan, 24 Mar. 1827; Lease to William McGarry, 29 Feb. 1845; Kingston papers: Leases to various tenants, 1815–45 (in the possession of Moore, Keily, and Lloyd, Solicitors, 31 Molesworth St., Dublin). For the earl of Listowel's leases, see *C.E.*, 2 Feb. 1846.
[300] 7 Geo. 4, c. 29.
[301] *Devon comm. digest*, i, 433.
[302] Guildford Muniment Room, Midleton papers: T. Foley to H. Marshall (extract and copy), 18 July 1844.

of farmers, however, would have dared to risk the possibly fateful consequences of a full-scale legal battle with their landlords. Aided by the much slower population growth of the 1830s and early 1840s, the spreading landlord policy of vigilance and timely warning as well as the growing determination to evict recalcitrant tenants probably halted the previous trend toward partition by 1845.

Investment in long-term agricultural improvements, including dwelling houses, farm offices, and drainage, was seriously neglected between 1815 and 1845. Before 1815 landed proprietors had almost entirely delegated the responsibility for investment to either middlemen or tenant farmers (whenever the latter held directly from the proprietor). Both of these groups generally enjoyed leases with terms long enough to afford more than ample security for a reasonable return on investment of a permanent character.[303] The withholding of capital from investment in agriculture after 1815 was usually attributed to the middleman system and to the widespread feeling of insecurity generated by yearly tenancies.

If . . . the farms are now without roads—if agriculture is backward, the soil impoverished, and the resident tenantry ill clothed and ill housed [said the land agent Christopher Gallwey in 1844], I may justly attribute such evils to the conduct of these middlemen, who, deriving a large profit from the lands, returned no part of that profit to the renovation or increase of its resources.[304]

Whether because the tide was running increasingly against the renewal of their leases, or simply because they were relatively poor gentlemen, middlemen had failed to spend much money on improvements. The commissioners of woods and forests complained bitterly in 1834 of the middlemen's neglect of the Kingwilliamstown estate. During a ninety-nine-year tenure,

not a single shilling had been expended by the crown lessees in any substantial improvement: the entire property was precisely in the same condition in which it had been demised a century before, without roads, drains, plantations, fences, or other works to adapt it for cultivation.[305]

The O'Donovan leased a large farm on his 2,700-acre estate near Skibbereen to Michael Atteridge for two lives in 1840. When Atteridge sought a temporary abatement in October 1843 to compensate for low prices,[306] The O'Donovan made a small

[303] Cullen, *Anglo-Ir. trade*, pp. 6–7.
[304] *Devon comm. evidence*, pt iii, p. 735.
[305] *Copies of papers relating to experimental improvements in progress on the crown lands at King William's Town, in the barony of Duhallow, in the county of Cork . . .* , p. 60.
[306] The O'Donovan papers: Rental of The O'Donovan's estate, Carbery only, 1839–69; A. Atteridge to The O'Donovan, 29 Oct. 1843 (in the possession of The O'Donovan, Hollybrook House, Skibbereen, Co. Cork).

reduction but added in a letter to Michael's father, Arthur Atteridge:

I was led to expect that either by his residence on . . . [this land] or by his holding a portion of it in his own occupation, he would have furnished an example of improvement and good farming to his neighbours and country. In this it appears I have been altogether disappointed. [307]

Sir John Benn-Walsh's estates suffered similarly from the middle-men's neglect. The Killarida farm was held upon the written promise of a lease for three lives, with power to nominate two more when these dropped, but on the explicit condition that £400 would be spent on improvements, chiefly embankments of riverine land. No money, however, was ever laid out between 1778 and 1851. [308] And the Derrindaff farm, held by a middleman named Wall upon a 1790 lease at an annual rent of £180, was a 'perfect illustration of the evils of the middlemen's rule' when Benn-Walsh first saw it in 1822:

Wall had never resided on the farm a bit more than I had myself. He had sublet it to about twenty occupying tenants at a rent of . . . £250. . . . The idea of improving the farm was never in his head for a moment, or in those of the tenants. [309]

While the middleman system clearly led to the neglect of perma-nent improvements, it is much less certain that yearly tenancies had the same result. Admittedly, annual tenancy became the more common type of tenure between 1815 and 1845. Only sixty-three of the 172 farms in the parish of Kilmurry near Macroom were held on lease by the early 1840s; the remaining 109 were all held from year to year. [310] Short leases for a concurrent term of twenty-one years and one life were common enough on the duke of Devon-shire's estates, but, said the chief agent in 1844, 'more in number hold as yearly tenants than under leases'. [311] The earl of Mountcashel, the owner of a large estate near Fermoy, asserted that many tenants held by lease in his district, 'but a great number from year to year'. [312] The reasons for the prevalence of annual tenancy are fairly obvious. The number of smallholders had multiplied enormously since 1800. Few middlemen or landowners considered it prudent to grant leases to such poor and slovenly tenants, who, in any case, could scarcely

[307] Ibid.: The O'Donovan to A. Atteridge, 1 Nov. 1843.
[308] Ormathwaite papers: Journal of Sir John Benn-Walsh, 23 Aug. 1851 pp. 133–4.
[309] Ibid.: Journal, 12 Sept. 1855, pp. 154–5.
[310] Freeman, *Pre-famine Ireland*, pp. 146–7.
[311] *Devon comm. digest*, i, 278.
[312] Ibid., i, 287.

have afforded the expensive luxury of taking out a lease. As the middleman system was eradicated after 1815, the head landlords gained a set of direct tenants who agreed to hold their land as yearly tenants. Because their estates had suffered grievously from the prevalence of long leases in the past, many landowners reacted strongly against all leases after 1815. Asked before the Devon commission how his large estate near Kanturk was principally let, Richard Longfield replied: 'Generally on lease; but I think there is a degree of objection now and dislike to letting on lease that formerly did not exist. Many of the farms let on very old leases are in a very bad state.'[313] Even though Charles Bailey had strongly urged Viscount Midleton that 'leases for 7, 10, or 14 years should be granted to good and responsible tenants' once the many old leases for lives had expired,[314] nothing was done to implement such a policy during the early 1840s. Lord Midleton was reluctantly willing to grant short leases for terms of either seven or fourteen years 'in consideration of his non-residence', but they would be leases replete with penal covenants to guard against a repetition of past abuses.[315] His agent Thomas Foley regarded this as highly impractical, however, because few tenants would incur the expense of perfecting any lease for a term of only fourteen years. Foley was firmly convinced that

taking into consideration the generally impoverished state of the land in this country, a term of 14 years would not hold out sufficient inducement to a solvent tenant to improve his farm or afford him time to be repaid his expenditure in case he should do so.

Foley therefore recommended a minimum term of twenty-one years.[316] This simply brought the whole matter to a standstill.

Although the swelling number of annual tenancies probably retarded investment in permanent improvements to some extent after 1815, the importance of this factor has been exaggerated.[317] Cottiers and smallholders, who least enjoyed security of tenure, and who doubtless felt increasingly insecure as they anxiously watched the consolidation of holdings taking place all around them, were not

---

[313] Ibid., i, 274.

[314] P.R.O.I., ref. no. 978, Midleton papers: Charles Bailey's summary report on the valuation of the Midleton estates, 6 Apr. 1840.

[315] Guildford Muniment Room, Midleton papers: 'Observations as to the non-payment of the rents and the better collection of them for the future, addressed to Mr Foley by Lord Midleton's desire', June 1844; H. Marshall to T. Foley (extráct and copy), 7 July 1844.

[316] Ibid.: Foley to Marshall (extract and copy), 18 July 1844.

[317] E.g., by Green, 'Agriculture', pp. 91–2.

discouraged by this from reclaiming great tracts of waste land between 1815 and 1845.[318] Landlords were often criticized for raising the rent whenever yearly tenants increased the value of their holdings through their own improvements. But many of them took steps to reassure farmers that their industry would not be penalized in this way. One of the duke of Devonshire's tenants offered in 1840 to construct a new slated barn and a labourer's house if the agent 'would say that the thing should not be valued upon him'. W. S. Currey promptly reminded him that 'such buildings were never valued on the duke's tenants, and he was satisfied with this and will build'.[319] Another tenant on Devonshire's Bandon estate claimed in 1841 that he had spent £350 to improve his farm and complained that he now had to face the revaluation carried out as a matter of course every twenty-one years. The agent expressed surprise at this complaint, for 'he must be aware that it was not usual to take any unfair advantage of a tenant's improvements, and he had better furnish me with as exact an account as he can of his expenditure in detail, which he says he will do'.[320] Shortly after becoming agent of W. H. Massy's sadly neglected estate near Macroom in 1842, James Carnegie learned that the tenants 'had no leases of their lands, and should therefore feel unwilling to go to any expense for another'. To stimulate improvement, Carnegie reportedly put a lease 'into the hands of mostly every tenant on the estate'.[321] And Lord Lisle informed his tenants near Kanturk in May 1845 that he had explicitly instructed his agent to 'have leases immediately prepared for such of you as may not have already got them, as I deem it but fair my tenants should have security for their improvements'.[322]

Falling farm incomes after 1815 were probably a far more important factor in hindering investment than the swollen number of annual tenancies. With or without a lease, tenants needed to be prodded sharply before they would spend money on long-term improvements while their economic prospects remained bleak. James Carnegie, who managed several Cork estates in addition to W. H. Massy's, utilized a drastic device. He gave leases for a concurrent term of three lives and thirty-one years but fixed extremely high rents. 'Suppose I value a farm at £50 a year rent', he asserted in 1844, 'I let it at £100 a year; then I state the improvements to be

[318] Crotty, *Irish agricultural production*, p. 54.

[319] Lismore papers, N.L.I., MS 7122: Particulars of lettings, 1839–47, p. 18.

[320] Ibid., MS 7127: Bandon memorandum book, 1839–43, p. 75.

[321] *C.E.*, 19 Aug. 1842. See also ibid., 16 Dec. 1842.

[322] Viscount Lisle to tenants of Kanturk estate, 7 May 1845, quoted ibid., 14 May 1845.

made every year, and if they are made then I take £50 a year.' Asked if he had given many such leases, and if tenants accepted them willingly, Carnegie replied firmly that 'every lease since I have had the management of the property has been of that description'. He confessed that some tenants were at first 'very much opposed to them and thought them too stringent, but now they are satisfied'. [323]

While improvements by tenants languished, it became increasingly common for landowners to improve their estates through either direct cash outlays or allowances to their tenants during the two decades before the famine. This gradual shift from an attitude of apathy to one of rising interest in the opportunities for profitable investment largely resulted from the crumbling of the middleman system. As long as his estate had been leased beyond his power to exact a reasonable return in the form of higher rents, no landowner could have invested with much hope of realizing a solid profit. Once he threw off his bondage to the middleman, however, his acquisitiveness quickened perceptibly. One rule followed on the earl of Kenmare's estates when middlemen's leases expired was that 'all permanent improvements should be provided for by his lordship out of the rents paid by the tenants'. [324] When the first of a series of leases to middlemen on his Cork and Kerry estates terminated in the early 1820s, Sir John Benn-Walsh promoted improvements without, however, sinking very much capital.

I began by dividing it into fields of about five acres, & dividing the farms afresh by large bounds ditches & dikes. I think the farms were 17 in number, for we did not venture to eject many of the occupying tenants. This was the first great commencement of improvement. The land was partially drained by these deep ditches (under draining was then unknown). . . . I built good comfortable cabins for almost all the farms at a cost of about £20 a cabin, to which I added barns for £15. . . . The next start the farm made was the introduction of thorough under draining by Bruce the Scotchman [*sic*] I brought over. . . . Another great source of improvement was the high road from Listowell [*sic*] towards Kanturk, which was made through the farms & from which I made little farm roads to each of the holdings. [325]

Benn-Walsh pursued a similar policy of modest development on the remainder of his estates once he had eradicated the negligent middlemen. [326] Other landowners were less rigidly frugal. After having persuaded his tenants to surrender their long leases, Lord

---

[323] *Devon comm. digest*, i, 273.

[324] *Devon comm. evidence*, pt iii, p. 736.

[325] Ormathwaite papers: Journal of Sir John Benn-Walsh, 12 Sept. 1855, pp. 158–61.

[326] Ibid.: Journal, 26 Aug. 1844, p. 189; Journal, 10 Aug. 1849, p. 219.

Arden made allowances amounting to £6,500 for buildings and other improvements between 1825 and 1844.[327]

Perhaps the most remarkable instance of heavy investment subsequent to the termination of middlemen's leases occurred on the earl of Egmont's estates, managed since 1824 by the crown solicitor Edward Tierney. Tierney commented in April 1832 that while the earl's formerly neglected estates had been vastly improved in recent years, much work yet remained that could not be accomplished until certain leases, dependent upon old lives, had expired.[328] Nevertheless, Tierney spent as much as £24,000 on buildings, drainage, plantations, and other permanent works between 1831 and 1841.[329] Most of this enormous sum was sunk in buildings. Two of Egmont's tenants stated before the Devon commission that Tierney had defrayed practically the whole expense of constructing about forty sets of dwelling houses and farm offices at an average cost of £500. To eight of the most industrious tenants, he had given allowances amounting to over £4,000.[330] Enterprising tenants on the duke of Devonshire's estates also received substantial encouragement. The agent at Bandon recorded in July 1840 that an unusually industrious tenant named Gash had been allowed £150 towards farm buildings and given a £200 loan to enable him to enlarge and alter his dwelling house. In addition, Gash was now 'going to build a cow house for 17 or 20 cows and will tonslate it and also the part of the old house retained as a dwelling house, if he gets an allowance of £100 instead of £80—agreed to'.[331] The Devonshire estate accounts show that during the 1830s approximately £1,200 was paid annually in compensation for tenants' improvements, and that about £3,900 was expended each year for 'general works'.[332]

The subject of permanent improvements remained at the discussion stage on Viscount Midleton's estates almost until the famine, as it probably did on many other properties from which middlemen had only recently been eliminated. The agent Thomas

[327] *Devon comm. evidence*, pt iii, pp. 142–3.

[328] Barry papers, *Egmont v. Darell, documents of respondents*: E. Tierney to Currie, Horne, and Woodgate, 14 Apr. 1832, pp. 185–6.

[329] Ibid., Printed copy of affidavits filed by petitioner in the English court of chancery, *Egmont v. Darell* (1861): Affidavit of C. P. Brassington and J. J. Byrne, 5 Dec. 1861, pp. 79–81 (hereafter cited as *Egmont v. Darell, petitioner's affidavits*).

[330] *Devon comm. digest*, i, 145–7.

[331] Lismore papers, N.L.I., MS 7127: Bandon memorandum book, 1839–43, p. 38.

[332] Ibid., MS 6929: Rent receipts and disbursements, 1818–90. The total annual rental of the Devonshire estates was about £35,000 during the 1830s.

Foley wished Lord Midleton to build slated dwelling houses and out-offices whenever he made a new letting, sharing the cost with the tenant by taking a fine for a twenty-one-year lease.[333] Foley condemned the allowance system under which the tenant paid for both materials and labour and was then permitted to deduct part or all of this expenditure from his rent.

> There is an objection [Foley pointed out in September 1844] to allowing the tenants to provide timber & slates, as they invariably get them of inferior quality & at retail prices; it is far better for the landlord to provide them ... —in the article of slate alone there would be a saving of at least £30 per cent.[334]

But Lord Midleton's views, as expressed by his London solicitor, clashed directly with Foley's. Midleton adamantly insisted that all buildings be erected 'on the lowest terms & in the easiest manner', according to the allowance system.

> This is the mode that has been generally recommended for the improvement of Irish estates, & it is the mode already practised as being the most economical on some of the best managed estates in Ireland. ... It is obvious that on a large estate in a country so backward in point of buildings as Ireland is, it would be impracticable for the proprietor to *take upon himself* to erect *all the buildings required* upon his estate in such a mode as he might *wish* to see them built. ...[335]

Because they were careering towards bankruptcy by the early 1840s, many Cork landowners could scarcely afford costly estate improvements. The finances of an unusually large segment of the landowning class were hopelessly chaotic. George Hodder's Fountainstown estate, worth about £1,100 per annum, was already incumbered with debts amounting to over £13,000 in the early 1820s.[336] W. H. Newenham's property near Carrigaline, worth between £3,000 and £4,000 per annum, was also loaded with enormous charges amounting to more than £47,500 in 1833. The annual interest on these charges alone consumed more than two-thirds of Newenham's entire rental.[337] Those portions of the earl of

---

[333] Guildford Muniment Room, Midleton papers: T. Foley to H. Marshall (extract and copy), 18 July 1844.

[334] Ibid.: Foley to Marshall (extract and copy), 16 Sept. 1844.

[335] Ibid.: Marshall to Foley (extract and copy), 30 Oct. 1844. The debate continued for several months before Foley finally had to yield (ibid.: Foley to Marshall (extract and copy), 27 Dec. 1844; Marshall to Foley (extract and copy), 15 Jan. 1845; Foley to Marshall (extract and copy), 21 Jan. 1845).

[336] Hodder papers: Draft settlement of the Hodder family estates, 1822.

[337] Newenham papers: Rental and account of W. H. W. Newenham's

Bantry's Cork estates offered for sale in 1851, comprising some 67,000 acres of largely mountainous land worth about £9,000 per annum, were incumbered to the extent of nearly £80,000 in 1845.[338] A considerable number of small estates had already been transferred to the courts before the famine, mostly with a view to eventual sale to pay off importunate creditors. The courts of chancery and exchequer were responsible for the administration of no less than 135 small Cork properties with an aggregate rental of £74,000 in 1844.[339]

There was certainly no shortage of landed proprietors who had simply squandered their resources. R. H. H. Becher, who possessed a large estate near Skibbereen, was virtually a ruined man by the early 1840s, largely because of celebrated litigation with the wealthy earl of Bandon over the ownership of certain land. Their bitter feud limped along in the courts for nearly twenty years and, after finally being appealed to the house of lords, ended in a judicial compromise by which Becher gained about £500 a year. Each side paid its own costs, which reportedly amounted to £20,000 a side. Not surprisingly, Becher was 'obliged to mortgage and remortgage his property to defray the costs of the litigation and to meet family claims, from which incumbrances he never regained his former footing'.[340] Daniel Conner, sen., whose estate near Dunmanway was worth about £4,500 per annum, heedlessly arranged an enormously expensive family settlement in 1844 under which the yearly outlays reached £2,270. He charged his property, already heavily burdened by prior debts, with portions of £2,000 for each of his five daughters.[341] His relative, the incumbered estates court judge Mountifort Longfield, told Daniel Conner, jun., in May 1852: 'I saw the settlement of 1844 at last. It would be a reasonable settlement if

---

[338] Bantry papers: Petition to the incumbered estates court, 1851 (in the possession of Mrs C. E. M. Shelswell-White, Bantry House, Bantry, Co. Cork).

[339] *Return from the registrar's office of the court of chancery in Ireland, of the number of causes, description of property, rental of estates, arrears of rent, when receiver was appointed, and when receiver last accounted; . . . similar return from the chief remembrancer's office in reference to estates under the court of exchequer in Ireland,* H.C. 1847–8 (226), lvii, 213.

[340] *C.E.,* 4 Sept. 1882. See also ibid., 20 Oct. 1851.

[341] Conner papers: Incumbered estates court rental and particulars of the Conner estates, 9 July 1852.

---

estate, 1817–33, 'A statement of the debts due on the estate of W. H. W. Newenham', 1 Jan. 1833 (in the possession of Mr W. P. Worth Newenham, Coolmore, Carrigaline, Co. Cork).

the estate was worth three times as much as it is worth.'[342] In an earlier letter, Longfield expressed amazement at the sums spent by Conner since 1844, which he placed at three times Conner's annual income; he charged that Conner had 'concealed the state of his affairs and procured his friends who confided in his honour to become security for him'.[343] The earls of Kingston provide the most spectacular example of improvidence between 1815 and 1845. They accumulated huge debts on the strength of an annual rental of almost £40,000 drawn from vast estates comprising some 75,000 acres in three counties.[344] Their great mansion, Mitchelstown Castle, reportedly cost £220,000 to build during the 1820s. For some unearthly reason, another £32,000 had to be found to finance the research for, and publication of, Viscount Kingsborough's work on Mexican history.[345] While touring Ireland in 1835, Alexis de Tocqueville visited Mitchelstown and inquired about the earl of Kingston. He learned that the earl had gone mad in 1833:

He found himself burdened with £400,000 of debts without hope of ever being able to pay them off. The money had been lent him by catholic merchants in Cork on mortgage of the huge estates which I had seen, and absorbed almost all his income.

The wild extravagance of the earls of Kingston apparently was not unique among Irish aristocrats. 'It is like that almost everywhere in Ireland', claimed de Tocqueville.[346]

Improvidence, however, was only one aspect of the complex question of increasing indebtedness among landowners after 1815. Not only did the middleman system prevent many of them from realizing the full rental value of their estates, but landowners also tended to anticipate the termination of old leases by creating incumbrances that could only be supported properly once these leases had actually expired. When the rents of many landowners fell after 1815, financial burdens that had been taken up lightly in more prosperous times now pressed heavily upon them. The earl of

[342] Ibid.: M. Longfield to D. Conner, jun., 18 May 1852.

[343] Ibid.: Longfield to Conner, 27 Oct. 1851.

[344] Earl of Kingston papers, N.L.I., MS 3276: Rental of the Limerick and Tipperary estates of the earl of Kingston, 1840–2; J. Kegan, *A young Irishman's diary (1836–1847), being extracts from the early journal of John Kegan of Moate*, edited with preface and notes by the Rev. Wallace Clare (n.p., 1928), pp. 35–7; A. M. Sullivan, *New Ireland* (3rd ed., London, 1877), i, 273–81.

[345] For a brief sketch of the vicissitudes of the earls of Kingston and their estates, see *C.E.*, 23 July 1868.

[346] A. de Tocqueville, *Journeys to England and Ireland*, ed. J. P. Mayer, trans. G. Lawrence and K. P. Mayer (London, 1958), pp. 158–9.

Mountcashel asserted in 1846 that when rents rose sharply during the French wars, landowners, 'supposing this increase of income permanent, charged their estates with larger settlements by their wills and deeds than they otherwise would have done, could they have foreseen the immense fall in rents which took place soon after the peace'. [347] Mountcashel also claimed that rents had declined almost immediately, whereas the interest payable on incumbrances had long continued unchanged. [348]

Defective laws with respect to the registration and priority of charges also facilitated the accumulation of debt and obstructed the sale of incumbered property. There was no single, simple, and complete register of settlements, mortgages, and judgments. Instead, there were separate registers in different courts and in the registry office of deeds. Under these unfavourable circumstances, searching for incumbrances usually led to prolonged delays and almost endless difficulties. Borrowers could therefore quite easily conceal or even purposely misrepresent the true state of their financial affairs without their fraud being detected. And lenders could often be persuaded to advance their capital without having accurate and detailed knowledge of the borrower's actual position. Lord Audley's estate between Skibbereen and Skull illustrates these conditions almost perfectly. His whole property, with the exception of some mines, had been leased to a single middleman for ninety-nine years in 1755 at the low rent of £527; a separate letting of the mines had raised the annual rental slightly to £577. By 1829 his incumbrances of over £25,000 far exceeded the value of the security. Yet, by concealing this information from his more than eighty different creditors, Lord Audley was able to increase the total charges against his insignificant estate to the incredible sum of nearly £90,000 before his death in 1837. [349] Admittedly, Lord Audley was an adept at the art of concealment. Under the prevailing system of registration, however, the sixth incumbrancer was legally as certain of recovering his investment as the first, provided only that the security was adequate. This obvious defect in the law encouraged 'the piling up of debts until the estates were mortgaged almost to their entire value'. [350] Because of the complexities and inadequacies of the registration system, proving title was extremely difficult and expensive when

[347] *C.C.*, 16 Apr. 1846.
[348] Ibid.
[349] Hancock, *Distress at Skull and Skibbereen*, pp. 5–8.
[350] S. H. Cousens, 'The regional pattern of emigration during the great famine, 1846–1851' in *Transactions and Papers of the Institute of British Geographers*, no. 28 (1960), p. 127.

estates were heavily incumbered. A great obstacle was thus erected to the sale of such estates before the famine. Although the fateful events of 1845–9 pushed the incumbered landowners of Cork over the brink of disaster, it was as clear as their best-polished silver by the early 1840s that the long-awaited day of reckoning with their creditors was close at hand. Only an economic miracle could have saved most of them. Instead, they were overwhelmed by the great famine, and the efficient court for bankrupt landowners to which the famine gave birth in 1849 helped them or their creditors to reorganize or liquidate what remained of their assets.

II

THE GREAT FAMINE, 1845–51

~~~~~~~~~~~~~~~~~~~~~~~~~~~~~~~~~~

THE POTATO BLIGHT, caused by the fungus *Phytophthora infestans,* was first noticed in gardens near Cork city in the second week of September 1845, but the extent of the dreaded disease could not be estimated until general digging commenced during the first week of October. [1] Initially, there was widespread alarm that the staple food for more than half the population had been largely destroyed. Cries were raised to 'keep the corn at home and keep it at the present price', [2] to close the distilleries and breweries, and to employ the people on public works, since they were faced with 'one of the most awful calamities that has ever threatened this country'. [3] The panic proved unjustified, however, and a less anxious mood prevailed in most places by the end of November. [4] It was now clear that some areas had suffered far more than others, with the worst reports coming from the districts of Skibbereen, Kinsale, Kanturk, and Fermoy, where from one-third to one-half of the crop was described as unfit for human consumption. [5] According to the constabulary returns of December 1845, only slightly more than one-fifth of the potato crop had been lost in County Cork as a whole. [6] Furthermore,

[1] *C.E.*, 10, 15 Sept. 1845; C. Woodham-Smith, *The great hunger: Ireland, 1845–1849* (New American Library ed., New York, 1964), pp. 88–96.

[2] *C.E.*, 29 Oct. 1845.

[3] Ibid., 13 Oct. 1845. See also ibid., 10, 20 Oct. 1845.

[4] West Sussex County Record Office, Chichester, Cowdray archives, MS 1914: P. Smith to earl of Egmont, 12 Nov. 1845; *C.E.*, 5, 21 Nov. 1845.

[5] *C.E.*, 13 Oct., 28 Nov., 10 Dec. 1845; 6 Feb., 6 Mar., 6 Apr. 1846.

[6] *Correspondence explanatory of the measures adopted by her majesty's government for the relief of distress arising from the failure of the potato crop in Ireland* [735], H.C. 1846, xxxvii, 41, p. 5.

some of the diseased potatoes could still be fed to pigs, and, luckily, the acreage under this crop had been somewhat greater in 1845 than in the previous year.[7]

Hopes were high for the success of the 1846 crop, which was planted earlier than usual in a desperate attempt to shorten the 'hungry months' between the old and the new potatoes. Unfortunately, farmers often refused to give conacre land to any unbound labourer who could not pay half or all of the rent in advance, a condition which many distressed labourers simply could not fulfil.[8] Partly as a result, the total area under potatoes in Cork, as compared with the previous year, is estimated to have declined by about 20 per cent in 1846.[9] In the end, however, this mattered little. By the second half of July, it was only too obvious from both the blackened leaves and the indescribable stench rising from field after field of potatoes that the crop would be a certain disaster. A shrill chorus of despondent reports from all over the county testified to the universality and utter destructiveness of the blight.[10]

The failure of 1846 completely disrupted the traditional relationship between farmers and their bound labourers, and helped to set the stage for an even worse disaster in 1847. Once their potato gardens were hopelessly blighted in 1846, the labourers repudiated those agreements which obliged them to work for the farmers in return for a cabin, a patch of ground, and a few privileges. Only money wages seemed to offer an escape from starvation, and they cried out for cash payment. This the farmers generally refused, causing the labourers to abandon their plots for either the public works or the workhouses.[11] Conacre arrangements were also thoroughly upset. More than ever in the spring of 1847, after the wholesale default of the previous autumn, farmers were inclined to insist upon payment in advance for conacre. Yet never were unbound labourers less able to satisfy this requirement. Besides the nearly total inability of unbound workers to pay in advance, the abandonment of their plots by the bound labourers, and the rapidly spreading demoralization, there was the stark fact that almost all the sound potatoes dug in the autumn of 1846 had been eaten by the following spring, and few remained for seed. Together, these factors produced an enormous decline in potato acreage from over 321,000 in 1846 to

[7] Bourke, 'Extent of the potato crop', pp. 7–9.

[8] *C.E.*, 16 Apr., 15 July 1846.

[9] Bourke, 'Extent of the potato crop', pp. 7–9.

[10] *C.E.*, 8 June, 15, 29 July 1846; Minute book, Dunmanway board of guardians, Jan.–Nov. 1846, 1 Aug. 1846, p. 228.

[11] *C.E.*, 14, 26, 28 Aug., 25 Sept., 9 Nov. 1846; *C.C.*, 27 Aug. 1846.

less than 40,000 one year later. Although the blight scarcely appeared in 1847, and though the yield in Cork was an average one of about six tons per acre, potato production was only about half of what it had been in the calamitous year of 1846.[12]

Falsely encouraged by the absence of blight in 1847, and ignoring the persistent warnings of landowners, agents, and relief officials, farmers made a limited attempt to restore the potato crop in the following year.[13] 'Wherever we turn our eyes,' remarked one observer in late February 1848, 'we see very extensive preparations for the planting of potatoes.'[14] 'Such has been the quantity sown that the whole country', claimed the *Southern Reporter* in June, 'appears like one vast potato field shooting up into verdure.'[15] Hoping against hope, many contemporaries sadly deceived themselves. There was increased exertion only by comparison with 1847. Starvation and epidemic diseases had by now advanced so far, and sound seed had become so scarce, that only between one-third and one-fourth of the pre-famine potato acreage was achieved in 1848.[16] What was worse, the blight returned to all parts of Cork, though not in so virulent a form as in 1846. Once again, Skibbereen and the southwestern seacoast were among the most devastated areas.[17] In the county as a whole the yield had fallen from 6 to only 3⅓ tons per acre, and with the sole exception of 1847, potato production was lower than in any other year between 1846 and 1851. As Table 7 shows, no significant change occurred in the three years following 1848; the acreage under potatoes remained extremely low.[18] The blight reappeared, helping to perpetuate disease, death, and emigration.

[12] *Returns of agricultural produce in Ireland in the year 1847,* pt i: *Crops,* p. ix; Bourke, 'Extent of the potato crop', pp. 7–9.

[13] *C.C.,* 14 Mar. 1848.

[14] *Southern Reporter and Cork Daily Commercial Courier* (hereafter cited as *Southern Reporter*), 29 Feb. 1848. See also Minute book, Dunmanway board of guardians, 1847–8, 12 Feb. 1848, pp. 188–9.

[15] *Southern Reporter,* 15 June 1848.

[16] *Returns of agricultural produce in Ireland in the year 1848* [1116], H.C. 1849, xlix, 1, pp. 134–7.

[17] *C.E.,* 11, 18 Aug. 1848.

[18] Bourke, 'Extent of the potato crop', pp. 7–9; *Returns of agricultural produce in Ireland in the year 1847,* pt i: *Crops,* pp. viii–ix; *Returns of agricultural produce in Ireland in the year 1848,* pp. x–xi; *Returns of agricultural produce . . . 1849* [1245], H.C. 1850, li, 39, pp. x–xi; *Returns of agricultural produce . . . 1850* [1404], H.C. 1851, l, 1, pp. xii–xiii; *Census Ire., 1851,* pt ii: *Returns of agricultural produce in 1851* [1589], H.C. 1852–3, xciii, 1, pp. xix–xx.

TABLE 7   Estimated (1844–6) and official (1847–51) potato production
in Cork

year	acreage (in thousands)	yield (in tons per acre)	production (in thousands of tons)
1844	369	6·25	2,306
1845	394	4·0	1,576
1846	321	1·5	482
1847	40	6·0	239
1848	103	3·3	341
1849	82	5·2	425
1850	101	4·2	422
1851	100	4·6	462

AGRICULTURAL PRODUCTION, PRICES, AND EXPORTS

While potato production between 1846 and 1851 was only a fraction
of the pre-famine volume, the level of grain output was apparently
well maintained, with the major exception of the drastic decline in
wheat. The number of both sheep and pigs fell sharply, but this drop
was more than offset by substantial increases in the number of cattle
as well as in butter exports. Table 8 illustrates these facts. [19]
The decline in wheat production and in the number of both pigs
and sheep is not difficult to explain. Poor wheat yields in 1848 and
1850 as well as a serious slump in wheat prices from 16s. per
hundredweight in 1846 to only 8s. ½d. per hundredweight in 1851 had
the effect of reducing the acreage under this crop from 166,000 in
1847 to only 52,000 in 1851. [20] Pigs and sheep were clearly the victims
of famine conditions. The export figures graphically demonstrate
that labourers and smallholders responded to the partial potato
failure of 1845 and to the disastrously small crops of succeeding years
by selling their pigs and sheep in extraordinary numbers without
possessing the ability to replace them. The export of pigs from the

[19] *Census Ire., 1841*, p. 455; *Returns of agricultural produce in Ireland in the
year 1847*, pt i: *Crops*, pp. viii–ix; *Returns of agricultural produce in Ireland in the
year 1847*, pt ii: *Stock* [1000], H.C. 1847–8, lvii, 109, pp. 4–5; *Returns of
agricultural produce in Ireland in the year 1848*, pp. x–xi, 146–7; *Returns of
agricultural produce ... 1849*, pp. x–xi, 154–5; *Returns of agricultural produce ...
1850*, pp. xii–xiii, xvii–xviii; *Census Ire., 1851*, pt ii: *Returns of agricultural
produce in 1851*, pp. xix–xx, 640; C.B.M. MSS, C. 38: Account of the total
annual quantity of butter in casks, firkins, and kegs passed through the
weigh-house, 1770–1869.
[20] *Returns of agricultural produce in Ireland in the year 1847*, pt i: *Crops*,
p. viii; *Census Ire., 1851*, pt ii: *Returns of agricultural produce in 1851*, p. xix;
Irish Farmers' Gazette, 1 Nov. 1879.

TABLE 8 Cork grain production and livestock numbers and Cork butter market receipts, 1841–52

	1841	1847	1848	1849	1850	1851
	(in thousands of cwt)					
oats	—	1,677	1,408	1,457	1,722	1,763
wheat	—	1,592	765	923	654	766
barley	—	725	610	754	746	737
	(in thousands)					
cattle	178 [21]	206	227	231	237	247
sheep	253	207	192	159	166	183
pigs	178	75	85	93	109	129
	1841–2	1847–8	1848–9	1849–50	1850–1	1851–2
	(in thousands of cwt)					
butter	230	281	322	342	307	317

port of Cork plummeted from more than 73,000 in 1845 to less than 9,000 in 1849, while shipments of sheep plunged from 88,000 in 1847 to less than 6,000 by 1851. [22] Besides export without replacement, two additional factors contributed to the sharp contraction of sheep flocks: the difficulty of protecting them from theft and slaughter by starving labourers and cottiers at night on open pastures, [23] and a virulent liver-fluke epidemic brought on by heavy rainfall in the summer of 1848. [24] The dire consequences of the potato failure for the stock of pigs and sheep of the poorest members of Cork's agricultural community are starkly reflected in Table 9. [25] Labourers

[21] There were 150,588 cattle in County Cork in 1841 according to the census of that year, but this figure probably represents only 80 to 84 per cent of the correct total, which lay between 174,700 and 180,700 (Bourke, 'Agricultural statistics', pp. 381–2). Thus a rounded average of 178,000 cattle is displayed in Table 8.

[22] *Report of the commissioners appointed to inquire into the state of the fairs and markets in Ireland*, pt ii: *Minutes of evidence* [1910], H.C. 1854–5, xix, 1, p. 196.

[23] See the discussion of food stealing below, pp. 87–91.

[24] Lismore papers, N.L.I., MS 7183, Letter book, 1842–50: F. E. Currey to A. Swanston, 29 Oct. 1848, pp. 16–18; Crotty, *Irish agricultural production*, p. 48.

[25] *Census Ire., 1841*, pp. 454–5; *Returns of agricultural produce in Ireland in the year 1847*, pt ii: *Stock*, pp. 4–5; *Returns of agricultural produce . . . 1849*, pp. 154–5; *Census Ire., 1851*, pt ii: *Returns of agricultural produce in 1851*, p. 640. The real size of holdings in 1841 was understated in the census of that year, perhaps by as much as one-half in each category. Therefore, as Bourke suggests, the classifications given in the 1841 census have been doubled

and smallholders were practically wiped out, and even farmers with holdings of between fifteen and thirty acres suffered heavy losses. Large farmers holding more than thirty acres, on the other hand, not only escaped almost unscathed but in fact strengthened their position during the famine years.

TABLE 9   Number of pigs and sheep on agricultural holdings in Cork, 1841–51

size of holding	1841	1847	1849	1851
		pigs		
2 acres or less	56,092	—	—	—
1 acre or less	—	3,207	3,585	5,360
above 2 to 10 acres	17,334	—	—	—
above 1 to 15 acres	—	5,293	6,583	8,248
above 10 to 30 acres	26,652	—	—	—
above 15 to 30 acres	—	10,936	12,792	16,808
above 30 acres	77,439	55,499	70,356	99,009
total no. of pigs	177,517	74,935	93,316	129,425
		sheep		
2 acres or less	46,035	—	—	—
1 acre or less	—	4,397	1,060	1,209
above 2 to 10 acres	23,326	—	—	—
above 1 to 15 acres	—	21,198	10,604	8,713
above 10 to 30 acres	48,779	—	—	—
above 15 to 30 acres	—	35,468	22,583	21,636
above 30 acres	134,755	145,979	124,824	151,524
total no. of sheep	252,895	207,042	159,071	183,082

In sharp contrast to the decline in the number of both pigs and sheep in Cork stands the substantial increase in the number of cattle from about 178,000 in 1841 to over 247,000 by 1851.[26] Whether dry cattle accounted for most or all of this increase is not completely certain, because the available figures fail to distinguish between dry cattle and cows. But Raymond Crotty has recently estimated that in Ireland as a whole dry cattle almost doubled in number between

[26] See above, p. 77.

('Agricultural statistics', p. 379). But the number of livestock included in the categories of the 1841 census have been attributed in Tables 9 and 10 to the enlarged classifications.

1841 and 1851, while the number of milch cattle remained practically stationary.[27] The receipts of the Cork butter market, as shown in Table 8, indicate, however, that butter exports rose steeply in the 1840s and expanded even during the famine years. The expansion of butter exports might suggest that Cork farmers were rapidly adding to their dairy stock. But at least after 1845, a large reduction in the domestic consumption of butter, arising from death, emigration, and the intense pressure of both rents and poor rates, must have helped greatly to swell the export figures. Indeed, it would not be surprising if the general Irish trend with respect to the ratio of dry cattle to milch cattle during the 1840s were closely mirrored by developments in County Cork. In any case, the more than 20 per cent rise in total cattle numbers in Cork between 1847 and 1851 alone is certainly remarkable. This increase, however, was entirely confined to holdings of over thirty acres. A significant decrease occurred on holdings of fifteen acres or less, and the number of cattle on farms of between fifteen and thirty acres merely remained about the same throughout the famine, as indicated by Table 10.[28]

TABLE 10   Number of cattle on agricultural holdings in Cork, 1841–51

size of holding	1841	1847	1849	1851
2 acres or less	4,181	—	—	—
1 acre or less	—	1,135	1,124	1,338
above 2 to 10 acres	10,094	—	—	—
above 1 to 15 acres	—	13,692	11,337	10,894
above 10 to 30 acres	26,197	—	—	—
above 15 to 30 acres	—	28,633	28,407	28,984
above 30 acres	110,116	162,156	190,412	205,995
total no. of cattle	150,588*	205,616	231,280	247,211

*'Calves of the current year' excluded.

Though a variety of adversities afflicted even the largest farmers during the second half of the 1840s, there was some consolation in the fact that agricultural prices held up well between 1846 and 1848, much better in fact than during the following three years, as Table 11 illustrates.[29] Potatoes naturally were double or triple their ordinary price since they were almost unobtainable. The high price of corn in

[27] Crotty, *Irish agricultural production*, p. 48.
[28] See above, p. 77, n. 25, and the sources cited there.
[29] T. Barrington, 'A review of Irish agricultural prices' in *Stat. Soc. Ire. Jn.*, pt ci, xv (Oct. 1927), p. 251.

1846 was obviously the result of the small supplies of foreign grain entering the country. Not until early 1847 did foreign supplies begin to arrive in large quantities. [30] Cork farmers helped to create an inflated market in 1846 by forestalling. The earl of Egmont's agent complained in late January that a great many of the earl's tenants near Kanturk and Churchtown had neglected to pay the second gale of rent in 1845, 'having kept their corn unthreshed in expectation of very high prices in consequence of the potato failure'. [31] The extraordinary grain prices of 1846 were not maintained in the following year, but still tillage farmers could not justly complain on that account. After 1848, however, grain prices fell sharply, and wheat prices in particular declined catastrophically. This overwhelmed many small tillage farmers who had managed to survive the earlier potato failures, particularly farmers in the baronies of Barrymore and Imokilly between the Blackwater and the sea coast. Wheat prices did not even respond to the poor crop yield of 1848, caused by a cold, rainy summer that brought smut and maggot in its wake. [32] With the loss of the protected British market after the repeal of the corn laws in 1846, wheat growing, always unsuited to the damp Irish climate, became highly unrewarding.

TABLE 11   Index numbers of Irish agricultural prices, 1840–51

(base 1840 = 100, except store cattle, base 1845 = 100)

year	wheat	oats	barley	butter	pork	mutton	beef	store cattle 1-2 yrs	2-3 yrs
1840	100	100	100	100	100	100	100	—	—
1845	98	118	118	92	92	120	103	—	—
1846	131	187	175	105	117	120	104	129	170
1847	98	107	116	99	149	125	105	157	190
1848	87	96	100	87	115	120	110	143	180
1849	66	83	85	74	88	105	79	97	150
1850	73	101	87	74	92	100	81	89	130
1851	66	89	85	83	94	105	86	100	135

During 1849, in fact, the price of every agricultural product declined significantly, especially that of young store cattle, which had performed remarkably well during the first three famine years. This hit the dairy farmers hardest, and they were really the typical farmers in County Cork. Between 1846 and 1850 the prices of butter

[30] C. E. Trevelyan, *The Irish crisis* (London, 1848), pp. 71–3.
[31] Cowdray archives, MS 1914: P. Smith to earl of Egmont, 2 Jan. 1847.
[32] *C.C.*, 22 July 1848.

and young stock fell by more than 25 and 30 per cent respectively. Discouragement swept over those solid farmers who had largely escaped many of the difficulties which had pushed thousands off the land. 'I cannot describe the unfortunate state of the country', the land agent John Waller Braddell told Sir Denham Jephson-Norreys in May 1849. 'I do not know what will become of us. This was fair day [in Mallow]. It was a wretched fair. Cattle for a song & no one to buy.'[33] Even though the grain harvest of 1849 was excellent, it was rightly said that 'the low price of all agricultural produce still casts a gloom on the farmers' prospects'.[34] The outbreak of the Crimean war finally revived corn and butter prices in 1853, but cattle prices, particularly those of young stores, did not respond until 1854 and 1855.[35] Only then did the possibility of a new era of prosperity stir the farmer's imagination.

Besides their serious losses arising from non-payment of conacre rents, the deterioration and destruction of livestock, the deficient crops of 1848, and then falling prices, farmers also suffered from yet another unfavourable turn of economic events. Drastic reductions in grain exports took place during the famine. With the enormous deficiencies in the potato crop, grain normally exported was diverted to home consumption, partly in order to provide food for livestock. Before the famine, livestock had consumed as much as one-third of all the potatoes produced in Ireland, that is, about 5 million out of the estimated 15 million tons grown annually. Pigs accounted for more than one-half of livestock consumption of potatoes, and another two-fifths were fed to cattle during the winter and early spring.[36] Without the potato, pig breeding became impossible or much less profitable and was sharply curtailed after 1845. Cattle raising, on the other hand, strongly expanded, but only because farmers used much more of the oat crop as cattle feed.

Human needs, however, exerted a much greater restraining influence over the course of grain exports. It is impossible to determine exactly what proportion of the grain retained was sold to feed the starving labourers and what proportion was consumed on the farm by the farmer's family, his help, and his livestock. No doubt

[33] Jephson-Norreys papers: J. W. Braddell to Sir D. Jephson-Norreys, 15 May 1849, in folder marked 'Mallow workhouse and poor law commissioners, 1847–50' (in the possession of Commander M. C. M. Jephson, Mallow Castle, Mallow, Co. Cork).

[34] *C.E.*, 17 Oct. 1849.

[35] *Irish Farmers' Gazette*, 1 Nov. 1879; Barrington, 'Agricultural prices' p. 251.

[36] P. M. A. Bourke, 'The use of the potato crop in pre-famine Ireland' in *Stat. Soc. Ire. Jn.*, xxi, pt vi (1968), pp. 83–7.

some farmers with a large grain surplus for the market profited from the increased domestic demand, at least until 1848. But the necessity to consume much more grain on the farm had serious adverse effects on the incomes of most farmers. One Cork poor-law guardian observed in January 1847 that even 'respectable farmers' with holdings of more than thirty acres were 'suffering severely at present, as are obliged to consume in their families and in their stables the corn which in former years procured clothes and other comforts for them'.[37] This diversion to domestic consumption of grain normally exported must be considered one of the most important factors which lowered farm incomes between 1846 and 1851. The extent of the diversion is illustrated by Table 12, which sets out Irish exports of corn, meal, and flour to Britain from 1843 to 1849.[38]

TABLE 12   Irish exports of corn, meal, and flour to Great Britain, 1843–9 (in long tons)

year	wheat	barley	oats	wheat meal & flour	oatmeal	total
1843	48,119	22,090	260,333	28,673	85,331	444,546
1844	50,069	18,133	251,645	41,978	57,549	419,374
1845	93,180	18,619	279,993	71,119	52,959	515,870
1846	46,683	18,571	159,808	36,178	27,715	288,955
1847	30,935	9,505	82,186	10,550	16,527	149,703
1848	36,197	15,961	158,463	28,015	46,812	285,448
1849	25,466	8,918	111,090	23,027	35,941	204,442

THE PLIGHT OF THE LABOURERS AND COTTIERS

Although corn exports declined drastically beginning in 1846, the fact that any food left the country while a large segment of its people lay on the verge of starvation was indeed deplorable and unjustifiable in social terms. By the spring of 1846 potatoes, when still obtainable,

[37] *C.C.*, 21 Jan. 1847. See also *Correspondence from July 1846 to January 1847, relating to the measures adopted for the relief of distress in Ireland and Scotland*, commissariat series [761], H.C. 1847, li, 1, pp. 363–6.

[38] P.R.O., Customs 5: Ledgers of imports, England, 1843–9, nos 32–5, 37, 39, 41 (special abstract, 'Corn exported from Ireland to Great Britain', on last pages of each ledger). In converting quarters of the various cereals and hundredweights of meal and flour into long tons (2,240 lb.), the conversion rates now in use have been adopted. The figures of Irish exports of grain and meal to Great Britain from 1815 to 1849 published by G. R. Porter are inaccurate (G. R. Porter, *The progress of the nation in its various social and economic relations from the beginning of the nineteenth century* (rev. ed., London, 1851), p. 345).

had risen in price to famine level. In Cork city potatoes brought by small hookers from Kinsale in March were sold to speculators on the quays for 7*d.* per weight of twenty-one pounds and then resold in the city's markets for 9½*d.* to 11*d.* [39] At the same time in the market at Kilworth they could be obtained at 4½*d.*, though none were free from taint, whereas in March of 1845 good-quality potatoes had cost as little as 2½*d.* Already, labourers in the Kilworth district were living on black, half-rotten potatoes, and those in casual employment rarely ate food more than once a day. [40] This soon became the condition of even those labourers with steady work at the best wages. [41]

Deaths from starvation were partly averted by the prompt action of Sir Robert Peel's government, which secretly purchased about £150,000 worth of Indian corn in the United States and Britain, and judiciously used it to curb private speculation. Sales of this grain at the government's depot in Cork city began at the end of March 1846; some 300 tons were purchased weekly by over fifty local relief committees during June and July. Sub-depots were also set up at Castletownsend, Bantry, and Castletown-Berehaven. [42] The relief committees sold the Indian meal at reduced prices. In Cove, for example, the completely destitute could obtain a stone (fourteen pounds) of meal for as little as 4*d.*, while those who had work but earned less than 1*s.* per day or had families of five or more persons paid 1*s.* per stone. [43] In Mallow the relief committee's price was higher—1*s.* 4*d.* per stone. Yet one committee member asserted: 'We could sell any quantity at this rate but have not gone further as yet than 2 tons a day. On some occasions we have to send for the police to protect the sales-people.' [44] In order to enable the poor to earn money to buy meal, public works, mainly road building, were started in April. About 12,800 persons were employed at average wages of 10*d.* per day by the end of July, chiefly in the baronies of Duhallow, Fermoy, and Kinalea. Actually, there was much less

[39] *C.C.*, 17 Mar. 1846.
[40] Ibid., 19 Mar. 1846.
[41] Cork Public Museum: Minute book, Cove famine relief committee, 1846–7, 13 Apr. 1846, p. 15.
[42] *Correspondence explanatory of the measures adopted by her majesty's government for the relief of distress arising from the failure of the potato crop in Ireland*, pp. 63–4, 115, 205; T. P. O'Neill, 'The organization and administration of relief, 1845–52' in Edwards & Williams, *Great famine*, pp. 214, 216, 221.
[43] Minute book, Cove famine relief committee, 1846–7, 17 July 1846, p. 53.
[44] Mr Gibson to Sir D. Jephson-Norreys, 23 May 1846, quoted in *C.C.*, 28 May 1846.

distress in Cork at this time than in the smaller neighbouring counties of Kerry, Limerick, and Tipperary. In Limerick alone, as many as 67,000 persons were being relieved through the public works. [45]

These measures helped materially to alleviate distress, but perhaps only a fifth of the 1845 potato crop had been destroyed by the blight. The 1846 crop, on the other hand, was almost a total loss. In spite of this, Lord John Russell's government decided in August 1846 to reverse Peel's policy of restraining speculation through the purchase and sale of foreign grain. [46] The new policy proved a horrible mistake. The public works begun by Peel's government were also ordered to be gradually discontinued beginning on 8 August 1846, though no action was taken in many places because the local authorities could not bring themselves to face the awful consequences. [47] Moreover, invaluable time was squandered in laying the plans for, and in beginning, new works, while destitution increased rapidly as more and more labourers were either thrown out of work by the farmers or unwilling to continue in employment if denied money wages. [48]

The announcement of the policy of non-interference with the grain trade on the east coast, including all of County Cork except a small corner in the southwest, made an already critical situation even worse. It helped within one month to raise the retail price of Indian meal in Cork by nearly one-third, from less than £10 to £13 per ton. [49] During October it moved up to £14 or £15, and by December Cork merchants who had purchased Indian corn at £10 15s. per ton were reselling it to relief committees and retailers at from £16 to £17—'a whacking profit at the expense of the poor'. [50] Because the government obstinately refused to undercut the average retail price in the nearest market town, its officials disposed of Indian meal in the special depots at the rate of £19 per ton, though it had cost less than £13. [51] In these circumstances, the wages paid on the public works merely mocked the destitution of the labourers. A moderately

---

[45] *Correspondence explanatory of the measures adopted by her majesty's government for the relief of distress arising from the failure of the potato crop in Ireland*, p. 356.

[46] O'Neill, 'Administration of relief', pp. 223–4; Woodham-Smith, *Great hunger*, p. 86.

[47] O'Neill, 'Administration of relief', pp. 221, 227–32; Woodham-Smith, *Great hunger*, p. 85.

[48] Minute book, Cove famine relief committee, 1846–7, 31 Oct. 1846, p. 74.

[49] P.R.O.I.: Distress papers, D5858.

[50] *C.E.*, 14 Dec. 1846. See also P.R.O.I.: Distress papers, D6190.

[51] O'Neill, 'Administration of relief', p. 226.

efficient worker was judged capable by the board of works of earning 10*d.* to 1*s.* per day at task labour, but in many parts of Cork wages did not exceed 8*d.* [52] Unable in many cases to purchase enough food even at the reduced prices offered by the relief committees, labourers slowly starved to death. Perhaps five or six pounds of meal daily would have sufficed to keep the labourer and his family of five alive, [53] but in late 1846 and early 1847, as the price of meal soared, wages became less and less adequate to achieve this irreducible minimum. [54] In the district of Skibbereen in December 1846 a labourer earning the prevailing public-works wage of 8*d.* per day was able to purchase only a little more than four pounds of meal daily at the price of almost 2*d.* per pound charged by the local relief committee. [55] It was scarcely surprising that desperate labourers in the districts of Dunmanway, Clonakilty, Bandon, and Mitchelstown assaulted the pay clerks during November and December, and generally demanded wages of at least 1*s.* per day. [56]

Starvation and epidemic disease began to take a terrible toll in several parts of Cork early in 1847. The southwestern districts of the county were undoubtedly the worst ravaged. Elihu Burritt, an American scholar and philanthropist who visited Skibbereen in February, was revolted by the prevalence of hunger edema. He saw men working on the roads 'with their limbs swollen to almost twice their usual size'; the body of a twelve-year-old boy was 'swollen to nearly three times its usual size and had burst the ragged garment that covered him'; the arms of a two-year-old were 'not much larger than pipe stems, while its body was swollen to the size of a full-grown person'. [57] Living men, women, and children, hideous skeletons racked by fever, buried themselves in the watchhouse of Skibbereen's graveyard. [58] An English midshipman who came ashore at Skull for a day described without embellishment the ghastly nightmare of the famine in a letter to his family in late February:

[52] Ibid., p. 228.

[53] *First annual report of the commissioners for administering the laws for relief of the poor in Ireland, with appendices* [963], H.C. 1847–8, xxxiii, 377, p. 17.

[54] *C.E.*, 6, 9 Nov. 1846; 12, 17 Feb. 1847; P.R.O.I.: Distress papers, D9842; Cowdray archives, MS 1914: P. Smith to earl of Egmont, 9 Dec. 1846.

[55] *C.E.*, 14 Dec. 1846.

[56] *Correspondence from July 1846 to January 1847, relating to the measures adopted for the relief of the distress in Ireland*, board of works series [764], H.C. 1847, l, 1, pp. 61–4.

[57] E. Burritt, *A journal of a visit of three days to Skibbereen and its neighbourhood* (London, 1847), p. 10.

[58] Ibid., p. 7.

We proceeded to East Skull on quitting Shirkin. Inland we passed a crowd of 500 people half naked and starving. They were waiting for soup to be distributed amongst them. They were pointed out to us, and as I stood looking with pity and wonder at so miserable a scene, my conductor, a gentleman residing at East Skull, and a medical man, said to me: 'Not a single one of those you now see will be alive in three weeks; it is impossible'. The deaths here average 40 to 50 daily. 20 bodies were buried this morning, and they were fortunate in getting buried at all. The people build themselves up in their cabins, so that they may die together with their children and not be seen by passers-by. Fever, dysentery, and starvation stare you in the face everywhere—children of 10 and 9 years old I have mistaken for decrepit old women, their faces wrinkled, their bodies bent and distorted with pain, the eyes looking like those of a corpse. Babes are found lifeless, lying on their mothers' bosoms. I will tell you one thing which struck me as peculiarly horrible; a dead woman was found lying on the road with a dead infant on her breast, the child having bitten the nipple of the mother's breast right through in trying to derive nourishment from the wretched body. Dogs feed on the half-buried dead, and rats are commonly known to tear people to pieces, who, though still alive, are too weak to cry out. I went into one of the only shops in the place to try and get some bread to give away. I was obliged to leave immediately, for I could not stand the stench. On looking again, I discovered the reason—one body lay stretched on a door. And I saw the outline of a form, although covered with a heap of rags, I perceived was also dead. Instead of following us, beggars throw themselves on their knees before us, holding up their dead infants to our sight.[59]

Because the towns were centres for the administration of relief, the famine-stricken and disease-ridden population of the rural areas flocked into them.[60] Cork city received the brunt of this desperate migration beginning in October 1846, and the influx during the last two months of the year from all parts of the county was described as 'overwhelming'.[61] Fully one-third of the 5,400 inmates of the Cork union workhouse at the beginning of February 1847 were said to be 'strangers to the union'.[62] Every day for the next three months the flood poured in. The *Cork Constitution* declared in late April:

The incursion of rustic paupers into the city continues unabated, the only change being that it is less observable, as they wait on the outskirts of the town till dark, when they may be seen coming in in droves, the bedclothes strapped to the shoulders of the father, while the children carry pots, pans,

[59] From *The Times*, quoted in *C.C.*, 11 Mar. 1847.

[60] *C.E.*, 10 Feb. 1847, 6 Dec. 1848; *C.C.*, 2 Feb. 1847; Minute book, Fermoy board of guardians, 1847–8, 23 June 1847, p. 245; Minute book, Midleton board of guardians, Mar.–Dec. 1848, 29 Apr. 1848, p. 52.

[61] Sir W. P. MacArthur, 'Medical history of the famine' in Edwards & Williams, *Great famine*, p. 294.

[62] *C.C.*, 2 Feb. 1847. See also ibid., 30 Jan. 1847.

jugs, old sacks, and other articles. On an average about 300 of these miserable creatures come into the city daily, who are walking masses of filth, vermin, and sickness.[63]

By late April some 20,000 paupers had reportedly invaded Cork from country districts as far away as Castletown-Berehaven and the borders of Kerry; as many as 500 a week were dying within the city limits.[64] The incursions represented such a grave threat to public health and civil order that on 26 April Cork's mayor, Andrew F. Roche, issued a proclamation ordering the magistrates to drive all 'strolling beggars, vagabonds, and idle persons seeking relief' out of the city at once.[65] In addition, twenty-two special armed constables were assigned to guard the city's entrances and to turn back the horde of rural refugees.[66] This latter measure was partly effective, and the constables were employed again in 1848.[67]

The desperate plight of labourers and cottiers produced not only a wave of migration to the towns but also food riots and food stealing of an unprecedented character. This is an aspect of the great famine which has failed to receive sustained treatment from historians but repays closer study, particularly for the insights it provides into class relationships. The sole business of a magistrate at the Kildorrery petty sessions on one day in October 1846 consisted of hearing farmers' complaints against labourers caught stealing turnips; the farmers loudly objected when the compassionate magistrate dismissed all cases.[68] In order to protect their crops, some farmers 'provided themselves with guns, and it was their custom to travel through their gardens before bedtime and fire a shot or two to intimidate the poor people'.[69] Intimidation occasionally gave way to homicide. A farmer named Hawkins near Courtmacsherry shot and killed a turnip thief in one of his fields in March 1847; and an armed watchman seriously wounded another at Rochemount near Cloyne in the following November.[70]

Far more serious than the pilfering of growing crops, however, was the theft and destruction of livestock. Reports of cattle and sheep stealing came in profusion from all parts of the county between late 1846 and 1849. In the Mallow district during November

[63] Ibid., 24 Apr. 1847.
[64] Ibid. See also ibid., 8 May 1847.
[65] Ibid., 29 Apr. 1847.
[66] Ibid., 1 May, 8 June 1847.
[67] *C.E.*, 1 Oct. 1847; 29 Sept., 22 Nov. 1848; *Southern Reporter*, 1, 3, 22 Feb., 11 Mar. 1848; *C.C.*, 22 Feb., 14 Sept. 1848.
[68] *C.E.*, 30 Oct. 1846.
[69] Irish Folklore Commission: MS 1071, p. 107.
[70] *C.E.*, 22 Mar., 21 Nov. 1847.

1846 the killing of cows and sheep was 'a favourite pastime with the idle and the vicious'. [71] Near Cork city in the same month sheep rearers were 'almost nightly subjected to the depredations of these starving men'. [72] By April 1847 the robbery of sheep, poultry, and other produce had reportedly increased to 'an astonishing extent' in the northwestern part of the county. [73] On the other side of Cork near Mitchelstown, cattle stealing was so frequent in May 1849 that 'the poor farmers must keep a man employed every night to watch their property'. [74] Near Kildorrery sheep stealing by distressed labourers was rampant at about the same time, and 'from the manner that the poor farmers are exposed to this sort of plunder, and the very heavy poor rates they are subject to, they refuse to give any sort of relief to the poor creatures who crawl about demanding it'. [75] The land agent John Waller Braddell wrote to Sir Denham Jephson-Norreys on 15 May 1849 from Mallow:

As to think of protecting property here, it is useless; robberies are committed on the unfortunate farmers to the most glaring extent. Sheep and hay are taken every night, and although hundreds are caught with hay, they defy you to prove that it has been stolen. [76]

Gangs of cattle thieves sometimes ranged over the countryside at night. Three desperate men in the locality of Coachford were said in September 1847 to have 'devastated the country round in right sweeping style, bringing home the spoils of a whole barony'. [77] And in May 1849 the police succeeded in breaking up and arresting 'a notorious gang of cattle stealers', five in number, near Skull. [78]

Sheep and cattle stealing were regarded as so subversive of the social order that famished labourers convicted of these offences for the first time were sentenced to transportation to penal colonies in Australia for terms of seven, ten, or fifteen years. The first six men convicted of sheep stealing at the Cork spring assizes in March 1846 received ten-year terms, but seven years became the ordinary penalty. [79] Such draconian measures were considered essential to protect the industrious farmers of the country, and had their firm

[71] Ibid., 18 Nov. 1846. See also ibid., 2 Dec. 1846.
[72] Ibid., 20 Nov. 1846.
[73] Ibid., 12 Apr. 1847.
[74] Ibid., 9 May 1849.
[75] Ibid., 14 May 1849.
[76] Jephson-Norreys papers: J. W. Braddell to Sir D. Jephson-Norreys, 15 May 1849, in folder marked 'Mallow workhouse and poor law commissioners, 1847–50'.
[77] *C.E.*, 27 Sept. 1847.
[78] Ibid., 14 May 1849.
[79] Ibid., 24 Mar. 1846.

support. After the potato failure of 1846, the criminal business of quarter sessions around the county came to consist almost entirely of offences against property, mostly occasioned by great hunger and abject want. Of the 4,077 defendants tried at quarter sessions in County Cork during 1848, almost 500 were charged with stealing sheep or cattle, and 333 received various terms of banishment. [80] The prosecuting assistant barristers, protested the *Cork Examiner* in March 1849, looked upon transportation as a panacea for Irish misery. Before the famine some 600 men in Ireland were annually sentenced to transportation. But in 1847 and again in 1848 this number more than tripled to about 2,000, and at the first quarter sessions in 1849 alone almost 600 received sentences of banishment. [81] It is not unlikely, however, that a considerable number of labourers deliberately courted transportation to Australia as a preferable alternative to continued destitution in their homeland.

Food riots and similar disturbances were part of the same pattern of desperation and despair. The workhouses and meeting places of relief committees in the towns and villages were focal points for venting the anger and frustration provoked by rising unemployment and food prices. Hundreds of hungry men marched into the small town of Unionhall in southwest Cork in late August 1846, demanding both food and work from the Myross relief committee and vowing ominously that they would not allow themselves to starve. [82] Early in September, on the scheduled meeting day of the Mallow relief committee, 'the road leading [into Mallow] from Doneraile presented one moving mass of human beings . . . headed by a tall and able-bodied man, bearing in his hand a wand with a tainted potato on the top, emblematic of their blighted prospects'. [83] Large crowds of men, women, and children from the surrounding parishes stormed into Macroom at the end of the same month, shouting 'work or food' and striking terror into the townspeople and shopkeepers; a local landlord who marched in their midst, aided by the parish priest of Macroom, barely succeeded in dissuading them from looting. [84] The earl of Egmont's agent reported in December that since there were as yet no public works in Castlemagner parish, 'the people were in awful distress & came in crowds several times, *threatening to plunder* if they did not get food or work' from the relief committee. [85]

[80] Ibid., 26 Jan. 1849.
[81] Ibid., 14 Mar. 1849.
[82] Ibid., 24 Aug. 1846.
[83] Ibid., 4 Sept. 1846.
[84] Ibid., 2 Oct. 1846.
[85] Cowdray archives, MS 1914: P. Smith to earl of Egmont, 9 Dec. 1846.

Largely balked in their demands for assistance, the labouring poor took matters into their own hands. As early as September 1846 risings were reported imminent in various places. [86] Sporadic outbreaks soon began to occur. Mobs from the country raged into the towns of Cloyne, Castlemartyr, Midleton, and Cloheen, where they sacked bread shops and provision stores. [87] The troops were called from Cork city when a large crowd in Castlemartyr, after seizing all the food they could lay their hands on, moved to the gates of the earl of Shannon's demesne at the head of the town and 'threatened to pull down the castle over the head of his lordship and [vowed] that they would return the following day in increased numbers to carry out their threat'. [88] Almost simultaneously, a mob which had emptied the bread shops in Fermoy left the town and proceeded along the road to Mitchelstown, stopping at the earl of Mountcashel's demesne gate; just as they were about to destroy it, troops arrived and dispersed them. [89] The most serious of these early riots occurred in and around Youghal during the last week of September 1846. Flour and bread shops were ransacked. Corn merchants' stores were surrounded, and grain deliveries from the country intercepted and taken out of the town by force. Ships in the harbour were boarded and the export of grain was stopped. [90] On Friday, 25 September, 'an immense number of people from both sides of the Blackwater' gathered on the hills above Youghal, apparently 'determined to sack and pillage the town'. Only the timely intervention of local clergymen prevented a bloody encounter with the authorities, for the magistrates had firmly decided to stop the would-be attackers from entering the town. [91] Together, troops and priests finally managed to quell the disturbances, bringing several days of violence to an end.

Similar outbreaks continued into the autumn of 1847. Early in February a mob of over 600 labourers crudely armed with spades and shovels broke through the outer gate of Cork city and began attacking the bread shops. The police, charging with fixed bayonets, succeeded after a long struggle in dispersing them; the head constable described it as 'the worst riot and the most determined mob he had ever encountered in Cork'. [92] Over the next few months these scenes were repeated. In the third week of June, a crowd of labourers was refused employment on the Cork, Blackrock & Passage railway

[86] *C.E.*, 16 Sept. 1846.
[87] Ibid., 25, 28 Sept., 6 Nov., 2 Dec. 1846.
[88] *C.C.*, 26 Sept. 1846.
[89] Ibid.
[90] Ibid., 24, 26 Sept. 1846.
[91] *C.E.*, 28 Sept. 1846.
[92] *C.C.*, 6 Feb. 1847.

then under construction; they paraded through Ballintemple and into Cork city, sacking bread shops in both places. [93] Movements of grain, even though heavily guarded by the police or the military, were unsafe from attack. Cars laden with Indian meal on their way to Araglin under police escort in late June were waylaid a few miles outside Kilworth by a throng of starving people, who carried away some of the meal before the military arrived from Fermoy. [94] In early October a famished crowd actually prevented a body of troops from removing Indian meal to Kanturk from the relief stores in the village of Boherboy.[95] Soup establishments, provision stores, and bread shops were attacked by raging mobs at Carrigtohill, Castlemartyr, Killeagh, and Clonakilty in May; at Killeagh, where the riot act was read, the crowd screamed that they would prefer to be shot than to die of starvation.[96] Corn mills were robbed at Five Mile Bridge and Donaghmore in June.[97] The soup depot at Clonakilty was plundered in early July and troops were summoned.[98] Hungry crowds that had been refused admission to the temporarily closed Bantry workhouse in early September pillaged the potato and turnip gardens adjoining the house before the military reached the scene.[99]

From these food disturbances, certain facts stand out clearly. There was little or no bloodshed, partly because the police and military authorities exercised great forbearance in mastering the hunger-crazed, violence-prone crowds. Moreover, the catholic clergy played a conspicuous part in discouraging plunder and violence, especially during the autumn of 1846, when public works were agonizingly slow in starting. In the chapels, in the streets, and on the roads, the clergy preached incessantly the virtue of patience in suffering to their people. [100] Though few parts of Cork were completely immune from disturbance, riots seem to have been substantially more frequent in the eastern than in the much more distressed southwestern districts of the county. Lastly, rioting was mainly confined to late 1846 and to 1847. Within a year of the total failure of the potato crop in 1846, the labouring population became so demoralized, shattered in spirit as well as in body, that they were no longer capable of carrying out effective mass protests, and the food riots degenerated into the furtive food stealing of 1848 and 1849.

---

[93] *C.E.*, 21 June 1847. See also *C.C.*, 22 June 1847.
[94] *C.E.*, 21 June 1847.
[95] Ibid., 8 Oct. 1847.
[96] *C.C.*, 11, 18, 22 May 1847.
[97] Ibid., 5 June 1847.
[98] Ibid., 8 July 1847.
[99] *C.E.*, 10 Sept. 1847.
[100] Ibid., 24 Aug., 4, 25, 28 Sept. 1846.

RELIEF MEASURES

Food riots and food stealing were understandable responses by the starving masses to glaring shortcomings in the provision and administration of relief. By failing both to exercise the necessary control over the grain trade and to ensure adequate wage payments on the public works during the autumn of 1846, the British government substantially advanced the prospect of wholesale starvation and epidemic disease among labourers and cottiers in early 1847. Belatedly recognizing its catastrophic errors, the government resolved in January 1847 to provide through public 'soup kitchens' direct food relief—gratuitous in cases of complete destitution—to all distressed persons outside the workhouses. Such an abrupt change in policy was made more palatable by the gradual reduction in public-works employment which it made possible and by the fact that it was to be temporary, continuing only until permanent reforms could be effected in the Irish poor-law system. [101] The new policy was largely inspired by the success of similar private relief schemes under which cooked food—usually 'stirabout', a thick soup of Indian meal and rice steamed—was sold at reduced prices or distributed free. In County Cork private soup kitchens were already combating hunger in late 1846 at Cove, Kanturk, Clonakilty, and Skibbereen, among other places. [102] The Society of Friends had also been operating soup kitchens in Cork city since November 1846 to alleviate the distress of the invading country paupers. [103] But the unsatisfied demand was enormous, especially in remote rural districts, and in such localities the newly established public soup kitchens had a great and immediate impact. 'Soup is keeping thousands alive', declared one West Cork landlord in January 1847. 'It was a blessed plan. In a village near my residence they gave out daily 700 quarts, at $\frac{1}{2}d$. per quart, at a loss under 10s. per day. It is an amazing relief to the creatures on the roads.' [104] By July every poor-law union in the county possessed a relief committee organized under the 'soup kitchen act', [105] and local soup committees had been formed in

[101] O'Neill, 'Administration of relief', pp. 235–41.

[102] Minute book, Cove famine relief committee, 1846–7, 27 Nov. 1846, p. 85; *C.C.*, 2, 5, 7 Jan. 1847; 'Charity souphouse at Skibbereen, 1846' in *Cork Hist. Soc. Jn.*, ser. 2, li, no. 174 (July–Dec. 1946), pp. 189–90.

[103] O'Neill, 'Administration of relief', p. 235. By April 1847 over 9,000 persons daily received a quart of soup at the seven large kitchens then operating in Cork city (*C.C.*, 17 Apr. 1847).

[104] *Correspondence from January to March 1847, relating to the measures adopted for the relief of the distress in Ireland*, board of works series, pt ii [797], H.C. 1847, lii, 1, p. 19.

[105] 10 & 11 Vict., c. 7.

almost every electoral division. At the peak of their operations on 3 July, the government kitchens distributed soup rations to almost 3,021,000 persons throughout Ireland.[106]

While the strategy of massive distribution of food prevented the fearful mortality from rising even higher, the success it achieved largely resulted from the sudden arrival of huge quantities of foreign grain, amounting to nearly 2,850,000 tons, during the first six months of 1847.[107] Corn imports at Cork first became heavy during the second half of February. The Cork grain merchant Nicholas Cummins reported to Charles Trevelyan, the permanent head of the treasury, on 24 February that 'the stocks of bread stuffs generally are accumulating here to a much larger amount than some of our dealers would have it believed'.[108] In the following month there was even talk of a glutted market, and on 26 March Cummins told Trevelyan, 'I cannot estimate the fleet this day in our harbours at less than 250 sail, nor the contents at much under 50,000 tons'.[109] These extremely heavy imports led to a drastic reduction in the price of Indian corn from a peak of £19 a ton in mid-February to £13 at the end of March and to only £7 10s. by the end of August.[110] Abundant supplies and low prices permitted the local relief committees to operate their soup kitchens with maximum efficiency and effect.

The soup kitchens, however, were meant to be only temporary. They were replaced by a new permanent system of relief under legislation passed in June and July 1847, though direct food relief did not cease altogether until early September.[111] This new system had to contend with two more winters of disease and awful mortality almost as bad as that of 1846–7, caused by the grievous underplanting of the land with potatoes in 1847 and by the return of the destructive blight in 1848. For the first time the right of all destitute persons to relief either in or out of the workhouse was recognized by the poor-law amendment act of June, although this theoretical departure from the cherished principle of the workhouse test often meant little in practice. Relief outside the workhouse in the form of food was sanctioned in emergencies, but it was generally expected that the tight-fisted local poor-law guardians would do everything in their

[106] Sir G. Nicholls, *A history of the Irish poor law in connexion with the condition of the people* (London, 1856), p. 339; O'Neill, 'Administration of relief', pp. 239, 241.
[107] Nicholls, *Irish poor law*, p. 318.
[108] Quoted in Trevelyan, *Irish crisis*, pp. 71–2.
[109] Quoted ibid., p. 73.
[110] Nicholls, *Irish poor law*, p. 318.
[111] 10 & 11 Vict., c. 31; 10 & 11 Vict., c. 90.

power to apply the workhouse test to all applicants for relief.[112] Events unfortunately confirmed this expectation. Despite a gradual increase in accommodations, the workhouses continued to be overcrowded, often hopelessly, between 1847 and 1849. Those at Kanturk and Skibbereen were probably the worst examples of this evil in County Cork. The main Kanturk workhouse and its three auxiliary buildings could have safely accommodated perhaps 1,000 persons, but at the end of November 1847, there were more than 1,850 inmates.[113] The situation at Skibbereen was sheer madness; there the main workhouse, originally meant to contain only 800 persons, had almost 2,800 inmates in December 1848, though only three small timber sheds were added to make room for them.[114]

The exceptional instances of Skibbereen and Kanturk apart, overcrowding was probably at its worst in early 1847. In the Fermoy workhouse in March, there were over 1,800 inmates in a building accommodating only 800, and there was no fever hospital.

A pestilential fever [the guardians reported on 10 March] is now raging through the house, every room of which is so crowded as to render it impossible to separate the sick from the healthy. . . . All the horrors of disease are aggravated by the foul air engendered by a multiplicity of impurities unavoidable where fifty patients are crowded into a room too small for twenty. . . . On the first of January last the number in the house was 1,377, from which date to the 8th of March inst. the admissions exceeded the discharges by 917, making a total of 2,294, of whom 543 died. . . . By reason of this overcrowding of the house, the supply of bedding is so short as to render it necessary to place 4 or 5 in many of the beds, & on this day 30 children labouring under disease were found in 3 beds.[115]

In other workhouses as well, the necessity of separating the sick from the healthy was often disregarded in the first few months of 1847.[116] Some improvement was possible after the guardians were empowered to rent houses and stores and to build special fever hospitals and dispensaries.[117]

---

[112] 10 & 11 Vict., c. 31, ss. 1–2; Nicholls, *Irish poor law*, pp. 335–6.
[113] The poor-law commissioners dismissed the unpaid Kanturk guardians in November 1847 for having admitted 500 more paupers to the workhouse than the number sanctioned; paid vice-guardians were appointed in their stead (*C.E.*, 1 Dec. 1847).
[114] Ibid., 8 Dec. 1848.
[115] Minute book, Fermoy board of guardians, 1847–8, 10 Mar. 1847, pp. 26–9.
[116] *C.C.*, 5 Jan. 1847; Minute book, Dunmanway board of guardians, 1846–7, 16 Jan. 1847, pp. 61–2; Minute book, Bantry board of guardians, 1846–7, 19 Jan. 1847, p. 5.
[117] 10 & 11 Vict., c. 22; MacArthur, 'Medical history', pp. 295–8.

The underlying causes of high mortality rates within public relief institutions during the winters of 1847–8 and 1848–9 were very much the same as they had been in that of 1846–7. The workhouses and fever hospitals were often the last refuge of those so hopelessly weakened by starvation or so completely overwhelmed by disease that food and medical attention were practically useless. For a complex of reasons, including the dislike of workhouse discipline, the strength of family ties, and the dread of contracting fatal disease, the destitute generally delayed entering the workhouse as long as they possibly could.[118] Many entered only to assure themselves a decent burial. 'The weekly admissions', Dr Eugene O'Neill informed the Fermoy guardians in early March 1847, 'are chiefly confined to the sick & the dying.' Of those paupers admitted at the last meeting of the board, he continued, 'many died a short time after being taken into hospital'.[119] When the number of deaths in Bantry workhouse rose alarmingly to almost fifty in a single week in April, there was a ready explanation: 'The majority of deaths occurred among young infants, children with broken down constitutions, persons brought into the house in a dying condition, & very old persons whose deaths were accelerated' by dysentery or diarrhoea.[120]

The extremely low standards of both sanitation and nursing care also contributed to the high mortality in the workhouses. The Dunmanway facility could scarcely have been 'more dirty or more disorderly', reported a visiting assistant poor-law commissioner in January 1847. He was shocked to find 'the sewers in the yard not swept, the ventilation not attended to, and the smell throughout the house most offensive'.[121] Conditions in Bantry workhouse were chaotic. 'The filth of the wards appropriated to patients suffering from dysentery & consequent effluvia is past endurance', protested the medical officer in March.[122] Beds were dirty and infrequently changed. Incoming paupers had to wash themselves in a few gallons of filthy cold water. Infirmary patients who were seriously ill were not restrained from getting out of bed at night, exposing themselves to cold, or eating improper foods like salt herrings introduced surreptitiously.[123] In certain workhouses the food was either inadequate to maintain health or unsuited to the special requirements

---

[118] Minute book, Mallow board of guardians, 1847–8, 8 Oct. 1847, p. 189; *C.E.*, 23 Oct. 1848.
[119] Minute book, Fermoy board of guardians, 1847–8, 3 Mar. 1847, p. 5.
[120] Minute book, Bantry board of guardians, 1846–7, 6 Apr. 1847, p. 5.
[121] Minute book, Dunmanway board of guardians, 1846–7, 16 Jan. 1847, pp. 61–2.
[122] Minute book, Bantry board of guardians, 1846–7, 2 Mar. 1847, p. 5.
[123] Ibid., 6 Apr. 1847, p. 5; 20 Apr. 1847, pp. 5–10.

of sick paupers. Dr Thomas Holmes implored the Dunmanway guardians more than once in April 1847 to provide milk and white bread for dysentery patients, whose disease was severely aggravated by a cheap diet of coarse brown bread and thin porridge.[124] But the niggardly guardians strongly disagreed with the argument that 'sick paupers should be supplied with food & drinks of a much more costly description than the hard-working labourers or mechanics or small shop-keepers or farmers can afford to themselves when afflicted by sickness'.[125] At Bantry workhouse, the inmates were being fed only once a day in early February 1847 because the guardians were short of funds. Conditions did not improve in succeeding months. By late April there was a 'total want of an adequate supply of whey to the fever hospital patients', who were 'eternally crying out for drink'; the supply of new milk used for whey was 'too scanty'; and the meat was not only irregularly supplied but of 'extremely bad quality'. 'Indeed, the meat is so bad', declared the medical attendant, 'that I never order it for the patients, & their convalescence must be greatly retarded for want of proper nourishment.'[126] By the end of May the Bantry workhouse was completely without food, firing, or any of the necessities of life because the guardians were temporarily bankrupt.[127]

The parsimonious manner in which relief outside the workhouse was administered also drove up the death rate during the famine years. Outdoor relief could be given under the poor-law amendment act of June 1847 to those disabled by old age, sickness, or serious accident, as well as to widows with two or more dependent children.[128] But the scale of outdoor relief was barely sufficient to maintain health and almost never exceeded the one pound of meal which the board of health in Ireland questionably claimed was 'the quantity of cereal food necessary to supply daily sustenance for an adult'.[129] Moreover, while the sheer pressure of destitution forced a few boards of guardians to extend outdoor relief to able-bodied men, not covered by the law of June, other boards doggedly insisted upon the application of the workhouse test to almost all applicants for

[124] Minute book, Dunmanway board of guardians, 1846–7, 3 Apr. 1847, pp. 171–2; 10 Apr. 1847, pp. 189–90.
[125] Ibid., 5 June 1847, p. 267.
[126] Minute book, Bantry board of guardians, 1846–7, 20 Apr. 1847, pp. 5–10.
[127] Ibid., 25 May 1847, p. 9.
[128] 10 & 11 Vict., c. 31, s. 1.
[129] *First annual report of the commissioners for administering the laws for relief of the poor in Ireland, with appendices*, p. 17. See also Minute book, Fermoy board of guardians, 1847–8, 8 Dec. 1847.

relief.[130] The Mallow guardians were conspicuous in this respect. They repeatedly refused to listen to those local parish priests who pointedly told them that many of the poor were either 'dying of starvation or driven to commit crime in order to procure that relief obstinately denied them by the Mallow board'.[131] Defending themselves in June 1848, the guardians claimed that though they 'had been subjected to great abuse & vituperation for not squandering the property of the ratepayers in giving outdoor relief', such relief had actually been unnecessary. In their myopic view, the loud outcry against them arose simply because 'a very large number of destitute persons prefer begging & strolling about these districts in which outdoor relief is distributed [some was given in the adjacent union of Fermoy] to submitting to the discipline of the house'.[132] Similarly, the Dunmanway guardians tersely remarked in April 1849 that because of 'the evils & impositions under out-door relief last year in defiance of the utmost vigilance', they were firmly determined 'never to have recourse to it again, as long as accommodation can be procured to keep the workhouse test'.[133]

The stern refusal to give outdoor relief in early 1849, while a cholera epidemic was raging, contributed significantly to mortality from starvation in some unions, for the poor had a tremendous fear of contracting this usually fatal disease if they entered the workhouse.[134] Despite the high rate of indigence in Fermoy union, 'not a morsel of out-door relief is given to any human being, no matter how deplorable his condition', claimed one incensed critic in April 1849. 'No, the plan is to starve them out of their wretched habitations and thus coerce them to the Fermoy bastile and its adjuncts, where inevitable death stares them in the face.'[135] Only after the menace of cholera had receded in June did the excessively frugal Fermoy guardians

[130] The Kanturk and Bantry boards did provide outdoor relief in 1849 which went far beyond that required by law: almost 20,000 persons were enrolled on the outdoor-relief lists of Kanturk union in February, and more than 17,000 on those of Bantry union in June (*C.E.*, 19, 26 Feb. 1849; Minute book, Bantry board of guardians, 1848–9, 16 June 1849, p. 298).

[131] Rev. R. Green to poor-law commissioners, 17 July 1848, quoted in Minute book, Mallow board of guardians, 1848–9, 21 July 1848, pp. 94–5. See also Minute book, Mallow board of guardians, 1847–8, 8 Oct. 1847, p. 189.

[132] Minute book, Mallow board of guardians, 1848–9, 30 June 1848, p. 76.

[133] Minute book, Dunmanway board of guardians, 1848–9, 28 Apr. 1849, p. 178.

[134] Minute book, Bantry board of guardians, 1848–9, 21 July 1849, p. 347; MacArthur, 'Medical history', pp. 306–7.

[135] *C.E.*, 9 Apr. 1849.

authorize relieving officers to provide food outside the workhouse for some classes of destitute able-bodied persons.[136]

One provision of the poor-law amendment act of June 1847 became notorious because of the way in which it both promoted forced starvation and facilitated the clearance of paupers from overcrowded estates. An ill-considered gesture on behalf of Irish landlords, it is known as the 'quarter-acre' or the 'Gregory clause', named for William Gregory, M.P. for Dublin city, who suggested it. The provision stipulated that occupiers of more than a quarter of an acre of land were not to be considered destitute, nor were they to obtain relief out of the poor rates so long as they persisted in clinging to holdings that exceeded this maximum.[137] Labourers and smallholders who somehow managed to gain admission to a workhouse without meeting the statutory requirement were regularly discharged whenever they were discovered by the local landlord-guardians.[138] But many landlords perverted the intent of the Gregory clause either by demanding that destitute occupiers relinquish everything before entering the workhouse or by destroying their cabins once they had been admitted on the basis of their partial surrenders.[139] Boards of guardians occasionally assisted these estate-clearing proprietors. The *Cork Examiner* angrily charged in late February 1848 that the Midleton guardians and those of some other unions had secretly ordered relieving officers to withhold tickets of admission to the workhouse unless paupers gave up their cabins as well as all their land; the newspaper also claimed that 150 paupers recently discharged from Midleton workhouse had discovered that their dwellings in the parish of Clonpriest were levelled while they were inmates.[140]

Confronted by these threats, occupiers anxious to obtain relief frequently attempted to evade the law. Holdings were often transferred to friends or relatives who were better off, with the parties to these collusive arrangements agreeing that the distressed occupier would repossess the land upon leaving the workhouse.[141] Collusive practices were especially common in unions with heavy concentra-

---

[136] Ibid., 6 June 1849.

[137] 10 & 11 Vict., c. 31, s. 10; O'Neill, 'Administration of relief', p. 253.

[138] Minute book, Fermoy board of guardians, 1847–8, 19 Jan. 1848, p. 658; Minute book, Mallow board of guardians, 1848–9, 18 Nov. 1848, pp. 242–4.

[139] *First annual report of the commissioners for administering the laws for relief of the poor in Ireland, with appendices*, p. 13.

[140] *C.E.*, 23 Feb. 1848.

[141] *First annual report of the commissioners for administering the laws for relief of the poor in Ireland, with appendices*, p. 13.

tions of smallholders, such as Fermoy, where almost 60 per cent of the tenements were five acres or less in 1844.[142] But vigilant local guardians quickly became aware of the subterfuge and took counter-measures that were usually effective.[143] Some landholders tried to avoid the consequences of the Gregory clause by sending their wives and children to the workhouse when distress overwhelmed them. But the guardians, ever anxious to preserve the workhouse test, were extremely reluctant to relieve portions of families. Commenting on the returns from Mallow workhouse in early March 1848, the poor-law commissioners remarked that 'nearly all the applicants for relief who were rejected last week were women & children whose husbands did not apply for admission'.[144]

Destitute small tenants also resorted to bogus desertion in a desperate effort to secure relief for their families and yet retain their holdings. No doubt the number of deserted mothers and orphaned children increased enormously during the famine years, but many cases were bogus and are properly seen as attempts to escape the loss of home and land despite the quarter-acre clause.[145] The Bandon guardians bitterly complained in July 1847 of 'the very frequent & gross imposition practised on the union by several parents sending their children into the workhouse *as orphans*'.[146] And the Mallow guardians strongly objected to the poor-law commissioners in June 1849 that

30 individuals having 23 children have this day applied for admission to the workhouse, stating that they had been deserted by their wives or husbands respectively, an increasing evil for the prevention of which the legal remedies are not found efficacious.[147]

The poor-law commissioners advised local boards in late May 1848, after the effect of the Gregory clause in promoting forced starvation had become all too clear, that the wives and children of men holding more than a quarter of an acre could be relieved without violation

---

[142] *Devon comm. evidence*, pt iv, pp. 280–3.

[143] Minute book, Fermoy board of guardians, 1847–8, 1 Dec. 1847, p. 552.

[144] Minute book, Mallow board of guardians, 1847–8, 3 Mar. 1848, p. 360. See also ibid., 13 Aug. 1847, p. 122.

[145] Minute book, Fermoy board of guardians, 1847–8, 27 Oct. 1847, pp. 486–7; Minute book, Mallow board of guardians, 1847–8, 10 Mar. 1848, p. 367; Minute book, Midleton board of guardians, Mar.–Dec. 1848, 28 Oct. 1848, p. 183.

[146] Minute book, Bandon board of guardians, 1847–8, 24 July 1847, p. 308.

[147] Minute book, Mallow board of guardians, 1849–50, 15 June 1849, p. 100.

of law. [148] The commissioners explained that they were not urging systematic or indiscriminate relief to such persons, but rather that women and children must not be allowed 'to die of starvation or to suffer extreme privation' because of the refusal of family heads to qualify themselves for public assistance. [149] This already was or now became the policy of the guardians in some unions, such as Dunmanway and Cork, but in others the landlord-dominated boards did not closely adhere to it. [150] In Bandon union, for example, the guardians directed the master of the workhouse in September 1848 to discharge all persons whose fathers, husbands, or mothers were outside the house, but to 'use a discretion in case of children who were too young & not strong enough to be sent away'. [151] The vicious aspect of the Gregory clause was that it clashed head on with the traditional attachment of the Irish countryman to the soil of his ancestors, an attachment so strong that many of the smallest landholders were prepared to face death rather than relinquish it. [152]

LANDLORDS AND TENANTS DURING THE FAMINE: RENTS

Besides the clearance of paupers which the Gregory clause facilitated, the great famine presented landowners with other opportunities, principally those of ousting bankrupt middlemen, weeding out struggling or broken tenants, and enlarging the farms of those who remained. But while there were opportunities, there were also great difficulties confronting landlords. Collecting rent and meeting increased charges for both poor rates and employment were undoubtedly the two most serious problems. Indeed, lost rents and the completely without food, firing, or any of the necessities of life already heavily loaded with debt, nearer to bankruptcy.

After the potato crop failed totally in 1846, farmers urgently pressed their claims for liberal reductions in rent. [153] They had lost

[148] Minute book, Bantry board of guardians, Jan.–Nov. 1848, 27 May 1848, pp. 199–200; *Second annual report of the commissioners for administering the laws for relief of the poor in Ireland* [1118], H.C. 1849, xxv, 87, pp. 117–19.

[149] Minute book, Bantry board of guardians, Jan.–Nov. 1848, 10 June 1848, pp. 219–20.

[150] Minute book, Dunmanway board of guardians, 1848–9, 3 Mar. 1849, p. 96; 21 Apr. 1849, p. 68; *C.C.*, 15 June 1848.

[151] Minute book, Bandon board of guardians, 1848–9, 23 Sept. 1848, p. 288. See also ibid., 22 July 1848, p. 197.

[152] *First annual report of the commissioners for administering the laws for relief of the poor in Ireland, with appendices*, p. 14; *Second annual report of the commissioners for administering the laws for relief of the poor in Ireland*, p. 4.

[153] Anti-rent notices appeared in some places. See, e.g., *C.C.*, 10 Sept. 1846.

not only their own crop but also their conacre rents, or at least the portion which had not been paid in advance; they would soon have to consume on the farm a large part of their corn, and there would also be heavy poor rates.[154] At this early stage, however, landlords were generally unsympathetic to these appeals, partly because they firmly believed that farmers had been fully compensated for the loss of the potato by the high price of corn in 1846 and early 1847.[155] Many proprietors were also incensed at the farmers for dismissing their labourers and farm servants, for by these dismissals the farmers appeared to be contemptuously unloading their own responsibilities upon the landlords, thus forcing them to provide for the labouring population that employment which farmers refused to give.[156] John Dillon Croker of Quartertown near Mallow was extremely bitter over the actions of those he called 'the middle farmers'. On the one hand, declared Croker in December 1846, these men were 'making large deposits in the different banks' while on the other hand they were discharging their labourers, 'thus bringing ruin on that class and consigning the property of landed proprietors to a similar fate'.[157] Nicholas P. Leader, the owner of an estate near Kanturk, denounced the farmers for dismissing their labourers in equally strong terms at a meeting of landlords and tenants in that town in January 1847. 'If poverty caused the farmers to act thus,' insisted Leader, 'no person would blame them, but there never was a year in Duhallow when the farmers had more money in their pockets than the present.'[158]

As a consequence of this intense ill-feeling, relatively few substantial reductions of rent were made in either 1846 or 1847.[159] Landlord insistence upon the collection of the full rent was impressively demonstrated in newspaper accounts of land agents and

[154] Ibid., 2, 4, 9 Feb. 1847.

[155] *C.E.*, 28 Aug., 25 Nov. 1846.

[156] Ibid., 30 Nov., 14 Dec. 1846.   [157] Ibid., 23 Dec. 1846.

[158] *C.C.*, 7 Jan. 1847. See also Cowdray archives, MS 1914: earl of Egmont to P. Smith, 8 Jan. 1847.

[159] Viscount Doneraile promised abatements of from 15 to 20 per cent on two gales, but only if his tenants would grant proportionate allowances to their labourers and conacre tenants (Doneraile papers: Draft copy of abatements on the Doneraile estates proposed by the agent, William Hill, 29 Oct. 1846). The duke of Devonshire remitted £5,255 of his annual rental of almost £44,000 in 1846, solely on account of the potato failure (Lismore papers, N.L.I., MS 6929: Rent receipts and disbursements, 1818–90). Viscount Midleton gave reductions ranging from 15 per cent where the rent was more than £100 to 40 per cent where the rent was less than £10 (*C.E.*, 8 Jan. 1847; *C.C.*, 12, 14 Jan. 1847). Other landowners, though far from a majority, reduced their rents by 25 per cent, and in a few reported instances by 50 per cent, on one or two gales in 1846 and 1847 (*C.E.*, 2, 11, 18 Dec. 1846; 16 July, 25 Aug., 22 Oct., 26 Nov. 1847).

bailiffs who distrained farmers' crops and livestock. Many observers regarded the action of the duke of Devonshire's agent in 'filling' the Dungarvan pound with distrained cattle in April 1847 as especially ominous, because it was allegedly 'the first time the noble house of Cavendish ever seized a beast for rent'.[160] Even the chief agent considered distraint 'a strong proceeding', but he quickly consoled himself with the thought that the lesson would 'not be without a good effect on others where it was needed'.[161] The earls of Bantry and Kenmare as well as a host of smaller proprietors resorted to this forcible method of rent collection during the famine years, especially in 1847[162] Among West Cork landlords, the Rev. Maurice Townsend was notably vigorous in this respect. His subordinates made daily raids for produce in October 1847, bringing their prizes into Skibbereen. Indeed, one witness declared that the roads leading into the town carried an 'uninterrupted stream of corn laden carts and cattle under the strong escort of [Townsend's] bailiffs'.[163] The *Cork Examiner* aptly summarized the situation in the autumn of 1847: 'The accounts that reach us from all parts of the country are but repetitions of landlord incursions on the crops and stock of the luckless farmers. . . '.[164]

Landlord seizures naturally led to tenant countermeasures. Rarely, however, did these countermeasures take such semi-permanent form as the protective society organized in Skibbereen in late 1847 to defend tenants from persecution by the landlords of the district.[165] For the most part, tenant responses were simply *ad hoc*. Seizures of goods to enforce payment of rent were forbidden on Sunday by law, and harried tenants sometimes gathered their friends to cut and remove a whole crop on such a day to some secure place.[166] Though actions aimed at preventing a landlord or agent from distraining were illegal and punishable upon conviction by a fine double the value of the goods removed, the law's remedies were often worthless in practice to the aggrieved landlord.[167] In any case, tenants determined to resist their landlords scarcely worried about whether their actions were lawful or not. Hastily collected

[160] *C.E.*, 14 Apr. 1847.
[161] Lismore papers, N.L.I., MS 7183, Letter book, 1842–50: F. E. Currey to W. Currey, 11 Nov. 1848, p. 65. See also *C.E.*, 17 May 1848.
[162] *C.E.*, 28 Dec. 1846; 3 Jan., 14 Apr., 17 Sept. 1847; 12 Feb. 1849.
[163] Ibid., 1 Nov. 1847.
[164] Ibid., 20 Sept. 1847.
[165] Ibid., 19 Nov. 1847.
[166] *C.C.*, 21 Sept., 11 Nov. 1848; *C.E.*, 3 Oct. 1849, 7 Oct. 1850.
[167] 15 Geo. 2, c. 8, ss. 3–4.

groups of tenants often attempted to obstruct seizures or to rescue distrained cattle and crops. One resolute proprietor, W. J. Bleasby, had to call out a strong constabulary force in September 1847 to help him in executing a distress notice on a large farmer near Cork city who had previously assembled a numerous crowd to prevent the sheriff from removing some of his corn.[168] Sometimes these confrontations led to violence. The widow Callaghan's farm on the Colthurst estate near Ballincollig was the scene of a serious affray at the end of September 1849. Almost 300 persons drawn from distant parishes and armed 'with pikes, scythes, and other weapons' gathered on the farm, drove off the keepers guarding the corn for the landlord, and began to carry it away. When the police arrived, a mêlée ensued in which several persons were wounded and more than twenty arrested.[169] In at least one instance, resistance to distraint resulted in murder. The bailiff of John Perrier's property near Macroom was brutally stoned to death by about twenty enraged country people after attempting to seize the cattle of two of Perrier's tenants for arrears of rent in December 1849.[170]

In other parts of Ireland, especially Connaught, landlords who persisted in hunting down their rents found that large numbers of their tenants sold their crops and stock surreptitiously and simply ran away. Cork proprietors, however, were largely spared this problem of disappearance. Though a frustrated rate collector in Kinsale union reported in September 1848 that as many as sixteen tenants had vanished from one local property, 'taking with them all their moveables', similar accounts from other parts of the county are remarkably infrequent.[171] The earl of Bantry, an indulgent landlord residing on an estate deluged with cottiers and paupers, remarked thankfully in January 1848 that none of his tenants had absconded.[172] And Sir John Benn-Walsh, an exacting proprietor in Cork and Kerry, recorded a case of flight in his journal in August 1849 but observed, 'He is the only one of my tenants who has yet played me this trick, so common now in all the distressed districts'.[173] Of course, the early-warning system activated by the runaway smallholders of Connaught enabled Cork agents to take strong precautions with defaulting tenants. They made such tenants find

[168] *C.E.*, 10 Sept. 1847. See also ibid., 27 Aug., 22 Nov. 1847.
[169] Ibid., 10 Oct. 1849. See also ibid., 1 Oct. 1849.
[170] Ibid., 7, 10 Dec. 1849.
[171] *C.C.*, 26 Sept. 1848. See also *C.E.*, 1 Jan., 19 Oct. 1849.
[172] Bantry papers: earl of Bantry to Viscount Berehaven, 26 Jan. 1848 (copy).
[173] Ormathwaite papers: Journal of Sir John Benn-Walsh, 15 Aug. 1849, pp. 221–2.

securities for the application of the harvest money or the proceeds from livestock sales to the payment of rent and arrears, they placed keepers on the uncut or unsold harvest, or they promptly distrained once the harvest had been saved.[174] These stern measures seem to have been fairly effective, and it was more common for struggling tenants intending to emigrate to seek compromises with their landlords rather than to abscond with the rent.[175]

By 1849 the decline in agricultural prices, the poor wheat harvest and liver-fluke epidemic of the previous year, and the other factors depressing farm income inclined landlords to moderate their rent demands. A distinct shift in both attitude and action now became apparent among the majority of proprietors and estate agents. 'It is useless to expect anything from the cabins & small holdings, they have it not', wrote the agent John Waller Braddell to Sir Denham Jephson-Norreys in mid-May 1849. 'You must look upon part of your property as valueless at the present moment.'[176] Though the *Cork Examiner* claimed in October 1849 that reductions in rent were as yet neither substantial nor universal, the increasing frequency of the announcements in its own pages makes it clear that large abatements became all but universal during the course of the year.[177] Following the lead given by the agents of the duke of Devonshire and by the receivers for the large number of Cork estates under the administration of the courts, landlords commonly granted temporary abatements of 20 or 25 per cent.[178] A few proprietors, such as the duke of Devonshire and the earls of Bantry and Donoughmore, made reductions of this magnitude every year between 1849 and 1853.[179] On the majority of estates they were very prevalent from 1849 to 1851, but much less so in 1852, when there was considerable anxiety to rescind them.[180] In tillage districts, however, falling corn

---

[174] Lismore papers, N.L.I., MS 7183, Letter book, 1842–50: F. E. Currey to A. Swanston, 2 Oct. 1849, pp. 50–1; Currey to Swanston, 8 Oct. 1849, pp. 53–6; *C.E.*, 3 Jan. 1848.

[175] *C.E.*, 19 Oct. 1849.

[176] Jephson-Norreys papers: J. W. Braddell to Sir D. Jephson-Norreys, 15 May 1849, in folder marked 'Mallow workhouse and poor law commissioners, 1847–50'. See also ibid., Braddell to Jephson-Norreys, 9 Aug. 1850.

[177] *C.E.*, 8 Oct. 1849.

[178] Ibid., 26 Mar., 6, 9 Apr., 30 May, 8 June, 6, 18 July, 1, 3 Aug., 1, 8, 15, 24 Oct., 19 Nov. 1849.

[179] Lismore papers, N.L.I., MS 6929: Rent receipts and disbursements, 1818–90; *C.E.*, 23 May 1853, 29 Oct. 1860.

[180] *C.E.*, 4, 25 Jan., 12 June, 2 Oct., 11 Dec. 1850; 31 Mar., 10 Oct. 1851; 5 May 1852.

prices and low potato yields often forced reluctant landlords to continue these abatements even then. [181]

Reductions in rent were vital if proprietors wished to keep their farms tenanted. For it became increasingly difficult from 1849 to find solvent tenants for lands which the previous occupiers had surrendered or, more usually, from which they had been dispossessed. This situation resulted not so much from the deeply rooted tradition against taking evicted farms but rather from dismal agricultural prospects. Because of the bleakness of the times, there was little inquiry in 1849 from respectable tenants for several vacant holdings on the duke of Devonshire's Bandon estate, and the duke's managers were very hard pressed to maintain the rents of previous lettings when making new ones. [182] Yet conditions around Bandon were hardly so bad in these respects as they were near Bantry and between Skibbereen and Skull, where thousands of acres reportedly lay derelict in December 1849. In the latter southwestern district, one landlord alone was unable to find tenants for 1,500 acres which he had on hand, though he had offered to reduce the acreable rent by as much as one-third and to give twenty-one-year leases. [183] Even in the relatively prosperous Midleton district, it was extremely difficult to relet farms that had fallen vacant. In a letter to the trustees of Viscount Midleton's estate in late February 1852, the agent gloomily reported:

I have advertized these lands [Ballydekin, Broomfield, and Garryduff] to be let by handbills and postings in the Cork papers but . . . have received no offers for them except those which I now enclose, and these I consider too low even in the present depressed times. . . . [184]

The decline in rent receipts between 1845 and 1853 arising from abatements, unpaid rents, and lost arrears rarely exceeded two years' rent for individual estates. Yet the loss of even a year's rent over that short span of time was generally regarded as a serious, if not a shattering, blow. Table 13 demonstrates that large landlords generally suffered losses of this magnitude. [185]

[181] Guildford Muniment Room, Midleton papers: T. Foley to J. Tatham, 18 Jan. 1852 (copy).

[182] Lismore papers, N.L.I., MS 7183, Letter book, 1842–50: F. E. Currey to A. Swanston, 29 Mar. 1849, pp. 32–3; Currey to Swanston, 19 Apr. 1849, pp. 34–5.

[183] *C.E.*, 31 Dec. 1849.

[184] Guildford Muniment Room, Midleton papers: T. Foley to R. Bray, 28 Feb. 1852 (copy). See also ibid.: T. Foley to J. Tatum, 18 Jan. 1852 (copy).

[185] Lismore papers, N.L.I., MS 6929: Rent receipts and disbursements, 1818–90; Kenmare papers: Rental of the earl of Kenmare's estates, 1830–50

TABLE 13   Rents due to and rents collected by various Cork landlords, 1845–53

estate	years	rents due	rents collected	% collected	abate-ments
		(to the nearest hundred)			
Devonshire	1846–53	£359,200	£300,300	84	£34,000
Kenmare	1845–50	146,400	123,400	84	—
Bandon	1845–8	94,200	75,500	80	8,400
Midleton	1845–8	63,000	59,600	95	—
Doneraile	1847–53	53,100	39,300	74	7,900
Jephson-Norreys	1846–53	30,200	27,300	90	—
Bowen	1848–53	20,800	16,900	81	—
Kingwilliamstown	1845–51	4,500	3,900	87	—

Three of these proprietors, however, did not fare as well as the figures in Table 13 indicate. Though little ground was lost on Viscount Midleton's estates in the collection of current rents between 1845 and 1848, the heavy arrears of some £14,000 in May 1845 could not be reduced.[186] In fact, by 1850 the arrears had grown to over £18,000, or close to one year's rental income, and additional losses occurred as a result of the large abatements of 25, 20, and 20 per cent granted on the year's rent due in the autumn of 1849, 1850, and 1851 respectively.[187] Abatements did not have serious adverse effects on the financial position of either Sir Denham Jephson-Norreys or Robert Cole Bowen, and Jephson-Norreys in particular managed to gather a very high proportion of the rents owed to him. But both landlords experienced significant declines in the amount of their annual rentals. Why these declines occurred is

[186] Warrens, London, Midleton papers: Proof and explanation of the account for Viscount Midleton's estates, Mar. and May 1845, no. 13.

[187] House of Lords Record Office, London: Viscount Midleton estate act (1850), no. 601, p. 108; Guildford Muniment Room, Midleton papers: T. Foley to J. Tatham, 18 Jan. 1852 (copy).

(in the possession of Mrs Beatrice Grosvenor, Killarney, Co. Kerry); Doherty papers: Rental of the earl of Bandon's estates, 1826–48; Midleton papers: Account of rents received on Viscount Midleton's estates, 1838–48 (in the possession of Warrens, Solicitors, 5 Bedford Square, London); Doneraile papers: Rentals of Viscount Doneraile's estates, 1847–53; Jephson-Norreys papers: Rental of the Jephson-Norreys estate, 1846–55; Bowen papers, Tipperary County Library, Thurles: Rental of Robert Cole Bowen's estates in the counties of Cork and Tipperary, 1847–53; *A copy of any reports on the experimental improvements on the crown estate of King William's Town in the county of Cork, submitted to her majesty's commissioners of woods and forests since the 8th day of August 1844 . . .* , p. 10.

not exactly clear, but they could easily have resulted from new lettings at reduced rents, from inability to relet holdings after evictions had taken place, or from the addition of vacant farms to the landlord's demesne. Whatever the precise reasons, the annual rental on the Jephson-Norreys estate fell from £4,200 to £3,500 between 1847 and 1853, and on the Bowen properties from £3,700 to £3,200 between 1848 and 1853.[188] In contrast to Bowen and Jephson-Norreys, the earl of Kenmare experienced a modest increase in the amount of his annual rental from £23,700 in 1845 to £25,400 in 1850, largely as a result of the expiration of a few middlemen's leases.[189] The earl's losses arising from uncollected rents were not negligible, but they would certainly have been much greater if his domains in Cork, Kerry, and Limerick had generally been let directly to the army of smallholders who actually occupied them. As late as 1850, however, nineteen of the twenty-three townlands on his Kerry estate in Killarney union were still in the hands of middlemen, who apparently paid their moderate head rents punctually—a rare occurrence during the famine—and received no reduction from Kenmare.[190] The duke of Devonshire, the earl of Bandon, and Viscount Doneraile all found it necessary to grant significant abatements to their occupying tenants, and yet each of them suffered a cumulative loss in rent receipts within the period specified in Table 13 which equalled or surpassed in relative terms the loss incurred by the earl of Kenmare. Especially notable for its moderate decline in rent receipts was the crown estate of Kingwilliamstown, administered by the commissioners of woods and forests. But after spending such large sums for permanent improvements, the managers of the property expressed keen disappointment in the revenues in 1851, for they had fixed the rents of the consolidated and enlarged holdings at a reasonable level in 1839 and yet had seen the arrears almost double from £640 to £1,270 between 1846 and 1851.[191]

EMPLOYMENT

Even while their revenues diminished markedly, landowners were continually pressed to relieve distress during the famine by providing

[188] Jephson-Norreys papers: Rental of the Jephson-Norreys estate, 1846–55; Bowen papers: Rental of Robert Cole Bowen's estates in the counties of Cork and Tipperary, 1847–53.

[189] Kenmare papers: Rental of the earl of Kenmare's estates, 1830–50.

[190] *C.E.*, 31 Dec. 1849.

[191] *A copy of any reports on the experimental improvements on the crown estate of King William's Town in the county of Cork, submitted to her majesty's commissioners of woods and forests since the 8th day of August 1844* . . . , p. 10.

employment on a greatly extended scale. The frequency and sharpness of the complaints made by members of their own class suggest, however, that this was a responsibility for which most proprietors showed little enthusiasm. The Fermoy guardians, shocked by the lassitude of many landlords in their union, implored them in September 1847 'in the most impressive language they can command to give employment . . . in preference to throwing their labourers on the union for support, for which they must immediately pay out of their own pockets'.[192] The Bantry guardians complained bitterly in July 1848 that destitution 'always existed in this wretched district in consequence of the almost entire disregard of that protective power that should be extended toward the poorer classes'. They strongly urged that coercive measures be adopted 'to make those parties to improve their properties who have tracts of country which might be increased in value 25 to 30 per cent, & where a mass of pauperism exists'.[193] Hoping that the pressure of public opinion would help to correct similar neglect, the Dunmanway guardians had resorted in February 1848 to publishing both the names of landlords who failed to borrow money under the land-improvement acts and the number of paupers receiving workhouse relief from particular estates within their union.[194]

There were, however, a considerable number of proprietors, though a small proportion of the total, who regarded the provision of employment as an urgent task, whether out of self-interest or generous humanitarian feelings. Some of the great landlords were conspicuous in this respect. But for the munificence of the earl of Kingston, observed a local parish priest in November 1847, the Mitchelstown district would surely have been another Skibbereen; Kingston was spending nearly one-fifth of his annual rental of some £40,000 to alleviate distress on his estates.[195] The earl of Shannon was singled out in January 1848 for having been 'indefatigable during the last two years of famine in his endeavours to promote the comfort and happiness of the poor on his property'.[196] As many as 400 labourers were employed on his Castlemartyr estate, and several hundred pounds were expended each week for wages, food, and related items; Shannon had applied in 1847 for a loan of £12,000 from the government in order to relieve distress on both his Castle-

[192] Minute book, Fermoy board of guardians, 1847–8, 15 Sept. 1847, p. 405.
[193] Minute book, Bantry board of guardians, Jan.–Nov. 1848, 29 July 1848, p. 290.
[194] *Southern Reporter*, 3, 26 Feb. 1848.
[195] *C.E.*, 27 Nov. 1847, 15 May 1848.
[196] *Southern Reporter*, 20 Jan. 1848.

martyr and Clonakilty properties.[197] There was reportedly not a single able-bodied labourer without work in Magourney parish in December 1848 because Sir George and Charles Colthurst were giving employment to over 200 men in the Ballyvourney district.[198] A local parish priest maintained in October 1849 that during the previous three years Sir George Colthurst had spent over £5,000, or more than one year's rental income, for buildings, drainage, fences, and roads on his Ballyvourney estate.[199] Viscount Midleton received repeated praise from the Cove relief committee for furnishing work at ample wages to 'hundreds of labourers & tradesmen' on his costly improvement projects in that locality.[200] At least £20,000, or about one year's income from all of Midleton's estates, was laid out for improvements between 1845 and 1848; more than half of this large sum was devoted to the building of a sea wall and esplanade at Ringmeen.[201] On the duke of Devonshire's properties expenditure for permanent improvements and repairs as well as for the alleviation of distress increased sharply during the famine years. Altogether, Devonshire spent £87,000, or almost two year's rental income, for drainage (£11,700), compensation for improvements by tenants (£4,500), charities and subscriptions (£18,400), and estate works and repairs at Lismore, Bandon, Youghal, and Dungarvan (£52,400) between 1845 and 1852.[202]

Such lavish outlays by these Cork landowners during the famine were highly exceptional. This fact becomes clear from an examination of the list of proprietors who borrowed money from the government at a low rate of interest after the land-improvement acts came into operation in 1847.[203] The goal of this legislation was to enable landowners to provide productive employment through the improvement of their estates as a substitute for the unproductive employment, mainly stone breaking, offered to the destitute under the poor laws. Although more than 250 Cork proprietors took advantage of the land-improvement acts during the famine years, less than one-fourth of them applied for sums in excess of £1,000. The policy of the board of works was partly at fault, for the full

[197] *C.E.*, 28 Dec. 1846, 21 Jan. 1848.

[198] Ibid., 6 Dec. 1848.   [199] Ibid., 24 Oct. 1849.

[200] Minute book, Cove famine relief committee, 1846–7, 5 Feb. 1847, p. 105. See also ibid., 14 May 1846, p. 33.

[201] Guildford Muniment Room, Midleton papers: Account of expenditures on Ringmeen building estate and others, 1844–8; P.R.O.I., ref. no. 978, Midleton papers: Rentals of Viscount Midleton's estates, 1847.

[202] Lismore papers, N.L.I., MS 6929: Rent receipts and disbursements, 1818–90.

[203] 9 Vict., c. 1; 9 & 10 Vict., c. 85, 96, 101, 108; 10 & 11 Vict., c. 106.

amount of any application was rarely sanctioned. Thus only about twenty of the more than sixty Cork landowners who applied for them actually received loans of more than £1,000. Government policy, however, had little to do with the fact that of the £176,000 sanctioned by the board of works, only £106,000 was spent by Cork proprietors.[204]

In general, landlords were either unable or unwilling to provide more employment—unable because they were already loaded with debts and saw their incomes dwindling, unwilling because, whether they did or not, they could not escape heavy rates. Poor rates were levied on the smaller administrative units known as electoral divisions rather than on the poor-law union as a whole, with the aim of encouraging proprietors to furnish employment and in that way to keep their assessments low. Many landowners, however, were inclined to throw off the burden of giving work if they found themselves unable substantially to reduce their own rates, either because their property spanned several electoral divisions in which the other owners refused to share the burden, or because neighbouring proprietors were clearing their estates of pauper tenants and thus contributing to the need for more relief. A landlord like the duke of Devonshire, whose estates were at once compact and not situated in or near districts where high rates of indigence prevailed, and who regularly provided substantial employment, was not saddled with heavy rates. In fact, Devonshire paid only about 7 per cent of his princely rental income in rates and taxes between 1846 and 1853.[205] But other proprietors were not nearly so fortunate. John Dillon Croker, who resided on his 1,000-acre estate near Mallow, railed in January 1848 against local absentee landlords whose grievous neglect of duty compelled him to pay almost £200 in rates on his demesne and on land held by tenants. Croker firmly believed that before the year was over, as much as 40 per cent of his income would be consumed by poor rates.

The consequence that must follow [Croker declared] will be my being incapacitated from employing the number of hands I now do, and [I] must lay all my grounds under grass and only keep such a number of servants as will attend to my cattle and sheep.[206]

[204] *Twenty-fourth report from the board of public works, Ireland: with the appendices, 1855* [2140], H.C. 1856, xix, 357, pp. 104–7. Some landowners, of course, privately financed estate improvements, but the expenditure under this legislation probably provides a good indication of the small volume of activity.

[205] Lismore papers, N.L.I., MS 6929: Rent receipts and disbursements, 1818–90.

[206] *C.C.*, 18 Jan. 1848.

The earl of Bantry and Viscount Berehaven, who together applied for government loans amounting to nearly £13,000 (the board of works sanctioned £9,000), actually spent less than £3,000.[207] Their agent, the Rev. Somers Payne, publicly explained in April 1849 that the remainder was returned because

> they found that such was the operation of the [poor] law that, although they employed large numbers of the people, it was impossible to lower their own rates, and that they were taxed as heavily as those who did not employ a single man.[208]

The pressure of rates became so intolerable for landowners in some unions that they resisted paying them. Charles Roche, a rate collector in Mallow union, reported to the guardians in September 1847 that 'many of the gentlemen' doggedly refused to pay their assessments, forcing him to take legal proceedings for recovery.[209] John O'Sullivan, a rate collector in Bantry union, encountered similar opposition. Nearly half the unpaid rates in his division, O'Sullivan informed the guardians in June 1847, arose from the default of two large estates, one under the management of the court of chancery, the other belonging to Samuel Hutchins, one of the Bantry guardians no less. Though threatened with a lawsuit, Hutchins still refused to pay and 'has left this part of the country'.[210] Henry Puxley, the wealthy owner of valuable copper mines in the Castletown-Berehaven district, balked at paying £1,200 in rates on his mines, which were valued at £8,000; he went to court and succeeded in February 1848 in obtaining a reduction of his valuation to £3,000 and of his rates to about £450.[211] Following Puxley's legal victory, a great number of appeals, mostly unsuccessful, were lodged by other dissatisfied proprietors against the poor rates in Bantry union.[212]

THE CLEARANCES

The burden of poor rates as well as the procedure for assessing them induced landlords to clear their estates of pauper tenants. Since the

---

[207] *Twenty-fourth report from the board of public works, Ireland: with the appendices, 1855*, p. 104.

[208] *Southern Reporter*, 14 Apr. 1849.

[209] Minute book, Mallow board of guardians, 1847-8, 17 Sept. 1847, pp. 156-7.

[210] Minute book, Bantry board of guardians, 1846-7, 22 June 1847, pp. 9-10.

[211] Minute book, Bantry board of guardians, Jan.-Nov. 1848, 19 Feb. 1848, pp. 57-8.

[212] Minute book, Bantry board of guardians, 1848-9, 23 June 1849, p. 309; 21 July 1849, p. 346.

rates were levied on electoral divisions, the evicting landlord could hope that if those whom he drove from his property did not enter the workhouse but rather sought refuge in other electoral divisions, in the towns, or in emigration, he would escape any contribution to their support. [213] Even more important in promoting clearances was the liability of the landlord from August 1843 for all the rates of holdings valued at £4 or less. [214] Whatever profit the landlord had derived in rent from such holdings was now seriously diminished by his chargeability for their rates, previously shared equally with the tenant; and when the occupiers stopped paying him rent, the landlord reacted predictably and dispossessed them. Looking back in 1866 to the famine, Sir Denham Jephson-Norreys remarked that the £4 rating clause 'almost forced the landlords to get rid of their poorer tenantry; in order that they should not have to pay for these small holdings, they destroyed the cottages in every direction'. [215]

Although there were some clearances in 1846, the great eviction campaigns began in earnest in 1847 under the combined influence of the stoppage of rents among smallholders, very heavy rates, and the notorious quarter-acre clause. While evictions apparently reached a peak in County Cork in 1850, they remained very numerous until 1852, after which there was a marked decline. No official attempt was made to record evictions until 1849, though for the previous three years the number of ejectments granted by the courts as well as the number of persons affected by these ejectments were both reported. Many tenants served with ejectment decrees, however, were not permanently evicted. Some who had been served later redeemed their holdings by paying rent, while others who failed to redeem, and who on that account were formally evicted, were subsequently readmitted to occupancy on the sufferance of the landlord. Given the acute distress, redemption of holdings by tenants under notice of ejectment probably did not occur often between 1846 and 1848, perhaps in no more than 20 per cent of the cases. But if one were to judge by the figures for subsequent years, re-admission took place much more frequently, perhaps in 40 per cent of the cases—the exact proportion between 1849 and 1853. In Table 14, therefore, the numbers of persons evicted without readmission between 1846 and 1848 are approximations derived by reducing the numbers of persons affected by ejectments by 60 per cent in each of these three years. [216]

[213] 6 & 7 Vict., c. 92, ss. 12–13; Nicholls, *Irish poor law*, pp. 292, 297–8.
[214] 6 & 7 Vict., c. 92, ss. 1–2; Nicholls, *Irish poor law*, p. 291.
[215] *C.C.*, 2 June 1866.
[216] *Returns from the courts of queen's bench, common pleas, and exchequer in*

TABLE 14   Estimated (1846–8) and reported (1849–53) evictions without readmission in County Cork

year	families (no.)	persons (no.)	year	families (no.)	persons (no.)
1846	—	974	1850	706	3,340
1847	—	2,436	1851	335	1,870
1848	—	2,808	1852	373	2,046
1849	560	2,938	1853	120	696

Total no. of persons evicted, 1846–53: 17,108

Several of the largest early evictions in County Cork were carried out by 'improving' landlords who owned town property, and assumed the character of 'slum clearance' or 'urban renewal'. Some 400 persons were scheduled for dispossession from dilapidated cottages in Churchtown in May 1846, in order to make way for a new market that Sir Edward Tierney planned to construct.[217] Viscount Midleton's road works in Cove necessitated the destruction of so many cabins that nearly 350 persons had reportedly been left homeless by November 1846.[218] On the outskirts of Charleville, the earl of Cork's agent had demolished by July 1847 almost fifty 'miserable mud cabins' previously occupied by over 400 persons; the cabins were to be replaced by 'respectable slated houses' in accordance with the earl's policy of gradually renovating the entire town.[219]

On agricultural estates, even proprietors with a reputation for indulgence, such as the earls of Kingston, Kenmare, and Cork, had recourse to large-scale evictions.[220] Before the famine many improving

[217] *C.E.*, 20 May 1846.
[218] Ibid., 21 Jan., 2 Mar., 6 Nov. 1846.
[219] Ibid., 28 July 1847.
[220] Ibid., 14 Apr., 28 Nov. 1848; 12 Feb., 29 Aug. 1849.

Ireland, of the number of ejectments brought in those courts respectively for the last three years, beginning with Hilary term 1846 and ending with Hilary term 1849, both included; specifying the number in each term and year, and the counties in which they have been brought, and the number of persons served in each ejectment, according to the affidavits of service, distinguishing the number brought for non-payment of rent and the number brought for over-holding: and, from the assistant barrister's court of each county in Ireland, of the number of civil bill ejectments entered in each of such courts for a similar period, together with the number of defendants in each civil bill ejectment, and distinguishing the number sued for non-payment of rent, and the number for overholding, and the number for desertion, H.C. 1849 (315), xlix, 235, pp. 236–40; Return by provinces and counties (compiled from returns made to the inspector general, Royal Irish Constabulary), of cases of evictions which have come to the knowledge of the constabulary in each of the years from 1849 to 1880 inclusive, H.C. 1881 (185), lxxvii, 725, pp. 8–10.

landowners were satisfied with something less than wholesale clearances of cottiers when the leases of middlemen expired: they rearranged farms and added land to already large holdings, but they often placed the more industrious smallholders on better ground while transferring the less promising ones to poorer plots or relegating them to the position of a labourer.[221] This restraint, however, was rarely in evidence after the potato failures. Now when old leases to middlemen terminated, head landlords commonly conducted sweeping clearances of cottiers.[222] Clearly, such landowners and their agents regarded cottiers as the middleman's responsibility and had few scruples about getting rid of them as quickly as possible. Robert D. Beamish received unwelcome notoriety in May 1847 for ordering the demolition of the houses of twenty-one families, including 117 persons, on the townland of Highfield near Skibbereen.[223] Beamish indignantly denied that either he or his agent, the Rev. Sommerset Townsend, had been guilty of 'any act of oppression or cruelty'; only eight of those evicted were his own tenants. 'The others', explained Beamish, 'were brought upon the lands in direct opposition to my wishes.'[224]

Sometimes middlemen were impelled to begin clearances after the head landlord had consistently refused to reduce their rents in spite of the inability of the subtenants to pay the middlemen.[225] Dr John O'Neill and Thomas Webb jointly held the lands of Kilbarry, containing about 1,000 acres and located between Mallow and Buttevant, from Sir Riggs Falkiner upon a lease of lives renewable forever. After examining the crops of the Kilbarry tenants, O'Neill regretfully informed Valentine Barry, Falkiner's solicitor, in August 1847 that with only a few exceptions, all of them would be completely unable to pay rent that year. He had reduced his own rents by 25 per cent; this was insufficient, but he could do no more by himself. 'Unless they are befriended by Sir Riggs Falkiner,' warned O'Neill, 'I fear they will go to the wall.'[226] O'Neill reluctantly continued the previous allowance in both 1848 and 1849, but Falkiner gave him no help, the Kilbarry tenants did not pay even

[221] Ibid., 25 Feb., 7 Mar. 1845; 3 Feb. 1846; 22 Dec. 1847; 4 Feb. 1848.

[222] Ibid., 20 Apr., 6 May, 8 June 1846; 24 May 1847; 15 Aug., 5 Oct. 1849; 25 Sept. 1850; 6, 15, 20 Jan. 1851; 17 May 1852.

[223] Ibid., 31 May 1847.

[224] Ibid., 7 June 1847. See also ibid., 10, 17, 24 Nov. 1847; 19 Jan. 1848.

[225] Few landowners granted abatements that applied to middlemen (Guildford Muniment Room, Midleton papers: T. Foley to J. Tatham, 12 Feb. 1852, copy; *C.E.*, 23 Apr. 1847).

[226] Falkiner papers: Dr J. O'Neill to V. Barry, 24 Aug. 1847, copy (in the possession of P. W. Bass and Co., Solicitors, 9 South Mall, Cork).

their abated rents, and O'Neill's income was so reduced that he completely neglected to pay the head rent. [227] By 1850 the patience of Falkiner's agent Matthew Leslie was exhausted, and he pressed for the immediate payment of both the current rent and the heavy arrears.

O'Neill and Webb responded by suing the Kilbarry tenants *en masse* at the June quarter sessions. [228] Hoping to prevent the forfeiture of his lease, O'Neill offered to pay part of what he owed at once and to take

all the waste lands into my possession and send a nephew of mine, who is a first rate agriculturalist, . . . to take care of and cultivate [them] to account, and any other lands the tenants cannot farm to their own or the landlord's benefit. [229]

He also visited Kilbarry and drew up a list of 236 paupers, most of whom were receiving outdoor relief, and seventy-nine 'farmers'.

When you and Mr Leslie look over this list [O'Neill told Valentine Barry], I am certain that you will agree with me that it's absolutely necessary to have the miserable sheds in which most of these unfortunates dwell done away with, so as to remove so heavy a burthen from the lands and induce the more than half starved inmates to seek an asylum in the poorhouse. [230]

O'Neill reminded Leslie that he had 'again and again asked for an abatement of the head rent for the purpose of enabling the unfortunate tenants to retain their position'. [231] Now all the tenants, with the exception of three, were bankrupt and could not pay even one gale of rent in 1850. Despite the fact that he had given them over £1,000 in abatements and had cancelled their arrears, still O'Neill found that 'they cannot get on, and I fear they must be sent away'. [232] The final arrangements for the evictions showed a strange mixture of diluted sympathy and criminal cynicism. O'Neill did not propose to assist any of the occupiers to emigrate. But fearing that so large a clearance might provoke a disturbance, he advised Falkiner's solicitor to show a little concern. He informed Barry in early January 1851:

[227] Ibid.: C. Daly to Barry, 30 Nov. 1849.
[228] Ibid.: T. Webb to M. Leslie, 30 May 1850; Copy of account of arrears due to the representatives of Sir Riggs Falkiner from John O'Neill, M.D., and Thomas Webb, Esq., 29 Sept. 1847–29 Sept. 1849, and continuation of account.
[229] Ibid.: O'Neill to Leslie, 1 Apr. 1850 (copy).
[230] Ibid.: O'Neill to Barry, 13 June 1850.
[231] Ibid.: O'Neill to Leslie, 1 Apr. 1850 (copy).
[232] Ibid.: O'Neill to Barry, 24 Oct. 1850.

We got possession from eighty four heads of families, whose children and relatives numbered three hundred and sixteen; as the weather was very bad, we deemed it right to give the unfortunates a little further time to seek for a home in some other quarters. I propose giving such of them as had very bad houses the timber and thatch, and I think they should be got quit of as quietly as possible. I will give the wretched creatures who lived in my part of the lands a few shillings. If you will give some trifle to such as lived on Mr Webb's portion of the farm, I should hope we will part with all of the unnecessary folk, over 200 in number, without causing any commotion in that district. [233]

The evictions, of course, did not relieve the financial embarrassment of O'Neill and Webb. Owing slightly more than £1,300 in head rents by the end of 1851, they were finally forced to surrender their lease of lives renewable forever in exchange for one of twenty-one years. [234]

It was extremely rare, however, for landowners to permit such an accumulation of arrears before ousting middlemen from their estates. In fact, the ranks of the remaining middlemen in County Cork were greatly thinned during the famine, since proprietors invariably exacted the full head rent and promptly evicted those who could or would no longer pay. [235] For most landowners who had largely ridded their properties of middlemen before 1845, the insolvencies of the famine years merely allowed them to finish quickly an eradication process that was already far advanced. But for some proprietors, these years brought either a long desired release from, or a wholesale disillusionment with, a system which now had no redeeming features whatsoever. The O'Donovan was one Cork landowner whose disillusionment with middlemen occurred very late, but as one middleman after another on his estate near Skibbereen fell hopelessly into arrears between 1846 and 1850, they were jettisoned, sometimes after costly delays, and the lands let to the occupying tenants. [236]

Landowners and estate agents in the west of Ireland often pursued a policy of colonizing evicted lands with farmers whom they brought over from England or Scotland. [237] Some Cork proprietors

[233] Ibid.: O'Neill to Barry, 5 Jan. 1851.

[234] Ibid.: O'Neill to Leslie, 31 Aug. 1850 (copy); C. Daly to Barry, 26 July 1853; Copy of account of arrears due to the representatives of Sir Riggs Falkiner from John O'Neill, M.D., and Thomas Webb, Esq., 29 Sept. 1847–29 Sept. 1849, and continuation of account.

[235] For accounts of the eviction of middlemen, see, e.g., *C.E.*, 23 Apr., 19 May, 23, 28 July 1847; 10 July 1848; 5 Oct., 7 Nov. 1849; 6 Jan. 1851.

[236] The O'Donovan papers: Rental of The O'Donovan's estate, Carbery only, 1839–69, pp. 1–3, 5–6, 21–3, 25–8, 41–2, 45–6, 75–6.

[237] Cullen, *Life in Ire.*, p. 145.

had a similar aim. 'We are given to understand on the very best authority', declared the *Cork Examiner* in May 1849, 'that several landlords in this county have deliberately expressed their determination of getting rid of their present tenants . . . and of substituting a race of English farmers in their stead.'[238] Little, however, seems to have come of these resolves, partly because agricultural prospects in Ireland were not sufficiently tempting to induce large numbers of English and Scottish tenants to settle there. In one much publicized case, Captain Eustace was unable to persuade an English farmer to take on reasonable terms a 150-acre holding at Ballydoyle near Castletownroche, which he had recently cleared of pauper tenants.[239]

One of the most remarkable facts connected with the clearances in Cork is that they provoked so little resistance or agrarian outrage. Only one case of outrage that arose from the taking of an evicted farm was reported in the local newspapers, though others undoubtedly took place.[240] Only one attempted murder of an evicting landlord received similar notice.[241] And only one shooting at the scene of an eviction was recorded: in September 1847 a protestant farmer named John Norris, whose house on the earl of Shannon's estate at Brownstown near Courtmacsherry was ordered levelled, shot the man removing the first slate.[242] At the start of the clearances many ousted tenants forcibly retook possession of their cabins, but this was soon made impossible by the unroofing, burning, or levelling of their dwellings.[243] Evicting landlords generally hired a 'crowbar brigade' to demolish the houses; this was done on Viscount Midleton's estate by contract at 3*s.* per house.[244] Whenever they expected serious opposition, landlords and agents enlisted the armed assistance of the police or the military in order to overawe those to be dispossessed.[245] Tenants who surrendered quietly received various forms of compensation. Their arrears were cancelled; they were allowed to carry away the timber and thatch of their cabins; they were made a present of their remaining crops or stock and were given small sums of money, usually only a few pounds at most and not enough for anyone to book passage on an emigrant ship.[246] Starvation

[238] *C.E.*, 16 May 1849. See also ibid., 6 Apr. 1849.
[239] Ibid., 28 Apr., 16, 20 May, 18 June 1849.
[240] *C.C.*, 4 Aug. 1846. [241] Ibid., 10 June 1847.
[242] *C.E.*, 24 Sept. 1847.
[243] Ibid., 24 Mar., 19, 31 May 1847; 10 July, 27 Oct. 1848; 25 Sept. 1850; 15, 20 Jan. 1851.
[244] P.R.O.I., ref. no. 978, Midleton papers: Rental of Viscount Midleton's estates, Sept. and Nov. 1847. See also *Southern Reporter*, 15 Feb. 1848.
[245] *C.E.*, 22 Nov. 1848, 27 Apr. 1849.
[246] Ibid., 20 May 1846; 28 July 1847; 21 May, 5 Oct. 1849; 10 Dec. 1863.

and epidemic diseases had, in any case, completely undermined the cottiers' will to resist by the summer of 1847, when the evictions began on a large scale.

Even if one grants that most estates could not have been improved without at least some clearance, it is still difficult to believe that so many proprietors and agents were insensible to the awful suffering of those whom they evicted with hardly any provision for their future. They must, they seemed to reason, have their rents and no more poor rates. They must have larger holdings in order to pave the way for more efficient dairy and livestock farming. Often flying in the face of reality, they clung tenaciously to the threadbare argument that cottiers were not really evicted but surrendered their holdings voluntarily. 'The lands taken up', observed Captain Eustace's agent John Smith in May 1849, 'were held by tenants who had neither skill nor energy to work them; and when it pleased Providence to afflict our country with the potato blight, it became evident that a new course of tillage was the only remedy.'[247] The Rev. Maurice F. Townsend's agent Thomas H. Marmion, who presided over the largest recorded clearance of a Cork estate during the famine, was equally callous. Responding to a carefully documented newspaper account of the eviction of 154 families, including nearly 850 persons, from about twenty townlands near Skibbereen over a two-year period,[248] Marmion published this businesslike apologia in August 1849:

I have taken the trouble to look through this list [of evicted tenants] and find, out of those names, several were never tenants at any time; others of them are still in possession; the majority, being totally unable to crop their lands or pay rates, voluntarily surrendered and were allowed to take away their stock and any other property they had. All were heavily in arrear, and I was obliged to pay their poor rate and county cess.[249]

Also very revealing of landlord psychology in these clearances were the private comments of Sir John Benn-Walsh. After visiting his Cork and Kerry properties in August 1851, Benn-Walsh noted in his journal that he was leaving Ireland 'with far more hope & in better spirits than on any of the three former occasions since the potato failure'. His poor rates had markedly declined, his improvements had not only increased the value of his farms but given his tenants courage, and his estates had been 'very much weeded both of paupers & bad tenants'.

247 Ibid., 21 May 1849.
248 Ibid., 13 July 1849.
249 Ibid., 1 Aug. 1849.

This has been accomplished by Matthew Gabbett [the agent] without evictions, bringing in the sheriff, or any harsh measures. In fact, the paupers and little cottiers cannot keep their holdings without the potato and for small sums of £1, £2, and £3 have given me peaceable possession in a great many cases, when the cabin is immediately levelled. Then to induce the larger farmers to surrender their holdings when they became insolvent, I emigrated several, either with their whole families or in part. This was expensive, but it enabled me to consolidate & make comfortable sized farms from [a rent of] £30 & £40 up to £140 per ann[um]. [250]

The great clearances of the famine years, combined with the death or emigration of landholders, did indeed enable Cork proprietors to consolidate holdings on an extensive scale, as Table 15 illustrates. [251]

TABLE 15   Number and percentage of holdings in Cork according to farm size, 1844–51

year	1 acre or less (no.)	(%)	1–5 acres (no.)	(%)	5–15 acres (no.)	(%)	over 15 acres (no.)	(%)
1844	8,052	13·9	7,468	12·8	13,197	22·7*	29,400	50·6*
1847	6,720	12·9	4,805	9·2	10,557	20·3	30,001	57·6
1849	4,342	10·4	2,943	7·0	7,003	16·7	27,575	65·9
1851	5,727	14·0	2,855	7·0	6,136	15·0	26,161	64·0
% decline, 1844–51		28·9		61·8		53·5		11·0

*Estimate.

Holdings of under one acre declined much less in number than those of from one to five and from five to fifteen acres, but this merely reflects the fact that many former cottiers had been reduced to the position of day labourers. Table 15 also demonstrates that there was very little difference in the impact of the famine and the ensuing clearances on the two smallholding classes, regardless of whether they held more or less than five acres. Lastly, the fall in the number of holdings exceeding fifteen acres testifies to the frequent failures even among those farmers who had been relatively much better off, but who now, for the reasons discussed earlier, found their incomes

[250] Ormathwaite papers: Journal of Sir John Benn-Walsh, 2 Sept. 1851, pp. 147–9.
[251] *Devon comm. evidence*, pt iv, pp. 280–3; *Returns of agricultural produce in Ireland in the year 1847*, pt ii: Stock, pp. 4–5; *Returns of agricultural produce . . . 1849*, pp. 154–5; *Census Ire., 1851*, pt ii: *Returns of agricultural produce in 1851*, p. 640.

declining sharply. In general, these failures and the consequent evictions were confined to those with holdings of between fifteen and thirty acres, the number of which fell from 11,433 to 8,215 between 1847 and 1851, or by almost 30 per cent. Obviously, the average size of the farms exceeding thirty acres, which also declined slightly in number, greatly increased.

STARVATION, DEATH, AND EMIGRATION

While the drastic decline in small holdings was one important result of the great famine, the sharp fall in population was another. Between 1841 and 1851 the population of County Cork declined from 854,118 to 648,903, or by almost 24 per cent. Excluding the population of Cork city, which through the migration of paupers from rural districts had increased slightly from 80,720 to 85,745, the demographic loss amounted to 27 per cent. [252] Moreover, if a census had been taken in 1846 and compared with that of 1851, the result would have shown an even more startling decline, since the population was unquestionably rising up to 1846. On the assumption that the rate of demographic increase between 1831 and 1841 of 5·35 per cent was maintained up to 1846, there were about 877,000 persons living in Cork when the potato failed totally. [253] The 1851 census recorded 132,433 deaths in the county from 1846 to 1851, but this figure is certainly an underestimate. [254]

In a recent article on the regional pattern of mortality in Ireland during the great famine, S. H. Cousens estimated that the excess deaths, that is, the mortality attributable to starvation and disease arising from the potato failures, amounted to 113,425 in County Cork between 1846 and 1850. [255] Cousens's map of excess mortality in 1847 shows that Cork and Leitrim were the two most distressed counties in Ireland, with excess-mortality rates of more than fifty per thousand of the total population. [256] By contrast, 1848 and 1850 were years of much less distress in Cork, for the rate was below thirty and twenty per thousand respectively. [257] In 1849, however, Cork was

---

[252] *Census Ire., 1841*, pp. 169, 190; *Census Ire., 1851*, pt i, vol. ii [1550, 1551], H.C. 1852-3, xci, 429, 499, pp. 110-11, 115, 161, 164.

[253] *Return of the population of the several counties in Ireland, as enumerated in 1831*, H.C. 1833 (254), xxxix, 1, p. 158; *Census Ire., 1841*, pp. 169, 190.

[254] *Census Ire., 1851*, pt v, vol. ii [2087-II], H.C. 1856, xxx, 1, pp. 355, 365, 375.

[255] S. H. Cousens, 'Regional death rates in Ireland during the great famine, from 1846 to 1851' in *Population Studies*, xiv, no. 1 (July 1960), p. 67.

[256] Ibid., p. 66.

[257] Ibid., pp. 71, 73.

again one of the most distressed Irish counties, with only Limerick, Clare, Galway, and Offaly registering substantially higher excess-mortality rates.[258] Over-all, Cork was one of five Irish counties (along with Mayo, Galway, Clare, and Kerry—all abutting the Atlantic) with an average excess mortality of more than one-eighth of the total population between 1846 and 1850.[259]

While Cork's relative standing in the country-wide scale of excess mortality has thus been carefully delineated, the geographical incidence of the famine within the county cannot be charted with the same precision. The 1851 census does provide data on deaths occurring in the workhouses of most Cork poor-law unions between 1841 and 1851, but no pattern consistent with reliable external evidence emerges when the census figures are used to calculate mortality by poor-law unions.[260] The configuration of distress is clearly visible, however, in Table 16, which shows the proportion of the population in receipt of poor-law relief both inside and outside the workhouses of the county between 1847 and 1850.[261]

TABLE 16 Percentage of the population receiving poor-law relief in Cork unions, 1847–50

union	1847–8 (%)	1848–9 (%)	1849–50 (%)	average, 1847–50 (%)
Kanturk	39·3	56·1	45·7	47·0
Bantry	46·1	54·1	22·0	40·7
Skibbereen	31·4	56·6	22·1	36·7
Fermoy	40·7	40·6	19·4	33·5
Macroom	41·1	20·2	11·4	24·2
Dunmanway	36·0	25·1	10·3	23·8
Midleton	13·8	22·4	21·7	19·2
Cork	12·5	19·9	20·0	17·5
Kinsale	11·0	18·6	10·4	13·3
Mallow	9·0	15·1	11·7	12·0
Bandon	8·8	13·3	6·4	9·5

With the major exception of Mallow union, the geographical incidence of poor-law relief closely coincides with that of the decline

[258] Ibid., p. 72.   [259] Ibid., p. 70.
[260] *Census Ire., 1851*, pt v, vol. ii, pp. 94–5.
[261] *Second annual report of the commissioners for administering the laws for relief of the poor in Ireland*, pp. 171–4; *Third annual report of the commissioners for administering the laws for relief of the poor in Ireland* [1243], H.C. 1850, xxvii, 449, pp. 82–4; *Fourth annual report of the commissioners for administering the laws for relief of the poor in Ireland: with appendices* [1381], H.C. 1851, xxvi, 547, pp. 161–5.

of the smallest holdings. The five unions with the highest proportions of their populations in receipt of poor-law relief—Kanturk, Bantry, Skibbereen, Fermoy, and Macroom—also showed the greatest declines in the number of holdings of five acres or less between 1844 and 1851. Conversely, five of the six unions with the lowest proportions of their populations in receipt of such relief—Dunmanway, Midleton, Cork, Kinsale, and Bandon—showed either small declines or increases in the number of the smallest holdings, as illustrated by Table 17. [262]

TABLE 17 Number of holdings of five acres or less in Cork poor-law unions, and percentage change, 1844–51

union	no. in 1844	no. in 1851	% change, 1844–51
Fermoy	7,096	958	−86·5
Skibbereen	1,447	549	−62·1
Mallow	769	295	−61·6
Bantry	871	402	−53·8
Kanturk	835	560	−32·9
Macroom	342	262	−23·4
Midleton	1,160	974	−16·0
Dunmanway	123	122	−0·8
Kinsale	336	363	+8·0
Bandon	820	1,030	+25·6
Cork	1,721	3,441	+99·9
co. total	15,520	8,956	−42·3

The impact of the famine in Mallow union was certainly greater than is indicated by the very small percentage of the population that received poor-law relief there. More than half its population—a very high proportion relative to other unions—was composed of landless labourers, and this group was hit hardest by the potato failures. [263] Moreover, Mallow's smallholding class was reduced by over three-fifths, as Table 17 shows. Two factors help to reconcile the in-

[262] In the parliamentary return from which the figures for 1844 in Table 17 are derived, the number of persons holding in common or by joint tenancy was separately distinguished in the case of six Cork poor-law unions. Each of these persons was considered to have had a holding of five acres or less, and their holdings have been included as such in Table 17 (*Devon comm. evidence*, pt iv, pp. 280–3; *Census Ire., 1851*, pt ii: *Returns of agricultural produce in 1851*, pp. 699–727).

[263] For the geographical distribution of landless labourers within the county, see below, p. 126.

consistent positions of this union with respect to public relief on the one hand and the desperate plight of its labouring and smallholding classes on the other. The landlord demesnes that surrounded the town of Mallow drew heavily on the large pool of agricultural labour within the union. [264] Also, the construction of the Dublin to Cork route of the Great Southern & Western railway through almost the entire length of Mallow union during the famine created a strong local demand for labour that was usually absent elsewhere. [265] Thus labourers and smallholders were not thrown nearly so much on poor-law relief to survive as they were elsewhere. Yet a third factor was also important. The niggardly fashion in which the Mallow guardians discharged their obligations towards the poor kept down the relief rolls on the one hand while exacerbating the distress of the labourers and smallholders on the other. [266]

The ravages of the famine were almost certainly more severe in Skibbereen than in any other Cork union, even though a smaller proportion of the population received public relief than in either Kanturk or Bantry unions, and even though the smallest landholders were not ruined to the same extent as in Fermoy union. The awful mortality in the Skibbereen district may have received a disproportionate amount of attention from properly horrified contemporaries, [267] but clearly, the primitive economy of the area, its bottom-heavy social structure, and the almost complete absence of retail trade facilities doomed its inhabitants to catastrophe. Next to Bantry, Skibbereen was the poorest union in the county in terms of physical assets *per capita*: the poor-law valuation of its land and buildings was less than £1 per head of its population, while in Mallow and Midleton unions the valuation per head was about double this amount. [268] Most of the county had a population density of 200 to 300 per square mile, but in Skibbereen union, especially in the coastal region, the population density was more than 400 per

[264] Freeman, *Pre-famine Ireland*, pp. 229, 231.

[265] Minute book, Mallow board of guardians, 1848–9, 29 Dec. 1848, pp. 288–9.

[266] See above, p. 97.

[267] Besides Elihu Burritt's work quoted and cited above, other contemporaries published vivid accounts of their visits to Skibbereen. See marquis of Dufferin and Ava and G. F. Boyle, *Narrative of a journey from Oxford to Skibbereen during the year of the Irish famine* (2nd ed., Oxford, 1847). But the social catastrophe that overtook the Skibbereen district received its greatest notoriety from the melancholy sketches and reports that appeared in the *Illustrated London News* beginning in December 1846. See especially *Illustrated London News*, 30 Jan., 13 Feb. 1847.

[268] *A return of the valuation of each electoral division in Ireland with its population in 1841*, H.C. 1847 (159), lvi, 379, pp. 19–20.

square mile. [269] Over 50 per cent of the landholders in this union had small farms of from five to twenty acres in 1844—a greater proportion than in any other Cork union. [270] The degree of dependence upon the unreliable potato, both for food and as a cash crop, apparently exceeded that of all other unions in the county. Skibbereen had long been remarkable, declared one writer in September 1846, 'for the vast quantity of potatoes which it produced annually; in fact, the population was so great and at the same time so poor that the extent of ground sown was incapable of producing any other crop sufficient to support them'. [271]

Moreover, the prevalence of the middleman system which had fostered subdivision made most estates in the Skibbereen district ripe for clearances. James George, a husbandry instructor appointed by the Royal Agricultural Improvement Society of Ireland during the famine, reported in August 1849 that more than half of Skibbereen union had been let around 1800 'in large tracts to tenants on terminable leases at moderate fixed rents'; these tenants had either possessed or assumed the power of subdivision, and since 1846 their leases had been falling 'into the hands of the principal landlord, or owner in fee, who had to receive back the land in a worn out state, all covered over with cabins and a pauper tenantry'. [272] Not surprisingly, some of the largest estate clearances in Cork during the famine took place in Skibbereen union, and reports in local news-papers indicate that evictions there were more numerous than in any other district. [273] Also, there were very few demesnes or resident landlords to provide employment. [274] Under all these adverse circumstances, it is understandable that Skibbereen suffered a population loss of over 36 per cent between 1841 and 1851—a heavier loss than that of any other poor-law union in the county. [275]

As in Skibbereen union, so too in Cork as a whole, excess mortality accounted for most of the population loss experienced during the famine years. But emigration was responsible for almost half of the county-wide decline. If Cork's total population had in fact reached about 877,000 by 1846, and then fallen to about 649,000 by 1851, with over 132,000 deaths recorded in the interim

[269] Freeman, *Pre-famine Ireland*, pp. 225–6.
[270] *Devon comm. evidence*, pt iv, pp. 280–3.
[271] *C.E.*, 23 Sept. 1846. See also ibid., 6 July 1849.
[272] James George to honorary secretaries, Central Relief Committee, 1 Aug. 1849, quoted ibid., 8 Aug. 1849.
[273] Ibid., 24 Mar., 19, 31 May 1847; 27 Oct., 27 Nov. 1848; 27 June, 13 July, 1, 15 Aug., 7 Nov. 1849.
[274] Freeman, *Pre-famine Ireland*, p. 237.
[275] See table 20 below, p. 129.

and little migration to other counties, then perhaps the total emigration during that period was somewhat more than 95,000, or about 11 per cent of the 1841 population. This figure of 95,000 emigrants coincides with the sophisticated estimate of S. H. Cousens, who calculated that emigration from County Cork amounted to between 10 and 12·4 per cent of its 1841 population.[276] The exodus from Cork was proportionately much less than that from several other Irish counties—Mayo, Roscommon, Sligo, Monaghan, Cavan, Longford, and Leix—from which about 20 per cent of the population is estimated to have fled.[277] The recorded emigration from the port of Cork, even though it was an embarkation point for emigrants from other southern counties, falls considerably short of the number reliably estimated to have left County Cork. But as early as April 1846, vessels were reportedly 'taking in emigrants at the Shannon, Bantry, Skibbereen, Kinsale, Youghal, Dungarvan, Waterford, and at all the large ports round the coast'.[278] The total failure of the potato crop in August 1846 initiated a huge exodus during the following spring and summer, and more than twice as many emigrants departed from the port of Cork in 1847 than in the previous year. The tide of emigration ebbed considerably between 1848 and 1850, as it was extremely difficult for the labourers and cottiers engulfed by the famine to acquire sufficient means to flee. But in 1851, with a marginal improvement in conditions, more people left from the port of Cork than in any year since 1847. Table 18 gives the recorded number and destination of emigrants between 1845 and 1851.[279]

As previously noted, Cork's rate of emigration was moderate in comparison with that of certain other Irish counties. The main reason for this was the relatively large proportion of landless labourers in its population.[280] A fair estimate can be made of the proportion of landless labourers both to those whose holdings were valued at above £4 (i.e., the ratepayers) and to those whose holdings were valued at or below £4 for poor-law purposes. Table 19 gives for Cork's eleven poor-law unions the respective percentage of the population in each of these three classes in 1846; the table shows

[276] Cousens, 'Regional pattern of emigration', p. 121.
[277] Ibid.
[278] *C.C.*, 2 Apr. 1846.
[279] *Twelfth general report of the colonial land and emigration commissioners, 1852* [1499], H.C. 1852, xviii, 161, pp. 82–3.
[280] Cousens has shown that the relatively moderate rate of emigration from the southern counties as a whole was largely a result of the heavy concentration of labourers within this region ('Regional pattern of emigration', p. 131).

TABLE 18   Recorded emigration from the port of Cork to foreign lands, 1845–51

year	To: United States	Canada	Australia	other	total
1845	358	4,473	—	—	4,831
1846	1,383	5,683	—	—	7,066
1847	4,360	13,159	—	—	17,519
1848	8,600	3,021	—	6	11,627
1849	7,846	1,869	—	6	9,721
1850	6,026	2,071	—	2	8,099
1851	7,753	4,709	—	—	12,462
total	36,326	34,985	—	14	71,325

TABLE 19   Percentage of the population with holdings valued for poor rates or without land in Cork unions, 1846

union	valued above £4	valued at or below £4	without land
Macroom	32	14	54
Dunmanway	41	5	54
Mallow	29	20	51
Bandon	38	13	49
Skibbereen	42	16	42
Bantry	25	35	40
Kanturk	43	17	40
Kinsale	54	11	35
Cork	43	27	30
Fermoy	46	36	18
Midleton	61	24	15

that in as many as seven of the eleven unions landless labourers constituted 40 per cent or more of the population. [281]

As a rule labourers lacked the means to emigrate, especially with

[281] *A return from the poor law commissioners, showing the name of each union in Ireland; the name of the county in which situated; the name of each electoral division in each union; the total numbers of occupiers in each electoral division on whom the rate is made; the total estimated extent of statute acres in each electoral division, the rate for which is made on the occupier; the total number of hereditaments not exceeding £4 in each electoral division, for which the rate is made on the immediate lessor; the total estimated extent, statute acres, in each electoral division, the rate for which is made on the immediate lessor; the total estimated extent of bog or waste not rated, in each electoral division*, H.C. 1846 (262), xxxvi, 469, pp. 34–5 (hereafter cited as *Return of the poor-law valuation of holdings*).

their families. Steerage passages to Canada in 1846 ranged from 50*s.* to 60*s.*, and to the United States, from 70*s.* to £5. For a short time in early 1847, at the height of the great rush to leave the country, fares almost doubled, but thereafter the rates became standardized at about 75*s.* for the cheapest passage to New York and at 65*s.* to the Canadian ports.[282] Thus for a labourer to emigrate with his wife and a family of three children might cost £15, and this was as much as he generally earned in a year before 1845.[283] Comparatively few labourers were observed among those leaving after the partial potato failure of 1845. 'The large mass of emigrants', commented the *Cork Constitution* in April 1846, 'are parties having the appearance of respectable farmers, all of whom are taking with them sums of money from £500 [down] to £10.'[284] The flight of small farmers and shopkeepers continued into 1847, but contemporaries noticed a much larger number of labourers departing than in 1846.[285] In 1848, however, there seems to have been a return to the pattern of 1846. The *Cork Examiner* remarked in November that 'the emigrants of this year, unlike those of the past, are of the more substantial class of peasantry'.[286]

While the heavy concentration of labourers in many parts of Cork was undoubtedly the most important reason for the county's relatively modest emigration, other factors also worked in the same direction. One such factor was the general absence of consistently high poor rates. The amount of taxation levied to support the destitute, especially where a large proportion of the ratepayers had holdings valued at between £4 and £5, often induced small tenants in certain other parts of Ireland to seek an escape in emigration.[287] But in Cork the average poor rate between 1847 and 1851 exceeded 3*s.* in the pound in only three of the eleven poor-law unions— Kanturk, Bantry, and Skibbereen.[288] Moreover, the extent of pauperism among the smallholders of these three unions had a tendency to counteract the influence of high poor rates. And unlike

---

[282] O. MacDonagh, 'Irish emigration to the United States of America and the British colonies during the famine' in Edwards & Williams, *Great famine*, p. 328.

[283] Green, 'Agriculture', p. 96.   [284] *C.C.*, 2 Apr. 1846.

[285] Ibid., 30 Mar., 1 June 1847; *C.E.*, 14, 23 Apr. 1847.

[286] *C.E.*, 6 Nov. 1848.

[287] Cousens, 'Regional pattern of emigration', pp. 132–3.

[288] *A return . . . of the valuation of each electoral division in Ireland with its population in 1841, and the total poundage directed to be raised by any rate or rates made upon every such electoral division during the year ending the 31st day of December 1847*, H.C. 1847–8 (311), lvii, 183. See also the similar returns for the years 1848 to 1851: H.C. 1849 (198), xlix, 243; H.C. 1850 (254), li, 425; H.C. 1851 (382), l, 631; H.C. 1852 (323), xlvii, 341.

the counties of Monaghan and Cavan, where over 15 per cent of the population was rated at between £4 and £5, and where the average poor rate between 1847 and 1850 was more than 3s. in the pound, [289] the county of Cork had less than 2 per cent of the population in this critical position. [290]

Assisted emigration was also very slight. While the counties of Clare, Limerick, and Kerry were prominent centres of landlord-assisted emigration, Cork lagged behind. It had no proprietors who could compare in emigration activity with the marquis of Lansdowne in Kerry or F. Spaight in Clare and Tipperary. [291] Some Cork landowners did actually encourage their distressed tenants to seek a new life abroad. George F. Colley spent a little more than £500 in aiding the emigration to Quebec of eighty-four persons from his estate near Rathcormack in 1847, providing not only their fares but also provisions for eight weeks and a small gratuity upon landing. [292] Viscount Midleton laid out about £1,150 to send pauper tenants to Quebec in June 1847, and the earl of Egmont dispatched several occupiers from his property to New York during the same year. [293] A few other Cork landowners, such as Sir John Benn-Walsh and Lady Carbery, spent considerable sums for assisted emigration during the famine. [294] But in the estate records that have been examined, expenditures under this head are very rare, and news-paper accounts of landlord assistance are equally scarce. Thus there is good reason to believe that this type of emigration, which one authority maintains 'can scarcely have exceeded 50,000 in extent' throughout Ireland between 1846 and 1852 (or less than 4 per cent of total overseas emigration), was even more uncommon in Cork than elsewhere. [295] Government activity was also insignificant. The commissioners of woods and forests did send 172 persons from the

[289] Cousens, 'Regional pattern of emigration', pp. 132–3.

[290] *Returns of parliamentary electors; also of tenements valued under the act 1 & 2 Vic., cap. 56, for relief of the poor in Ireland, 1842–3,* H.C. 1844 (533), xliii, 323, p. 6; *Return of the poor-law valuation of holdings,* pp. 34–5.

[291] For the activities of Lansdowne and Spaight, see Ormathwaite papers: Journal of Sir John Benn-Walsh, 21 Aug. 1849, pp. 228–9; W. S. Trench, *Realities of Irish life* (Boston, 1880), pp. 101–6; MacDonagh, 'Irish emigration', pp. 333–4.

[292] *C.E.,* 24 Mar. 1847; *C.C.,* 20 May 1847.

[293] P.R.O.I., ref. no. 978, Midleton papers: Rental of Viscount Midleton's estates, Mar. and May 1847; Cowdray archives, MS 1914: P. Smith to earl of Egmont, 10 Mar. 1847; Smith to earl of Egmont, 18 Mar. 1847.

[294] Ormathwaite papers: Journal of Sir John Benn-Walsh, 2 Sept. 1851, p. 148; *C.E.,* 10 Dec. 1863.

[295] MacDonagh, 'Irish emigration', p. 335.

crown estate of Kingwilliamstown in northwest Cork to the United States in 1849 and 1850.[296] But from the spring of 1848 to the end of March 1851 the guardians of Cork's poor-law unions altogether assisted the emigration of only about 720 persons, mostly female orphans, who went as servants to Australia.[297]

The distribution of emigrants within the county cannot be established precisely. But by comparing the population declines of Cork poor-law unions with the geographical incidence of destitution as measured by the proportion of the population that received poor relief (see Table 16), some tentative conclusions can be drawn about the volume of emigration from different parts of Cork. Table 20 presents the population changes between 1841 and 1851.[298]

TABLE 20   Population changes in Cork poor-law unions, 1841–51

union	population in 1841	population in 1851	% change, 1841–51
Skibbereen	85,222	54,477	−36·1
Bandon	100,381	64,682	−35·6
Dunmanway	31,603	20,438	−35·3
Mallow	64,364	42,145	−34·5
Fermoy	89,378	62,025	−30·6
Kanturk	85,321	59,328	−30·5
Kinsale	41,342	28,948	−30·0
Macroom	51,744	37,394	−27·7
Bantry	51,014	37,786	−25·9
Midleton	81,571	65,189	−20·1
Cork	163,492	168,576	+3·1
co. total	845,432	640,988	−24·2

Wherever a large decline in population took place without the existence of a high level of destitution, the loss is likely to have resulted from an unusual amount of emigration. Thus the unions of

[296] *A copy of any reports on the experimental improvements on the crown estate of King William's Town in the county of Cork, submitted to her majesty's commissioners of woods and forests since the 8th day of August 1844 . . .*, p. 10. See also E. Ellis, 'State-aided emigration schemes from crown estates in Ireland c. 1850' in *Anal. Hib.*, no. 22 (1960), pp. 368–79.

[297] *Third annual report of the commissioners for administering the laws for relief of the poor in Ireland*, pp. 133–4; *Fourth annual report of the commissioners for administering the laws for relief of the poor in Ireland: with appendices*, pp. 192–3.

[298] *Census Ire., 1911: Area, houses, and population: also the ages, civil or conjugal condition, occupations, birthplaces, religion, and education of the people, province of Munster, county and city of Cork* [Cd 6050–I], H.C. 1912–13, cxv, 153, p. 1.

Bandon, Dunmanway, Mallow, and Kinsale probably experienced relatively high rates of emigration. Other sources provide confirming evidence of a strong current of departures from these unions. Many small farmers in the Bandon district in December 1846 had reportedly surrendered their holdings and were 'only awaiting the sailing of emigration vessels in spring to leave forever'. [299] Large numbers of hard-pressed tenants on the earl of Bandon's extensive estate in the unions of Kinsale, Bandon, and Dunmanway apparently uprooted themselves between late 1846 and early 1849. For when the earl announced the remission of all arrears and a large abatement in April 1849, one writer declared that this step 'effectually checked the tide of emigration on his property' and 'prevented whole tracts from being left desolate'. [300] Popular enthusiasm for emigration was very strong in Mallow union. In fact, the local guardians were forced to suspend a state-aided emigration scheme in January 1849, so great was the rush of women who 'sought admission to the workhouse avowedly in order to be placed on the list as candidates for emigration'. [301]

The famine was in many ways a watershed in the economic and social history of Cork. Some of the forces that powerfully shaped post-famine development, it is true, appeared before 1845, such as the changes in market conditions for Irish agricultural produce, the movement for the reform of estate management, and the diminution in the rate of population growth. But not only did the years of the 'great hunger' witness a sharp accentuation of these earlier trends; they also saw certain novel changes of immense significance for the future. The cultivation of the potato declined permanently and drastically, and never was this crop so abundant in yield again as it had frequently, though very erratically, been prior to the catastrophic failures of the late 1840s. The growing of corn also contracted, but the raising of cattle expanded, for if subsistence agriculture was largely destroyed, commercial farming began to respond strongly and in a new way to altered market opportunities. The famine was also the real beginning of a fundamental change in the class structure of the population. Its ravages were of course greatest among those at or near the bottom of the social scale. Moreover, emigration from rural areas, once only a trickle, now became a torrent chiefly composed after the early 1850s of landless labourers and farm servants. In the process, farmers, who before were greatly out-

[299] *C.E.*, 14 Dec. 1846.
[300] Ibid., 6 Apr. 1849.
[301] Minute book, Mallow board of guardians, 1848–9, 19 Jan. 1849, p. 311.

numbered by the labouring classes, eventually reached a state of near numerical equality with them as a result of forces which the famine set in motion or accelerated. At the apex of the economic pyramid, the famine also claimed victims by forcing many landowners into bankruptcy. Their place was taken most often by others of gentry stock whose financial position before 1845 had not become critical, and who were thus able to survive several years of diminished income until the dawning of a new era of generally well-paid rents.[302] Landlord indebtedness soon ceased to be a major problem, and this factor facilitated landlord investment in agricultural improvements.

[302] This generalization concerning the gentry is based upon a systematic analysis of the social background of the purchasers of property in County Cork under the provisions of the incumbered estates act of 1849. The sources for this analysis were, first, the indexes to conveyances of the incumbered estates court from 1850 to 1858, which are available in the Public Record Office, Dublin; and, second, local directories, genealogical guides, and other contemporary works of reference. I hope soon to publish elsewhere a full treatment of the long misinterpreted question of land purchase between 1850 and 1880.

III

AGRICULTURE, 1851–91

~~~~~~~~~~~~~~~~~~~~~~~~~~~~~~~~~~~~~

THE NEW TRENDS in agriculture which had manifested themselves before and especially during the famine in Cork were confirmed in the following decades. After the great clearances of the famine years, the consolidation of holdings continued, but at a much slower pace, as illustrated in Table 21.[1] In 1851 slightly more than half of the holdings of over 1 acre were larger than 30 acres, whereas by 1891 the proportion of farms in this category was still less than three-fifths of the total. Although more than one-third of the total number

TABLE 21   Number of holdings of over one acre in Cork according to farm size, 1851–91

year	1–5 acres	5–15 acres	15–30 acres	30–50 acres	over 50 acres	total
1851	2,855	6,136	8,215	6,920	11,026	35,152
1861	2,817	5,622	7,290	6,843	11,616	34,188
1871	2,429	5,211	7,093	6,727	11,715	33,175
1891	2,315	4,687	6,520	6,686	11,856	32,064

[1] *Census Ire., 1851*, pt ii: *Returns of agricultural produce in 1851*, p. 640; *The agricultural statistics of Ireland for the year 1861* [3156], H.C. 1863, lxix, 547, pp. 16, 18; *The agricultural statistics of Ireland for the year 1871* [C 762], H.C. 1873, lxix, 375, pp. 16, 18; *The agricultural statistics of Ireland for the year 1891* [C 6777], H.C. 1892, lxxxviii, 285, p. 11. The annual series, *The agricultural statistics of Ireland*, is cited throughout the remainder of this work as *Irish agricultural statistics*.

of holdings were larger than fifty acres by 1891, the small farm of less than fifty acres, worked by the farmer and his family with the help of perhaps one or two hired labourers, remained the typical unit of production throughout this period.

The decline in tillage also progressed more slowly at first, until the wet seasons of the early 1860s, and then more rapidly thereafter. In 1851 about 30 per cent of the cultivated land of Cork was under tillage, whereas only about half as much land was being tilled by 1891. The corn crops, which grew poorly in the damp Irish climate and faced the devastating competition of American prairie wheat and maize pouring into the British market, declined in acreage from nearly 258,000 to only about 122,000, or by more than one-half, over the same period. Barley, formerly grown extensively for the large breweries and distilleries of Cork city and Dublin, especially in two particular districts of the county—between Aghada and Youghal in East Cork, and between the Old Head of Kinsale and Galley Head in West Cork [2]—fell from well over 45,000 acres in 1851 to less than 18,000 acres by 1891. Wheat declined even more drastically from almost 65,000 acres to only about 10,000 acres during the same period. What little wheat was grown was either sold to the bakers of Cork city and the country towns or consumed by farm families. Only the production of oats, which were largely used to feed cattle during the winter and early spring, was maintained on a significant scale, though the acreage also fell steadily from almost 146,000 in 1851 to less than 94,000 by 1891. The function of tillage in the structure of agriculture, already subordinate to livestock farming before the famine, became even more ancillary after it. Oats, potatoes, and perhaps another crop of oats were employed in rotation to break up worn-out grassland, which, along with meadow and clover, further extended its dominion. In 1851 about 70 per cent of the cultivated land of Cork had already come under pasture or hay, and this proportion increased to almost 85 per cent by 1891, as Table 22 shows. [3]

The continuation of this shift from labour-intensive tillage to labour-extensive livestock farming was a necessary adjustment to price trends and to the increasing scarcity of agricultural labour and its steeply rising cost. [4] Between 1851 and 1891 the total population of County Cork, as a result of emigration and the later age at marriage,

[2] *C.E.*, 13 Mar., 23 July 1888.
[3] *Irish agricultural statistics for 1871*, p. xxxix; *Irish agricultural statistics for 1881* [C 3332], H.C. 1882, lxxiv, 93, p. 34; *Irish agricultural statistics for 1891*, pp. 52, 57.
[4] Crotty, *Irish agricultural production*, p. 67.

TABLE 22   Acreage of crops and pasture in Cork, 1851–91 (in thousands)

year	corn crops	root & green crops	total tillage	hay	pasture	total crops & pasture
1851	258	154	412	107	852	1,371
1861	231	155	386	120	909	1,415
1871	181	147	328	139	1,001	1,468
1881	149	118	267	164	974	1,405
1891	122	107	229	170	988	1,387

fell from over 649,000 to about 438,000, or by practically one-third. The rate of decline was much greater in the 1850s and 1880s than in the intervening decades, but the cumulative loss since 1846 created a relative shortage of labour by the 1860s and was partly responsible for the more rapid conversion to pasture between 1861 and 1871 indicated in Table 22.[5] This scarcity of labour doubled the cost of agricultural labour by the early 1880s, and in some cases more than doubled it. An angry farmer furnished an interesting piece of supporting evidence in November 1880:

Before the potato disease, labour was cheap; men were grateful for employment and gave value for their wages. Now they make you submit to their own terms, for which they will return you half a day's work. Forty years ago a farmer paid and supported a servant boy for about £8 a year, a servant girl in like proportion. Now a boy cannot be less to his employer than £24, and a servant girl £19. Their support and pay came all from the land formerly, for which they gave thanks with a fair day's work. Now you must keep a grocery account open for them, that gives them tea twice a day, for which you receive not thanks, but impertinence.[6]

In the 1840s the weekly wage of a labourer not receiving his diet from the farmer who employed him was commonly 4s., whereas the same class of labourer, even in as poor a district as Castletown-Kinneigh, earned 8s. per week in the early 1880s.[7] During the great strikes of 1881, the labourers near Cork city who were not dieted and did not rent their houses from the farmers demanded 12s. per week, and in the Carrigaline district as much as 15s. per week.[8] In these

[5] One result of the labour shortage was the introduction on large farms from the late 1850s of threshing machines that replaced the flail and of reaping machines that replaced the sickle and the scythe (*C.C.*, 12 Sept. 1857, 13 Sept. 1866).

[6] From *Irish Times*, 24 Nov. 1880, quoted in Irish Land Committee, *The land question, Ireland*, no. 5: *Arrested progress, January 1881* (Dublin, 1881), p. 16.

[7] *C.E.*, 2 Aug. 1881.

[8] Ibid., 27 July, 10 Aug. 1881.

circumstances, labour-extensive livestock farming became a necessity.

The making of butter and the rearing of young cattle were the twin bases of agriculture in Cork and Munster during the second half of the nineteenth century. The emphasis on butter was much stronger at the beginning of this period than at its close. While there was little overall growth in the number of dairy cattle, there was a startling rise in the number of dry cattle, a difference which became more pronounced after 1876. The number of milch cattle increased by 17 per cent in Cork and 10 per cent in Munster between 1854 and 1876, while the number of dry stock rose by 30 per cent in Cork and 33 per cent in Munster during the same period. Between 1876 and 1891, however, while the number of cows fell by 7 per cent in Cork and 4 per cent in Munster, the number of dry stock increased even more rapidly than before, rising by 36 per cent in Cork and 30 per cent in Munster as a whole. As Table 23 indicates, the overall increase in the number of dry cattle in both Cork and Munster was approximately 75 per cent between 1854 and 1891.[9]

TABLE 23 Number of cows and dry cattle in Cork and Munster, 1854–91 (in thousands)

year	Cork			Munster		
	cows	dry cattle	total	cows	dry cattle	total
1854	161	138	299	537	521	1,058
1859	186	147	333	602	542	1,144
1871	182	164	346	585	654	1,239
1876	188	179	367	589	692	1,281
1881	178	208	386	552	745	1,297
1891	175	243	418	563	902	1,465
% increase, 1854–91	8·7	76·1	39·8	4·8	73·1	38·5

This remarkably divergent pattern of development was the outcome of the choice made by farmers primarily on the basis of the relative price movements of butter and store cattle. If it had not been for the failure of cattle prices to advance in the late 1860s, the eclipse of dairying would probably have proceeded much further before

[9] *Returns of agricultural produce in Ireland in the year 1854* [2017], H.C. 1856, liii, 1, pp. 116, 118; *Irish agricultural statistics for 1859* [2763], H.C. 1861, lxii, 73, pp. 116, 118; *Irish agricultural statistics for 1871*, pp. 116, 118; *Irish agricultural statistics for 1876* [C 1749], H.C. 1877, lxxxv, 529, p. 19; *Irish agricultural statistics for 1881*, p. 44; *Irish agricultural statistics for 1891*, p. 62.

TABLE 24   Percentage price movements of butter and store cattle, 1851–90

years	butter (%)	store cattle 1–2 yrs (%)	store cattle 2–3 yrs (%)
1851–5 to 1856–60	+18	+61	+65
1851–5 to 1866–70	+34	+61	+62
1851–5 to 1871–5	+45	+138	+124
1851–5 to 1876–80	+30	+148	+115
1851–5 to 1886–90	−5	+147	+91

1876. But the strong reinforcement of the divergent price trends between 1871 and 1890, as illustrated in Table 24, made the farmers' choice practically automatic. [10]

Within livestock farming in Cork, regional specializations had arisen. The typical butter pastures were found on upland and mountain farms. These uplands were generally unsuitable for fattening cattle because of the lightness of their soils and the sparse growth of grass outside the summer months. Farmers pursued dairying almost exclusively in the hilly or mountainous southwestern parts of the county. Extensive upland dairying districts surrounded the Nagle, Boggeragh, and Derrynasaggart mountains, which stretch in a broken chain all the way from Fermoy in the northeast to Ballyvourney in the northwest. Farmers in the extreme northwestern and northeastern parts of Cork, near the Mullaghareirk mountains beyond Newmarket and near the Galtees beyond Mitchelstown, also relied mainly on butter and calves. [11] On the other hand, land in the valleys of the Bride, Blackwater, Lee, Awbeg, and Funcheon rivers in east, central, and north Cork was largely devoted to grazing mixed with tillage.

Because of the scarcity of rich grazing land, upland farmers had to sell their calves and yearlings to lowland graziers. Young stock from northwest Cork were sent to be fattened in south Clare and east Limerick. It was said in December 1884 that graziers from the Golden Vale patronized the Dromcolliher fairs near Charleville because they found that young cattle hardily reared on nearby hilly ranges 'improve so much on the rich pasturages of eastern Limerick

[10] Crotty, *Irish agricultural production*, p. 356. Crotty is in error in computing the price index number of butter in the quinquennium of 1851–5 at 79; it should be 99 (Barrington, 'Agricultural prices', p. 251).

[11] *Report from the select committee on general valuation, &c., (Ireland); together with the proceedings of the committee, minutes of evidence, and appendix*, H.C. 1868–9 (362), ix, 1, p. 57; Freeman, *Pre-famine Ireland*, pp. 203–41.

that they prove a most remunerative investment'.[12] Young stock from northeast Cork were regularly sent to be fattened in Tipperary. The extent to which the pastures of south Clare and Tipperary served as fattening areas for the young cattle of the other Munster counties can be gauged from Table 25.[13]

TABLE 25   The cattle enterprise in Munster, 1854

county	no. of cows (in thousands)	no. of dry cattle over 1 yr (in thousands)	dry cattle over 1 yr per 100 cows
Clare	58	52	90
Tipperary	85	66	78
Kerry	104	58	56
Waterford	41	22	54
Cork	161	81	50
Limerick	88	37	42

The building of the first railways during the famine and the extension of the network in the 1850s and 1860s improved and strengthened the structure of agriculture. The Great Southern & Western line through Charleville and Mallow into Cork city as well as a line from Cork to Bandon were constructed during the famine.[14] Short lines from Cork to Midleton and from Queenstown to Carrigtohill were opened in the 1850s.[15] A branch of the Cork & Bandon line to Kinsale was completed in 1863,[16] and in 1866 two important railways were opened for traffic—the Cork & Macroom railway and the West Cork railway from Bandon as far as Dunmanway.[17] After the duke of Devonshire had reportedly spent £130,000 to bring a railway to his Irish seat, a fifteen-mile extension of the Mallow-Fermoy branch of the Great Southern & Western was completed to Lismore in 1872.[18] By this time railways criss-crossed the county, from Charleville in the north to Kinsale in the south,

[12] *C.E.*, 9 Dec. 1884. See also House of Lords Record Office, London: House of lords committee on the Cork & Limerick direct-railway bill, vol. iii of 1860, 13 Mar. 1860, pp. 80–2; 14 Mar. 1860, pp. 28–9.
[13] *Returns of agricultural produce . . . 1854*, pp. 113, 116, 118, 131, 141, 159–60, 164.
[14] *C.E.*, 13 Aug. 1852.
[15] *C.C.*, 20 Dec. 1856.
[16] *C.E.*, 18 May 1863.
[17] Ibid., 1, 11, 12, 25 May 1866.
[18] *C.C.*, 23 Sept. 1885. The railway from Mallow to Fermoy had been opened in 1860, as had the one from Cork to Youghal.

and from Lismore and Youghal in the east to Millstreet, Macroom, and Dunmanway in the west. Before the opening of these lines, the marketing of agricultural produce was both time-consuming and expensive. It had taken the dairy farmer residing near the Kerry border beyond Macroom at least three days to cart his butter to the market in Cork and return home, whereas the line from Macroom to Cork enabled him to do this within one day. [19] The carriers of butter and other produce from Skibbereen to Cork had taken eight days to go up and return in the late 1850s, but the time was cut by three-quarters with the opening of the West Cork railway to Dunmanway. [20] Some idea of the lower transport costs brought about by the railways was given in November 1856 by Daniel Conner, jun., who urged the extension of the Cork & Bandon line not only to Dunmanway but to Bantry and Skibbereen:

The carriage of goods from Dunmanway to Cork now costs 7s. the ton, 4s. to Bandon by car and 3s. by railway [to Cork]. The railway would bring [goods] for 5s. the ton and give a saving of 2s. the ton. Carriage from Skibbereen to Cork now costs 25s. the ton; the railway would only charge 8s. and thus give a saving of 17s. the ton. Carriage from Bantry to Cork is 30s. the ton; the railway would charge 8s. and give a saving of 22s. the ton. [21]

Besides the increased speed with which produce was marketed and the large reduction in the cost of carriage, there was no longer the great deterioration in the weight of livestock driven long distances by road to the fattening areas and the ports in hot weather.

DAIRY FARMING

Ideal climatic conditions for making butter, as it was then made, prevailed in Cork and the south of Ireland generally. More rain falls annually on the pastures of Munster than on any other area of similar size in Europe. Meteorological data collected in Cork between 1873 and 1886 showed that the average annual rainfall was 40·5 inches. [22] The heaviest rainfall occurs during the winter and spring, but the summer is also comparatively wet, and the growth of grass produced by the even heavier rains of September to November enabled farmers to make butter highly reputed for its keeping qualities. [23] Besides actual precipitation, the relative humidity is

[19] *C.E.*, 27 Aug. 1863.
[20] Ibid., 19 Sept. 1859.
[21] *C.C.*, 6 Nov. 1856. Skibbereen and Bantry were not connected by railway with Cork until the 1880s.
[22] Ibid., 6 Jan. 1888.
[23] Ibid., 2 May 1891.

high throughout the year, and 'there is a constant dampness of atmosphere very favourable for the growth of grass'.[24] Seasonal temperature variations are small. According to one official measurement, the lowest average monthly temperature, occurring in January, was 40·3°F., whereas the highest, occurring in July, was only 58·9°F.[25] The chief advantage of this narrow seasonal temperature range to butter makers lay primarily in the coolness of the peak-producing summer months, enabling farmers to turn out firm butter capable of holding its original quality longer and without the artificial cooling required in hotter climates.

Partly because of these climatic conditions, butter making in nineteenth-century Ireland was a seasonal occupation. Supplies were extremely low from late November to mid-April and practically nonexistent during the first three months of the year. This pattern can clearly be seen in Table 26, which gives the monthly receipts of salt butter at the Cork market in 1886.[26] This seasonal fluctuation in supplies naturally produced a corresponding seasonal fluctuation in butter prices, which became more pronounced with the large increase after 1870 in the volume of foreign butter imported by Britain. The constant demand for butter throughout the year in Britain created a situation in which the difference in Cork first-quality butter prices between the dearest and cheapest month was regularly as much as 50s. per cwt during the 1880s.[27]

All the leading advocates of the reform of Irish dairy farming used this fact, and the example of the conversion to winter dairying

TABLE 26   Monthly Cork market receipts of salt butter, 1886

month	no. of firkins and kegs	month	no. of firkins and kegs
Jan.	1,905	July	48,510
Feb.	1,820	Aug.	35,065
Mar.	3,861	Sept.	37,867
Apr.	13,836	Oct.	32,973
May	30,261	Nov.	35,073
June	43,966	Dec.	10,310

[24] Quoted in J. P. Sheldon, *Dairy farming, being the theory, practice, and methods of dairying* (London, 1888), p. 360.

[25] Crotty, *Irish agricultural production*, p. 69.

[26] 'The dairying industry in Ireland' in Coyne, *Ire.*, p. 239.

[27] In the thirty years from 1841 to 1870, the difference in price between the dearest and the cheapest month was more than 30s. per cwt in only eight years (T. J. Clanchy, *Guide to the buying of Irish butter* (Cork, 1870), p. 2).

which began in the Scandinavian countries during the 1870s, in order to persuade farmers in Ireland to move in the direction of an extended butter season. Raymond Crotty has shown, however, that the Irish farmers' stubborn resistance to such a radical change was not irrational.[28] Most cattle are traditional outwintered in Ireland because winters there are relatively mild, with at least some growth of grass. The additional cost of erecting cow stalls and food-storage sheds solely for winter use would have been considerable and did not appeal to farmers with small and mixed herds. Moreover, several factors helped to curtail the availability of roots, straw, and hay for winter use and to raise their cost to levels which farmers did not feel economically justified in assuming.[29] As a result, cows were expected to get along on a minimum of winterfeed.

The effects of the minimal winterfeeding of milch cattle on annual milk and butter yields can be appreciated if one compares several reliable estimates of milk yields with the results obtained where cows are known to have been fed in-house during the winter. It should first be noted, however, that although little attention was paid to pedigree dairy cattle before the late 1880s (farmers generally relied for good yields on cows bought haphazardly at local fairs without any knowledge of their antecedents), moderately high standards seem to have been achieved during the course of the century.[30] The most popular commercial cows in Cork and Munster were crosses either between the small, hardy native Kerries and the originally imported shorthorns or between the Devon and the Ayrshire breeds. There were scarcely any dairies composed of pure-bred Kerry cows, except those acquired by 'gentlemen who are fanciers of pretty animals'.[31] There is no doubt that milk yields varied widely according to the quality of the pastures. The possibility also exists that the increasingly widespread use of beef-type bulls after 1800 may even have depressed milk yields. For this reason, Crotty believes that 'the efficiency of Irish cows relative to dry cattle in 1850 was probably much greater than in later years'.[32]

[28] Crotty, *Irish agricultural production*, pp. 75–7.

[29] The corn-root crop ratio was already high in the second half of the century, and increased cultivation of roots would have added little to general soil fertility while increasing significantly the cost of production. Feeding was scarce and dear. Comparatively wet summers seriously limited the amount of land that could safely be devoted to meadows; hay saving was not only naturally difficult but also increasingly expensive as a result of a shortage of labour (ibid.).

[30] *C.C.*, 10 Oct. 1887.

[31] B. H. Becker, *Disturbed Ireland, being the letters written during the winter of 1880–81* (London, 1881), pp. 291–3. See also *C.C.*, 8 Oct. 1857.

[32] Crotty, *Irish agricultural production*, p. 73. See also *C.E.*, 13 June 1885.

In any case, the average milk yield of Irish cows in the 1880s was probably between 400 and 450 gallons per year. [33] Few records of milk or butter yields exist for earlier decades, but one that does tends to confirm contemporary estimates. In 1857 the thirty-three cows in the dairy of the Rev. Thomas Gollock at Leemount near Macroom produced an average of 162 pounds of butter, or about 486 gallons of milk (at the generally adopted conversion rate of one pound of butter to three gallons of milk). [34] When the yields of cows fed like Gollock's in the normal way are compared with those which resulted when cows received substantial amounts of in-house winterfeed, it is possible to form at least a general impression of the magnitude of the economic loss imposed by minimal winterfeeding. A. J. Campbell, who farmed about 300 acres at Ballynahow near Fermoy, had a dairy of twenty-two cows which he fed in-house until mid-April, allowing them to lie out altogether at the beginning of May. His cows produced an average of 203 pounds of butter (609 gallons of milk) in 1871. [35] The Munster Dairy School maintained a herd of thirty-five shorthorn and Ayrshire crosses, mainly purchased at local fairs, on its 126-acre farm just outside Cork city. The average milk yields per cow were 691 gallons in 1884, 717 gallons in 1885, and no less than 743 gallons in 1886. [36] Richard Barter kept a dairy of forty cows, consisting almost entirely of shorthorns, on his 700-acre farm near Blarney. He obtained an average yield per cow of 682 gallons during one year in the 1880s. [37]

THE DAIRYMAN SYSTEM

It had been common in the eighteenth century for landlords, middlemen, and wealthy farmers who owned herds of milch cattle to rent them for the year to landless peasants, who then became known as dairymen. Arthur Young discovered that the dairyman system was widespread in Munster when he made his famous tour in the late 1770s. Of the district around Castleisland in Kerry, Young noted: 'Great farmers hire vast quantities of land, in order to stock with cows, and let them to dairymen; one farmer, who died lately, paid

---

[33] For contemporary estimates of milk yields, see *C.C.*, 13 June 1885; *C.E.*, 6 Jan. 1887; Sheldon, *Dairy farming*, p. 357; W. L. Stokes, 'Irish creameries' in *Co-operative Wholesale Society Annual for 1897* (Manchester, 1897), p. 425.
[34] Gollock papers: Demesne account book, 1846–66, pp. 78–9.
[35] *C.C.*, 15 July 1872.
[36] Ibid., 20 May 1887.
[37] Sheldon, *Dairy farming*, pp. 360–1; *C.E.*, 13 June 1885.

£1,400 a year for this purpose; but £300 or £400 [is] common'. [38] The size of the herds rented to dairymen varied from some of twenty to fifty cows around Castlemartyr to others of up to sixty cows near Mallow. [39] Payment was generally made in both money and kind, and payments in kind included not only butter but also calves and pigs. [40]

The system continued as Young had found it with little modification up to and through the great famine. It is difficult to be certain whether it was as widespread in the 1880s as it had been in Young's time, but one experienced agriculturalist, William Bence Jones, of Lisselan near Clonakilty, asserted:

Since the famine the practice of letting cows to a dairyman has greatly increased. . . . Not only landowners adopt this plan, but also numbers of tenants, who let their cows to dairymen, instead of getting their own wives and daughters to do the dairy work. [41]

The practice must indeed have been very extensive among Cork farmers to provoke the following outcry in November 1881 from labourers in the Kilmichael district:

Resolved—that we look upon the present system of dairy farming, known as 'a dairy', to be the greatest hindrance to our prosperity, and we call upon all classes of farmers to give up this system, to farm their own farms, and to employ labour; and we furthermore call upon parties inclined to take such dairies once and for all not to do so, that labour may in consequence be brought into the market, and that we obtain a fair day's wages for a fair day's work. [42]

Bence Jones described in detail the operation of the system in West Cork during the 1880s:

The owner provides cows, utensils, and house and land for potatoes, to be manured by the dung of cows. The dairyman is allowed to keep two or three sheep and a horse or donkey, according to the size of the dairy. If he has money, he pays part of the rent at once; for the rest, or if he has no money . . . [at] all, he gives promissory notes with two thoroughly solvent securities. From the habit of the country there is no trouble in getting excellent security. The rent is quite safe. About 4 acres of ordinary land are allowed for each cow. [43]

---

[38] Young, *Tour*, i, 367.
[39] Ibid., i, 307, 329; Townsend, pp. 578–81.
[40] Young, *Tour*, i, 367–8.
[41] Quoted in Sheldon, *Dairy farming*, p. 360.
[42] *W.C.E.*, 26 Nov. 1881.
[43] Quoted in Sheldon, *Dairy farming*, p. 360.

The owner of the dairy also provided winter fodder. When fodder was extremely scarce in the spring of 1881, and farmers refused to give an additional supply, the dairymen frequently abandoned the cows and absconded. [44] Dairymen fed a few pigs on potatoes and skim milk and sometimes grew a corn crop as well as potatoes. [45]

The rent per cow depended on several factors—the price of butter and young cattle, the milk yield of the cows, the quality of the pasture, and the distance from the best markets. During the long run of high butter prices up to 1876, rents of from £9 to £12 per cow were fairly common, but the sharp decline in prices from 1877 would not support such rents; they fell to between £7 and £10 per cow during the 1880s. [46] One dairyman persuaded a tenant farmer on the Colthurst estate at Ballyvourney in 1884 to allow him to pay £9 in cash, together with 12 firkins of butter worth £3 10s. to £4 each. [47] Similar arrangements were probably not unusual as prices continued to decline drastically in the later 1880s.

In Young's time, dairymen had generally enjoyed the privilege of disposing of some or all of the calves from the cows they hired, and Townsend also stated in 1810 that dairymen in the barony of Imokilly possessed the additional source of profit of rearing calves and supplying Cork city with veal. [48] With the enormous increase in the price of young stock after 1850, it would not have been at all surprising to learn that this valuable privilege had gradually been withdrawn or curtailed. Dairymen must have retained it in many places, however, because calves were said to form the main business of the cattle trade at the September fairs in County Cork in 1883, 'as about this time dairy people must, according to contract, have the calves off the grass'. [49] At the Clonakilty November fair in 1888, there was an especially large supply of weanling calves, 'as about this time dairymen should get rid of them. These were in great demand and realized very high prices, some as high as £5.' [50]

Milk and butter yields also influenced the cost of renting cows. The time of calving, which generally took place between 25 March and 1 May, regulated the amount of butter obtainable from cow's whole milk; the earlier the suckling period ended, the sooner a

[44] *C.E.*, 8 Apr. 1881.
[45] Sheldon, *Dairy farming*, p. 357.
[46] *W.C.E.*, 27 May, 21 Oct. 1882.
[47] Kenmare papers, Letter book, 1883–4: S. M. Hussey to W. Erck, 19 May 1884, pp. 1004–7.
[48] Young, *Tour*, i, 368; Townsend, p. 614; Gollock papers: Demesne account book, 1824–6, 15 Mar. 1824, p. 15.
[49] *C.E.*, 4 Sept. 1883.
[50] *C.C.*, 6 Nov. 1888.

richer butterfat content could be expected of the milk. It was therefore part of the dairyman's contract with the owner of the herd that each cow must have calved before 15 May; otherwise, the rent had to be adjusted accordingly. [51] Cows which died or went dry before an agreed date were replaced by the owner, or a proportionate abatement was made in the dairyman's rent. [52] A similar arrangement had to be made if the average milk yield did not reach an acceptable minimum standard: 6 'pottles', or 12 quarts, of milk per day was the most widely recognized yardstick when cows were fed on grass and hay. If there was a deficiency, the owner made a proportionate reduction in the rent. [53] The quality of the pasture and the distance from the great butter market in Cork city were also important considerations in fixing rents. Dairymen in the Galtee mountain district, for example, found it difficult to obtain 1 or 1½ firkins of butter (less than 325 gallons of milk) per cow during the best of seasons and had the additional expense of hand-feeding almost from Michaelmas until the beginning of May. A rent of £7 or £8 per cow was really exorbitant in such a case. Dairies in districts with generally poor pastures, particularly in southwest and northwest Cork, were often let at less than £8 per cow in the 1880s. [54]

The relationship between dairymen and the owners of the cows was largely an exploitative one. It bore a striking resemblance in some respects to the conacre system of letting land for one potato crop. In neither system was there any real restraint on rent, unless unrestricted competition can be said to have afforded some small measure of protection. Dairymen rarely made a profit on the cows alone, certainly not if they paid as much as £10 per cow after 1876. 'Very few tenants', said Bence Jones, 'make anything like £10 a cow from those they do not let. It is a sort of mystery how dairymen manage to pay; yet not a few make money.' [55] Whatever profits there were for dairymen came mainly from the sale of weanling calves, bonhams, or lambs. The system may have given reasonable satisfaction to both parties before 1877, but it aroused much resentment when butter prices fell disastrously in the 1880s. Tenant farmers enjoying sizeable profit rents did not hesitate to dispossess

---

[51] Sheldon, *Dairy farming*, p. 357.

[52] Gollock papers: Demesne account book, 1824–6, 15 Mar. 1824, p. 15; Demesne account book, 1838–43, 29 Feb. 1840, p. 152.

[53] Townsend, pp. 546–7; *Munster Farmers' Magazine*, no. 10 (Sept. 1813), pp. 94–5.

[54] *C.E.*, 12 Nov. 1880; *W.C.E.*, 27 May, 21 Oct. 1882.

[55] Quoted in Sheldon, *Dairy farming*, p. 360. See also *W.C.E.*, 17 June 1882.

dairymen who defaulted in the payment of rent.[56] The land agent
Samuel Hussey recalled in February 1881 the case of a farmer named
Hennigan on the earl of Kenmare's Bantry estate who 'had the farm
which he held from Lord Kenmare at £37 a year sublet to a dairyman for £208'. Hennigan had earlier become chairman of the local
branch of the Land League. 'In 1877 the dairyman was ruined,' said
Hussey, '& so far from giving him any compensation, Mr Hennigan
sued his securities for the last shilling, & I believe every other Land
League chairman would do the same.'[57] Faced with such an exacting
policy on the part of the owners of the cows, dairymen from Cork and
Limerick assembled in Kilmallock in January 1881 and decided to
attempt to hold the line on rents. They sought to reduce competition
by prohibiting farmers with more than 20 acres of land from hiring
cows and to limit their own liabilities in the event of failure by
keeping deposits to £100 or less in the coming season. Dairy masters
who ignored these resolutions were threatened with public exposure,
which was often tantamount to violent retribution in the excited
climate of the 1880s.[58]

The disintegration of the dairyman system, caused partly by the
shifting emphasis within the structure of agriculture from butter to
beef and partly by the declining profitability of dairy farming after
1876, was a protracted process, but its beginnings may be seen in the
1880s. Both the size of dairies let and the geographical extent of the
system contracted. It was now extremely rare for dairymen to hire
more than thirty cows, and the average may indeed have been less
than fifteen.[59] And whereas examples of the system could be discovered before the famine in many parts of Cork, by the 1880s they
were difficult to find, except in the poorer western parts of the
county.

PRODUCTION AND PRICES, 1851–76

The recovery of Cork farmers from the effects of the great famine was
remarkably rapid. This was mainly attributable to dramatic
increases in the prices of butter and store cattle. The seven-month
(May to November) average price of first-quality Cork butter rose
from 75*s.* per hundredweight in 1851 to 109*s.* per hundredweight in
1859, or by slightly more than 45 per cent, and the average price of

---

[56] *C.E.*, 5 May 1881, 25 Sept. 1882.
[57] Kenmare papers, Letter book, 1880–2: S. M. Hussey to Lord
Hamilton, 7 Feb. 1881, pp. 157–8.
[58] *C.E.*, 7 Jan. 1881.
[59] See, e.g., the advertisements of 'dairies to be let' in *W.C.E.*, 24,
31 Dec. 1881; 23 Dec. 1882.

one-to-two-year-old stores increased from 70*s*. to 105*s*. over the same period, or by no less than 50 per cent. [60] Accumulating capital was freely invested in livestock. The number of cattle on Cork farms rose from 247,000 in 1851 to 333,000 in 1859, or by more than a third. Pig breeding was probably not as profitable as it had been in good years before the famine, because of the greatly reduced yields of the potato that consistently characterized this crop in the post-famine period. The production of pigs, however, did recover from the low level of output in 1851, and by 1859 their numbers had increased from 129,000 to 148,000. Sheep flocks, which had been sharply reduced in size because of both liver-fluke disease and stealing during the famine, began expanding again in 1851, and by 1859 sheep numbers had risen from 183,000 to 295,000. [61]

The extremely cold and wet seasons of 1860–2 and the unusually dry years of 1863–4 constituted, however, a fairly serious setback for Cork farmers. Heavy summer rains and floods were responsible for poor grain harvests in 1861 and 1862, [62] and the potato blight returned in alarming proportions for three years in succession. Serious deficiencies also characterized the root and green crops, and meadows that had been inundated with water in both 1861 and 1862 yielded a light hay crop in 1864 because of the parching summer heat. [63] The effects of unfavourable weather on the crops in County Cork are shown in Table 27. [64]

TABLE 27   Percentage deficiencies between expected and actual crop production in Cork, 1860–4

(N = at least normal yield; 26 = 26% below normal)

	oats	barley	wheat	potatoes	turnips	mangels	hay
1860	N	N	N	35	33	30	N
1861	26	31	36	60	34	39	17
1862	26	32	39	43	30	37	11
1863	N	N	N	8	10	20	6
1864	N	N	N	N	32	24	17

[60] T. J. Clanchy and Co., *Half-a-century's butter prices, showing the fluctuations and the cheapest and dearest months of each year for 50 years, as a guide to buyers and sellers of butter* (Cork, 1892), 1 p.; *Irish Farmers' Gazette*, 1 Nov. 1879.

[61] *Census Ire., 1851*, pt ii: *Returns of agricultural produce in 1851*, p. 640; *Irish agricultural statistics for 1861*, p. lxi.

[62] *C.C.*, 19 Aug., 3 Sept. 1861; 5, 11 Aug., 15 Sept. 1862.

[63] Ibid., 1 Aug. 1864.

[64] *Irish agricultural statistics for 1871*, p. xxxix. The average yield of each of the above crops between 1851 and 1860 has been taken to indicate the normal or expected yield.

The cottiers and smallholders were badly hurt by the potato failures, and there was a great deal of distress among them. [65] All farmers suffered from the scarcity and consequent high cost of fodder, and the condition of cattle and pastures seriously deteriorated. [66] Higher feeding costs and lower incomes, combined with the importunate demands of landlords, meal merchants, and shopkeepers, led farmers to dispose of livestock without replacing them until 1864 (and in the cases of cows and pigs, until 1865), as indicated in Table 28. [67]

TABLE 28   Number of cattle, sheep, and pigs in Cork, 1860–5 (in thousands)

year	cows	dry cattle	total cattle	sheep	pigs
1860	184	135	319	293	152
1861	178	125	303	302	149
1862	171	107	278	286	144
1863	165	105	270	262	143
1864	160	126	286	268	134
1865	162	145	307	314	159

Because of the fall in the number of milch cows, the bitterly cold spring weather that retarded the growth of vegetation in 1860 and 1861, and the drought of 1864, Cork Butter Market receipts declined from an average of 404,000 firkins a year between 1855 and 1860 to only 366,000 firkins a year between 1860 and 1865, or by nearly 10 per cent. [68] The profits of dairy farmers were further reduced by the first significant break in the trend of rising butter prices between 1861 and 1863, when the market for Irish butter in Australia collapsed. [69] The average price of first-quality Cork butter fell

[65] *C.E.*, 5 Oct., 9 Nov., 19 Dec. 1861; 18 Feb., 10 Mar., 2 May 1862; 17 Feb., 23, 26 Mar. 1863.

[66] It was reported in April 1860 that fodder was so scarce in the Charleville district that cattle were 'dying in dozens of starvation. On an average twenty hides of animals that have thus died are being brought into the town every day' (*C.C.*, 3 Apr. 1860).

[67] *Irish agricultural statistics for 1860* [2997], H.C. 1862, lx, 137, p. xlix; *Irish agricultural statistics for 1861* [3156], H.C. 1863, lxix, 547, p. lv; *Irish agricultural statistics for 1862* [5286], H.C. 1864, lix, 327, p. lv; *Irish agricultural statistics for 1863* [3456], H.C. 1865, lv, 125, p. liv; *Irish agricultural statistics for 1864* [3766], H.C. 1867, lxxi, 201, p. lvi; *Irish agricultural statistics for 1865* [2939], H.C. 1867, lxxi, 491, p. lx.

[68] C.B.M. MSS, C. 38: Account of the total annual quantity of butter in casks, firkins, and kegs passed through the weigh-house, 1770–1869.

[69] J. S. Donnelly, Jr, 'Cork Market: its role in the nineteenth century Irish butter trade' in *Studia Hib.*, no. 11 (1971), p. 131.

almost 10 per cent below the average of the previous five years. [70]
There is no doubt that farmers felt keenly the damaging effects of
these unfavourable turns in economic events. At a meeting of
tenants of the duke of Devonshire's Bandon estate in August 1862,
one of them remarked:

> It was well known that the past two years were, in this part of the country at
> all events, most unremunerative to the farmer; in fact, men of experience say
> they got a worse return from their land than in the midst of the famine. [71]

The period from 1865 to 1876 was generally one of unprecedented
prosperity for most Cork farmers, with only a few minor setbacks.
There was another break in the trend of rising butter prices in 1867
as a result of heavy foreign competition in the London market, but it
was brief and not very sharp. [72] A serious drought occurred in 1868,
and less serious ones in 1874 and 1876, [73] but dairy farmers were
compensated, especially in the last two years, by higher butter
prices. The wet year of 1872 was a bad one for tillage, above all for
the potato, which failed almost completely. 'We have had a dreadful,
wet season & no appearance of fine weather', the land agent Richard
Doherty, sen., told the Cork landlord James Oswald in August of
that year; 'the hay crop [is] in a very bad state & no chance appears
at present of saving it—the corn looks well but the potatoes bad
from the blight.' Doherty ended his letter, however, by saying
significantly, 'prices for stock of all kinds [are] very high & . . .
everything else [is] in prosperity'. [74] When store-cattle prices failed to
advance in the late 1860s, farmers compensated by an extraordinarily
rapid expansion in the size of their flocks of sheep, which increased
in number from 314,000 in 1865 to a nineteenth-century peak of
almost 437,000 just two years later. When store-cattle prices rose
again in the early 1870s, the less profitable sheep were quickly
displaced, as farmers stopped sending new calves to the shambles.
The number of dry cattle on Cork farms increased from 145,000 to
179,000 between 1865 and 1876—far above the level of the late
1850s; and the number of cows rose over the same period from
162,000 to 188,000—the peak of the nineteenth century. [75]

[70] T. J. Clanchy and Co., *Half-a-century's butter prices*, 1 p.

[71] *C.C.*, 5 Aug. 1862.

[72] O'Donovan, *Econ. hist.*, pp. 305–6; Donnelly, 'Cork Market', pp. 144–5.

[73] *C.C.*, 17, 27, 30 July, 22 Aug. 1868; 24 Mar. 1875; 18 Sept. 1876.

[74] Doherty papers, Letter book, 1871–3: R. W. Doherty, sen., to J. J.
Oswald, 26 Aug. 1872, p. 693.

[75] *Irish agricultural statistics for 1871*, p. lxx; *Irish agricultural statistics for 1881*, p. 49.

The great prosperity enjoyed by Cork farmers during this period was the result of the growing British dependence on imported food, combined with a relative shortage of foreign supplies of butter, beef, and mutton. Rising population and the industrial revolution pushed the British demand steadily upward. The population of England and Wales, which had already doubled during the first half of the century, doubled again between 1851 and 1911. The so-called golden age of Victorian prosperity, said to have lasted from 1850 to 1873, was marked by a clear reversal of the earlier trend in which wage increases had largely been cancelled by rising prices. Food prices now rose much less rapidly than those of industrial goods, and *per capita* consumption of tea, sugar, meat, and dairy products all increased substantially.[76] The industrial revolution was finally ushering in an indisputable rise in British living standards, and 'the working classes were taking the first great stride out of that poverty which had been their lot for a century past'.[77]

The great demand for liquid milk in the industrial cities and the traditionally large manufacture of cheese in Britain created a 'seller's paradise' for Irish butter, as the amount of milk available there for conversion into butter was almost certainly declining.[78] Even though British imports of foreign (non-Irish) butter more than quadrupled between 1853 and 1876, rising from 403,000 hundredweight to 1,659,000 hundredweight, Ireland remained Britain's largest individual supplier of butter. Irish butter exports (practically all to Britain) are estimated to have averaged 617,000 hundredweight a year between 1870 and 1875, whereas the exports to Britain of Ireland's nearest rivals, France and Holland, averaged 421,000 hundredweight and 340,000 hundredweight a year respectively.[79] The British demand for Irish livestock was stronger than that for butter, and Ireland's competitive position in this area was even better. As late as 1875, Irish exports of store and fat cattle to Britain were well more than double British cattle imports from abroad, and those of sheep almost equalled British sheep imports from all foreign countries together. With the exception of pig meat, the imports of which had grown as large as 2,639,000 hundredweight, British dead-meat imports were still of no consequence. Carcass-beef imports were as low as 216,000 hundredweight, and imports of mutton too insignificant for enumeration.[80] Because of these extremely

[76] J. Burnett, *Plenty and want: a social history of diet in England from 1815 to the present day* (Harmondsworth, Middlesex, 1968), p. 123.
[77] Ibid., p. 124.   [78] O'Donovan, *Econ. hist.*, p. 302.
[79] Donnelly, 'Cork Market', p. 132.
[80] O'Donovan, *Econ. hist.*, p. 316.

favourable factors of rising demand and relative scarcity of foreign supplies in Britain, the prices of the principal Irish agricultural exports soared between 1851 and 1876, as Table 29 shows.[81]

TABLE 29 Index numbers of Irish agricultural prices, 1851–76

(base 1840 = 100, except store cattle, base 1845 = 100)

years	butter	store cattle		mutton	pork
		1–2 yrs	2–3 yrs		
1851–5	99	93	115	98	94
1856–60	117	150	190	128	130
1861–5	121	171	204	143	128
1866–70	133	150	186	146	140
1871–5	144	221	258	171	135
1876	155	243	260	186	133
% increase, 1851–5 to 1871–5	45	138	124	74	44

PRODUCTION AND PRICES, 1876–91

Compared with the prosperity of the previous quarter of a century, the late 1870s and the 1880s were difficult, exasperating, and much less profitable years for Cork farmers. Bad seasons, foreign competition, and a short but sharp industrial depression in Britain between 1884 and 1887 not only took much of the profit out of farming but also helped to start and sustain the land war. The economic background of the land war is treated in greater detail in the concluding chapters of this work, and it is necessary here to be concerned only with agricultural production and prices. As Table 30 indicates, a recurrence of extremely wet and cold weather seriously damaged the crops from 1877 to 1879, and the blight again ravaged the potato for three years in succession.[82] On the whole, these crop deficiencies were less injurious than those of the early 1860s, and partly for this reason, they did not lead to a similar decline in livestock numbers, with the exception of pigs, which could not be bred with profit so long as the potato crop was a failure. Although the number of cows and sheep fell between 1877 and 1880, this was for the most part a

[81] Barrington, 'Agricultural prices', p. 252.
[82] *Irish agricultural statistics for 1881*, p. 39. The crop deficiencies in Table 30 represent the difference between the actual yield per acre of each crop in 1877, 1878, and 1879, and the average yield per acre between 1871 and 1876.

TABLE 30 Percentage deficiencies between expected and actual crop production in Cork, 1877–9

(N = at least normal yield; 22 = 22% below normal)

year	oats	barley	wheat	potatoes	turnips	mangels	hay
1877	22	14	N	37	17	19	N
1878	16	10	3	50	N	N	N
1879	8	31	24	47	31	32	N

wholly desirable and beneficial response to the greater economic returns from producing beef instead of butter or mutton. Even during the wet years, the number of dry cattle increased, and this trend continued in the 1880s, as Table 31 illustrates.[83]

TABLE 31 Number, of cattle, sheep, and pigs in Cork, 1875–90 (in thousands)

year	cows	dry cattle	total cattle	sheep	pigs
1875	187	184	371	341	148
1880	176	206	382	295	124
1885	177	226	403	303	156
1890	172	230	402	332	166

After the wet years of 1877–9, Cork farmers had to contend with the cold, rainless spring weather that characterized the 1880s and with the major droughts of 1884 and 1887. Milk and butter yields were reduced sharply and feeding costs increased greatly. In no less than seven of eleven years between 1881 and 1891, dairy farmers and graziers were afflicted by unusually severe weather in April and May. Cattle were said to be starving in Cork in 1881 'from the unprecedented continuance of hard, dry weather'. [84] In May 1885 it was reported that 'sleety showers and nightly frosts . . . have in a considerable measure retarded the progress of vegetation of all kinds. Grass everywhere is short, and farmers complain of its backwardness, being so sparsely supplied with provender after the past exceptional dry summer' of 1884. [85] In April 1887 the sub-agent of Viscount Midleton's estate told one of his correspondents: 'This year has been

[83] *Irish agricultural statistics for 1875* [C 1568], H.C. 1876, lxxviii, 413, p. 48; *Irish agricultural statistics for 1880* [C 2932], H.C. 1881, xciii, 685, p. 57; *Irish agricultural statistics for 1885* [C 4802], H.C. 1886, lxxi, 1, p. 50; *Irish agricultural statistics for 1890* [C 6518], H.C. 1890–1, xci, 277, p. 60.
[84] *C.E.*, 8 Apr. 1881.
[85] Ibid., 8 May 1885. See also ibid., 14 May 1885.

exceptionally severe on grass lands, being very dry with sharp frosts & no vegetation, & lands like Rostellan, that has [*sic*] not been turned up or renewed for years, has suffered especially from the cold & drought'. [86] In 1891 the total rainfall in Cork during the four months ending 30 April was only 6·63 inches, whereas the average rainfall for the same period in the previous eighteen years had been as much as 15·28 inches; the month of April in 1891 was 'chiefly remarkable for low temperatures, harsh winds, and deficient rainfall, all having the effect of retarding vegetation'. [87] Similar climatic conditions reduced the early make of butter and increased feeding costs between 1882 and 1884 and in 1888. [88]

Summer pastures which normally afforded rich feeding were scorched by serious droughts in 1884 and 1887. Nothing resembling the less serious drought of 1884 could be recalled for half a century. The *Cork Examiner* fixed the loss in income from butter at nearly £500,000, or about 8 per cent of the estimated total value of Irish production. [89] The much more damaging effects of the 1887 drought can be gauged from the fact that the total rainfall in Cork during that year was only 22·25 inches, as compared with an annual average rainfall of 40·5 inches during the previous fourteen years. [90] It was the driest year of the entire century, with the possible exception of 1826. The absence of rain and the almost tropical heat 'parched the land and dried up the springs and streams, causing great difficulty and loss to the farmers, whose anxiety was not alone how to provide the cattle with food, but with water'. [91] The turnip crop was largely destroyed, and the growing oat crop was frequently cut before it was fully ripe in order to feed the starving livestock. Thousands of cows ran dry early in the season, and milk yields declined drastically until September. Only a superior make of butter from the aftergrass prevented an even more disastrous year for dairy farmers. [92]

Estimates of the deficiency in butter production before autumn rains revived pastures varied from one-third to one-half. [93] R. K. McBride, a Cork landlord with a large demesne near Midleton, was informed by his agent James Penrose Fitzgerald in May 1888 that the previous year's account had barely shown a profit.

[86] P.R.O.I., ref. no. 978, Midleton papers, Letter book, 1886–8: J. J. Sullivan to Messrs Clarke, Rawlins, and Co., 23 Apr. 1887, p. 391.
[87] *C.C.*, 2 May 1891.
[88] *C.E.*, 1 May 1882, 5 June 1884; *C.C.*, 18 Apr. 1883, 17 Apr. 1888.
[89] *C.E.*, 4 Oct. 1884.
[90] *C.C.*, 6 Jan. 1888.
[91] Ibid., 30 Dec. 1887.
[92] Ibid., 11 Oct. 1887.
[93] *C.E.*, 17, 26 Aug. 1887.

Had last summer been an ordinary season, we should have done much better; owing to the drought, our summer yield of milk was only about half an average; fortunately, we had a good crop of oats & mangolds & were able to buy more winter cows; their produce saved us from making a loss on the year. [94]

Taking the season as a whole, the fall in butter production seems to have been less catastrophic, perhaps about 25 per cent. Cork Butter Market receipts declined to 277,000 firkins during the year ending 31 December 1887, as compared with 332,000 firkins during the previous twelve months. [95] Still, it was the worst year for dairy farmers since the famine. Butter prices hardly rose in response to scarcity now that increasing foreign supplies were always forthcoming in the British market.

TABLE 32   British imports of non-Irish butter and Cork butter prices, 1871–90

years (average)	British imports (thousands of cwt)	Cork prices (May–Nov. average) (shillings per cwt)
1871–5	1,368	126
1876–80	1,893	119
1881–5	2,286	109
1886–90	2,862	92

The beginning of the great expansion in British imports of foreign butter between 1877 and 1879 brought about a veritable collapse of Irish butter prices. The seven-month average price of first-quality Cork butter tumbled from 137*s.* per cwt in 1876 to only 100*s.* per cwt in 1879, a year of sluggish commercial and industrial activity in Britain. [96] A strong though extremely short-lived recovery took place in 1880, despite another substantial rise in imports, but an almost continuous, headlong, and alarming decline marked the following decade. As Table 32 indicates, British imports of butter and butter substitutes from abroad more than doubled between the early 1870s and the late 1880s, and the average price of first-quality Cork butter fell by almost 27 per cent. [97] Supplies from Holland, France, and the

[94] P.R.O.I., ref. no. 978, Midleton papers, Letter book, 1886–8: J. P. Fitzgerald to R. K. McBride, 8 May 1888, p. 1160.

[95] *C.E.*, 7 Apr. 1888.

[96] W. Ashworth, *An economic history of England, 1870–1939* (London and New York, 1960), pp. 244–5.

[97] *Annual statements of the trade and navigation of the United Kingdom with foreign countries and British possessions,* 1871–90 (London, 1872–91); T. J. Clanchy and Co., *Half-a-century's butter prices,* 1 p.

Scandinavian countries successfully challenged the traditional supremacy of Irish butter in the industrial centres of Britain. This challenge was not only a matter of quantity but also one of quality. When British retailers and consumers looked for neatness in packaging, exact weights, freshness, and uniformity of colour, texture, and taste, they were more likely to find these attributes in foreign, not Cork or Irish, butter, and even in foreign butter substitutes. [98]

The United States and Holland were linked in a growing trade in butter substitutes from the early 1870s. Shortly after the invention in 1869 of beef-fat oleomargarine by a French food analyst, Mège-Mouries, American stockyard interests were exporting it in large quantities to Rotterdam. Enterprising Dutch merchants mixed the oleomargarine with from 10 to 30 per cent of the finest Danish butter and then re-exported this new article, which became known as butterine, to London, Hull, and Grimsby for sale to the working classes. [99] Because butterine was wholesome, tasty, and above all cheap, it was readily accepted in place of the genuine article, and its sale in Britain increased at a truly phenomenal rate. By 1886 imports of Dutch butterine had risen to 888,000 hundredweight, worth more than £3 million, and they further increased to the enormous quantity of 1,305,000 hundredweight in 1892. Butterine imports accounted by the latter year for almost 40 per cent of British imports of butter and butter substitutes from abroad and in quantity, if not in value, were probably about double Irish butter exports to Britain at that time. [100]

Cork farmers and merchants regarded butterine as the chief cause of their woes. W. J. Lane, a Cork butter exporter, asserted in June 1885 that the main competition of Irish butter was now 'rather with the produce of the butterine factories than with the butter shipped from France, Denmark, Germany, and Sweden'. Lane also claimed that higher prices were being paid for butterine in Dublin and England than for Irish butter of secondary quality, and most Irish butter, said Lane, was of this description. [101] James Hudson, called 'the butter king of London' because of the extent of his wholesale and retail activities, observed in September 1886 that the consequences of the butterine trade had been 'felt very severely by

[98] Donnelly, 'Cork Market', pp. 146–54.
[99] *C.C.*, 23 Sept. 1886; J. Howard, 'Butterine legislation' in *C.E.*, 20 May 1887; Burnett, *Plenty and want*, pp. 141–2.
[100] *Annual statements of the trade and navigation of the United Kingdom with foreign countries and British possessions*, 1886–92 (London, 1887–93).
[101] *Report from the select committee on industries (Ireland); together with the proceedings of the committee, minutes of evidence, and appendix*, H.C. 1884–5 (288), ix, 1, p. 728 (hereafter cited as *Industries committee evidence*).

the producers of the lower class of Irish butter—for this reason, that the genuine article is inferior in appearance and in taste to the manufactured'.[102] The *Cork Examiner* asserted in June 1887: 'This roguish compound is beating Irish butter out of the market. While our farmers are making earnest efforts to improve the make, they see the price tumbling under the competition of this specious rival.'[103] In the absence of legal restrictions on the sale of butterine as butter or in studied imitation of butter, the contest between the genuine article and its 'specious rival' was very uneven. Butterine manufacturers went to great lengths to copy exactly the colour, shape, and packaging of Irish and foreign butters sold in Britain, and retailers often sold butterine over the shop counter as pure butter. One of the largest London wholesale houses actually advertised in 1885 in the *Grocer*, the journal of the provision trade, that it sold butterine as 'finest Irish firkins', and a Dutch firm offered in one of its trade circulars to imitate any well-known brand, such as 'Irish firkins' or 'Irish rolls'.[104] Largely as a result of pressure from Cork export merchants and Irish members of parliament, legislation restricting the sale of butterine as butter was passed in late 1887 and came into effect at the beginning of 1888.[105] It did not restrain the growth of imports, however, and was much less stringent than similar legislation passed about the same time in other countries, especially Denmark and Sweden. Complaints that even its weak provisions had not been strictly enforced were common.[106]

Irish butter producers also encountered formidable rivalry from France as a result of a new development in the dairy industry there. Using Dutch butter-blending machinery, French merchants increasingly purchased fresh butter in lumps a few times a week from the small dairy farmers of Normandy, classified it according to quality, mixed it carefully, packaged it attractively, and dispatched it to London within a few days of its local sale. This factory-blended butter completely ousted Irish butter from the London market during the 1870s and soon became a serious competitor throughout England. Contrasting the Normandy and Irish systems of production, James Hudson remarked in September 1886:

Thus butter which we deliver to our customers throughout the metropolis on Thursday was milk in the cow in France on Monday, and the whole of it is eaten in London before the Irish farmers begin to churn the cream from the cows milked [at] the same time.[107]

[102] *C.C.*, 23 Sept. 1886.   [103] *C.E.*, 2 June 1887.
[104] *Industries committee evidence*, p. 731.   [105] 50 & 51 Vict., c. 29.
[106] *C.E.*, 1 June 1887; 7 Feb., 16 May 1888.
[107] *C.C.*, 23 Sept. 1886.

The Scandinavian countries, however, made the most rapid strides in increasing the quantity and improving the quality of their butter exports to Britain. Danish supplies trebled between 1871 and 1890, increasing from an average of 189,000 hundredweight a year between 1871 and 1875 to an average of 598,000 hundredweight a year between 1886 and 1890; imports from Sweden grew even more rapidly, rising from an average of only 22,000 hundredweight a year in the early 1870s to an average of 190,000 hundredweight a year in the late 1880s.[108] Butter-making in these countries, within the space of little more than a decade, was largely transferred from the farms into large, central, co-operative creameries, where separation and churning were done by machine; the producing season was also extended through the winter and spring months by the in-house feeding of milch cattle on roots and artificial food such as colza cake.[109] Danish merchants also carefully attended to the requirements of the English market. One prominent example of their marketing acumen was the introduction of a heatproof butter truck to carry Danish butter at an even temperature of 58° to 68°F. from the port of Newcastle to inland centres as early as 1880.[110]

Perhaps the most serious aspect of butter prices in the 1880s and 1890s, apart from the extraordinary decline itself, was the increasingly low level of prices during the summer months, when Irish production was at its seasonal peak.[111] Denmark more than doubled its exports to Britain in the short space of five years, from 401,000 hundredweight in 1886 to 825,000 hundredweight in 1890; with the adoption of winter dairying in Denmark, these exports were spread more evenly over the entire year. This fact, together with the year-round availability of an alternative source of supply in butterine from Holland and the arrival of butter in the 1890s from Australia and New Zealand (where their summer corresponded with the European winter), meant that it was possible to meet the continuous demand for butter in the British market.[112] But it also meant that Ireland, whose butter exports to Britain practically ceased for almost five months of the year, had to recapture her share of the market and to reconvert British consumers, who naturally tended to show a preference for the more evenly supplied foreign butter and

[108] *Annual statements of the trade and navigation of the United Kingdom with foreign countries and British possessions*, 1871–90.
[109] For a comparative analysis of the dairy industries of Ireland and Denmark, see Crotty, *Irish agricultural production*, pp. 72–7.
[110] *C.E.*, 2 Sept. 1880.
[111] T. J. Clanchy and Co., *Half-a-century's butter prices*, 1 p.
[112] *Annual statements of the trade and navigation of the United Kingdom with foreign countries and British possessions*, 1886–92.

butterine, by substantially undercutting prevailing market prices at the beginning of each season. Thomas O'Connell of O'Connell Brothers, the Cork butter exporters, made this point in January 1890, when he said, 'Irish butter will have to fall 1*d*. in the lb. under foreign in April or May next before the public, whose palate has been educated to the flavour of its foreign rival, will buy it'. 'It is this', O'Connell lamented, 'that has enabled the foreigner to take such a hold upon the British market.' [113]

TABLE 33   Index numbers of Irish agricultural prices, 1876–90

(base 1840 = 100, except store cattle, base 1845 = 100)

years (average)	store cattle		mutton	pork	butter
	1–2 yrs	2–3 yrs			
1876–80	231	247	176	138	129
1881–5	219	232	162	131	107
1886–90	230	220	141	113	94
% decline, 1876–80 to 1886–90	—	10·9	19·9	18·1	27·1

Fortunately for Cork farmers, foreign competition affected live-stock prices less seriously than those of butter. Store-cattle prices remained high between 1877 and 1890, with the major exception of a sharp downturn between 1884 and 1887 as a result of one of the more intense cyclical recessions in British industrial activity. [114] But mutton and pork prices fell substantially under the impact of heavy increases in British imports of mutton, bacon, and hams, especially after the introduction of continuous refrigeration in steamships from about 1885, as Table 33 shows. [115] A much greater fall in Irish live-stock prices might have been expected to result from the growth in British imports of dead meat and live cattle from abroad (see Table 34). [116] But the declining prices of the so-called great depression meant greatly increased purchasing power for the urban masses. The greater quantity, variety, and purity of the food consumed by British

[113] *C.E.*, 20 Jan. 1890.
[114] J. H. Clapham, *An economic history of modern Britain* (Cambridge, 1926–38), ii, 454; iii, 6–7, 29.
[115] Crotty, *Irish agricultural production*, p. 356; Barrington, 'Agricultural prices', p. 252.
[116] *Agricultural returns of Great Britain, with abstract returns for the United Kingdom, British possessions, and foreign countries, 1892* [C 6743], H.C. 1892, lxxxviii, 1, pp. 102–3; O'Donovan, *Econ. hist.*, p. 216.

TABLE 34 British imports of non-Irish livestock and
meat, 1875–90 (in thousands)

year	cattle (no.)	beef (cwt)	sheep (no.)	mutton (cwt)	bacon and hams (cwt)
1875	264	216	986	—	2,639
1885	373	903	751	573	6,459
1890	643	1,855	358	1,656	8,108

workers has led one scholar to assert that 'there is a good case for selecting the 1880s as one of the decisive periods in the improvement of the standard of living of the working classes'.[117] Moreover, the most rapid phase in the expansion of British meat imports did not begin until the 1890s, with the arrival of frozen beef and mutton from the Argentine, Australia, and New Zealand.[118] Even then, the prices of Irish store cattle and sheep (to a lesser extent) were partly sheltered by the fact that 'this frozen meat was not indeed of a quality to compete effectively with home-killed meat of a good standard'.[119]

THE LANDLORDS AND AGRICULTURE: SUBDIVISION OF FARMS

Even though the forces which had promoted subdivision of farms before the great famine—the fruitfulness of the potato, the relatively early age at marriage, rising population with too little emigration, and the prevalence of the middleman system—were no longer operative after 1851, the problem still existed. Professor Connell has argued that the famine 'demonstrated beyond all dispute the folly of endless subdivision: it left people disillusioned with life on the tiny farms of Ireland'.[120] No doubt this is largely true. But the part which the landlords played in actively discouraging this abuse was also important. Increasingly in the 1830s and early 1840s, as has been shown in Chapter I, tenants who had subdivided their farms were punished for what had come to be regarded as a criminal act. The continuous decline in the number of holdings and the increase

[117] Burnett, *Plenty and want*, p. 125.
[118] C. S. Orwin and E. H. Whetham, *History of British agriculture, 1846–1914* (London, 1964), p. 260.
[119] Ibid., p. 261.
[120] K. H. Connell, 'Peasant marriage in Ireland: its structure and development since the famine' in *Econ. Hist. Rev.*, ser. 2, xiv, no. 3 (Apr. 1962), p. 522.

in their average size after 1851 must not be allowed to obscure the continued efforts of landlords and agents to prevent and correct subdivision and to keep farms intact.

Subdivision as a significant economic problem after 1850 was confined almost exclusively to West Cork, where resistance to emigration persisted far longer than elsewhere. Thomas Scott, the agent of the Cave estate near Skibbereen, told the tenants in April 1855: 'You ought [to] . . . send out your sons and daughters into the world and retain your farms unbroken, instead of trying, as you do now, [to see] on how small a plot of earth you can contrive to exist'.[121] Thomas R. Wright, the agent of the Clinton estate near Castletown-Berehaven, informed the tenants by circular in December 1864 that after managing the property for more than a year, he had been

painfully struck with your small holdings, uncomfortable dwellings, and family quarrels, and I naturally inquired into the cause, which I ascertained arose in almost every instance from the system of dividing and subdividing the farms on the marriage of sons and daughters, or the death of the original holder.[122]

In January 1878 the agent Samuel Hussey required the bailiff of the earl of Kenmare's Bantry estate to report to him 'if any tenant has divided his farm or may do so before the 1st March, as whoever does so must be served with a notice to quit'.[123] As in West Cork, so in much of Kerry, the resistance to emigration frequently led to attempts to subdivide farms. Sir John Benn-Walsh made the following record in his journal in September 1855:

I had a long visit from priest Hartnett & Mr Ambrose Madden on the disposition of the late Edmund Walsh's farm at Ballyduhig. The case is a good example of the embarrassments which are constantly arising in the management of Irish property from the quasi tenant right which the tenants are always trying to establish. Edmund Walsh was a good, improving tenant of rather a superior class. . . . He had a nephew, Ambrose Madden, a respectable, active man, whom he placed great confidence in. A few months ago he died, leaving four girls & two boys, minors, the mad mother, & left a will appointing five ex[ecut]ors & leaving his property to his children & to Ambrose Madden, share & share alike. The priest called on me two days ago, making a very pathetic & earnest appeal to me to continue the farm to the minors & adopt the will. I should thus have six children, represented by five ex[ecut]ors, to manage my farm. I said that this was

[121] *C.E.*, 23 Apr. 1855.
[122] T. R. Wright to tenants of Lord Clinton, 14 Dec. 1864, quoted in *C.E.*, 16 Mar. 1866.
[123] Kenmare papers, Letter book, Jan.–Aug. 1878: M. Leonard to E. Godfrey, 19 Jan. 1878, p. 97.

impossible, that I must put an end to their tenancy, but that I would give the farm to Ambrose Madden, his nephew.[124]

George Trench, the agent of the Talbot-Crosbie estate near Ardfert, writing as late as 1881, stated emphatically that 'resisting and correcting' subdivision 'involved for the landlords of Ireland the long and odious task which constitutes their principal difficulty to this day'.[125]

Subdivision in the period after 1850 was most frequently attempted on the occasion of the marriage of a son or daughter. R. J. Mahony, a large landowner in Kerry, claimed in 1880 that English landlords

> would be surprised if the occupiers of their farms proposed to provide for their eldest sons by getting them married and settled down on a part of their father's holding. Yet such is here the general . . . practice. A man gets his son married as soon as he can, and establishes him either in his own house or in one of his farm offices, and gives him half the farm. The consequence is that new offices are required for both father and son.[126]

Successive agents had grappled with this very problem on the Clinton estate in West Cork. In 1855 the agent Thomas O'Kearney White had notified the tenants—most of whom were little better than cottiers—that anyone who attempted to subdivide his farm would not be allowed to remain on the property.[127] White's warning apparently had little effect, for in December 1864 the newly appointed agent Thomas Wright again threatened the tenants.

> I am determined to put an end to a system so injurious to you and your landlord, and therefore I think it due to you and to myself to warn all of you against dividing your lands on the marriage of either son or daughter, . . . or on your death to portion out your farm amongst your children; in the latter case no person can be recognized as tenant but the widow, if she survives, or the eldest son, if he be industrious and well-behaved, and in the former case, namely, in the case of division on the marriage of son or daughter, . . . the most summary steps will be taken by ejectment to turn all the parties out of possession, and in no case after the ejectment shall have been brought will any terms be given.[128]

[124] Ormathwaite papers: Journal of Sir John Benn-Walsh, 12 Sept. 1855, pp. 151–4.

[125] G. F. Trench, *The land question: are the landlords worth preserving? Or forty years' management of an Irish estate* (Dublin, 1881), pp. 15–17.

[126] R. J. Mahony, *A short statement concerning the confiscation of improvements in Ireland, addressed to the right hon. W. E. Forster, M.P., chief secretary to the lord lieutenant of Ireland, by a working landowner* (Dublin, 1880), p. 9.

[127] *C.E.*, 31 Aug. 1865.

[128] T. R. Wright to tenants of Lord Clinton, 14 Dec. 1864, quoted in *C.E.*, 16 Mar. 1866.

Wright soon found it necessary to execute his threat. In 1865 Daniel Dowling, whose family had reportedly held land in the townland of Letter for 200 years, divided his small farm among his three sons, contrary to verbal and written warnings of the consequences from Wright. Quarrels soon developed, neither the father nor the sons would pay any rent, and the agent evicted all four of them, causing a great local uproar. [129] Wright also refused to allow 'any son-in-law to come into your house to reside with you on his marriage', and when Denis Neil violated this estate rule, aimed at preventing clandestine subdivision, he was served by the agent with a notice to quit. [130]

On two estates—one in Kerry, the other in West Cork—where subdivision had long been absolutely prohibited under pain of eviction, the landlords used this ultimate remedy more than once in the 1850s and 1860s. Sir John Benn-Walsh detected in 1855 'one of those clandestine sublettings & division[s] of a farm which it is the great difficulty of a landlord to prevent. Old Mathew Dillane has married his son & given him half the farm.' [131] In 1857 Laurence Buckley, the tenant of Tullamore demesne, 'promised to subdivide his farm' with his younger son (his elder son already held another farm from Benn-Walsh) and was evicted the following year, after the family had failed to come to an arrangement under which the father would have had to retire. [132] 'Both old Sheahan and Keefe', Benn-Walsh noted of two more of his Kerry tenants in August 1861, 'divided their farms with their sons, so I evicted them.' Although Sheahan was 'forgiven' and merely removed to a smaller holding, Benn-Walsh completely 'got rid of the Keefes, who were always a turbulent, bad lot'. [133] William Bence Jones experienced similar difficulties on his Lisselan estate near Clonakilty. In the early 1860s, one of the tenants divided a forty-acre holding with his elder son, and when the latter became unable to pay rent, Jones dispossessed him but returned the land to his father on the express condition that he would transfer the entire farm to a second son when he retired. [134] In 1864 Jones evicted Edmund Lucey, who had secretly divided his 118-acre farm between two of his four sons. [135]

Penal rents were another device used by landlords and agents to discourage subdivision. When the McGraths divided a large farm on

129 Ibid., 31 Aug. 1865.
130 Ibid., 16 Mar. 1866.
131 Ormathwaite papers: Journal of Sir John Benn-Walsh, 1 Sept. 1855, p. 161.
132 Ibid.: Journal, 27 Aug. 1857, p. 148; Journal, 3 Sept. 1858, pp. 193–4.
133 Ibid.: Journal, 31 Aug. 1861, p. 215.
134 Jones, *Life's work*, p. 229.
135 *W.C.E.*, 17 Sept. 1881.

the earl of Kenmare's Bantry estate at Laharan in 1878, the agent Samuel Hussey served them with a notice to quit. But Hussey indicated in January 1880 that he was prepared to make a settlement

on the following conditions, viz, that they agree to [the resident agent] Mr Barrett's *division* of the farm, pay at the rate of £103–5 a year for the lands from 29 Sept. 1877 [a substantial increase in rent] & all the law costs which we had to incur by there [*sic*] taking defence to the ejectment. [136]

On his own estate near Dingle, County Kerry, Hussey had given a lease of a small farm to Patrick Kennedy of Ballingarraun, providing for the payment of a penal rent of £10 per annum in the event of subdivision. Kennedy divided the holdings between his two sons, who quarrelled and refused to pay rent. When Hussey evicted them and destroyed one of the houses on the farm, he was publicly denounced. But he vehemently defended his action in a letter to *The Times* in October 1880.

The moment I heard of the subdivision, I proceeded to enforce the penalty, & as regularly as it was enforced, so regularly did I tender it back, if one brother would leave & restore the farm to one holding as it originally stood, & whatever of the £10 penal rent I may have received, I am about to expend on the farm for the benefit of the brother who remains, to remedy the deterioration caused by subdivision. No landlord in Ireland in his senses would consider an increased rent of £10 as compensation for subdivision. On another farm I have been offered 50 p[er] c[ent] increase on a fair rent f I allowed it, & I declined. . . . I had no object but to stop subdivision—the curse of Ireland—and that I did & will, as long as my property is left me. . . . [137]

Although they vigorously resisted the division of small holdings, landlords and agents sometimes tolerated the break-up of large farms. When a tenant on Sir George Colthurst's estate at Ballyvourney sought permission in 1878 to give a portion of his farm, which he had acquired from another tenant, to a prospective son-in-law, Samuel Hussey reported the request to the landlord and commented, 'Of course, an additional tenant there is a nuisance, especially when you have built a good house for . . . [him], but then I know you take a great interest in him'. [138] Hussey was also prepared to approve in January 1879 the division of Jeremiah Callaghan's

[136] Kenmare papers, Letter book, 1879–80: S. M. Hussey to A. Hutchins, 10 Jan. 1880, p. 921.

[137] Ibid., Letter book, Jan.–Oct. 1880: Hussey to editor of *The Times*, 22 Oct. 1880, pp. 984–7. See also ibid.: Hussey to editor of *The Times*, 11 Oct. 1880, pp. 946–7.

[138] Ibid., Letter book, Jan.–Aug. 1878: Hussey to Sir G. St J. Colthurst, 11 Feb. 1878, pp. 218–19.

farm on the earl of Kenmare's Bantry property, 'provided Mr Barrett approves of the bounds struck out, & that the son builds a good, substantial house on the new division, for which he must agree not to make any claim on Lord Kenmare for now or at any future time'. [139] Divisions of large farms were permitted on other estates in West Cork. The Bandon land agent Richard Doherty, sen., saw no reason to object in February 1880 to the break-up of Cloonties (worth about £110 per annum) on the Moorehead property; two brothers were proposing for it. [140] The Hurleys were anxious to have their farm on James J. Oswald's estate divided, and 'I think it would be as well to do it,' Doherty told their landlord in January 1881, 'as the farm is very large, & though they hand in separate rents, they up to this got but one rec[eip]t. I don't expect any difficulty with them.' [141]

Because there were undoubtedly several other factors at work in keeping farms at a viable economic size, especially the later age at marriage and the emigration outlet, it would be wrong to over-emphasize the importance of the landlord contribution to this aspect of agricultural development. But on the basis of the evidence, it seems fair to conclude that the tendency of small farmers to subdivide in southwest Cork, where the alternative recourse of emigration was not fully accepted even in the 1880s, [142] could easily have got out of hand in the absence of landlord opposition.

DEMESNE FARMING AND INVESTMENT IN AGRICULTURE

Besides resisting the subdivision of small holdings, Cork landlords and agents pursued other policies which promoted economic progress. There was in fact a distinct quickening of landlord interest and investment in agriculture after 1850. Many factors contributed to this development. Whereas low farm incomes had naturally resulted in the accumulation of large arrears of rent on many Cork estates before and during the famine, the post-famine increase in farm incomes meant that with the exception of a few years in the 1860s, rents were paid punctually and in full until the late 1870s. The middlemen who had formerly been a formidable barrier to investment in estate improvements were virtually eliminated shortly

---

[139] Ibid., Letter book 1878–9; Hussey to Very Rev. Canon O'Regan, 31 Jan. 1879, p. 685.

[140] Doherty papers, Letter book, 1880–6: R. W. Doherty, sen., to Mrs A. Moorehead, 26 Feb. 1880, p. 38.

[141] Ibid.: Doherty to J. J. Oswald, 11 Jan. 1881, p. 229.

[142] See below, Chapter VI, pp. 230–2.

before and during the famine. The incubus of a largely bankrupt or debt-ridden landlord class was cast off by the operation of the incumbered estates court in the 1850s. Although the widely expected influx of English capital never materialized, and although the new purchasers in Cork could hardly be characterized as monied men, the overall effect of the incumbered estates act of 1849 was favourable to greater interest and investment.

One revealing indication of this new or heightened interest in agricultural improvement was the large number of Cork landowners who became demesne farmers after clearing their estates of cottiers or after having a large amount of land thrown on their hands when tenants failed during the famine. Once the corner of prosperity had been turned in the early 1850s, many of them persisted in this increasingly lucrative endeavour instead of reletting the land to new tenants. Most landowners who had turned to demesne farming reared improved breeds of cattle and sheep, furnished an example of 'high farming' to the surrounding tenants, and sometimes realized good profits. The earl of Shannon, for example, was a noted agricultural enthusiast, and the annual auctions of sheep—mostly Border Leicesters and Shropshire Downs—on his demesne at Castlemartyr were said in 1863 to be 'perhaps the best attended sales of regular occurrence in the south of Ireland'.[143] Richard Welsted began holding his famous annual sales of young shorthorns at Ballywalter in the early 1860s. He had hired shorthorn bulls from the celebrated herd of the Booths at Warlaby in Yorkshire. It was said in 1881 that Welsted

has been one of the most successful shorthorn breeders in the three kingdoms, and not a little of the improvement made in recent years in the dairy stock of our large southern farmers is due to the exertions of this gentleman in providing good strains of shorthorns.[144]

Viscount Doneraile apparently began farming a large demesne about 1850 and specialized in fattening cattle rather than in raising sheep or in dairying; he rarely made much money, however, because of his high labour bills and his failure to spend enough on feed and fertilizers.[145] But other Cork landowners realized fair or excellent profits. Sir Denham Jephson-Norreys's net profits from the dairy herd on his 360-acre Scarteen demesne averaged over £460 per annum between 1861 and 1868; he found a ready market for the

[143] *C.E.*, 17 Sept. 1863. See also ibid., 4 Oct. 1861, 17 June 1863.
[144] Ibid., 13 Oct. 1881.
[145] Doneraile papers: Demesne accounts, 1850–73.

sale of milk in the town of Mallow.[146] During the famine and gradually thereafter, William Bence Jones increased the size of his demesne from 500 to 1,000 acres of his 3,800-acre Lisselan estate. At first he 'resolved to try sheep largely, as not requiring outlay for buildings', but he soon discovered that dairying and the rearing of young cattle produced better returns. Jones constructed a superior dairy, where lightly salted butter was made up in small rolls which he sent directly to London retailers.[147] He greatly extended his use of artificial fertilizers and feeding stuffs, and by 1878–9 his outlay on these items alone exceeded £1 per acre. He claimed that in 1879–80, a very bad year for farmers, his demesne had returned a net profit of 38s. per acre.[148]

In any analysis of the scale of expenditure for estate improvements of Irish landowners as compared with that of their English counterparts after 1850,[149] some basic facts of a contrasting nature must be emphasized. The estates of Irish landlords did not contain great deposits of coal, iron, or copper, from the profits of which agricultural improvements might partly have been financed.[150] Nor were there any Irish landlords, with the exception of a few in Ulster, whose property values were greatly enhanced by the mushroom growth of industrial towns outside their gates or by the coming of the railways. Only a handful derived lucrative ground rents from urban properties, and never on a scale to match those of many English landowners. Moreover, Irish agriculture required landlords to invest comparatively much less fixed capital, especially in the form of farm buildings, because of the almost exclusive concentration on pasture, the character of the climate, and the preferences of farmers.

[146] Jephson-Norreys papers: Summary of farm accounts of the Scarteen demesne, 1861–8, in folder marked 'Farm accounts and general, 1817–88'.

[147] Jones, *Life's work*, pp. 9–10, 294, 312–15.

[148] Ibid., p. 317.

[149] The half-dozen years after the repeal of the corn laws witnessed in England the initiation of a new age of agricultural improvement by the owners of the great estates. There was a tremendous surge of capital investment, which was primarily regarded as a rescue operation that would ward off or mitigate permanent reductions in rent (F. M. L. Thompson, *English landed society in the nineteenth century* (London and Toronto, 1963), pp. 243–53).

[150] A notable exception in Cork was the Berehaven copper, lead, and barytes mines belonging to Henry L. Puxley, who also owned a 7,300-acre estate of no great agricultural value in this poor and mountainous district. There are no reliable records of Puxley's profits from the mines, which were mostly sold in the 1860s. But it was reported in February 1889 that '£2,000 per month used to be paid to miners and labourers by Mr Puxley, when he worked the Berehaven mines formerly, and he cleared for many years £30,000 to £37,000 per annum profit' (*C.C.*, 6 Feb. 1889).

Nevertheless, many landlords in County Cork began or, in some cases, continued to spend large sums on permanent improvements after 1850. Several of the great landlords were conspicuous in this respect. Through his lavish outlays over a period of thirty years, Sir George C. Colthurst greatly altered the physical appearance of his Ballyvourney estate. When Samuel Hussey became his chief agent in 1850, there were 'only three slated houses on the property, hardly any out-buildings, only seven miles of road under contract, and about twenty acres planted'; by 1880 there were 'over one hundred slated houses, about sixty miles of roads, and over four hundred acres planted'. [151] On each of the four Colthurst estates in Cork except one, there were large outlays for farm buildings, drainage, labourers' dwellings, and plantations between 1849 and 1880: £15,000 on the Ballyvourney property, worth £5,000 per annum; £11,000 on the Rathcool estate, worth only £1,500 per annum; and £8,000 on the Blarney estate, worth £4,000 per annum (exclusive of £3,500 in landlord allowances for improvements made by tenants). [152]

The traditional policy on the carefully managed Devonshire estates in Cork and Waterford, worth about £46,000 per annum in 1850, had been to co-operate with the tenants in executing permanent buildings, drainage, fences, and other necessary improvements, and this policy was carried out liberally after 1850. Almost £23,000 was spent on drainage between 1848 and 1880. Even though slated dwelling houses and out-offices were common on the Devonshire estates by the 1850s, the agent F. E. Currey invested almost £35,000 in 'farm improvements' between 1860 and 1879. The 'general works' account, which included expenditures for Lismore Castle and demesne as well as for town properties in Bandon and Lismore, indicated that more than £150,000 had been disbursed over the same period. In addition, Devonshire reportedly contributed more than £200,000 in subsidies and shares towards the construction of railways in Cork and Waterford. [153]

Because of the prevalence of middlemen, there had been little investment in improvements on the vast estates of the earl of Kenmare in Cork, Kerry, and Limerick before 1850, but as old leases expired,

[151] S. M. Hussey, *The reminiscences of an Irish land agent, being those of S. M. Hussey*, compiled by Home Gordon (London, 1904), p. 71.

[152] *Report of her majesty's commissioners of inquiry into the working of the Landlord and Tenant (Ireland) Act, 1870, and the acts amending the same*, vol. iii: *Minutes of evidence*, pt ii; *appendices* [C 2779], H.C. 1881, xix, 1, p. 924 (hereafter cited as *Bessborough comm. evidence*).

[153] Lismore papers, N.L.I., MS 6929: Rent receipts and disbursements, 1818–90; F. Dun, *Landlords and tenants in Ireland* (London, 1881), pp. 54, 58–9.

Kenmare spent large sums on the lands. Expenditures on drainage and related works amounted to £25,000 between 1854 and 1878. Over the same period, dwelling houses and farm offices costing more than £15,000 were constructed for 123 tenants, and allowances averaging £1,250 per annum were given to tenants for their own improvements when they paid their rents. Between 1870 and 1880 some 300 labourers were comfortably housed in concrete cottages and provided with half- or quarter-acre allotments at a cost of over £6,000. (The earl spent huge sums in the 1870s on his new mansion, his demesne farm, and the town of Killarney; the money paid in wages alone amounted to over £50,000, and the materials for Killarney House probably cost as much if not more.) In order to ward off the reductions in rent which would otherwise have been necessary during the wet seasons at the end of the decade, Kenmare laid out or allowed to the tenants more than £33,000 between 1878 and 1881, exclusive of expenditures on his mansion and demesne. Not surprisingly, the Kenmare estates had to be placed in the hands of trustees in 1882. A rash of borrowing from the Standard Life Assurance Office between 1876 and 1881, amounting to no less than £146,000, brought the total charges on the estates to over £236,500. (Kenmare's rental was about £38,000 in 1880.) [154]

Considerable evidence exists to show that many other Cork landlords made substantial outlays for improvements, although that evidence is often incomplete or imprecise. On the estates of the earl of Bandon, who was one of the richest landowners in the county, with a rental of £26,000 per annum, allowances of over £3,400 were made to the tenants for their own improvements each year between 1857 and 1861. [155] After succeeding to his estate in 1868, Charles W. T. Ponsonby spent £9,500 in the next six years:

Some hundreds of acres were thoroughly drained, ten miles of open main drains were cut to enable tenants to drain for themselves, houses and offices were built [by the tenants, with stone, timber, and slate supplied free by the landlord], roads improved, and 120 acres of rough land planted. [156]

[154] Kenmare papers, Letter book, 1879–80: S. M. Hussey to [illegible] Williamson, 9 July 1879, p. 285; Letter book, 1880–2, Hussey to W. Thompson, [?] Nov. 1880, pp. 41–2; Hussey to J. A. Godley, 6 June 1881, pp. 450–5; Rental and account for July–Dec. 1880; Draft articles of agreement for trustees, 1882. See also *C.E.*, 24 June 1881; Dun, *Landlords and tenants*, pp. 76–7.

[155] Bandon papers: Rental of the earl of Bandon's estates, 1857–61 (in the possession of Rev. Thomas A. O'Regan, C.C., Kilbrittain, Co. Cork).

[156] From *The Times*, quoted in *C.C.*, 30 Dec. 1887. Ponsonby told William Hurlbert in 1888: 'Since I came into my property in 1868, I have laid out upon it in drainage, buildings, and planting . . . over £15,000, including

On the earl of Cork's Charleville property, a dairy estate worth £7,000 per annum, the agent Daniel Leahy reported that £3,500 had been expended during the 1870s in the construction of complete homesteads, consisting of two-storey dwelling houses, cow barns, and dairies.[157] Michael O'Gorman, for whom one of these homesteads was provided at a cost of £340, happily pointed out in April 1873 that other tenants could 'gratefully acknowledge similar bountiful treatment, and ... [their] beautiful and commodious slated dwellings and out-offices can be seen from the public road from Charleville to Croom, and from Charleville to Bruree, ornamenting that portion of his lordship's estate'.[158] The O'Donovan asserted before the Bessborough commission in 1880 that he had built houses for all but a few of the sixty tenants on his 2,700-acre estate, worth £1,740 per annum, by providing timber, slate, and lime; on each of five large farms, he had spent from £300 to £450.[159] William Uniacke Townsend, the agent of the Oliver estates in Cork and Limerick, declared in December 1880 that the accounts had shown that during the previous thirty-three years more than £29,000 was spent 'amongst the [700] tenants'.[160] During Charles Garfit's long term as agent of the 11,800-acre Cork estates of Arthur Hugh Smith-Barry ending in 1881, large allowances were made to the tenants for buildings, drainage, and fences; fifty labourers' cottages were constructed; and every farm, according to Garfit, was provided with accommodations appropriate to its size.[161] The trustees of Lord Carbery's estate, worth perhaps £8,000 per annum, reportedly spent over £7,000 between 1874 and 1886 on various improvements in the town and immediate neighbourhood of Baltimore.[162] One of the tenants gratefully acknowledged in June 1877 that 'comfortable dwelling houses, out-offices, and labourers' cottages are ... [being built] for those who desire it, and the great bulk of the ready money required comes from the pocket of the landlord'.[163]

On most Cork estates, permanent agricultural improvements were the result of a co-operative effort between landlord and tenant. When the landlord provided the capital for building materials and

[157] *Bessborough comm. evidence*, pt ii, pp. 845, 847.
[158] *C.E.*, 4 Apr. 1873.
[159] *Bessborough comm. evidence*, pt ii, p. 906.
[160] *C.E.*, 6 Dec. 1880.
[161] *W.C.E.*, 3 Dec. 1881; *C.C.*, 14 Feb. 1882.
[162] *C.C.*, 1 Feb. 1888.
[163] *W.C.E.*, 23 June 1877.

---

about £8,000 of loans from the board of works' (W. H. Hurlbert, *Ireland under coercion: the diary of an American* (2nd ed., Edinburgh, 1888), ii, 357).

labour, the tenant was usually charged 5 per cent, but more often timber, slate, stone, and lime were given without expense, and the tenant performed the work himself. The tenant's expenditures for drains, fences, and fertilizers were taken into consideration by the landlord when the rent was paid.[164] Of course, there were wide differences in the amount of encouragement given tenants to execute improvements as well as in the liberality with which these improvements were treated by the landlord. In order to avoid giving the landlord any pretext for an increase of rent, many tenants preferred to do what they could without seeking assistance from the estate office.[165] But the popular impression that Irish farmers alone executed almost all permanent agricultural improvements is certainly untrue for County Cork between 1850 and 1880. When agrarian relations became embittered in the 1880s and landlord incomes declined, landlord investment naturally waned. Undoubtedly, much greater expenditures by landowners, especially for drainage and dairies, would have been economically beneficial, and no claim is made here that the landlords of Cork did nearly as much as they could or should have done in these respects. But where the work of improvement was a combined effort, it seems fair to conclude that the landlords were often, perhaps most often, the senior partners in that effort.

LAGS AND RESISTANCES

In spite of the substantial progress which had been made in improving the quality of farming in Cork between 1851 and 1891, there were still many significant lags. Livestock breeding required much greater attention than farmers had so far devoted to it. Instead of using shorthorn bulls, Shropshire or Leicester rams, and white Yorkshire boars, farmers too often bred cattle, sheep, and pigs in-and-in, 'till their degeneracy is notoriously apparent'.[166] The inspectors of the congested districts board reported in the early 1890s that all kinds of livestock in southwest Cork were a mixture of

[164] The feature of co-operation in the making of agricultural improvements was brought out by the results of the Irish Land Committee's questionnaire, which showed that on 224 of 354 estates in Munster (63·3 per cent), the existing improvements in 1880 were the result of contributions from both landlord and tenants; on fifty-four estates (15·2 per cent), the improvements were the work of the landlord alone; and on seventy-six estates (21.5 per cent), the work of the tenants alone (Irish Land Committee, *The land question, Ireland*, no. 3: *Facts and figures* (Dublin, 1880), Table 6).
[165] Dun, *Landlords and tenants*, pp. 74–5.
[166] Mahony, *Confiscation of improvements*, p. 10.

various breeds and had lost all their distinctive characteristics.[167]

Pastures needed to be upgraded. The *Irish Farmers' Gazette* had been critical in 1860 of the widespread failure to top-dress pastures with superphosphates and bone manures,[168] and this was still a fair criticism thirty years later. When land was laid down to pasture, the sweepings of the hayloft sometimes took the place of good grass seed. Farmers tended to pay as little as possible for purchased seed. Sir Daniel V. O'Sullivan, a Cork butter exporter, said in February 1885 that he had been 'surprised to hear that the Danish farmers paid 50 to 75 per cent more for seed than the Irish farmers, but the truth was . . . that the Irish farmers in the long run paid far more and got far worse value'.[169] The *Farmers' Gazette* remarked in the same month:

We have ourselves, over and over again, heard seedsmen strongly advising farmers who were asking for rye-grass seed to buy good, heavy seed instead of light stuff that looked and handled more like chaff than seed, but in vain— they would have the cheapest; 'twas good enough for them'.[170]

Much naturally good pasture, it seems, was not properly maintained and produced mostly coarse grasses with a full complement of weeds.

Although the quality of the butter produced on Cork farms had gradually improved since the late 1850s, more than 60 per cent of the butter inspected at the Cork market as late as 1885 was undeserving of the brand of ordinary first quality.[171] This was partly the result of one of the most serious shortcomings of Cork farming— the absence of proper dairies and clean cow barns. The Cork Farmers' Club estimated in 1867 that as much as one-half of the butter sent to the Cork market was being sold at reduced prices because large numbers of tenant farmers had 'neither suitable cow houses nor houses fit either to have milk in or to make butter, and no matter what care may be taken in the after management of the butter, all will fail unless these houses are provided'.[172] The Cork butter exporter W. J. Lane declared in 1885:

Without proper dairy and cow-house accommodation, no amount of education would enable the Irish farmer to produce good butter. They are practically without one or the other at present, that is, as these buildings are understood in dairy countries on the continent and in America.[173]

[167] Congested districts board, *Base-line reports to the congested districts board, 1892–8*, pp. 687–96 ('confidential' printed reports collected in one volume, deposited in Trinity College Library, Dublin).
[168] *Irish Farmers' Gazette*, 22 Sept. 1860.   [169] *C.E.*, 5 Feb. 1885.
[170] Quoted ibid., 23 Feb. 1885.   [171] *C.E.*, 27 Jan. 1887.
[172] *Cork Daily Herald and Advertising Gazette*, 16 Sept. 1867.
[173] *Industries committee evidence*, p. 730.

The lack of suitable buildings resulted in lowering the quality of Cork and Irish butter in several ways. As Lane remarked:

Milk, cream, and butter are most susceptible of taint from any kind of bad odours or impure air. The most frequent complaint against secondary Irish butter is its peaty or smoky flavour. This is contracted by having the milk set, and the butter made, in the ordinary dwelling rooms of small farmers. Impurities also attach to the milk owing to the filthy condition of the cow from bad stabling.[174]

On farms without dairies, Professor J. P. Sheldon pointed out in 1888, 'the milk is usually kept in the barn and becomes spoiled from the dirt which falls into it from the roof. The clay floor also absorbs spilt milk, which sours and gives forth offensive smells.'[175] Even when farmers had constructed dairies, they often did not keep them sufficiently clean or properly ventilated. Dung heaps placed near the dairy, and potatoes, turnips, or clothing stored inside it, injured the taste of the butter; sometimes the milk and butter vessels, the shelves, and the floors were not scoured regularly. Small farmers often housed their cows for part of the winter in their summer dairies and then neglected to re-earth the floors.[176]

The small scale of production also had the effect of lowering the quality of the butter, which too often had become sour by the time a firkin was full. Table 35 shows that the size of the average dairy herd on all Cork holdings of more than five acres in 1871 was only about six cows per farm.[177]

TABLE 35 Distribution of milch cattle in Cork according to farm size, 1871

farm size (acres)	cows (no.)	stock holders (no.)	cows per farm
5–15	8,689	5,211	1·7
15–30	21,850	7,093	3·1
30–50	32,361	6,727	4·8
over 50	118,004	11,715	10·1
total	180,904	30,746	5·9

With so many small producers, it was impossible to obtain uniformity of colour, texture, or taste. When one of the largest Cork

[174] Ibid.
[175] Sheldon, *Dairy farming*, p. 357.
[176] *Grocer*, 21 Mar. 1868.
[177] *Irish agricultural statistics for 1871*, pp. 116, 118.

butter merchants was asked to explain why so many firkins of inferior butter were inspected in the Cork market, he replied, 'Today I have in the market about 200 firkins, and they are from about 170 different farms, and the wonder is they are so good and near alike as they are'.[178]

[178] Cork Corporation, *Report of the law and finance committee of the Cork Corporation on the Cork Butter Market* (Cork, 1884), p. 239.

IV

THE LAND QUESTION AND
ESTATE MANAGEMENT, 1850–80

~~~~~~

THE BUSINESS OF LAND AGENCY

ESTATE AGENTS in nineteenth-century Ireland traditionally enjoyed a much greater measure of autonomy in the management of landed property than did their counterparts in England. In fact, the position of land agent had partly fallen into disrepute because indifferent landowners had permitted their agents grossly to abuse the wide discretionary powers entrusted to them. The figure of the unscrupulous agent who encompasses the ruin of the fox-hunting, hard-drinking nobleman or squire was not merely the literary invention of William Carleton.[1] There was at least a certain kinship to reality in the stereotype.

The frightful financial mismanagement of Viscount Midleton's estates before 1840 demonstrated how much injury could be done when an incompetent agent was left unchecked for a long period by a landlord preoccupied with other matters. After succeeding to the title and estates of his father in 1836, the new Lord Midleton promptly ordered a rigorous investigation into the chaotic state of his Irish affairs. The late Lord Midleton, an absentee landlord for some fifty years, had employed a resident agent named Thomas Poole, who served in that capacity from 1806 to 1836. While Poole was in charge, arrears of no less than £70,000 were allowed to accumulate.[2] Records were so carelessly kept that 'very many sums

[1] W. Carleton, *Valentine McClutchy, the Irish agent, or chronicles of the Castle Cumber property* (3 vols, London, 1845).
[2] *Devon comm. evidence*, pt iii, p. 196.

173

amounting to upwards of £2,000 have been received by him of the tenants, without debiting himself with such receipts in his accounts'. [3] Poole was also accused of allowing William Welland, an Englishman who served as surveyor and assistant agent, to become tenant of 'many townlands, farms, plots of land, and houses, generally of the best quality, at rents grossly below the value'.[4] Charles Bailey, who conducted this damaging inquiry into Poole's stewardship, firmly believed that the painful history of the Midleton estates once again clearly proved the necessity of never permitting any agent to become a tenant as well.

The reporter has witnessed many lamentable instances of men who well performed their duty as agents until they became tenants, when ... they have at once not only sanctioned but suggested changes for the benefit of the tenants generally, to the prejudice of the employer and landlord. 'No man can serve two masters', and when an agent makes himself a tenant he creates in himself the more powerful master; and to serve the mammon of his own pocket, he gets weaned by degrees from that zeal and singleness of mind which he before possessed in the service of his employer, and without which an agent's services are worse than worthless.[5]

Some landlords reposed such complete trust in their agents that they never troubled to inquire at all closely into the financial aspects of their property. Such neglect could prove disastrous. The earl of Mountcashel owned valuable estates in Cork (where he lived at Moore Park outside Fermoy) and in Antrim. The resident agent of the earl's northern estates, inauspiciously named Alfred Cleverly, also supervised the management of his Cork property. Cleverly's father had been one of Mountcashel's most intimate friends, and the earl had known Cleverly himself since childhood and had taken a great interest in his early career in the East India Company's service. Writing in July 1851, Mountcashel summarized his reasons for appointing Cleverly his chief agent in 1846 or 1847.

I did so because I had more confidence in you than in anyone else, and I had already experienced heavy losses by the bad management and want of zeal of my former agents. .... Amongst the many thousands of my acquaintances and my friends, there are some I can trust in small things, a few in large, but there is no one I would with perfect confidence entrust with everything that I possess but yourself.[6]

---

[3] P.R.O.I., ref. no. 978, Midleton papers: Charles Bailey's summary report on the valuation of the Midleton estates, 6 Apr. 1840.

[4] Ibid. [5] Ibid.

[6] Newenham papers, Copy of rolls court pleadings, *Mountcashel v. Newenham* (1857): earl of Mountcashel to A. Cleverly, 21 July 1851, pp. 47–50.

Unfortunately, Mountcashel had completely mistaken his man. In July 1852 the earl belatedly boasted to his son-in-law, Edward Newenham: 'At last I have caught the bird, and he is at present safe in the care of the officials. . . . He was a most slippery fish, and it took a great deal of management to make sure of him.'[7] Mountcashel claimed that during his brief agency, Cleverly had heartlessly embezzled no less than £24,000 and then destroyed all the accounts. Nor was that all. Moaned Mountcashel:

He took my carriages and horses and plate and gold snuff boxes and trinkets consigned to his care to send to the south [of Ireland], he brought them up to Dublin, put them into the house of a Mrs Gilbert on Westland Row. Without my authority, he broke open my boxes, took my plate, gold snuff boxes, and trinkets. I never saw one. I bought one afterwards in a shop; he made away with my yacht; everything of mine he could lay his hands on he swindled me of.[8]

Obviously, a landowner who relied less on others and kept in closer personal touch with his affairs would scarcely have suffered such serious losses from the peculations of a land agent. Cleverly's theft of so much of his property without detection can largely be explained by the earl's prolonged absence from his northern estates.

The relationship between the earl of Egmont and his agent Edward Tierney also illustrates the extremely wide discretionary authority exercised by many Irish land agents. The earl's remoteness from personal supervision of his Cork property is shown by the instructions given Tierney upon his appointment in August 1823. The new agent was simply told, 'Employ proper persons at Churchtown and Kanturk to look after the tenants and farms, and to communicate with you upon the subject, so that you can at all times be enabled to have every necessary information'.[9] Clearly, Egmont envisaged Tierney as a substitute landlord, even though as a crown solicitor riding circuit a good part of every year, his agent would also be partly an absentee. In the planning and execution of extensive permanent improvements to Egmont's Cork estates, Tierney acted with substantial independence, merely informing the earl of what was to be done. A typical letter from the earl showed him to be concerned as much with his immediate financial needs as with the long-term improvement of his property.

I received the letters you sent me on the subject of the improvement at Kanturk by this morning's post. I enclose you Mr Teed's letter on the

[7] Ibid.: earl of Mountcashel to E. Newenham, 22 July 1852, pp. 62–4.
[8] Ibid., pp. 52–3.
[9] Barry papers, *Egmont v. Darell, documents of respondents*: earl of Egmont's instructions for Edward Tierney, 7 Aug. 1823, pp. 73–4.

subject as well as my son's; what would you wish to be done on the subject? I hope you will be able to send me some money; I have only a few pounds in the house. I hope Mrs Tierney and yourself are well.[10]

Egmont's relationship with Tierney also displays another feature often associated with land agency in pre-famine Ireland—the use of the agent's personal coffers as a source of ready cash by the landlord. When so many Irish landowners were mortgaged far beyond their resources, it was not uncommon for them to engage as agents wealthy or well-connected gentlemen on the principle, 'I will make you my agent if you will lend me your money'. Egmont certainly conformed to this pattern. He was acutely embarrassed by debts. Creditors in England held mortgages and judgments exceeding £250,000 against his Somerset estates. Unless drastic measures were adopted immediately, sales of the Irish as well as the English estates might become necessary to satisfy their claims. Shortly after Tierney's appointment, the earl named his son and heir Viscount Perceval, a Lincoln's Inn solicitor, John Godfrey Teed, and Tierney as co-trustees to arrange his confused affairs and conveyed to them all his property for the benefit of his creditors.[11] Both Tierney and Teed had wealthy brothers whose money could be made available to the trustees as the need arose.

Gradually, Edward Tierney and his brother, Sir Matthew, the well-known physician to King George IV, acquired a stranglehold over the ancestral estates of the Percevals. By December 1828 Sir Matthew had already lent the better part of £15,000 on assignments of charges of persons who were pressing for payment of their debts, and who 'would now be in possession of the estates for payment, with enormous expense, if . . . [he] had not advanced his money'.[12] The claims of other importunate creditors were treated in similar fashion, so that by October 1835 nearly £22,000 was owed to Sir Matthew, along with an additional sum of over £10,000 willingly provided since 1823 by Edward Tierney to meet the repeated demands of the earl and Lord Perceval for ready cash.[13] After an abortive attempt to dispose of the Cork estates in 1832, the Somerset property was sold, but the creditors entitled to the benefit of the trust received only 11s. 6d. on every pound. To raise a sum sufficient to satisfy remaining debts, the Cork estates were then mortgaged in 1836 to secure £94,000, and Sir Matthew obtained the principal charge of

10 Ibid.: earl of Egmont to E. Tierney, 1 Feb. 1829, p. 75.
11 Ibid.: Extracts from Vines's and Adey's bill of costs, 28 Oct. 1823, p. 46.
12 Ibid.: E. Tierney to C. F. Adey, 10 Dec. 1828, pp. 171–4.
13 Ibid.: E. Tierney to W. Woodgate, 17 Oct. 1835, pp. 206–8.

£50,000. [14] As remuneration for his services as a trustee, Edward Tierney was also promised £3,500. [15] With their enormous interests in Egmont's affairs, the Tierneys recognized the absolute necessity of carefully safeguarding their position. It was therefore stipulated by deed in November 1836 that as long as he was still owed any money, Edward Tierney could not be removed from the management of Egmont's Irish estates. [16] In effect, the Percevals had abdicated all power and control over their financial affairs, and as events soon proved, Tierney was well along the road to gaining full possession of all their remaining assets.

When he succeeded to his diminished inheritance in early 1836, Viscount Perceval was already a confirmed alcoholic. Instead of claiming his father's title, he adopted an assumed name and lived in obscurity in Wiltshire. Until his death in September 1841, Perceval was said to be totally directed and controlled by Tierney, who not only managed the family's estates with such independence that he seemed their owner but also acted as Perceval's general and legal agent, exercising complete supervision over all his affairs. [17] Tierney attempted repeatedly to bring him to some sense of his responsibilities, but Perceval refused to answer letters, keep appointments, or journey to Dublin to consult with his agent. [18] During his last illness, however, Perceval drafted a will in which he devised all his property in both England and Ireland to Tierney. Under this will, the validity of which was contested only twenty years later, Tierney acquired property reputedly worth about £250,000. [19] When this became known, he immediately attempted to demean its importance by emphasizing that the Cork estates were incumbered to their full value. Probably to discourage a lawsuit by indignant members of the Perceval family, he induced the *Dublin Evening Packet* to deny categorically an earlier report that the bequest had brought him a vast accession of property. 'We regret to hear', quipped the *Packet*,

[14] Ibid., *Egmont v. Darell, petitioner's affidavits:* William Woodgate's affidavit, 26 Nov. 1861, pp. 26–35.

[15] Ibid., *Egmont v. Darell, documents of respondents:* Viscount Perceval to E. Tierney, 13 Jan. 1836, p. 144.

[16] *C.E.*, 4 Aug. 1863.

[17] Barry papers, *Egmont v. Darell, petitioner's affidavits:* John Parkinson's affidavit, 18 Nov. 1861, pp. 9–26; William Woodgate's affidavit, 26 Nov. 1861, pp. 26–35.

[18] Ibid., *Egmont v. Darell, documents of respondents:* E. Tierney to 'Henry Lovell' (Viscount Perceval), 11 Nov. 1841, pp. 221–2.

[19] In 1863 the then earl of Egmont settled a chancery case begun two years earlier, contesting the validity of the 1841 will, and recovered the Percevals' Cork estates by paying outside the court a reported £125,000 to the legal heirs of Sir Edward Tierney (*C.E.*, 6 Aug. 1863).

'that the mountain is little better than a molehill.' [20] Needless to say, the Perceval-Tierney case is an extreme one, for which it would be difficult to find a parallel. Tierney's managerial autonomy, however, was certainly duplicated by the agents of many other absentee landowners, and analogies for the financial dependence of the Percevals upon the private pocket of their agent could probably be found among the hundreds of other heavily incumbered landlords of pre-famine Ireland.

The wide administrative independence of Irish land agents largely derived from their high social status. Besides the agencies of Tierney and Cleverly, those of Colonel Henry Boyle Bernard for the earl of Bandon, Colonel W. S. Currey for the duke of Devonshire, the knight of Kerry for Sir George Colthurst, and the Rev. Somers Payne for the earl of Bantry illustrate the elevated social position of the agents of Cork landowners before the famine. [21] This pheno-menon partly resulted from the ingrained and perdurable class prejudice of the 'protestant ascendancy' landlords. In July 1816 William R. Townsend, a noted writer on Irish agricultural subjects, forcefully condemned the idea of 'keeping as an agent one of the lower orders, one of the people's selves,' because such a person was 'incapable of improving the farms or farmers' and 'generally both corrupt and oppressive'. [22] Social respectability was also considered desirable because of the political duties peculiar to the Irish land agent, who often managed property where the landowner himself was an absentee either all the time or for part of each year. Besides attending to the duties of all land agents—receiving rent, drawing up agreements with tenants, and superintending improvements—Irish agents ordinarily served as resident magistrates and represented the landowner at poor-law-union meetings, at road sessions, and on grand juries. [23] A more prosaic reason operated against the chances that a person from 'the lower orders' might become an agent. The moderate financial rewards of the profession attracted an increasing number of the younger sons of Irish protestant families, largely because, as one observer put it, 'there seemed nothing else in Ireland for them to do'. [24]

[20] *Dublin Evening Packet*, 18 Jan. 1842.

[21] Doherty papers: Rental of the earl of Bandon's estates, 1826–48; Earl of Bantry papers, N.L.I., MS 8599 (2): Correspondence, mainly with J. W. Payne, in respect of the estates of the earl of Bantry in Co. Cork, together with financial accounts, eviction notices, etc., 1840–81; *Devon comm. evidence*, pt iii, p. 187; Hussey, *Reminiscences*, p. 38.

[22] *Munster Farmers' Magazine*, no. 18 (July 1816), pp. 99–106.

[23] Hussey, *Reminiscences*, p. 39.

[24] Becker, *Disturbed Ire.*, p. 315.

If anything, the elevated social status of land agents became even more pronounced between 1850 and 1880, when they were drawn almost exclusively from three overlapping sources: the landowner's family, the legal profession, and the landed gentry. Much more often than in England, landlords kept the trusted office of estate agent within the ambit of the family. Younger brothers frequently appear in the records as managers of family properties, large as well as small. John Wrixon Becher administered the 19,000-acre estates of his brother Sir Henry; the brother of The O'Donovan collected rent on the latter's 3,600-acre property near Skibbereen; and Richard Harris conducted the business of a 600-acre estate owned by his brother George until 1878, when the landlord's son-in-law, a National Bank manager, took over the agency. [25] Sons often acted as agents for their fathers, sometimes under special circumstances. Attempting to salvage something from the wreck of his father's affairs, Daniel Conner, jun., took over the administration of his family's 8,400-acre property near Dunmanway in the early 1850s. [26] When the previous agent was murdered in 1862 while collecting the rents of another landlord, D. W. Jephson-Norreys assumed the management of the 700-acre Mallow estate belonging to his father Sir Denham. [27] Not only did other sons conduct their fathers' affairs as a matter of course, [28] but cousins and other relatives frequently performed the duties of an agent for landed members of their families. [29]

[25] *C.E.*, 16 Mar. 1865, 2 Apr. 1881; The O'Donovan papers: Rental of The O'Donovan's estate, 1839–69, Carbery only. Colonel Henry Boyle Bernard managed the 46,000-acre estates of his brother the earl of Bandon from 1856 until 1877, and James Penrose Fitzgerald apparently began his career as an agent on the 5,300-acre Whitegate property of his brother Robert (Doherty papers, Letter book, 1876–9: R. W. Doherty, sen., to J. J. Oswald, 25 Apr. 1877, p. 253; P.R.O.I., ref. no. 978, Midleton papers, Letter book, 1873–80: J. P. Fitzgerald to J. R. Stewart, 18 Nov. 1879, p. 401).

[26] Conner papers: M. Longfield to D. Conner, jun., 15 July 1853.

[27] Jephson-Norreys papers, Letter book, 1863–70: D. W. Jephson-Norreys to W. H. Jephson, 27 June 1863. The previous agent John Waller Braddell was shot and killed in the town of Tipperary while collecting rent for the Limerick landowner, Colonel Hare (*C.E.*, 31 July 1862; *C.C.*, 1, 2 Aug. 1862).

[28] George S. Ware, a Mallow solicitor, conducted the business of his father Nathaniel's 1,700-acre estate; H. F. Townsend managed the 600-acre property owned by his father, the admiralty judge John Fitzhenry Townsend; and Pasco Savage French apparently began his professional career on the 5,300-acre estates of his father Sampson (*C.E.*, 11 Nov. 1880, 29 July 1881; R. J. Hodges, *Cork and County Cork in the twentieth century* (Brighton, 1911), p. 199).

[29] G. W. Brasier-Creagh acted for the Creagh minors; Samuel Hussey for the Blennerhassetts and the Hicksons; Samuel N. Hutchins for

Although members of the legal profession were less involved in estate management than might have been expected, at least before 1850, there was an increasing tendency to appoint lawyers as land agents, especially from the 1870s.[30] A legal education came to be considered one of the most suitable qualifications for such a position. In a business where the technicalities of leases, mortgages, strict family settlements, and ejectment decrees were staple matters of concern, this development is thoroughly understandable. More surprisingly, however, lawyers served as agents for many of the great Cork landowners, even though the supervision of two hundred or more tenants would normally be expected to demand an almost total commitment of one's energies. Thomas Foley, a Cork city solicitor, succeeded the badly discredited Thomas Poole as Viscount Midleton's agent in 1838.[31] Michael Bourke, a Fermoy solicitor, was both the law and land agent of the earl of Mountcashel's Cork estates from 1847 to 1855, when he resigned amid apparently unfounded charges of wrongdoing by the earl.[32] Thomas R. Wright, a Clonakilty solicitor, assumed the management of the 13,600-acre properties of Lord Charles Pelham-Clinton in 1863 and immediately redoubled the previous agent's efforts to eradicate subdivision.[33] James Russell, a solicitor on the South Mall in Cork city, replaced J. N. Beamish as manager of the 8,100-acre Ballyedmond estate of Richard H. Smith-Barry in 1870, when Beamish prudently retired after receiving a threatening letter.[34] Richard Doherty, sen., a Bandon solicitor, became the earl of Bandon's new land agent in 1877, succeeding the earl's uncle and Edward A. Applebe, whose

[30] Of the thirty-two 'house and land agents' in Cork city listed in a local directory for 1867, at least thirteen were also solicitors; but with only a few exceptions, these solicitors were simply house agents. By 1875 the number of Cork city solicitors serving as land agents had increased modestly. Of the twenty-six 'house and land agents' enumerated in a local directory published in that year, ten were solicitors as well, and at least six of these ten were land agents (*Henry and Coghlan's general directory of Cork for 1867, with which is incorporated Wynner & Co.'s business directory of the principal towns in the province of Munster* (Cork, 1867), pp. 239–40, 258; *Guy's county and city of Cork directory for the years 1875–1876* (Cork, 1875), pp. 617, 634–5).

[31] *Devon comm. evidence*, pt iii, p. 196.

[32] *C.C.*, 5 June 1858.

[33] *C.E.*, 16 Mar. 1866.

[34] Ibid., 9 Mar. 1870.

Emanuel Hutchins; W. Longfield for Mrs Henry Longfield; John Meade for William R. Meade; and William Downes Webber for William Tankerville Webber. This information was gathered from brief references to collections of rent in local newspapers.

conduct of affairs had apparently been sadly inefficient.[35] And Hatton R. O'Kearney, another South Mall solicitor and a butter merchant besides, replaced Daniel F. Leahy (likewise a butter merchant) as chief agent of the earl of Cork and Orrery's 19,700-acre estates in 1883.[36] While some aggressive solicitors in country towns, such as Doherty and Wright, served as managers of great estates, most cared only for small properties as adjuncts to their legal business.[37]

Land agents were recruited not only from the ranks of the legal profession but also from among the landed gentry. In fact, one of the outstanding characteristics of those who administered large estates between 1850 and 1880 was that they had either purchased or inherited considerable landed property themselves. On the whole, the same could probably not be said of Cork land agents before the famine. Table 36 lists alphabetically twenty-three agents in County Cork who owned more than 500 acres in 1878.[38]

As in other businesses, so too in land agency, family succession was common; sons followed their fathers as agents on many estates. Three generations of Curreys, Leahys, and Paynes served respectively the dukes of Devonshire, the earls of Cork and Orrery, and the earls of Bantry.[39] Thomas Gallwey, trained as a barrister, succeeded his father Christopher as the earl of Kenmare's agent, and William B. Leslie followed his father Matthew as agent for the earl of Shannon and the Falkiner family.[40] Among solicitor-land agents, Richard

---

[35] Doherty shared his agency business with his eldest son, and his legal business with his second son (Doherty papers, Letter book, 1876–9: R. W. Doherty, sen., to J. J. Oswald, 25 Apr. 1877, p. 253).

[36] *C.E.*, 11 Jan. 1884, 13 Jan. 1886.

[37] Thomas Rice, a Fermoy solicitor, administered the 3,000-acre estate of Admiral George Evans and Captain John Evans; Messrs Hodnett and Verlin of Youghal, the 1,100-acre property of Sir Edward Synge; Thomas Downes of Skibbereen, the 1,000-acre estate of James MacCarthy-Morrogh; and Richard Ashe of Macroom, the 500-acre property of Robert B. Warren and the earl of Bantry's Macroom estate (Doherty papers, Letter book, 1876–9: R. W. Doherty, sen., to R. Ashe, 7 May 1877, p. 268; *C.E.*, 10, 13 Dec. 1880; 16 Apr. 1881; *C.C.*, 27 Feb. 1888).

[38] U. H. H. de Burgh, *The landowners of Ireland: an alphabetical list of owners of estates of 500 acres or £500 valuation and upwards in Ireland, with the acreage and valuation in each county; and also containing a brief notice of the education and official appointments of each person, to which are added his town and country addresses and clubs* (Dublin, 1878), *passim*. The local newspapers supplied the information on land agencies.

[39] *Devon comm. evidence*, pt iii, p. 187; *Minutes of evidence taken before her majesty's commissioners on agriculture*, vol. i [C 2778–I], H.C. 1881, xv, 25, p. 825 (hereafter cited as *Richmond comm. evidence*); *W.C.E.*, 23 June 1883; *C.C.*, 21, 24 Aug. 1886.

[40] *C.E.*, 17 Dec. 1851; Falkiner papers: W. Despard to T. Barry, 25 Apr. 1863; T. Barry to W. B. Leslie (copy), 4 Feb. 1864.

TABLE 36 Cork land agents owning over 500 acres, 1878

agents	estates managed	acreage	valuation*
J. Newman Beamish	Capt. James H. Smith-Barry	671	£189
Col. Henry Boyle Bernard	Earl of Bandon	1,038	515
Michael Bourke	Earl of Mountcashel	526	402
G. W. Brasier-Creagh	Creagh minors	2,873	1,356
John H. Bryan	Maj. Bennett W. Gillman	683	—
James D. Curtayne	Daniel C. Coltsman	1,165	53
Peter Fitzgerald	Partner, Hussey and Townsend	8,066	3,850
Pasco Savage French	Judge Mountifort Longfield	2,849	1,746
Toler Roberts Garvey	Rev. Hans T. Hamilton	2,927	1,921
Samuel M. Hussey	Partner, Hussey and Townsend	4,272	1,590
Daniel F. Leahy	Earl of Cork and Orrery	2,364	1,455
Henry Longfield	Viscount Doneraile	588	415
Adam N. Meade	William E. Gumbleton	529	658
Henry Newman	Thomas Hicks	877	348
James H. Payne	Sir Augustus Warren	621	362
John W. Payne	Earl of Bantry	621	523
Rev. Somers H. Payne	Earl of Bantry	653	548
Horatio Townsend	Partner, Hussey and Townsend	998	603
Capt. Henry Trench	Earl of Egmont	1,370	735
Thomas Ware	Capt. Caulfield Beamish	1,122	618
Capt. Frederick H. Warren	Daniel Conner	566	496
William Downes Webber	Earl of Kingston	3,950	1,944
Thomas R. Wright	Lord Charles Pelham-Clinton	1,257	913

*The government valuation provides some indication of the letting value of these properties. It was generally accepted that the valuation was about 30 or 35 per cent below the rents in County Cork in the 1870s.

Doherty, sen., and his son acted for the earl of Bandon, and Thomas R. Wright and his sons for Lord Charles Pelham-Clinton. [41] The Husseys and the Townsends—the giants of the land-agency business in the south of Ireland during the second half of the nineteenth century—provide an interesting example in this respect. Samuel Hussey began his long and distinguished career in 1845 as an assistant to his brother-in-law the knight of Kerry, who managed Sir George Colthurst's estates. [42] Later Hussey and the knight of Kerry joined the Townsend brothers, Horace and Robert, in establishing the famous land-agency firm of Hussey and Town-

[41] Doherty papers, Letter book, 1881–4: R. W. Doherty, jun., to G. Atkins, 7 Feb. 1883, p. 657; Hodges, *Cork*, p. 304.
[42] Hussey, *Reminiscences*, p. 38.

send.[43] By the 1880s Samuel Hussey's son Maurice had been launched on a promising career and collected rent from some 4,500 tenants in the west of Ireland.[44]

If Irish land agents were similar to their English counterparts in that both often enough followed in their fathers' footsteps, the two differed radically in social origins and educational background. The English 'tended to be sons of tenant farmers and yeomen; of land agents, builders, and surveyors; and of mining engineers. In a word they were sons of practical men, often familiar from youth with the varied business of land management.'[45] The Irish, on the other hand, were the sons of lawyers, protestant clergymen, British army officers, and sometimes merchants, but above all they were the sons of the landed gentry. While English land agents were 'products not of Oxford or Cambridge nor for that matter of London colleges or Scottish universities', but rather practical men whose knowledge derived from 'a life bred to the soil',[46] Irish agents generally received an entirely different education befitting their higher social standing. Pasco Savage French, who managed the Longfield estates near Cloyne among others, attended Westminster and took his degree at Christ Church, Oxford.[47] Thomas H. Marmion, the agent of the Townsend estates near Skibbereen, was educated at Kingston School, County Dublin, and Queen's College, Cork.[48] James Russell, Captain Richard H. Smith-Barry's agent, and William Downes Webber, the earl of Kingston's agent, were both educated at private schools before entering Trinity College, Dublin.[49] And Robert Townsend, a partner in the famous land-agency firm, attended an English grammar school in Crewkerne, Somerset, and then went on to Trinity College, Dublin.[50]

[43] Colthurst papers: Legal document relating to the firm of Hussey and Townsend, 1885 (in the possession of Sir Richard LaTouche Colthurst, Turret Farm, Blarney, Co. Cork).

[44] *Second report from the select committee of the house of lords on land law (Ireland); together with the proceedings of the committee, minutes of evidence, and appendix*, H.C. 1882 (379), xi, 547, p. 97 (hereafter cited as *Cairns committee evidence*).

[45] D. Spring, *The English landed estate in the nineteenth century: its administration* (Baltimore and London, 1963), p. 100.

[46] Ibid., pp. 101–2.

[47] Hodges, *Cork*, p. 199.

[48] Ibid., p. 246.

[49] Ibid., pp. 279, 298.

[50] Ibid., p. 294. Two other members of this firm did not receive a university education but came from socially accepted families. Samuel Hussey's father had been a barrister in the Four Courts in Dublin before he succeeded to a small estate near Dingle, County Kerry, by the death of an

Having received a university education, most Cork land agents must have acquired a theoretical knowledge of their profession quite informally—from books, journals, and discussions at meetings of agricultural societies or the local magistracy. Their practical training, especially in farming, must have been much more limited at the outset than that of their English counterparts. Of course, those whose fathers had been agents as well no doubt received invaluable experience from an early age. Similarly, solicitors who had previously acquired a thorough knowledge of the legal aspects of estate administration must have slipped quite easily into their new role. Some novices learned their profession by joining the staff of an established agent as an assistant. When seeking a recommendation for a vacant agency in January 1864, E. Maunsell informed Daniel Conner, jun., that after graduating from Trinity College, he had 'been in the employment, as apprentice, of Messrs Stewarts & Kincaid, 6 Leinster St., Dublin, since the 1st June last, before which time I was in the habit of assisting my brother', also an estate agent.[51] Most agents who had reached or passed their prime by the 1870s, however, probably did not begin in this way. But almost all those who entered the profession in the 1870s and later, obtained their practical experience in business methods and farming as apprentices in firms that specialized in the management of landed estates.[52]

Land-agency firms, or even a single agent, often administered several estates from one central office. Dublin spawned the greatest number of agents or firms of agents in general business, who acted indifferently for large and small landowners all over the country. At least two of the most prominent of these firms managed properties in County Cork—Gurnett, Mahony, and Company, and Messrs Stewart and Kincaid.[53] These Dublin establishments and similar ones in Cork city placed their major emphasis upon the inexpensive and efficient collection of rent, rather than upon the propagation of advanced farming techniques or the promotion of estate improvements. J. G. MacCarthy, the proprietor of the Munster House and Land Agency Office on the South Mall, specifically advertised in 1867 his firm's 'systematic' and cheap arrangements for collecting the rents of absentees, trustees, ladies, and 'persons not skilled in the

---

[51] Conner papers: E. Maunsell to D. Conner, jun., 27 Jan. 1864.
[52] Hussey, *Reminiscences*, pp. 41–2.
[53] *C.C.*, 21 Sept. 1880; *C.E.*, 28 Mar. 1881.

---

elder brother; and William Beamish's father, Rev. Adam Newman Beamish, was the rector of Templenacarriga, Co. Cork (Hussey, *Reminiscences*, pp. 10, 12; Hodges, *Cork*, p. 164).

management of property'; the announced agency fee was only 2½ per cent on rentals of over £2,000 per annum. [54] Few land agents with any pretensions to being more than simply rent receivers would have considered such a fee a reasonable remuneration for their manifold responsibilities.

Without reducing themselves to mere rent collectors, many agents successfully managed a few estates of moderate size or several smaller properties. In the early 1860s John Waller Braddell's multiple agencies took him to two small and two fairly extensive estates in four different southern counties. [55] Michael Bourke, the Fermoy solicitor, administered at least three small properties of less than 1,000 acres, including those of Sir George Abercromby (the owner of the town of Fermoy), Colonel Alfred Davis, and the Rev. John S. Walker. [56] Before assuming the difficult management of the earl of Bandon's vast estates in 1877, Richard Doherty, sen., had for many years conducted the agencies of numerous small landowners in Cork, including the Fitzpatricks, the Gillmans, the Mooreheads, the Notters, and the Oswalds. [57] J. D. Cornwall administered six small properties ranging in size from 800 to 1,600 acres in the early 1880s. [58] Occasionally, a single agent extended his supervision over two great estates in the same vicinity. By 1880 John Warren Payne, originally the earl of Bantry's agent, had also taken charge of Henry L. Puxley's 9,200-acre estate near Castletown-Berehaven; and James H. Payne, William H. Massy's agent, had come to conduct the affairs of Sir Augustus Warren's 8,000-acre property near Macroom. [59]

While many individual agents and firms commonly supervised several estates, an acceleration of this trend towards the consolidation of agencies occurred in the 1870s, and especially during the land war of the 1880s, when tenants widely refused to pay their accustomed

---

[54] *Henry and Coghlan's general directory of Cork for 1867*, p. 8.

[55] Bowen papers, N.L.I., box 30, iv: Leases to various tenants, 1850–60; *C.C.*, 4 July 1857, 1 Aug. 1862; Jephson-Norreys papers, Letter book, 1863–70: D. W. Jephson-Norreys to W. H. Jephson, 27 June 1863.

[56] *C.C.*, 2 Sept. 1856.

[57] Doherty resigned several of these small agencies after the death in 1880 of his younger son, who had assisted him in conducting them (Doherty papers, Letter book, 1880–6: R. W. Doherty, sen., to J. L. Notter, 7 Sept. 1880, p. 158; *W.C.E.*, 12 May 1883).

[58] *Bessborough comm. evidence*, pt ii, p. 862.

[59] Ibid., pt ii, p. 927; *C.E.*, 1 Oct. 1880. Under similar circumstances, John E. Barrett administered his own small property, the earl of Kenmare's Cork estate, and the properties of the Beamish minors, Lady White, and the Messrs Gumbleton. All five were near Bantry (*Bessborough comm. evidence*, pt ii, p. 929; *C.E.*, 17, 23 Sept., 4 Nov. 1880).

rents.[60] The remarkable growth in James Penrose Fitzgerald's business provides an excellent illustration of the demand created for experienced land agents by the increasing difficulty of collecting rent. Fitzgerald began his career on his brother's 4,600-acre White-gate estate sometime before 1870 and then succeeded Captain E. C. Bayly in the management of Viscount Midleton's 6,200-acre property in 1877.[61] In the early 1880s Fitzgerald greatly enlarged the number of his concerns, adding the small estates of Robert Atkins, the Misses Austen, Dr Peter McBride, Captain R. K. McBride, J. Augustus Smith, and H. G. Warren.[62] Already in charge of two extensive properties and a half-dozen small ones, he then assumed temporarily the agency of the great Kingston estate in late 1883.[63] Fitzgerald was extremely able and energetic, although harried and in need of an occasional holiday in Switzerland or the Austrian Tirol in order to recover from his exhausting schedule. He had greatly overextended himself, however, if he wished even casually to know the tenants on the estates he managed, or to understand how they lived, farmed, and paid rent in the early 1880s.

In the amalgamation of land agencies, Cork city firms also played a prominent role. Among the leading establishments were J. H. Carroll and Sons, W. Guest, Lane, and Company, and Warren and Micheili,[64] but towering above these and all the others was the firm of Hussey and Townsend. By 1880 this firm of five partners administered as many as eighty-eight estates throughout the south of Ireland.[65] Although many of these properties had passed under its control gradually since the 1850s, the scope of the firm's activities widened greatly after 1870, when some of its largest acquisitions were made. Samuel Hussey replaced Thomas Gallwey as agent of the earl of Kenmare's 119,000-acre estates in Cork, Kerry, and Limerick in 1874.[66] Horace Townsend succeeded Charles Garfit as

[60] Hussey, *Reminiscences,* p. 40.

[61] P.R.O.I., ref. no. 978, Midleton papers, Letter book, 1867–72: J. P. Fitzgerald to E. Roche, 2 Jan. 1871, p. 165; Rentals of Viscount Midleton's estates, 1876–7.

[62] Ibid., Letter book, 1882–5: Fitzgerald to R. K. McBride, 1 Dec. 1882, pp. 305–6; Fitzgerald to H. G. Warren, 2 Dec. 1882, p. 307; Letter book, 1883–4: Fitzgerald to P. McBride, 3 Nov. 1883, p. 18; Letter book, 1884–6: Fitzgerald to W. Jackson, 8 Dec. 1884, p. 116.

[63] Ibid., Letter book, 1883–4: Fitzgerald to H. A. Cholmondeley, 20 Nov. 1883, p. 44; Fitzgerald to Cholmondeley, 2 Jan. 1884, p. 100.

[64] Hodges, *Cork,* pp. 176, 214, 235.

[65] Dun, *Landlords and tenants,* p. 65.

[66] Kenmare papers: S. M. Hussey's report, Rental and account, July–Dec. 1874.

manager of Arthur H. Smith-Barry's 28,000-acre properties in Cork and Tipperary in 1880. [67] The firm also acquired authority over the earl of Dunraven's 15,500-acre estates, mostly situated in Limerick, in the same year, after the previous agents had proved inadequate in extracting rent from the earl's hard-pressed tenants. [68] Samuel Hussey, the greatest Irish land agent of his time, reported in 1882 that he personally received rent amounting to almost £81,000 annually from over 4,600 tenants in Kerry and in some adjacent parts of Cork and Limerick. In addition, the firm in which he was the senior partner collected £130,000 per annum from another 4,500 tenants all over Munster. [69] If their agency fees on total rents received were 5 per cent, then Hussey and his partners together enjoyed a gross annual income of more than £10,000, which must have placed their firm in the front ranks of Irish business organizations at this time.

Estate administration in Cork as well as in many other parts of Ireland was frequently impersonal and remote because of the non-residence of the landowner or his agent, and sometimes of both of them. The elevated social position and the educational background of Cork land agents created a wide gulf between them and the occupying tenantry. There was a notable lack of sufficiently practical men who were keenly aware and possessed a real understanding of the ordinary farmer's problems. Too often, the principal emphasis was placed upon the prompt and efficient collection of rent, largely to the exclusion of fruitful concern for fostering an improved system of agriculture. The phenomenon of multiple agencies, and especially the growth of land-agency firms, only served sharply to accentuate these characteristics of estate administration.

RENT

'The real or fancied excess of rent', declared Finlay Dun in 1880, 'has been the chief cause of the land grievance.' [70] Few would wish to quarrel with Dun's remark or with the conclusion of the most recent examination of the level of rent in pre-famine Ireland. 'There is no doubt', in Crotty's view, 'that land rents in Ireland were high by almost any standard.' [71] Whether the same can be said of land rents between 1850 and 1880 deserves careful study, not only

---

[67] Ibid., Letter book, Jan.–Oct. 1880: S. M. Hussey to Mrs G. Colthurst, 20 Aug. 1880, p. 748.
[68] *C.E.*, 16 Dec. 1880.
[69] *Cairns committee evidence*, p. 97.
[70] Dun, *Landlords and tenants*, p. 262.
[71] Crotty, *Irish agricultural production*, p. 51. See also ibid., pp. 294–307.

because of their critical impact on the economy as a whole, but also because of what was considered their exacerbating effect on Irish grievances. Crotty has insisted that the full commercial rent of the pre-famine period continued to be exacted without substantial modification until the land legislation of 1881 sharply curtailed landlord incomes. [72] Connell has argued—somewhat in the same vein—that the characteristic features of social life in Ireland before 1845 were 'rooted in a mercenary landlordism', and that 'they outlasted the famine, not simply as their old momentum ran down, but while landlordism retained sufficient of its old spirit, freely though it discarded old personnel and old policies'. 'It was the land legislation', concludes Connell, 'that eventually subdued rent, first restraining it, and then making it a falling real charge.' [73]

Not everyone agreed, however, that Irish rents remained excessive after the famine. Michael Ryan, a large farmer and corn miller at Bruree, County Limerick, told a house of lords committee in 1860 that

the landlords on our side of the country since the famine have reduced the price of land . . . ; they find that by giving the tenants an opportunity of living, they are a great deal better off than they were by getting a rack rent. [74]

Samuel Hussey bluntly declared to the duke of Argyll in 1880: 'The rental of arable land in Ireland is less than in 1840; since that time it has doubled in Scotland'. [75] Hussey was surely wrong in claiming that the total rental of Ireland had declined between 1840 and 1880, but his bitter comment may at least be taken to indicate the severe difficulties faced by even the most experienced Irish land agents in raising rents. The Bessborough commission, set up by Gladstone's government in 1880 to investigate the Irish land question, received many complaints—some legitimate, others baseless—of both excessive rents and exorbitant increases in rent. [76] But one of the members of that commission, Arthur MacMorrough Kavanagh, could only conclude from the voluminous testimony given on both the landlord and tenant sides that most Irish farmers had no real

[72] Ibid., p. 62.
[73] K. H. Connell, 'The land legislation and Irish social life' in *Econ. Hist. Rev.*, ser. 2, xi, no. 1 (Aug. 1958), p. 4.
[74] House of Lords Record Office, London: House of lords committee on the Cork & Limerick direct-railway bill, vol. iii of 1860, pp. 52–3.
[75] Kenmare papers, Letter book, Jan.–Oct. 1880: S. M. Hussey to duke of Argyll, 2 July 1880, pp. 589–96.
[76] *Report of her majesty's commissioners of inquiry into the working of the Landlord and Tenant (Ireland) Act, 1870, and the acts amending the same* [C 2779], H.C. 1881, xviii, 1, pp. 7–11 (hereafter cited as *Bessborough comm. report*).

grounds for complaint. 'The weight of evidence', wrote Kavanagh in January 1881, 'has . . . undoubtedly proved that the properties of the majority of extensive landowners, which comprise the largest portion of agricultural and pastoral land in Ireland, have been well and humanely managed', and that on such estates 'the lands are let low, and the rents rarely raised.' [77]

Those contemporaries who believed that rents in Ireland did not climb rapidly in the post-famine years have recently received strong support from Barbara Solow's painstaking analysis of the assessments of Irish land for income-tax purposes and of the relationship which these assessments bore over time to the actual letting value of land. [78] Her careful study of this evidence led Mrs Solow to conclude that 'Irish agricultural rents rose about $12\frac{1}{2}$ per cent between 1865 and 1880, much in line with the course of rent elsewhere in the United Kingdom and in accordance with rises in agricultural income during the period'. [79] It seems that most of the rents existing in 1880 had in fact been fixed before 1865, but this of course only strengthens the case for the generally moderate level of rents well before the land legislation of the 1880s. On the basis of a survey of almost 1,300 estates, the Irish Land Committee reported in 1880 that over 40 per cent of the rents prevailing in that year had been fixed before 1851, while another 30 per cent had been agreed upon in the following decade.[80] The land committee was, it should be noted, a propagandist body for the landlords, and grazing lettings for one year or less, the rents of which had risen most since 1850, were specifically excluded from its published data.[81] But if the committee's survey accurately indicates the dates within which the overwhelming portion of Irish land rents was determined (and there is good reason to believe that it does), then it would follow that tenant farmers, not landlords, received the lion's share of the benefits accruing from price and production increases between 1851 and 1876.[82]

Not only could tenants enjoying an enormous rise in prices pay rent much more easily during this period, but landlords generally refused to exploit the stiff competition for farms to anything like the same extent as previously. Admittedly, peasant land hunger had not disappeared in County Cork; men prepared to deprive a neighbouring tenant of his holding by offering a higher rent than he was

[77] *Bessborough comm. report*, p. 55.
[78] Solow, *Land question*, pp. 58–69.
[79] Ibid., p. 76.
[80] Irish Land Committee, *The land question, Ireland*, no. 3: *Facts and figures*, Table 3; see also *Bessborough comm. evidence*, pt ii, p. 1292.
[81] *Bessborough comm. evidence*, pt ii, p. 1288.
[82] See above, pp. 145–50.

willing to pay could be found on practically every estate. On the Conner property near Dunmanway, for example, Florence McCarthy proposed in 1871 to pay £60 per annum along with a £200 fine for a farm currently held at a lower rent by Patrick Crowley.[83] When it appeared that the landlord was ready to settle with Crowley, McCarthy became frantic.

Together with what I promised you for Patrick Crowley's farm of Aultagh, I will give you 50£ more in four year's time & give you solvent securities for it or even pay it at present. . . . I will also promise you to reclaim your land to such a degree that . . . before half the lease is expired, the principle [*sic*] part of it will be worth £4 an acre. Please accept me as tenant. I will pay you the whole amount at present.[84]

Overcoming the obvious temptations, Conner kept Crowley as tenant. A few landowners, however, continued to take full advantage of the competition for land. When one of Sir John Benn-Walsh's tenants violated an estate rule by dividing his large holding with a younger son in 1857, Benn-Walsh evicted him. After the evicted tenant's eldest son had declined the landlord's offer of the farm for £200 per annum, Benn-Walsh advertised it, received no less than fourteen proposals ranging from £240 to £280, and finally accepted one for £270 from a working farmer named Dowling.[85] The sequel to this case of 'canting' was scarcely surprising. Dowling, noted the landlord sadly in August 1864, 'turned out a grumbling, indolent tenant, wanted an abatement of £70, & I got rid of him and let the farm to a son of widow Conner of . . . [Kylebiwee] for £250'.[86]

Most landlords and agents, however, had already learned from long experience that letting their farms to the highest bidder did not always make sound economic sense. Even Benn-Walsh was inclined to conform to the common estate policy of keeping an evicted farm whenever possible within the former tenant's family at a reasonable rent. On the Devonshire estates, preference was invariably given to another member of the family at a fixed valuation whenever it became necessary to remove an insolvent tenant, no matter how many proposals above this valuation had been received for an evicted farm; nor were offers above the valuation accepted from outsiders when no relative took the farm.[87] On Robert Fitzgerald's

[83] Conner papers: Proposal of Florence McCarthy, 15 Oct. 1871. See also ibid.: F. McCarthy to D. Conner, jun., 15 Oct. 1871.

[84] Ibid: McCarthy to Conner, undated, *c.* Nov. 1871.

[85] Ormathwaite papers: Journal of Sir John Benn-Walsh, 3 Sept. 1858, pp. 193–4.

[86] Ibid: Journal, 19 Aug. 1864, pp. 204–5.

[87] *C.E.,* 1 Oct. 1863.

property, a tenant wishing to sell the interest in his lease was told by the agent in 1872 that he should obtain privately the best offer he could, and not resort to advertisement in the press. [88] On the earl of Bandon's estates, the desire to let vacant farms to adjoining tenants in order to consolidate small holdings kept rent demands lower than if they had automatically been given to the highest bidder. [89] Much more attention seems to have been paid than formerly to a prospective tenant's qualifications as a good farmer rather than as simply a rent-producing machine. [90] Canting ceased to be a prevalent method of letting vacant farms, and even when it was still practised, extravagant bids were now regularly rejected out of hand. [91] Increasingly, landlords and agents much preferred tenants with the capital requisite to stock and work enlarged holdings, rather than those who simply tendered the highest rent. Increases of rent were generally not made arbitrarily or unexpectedly, but only after the revaluation of an entire estate, the termination of a lease, or occasionally the transfer of a holding to a son or son-in-law upon marriage.

While the reluctance of landlords shamelessly to exploit peasant land hunger may partly reflect careful calculation of economic interest, the stability of rents on many Cork estates defies a largely economic explanation. On at least five extensive properties, the rise in rents was either non-existent or insignificant, despite the marked increase in both agricultural prices and production. The rents of the tenants on Lord Charles Pelham-Clinton's estates near Castletown-Berehaven had not been increased since the early 1850s, when Clinton purchased most of his property in that district from the earl of Bantry. His tenants grumbled when Clinton withdrew the temporary abatement of 25 per cent given by Lord Bantry during the famine, and also when he demanded heavy old arrears. They complained too of having to pay Clinton the same rents formerly exacted by middlemen after old leases expired. Yet one overarching fact remains. Although he had purchased the estates for, some said, £10,000 or £12,000 more than they were worth, Clinton did not charge more rent in 1882 than his tenants had paid to Lord Bantry or the middlemen before 1845. [92] Bantry's remaining estates, amounting to over 73,000 acres with a high proportion of worthless

[88] P.R.O.I., ref. no. 978, Midleton papers, Letter book, 1867–72: J. P. Fitzgerald to [illegible], 5 Nov. 1872, p. 178.

[89] Dun, *Landlords and tenants*, p. 73.

[90] P.R.O.I., ref. no. 978, Midleton papers, Letter book, 1867–72: J. P. Fitzgerald to E. Roche, 2 Jan. 1871, p. 165; Letter book, 1882–5, Fitzgerald to R. W. Doherty, sen., 18 Aug. 1882, p. 157.

[91] *C.E.*, 19 Apr. 1881.

[92] Ibid., 23 Nov. 1853, 29 Oct. 1860; *C.C.*, 18 Aug. 1882.

waste and mountain land, are another case in point. His accounts largely confirm the assertion made in 1882 that the rents had not been raised in thirty or forty years. [93] His estate revenues increased from £11,500 to only £12,000 between 1865 and 1882, or by less than 5 per cent. [94]

The four Colthurst properties in Cork, extending to over 31,000 acres, provide a further example of the remarkable moderation of rent demands on some great estates, and in this instance, despite the landlord's lavish expenditure on permanent improvements. The rentals of the Ardrum and Garryadeen estate as well as of the Blarney property inherited in 1862 were actually lower in 1881 than in 1849. The Ballyvourney estate, according to the agent Samuel Hussey, had been worth £5,000 in 1844 and was still 'within a few pounds of the same amount' in 1881, notwithstanding the fact that during the intervening years the landlord spent £20,000 on improvements, all allegedly without charging interest. Only on the Rathcool property, where £11,000 was expended, had the rents been increased substantially, from £930 in 1847 to about £1,500 in 1881. Altogether, however, the Colthurst estates yielded only about 10 per cent more revenue by the latter year than they had at the time of the famine. [95] William Downes Webber, a former agent of the 25,000-acre Kingston estate near Mitchelstown and since 1873 the husband of the dowager countess of Kingston, mounted a strong case in 1881 for the moderation of their rental: 'While the price of the principal products has nearly doubled in the last forty years, the increase of the rents has scarcely exceeded 10 per cent, most of which occurred before 1867, when the majority of leases were granted'. [96] And Viscount Doneraile's 8,400-acre Cork properties, which included the towns of Buttevant and Doneraile, afford still another striking illustration of rent stability. His accounts show an insignificant increase from £7,700 to £7,900 between 1849 and 1881. [97]

The stability of rents found on these five great estates was duplicated on much smaller properties, although probably not so often, if only because their owners could less well afford generosity. The Rev. T. Jasper Smyth, rector of Rathbarry, informed his

[93] *C.C.*, 18 Aug. 1882.

[94] Bantry papers: Rentals of the earl of Bantry's estates, 1864–5, 1881–2.

[95] Colthurst papers: Abstract rentals of the Colthurst estates, 1845–51; *Bessborough comm. evidence*, pt ii, p. 924; Kenmare papers, Letter book, 1883–4: S. M. Hussey to W. Erck, 23 May 1884, pp. 1018–19.

[96] W. D. Webber to editor of *The Times*, 4 June 1881, quoted in *C.E.*, 9 June 1881.

[97] Doneraile papers: Rentals of Viscount Doneraile's Cork estates, 1849–81.

assembled tenants in 1881 that he had carefully examined the estate accounts since 1821 and found that during this sixty-year period, 'in no single instance have the rents been raised, nor is there a record of a single tenant being evicted for non-payment of rent'. [98] The rental of the 2,200-acre Falkiner properties in Cork and Tipperary seems to have increased from slightly less than £4,000 to £4,170, or hardly at all, between 1836 and 1882. [99] There had even been a reduction in rent on Captain William Fagan's 600-acre estate, it was asserted in 1881, of no less than 30 per cent since 1840, 'besides a very large amount expended in building, making roads, liming, etc., all at his own expense'. [100] The rental of Robert Cole Bowen's 1,700-acre property near Kildorrery had been slightly more than £1,000 in 1848 but remained at about £850 between 1854 and 1881. [101] It was reliably reported in 1882 that the rents on the 1,200-acre estate of H. G. Gillman had not been raised since 1850. [102] And while he took fines when giving leases, Sir Joseph N. McKenna (M.P. for Youghal, 1865–8 and 1874–80) declared in 1881 that he had never increased the rents on any of his properties nor dispossessed any tenant owing less than four years' rent during the twenty-five years he had been an Irish landlord. [103]

In stark contrast to these large and small estates where almost a moratorium on rent increases was observed, there were the properties of Thomas L. Cave and Sir John Benn-Walsh, where the advances of rent were extremely large. Cave purchased the 3,200-acre Audley estate near Skibbereen in 1853, when he paid about £16,000 for a property with an official net rental of only £230, but with a poor-law valuation of £940 in 1849. [104] Under these circumstances, it is scarcely surprising that the agent Thomas Scott rearranged the scattered holdings into compact farms and raised estate revenues considerably. But he was probably as astonished as everyone else when he told the tenants in April 1855 that they had not only cleared off all old arrears and met current rents promptly, but had also agreed to pay an average increase of more than 50 per cent. [105]

[98] *W.C.E.*, 19 Nov. 1881.

[99] Falkiner papers: Rentals of the Falkiner estates, 1835–6, 1881–2.

[100] *C.E.*, 12 Feb. 1881.

[101] Bowen papers, Tipperary County Library, Thurles: Rentals of Robert Cole Bowen's estates in the counties of Cork and Tipperary, 1847–83.

[102] *W.C.E.*, 3 June 1882.

[103] *C.E.*, 12 Feb. 1881. McKenna owned nearly 1,600 acres near Youghal in Cork and about 1,400 acres in other counties.

[104] P.R.O.I.: Incumbered estates court index to conveyances, vol. iii, Aug. 1852–July 1853, no. 3828.

[105] *C.E.*, 23 Apr. 1855.

Like many other purchasers in the incumbered estates court, Cave no doubt sought quickly to realize some of his large investment.[106] Rents also rose rapidly over a relatively short period on the 11,000-acre Cork and Kerry estates of Sir John Benn-Walsh. There was an advance of 13 per cent between 1840 and 1847, and a further rise of no less than 50 per cent between 1847 and 1866.[107] Benn-Walsh had long been unable to make money from his Irish property because of numerous long leases to middlemen. Once the middlemen had been ousted completely and the famine had passed, he saw his estates 'coming round'. After finishing one of his periodic visits in 1852, he recorded his fixed determination that 'if politics will but let us alone, & no tenant right or other device of socialism & Jacobinism marr our prospects, we shall yet regain our property'.[108] In Kerry in 1858 and in Cork in 1860, he attempted to do precisely that by advancing the rents significantly. He based the increase upon the number of stock the tenants already possessed as well as upon his agent's conviction that stocking ratios could be greatly improved under the spur of higher rents.[109] Although a portion of the 50 per cent rise in rents between 1847 and 1866 resulted from the expiration of middlemen's leases and from landlord expenditure on permanent improvements, Benn-Walsh took full advantage of price increases.

Landlords such as Cave and Benn-Walsh, however, appear to have been exceptional. Much more typical were landowners whose rent increases ranged from 20 to 30 per cent and were therefore well within the limits of the price and production increments of the time. The duke of Devonshire's Irish domains extended to over 60,000 acres, of which nearly 33,000 were located in Cork, around Bandon and between Fermoy and Tallow. The duke's agents fixed his rents upon the basis of a careful valuation supposedly conducted every twenty years. When the estates were last revalued before the famine, the rental grew from £37,000 in 1841 to £42,700 in 1842, or by slightly more than 15 per cent. The expiration of numerous middlemen's leases in the 1840s, and the interest charged on drainage and buildings executed by the landlord, helped to augment the rental to almost £48,000 in 1860, or by an additional 13 per cent. In 1859

[106] For a celebrated case of the raising of rent by another incumbered estates court purchaser, Herbert Gillman, who insisted that he must realize 6 per cent on his investment in property near Queenstown, see ibid., 19, 29, 30 Oct. 1872; 1 Jan. 1891.

[107] Ormathwaite papers: Account of the property and income of Sir John Benn-Walsh, 1829–66.

[108] Ibid.: Journal of Sir John Benn-Walsh, 18 Oct. 1852, p. 22.

[109] Ibid.: Journal, 9 Sept. 1858, pp. 200–1; Journal, 10 Sept. 1858, pp. 201–2; Journal, 6 Sept. 1860, pp. 197–8.

and 1860 Devonshire sold some land, principally his urban property in Youghal, worth about £3,600 per annum, and these sales were reflected in the decline of his revenues to £43,500 in 1862. The customary revaluation was deferred, no doubt because of the severe agricultural depression of the early 1860s, and was then apparently never carried out. No further important sales of property occurred before 1881, when Devonshire's rental stood at £44,800, or scarcely higher than it had been twenty years earlier. Many ducal tenants had remained at the same rents since 1842.[110] Equally moderate increments in revenues could be observed on other estates. After huge incumbrances had forced the sale of most of his property, Viscount Midleton's remaining agricultural land yielded an income of £4,100 in 1854. In 1861 and annually from 1874, Midleton increased his land rents until they amounted to £5,200 in 1881, or about 25 per cent more than in 1854.[111] Despite the intense competition for farms on the Conner estate mentioned earlier, the landlord added only about 30 per cent to his rent roll between the early 1850s and the early 1880s.[112]

Advances of rent such as those of Conner, Midleton, and Devonshire may seem inoffensive enough to have been absorbed easily by their tenants. Similar increases on the estates of the earl of Kenmare and Nathaniel Buckley, however, provoked bitter clashes between the agents and the tenants. The wider context within which rents were raised could be crucial in determining the tenants' willingness to agree to them. There had been a long tradition of liberal management and moderate rents among the catholic earls of Kenmare, and agrarian crime was almost unknown on their vast domains in Cork, Kerry, and Limerick. Although arrears of more than £10,000 accumulated during the agricultural crisis of the early 1860s, there were scarcely any evictions. A large part of the 16 per cent rise in rents between 1850 and 1874 was attributable to the termination of old leases to middlemen, with whom the Kenmare estates were saddled much longer than many others.[113] When Samuel Hussey became Kenmare's chief agent in 1874, however, he immediately began raising revenues from all sources in order to provide the funds

[110] Lismore papers, N.L.I., MSS 6799–817: Rentals of the duke of Devonshire's Youghal estate, 1843–60; MS 6929: Rent receipts and disbursements, 1818–90; Sales of property, 1861–79; Circular advertisement of the sale of the Youghal estate.

[111] P.R.O.I., ref. no. 978, Midleton papers: Rentals of Viscount Midleton's estates, 1854–86.

[112] Conner papers: Rentals of the Conner estates, 1853–4, 1883–4.

[113] Kenmare papers: Rentals of the earl of Kenmare's estates, Nov. 1841–Nov. 1850; May–Nov. 1865; July–Dec. 1874.

necessary for the construction of the earl's great new £100,000 mansion, Killarney House. In his first six months alone, Hussey increased receipts by over £6,000 through the simple expedients of reducing arrears, ousting a few middlemen, and collecting some long-forgotten rents. [114] In 1875 he gained £800 by leasing the bogs, which the tenants had previously enjoyed free of rent, and happily reported to Lord Kenmare that the departure of four more middlemen and the service of numerous notices to quit would soon augment the rental by another £600. [115]

Thus far, Hussey's operations had added about £3,000 to the earl's permanent annual income almost without touching current agricultural rents. New agreements with several of the larger Kerry tenants in 1876, however, yielded some £1,300. Hussey proudly informed Kenmare in early 1877 that he was also

in negotiation with the Co. Limerick tenants about taking out leases at an increased rent, which I trust will end amicably, & this summer I shall also do the same on the Bantry estate, but as the greater portion of that estate is leased, the increase will not be much. [116]

Although Hussey apparently had little trouble in Cork, raising the rents of the Limerick tenants proved extremely difficult, now that agricultural prospects had dimmed considerably as a result of bad harvests and lower prices in 1877 and 1878. Notices to quit had to be served when ordinary persuasion failed, but the local bailiff at Hospital would have nothing to do with serving them, because he greatly feared that the tenants 'would do away with him before the notices expired'. [117] Only after Horace Townsend, Hussey's land-agency partner, had personally delivered these notices did many of the Limerick tenants grudgingly submit to a total advance of £700. [118] Even then, not everyone succumbed at once to the threat of eviction, and in April 1878 Hussey carefully instructed the Hospital bailiff to warn the recalcitrants for the last time that their tenancies would be terminated automatically unless they accepted his final offer. [119] As late as November, however, some diehards still held out, and Hussey told Lord Kenmare, 'I fear I shall have to bring ejectments against ten of the Hospital tenants; it is dangerous

[114] Ibid.: S. M. Hussey's report, Rental and account, July–Dec. 1874.
[115] Ibid.: S. M. Hussey's reports, Rentals and accounts, Jan.–June, July–Dec. 1875.
[116] Ibid.: S. M. Hussey's report, Rental and account, July–Dec. 1876.
[117] Ibid., Letter book, Jan.–Aug. 1878: M. Leonard to H. Townsend, 5 Mar. 1878, pp. 346–7.
[118] Ibid.: S. M. Hussey to earl of Kenmare, 22 Mar. 1878, pp. 437–9.
[119] Ibid.: Hussey to M. Riordan, 1 Apr. 1878, p. 488.

work'. [120] In retrospect, Hussey pronounced himself satisfied with the £1,100 gained in Limerick (22½ per cent) and Cork (27 per cent), for as he emphasized, the previous season had been bad for farmers almost everywhere, and no other landlord in the Hospital district of Limerick had been able to raise rents for two decades. [121] After almost six years of single-minded effort, however, Hussey had only succeeded by 1880 in augmenting Kenmare's permanent annual rental by less than £5,000, or about 17 per cent, even though the estates had been generously let before 1874. [122]

While Hussey's efforts to raise Kenmare's revenues did not end in violence, those of another agent on the Buckley estate quickly produced agrarian outrage. The 20,800-acre property of the millionaire Lancashire cotton manufacturer Nathaniel Buckley lay astride the Galtee range near Mitchelstown, County Cork, but in Tipperary and Limerick. Until the property was purchased in the incumbered estates court in the early 1850s by the Irish Land Company, composed of a group of speculating Manchester business-men, it had formed part of the unsettled estates of the earls of Kingston. At the very beginning of the century, tenancies at nominal rents of a few shillings per acre had been created on the mountainous portions of these estates, no doubt with the understanding that the occupiers would in time be required to pay reasonable rents for the lands which their long, arduous toil would gradually bring under cultivation. Neither the earls of Kingston nor the Irish Land Company altered the original lettings, but after Buckley purchased the property from his fellow directors in 1871, he finally ordered a new valuation. [123]

To conduct the valuation, Buckley's agent Patten Smith Bridge [124] selected another land agent and practical farmer named Walker from King's County. He carefully instructed Walker to exclude from consideration waste lands, recent improvements executed within the

[120] Ibid., Letter book, 1878–9: Hussey to earl of Kenmare, 25 Nov. 1878, pp. 394–6.

[121] Ibid.: S. M. Hussey's report, Rental and account, Jan.–June 1878.

[122] Between 1850 and 1880 the total rental of the Kenmare estates grew from £28,700 to about £38,000, or by 33 per cent (ibid.: Rentals of the Kenmare estates, Nov. 1841–Nov. 1850; Jan.–June, July–Dec. 1880).

[123] Central Tenants' Defence Association, *Full and revised report of the eight days' trial in the court of queen's bench on a criminal information against John Sarsfield Casey at the prosecution of Patten Smith Bridge from November 27th to December 5th, 1877* (Dublin, 1877), pp. 20–1 (hereafter cited as *Bridge v. Casey*).

[124] Bridge had served as the earl of Kingston's agent from 1855 to 1867. 'I found the estate in the greatest confusion', declared Bridge, 'and left it in perfect order' (*W.C.E.*, 7 Apr. 1877).

previous five years, and farm buildings or dwelling houses, but to include all mountain land reclaimed since 1800.[125] When Walker completed a three-month, field-by-field survey in August 1873, Bridge accepted his recommendation to increase the gross rental of 512 tenancies from £4,200 to £5,500, or by 25 per cent after the deduction of the county cess (or tax) paid by the landlord.[126] Bridge notified each tenant of his new rent in February 1874 and posted a terse announcement throughout the estate:

The tenants are hereby noticed that it will be necessary . . . to signify to the agent during the month of November whether they will submit to Mr Walker's valuation and enter into a new arrangement. Any tenants who do not come will be considered as having refused to do so.[127]

The new arrangement included leases for a term of thirty-one years to all who wanted them and permission for anyone objecting to the new rent to sell his interest, either to another Buckley tenant or to an outsider, subject of course to Walker's valuation.[128]

These terms, however, at first proved completely unacceptable to about 200 of Buckley's tenants, and notices to quit were said to have rained like snowflakes on the peaks of the Galtees. As late as 1877, there were still almost fifty unsettled cases on the estate, although apparently no evictions had yet occurred.[129] These recalcitrants had been emboldened by two unsuccessful attempts to murder the agent, a famous libel trial against a prominent supporter of the tenants, and attendant newspaper publicity which made the Buckley estate a byword for mercenary landlordism throughout the country. In late March 1875 an enraged tenant named John Ryan tried to kill Patten Smith Bridge within the grounds of his residence, Galtee Castle, but wounded him only slightly.[130] Almost exactly one year later, Bridge was attacked again, and this time took nine balls, one in the throat, but once more survived; his driver was killed, and a policeman seriously wounded.[131] While public excitement over this second outrage was at its height, the Mitchelstown Fenian, John Sarsfield Casey, wrote two famous letters to the *Cork Examiner* and the

[125] *Bridge v. Casey*, p. 54.
[126] Ibid., pp. 20–1.
[127] Ibid., p. 35.
[128] Ibid., pp. 18, 38.
[129] *C.E.*, 5 Jan. 1878.
[130] Ryan held a 37-acre farm on an old lease of 1798 which had recently expired. His rent had been raised from £30 to £44. Besides refusing to pay the new rent, he would neither sell his interest nor accept £200 compensation for the surrender of his holding. He was never apprehended and probably emigrated (*C.C.*, 24 Mar. 1875; *Bridge v. Casey*, p. 19).
[131] *C.E.*, 2 Apr. 1876.

Freeman's Journal, in which he demonstrated without difficulty that Bridge had imposed the largest individual increases of rent on precisely those holdings which had previously carried the smallest rent. Many cottiers saw their rents double or even triple.[132] After recovering from his wounds, Bridge alleged that he had been libelled by Casey's letters and brought an unsuccessful suit for damages in the court of queen's bench in late 1877. What the eight-day trial brought out most clearly was not Casey's vindictiveness or Bridge's oppressiveness, but rather the enormous labour involved in reclaiming these Galtee mountain farms and the willingness of tenants to eke out a miserable living in such an unrewarding place.[133] The compassionate articles written for the *Freeman's Journal* by William O'Brien, who shortly became one of the leading members of the Irish parliamentary party, amply demonstrated that the prosperity of the 1870s had little affected the smallholders on the Buckley estate.[134] Indeed, the unfortunate truth to which O'Brien's articles and Casey's letters unintentionally pointed was that many of these mountain farmers would have remained at nearly the subsistence level even if a moratorium on all rent had been declared.

The weight of the evidence indicates that in County Cork the excess of rent which Finlay Dun declared to be the chief cause of the land grievance in 1880 was as much fancied as it was real; or putting the matter another way, it was made a grievance by the events of 1877–9 as much as it was a grievance before then. Most landlords had pursued since the famine a policy of live and let live—Irish landlords always had to overcome their ill repute. Many landowners evinced an earnest desire to improve the material condition of the people and as for rent, left well enough alone; some were restrained by an increasingly powerful public opinion which focused attention on landlord abuses; and a few were checked by the fear of violent retribution. Yet, it is not difficult to understand either how or why rent became a burning issue in the late 1870s. A few landowners, such as Sir John Benn-Walsh or the notorious William Bence Jones,[135] believed wholeheartedly in driving their tenants to extraordinary effort by stiff commercial rents. Under appropriate conditions, such men could be cited as typical examples of abusive landlordism, when, in fact, they were quite unrepresentative of their

[132] For Casey's letters, see *C.E.*, 13 Apr. 1876; *Freeman's Journal*, 26 Apr. 1876.

[133] *Bridge v. Casey*, p. 53.

[134] O'Brien's articles were reprinted in *Christmas on the Galtees: an inquiry into the condition of the tenantry of Mr Nathaniel Buckley by the special correspondent of the 'Freeman's Journal'* (Dublin, 1878).

[135] See below, Chapter VI, pp. 272–5.

class. More importantly, there were several thousand smallholders in Cork, especially in the extreme southwest, whose position was analogous to that of the Buckley tenantry. Seemingly inoffensive increases in rent could encroach upon their normally slender margin above subsistence, and a substantial fall in prices or a series of bad harvests would have much the same effect. In either case, reductions in rent, and strikes to achieve them, could be expected to possess an attractiveness out of all proportion to their limited beneficial results. On some estates, the recency of advances of rent made them particularly irksome when economic conditions deteriorated in the late 1870s. The first two-thirds of the decade had been an extremely prosperous time for farmers, and some landlords had been quick to capitalize on this by raising rents.[136] The three bad seasons of 1877–9, however, generated enormous pressure for the rescinding of these rent increases. The landlords concerned were naturally reluctant to comply, and many others were agonizingly slow to grant abatements enabling their tenants to weather the severe agricultural crisis.[137] While all these factors helped to make the question of rent a burning issue by 1880, the most important was that a period of prosperity unknown since the Napoleonic wars had been followed by a series of bad seasons which threatened to bring a 'revolution of rising expectations' to an abrupt halt.

LEASES AND SECURITY OF TENURE

Just as the problem of excessive rent diminished sharply after the great famine, so too did that of insecurity of tenure. Before 1845 the manifest anxiousness of landlords to consolidate small holdings and the growing prevalence of annual tenancy had combined to create a high degree of insecurity of tenure. This insecurity was of course greatly increased by the wholesale clearances of the famine years. But the number of evictions drastically declined after 1854, and from 1855 to 1879 an average of only about thirty tenants and their families per year were evicted without readmission in County Cork.[138] Since there were so few evictions after 1854, even yearly tenants gradually came to feel very secure in the possession of their

---

[136] *C.E.*, 10, 13 Dec. 1880; 3 Jan., 23 Mar., 29 July 1881; *Bessborough comm. evidence*, pt ii, pp. 897–8.

[137] See below, Chapter VI, pp. 255–6.

[138] *Return by provinces and counties . . . , of cases of evictions which have come to the knowledge of the constabulary in each of the years from 1849 to 1880 inclusive*, pp. 10–23. It is assumed that one-third of the tenants evicted between 1871 and 1879 were readmitted to their holdings as caretakers (Solow, *Land question*, pp. 56–7).

holdings. But the paucity of leaseholds in the immediate post-famine years possessed disadvantages, not only for tenants but for landlords as well. While landowners naturally wished to avoid a recurrence of the great evils produced by long leases to often non-resident middlemen, there was some feeling that this objective could best be achieved not by yearly tenancies, but by granting to occupying tenants short leases that contained suitable husbandry covenants. Without proper covenants stringently enforced, it would be much more difficult for landlords and agents to promote agricultural improvement.[139] Perhaps the graziers of the great Irish midland plain did not really need leases to produce efficiently. Having a relatively low level of fixed investment, they required merely the assurance that the grasslands would be theirs until the end of the grazing season.[140] The dairy farmers of Cork and Munster, however, faced higher fixed costs—for milch cows, additional byre accommodation, extra labour, and more winterfeed. Consequently, leases would have encouraged them to sink more of their capital with the assurance of reaping the expected rewards.

A significant shift in attitudes towards leases occurred on many estates after the famine. Daniel Conner, jun., who granted leases for terms of twenty-one or thirty-one years to most of his tenants with large holdings in 1850 and 1851, obviously aimed at fostering a better system of farming. The covenants of his leases read as if they were 'the ten commandments of good husbandry'. No more than one of every four acres could be broken up and converted into tillage in any one year, and whenever an acre of grassland was broken up, it had to be dressed with twenty barrels of lime or ten carts of sand, under a penalty of £1 per acre for non-performance. No more than one corn crop could be taken without an intervening green or root crop, and after three years of tillage, the land was to be laid down in grass and left so for four years. No green or root crop (except potatoes), fodder, or manure grown or made on the farm was to be removed; everything had to be consumed or laid out upon it. No portion of the holding could be sublet, not even to a dairyman for the butter-making season. No more than one labourer's house could be built on a farm of less than fifty acres, and only one family was allowed to reside in that house, under a penalty of £5 per annum.[141] The motivation for a change in policy on the duke of Devonshire's

[139] See above, Chapter I, pp. 63–6.
[140] Crotty, *Irish agricultural production*, pp. 60–1.
[141] Conner papers: Leases of 21 or 31 years to various tenants, 29 Sept. 1850, 29 Sept. 1851; Lease of part of Shanlaragh to Michael Cahalane for a term of 31 years, 29 Sept. 1871.

estates was very similar. The duke's chief agent F. E. Currey explained to Finlay Dun in 1880 that while most of the smaller tenants had held without a lease prior to 1860, it had since then been

found desirable to guard against abuses, and especially against subdivision, subletting, the removal by the way-going tenant of his last crop, and irregularities of cropping. Printed agreements for yearly tenants and leases for thirty-one years are now given . . . .[142]

The interests of a more efficient agriculture were occasionally subservient to, or coincidental with, a landlord's financial needs in this alteration of estate policy towards leases. Lord Fermoy was said to have required his Carrignavar tenants to take out leases at increased rents in the 1850s, in order to give a boost to the depleted finances of the Roche family, whose fortunes nonetheless collapsed under the weight of enormous debts in the late 1870s.[143] Nearly 400 leases for a term of three lives or thirty-one years were granted at existing rents by the highly popular earl of Kingston in December 1867, when his 25,000-acre estate lay in grave danger of being forced to a sale by importunate creditors.[144] The sorely pressed Kingston had 'called on his tenants to aid him by paying him one year's rent, along with the year's rent due'. They 'cheerfully complied, raised it in the bank, and saved the earl. . . '.[145] Anxiously casting about for ways to raise money for the construction of his elaborate new mansion in the early 1870s, the earl of Kenmare happily hit upon the well-worn device of taking fines on new leases. He offered tenures of one life or forty-one years to all those willing to pay the equivalent of two or three years' rent; as a result, he managed to extract some £11,000 from about 170 tenants on his Cork and Kerry estates in 1872 and 1873.[146] After purchasing a small property in chancery in 1876, the land agent Major Richard L. Warren attempted to take substantial fines in consideration of his granting the tenants a rebate on a new valuation which would have raised their rents. When he failed in this, Warren required them to accept thirty-one-year leases at his valuation.[147] While some tenants gladly

[142] Dun, *Landlords and tenants*, p. 56.
[143] *C.E.*, 16 June 1881.
[144] Kingston papers: Landed estates court title book for the dowager countess of Kingston's estate, 1875 (in the possession of W. E. O'Brien and Co., Solicitors, Mitchelstown, Co. Cork).
[145] *C.E.*, 15 June 1881.
[146] Kenmare papers: Leases to various tenants on the Kenmare estates in Cork and Kerry, 1872–3; Account of the sums received by Thomas Gallwey, agent, for fines and costs of leases, 5 July 1874.
[147] *C.C.*, 20, 21 Feb. 1882.

availed themselves of the opportunity to buy a lease, fines became extremely unpopular at the beginning of the land war, partly because they were a thinly disguised substitute for higher rents. At a Land League meeting in Cork city in April 1881, the South Mall solicitor and land agent Walter Thornhill was roundly condemned for having exacted fines equivalent to one year's rent when he granted leases for a term of forty-one years or one life on the Goode estate near Bandon.[148] Another solicitor-agent, William Hodnett of Youghal, was publicly taxed with the allegation that the profits of his law partner consisted largely of the fines which tenants 'from time to time were obliged to pay on being compelled to take leases'.[149]

Many other landowners, both large and small, regularly granted leases with apparently no cost but the drafting fee. George Twiss not only reduced rents when he came into possession of his 800-acre Cork estate in the late 1850s, but also issued, it was said, new and long leases to the tenants.[150] Almost all of Sir Samuel Falkiner's tenants possessed leases by the 1860s, although under the conditions of a strict family settlement then in force, these agreements could only be for a term no longer than twenty-one years.[151] Leases were invariably given on the earl of Cork and Orrery's estates, according to the agent Daniel F. Leahy, despite the fact that the holdings were generally small, over 400 having been valued at less than £20.[152] Considerable uneasiness prevailed in late 1871 in the Charleville district, where one of the earl's estates was situated, over the illness of the prince of Wales.[153] The farmers were not being patriotic; about 80 per cent of them held for the life of the prince of Wales. The land agent Henry R. Marmion issued no less than 300 leases to tenants on the Rev. Maurice Townsend's 8,700-acre estate near Skibbereen in 1869; farming leases ran for sixty-one years, and building leases for 300 years.[154] Many incumbered or landed estates court purchasers were also numbered among the owners of property on which the tenants enjoyed leases, such as Richard Doherty, sen., McCarthy Downing, M.P., Richard Rice, sen., and

[148] *C.E.*, 4 Apr. 1881.
[149] Ibid., 16 Apr. 1881.
[150] Ibid., 16 July 1862.
[151] Falkiner papers: Abstract from the will of Sir Riggs Falkiner, 10 Oct. 1849, concerning the leasing power given tenants for life; Schedule of tenants, modes of tenure, and rents on the Falkiner estates, undated, but post-1861.
[152] *C.E.*, 21 Apr. 1881, 16, 18, 23 Jan. 1882.
[153] Ibid., 19 Dec. 1871.
[154] *Bessborough comm. evidence*, pt ii, pp. 915–16.

R. H. E. White.[155] Even before the land act of 1870 gave a greatly heightened and somewhat sinister popularity to leases among landowners, a significant proportion of Cork tenants had gained formal security of tenure. According to a parliamentary return in 1870, over 20,000 of the 48,000 holdings (42 per cent) in the poor-law unions of the county were held under lease.[156]

Gladstone's land act of 1870 was a well-meaning attempt to check the exceptional landlord abuses of excessive rents and un-warranted evictions by providing the occupiers of the land of Ireland with greater security of tenure. The act was largely inspired by the alleged success of the so-called Ulster custom in promoting agri-cultural prosperity in the north of Ireland. This custom gave northern farmers security of tenure as long as they paid a fair rent, and guaranteed to them the fruits of their own improvements if they surrendered possession by allowing them to sell the interest in their holdings, or their goodwill, to another tenant. The 1870 land act gave the force of law to this custom in Ulster and to well-established analogous usages in the other three provinces. Where a correspond-ing usage did not exist, the legislation sought to provide equivalent benefits in the form of landlord-paid compensation for both 'capricious eviction' and 'permanent agricultural improvements'.[157]

As Barbara Solow has convincingly demonstrated, the 1870 land act could not begin to solve Ireland's real agrarian problems, especially the plethora of small, inefficient units of production, because its author wrongly diagnosed the ills of the agricultural economy. The rate of eviction was already low (too low for reason-able agricultural efficiency), rents were generally moderate, and the prevalence of yearly tenancy did not constitute a significant obstacle to tenant investment in farm improvements. In one respect the act was beneficial: it largely eliminated the confiscation by some proprietors of the value of improvements executed by an evicted or departing tenant. But in other respects the act disappointed tenants: it removed neither the minor evil of exorbitant increases of rent nor the annoying landlord restrictions on the sale of goodwill.[158]

Gladstone's measure was partly designed to reduce the often well-

[155] Doherty papers, Letter book, 1880-6: R. W. Doherty, sen., to Mrs A. Moorehead, 15 Mar. 1881, p. 265; *C.E.*, 2 May 1881; *W.C.E.*, 17 June, 16 Sept. 1882.

[156] *Returns showing the number of agricultural holdings in Ireland and the tenure by which they are held by the occupiers* [C 32], H.C. 1870, lvi, 737, pp. 18-20.

[157] 33 & 34 Vict., c. 46, ss. 1-4. A convenient source, with text and commentary, is W. O'Connor Morris, *The Irish land act* (Dublin, 1870). Further references to provisions of the act give the relevant page(s) in Morris.

[158] Solow, *Land question*, pp. 51-88.

warranted opposition of many Irish proprietors to leasehold tenancy. [159] And the act did let loose in Cork and elsewhere in Ireland a flood of new leases, some of which contained covenants that were doubtfully legal and positively damaging to the interests of the tenants. The large farmer was presumed capable of protecting himself and could 'contract out' of the land legislation of 1870. As long as his holdings under one landlord were valued at not less than £50 for purposes of taxation, he could sign an agreement to forego any claim he might later have. [160] The agent William B. Leslie firmly rejected in March 1873 a solicitor's proposal to exclude the £50 landholders on the Falkiner estates from claims for compensation. Leslie did not

think it beneficial to the landlord's interest to seek to deprive the tenant of the value of buildings erected by him—as from long experience I have always found it a gain in every way to allow the tenant the value of his expenditure. [161]

Many other landowners and agents, however, eagerly seized upon this loophole. The new printed form of lease which Samuel Hussey authorized for use on the earl of Kenmare's estates after 1873 specifically excluded £50 landholders from lodging any claim under the land act. [162] A similar exclusionary covenant was inserted when appropriate in the leases granted by the earl of Cork during the 1870s. [163]

While £50 landholders were rare enough to have given only a small incentive to the issuance of leases after 1870, other provisions of the act greatly encouraged the spread of leasehold tenancy. Any tenant who after 1 August 1870 accepted a lease for a term of thirty-one years or longer was automatically debarred from claiming compensation for disturbance or for improvements, with the exception of buildings, reclamation, unexhausted manures, and un-harvested crops. [164] By granting leases for the stipulated term, landlords could thus gain complete immunity from claims for such improvements as surface drainage, fences, and irrigation, as well as for disturbance. As if this did not furnish more than sufficient

[159] For a cogent statement of this opposition, see Jones, *Life's work*, pp. 48–50.

[160] Morris, *Land act*, pp. 147–8.

[161] Falkiner papers: W. B. Leslie to T. Barry, 27 Mar. 1873.

[162] Kenmare papers: Printed lease prepared for use on the earl of Kenmare's estates, unperfected and undated, but *c.* 1874. See also *C.C.*, 25 Feb. 1882.

[163] *C.E.*, 20 Nov. 1880.

[164] Morris, *Land act*, pp. 67–70, 96.

incentive, there was the singular question of compensation for buildings. When the landlord might now be called upon to reimburse tenants for what he considered either too lavish, very inferior, or completely unnecessary buildings, he naturally became more anxious than ever before to regulate or scrutinize their construction.[165] Much of the eagerness with which leases were urged upon tenants after 1870 is attributable to this desire to prevent the erection of unsuitable buildings, or to make the extent and cost of suitable improvements matters of agreement and record. Many landowners issued leases containing a clause similar to that of the lease standard on the duke of Devonshire's estates:

The Landlord and Tenant (Ireland) Act of 1870 notwithstanding, no remuneration will be made for buildings put up by the tenant unless with the consent of the landlord, or unless they have been paid for by the tenant at the period of his entry.[166]

The abrupt change of policy which occurred on William Bence Jones's 3,800-acre estate near Clonakilty well illustrates the great anxiety aroused among landlords by the land act's compensation provisions. With but one exception, Jones had never given a lease before 1870; seven of his forty tenants were leaseholders, but six of these held under thirty-one-year agreements granted in 1851, before Jones had purchased that part of his property in the landed estates court.[167] After the land act, however, he required every tenant to sign a thirty-one-year lease bulging with the strictest covenants. Answering a charge that he had merely sought to evade the land act by this requirement, Jones left no one in doubt that the prospect of having to pay compensation for buildings had largely goaded him to these leases.

I contract to make all permanent improvements the tenant asks for, and on the cost of which he will pay 5 per cent. I thus get houses, etc., well built in all respects, at less than first cost, and that cost far less for repairs, and so are a gain to both the tenants and me, instead of having to fight an outrageous

---

[165] Richard Doherty, sen., informed Amelia Moorehead in August 1872 that one of her yearly tenants was building a house 'fit for a gentleman' which would cost £150. 'He . . . has done it', wrote the agent, 'evidently to claim under the land act.' Doherty planned to serve him with a notice to quit, which would terminate his legal tenancy and thus prevent him from lodging the claim (Doherty papers, Letter book, 1871–3: R. W. Doherty, sen., to Mrs A. Moorehead, 16 Aug. 1872, pp. 706–7).

[166] Dun, *Landlords and tenants*, p. 57. See also *C.C.*, 25 Feb. 1882, 2 Mar. 1883.

[167] W. B. Jones, 'My answer to opponents' in *Contemporary Review*, xl (Sept. 1881), reprinted in full in *W.C.E.*, 17 Sept. 1881; *C.C.*, 6 Feb. 1882.

claim for unsubstantial houses with inferior timber and scamped at all ends.[168]

His tenants were not only prohibited from executing any permanent improvements without his written consent but even forbidden to request that Jones make them, unless at least ten years of their term were still unexpired. Furthermore, his leases strictly bound the tenant to cultivate the land as minutely prescribed; they even went so far as to pinpoint how long five different types of fertilizer remained unexhausted. This was hardly window dressing, for Jones had kept since 1870 an exact register of the quantity and type of manure put out each year by every one of his tenants. Meticulously, Jones inserted in his leases the respective improvements made by himself or the tenant; then in a sweeping, confiscatory conclusion, he declared,

all other fences and improvements belong to the landlord, and at the end of the lease it is agreed that the value of the improvements above mentioned, made by the tenant, will have been fully and over repaid to him.[169]

The tight-fisted spirit in which Jones valued his tenants' improvements and exploited every possible loophole in the land act in order to avoid paying compensation is exquisitely illustrated by the following extract from a lease to one of his tenants, Denis Hayes:

And in regard to buildings now existing on the farm, it is agreed that the dwelling house and stable at the end are the old dwelling house of the farm, which existed before the deceased became tenant, and was built with mud mortar. It was improved by being slated 20 years ago by Patrick Hayes, but this also, even the quoins [i.e., the corners of the walls], was done with mud mortar, and the timber is white deal. It is 50 ft. long. Timber and Benduff slates were then much cheaper than they are now. The store was built for the butter business when carried on by Patrick Hayes' wife, and since by his son Denis. It was built in 1848, and was not built for the use of the farm. The cowhouse was built by Denis Hayes in the year 1876, when he was not tenant of the farm. Ten feet of the back wall belonged to an old building, and is built of mud mortar. The rest with lime mortar, and slated, but with white deal for the roof. The bills for Benduff slates—£10 10s., and for timber from William Honnor—£8 3s. 8d., were produced. It is agreed that all fences, drains, and other improvements of all kinds were made and paid for by Mr Bence Jones, except such as may have been made over 30 years ago, and have many times overpaid themselves. All are now Mr Bence Jones' property.[170]

The manner in which Jones imposed leases on his unwilling tenants is instructive as well as entertaining. One of them, Joseph

[168] W. B. Jones to editor of *The Times*, quoted in *C.E.*, 5 Jan. 1881.
[169] Quoted in *C.C.*, 23 Feb. 1882.
[170] Quoted ibid.

Noonan of Liscubba, testified in 1882 that Jones had informed him that the land act required every tenant to have a lease, and that he would not let a farm without one. When Noonan replied that he would trust to the land act, rather than have to depend upon a lease, Jones, according to the tenant, went into a rage: 'Noonan, you are getting on with abominable nonsense; if you don't take the place, you will go out of the land; you must take this lease today; I will evict you'. Jones also reportedly balked at paying compensation if Noonan resorted to the protection of the 1870 act:

The dwelling house ... was built in 1843 ..., and he would not allow for it; the stall, stable, and barn were built in '53, and he would not allow for them; the other houses he would not allow for either; the only compensation that he would give was for two bits of reclaimed land.

Fearing that he would be treated no better by the county-court judge who administered the land act, and that in any case he would lose his farm, Noonan finally signed the obnoxious lease. Another tenant, John Walsh, testified that Jones had demanded in 1871 that he surrender twenty acres of his Monteen farm and take a thirty-one-year lease for the remainder at the identical rent. 'If you don't take the lease,' Jones allegedly bellowed, 'I don't care a pin for the compensation under the land act of '70, and I'll make an example of you.' Yet another tenant, Daniel Collins, who held a small farm also in the townland of Monteen, said he visited Jones, who read to him a portion of a lease which he refused to sign: 'Mr Jones got up out of his chair, bowed to me, and I thought he would break the floor with his stamping on it; I got afraid of him, and he said if I did not take the lease he would evict me. . . '. Like Noonan and Walsh, the frightened Collins capitulated to his tyrannical landlord.[171]

Jones obviously carried his anxiety over compensation for improvements to neurotic lengths, but the symptoms of his neurosis were visible in a host of other Cork landlords who adopted leases as one of the most reliable cures for the dreaded disease of legislative interference in the Irish land question. The extreme example of William Bence Jones entirely apart, the evidence of landlord enthusiasm for leases in the 1870s, matched by tenant aversion, is impressive. The tenants on H. J. Hungerford's 3,500-acre estate could hardly have been very enthusiastic when their landlord gave them a choice in 1876 between buying their holdings under the

[171] The above quotations have all been taken from the reported testimony of Noonan, Walsh, and Collins in their cases against Bence Jones before the chief land commissioners (*C.C.*, 23 Feb. 1882).

purchase clauses of the land act and agreeing to sixty-year leases at a moderate rise in rent of 12½ per cent.[172] In accepting the leases, they surrendered all their rights to compensation 'under the provisions of the Landlord and Tenant (Ireland) Act, 1870, or other or subsequent act or acts amending, altering, or extending same'.[173] These so-called compound leases were popularized by the extensive Cork land agent Richard G. Campion. On several properties which he managed in the Carbery district and near Castlelyons, Campion clumsily attempted through his leases to deprive tenants of the benefits of not only the 1870 act, but all future Irish land legislation.[174] Philip Wolfe duplicated Campion's effort on his 1,000-acre estate near Bantry. His tenants were required to promise in their leases to forego any claim for either disturbance or improvements 'under the provisions of the Landlord and Tenant Act, or any extension or amendment thereof, or any act of parliament containing similar or like provisions'.[175]

Frequently enough, tenants took strong exception to the higher rents associated with these leases as much as to the new agreements themselves. Over forty tenants on the former Wallis estate, now owned by R. H. E. White, adamantly denied in 1882 having ever signed their names to leases under which their rents had been raised some years earlier. But if they had not perfected their leases, they had probably signed equally binding agreements to take them.[176] That compulsion was often necessary is beyond question. Notices to quit were instrumental in persuading tenants to accept leases at higher rents on the estates of both Nathaniel Buckley and the earl of Kenmare.[177] Sampson Beamish also served notices to quit and sometimes ejectment decrees in the early 1870s in order to both increase his rental considerably and force his tenants to accept leases containing the most stringent covenants and excluding them from any benefit conferred by the land act.[178] And in the district between Skibbereen and Dunmanway, compulsion was reportedly employed on at least seven estates during the 1870s to induce the tenants to accept leases in which their rents were raised.[179] It is

[172] *C.E.*, 3 Jan. 1881.
[173] *C.C.*, 1 Mar. 1882.
[174] *C.E.*, 26 Apr., 3 May 1881; *W.C.E.*, 11 Mar. 1882.
[175] *C.C.*, 1 Mar. 1882.
[176] *W.C.E.*, 17 June 1882.
[177] See above, pp. 196–8.
[178] *W.C.E.*, 3 Dec. 1881. See also Doherty papers, Letter book, 1880–1: R. W. Doherty, jun., to J. Walsh, 19 May 1881, p. 641; Doherty to D. Crowley, 29 Aug. 1881, p. 803.
[179] *C.E.*, 1 Oct. 1881.

scarcely surprising that so many farmers displayed the great anti-
pathy towards leases which Finlay Dun claimed was characteristic of
the earl of Kenmare's tenants. Unfamiliar with the legal niceties
of the land legislation of 1870, but well aware of the conflicting
implications of the concoctions of their landlords, they wanted no
part of these novel agreements.

The desire of landowners to place their relations with tenants on a
contractual basis in the interests of better farming or extraordinary
revenue helped to make leaseholders of slightly more than 40 per
cent of the tenants in County Cork by 1870. During the following
decade, the efforts of landlords and agents to come to grips with the
financial dangers seen lurking in the 1870 land act perhaps added
another 20 per cent to the earlier figure. Wherever the balance was
finally struck, leaseholders formed a solid majority of Cork tenants
by the late 1870s, when a severe agricultural crisis began. Although
they had by then largely gained formal security of tenure, farmers
often held leases requiring them to pay rents fixed in prosperous
times. Their strivings to throw off the heavy burden of a seemingly or
actually unreasonable lease tended to rouse the entire tenant community into one chorus of discontent at the beginning of the land war.

'FREE SALE'

Besides approving the concept of security of tenure as long as the
rent was paid, the 1870 land act also attempted to encourage
another distinctive feature of the Ulster custom—the right of 'free
sale'. This right entitled a tenant having to surrender his holding to
obtain compensation for his permanent improvements by selling his
interest, or goodwill, to the entering tenant. The benefits of this
feature of the custom, as it existed in the north of Ireland, were
mixed. Finlay Dun observed in 1880 that the premium paid by the
incoming tenant often amounted to £30 or £40 an acre; Dun also
noted that such an investment, even if charged at only 4 or 5
per cent, might well more than double the rent.

If, as too frequently happens, the capital has to be borrowed at 7 to 10 per
cent, independently of any payment whatever to the landlord, it constitutes
a very full rent. So much of the tenants' capital being thus locked up,
diminishes the amount available for the profitable cultivation and stocking
of the land.[180]

While the economic assets of free sale were often overrated, it
certainly helped greatly to preserve agrarian peace. It softened the

[180] Dun, *Landlords and tenants*, p. 99.

rough break between the farmer and his home and land, and usually enabled him to migrate into a town, to another holding, or across the ocean, with enough money to start afresh. It generally protected the new tenant from the rancour and bitterness of the one whom he had supplanted. Many landlords, it is true, increasingly believed that free sale converted a moderate rent into a rack rent, but it also fully protected them from the loss of arrears of rent, which were always deducted from the premium paid for the goodwill. [181]

A practice analogous to free sale had become widespread in Cork and outside the north of Ireland generally before 1881, [182] but the monetary value of a departing tenant's goodwill could hardly be compared with the extravagant sums regularly given on many northern estates. All of the earl of Bandon's tenants were 'allowed to assign their possessory interest, which usually represents five years' rental, or ... about one-fifth of the value of the fee-simple'. [183] A tenant who surrendered his holding on the duke of Devonshire's estates was usually permitted to 'nominate a creditable, reliable successor, and on an average receives for his good will about five years' rent'. [184] Every facility was reportedly given a tenant wishing to dispose of his interest on the earl of Kenmare's estates. Although much higher sums were not unknown, a departing yearly tenant generally received the equivalent of two or three years' rent, whereas a leaseholder usually realized double that amount. [185] On the Kingston estate, where long leases were the rule, and moderate rents an old tradition, tenants who left often obtained premiums 'exceeding the fee-simple value of the land'. [186] And practically every tenant on the almost ninety estates managed by the firm of Hussey and Townsend was allowed to sell his interest, for which he received on the average about five years' rent. [187]

In addition to the vast difference in the amount of premiums, there were other significant variations in the sale of goodwill between Cork and, say, Antrim or Down estates. Cork landlords generally did not recognize free sale as a right won by long usage, but rather conceded it in an attenuated form as a privilege which

[181] For a succinct discussion, see R. B. McDowell, 'From the union to the famine' in T. W. Moody and J. C. Beckett (eds), *Ulster since 1800: a social survey* (London, 1957), pp. 28–9.
[182] Beckett, *Mod. Ire.*, p. 372.
[183] Dun, *Landlords and tenants*, p. 73.
[184] Ibid., p. 55.
[185] Ibid., pp. 79–80.
[186] W. D. Webber to editor of *The Times*, 4 June 1881, quoted in *C.E.*, 9 June 1881.
[187] Dun, *Landlords and tenants*, p. 66.

both leaseholders and yearly tenants had constantly to renew. They also exercised more frequently their unquestioned prerogative of objecting to a proposed purchaser. Richard Doherty, sen., informed Amelia Moorehead in March 1875 that one of her tenants, who had fallen heavily into debt to his brother and to a Cork butter merchant, had asked permission to sell his goodwill to a farmer named Hayes. Doherty strongly advised against this, because 'Hayes has a farm of his own & would not certainly attend to the two'.[188] James Penrose Fitzgerald flatly refused in January 1878 to accept as a tenant on his brother's estate a Whitegate victualler who had already given the departing tenant a large sum of money for her interest, apparently because the victualler was not respectable or solvent enough.[189] Captain Henry Trench, the earl of Egmont's agent, withheld recognition of Thomas Sampson as tenant of a fifty-acre farm which Sampson had purchased from his father-in-law for £500 in January 1879. The land was held under a lease which, as was customary, contained a strict covenant against assignment without the landlord's written consent. Either Sampson never bothered to obtain the requisite approval in advance, or Trench simply refused to give it.[190] Similarly, an interloper who had sent his rent to the Kenmare estate office had it returned to him, because, as the sub-agent firmly told him in October 1880, '*you purchased* Hayes' interest in his farm without the sanction of the earl of Kenmare or Mr Hussey, contrary to the well known, established estate rule & in direct defiance of a notice from the office'.[191]

Also in contrast to the general practice in the north of Ireland, Cork land agents carefully regulated all aspects and stages of these sales. The extent of this regulation is admirably illustrated by an example from Robert Penrose Fitzgerald's property. Discussing in November 1872 the case of one tenant who intended to leave, the agent stated:

The landlord gave his consent to Cox's disposing of the interest in his farm in the *usual* way, that is to say, he is to obtain privately & not by advertisement in the press, the best offer he can from any solvent & respectable tenant, the offer with the proposed tenant's name to be submitted to me; if approved of, Cox is then to hand me his lease, & I will have a new one on exactly the same terms made to the incoming tenant, who will of course pay

[188] Doherty papers, Letter book, 1874–6: R. W. Doherty, sen., to Mrs A. Moorehead, 13 Mar. 1875, p. 354.
[189] P.R.O.I., ref. no. 978, Midleton papers, Letter book, 1873–80: J. P. Fitzgerald to Mrs G. Rowan, 8 Jan. 1878, p. 42.
[190] *C.C.*, 30 Jan. 1882.
[191] Kenmare papers, Letter book, Jan.–Oct. 1880: M. Leonard to J. Connelly, 6 Oct. 1880, p. 926.

the legal expenses. I must also see that the whole of the purchase money is handed over by the incoming tenant to Cox or his authorized representative before possession is given of the lands; also possession of the whole farm, house, etc., will then be handed over by me to the tenant. [192]

There was nothing automatic about the landlord's acceptance of the prospective purchaser, whose offer came as the result of a strictly private search. The entering tenant was required to divulge the amount he had paid, and the agent had to be fully satisfied that there neither were nor would be any surreptitious additional payments.

Besides prohibiting advertisement of a farm in the press, Cork landlords and agents otherwise restricted the range of possible purchasers more often than in the north of Ireland. They sometimes insisted that the search for a buyer be confined to those who already happened to be tenants of the estate. Although the earl of Kenmare's sub-agent told one tenant in 1880 that he had been given permission to 'sell the interest in your farm to the highest bidder, which permission I understand you have availed of', [193] there is considerable doubt as to whether Kenmare's tenants could generally obtain the best offer, either on or off the estate, as it suited them. When another tenant requested official consent to sell his holding in the open market, he was promptly informed in the same year that 'Mr Hussey will not give you permission to sell your farm to a person off the property'. [194] The range of possible purchasers might be narrowed even further to exclude all but adjoining tenants, in order to promote consolidation. In April 1872 Richard Doherty, sen., told James Oswald: 'Condon, one of your tenants who has a small farm . . . , wants to sell his good will & go to America to his sons. Hart [another tenant] wanted me to allow him to be the successor. . . .' But since Hart's holding was a long distance from Condon's, Doherty demurred: 'I think if I could get it for a reasonable sum & hand it to Mr Scott if he will pay Condon, it would be better . . . , so as to have all the land at that side of the road in one gent's hands. . . '. [195] After he had assumed the management of the earl of Bandon's estates in 1877, Doherty demonstrated the same desire to 'dispose of farms vacated to neighbours and thus consolidate the

[192] P.R.O.I., ref. no. 978, Midleton papers, Letter book, 1867–72: J. P. Fitzgerald to [illegible], 5 Nov. 1872, p. 178.
[193] Kenmare papers, Letter book, Jan.–Oct. 1880: M. Leonard to J. Hayes, 13 Oct. 1880, p. 962.
[194] Ibid.: Leonard to P. Carroll, 24 Feb. 1880, p. 239.
[195] Doherty papers, Letter book, 1871–3: R. W. Doherty, sen., to J. J. Oswald, 13 Apr. 1872, pp. 444–5.

smaller holdings'.[196] As their selection was preordained, adjacent farmers probably paid less for a departing tenant's goodwill than an outsider straining to obtain a holding on the estate.

The landlord's right of reasonable objection, the prohibition of public advertisement, and the refusal to accept as tenants either strangers to the estate or non-adjoining farmers all could have the effect of diminishing the value of the departing tenant's interest. What could most seriously impair that value, however, was the actual selection of the entering tenant by the landlord or his agent. This mockery of free sale naturally incensed its victims, if not its beneficiaries.[197] One of the earl of Egmont's tenants, David Walsh, complained bitterly that Egmont's agent had chosen Henry O'Connor as the new tenant of a farm that he had vacated in 1879.

If Mr O'Connor left my farm alone, and let my goodwill be obtained in such a large holding of 130 acres, I should realize as much for my interest and goodwill of the place as would satisfy all claims and creditors, for 3 or 4 persons . . . asked for my permission and goodwill to take the place, but it was useless, for Mr O'Connor had made his terms with the earl of Egmont, and no other need apply.[198]

Although his rent had been as much as £300 per annum, Walsh obtained only £450 for his interest from O'Connor, and this was completely washed away by his debts. He protested that at the time he quit his holding, his goodwill had been worth at least £1,200.[199] Similarly, one of the dowager countess of Kingston's tenants became incensed when the agent prohibited him in 1880 from selling the goodwill of a portion of his farm—a yearly tenancy and separate letting from the rest—to anyone but another Kingston tenant named Donohue. When he learned that he had received preference over a second competitor, Donohue promptly reduced his offer from £140 to £75, which barely met the departing tenant's debts.[200] Another instance of selection led to agrarian outrage. When a farmer named John O'Connor fell into arrears and had to

---

[196] Dun, *Landlords and tenants*, p. 73.

[197] One Cork land agent reported in September 1879 that after he had given a tenant permission to sell his goodwill, this tenant's brother had come to him and said: 'I hear, sir, you have given my brother leave to sell his holding. Now I do not think it fair or right that he should sell it to anyone but me, and I ask you to stop the sale of it to anyone else.' When informed that the agent was merely granting the demand of the home rulers for free sale, the envious brother remarked that he 'would rather have the farm than their home rule' (*C.C.*, 16 Sept. 1879).

[198] *C.E.*, 6 Jan. 1881.

[199] Ibid.

[200] Ibid., 30 Dec. 1880.

surrender part of his land on Viscount Doneraile's estate, the agent Henry Longfield chose a gentleman farmer who lived near Buttevant, William Lysaght, as the approved purchaser of O'Connor's goodwill. Lysaght had already become extremely unpopular by purchasing the interest in a number of other farms in the district; he held three from Lord Doneraile alone by 1881. Heated disagreement arose between Lysaght and O'Connor, who was apparently dissatisfied with the amount given for his goodwill. After he had adamantly refused to alter Longfield's arrangement, Lysaght received a threatening note:

> If you put a foot on this ground to plough, you or your man will be [shot], as sure as God made you. . . . We have threatened you before; don't think it is the O'Connor's [who] will do it. Rory of the Hills. We defy the police.

When Lysaght's ploughman was shot and slightly wounded, the police ignored 'Rory's' advice and arrested John O'Connor and his brother Thomas. [201]

In addition to these serious restrictions on the sale of goodwill, landlords and agents imposed others in response to certain provisions of the 1870 land act. Gladstone's legislation, of course, was intended only to encourage free sale by offering the landlord complete immunity from demands for compensation for permanent improvements as long as he gave a departing tenant leave to dispose of his interest. [202] The reasoning behind this provision was straightforward: the landlord who evicted a tenant for non-payment of rent must either compensate him for his permanent improvements, or he must allow him to find that compensation in free sale. Other provisions, however, threatened the pocket of the landlord who gave his express or even implied consent to the payment of goodwill. For if he were ever obliged to evict a defaulting tenant who had made such a payment on entry, he could be required to reimburse the tenant for this outlay. [203] Landlords and agents commonly reacted by refusing thereafter to sanction the sale of annual tenancies, unless they obtained a specific promise that such a demand would not be pressed. The duke of Devonshire's contracts for yearly tenants strictly provided that 'no claim shall be entertained for compensation for money given as premium on coming into possession, excepting when specified in the agreements'. [204] Others took no chances and went the whole distance. James Penrose Fitzgerald

[201] Ibid., 24 Feb. 1881.
[202] Morris, *Land act*, p. 96.
[203] Ibid., pp. 66, 128.
[204] Dun, *Landlords and tenants*, pp. 57–8.

would not permit annual tenants on Viscount Midleton's estate to sell their goodwill after 1870. [205] Replying to a request from a yearly tenant on the Stoughton property in County Kerry, Samuel Hussey pointed out in May 1878 that 'since the passing of the land act of 1870, it is impossible for Mr Stoughton or any other landlord to allow any of their tenants [to] sell their farms'. [206] On the earl of Kenmare's estates, declared Hussey in August 1880, 'I have occasionally made a lease to a tenant to enable him to sell, but I have never allowed a yearly tenant to sell'. [207] Leasehold tenancies, however, continued to be sold on nearly all estates, although generally under tight safeguards. James Penrose Fitzgerald consented in July 1877 to an assignment of a lease by one of his brother's tenants, but with the distinct agreement that this assignment was 'not to create a right to compensation at the expiration of the lease in consideration of any money paid . . . for it'. [208] Equally concerned, Robert Cole Bowen adopted similar precautions; his leases specifically prohibited the tenant quitting his farm to 'have or make any claim for compensation under the seventh section of the Landlord and Tenant (Ireland) Act, 1870, in respect of any money or monies worth paid or given by him' when he entered into possession of his holding. For good measure, Bowen's leases declared categorically that neither the lands nor the premises mentioned therein were 'subject to the Ulster tenant right custom, or any other usage mentioned or referred to in the Landlord and Tenant (Ireland) Act, 1870'. [209]

Still other difficulties came to surround the sale of goodwill when the agricultural crisis began in the late 1870s. Tenants who suddenly desired to sell their goodwill were often only seeking a convenient way to dodge a host of small but petulant creditors. Understandably, landlords refused to co-operate in these crude attempts at deception. Samuel Hussey established a rule on the earl of Kenmare's estates

[205] P.R.O.I., ref. no. 978, Midleton papers, Letter book, 1873–80: J. P. Fitzgerald to [illegible], [?] Aug. 1879, p. 313.

[206] Kenmare papers, Letter book, Jan.–Aug. 1878: S. M. Hussey to J. Kelly, 31 May 1878, p. 775.

[207] Ibid., Letter book, Jan.–Oct. 1880: Hussey to marquis of Lansdowne, 16 Aug. 1880, p. 736. Hussey did in fact permit some yearly tenants on the Kenmare estates to sell their interests. The meaning of his denial is unclear, but he may have wished to say that yearly tenants could never sell without official leave, which might be refused or granted only under specific conditions.

[208] P.R.O.I., ref. no. 978, Midleton papers, Letter book, 1873–80: J. P. Fitzgerald to W. Sullivan, 17 July 1877, p. 32.

[209] Bowen papers, N.L.I., box 30, iv: Printed lease prepared for use on Robert Cole Bowen's estates, unperfected and undated, but post-1870.

that 'tenants who wish to part with their interests must make some provision to pay their creditors before he will give his consent to the assignment'. [210] Desperately trying to keep two steps ahead of the bill collector, tenants frequently neglected to request permission for these sales, and they or those whom they duped into parting with their money usually suffered the consequences. Hussey's reaction was no doubt typical. In March 1879 he told his employer Sir George Colthurst, 'Several farms have been sold at Ballyvourney without leave, so I must serve notices to quit'. [211] And a few months later, Hussey sent instructions to the resident agent of Lord Kenmare's Bantry estate, directing him 'in every case of a yearly tenancy [sold for debts] to serve a notice to quit', but noting that 'with regard to the leaseholders, nothing can be done'. [212] Landlords and agents strongly resisted the attempts of all kinds of creditors to supplant bankrupt tenants whose farms were carried to execution sales. After he had publicly warned that he would refuse to recognize the purchaser in one such instance, Richard Doherty, sen., became quite vexed in May 1879 when the sale took place despite his *caveat*.

The sale of Caverly's farm was contrary to the rules & customs on the earl of Bandon's estate. . . . I assure you the earl of Bandon does not & will not sanction the sale nor accept . . . [the purchaser] as tenant & is determined to take proceedings to enforce the rules & customs on his estate & thus show an example that his lands cannot be sold by execution sales nor in [any] other manner dealt with without his approval & consent. [213]

In summary, the sale of goodwill in County Cork was never a right in the strict sense: it was necessary to obtain the landlord's permission in advance, and in writing, and he could refuse to approve the proposed purchaser. The sale was also subject to the agent's interference: he could designate neighbours, exclude strangers, and even select individuals in some cases. After the passage of the land act in 1870, many yearly tenants were no longer allowed to dispose of their interests, and many others were deprived of any claim against their landlord for money given to departing tenants

[210] Kenmare papers, Letter book, 1879–80: M. Leonard to J. Donovan, 1 Oct. 1879, p. 562.

[211] Ibid., Letter book, 1878–9: S. M. Hussey to Sir G. St J. Colthurst, 4 Mar. 1879.

[212] The leases of Kenmare's tenants at Bantry apparently did not contain the customary clause against assignment without the landlord's written consent (ibid., Letter book, 1879–80: M. Leonard to J. E. Barrett, 3 July 1879, p. 252).

[213] Doherty papers, Letter book, 1876–9: R. W. Doherty, sen., to R. Notter, 31 May 1879, p. 538. See also ibid., Letter book, 1880–6: Doherty, sen., to J. J. Oswald, 20 Dec. 1880, pp. 216–17.

when they entered into possession. All these limitations made the privilege of restricted sale much less attractive than the full-blown right of free sale. Nevertheless, as the agricultural crisis deepened in the late 1870s, the pressure for the recognition of the unhindered right rather than its pale imitation increased apace. With both more failures and near failures, especially among smallholders, the number of those who wished to sell their goodwill multiplied at an alarming rate. The adamant refusal of some landlords to sanction the sale of yearly tenancies, before objectionable mainly in theory, now became a bruising grievance.

V

LIVING STANDARDS, 1851–91

~~~~~~

THE GREAT FAMINE was a watershed in Irish demographic history, marking the end of one period of rapid population growth and the beginning of another period of pronounced decline. Between 1851 and 1891 the population of Ireland fell from 6·6 to 4·7 million, or by 28 per cent.[1] This extraordinary development, unique among European countries during the second half of the nineteenth century, was brought about primarily by exceptionally heavy emigration and secondarily by the increasingly widespread postponement of marriage, which led to a sluggish rate of natural increase. Other European nations also witnessed a massive exodus during the years of what Marcus Hansen called the 'great Atlantic migration', but nowhere except in Ireland did the movement result in a large population decline.[2] The economic consequences of emigration were, moreover, perhaps nowhere as beneficial for those Europeans who remained at home as in Ireland during the half-century after the famine. Together, emigration, the postponement of marriage, and the great rise in British living standards, which so powerfully and profitably reoriented Irish agriculture towards livestock farming, caused dramatic improvements in the quality of Irish rural life between 1851 and 1876. Some of the most notable of these improvements, such as those in housing, diet, and education, even resisted permanent erosion during the agricultural depression of the late 1870s and the 1880s.

[1] *Census Ire., 1901*, pt i, vol. ii, no. 2 [Cd 1058–I], H.C. 1902, cxxiv, 179, p. 4.
[2] A. Schrier, *Ireland and the American emigration, 1850–1900* (Minneapolis and London, 1958), p. 3.

MARRIAGE AND DEMOGRAPHIC CHANGES

Of all Irish counties, Cork experienced the most drastic population loss between 1851 and 1891. In only forty years the number of its inhabitants plummeted from nearly 649,000 to less than 439,000, or by 32 per cent. The rate of decline was uneven from decade to decade—only one-third or one-fourth as high during the 1860s and 1870s as in the 1850s but more than twice as high during the 1880s as in the previous two decades.[3] Nor was the rate of decline uniform geographically within the county. Half of the eighteen Cork poor-law unions underwent smaller population losses ranging from 21 to 33 per cent, while the other half suffered larger declines ranging from 35 to 48 per cent. These variations followed a distinct geographical pattern. Cork union with its heavily urban character aside, the six poor-law unions in more prosperous East Cork suffered an aggregate population loss of over 43 per cent, whereas the eleven poor-law unions in less prosperous West Cork experienced a significantly lighter aggregate decline of only 32 per cent.[4]

As there was no considerable permanent migration from the county to other parts of Ireland, Cork's drastic population loss could only have resulted from emigration and a falling rate of natural increase (i.e., excess of births over deaths). From 1864, when the official registration of births, deaths, and marriages began, the birth rate fell steadily while the death rate remained fairly constant, with the result that by the 1880s the rate of natural increase was only about half as high as in the 1860s. Again, there were wide variations within the county that fell into a clear geographical pattern. There is a strong correlation between areas of relatively small natural increase and areas of relatively large population loss. The same east-west division reappears, only in sharper relief. The seven poor-law unions of East Cork possessed aggregate rates of natural increase of merely 8 and 5 per thousand in the 1860s and 1870s respectively, whereas the corresponding figures for the eleven poor-law unions of West Cork were 17 and 13 per thousand, or well more than double.[5]

A transformation in marriage customs lay at the root of both the sluggishness and the east-west divergence in the rate of natural increase. Before the famine, the people of rural Ireland tended to

[3] The exact rates of population decline were as follows: 1851–61, 16·0 per cent; 1861–71, 5·1 per cent; 1871–81, 4·2 per cent; and 1881–91, 11·5 per cent.

[4] *Census Ire., 1911: . . . county and city of Cork,* p. 4.

[5] *Census Ire., 1871,* pt i, vol. ii, no. 2 [C 873–II], H.C. 1873, lxxii, pt i, 119, p. 270; *Census Ire., 1881,* pt i [3148–II], H.C. 1882, lxxvii, 119, p. 270; *Census Ire., 1891,* pt i, vol. ii, no. 2 [C 6567–I], H.C. 1892, xci, 123, p. 270.

marry at a relatively early age, largely because of the ease with which small holdings could be acquired. [6] Love matches were then the rule, although the arranged match and the dowry system had already made their appearance. At this early stage, arranged matches were most common in the rich grazing counties of eastern Ireland such as Kilkenny, where in 1839 there was

> apparently very little love or sentiment between the interested pair, the whole affair being conducted and concluded by the parents and friends on both sides in quite a businesslike manner, just as they would dispose of their stock or swap a farm. [7]

But the dowry, or 'fortune', was at least known in many parts of Cork. In 1835 it was not unusual in the parish of Durrus near Bantry 'for a cottier who pays £8 or £10 a-year rent . . . to give his son or daughter a marriage portion of £20'.[8] In 1839 a farmer on the Conner estate near Dunmanway created a trust fund of £100 'in consideration of natural love and affection which he hath and beareth towards his daughter . . . and for the purpose of securing a fortune or marriage portion for her on the day of her marriage'. [9] Arranged matches were apparently well known on the Smyth estate near Youghal in 1845, although a local parish priest reported that daughters currently remained 'an incumbrance on the land, from the utter inability of their parents to pay the smallest portion that would procure a fitting match amongst persons of their own class in life'. [10] Nevertheless, as a rule, marriage was contracted at a comparatively early age before the famine, especially but not exclusively among the labouring classes. [11] In 1841, 12 per cent of all married women in Cork were under twenty-six years of age, whereas in 1891 only 5 per cent were under twenty-five. [12]

Even before the famine, however, landowners had reduced the tendency to marry early by forbidding farmers to divide their holdings

---

[6] Connell's thesis that early marriages were a leading cause of pre-famine population growth has been challenged by Drake, but the most recent contribution to the debate by Lee largely supports Connell's views. For an admirable summary of the debate, see B. M. Walsh, 'A perspective on Irish population patterns' in *Eire-Ireland*, iv, no. 3 (autumn 1969), pp. 4–5.

[7] Kegan, *Young Irishman's diary*, p. 24.

[8] *Poor inquiry, supplement to appendix E*, p. 164.

[9] Conner papers: Deed of trust between John Beamish, farmer, and Thomas Beamish and Michael Kearney, farmers, Aug. 1839.

[10] *C.E.*, 12 Sept. 1845.

[11] *Poor inquiry, supplement to appendix E*, p. 177; J. Lee, 'Marriage and population in pre-famine Ireland' in *Econ. Hist. Rev.*, ser. 2, xxi, no. 2 (Aug. 1968), p. 286.

[12] *Census Ire., 1841*, pp. 168–9; *Census Ire., 1891*, pt i, vol. ii, no. 2, p. 280.

among their sons, and the extent and effectiveness of these efforts increased as time passed.[13] Other pressures undermined early marriages during and after the famine. With the landlord policies of clearance and consolidation as well as the shift towards grassland farming, small holdings on which to start and support a family became extremely difficult to obtain. Now that potato yields had diminished and subdivision had proved self-defeating, an early marriage seemed much less desirable and emigration much more so. When succession to the family holding became limited to a sole heir, the other children were usually

reared to regard their own emigration as a very real possibility: the person thinking of emigrating is unlikely to marry, and it is easier for the boy waiting for the land to remain unmarried if his friends are single too.[14]

The sole heir was now obliged to postpone marriage, for 'there must be none of the folly of expecting . . . [the land] to support a second family before the first was dying, or dead, or dispersed'; he could marry only 'when his father decided, and he must marry a woman able to enhance the value of the land and ensure its succession—he must, in short, marry the bride of the old man's choice'.[15] Table 37 helps to demonstrate the extent to which marriage was postponed as the arranged match spread and took root throughout the county during the second half of the nineteenth century.[16]

TABLE 37 Percentage of married men and women in Cork who were under 30, 1861–91

year	men	women
1861	10·2	23·2
1871	9·4	20·1
1881	8·1	16·6
1891	7·1	15·1

As marriage was increasingly delayed, the number of marriages decreased even faster than population. Between 1871 and 1891 the crude marriage rate declined from 5·4 to 4·2 per thousand.[17] In some

[13] See above, Chapter I, pp. 59–62; Chapter III, pp. 158–63.
[14] Connell, 'Peasant marriage', p. 522.
[15] Ibid.
[16] *Census Ire., 1861*, pt v [3204–IV], H.C. 1863, lxi, 1, pp. 171, 187, 197; *Census Ire., 1871*, pt i, vol. ii, no. 2, p. 280; *Census Ire., 1881*, pt i, vol. ii, no. 2, p. 280; *Census Ire., 1891*, pt i, vol. ii, no. 2, p. 280.
[17] *Eighth annual report of the registrar-general of marriages, births, and deaths in Ireland, 1871* [Cd 968], H.C. 1874, xiv, 357, p. 42; *Twenty-eighth detailed annual report of the registrar-general (Ireland); containing a general abstract of the*

districts where the fall was sharper than in others, this aroused considerable anxiety among the clergy, partly because it jeopardized their income from marriage dues. [18] The curate of Cloyne complained loudly in December 1880 that on the two most extensive estates within his parish, 'each estate having more than 200 families of the agricultural classes resident on it, only two men of these classes . . . have got married in any of the four chapels of the parish for the last three and a half years'. 'I have no knowledge', he added, 'of more than one other of them getting married elsewhere.' [19] This complaint may well reflect not merely the phenomenon of later marriage but also the rise in celibacy, which was a more recent development. Although it was not reflected on a significant scale in the statistics until the very end of the century, abstention from marriage began seriously to affect the rate of natural increase in the 1880s. Compared with some other counties such as Londonderry, however, Cork had a rate of celibacy which was much less important than the simple postponement of marriage in reducing the rate of natural increase, as Table 38 shows. [20]

Even though the trend was towards arranged marriages at a later

TABLE 38   Percentage of women in Cork and Londonderry in the 45–54 age group who were unmarried and not widowed, 1841–1901

year	Cork spinsters	Londonderry spinsters
1841	11·2	16·8
1851	10·2	18·8
1861	11·8	20·9
1871	12·0	23·3
1881	13·3	23·4
1891	13·3	26·1
1901	18·6	30·1

[18] For performing a marriage, a priest usually received about 10 per cent of the girl's fortune (G. Pellew, *In castle and cabin, or talks in Ireland in 1887* (New York and London, 1888), p. 97).

[19] *C.E.*, 11 Dec. 1880.

[20] *Census Ire., 1841*, pp. 168–9; *Census Ire., 1851*, pt vi [2134], H.C. 1856, xxxi, 1, pp. 231, 251, 267; *Census Ire., 1861*, pt v, pp. 171, 187, 197; *Census Ire., 1871*, pt i, vol. ii, no. 2, p. 280; *Census Ire., 1881*, pt i, vol. ii, no. 2, p. 280; *Census Ire., 1891*, pt i, vol. ii, no. 2, p. 280; *Census Ire., 1901*, pt i, vol. ii, no. 2, p. 191; J. H. Johnson, 'Marriage and fertility in nineteenth century Londonderry' in *Stat. Soc. Ire. Jn.*, xx, pt i (1958), p. 104.

numbers of marriages, births, and deaths registered in Ireland during the year 1891, transmitted pursuant to the provisions of the 7 & 8 Vic., cap. 81, s. 56; 26 Vic., cap. 11; and 26 & 27 Vic., cap. 90 [C 6787], H.C. 1892, xxiv, 313, p. 44.

age, it was not uniform throughout County Cork. Marriage was contracted earlier in the west down to the 1870s, thus attesting to the strength of traditional folkways in the face of opposing economic pressures. None of the censuses between 1851 and 1891 indicate either the age at marriage or the fertility of marriages, but they do provide a rough indication of both by classifying the population according to age and marital status. Once again, the fundamental east-west division is thrown into relief by the proportion of fertile women (i.e., those aged fifteen to forty-four) who were married. At the same time that this proportion was falling slowly in the rural districts of East Cork during the 1850s, it was actually rising in West Cork. This rising trend in the west was gradually halted in the 1860s, but an imbalance still existed in 1871, when 51 per cent of the fertile women in the west were married, as compared to 44 per cent in the east. At one extreme stood Youghal union, where only 41 per cent of fertile women had husbands; at the other extreme stood Bantry union, where the corresponding figure was as high as 68 per cent. This clear east–west contrast in marriage customs largely explains the equally distinct contrast in the rate of natural increase between the two divisions discussed previously. In the next two decades, however, West Cork's marriage customs came to mirror those of East Cork more closely, so much so, in fact, that by 1891 there was scarcely any difference between them in the proportion of fertile women who were married. [21]

If marriages were increasingly fewer and later after the famine, they were also the subject of careful negotiation and cold calculation between the families of the intended bride and groom (whose love for one another now rarely mattered). Actual practice corresponded closely with what one old sage reputedly told a young lad who liked a girl with only one cow to her fortune better than her rival with two: 'Take the gyurl wid the two cows. There isn't the difference of a cow, begorra, betune any two women in the wor-r-ld.' [22] Not love, but the amount of the girl's dowry and the size and quality of the boy's farm, along with his title to the land, were the crucial considerations in the arrangement of the match. Before the 'bindings', or settlement, could be prepared by a solicitor in the nearest town about Shrovetide, [23] the landlord or his agent needed to be consulted in

---

[21] *Census Ire., 1851*, pt vi, pp. 231, 251, 267; *Census Ire., 1861*, pt v, pp. 171, 187, 197; *Census Ire., 1871*, pt i, vol. ii, no. 2, pp. 278–80; *Census Ire., 1881*, pt i, vol. ii, no. 2, pp. 278–80; *Census Ire., 1891*, pt i, vol. ii, no. 2, pp. 278–80.

[22] Quoted in Becker, *Disturbed Ire.*, p. 270.

[23] *Bessborough comm. evidence*, pt ii, p. 949; Irish Folklore Commission: MS 1429, pp. 246, 256–7.

regard to the change of tenancy, and to approve if a prospective son-in-law were to marry into a farm on the estate.[24] For the girl's parents were naturally anxious about the security of the boy's title to the land and its ability to bear the rent placed upon it. A lease was sometimes a necessity and always a good bargaining point for the prospective groom. When a tenant on the Brasier estate desired to have his son married, he applied to the landlord for a lease and a reduction in rent, surprisingly received both, and as a result, obtained a considerable fortune with his daughter-in-law.[25] One tenant on the Jones estate explained in 1882 why he took out a lease about twenty years earlier: 'I was unmarried then, and some people were match-making with me; they would not finish the match unless I had a lease, for they did not like the character of the landlord'.[26] Matchmakers did well to ascertain the landlord's intentions, because increases of rent occurred frequently when tenancies changed hands through marriage.

It is a fact too well known [complained the duke of Devonshire's tenants in a memorial in December 1885] that no parent was allowed the exercise of his right . . . to get his son or daughter married without the consent and sanction of the agent, which were invariably withheld unless the new tenant consented to a considerable increase of the rent. . . .[27]

An increase in rent, or the prospect of one, could easily upset a proposed match, as it did in one notorious case on the Egmont estate in 1879.[28]

Where the rent was moderate, the title well established, and the land in good heart, a substantial dowry had to be provided. Its amount partly depended on the social standing of the two families and the personal qualities of the intended couple but was mostly determined by the desirability of the boy's farm.[29] Among small farmers, the fortune was often paid partly in kind—in livestock or household goods. When one tenant on the Buckley estate whose rent

[24] Ormathwaite papers: Journal of Sir John Benn-Walsh, 25 Aug. 1864, pp. 214–15. See also Kenmare papers, Letter book, Jan.–Aug. 1878: S. M. Hussey to Sir G. Colthurst, 11 Feb. 1878, pp. 218–19; Letter book, 1878–9: F. Denny to C. O'Connell, 17 Feb. 1879, p. 756; S. M. Hussey to J. Good, 24 Feb. 1879, p. 793; P.R.O.I., ref. no. 978, Midleton papers, Letter book, 1883–4: J. P. Fitzgerald to G. Heard, 9 Jan. 1884, p. 119; *C.C.*, 21 Feb. 1882.

[25] *C.E.*, 4 Aug. 1881.

[26] *C.C.*, 23 Feb. 1882.

[27] Tenants' memorial to duke of Devonshire, 4 Dec. 1885, quoted in *C.C.*, 18 Dec. 1885; see also duke of Devonshire to R. H. Power, 15 Dec. 1885, quoted ibid.

[28] *C.E.*, 6 Feb. 1880.

[29] Connell, 'Peasant marriage', p. 504.

was only £17 10s. had his daughter married in the late 1860s, he dowered her with £80 in 'means' and money: 'I gave her a couple of in-calf cows, and when he [i.e., the son-in-law] would be in want of a couple of pounds, I would give it to him. I gave him £26 before I made the match.'[30] As this passage indicates, part of the fortune was often withheld until after the marriage took place, and such a practice sometimes led to inter-family feuds later on. Thus in 1882 the sheriff seized twenty-three cows on the farm of one apparently prosperous tenant near Mitchelstown in executing a superior-court writ brought by the tenant's son-in-law for recovery of a £200 dowry promised with his wife.[31] A man marrying into the farm of an only daughter or a widow was also expected to bring a fortune. When a widow with 135 acres (at a rent of £185 per annum) on the earl of Donoughmore's estate remarried in 1867, her second husband brought £700 into the farm.[32] Gerald Fitzgibbon's son-in-law paid him £500 to obtain the assignment of a fifty-acre holding (at a rent of £75 per annum) on the earl of Egmont's estate in 1879.[33]

Such sums as these may appear extravagant and exceptional, but with their increased prosperity, farmers were indeed fond of 'laying up nest eggs' to provide portions for their sons and daughters, as one agent remarked in 1865.[34] The amounts of their savings for the purpose of settling as many of their children as possible on the land were quite remarkable. These savings were largely reflected in the enormous rise in Irish joint-stock bank deposits from £8,263,000 in 1851 to a peak of £32,815,000 in 1876.[35] As early as the 1860s, circumstances favoured large dowries. Bence Jones asserted that while he knew of only two fortunes of £500, others of £100 were quite common on his estate and any sum less than £50 would be considered extremely low.[36] One farmer thought £200 a small price to pay for the interest in a thirty-four-acre holding (at a rent of £37 per annum) on the earl of Devon's estate in 1865, for as he said, 'It will not cost anything because I shall get a wife, and she will have 200*l*'.[37] The high prosperity of the early 1870s encouraged

[30] *Bridge v. Casey*, p. 55. See also ibid., p. 18.
[31] *C.E.*, 9 Feb. 1882.
[32] *C.C.*, 7 Mar. 1883.
[33] Ibid., 30 Jan. 1882. See also *C.E.*, 12 Apr. 1882.
[34] *Report from the select committee on Tenure and Improvement of Land (Ireland) Act; together with the proceedings of the committee, minutes of evidence, appendix, and index*, H.C. 1865 (402), xi, 341, p. 216 (hereafter cited as *Maguire committee evidence*).
[35] D. B. King, *The Irish question* (New York and London, 1882), p. 279.
[36] Jones, *Life's work*, p. 24.
[37] Quoted in *Maguire committee evidence*, p. 208.

larger dowries than ever before, and even when prices began to fall in the latter part of the decade, fortunes six or seven times the rent of the land with which they were joined were not unusual. [38] John Caniffe of Ballinadee must have been a very wealthy farmer to have been able to offer fortunes of £300 apiece to two of his younger daughters in 1881, after he had already given an equal amount to his eldest daughter upon her marriage. [39] But even moderately well-to-do farmers commonly did as much for at least one of their daughters. The land agent Samuel Hussey, whose wide experience made him a competent judge of such matters, declared in 1881 that Cork tenants paying rents of only £30 or £40 per annum regularly dowered their daughters with £300 or £400. [40] The arranged match, with its liberal fortunes, was thus not only an essential mechanism by which the farming community adjusted after the famine to altered economic conditions and landlord decrees against subdivision; it was also at once an important cause and a clear reflection of its increased material welfare.

THE EMIGRANT STREAM

More important than either later marriage or celibacy in reducing population and raising living standards was exceptionally heavy emigration. Almost 425,000 persons—more proportionately than from any other Irish county—officially emigrated from Cork between 1851 and 1891. The exodus was especially strong during the 1850s and 1860s, when nearly one-fourth of the population left the county; it subsided significantly in the 1870s only to gather momentum again in the 1880s, when nearly one-fifth of Cork's population emigrated. Males predominated among the emigrants by a margin of close to 10 per cent, except during the 1850s, when slightly more women than men left. [41] The movement of entire families assumed greater importance in times of agricultural crisis prompted by crop failures, such as during the early 1850s and 1860s. [42] In ordinary times, however, individuals—invariably young men and women in their twenties—formed the overwhelming majority of the emigrants. Even in the spring of 1881, after a great agricultural crisis had barely

[38] Kenmare papers, Letter book, 1882–3: S. M. Hussey to Colonel Dease, 18 Apr. 1883, pp. 823–4; *C.C.*, 30 Jan. 1882; *C.E.*, 23 Nov. 1882.

[39] Doherty papers, Letter book, 1880–1: R. W. Doherty, jun., to Fr Dunlea, 16 Aug. 1881, p. 764.

[40] Connell, 'Peasant marriage', p. 504.

[41] *Census Ire., 1891*, pt i, vol. ii, no. 2, p. 406.

[42] S. H. Cousens, 'The regional variations in population changes in Ireland, 1861–1881' in *Econ. Hist. Rev.*, ser. 2, xvii, no. 2 (Dec. 1964), pp. 311–13.

passed, 'very few families' were reported to be leaving Queenstown harbour, and in 1885 it was observed that the emigrants were 'all young men and young women; very few families [were] to be seen'.[43] 'One of the most alarming features of the present exodus', declared another observer in the spring of 1887, 'is the fact that nearly all the emigrants are young men and women of . . . [from] 18 to 30. The pick and flower of the land, so to speak, are going.'[44]

While the youthfulness of these emigrants could not be mistaken, their social status was often ill defined. Contemporary newspaper accounts frequently used omnibus terms, such as 'peasants' or 'agricultural classes', to describe them, or limited their comments to physical appearances, which then as now could be deceptive. It is clear, however, that when the complete destitution that had drastically curtailed the emigration of landless labourers during the famine receded in the early 1850s, this class began to leave in great numbers. In fact, the exceptionally heavy exodus from Cork and certain other Munster counties during the decade was mostly the product of 'a large labouring population, quite unable to obtain a foothold on the land at home, and whose only alternative to pauperism was emigration'.[45] This was especially true where holdings of thirty acres or more were most prevalent, as in the poor-law unions of Dunmanway, Macroom, and Millstreet, all three having more than 65 per cent of their holdings in this category in 1851.[46] After the 1850s, however, landless labourers comprised a somewhat smaller share of Cork's emigrants, if appearances corresponded with reality. 'The emigrants taken from this port appear to be of the better farming class', remarked one observer in the spring of 1860.[47] And the men leaving in 1864 were usually dressed comfortably, while the women were 'decked out in every absurdity of hat and hoops and feather and ribbon'.[48] For these well-dressed farmers' sons and daughters who had absolutely no desire to become hired labourers, there was much less room left in Ireland, now that landlords had resolutely set their faces against the subdivision of land which had brought such misery upon the country during the famine.

At all times, however, the labouring rather than the farming classes provided the overwhelming majority of emigrants, thanks in large measure to the remarkable development of a self-perpetuating

[43] *C.E.*, 18 Apr. 1881, 23 Apr. 1885.

[44] Ibid., 22 Apr. 1887.

[45] S. H. Cousens, 'Emigration and demographic change in Ireland, 1851–1861' in *Econ. Hist. Rev.*, ser. 2, xiv, no. 2 (Dec. 1961), p. 285.

[46] *Census Ire., 1851*, pt ii: *Returns of agricultural produce in 1851*, pp. 636–40.

[47] *C.C.*, 10 Apr. 1860.

[48] Ibid., 8 Mar. 1864.

system of emigrant remittances. These remittances 'came to assume such large proportions that the 40 per cent which arrived as prepaid passage tickets alone paid for more than 75 per cent of all Irish emigration in the fifty years following the famine'. [49] Both the *Cork Constitution* and the *Kerry Post* agreed in 1860 that because of the remittances arriving in every mail from friends in America, 'the class of persons who are leaving the south of Ireland for the new world this year are principally farm labourers and household servants', with only 'a limited proportion of the children of small farmers'. [50] Similarly, while there were many farmers' children among the emigrants waiting to depart from Queenstown in the spring of 1882, 'the great bulk seems to be provided by the agricultural labourers, who as a rule go upon prepaid tickets, their passages being paid by their friends in America'. [51] Again, when the season opened in the spring of 1885, all those leaving from Queenstown belonged to 'the agricultural labouring class, with a small sprinkling of farmers and mechanics'. [52] This continually heavy outflow of landless labourers and farm servants was primarily responsible for the fact that Cork experienced a greater intensity of emigration than any other Irish county during the second half of the nineteenth century. And it was also largely responsible for a radical alteration in the social composition of the population that remained at home. Whereas the 1841 census list of occupations in Cork had shown almost 149,000 labourers and servants along with 41,000 farmers, the 1891 census enumerated only about 34,000 labourers and servants along with 29,000 farmers. [53] This amounted to nothing less than a social revolution.

The uneven distribution of labourers within the county as well as other factors might have produced considerable variation in the geography of emigration. The earlier marriages and consequently higher rate of natural increase in West Cork meant of course that population pressure remained greater there than in the eastern part of the county. In six southwestern unions, population density regularly exceeded 600 per square mile of cultivated land, and in Castletown union, reached almost 1,400 per square mile—higher than anywhere else in Ireland with the exception of urban unions. In the rural eastern and northwestern parts of the county, on the

[49] Schrier, *American emigration*, p. 111.
[50] From *Kerry Post*, quoted in *C.C.*, 4 May 1860.
[51] *C.E.*, 29 Apr. 1882. See also ibid., 4 May 1883.
[52] Ibid., 23 Apr. 1885.
[53] *Census Ire., 1841*, p. 194; *Census Ire., 1891*, pt i, vol. ii, no. 2, pp. 287, 293. The 1891 census also listed 12,564 close relatives of farmers (sons, grandsons, brothers, nephews) who have not been included above.

other hand, densities ranged from 400 to 600 per square mile.[54] Not only were the people of West Cork more densely settled on the land, but their land was also less fertile and less productive. Almost 75 per cent of the holdings in the poor-law unions of the west were valued for rating purposes at less than £15 in 1870, whereas the corresponding figure for East Cork was under 55 per cent.[55] Some western unions did have an unusually high proportion of farms of thirty acres or more, and a rating pattern very similar to that of the eastern unions. Yet this was not necessarily a fair criterion of general prosperity, for it was precisely these western unions (Dunmanway, Macroom, Millstreet, and Kanturk) that possessed the highest concentrations of labourers, who were as a class the most sensitive to the 'push and pull' of emigration.[56] In the extreme southwest, the meagre livings dictated by infertile holdings should have almost equally disposed the occupiers to seek a better life across the ocean. More than 80 per cent of the holdings in the unions of Castletown, Skull, Bantry, Skibbereen, and Clonakilty did not exceed £15 in value in 1870. This depressing situation, repeated on a similar scale throughout much of the west of Ireland, prompted the outspoken land agent Samuel Hussey to suggest in 1883 that 'nearly 2 millions of Irish could be employed in the fertile lands of America or in the colonies without allowing an acre in Ireland to go out of cultivation'. Hussey seriously doubted whether any practical man would maintain that an Irish farmer could live in decent comfort and pay a fair rent on a holding valued for poor rates at less than £40.[57] Certainly, those tenants who did not attain half of Hussey's standard of decent comfort could only lead a makeshift existence as long as they remained at home. And yet resistance to emigration was widespread among them.

This resistance was demonstrated in the painful scenes surrounding emigrant departures in southwestern Cork as late as the 1880s. In many other regions of Munster by that time, the trains carrying emigrants to Queenstown moved off to the sounds of the fiddle and dancing feet on the station platform.[58] But those bringing emigrants up to Cork city from Skibbereen in 1882 still creaked out of the station amid 'the heart-rending wails of parents and friends'.[59] In spite of higher population density, less productive land, and heavy

[54] Cousens, 'Population changes, 1861–81', p. 310.

[55] *Returns showing the number of agricultural holdings in Ireland and the tenure by which they are held by the occupiers*, pp. 18–20.

[56] *Irish agricultural statistics for 1871*, pp. 76–99.

[57] Kenmare papers, Letter book, 1882–3: S. M. Hussey to editor of *The Times*, 30 Apr. 1883, pp. 867–8.

[58] *C.E.*, 24 May 1880, 7 May 1881.   [59] *W.C.E.*, 8 Apr. 1882.

concentrations of labourers in certain areas, the people of West Cork appear to have emigrated only in about the same proportion as people in the eastern part of the county. Although emigration was not recorded officially below the county level, both natural increase and overall population change were measured at the level of the poor-law union. The difference between natural increase and population change, which roughly equals the amount of emigration, was fairly uniform throughout Cork. In certain unions, and during certain decades between 1861 and 1891, the exodus rose above or fell below the average of the county, but in general, and over the whole period, what is remarkable is the uniformity between east and west. [60] Even during the 1880s, when movement from other parts of the west of Ireland was exceptionally heavy for the first time since the famine, [61] all the unions of West Cork conformed closely to the normal county pattern.

When the opposite might reasonably have been expected, this uniformity requires some explanation. Emigration from West Cork was not more intensive partly because of lack of means, and especially because of the often almost fanatical attachment of poor peasants to the smallest bit of ground in their ancestral parish. Yet movement was as heavy as from the more fertile, less densely settled eastern part of the county because of the periodic agricultural crises which always afflicted the poor the most. These agricultural crises provoked sudden bursts of emigration, of which there were five during the second half of the nineteenth century. In addition to the mass exodus of the 1850s initiated by the famine, spasms of movement from Cork occurred in the years of 1862–6, 1874–5, 1880–2, and 1887–91. [62] After a year of normal crop yields like that of 1859, the emigrants in the following spring included relatively more farmers' children from East Cork, who could most easily afford the lowest current steamship fare of £6 6s. (direct from Queenstown to the United States). [63] After a year of crop failure like that of 1879, remittances from family members or friends abroad increased sharply, thus making possible the emigration from the west of thousands of poor smallholders and labourers who could not or would not otherwise have left. [64] Of the

---

[60] See above, p. 220, n. 5, and the sources cited there.

[61] Cousens, 'Population changes, 1861–81', p. 303.

[62] *Census Ire., 1911: . . . county and city of Cork*, p. 383. The first and third of these periods were preceded by the serious grain and potato failures of 1860–62 and 1877–9; the second followed the serious potato shortages of 1871–3, while the fourth partly coincided with and partly followed an acute phase of the agricultural depression of the 1880s.

[63] *C.C.*, 10 Apr. 1860.

[64] Remittances rose steeply during all the sudden bursts of movement

emigrants leaving Skibbereen for Queenstown during one week in May 1880, the number who had received prepaid tickets from America was said to be extremely large.[65] In April 1882, when this wave of emigration was reaching its crest, it was asserted that more of those who had left in the previous four or five months possessed prepaid fares than ever before.[66] Yet 'American money', as distinct from 'passage money', made it possible for others in the west to maintain an otherwise hopeless position on uneconomic holdings and to persist in an irrational, if understandable, resistance to emigration. Many families eking out a bare subsistence from poor land in the Castletown-Berehaven district in 1890 'would be long ago evicted were it not for the help they got from their friends abroad'.[67] Indeed, it was said in 1891 that 'the people of the promontory from Glengarriffe to Castletownbere and Ballydonegan seem to live for the most part by American contributions'.[68] Without the periodic agricultural crises and the prepaid passages that poured in after them, the rate of movement from West Cork during the second half of the nineteenth century would have been much less than it actually was.

The *Cork Examiner* could argue persuasively in 1891 that Ireland was 'capable of supporting a far larger population in peace and comfort' if self-government were granted, and industrial development and land reform then carried out.[69] Yet, it is unquestionable that the country's far smaller population enjoyed much higher living standards precisely because of large-scale emigration. Some of the direct results were highly visible, others more obscure, yet perceptible. For Sir John Benn-Walsh in 1855, his Ballygroman farm near Cork city was a striking, though fair, illustration of 'the benefit which the emigration has effected for Ireland, in spite of the clamour of the priests & anti Malthusians'. Benn-Walsh now had 'but six tenants instead of eleven on the whole farm, besides having got rid of younger brothers & their families in every lot. The tenants are flourishing, the culture is improving, & the farm is doing well.'[70] After the 1850s, however, the enlargement of farms proceeded slowly.

[65] *C.E.*, 17 May 1880.
[66] Ibid., 29 Apr. 1882. See also ibid., 4 May 1883.
[67] Ibid., 26 May 1890.
[68] Ibid., 11 Feb. 1891.
[69] Ibid., 4 June 1891.
[70] Ormathwaite papers: Journal of Sir John Benn-Walsh, 1 Sept. 1855, pp. 145–6.

from Ireland except that of 1863–7 (Schrier, *American emigration*, pp. 157, 167–8).

Although holdings of fifty acres or less fell by 18 per cent between 1851 and 1891, almost half of this decline was concentrated in the first decade; holdings of more than fifty acres rose by 7 per cent over the same period, but almost three-quarters of this rise occurred in the 1850s.[71] Not all of this change in the structure of landholding, moreover, can be attributed to emigration. Cork and Wicklow experienced roughly the same proportional decrease in the number of holdings of fifteen acres or less during the second half of the century, even though Wicklow possessed one of the lowest emigration intensities, while Cork had the highest.[72] Only during the late 1840s and the early 1850s was there a strong, immediate relationship between consolidation and emigration in Cork.

On the other hand, emigration did make a significant contribution to the shift towards grassland farming, which was the exclusive basis of whatever agricultural prosperity Cork enjoyed. Without emigration, the tillage acreage in Cork would not have been cut in half between 1851 and 1891.[73] Those rural unions that lost the most people also saw the largest decrease in ploughed land, while those that lost the least people saw the smallest decrease in ploughed land.[74] In Fermoy, Mallow, Midleton, and Youghal unions, where the aggregate population declined by 36 per cent from 1851 to 1881, the tillage acreage fell by as much as 25 per cent. In Bantry, Dunmanway, Millstreet, and Skibbereen unions, where the aggregate population declined by 16 per cent, the tillage acreage fell by only 8 per cent.[75] Of course, the continuous shift towards pasture farming was also a conscious response to conditions in the British market, where relative price movements increasingly favoured livestock over tillage products.[76] These conditions were at least as important as emigration in accelerating the shift towards grassland farming.

Emigration also played a significant part in augmenting rural wealth. One of the best measures of this wealth in Cork during this period is the *per capita* value of livestock, especially cattle. While both the number and price of cattle rose steeply, population fell sharply. At current market prices, the cattle on the farms of the county increased in value from £2·2 million in 1854 to over £4·2 million in 1884, or by 90 per cent. Since there were many fewer people by the latter year, the *per capita* value of these cattle rose from £3·7 to £9·1

[71] See above, Chapter III, p. 132, n. 1 and the sources cited there.
[72] Schrier, *American emigration*, p. 68.
[73] See above, Chapter III, p. 134.
[74] Schrier, *American emigration*, pp. 70, 164.
[75] *Census Ire., 1851*, pt ii: *Returns of agricultural produce in 1851*, passim; *Irish agricultural statistics for 1881*, pp. 19–20.
[76] See above, Chapter I, pp. 45–8; Chapter III, pp. 133–5, 145–50.

over the same period, or by no less than 143 per cent. [77] Not all sections of the farming classes, however, shared equally in this extraordinary increase in rural wealth. Before the 1870s small farmers did surprisingly better than larger ones by extending their cattle herds at a faster rate. On farms of over thirty acres cattle rose in number by only 14 per cent from 1854 to 1871, whereas on farms of five to thirty acres, they increased by as much as 27 per cent. [78] From 1874 down almost to the First World War, however, this situation was reversed, with only the very largest farmers significantly extending their herds. As Schrier has aptly said of this later period, 'the cream of accumulating wealth floated to the top and only those at the apex of the economic pyramid enjoyed the pleasure of skimming it off'. [79]

Besides augmenting rural wealth, emigration reduced excessive competition for land. Schrier has argued that in post-famine Ireland the 'desire to own land reasserted itself in all its former vigor, and competition for its possession remained as keen as ever'. [80] His contention seems highly improbable in the case of Cork, where the number of holdings above one acre decreased by less than 10 per cent while population fell by more than 30 per cent between 1851 and 1891. Even before land rents were restrained by agitation and by the legislation of 1881 and 1887, the rent increases that had occurred on Cork estates had generally been moderate, and certainly far below what might have been justifiable in view of the enormous rise in both cattle and butter prices up to 1876. [81] This strongly implies that competition for farms had decreased since the famine, and that landlords no longer exploited the spirited competition that still existed, at least not to nearly the same extent.

THE LABOURERS' STRUGGLE

By drastically reducing their number, emigration greatly benefited the labouring classes. Any adverse effect on the demand for labour created by the decline of tillage was soon more than counter-balanced by the exceptionally heavy flight of labourers and farm

---

[77] H. V. Stuart, *Prices of farm products in Ireland from year to year for thirty-six years, illustrated by diagrams, with observations on the prospects of Irish agriculture, including the substance of letters addressed to the rt. hon. W. E. Gladstone, M.P., in February and March of this year* (Dublin, 1886).

[78] *Returns of agricultural produce . . . 1854*, pp. 116, 118; *Irish agricultural statistics for 1871*, pp. 116, 118.

[79] Schrier, *American emigration*, p. 72.

[80] Ibid., p. 68.

[81] See above, Chapter IV, pp. 187–200.

servants from the county. By the 1860s farmers were complaining loudly of the shortage of labour, especially during harvest. [82] Thereafter, new agricultural machinery became an increasingly popular subject and a common sight on the larger farms in Cork, much to the dismay of those labourers who remained at home. [83] Mowers, reapers, binders, and threshers were used extensively throughout most of the county by the 1880s, largely because of the labour shortage. [84] In spite of machinery, however, hands were still extremely scarce. Around Castletownroche in late August 1880, farmers protested vehemently over the high wages demanded by harvest workers. [85] Enough able-bodied labourers to satisfy the farmers could not be found in the Youghal district in 1882, and 'the present rate of emigration', it was sadly noted, 'will not improve matters'. [86] The board of guardians and the town commissioners of Killarney were decidedly opposed, in mid-April 1883, to the implementation of a government emigration scheme, because 'not a single additional man could be hired last week at Milltown or Killorglin by the contractors for the new railway to Farranfore'. [87]

Emigration-induced labour shortages led to a steep rise in money wages. As early as 1860, agricultural wages in Munster were reported to have climbed to 7s. per week, as compared with only 4s. in 1843 and 1844, [88] although there is scattered evidence that only landowners, and farmers near large towns, had granted an increase of this magnitude. [89] The poor-law inspectors reliably estimated in 1870, however, that the earnings of agricultural labourers and farm servants had doubled since 1849, except in the southwestern part of the county, where the advance was only 75 per cent. Male farm servants who were fed and lodged by their employers now received £8 to £10 per year, as compared with only £4 or £5 before the famine. Unbound labourers hired at the average daily rate could earn 8s. or 9s. if they worked a full six-day week. Although many still could not find work every day, it should be remembered that such labourers had received only 4s. per week at the most before 1845, when regular employment was exceedingly difficult to obtain. Bound

[82] *C.E.*, 11 Apr. 1867; *C.C.*, 31 Aug. 1867.
[83] *C.E.*, 29 June, 27 July 1860; 3 July 1867.
[84] Ibid., 18 Aug. 1885.
[85] Ibid., 26 Aug. 1880.
[86] Ibid., 26 Apr. 1882.
[87] Ibid., 18 Apr. 1883.
[88] *The Times*, 6 Sept. 1865.
[89] Regional Museum, Kinsale: Kilbrittain Castle account books, Sept. 1864–Dec. 1866; Bantry papers: Demesne accounts, May 1869; *C.C.*, 7 Sept. 1861; *C.E.*, 31 Jan., 11 Apr. 1867.

labourers who had been paid merely 2*s*. or 3*s*. a week before the famine when dieted by a farmer, or 3*s*. to 4*s*. when not, now obtained 3*s*. to 6*s*. with food, or from 7*s*. to 10*s*. without food.[90] Harvest earnings had risen more than proportionately; only about 6*s*. per week before 1845, they now ranged from 12*s*. to 18*s*.[91]

This steep rise in money wages, however, was partly offset by the diminished yield of the potato crop, which meant that labouring families needed to buy more Indian meal or flour, and that they could sell fewer pigs, poultry, and eggs, since they had much less potato refuse. Nor did the rents of potato gardens or conacre fall in proportion to the decline in yield, and in many cases they did not fall at all.[92] Even though its incidence had greatly diminished since 1845, there remained an unhealthy amount of casual employment. It still frequently happened that regular work could only be found for nine months of the year.[93] Furthermore, labourers had been compelled to crowd into the towns and villages, and thus had often to travel long distances in order to reach their place of work.[94] This undesirable situation, one of the strongest grievances of unbound labourers, originated in landlord fears of pauperism. Crippled by a poor-law regulation of 1843 that made them liable for all the rates of holdings valued at £4 or less, head landlords had liquidated such holdings *en masse* during the famine and had driven the labourers and cottiers into the towns. Then in order to prevent a recurrence, they widely adopted policies absolutely forbidding their tenants to sublet to labourers or severely restricting the number permissible on each farm.[95] As a result, large numbers of agricultural workers were forced to remain in insanitary, dilapidated town lodgings.

Much wretchedness therefore persisted despite the substantial progress that had been achieved, and this very progress no doubt served to accentuate the consciousness of the painful injustices still suffered. Organization and united action were sorely needed to exert strong public pressure against offending landowners and farmers as well as to obtain remedial legislation from Westminster. What was apparently the first organization in Ireland specifically

[90] *Reports from poor law inspectors on the wages of agricultural labourers in Ireland* [C 35], H.C. 1870, xiv, 1, pp. 1–2, 22–3.
[91] *C.C.*, 7 Sept. 1861, 31 Aug. 1867.
[92] *The Times*, 13 Oct. 1880; *C.E.*, 9, 21 July, 2 Aug. 1881.
[93] *Reports from poor law inspectors on the wages of agricultural labourers in Ireland*, p. 25.
[94] Ibid., p. 27; King, *Irish question*, p. 269; E. Strauss, *Irish nationalism and British democracy* (New York and London, 1951), p. 139.
[95] *C.E.*, 2 Mar. 1871, 9 July 1881; *Bessborough comm. evidence*, pt ii, pp. 902–3.

devoted to improving the lot of the agricultural worker was established in Kanturk in late 1869. [96] The guiding spirit of the Kanturk Labourers' Club was Philip F. Johnson, the owner of the Egmont Arms Hotel in Kanturk and a small tenant farmer. [97] Under Johnson's aggressive leadership, the 200 labourers who assembled at the Egmont Arms Hotel in January 1870 urged their confrères throughout the country to form similar clubs, and 'in every parish in Ireland to agitate the claims of the labourer, whose interests have hitherto been quite ignored by members of the legislature'. [98] The club's immediate impact outside Cork was slight, but within the county it aroused a sharp, though brief, tumult. In early July, following a period of general labour unrest in Cork city that included widespread strikes and several nights of rioting, crowds of agricultural workers broke or threatened to break mowing machines in the districts of Liscarroll, Charleville, and Ballinhassig, and demanded higher wages. [99] The first instance of organized discontent among the labourers of Cork apparently failed in its objectives, but it served greatly to alarm the farmers. One frightened member of the Mallow Farmers' Club erroneously claimed in February 1871 that militiamen were drilling the labourers throughout the country and also charged that P. F. Johnson was one of the 'Reds of Duhallow', an advocate of physical force to solve the labourers' problems. [100]

Johnson soon gave the farmers further reason for alarm. He was well aware of the growing strength and militancy of agricultural trade unionism in England during the early 1870s. He came to believe that his efforts to improve the condition of Irish farm workers would be considerably enhanced by collaborating with the National Agricultural Labourers' Union, formed in England in 1872 and presided over by Joseph Arch. For reasons of its own, the N.A.L.U. was interested in extending its activities to Ireland. Arch's body wished to minimize and regulate the migration of Irish workers to England for the harvest as well as to prevent them from being used as strike breakers by English farmers. This shared perception of the advantages of collaboration led to the formation of an Irish labourers' union, as a branch of the parent N.A.L.U., at a conference held in Kanturk in mid-August 1873. [101]

[96] *C.E.*, 4 Jan. 1870.
[97] *Bessborough comm. evidence*, pt ii, p. 840.
[98] *C.E.*, 12 Jan. 1870. The club's earliest specific goal was to obtain better housing and land allotments for local labourers, especially those on the earl of Egmont's estate (ibid., 15 Mar. 1870).
[99] Ibid., 5, 6, 7 July 1870.   [100] Ibid., 24, 28 Feb. 1871.
[101] P. L. R. Horn, 'The National Agricultural Labourers' Union in Ireland, 1873–9' in *I.H.S.*, xvii, no. 67 (Mar. 1971), pp. 340–3, 346.

The collaboration, however, was extremely short-lived. The major cause of strain was the issue of Irish home rule. Whereas Johnson and other Irish supporters of the labourers' cause believed strongly in the desirability of home rule, the English leaders of the N.A.L.U. were either equivocal or opposed. Once it became apparent that the political question could not be kept out of the Irish labourers' agitation, the N.A.L.U. quickly withdrew from the Irish arena. After N.A.L.U. support ceased in late 1873, the Irish farm-workers' movement limped along with diminished vitality until 1879, when it was completely eclipsed by the rise of the Land League. [102]

But in 1881 the labourers' movement was temporarily revived in Cork and other parts of Ireland. In fact, the farm-workers' agitation gathered such momentum that it threatened to arouse strife between labourers and farmers as intense as the struggle already raging between tenants and landlords. At a great convention held in the town hall of Limerick in May 1881, speakers such as Andrew Kettle, one of the more extreme Land League leaders, urged Irish labourers to follow in the footsteps of Arch's N.A.L.U. in England and to prepare to strike for an increase in wages. [103] The convention's organizers, chief of whom was P. F. Johnson, apparently hoped to reinforce the Land League agitation, despite the opinion widespread among labourers that the league served exclusively the selfish interests of farmers. Instead, the convention spurred the labourers to take the offensive against their immediate enemies. Strike fever flashed across the entire county in the summer of 1881. Large crowds of resolute labourers marched from farm to farm, demanding concessions and drawing away workers from those who rejected their demands. [104] Though haphazardly organized, the strikers were so well disciplined that surprisingly little violence occurred. Both psychologically and tactically, the farmers were at a disadvantage. They had recently received abatements in rent (of which the labourers wanted a share) from many landlords as a result of the league agitation. They enjoyed the prospect of beneficial land legislation then in its final stages of passage through parliament. And finally, with the harvest fast approaching, they had little room to manoeuvre.

The strikers' wage demands usually covered all types of farm workers, and although its full claims were not always met, each group won significant concessions. Unbound labourers obtained an increase of at least 1s., sometimes 2s., and their weekly earnings now

---

[102] Ibid., pp. 342–3, 345–50.
[103] *C.E.*, 20 May 1881.
[104] *W.C.E.*, 23, 30 July 1881; *C.E.*, 28 July, 3, 10 Aug. 1881.

ranged from 9*s.* to 12*s.*[105] Bound labourers rarely secured an advance
of more than 1*s.* per week but often received their privileges gratuitously, without the annoying reductions formerly made for cottage
and cabbage garden, coals, and the grass for one or two sheep.[106]
Farm servants usually gained only £1, so that their seasonal earnings
now ranged from £9 to £12.[107] But their wages rose steadily during
the following decade. At the great spring hiring fair held in
Kilmallock in 1890, farmers offered £15 or £16 for female servants
and £13 or £14 for male servants, whose cost of feeding was
higher.[108] This rapid rise is probably explained by the exceptionally
heavy emigration among this group. As one servant girl working on a
farm near Kilmallock said earlier, 'I have £1 a month here for nine
months, and as soon as that's up I'm going over the western ocean'.[109]

After the great outbreak of strikes in 1881, the labourers' agitation
in Cork receded into the background of a bitter land war between
farmers and landlords. The old acrimony over the exorbitant
conacre rents charged by most farmers, however, continued
unabated.[110] The 'carberies', or labourer-fishermen, in the Ballymacooda and Shanagarry districts complained bitterly in December
1882 that £4 an acre was still exacted for unprepared potato ground,
even though local farmers paid only £1 an acre for the same land
and took two corn crops after the potatoes on the strength of the
labourers' manure. As long as they prepared it properly, the carberies
demanded the land at the farmers' rent.[111] Immediately, the leaders
of the labour movement wanted all farmers holding over thirty acres
to provide their workers with half-acre allotments; these leaders
were willing that labourers pay as much for the land as farmers but
wanted the landowner to receive the rent.[112] Ultimately, they
sought to gain for the labourer a legal tenure of his house and
ground, independent of both landowner and farmer.[113] John
Sarsfield Casey, famous as 'the Galtee boy' for his efforts on behalf
of the Buckley tenants in 1876 and 1877, ominously warned farmers
in August 1884 that the day might soon dawn when labourers would

[105] *C.E.*, 21, 27 July 1881; *W.C.E.*, 30 July, 6 Aug. 1881.
[106] *C.E.*, 21, 27 July, 10 Aug., 10 Sept. 1881; *W.C.E.*, 30 July, 6 Aug. 1881.
[107] *C.E.*, 23, 27 July, 10 Aug. 1881.
[108] *C.C.*, 26 Mar. 1890.
[109] Irish Folklore Commission: MS 107, p. 462.
[110] For a classic expression of this embittered feeling, see the angry speech
of Patrick Barry, a labourer in the Ballycottin district, in *The Times*,
13 Oct. 1880. See also *C.E.*, 20 Feb., 15 Mar. 1882.
[111] *C.C.*, 5 Dec. 1882.
[112] *W.C.E.*, 1 July 1882.
[113] *C.E.*, 9 July 1881.

not be satisfied with merely half an acre; then 'a great cry would go forth, echoing the voice of Michael Davitt [an advocate of land nationalization], that the land should belong to no section of the people, but should become the property of the nation, as God ordained it'.[114] Most farmers ignored the warning and refused to provide allotments.[115]

The old resentment over the use of agricultural machinery also embittered relations between labourers and farmers in the 1880s. Agreements, either tacit or explicit, existed in numerous districts that farmers would refrain from using mowers and reapers as long as local labourers could find no employment during harvest.[116] Mowing gangs earned high wages—as much as 5s. per day per man— and the restriction on the hiring and use of machines penalized many farmers.[117] Some accepted the restriction for the sake of social peace, others would not. In the Charleville district in 1881, rick burning by labourers against farmers who had hired mowing machines reached serious proportions and was strongly condemned by the local branch of the Land League.[118] At Mitchelstown in 1885, a large crowd of labourers yelling, 'Cheers for landlordism, down with machines', interrupted a meeting of tenant farmers. One labourer who stormed into their meeting created a great uproar by shouting, 'If machines are not done away with, we'll burn the house of the persons that owns [sic] them'.[119] The *Cork Examiner* tried to convince the anti-machine labourers that they were only damaging their own cause, but bitterness against the offending farmers persisted.[120]

Probably the most contentious issue between labourers and farmers in the 1880s was that of decent housing. While many land-owners, most prominently the duke of Devonshire and the earl of Kenmare, had made serious efforts to provide adequate accommodation for their own labourers,[121] farmers had initiated little new building and often allowed existing cottages to fall into extreme disrepair. Labour leaders had long pressed strenuously for government intervention. A provision concerning labourers' housing was included almost as an afterthought in the 1881 land act, but it was

---

[114] Ibid., 16 Aug. 1884.

[115] Ibid., 16 Mar. 1886.

[116] Ibid., 2 July, 2 Aug. 1881; 21 Aug. 1890.

[117] The owners of the machines were generally prosperous farmers, who hired them out by the day to their less well-to-do neighbours (Pellew, *Castle and cabin*, p. 112).

[118] *C.E.*, 6, 8 Sept. 1881.

[119] Ibid., 14 July 1885.

[120] Ibid., 15 July 1885.

[121] Dun, *Landlords and tenants*, pp. 60, 77; *C.C.*, 23 Sept. 1885.

inadequate and required amendment.[122] The result was the labourers' cottages and allotments act of 1882, authorizing the land commission to order farmers whose rents had been fixed under the legislation of the previous year to improve existing or build new cottages for their workers. Farmers failing to comply with such an order within six months were liable to be tried summarily before the justices in petty sessions and fined £1 a week for as long as they remained in default.[123] New buildings could be financed easily with cheap loans from the board of works under the land-improvement acts.

In spite of judicial orders and the threat of heavy fines, procrastination and resistance were widespread among farmers. Part of the problem stemmed from the fact that if the labourers themselves failed to prosecute, the responsibility lay with the boards of guardians. These bodies, now largely composed of well-to-do farmers, were most dubious champions of the labourers' interests. They had already demonstrated as much by failing to perform their clear duty under the sanitary dwellings laws, which required the repair or demolition of houses deemed unfit for human habitation and mostly inhabited by labourers.[124] The guardians of Cork and Mitchelstown unions took proceedings against some farmers who had neglected to erect cottages as ordered,[125] but on the whole, enforcement appears to have been extremely lax. Indeed, by a shameless vote of fourteen to five, the Kanturk board of guardians rejected in October 1885 a resolution to prosecute farmers who had long ignored the orders of the land commission.[126] Farmers could also avoid prosecution by simply evicting their labourers. Although this vicious measure was not widely adopted, it was reported from Skibbereen in January 1886 that 'in order to avoid the necessity of having labourers' cottages erected on the lands, [farmers] are dismissing their labourers, many of whom have been in the same employment for a long term of years'.[127]

Local boards of guardians also possessed authority to arrange for the construction of new dwellings under the labourers acts of 1883 and 1887, but farmers could and did refuse to provide appropriate sites, even though they would have been well compensated.[128] The

---

[122] 44 & 45 Vict., c. 49, s. 19.

[123] 45 & 46 Vict., c. 60, ss. 3–4. The land commission was also empowered to order that farmers assign to their labourers allotments not exceeding half an acre, but the provision remained almost entirely inoperative.

[124] *W.C.E.*, 29 Apr. 1882.   [125] *C.E.*, 9 Apr. 1884, 7 Feb. 1885.

[126] *C.C.*, 23 Oct. 1885.

[127] *C.E.*, 28 Jan. 1886. See also *C.C.*, 10 Apr. 1888.

[128] *C.E.*, 4 June 1884; *C.C.*, 11 Aug. 1886.

guardians themselves seldom acted unless under pressure,[129] with the notable exception of their frequent attempts to harass landlords by selecting sites for dwellings on evicted farms, with the avowed object of reinstalling the evicted tenants as labourers.[130] The deliberate delays and chicanery merely exasperated the often ill-housed labourers. At Kilmallock in May 1887, a large crowd of them, armed with blackthorns, invaded the courthouse, where the local guardians were conducting an inquiry into a proposed plan for new dwellings. When anyone 'unfriendly to their cause, or who in any way opposed the scheme for the cottages, put in an appearance, he was subjected to very bad treatment'. Two farmers were severely beaten, and five labourers were arrested and charged with assault.[131]

With their long list of grievances against farmers over housing, machinery, potato-garden rents, and wages, it is scarcely surprising that labourers generally regarded them as cunning adversaries and class enemies. During a protest meeting of labourers at Shanagarry in October 1880, one of the demonstrators was heard to say:

They knew poor Pat O'Brien, as good a man as ever was in the parish, who had to go with his family into the poor-house because he would not be supported by a farmer who gave £300 to his daughter when she was getting married.[132]

To the Kanturk guardians, who had requested the government to provide employment after the partial potato failure of 1890, one distressed labourer blurted out: 'If the farmers get the handling of it, our portion will be very small. Before any employment will be given, I am quite sure some of my children will be dead.'[133]

IMPROVEMENTS IN HOUSING, DIET, AND EDUCATION

Although the dwellings of agricultural labourers, especially those forced to live in dilapidated town lodgings, still left much to be desired, the housing of the rural population as a whole had improved tremendously since the famine. The ubiquitous mud cabins in which nearly half of all Cork families had lived in 1841 were easily and rapidly demolished by the crowbar brigades of consolidating landlords during and after the famine. Over 80 per cent of the one-room hovels defined as fourth-class houses by the census commissioners

---

[129] *C.C.*, 14 Nov. 1885.
[130] Ibid., 8 Mar. 1886, 22 Mar. 1887; Pellew, *Castle and cabin*, p. 102.
[131] *C.E.*, 4 May 1887.
[132] *The Times*, 13 Oct. 1880.
[133] *C.C.*, 13 Dec. 1890. See also ibid., 18 Sept. 1890.

had disappeared from the landscape by 1861. In order to demonstrate the dramatic improvement in even the poorest type of accommodation ten years later, the commissioners divided fourth-class houses into small brick or stone cottages and mud cabins. Although 22 per cent of the houses in the county still consisted of merely a single room in 1871, only 6 per cent were made of mud. Even the more durable fourth-class cottages practically vanished in the next twenty years; they comprised a mere 3 per cent of all houses in 1891. As the worst kind of accommodation disappeared, labourers and cottiers often moved into more spacious dwellings consisting of two to four rooms, defined by the census as third-class houses, which in former years would have eminently satisfied many a small or medium farmer. Partly because the more prosperous farmers had come to disdain so visible a monument to their past adversity, and even more because of emigration, third-class houses also diminished greatly after 1851, falling by 52 per cent in the course of the next forty years. Yet, for the farming classes, these years formed an extraordinary era in home construction—one of the best indications of their increased material welfare. Table 39 shows that substantial dwellings with five to nine rooms—second-class houses in the language of the census—rose by 76 per cent between 1841 and 1891.[134]

TABLE 39 Number of dwellings in each category of house accommodation in Cork, 1841–91

year	first-class	second-class	third-class	fourth-class	total
1841	3,001	20,309	37,304	60,896	121,510
1851	3,624	24,464	39,860	16,197	84,145
1861	3,945	26,552	35,196	11,165	76,858
1871	4,325	29,318	24,621*	16,135*	74,399
1881	4,937	31,507	27,079	4,561	68,084
1891	5,520	35,668	19,184	1,887	62,259
% change, 1841–91	+83·9	+75·6	−48·6	−96·9	−48·8

* A real increase in fourth-class houses in 1871 is highly improbable. Since the census takers made a special effort to enumerate mud cabins in that year and to distinguish them from other fourth-class houses, they may have departed somewhat from their usual classificatory procedures.

[134] *Census Ire.*, *1841*, p. 190; *Census Ire.*, *1851*, pt vi, pp. 248–9, 264–5; *Census Ire.*, *1861*, pt v, pp. 184, 194; *Census Ire.*, *1871*, pt i, vol. ii, no. 2, pp. 265–6; *Census Ire.*, *1881*, pt i, vol. ii, no. 2, pp. 265–6; *Census Ire.*, *1891*, pt i, vol. ii, no. 2, pp. 265–6.

A more meaningful analysis of this improvement in housing conditions can be made by measuring the proportion of families inhabiting each of the four types of dwellings. When analysed in this way, the improvement is not so striking, especially in the category of third-class houses, as Table 40 illustrates. [135]

TABLE 40 Percentage of families occupying each category of housing in Cork, 1841–91

year	first-class	second-class	third-class	fourth-class
1841	2·8	19·0	30·2	48·0
1851	4·8	30·8	45·9	18·5
1861	6·5	36·6	43·3	13·6
1871	7·0	41·1	31·5	20·4
1881	8·6	47·2	37·9	6·3
1891	10·2	57·3	29·6	2·9

Although there were only about half as many third-class houses in 1891 as there had been fifty years earlier, the proportion of families living in such dwellings scarcely changed at all during that time. Nevertheless, the real significance of these figures lies in the fact that whereas in 1841 nearly half of all Cork families had lived very much like animals in windowless, smoke-choked shacks and sheds easily penetrated by wind and rain, by 1891 nearly three-fifths of the population resided in solid, snug farmhouses having plenty of access for light and air. Together, agricultural prosperity and the emigrant stream had radically changed the style and quality of rural life for the better.

Another yardstick of the increased material welfare of the rural community was the improvement in diet that took place unobtrusively during the second half of the nineteenth century. The potato lost much of its old dominance. The production of this root crop decreased from an average of more than 378,000 tons a year between 1851 and 1855 to an average of less than 284,000 tons a year between 1871 and 1875, or by 25 per cent. [136] Much of this fall can be attributed to the simple loss of one-fifth of the county's population between 1851 and 1871. Yet it should be remembered that after 1851 there was a substantial rise in all forms of livestock, which had consumed about one-third of the potatoes produced before 1845. Without the availability of alternative sources of food, a greater

---

[135] See above, p. 243, n. 134.
[136] *Irish agricultural statistics for 1871*, pp. xxix, lii; *Irish agricultural statistics for 1881*, pp. 34, 39.

decline in potato production than in population would have been extremely unlikely. No basic change in diet occurred in the 1850s, but the next two decades saw the importation of cheap foreign grain—mostly from American and Black Sea ports—on an unprecedented scale. As Table 41 demonstrates, wheat imports tripled while those of Indian corn, or maize, jumped more than fivefold between the early 1860s and the late 1870s. [137]

Introduced in order to meet the catastrophic emergency of the famine, Indian meal later became a principal item in the diet of labourers and small farmers. Whenever the potato failed, it became their staff of life. In May 1863 it was reported that the poor in the parish of Durrus near Bantry had been living altogether on meal for the previous three years. [138] Similarly, in March 1880 a local parish

TABLE 41   Cork imports of wheat and Indian corn, 1857–80

years (average)	wheat (qtr.)	Indian corn (qtr.)
1857–60	245,120	193,794
1861–5	705,178	373,784
1866–70	1,709,289	951,447
1871–5	2,311,832	1,238,807
1876–80	2,159,698	1,970,455

priest declared that the 'humane, merciful, and large-hearted shopkeepers of Castletown ... kept all the people of this barony alive [on meal] for the last three years against great odds'. [139] Even in times of plenty, however, 'yellow male' was widely used for a good part of the year—three to six months—as the main food. Although labourers sometimes ate coarse wheat bread made from inferior flour, 'a cheaper food, the Indian corn meal, at 1*d*. or 1¼*d*. per pound, made into "stirabout" with the sour milk of the dairies', was 'more extensively consumed by these hard-living people'. [140] Small farmers, unable to afford better, also depended heavily on stirabout. The earl of Shannon's agent William B. Leslie urged small farmers in 1882 to imitate the Scottish practice of making oatmeal the principal food, instead of the much 'less nutritious' Indian meal. [141]

[137] *Annual statements of the trade and navigation of the United Kingdom with foreign countries and British possessions*, 1857–80.
[138] *C.E.*, 18 May 1863. See also ibid., 7 Nov. 1861, 10 Mar. 1862.
[139] Ibid., 3 Mar. 1880.
[140] From *The Times*, quoted in *C.C.*, 7 Sept. 1861. See also *C.E.*, 27 Feb. 1880; *Bessborough comm. evidence*, pt ii, p. 894.
[141] *C.C.*, 4 Dec. 1882.

For the larger farmers, wheat bread as a regular article of diet was one of the chief rewards of their increased wealth, and even meat was no longer confined to special occasions. As one labourer said disgustedly of these well-to-do farmers in 1886, 'The mean devils, they would give you spuds and some milk and put you to the hardest work, and eat plenty of meat themselves and do the lightest.' [142]

For the labouring classes, with higher wages and steadier employment, milk was no longer the luxury that it had been before the famine. When dieted by a farmer, bound labourers invariably received two pints of buttermilk along with each meal of potatoes. Unbound labourers purchased their own milk, usually boiled skim, or 'skyblue', but sometimes more expensive, fresh whole milk, and carried it to work. [143] Among farmers, tea was becoming the immensely popular drink that it is today, but few labourers or servants as yet took it. While one farmer, outraged by the mounting cost of supporting his servants, remarked sarcastically in 1880, 'Now you must keep a grocery account open for them, that gives them tea twice a day', [144] a farm servant from Enniskeen was shocked at the suggestion: 'Tay [tea] or sugar, I say tay or sugar to ye, "mo lair" we'd be very happy I tell ye if we'd get tay at Christmas'. [145] But by the 1890s tea had crept into the breakfast diet in Cork's congested districts along the southwestern coast, while milk was taken at dinner and supper. [146]

Another aspect of the improvement in diet after 1850 was the great increase in the use of butter among all classes, as a result of which Irish consumption of butter at forty-one pounds *per capita* has become one of the highest in the world. [147] Although this pre-eminence was mostly achieved in the present century, its roots may be found in the second half of the last century. As the number of cows and their yield increased up to the late 1870s, so perforce did milk production. In Table 42, *per capita* milk consumption is assumed to have risen from thirty-six to forty-six gallons per annum, with the result that, despite the population drain, total milk consumption remained fairly constant between 1854 and the late 1870s. The amount of milk converted into butter, however, increased by 30 per cent. [148]

[142] Ibid., 11 Aug. 1886. [143] *C.E.*, 7 Feb. 1880.
[144] From *Irish Times*, 24 Nov. 1880, quoted in Irish Land Committee, *The land question, Ireland*, no. 5: *Arrested progress, January 1881*, p. 16.
[145] Irish Folklore Commission: MS 437, p. 302.
[146] Congested Districts Board, *Base-line reports to the congested districts board, 1892–8*, pp. 687–96.
[147] Evans, *Irish folk ways*, p. 81.
[148] With some revision in milk yield per cow and milk consumption *per*

TABLE 42   Estimated milk production and utilization, in Cork, 1854–80 (in millions of gallons,)

years (average)	total production	liquid-milk consumption	fed to calves	made into butter
1854–5	65·6	23·4	2·2	40·0
1856–60	73·0	22·7	2·1	48·2
1861–5	68·6	21·8	2·0	44·8
1866–70	74·1	22·3	2·6	49·2
1871–5	76·8	22·8	3·4	50·6
1876–80	79·0	23·3	3·7	52·0

Yet the export of butter showed remarkable stability after the early 1850s. This stability is attributable to the diversion of a growing share of the increased butter production to domestic consumption. While the extent of this diversion was small in relation to production, it was magnified by the decline in population. As Table 43 illustrates, the total consumption of butter in Cork rose by 42 per cent, and *per capita* consumption by as much as 81 per cent between the mid-1850s and the late 1870s. [149] Farmers were increasingly able to withhold butter from export to Britain, because, thanks to the rise in rural wealth, they could sell more of it at home and consume more of it within their own families. As cakes of wheat flour or maize meal, and bread made from mixtures of other flours and meals, came within the means of a much larger section of the people, it was only natural that the use of butter greatly expanded. [150]

Not only were the rural folk much better fed and housed than formerly, but they were also more educated. Until 1831 the education of catholics in Ireland was limited almost entirely to the instruction offered by free-lance schoolmasters in the 'hedge schools'. Although there were more than 10,000 hedge schools in the country in 1824,

---

[149] The figures presented in Table 43 are derived from Table 42 (320 gal. of milk equivalent to 1 cwt of butter in farm butter making) and from Cork market receipts, of which approximately 40 per cent came from within the county (C.B.M. MSS, C. 38: Account of the total annual quantity of butter in casks, firkins, and kegs passed through the weigh-house, 1770–1869; *C.E.*, 12 Mar. 1859; Cork Corporation, *Report of the law and finance committee of the Cork corporation on the Cork Butter Market*, p. 236).

[150] K. Danaher, *In Ireland long ago* (Cork, 1962), pp. 44–50.

---

capita, the bases for these calculations are those used by Professor J. Lyons ('Dairying industry', pp. 190–3). The numbers of cows in the years covered by Table 42 have been taken from the *Returns of agricultural produce in Ireland*, 1854–6, and from *The agricultural statistics of Ireland*, 1857–80.

TABLE 43 Estimated butter production, exports, and consumption in Cork, 1854–80

years (average)	total production (cwt)	exports (cwt)	total consumption (cwt)	per capita consumption (lb.)
1854–5	124,900	82,200	42,700	7·4
1856–60	150,700	101,000	49,700	9·3
1861–5	139,900	91,500	48,400	9·9
1866–70	153,900	98,100	55,800	11·8
1871–5	158,100	98,800	59,300	12·9
1876–80	162,600	101,800	60,800	13·4

with a total enrolment of over 400,000,[151] they barely scratched the surface of the mass illiteracy and ignorance produced by a century of deliberate English suppression of catholic education at all levels. Gradually, the state-supported system of primary education introduced in 1831 provided a thorough grounding in the three Rs for an ever-increasing proportion of Irish children.[152] Table 44 shows that, as a percentage of the population aged five to fourteen, the number of children receiving instruction in Cork primary schools doubled between 1841 and 1891.[153] The coming of the national schools made a tremendous impact on the hard-core illiteracy of the rural areas of

TABLE 44 Number and percentage of children attending Cork primary schools, 1841–91

year	no. aged 5–14	no. in school	% in school
1841	209,126	61,681	29·5
1851	166,085	55,338	33·3
1861	106,998	44,556	41·6
1871	123,035	61,976	50·4
1881	122,599	70,758	57·7
1891	101,324	62,093	61·3

[151] V. Rice, 'Education' in O. D. Edwards (ed.), *Conor Cruise O'Brien introduces Ireland* (London, 1968), p. 171. See also P. J. Dowling, *The hedge schools of Ireland* (rev. ed., Cork, 1969).

[152] D. H. Akenson, *The Irish education experiment: the national system of education in the nineteenth century* (London and Toronto, 1970), pp. 376–7.

[153] *Census Ire., 1841*, pp. 168–9, 192–3; *Census Ire., 1851*, pt iv [2053], H.C. 1856, xxix, 1, pp. 68–77; *Census Ire., 1861*, pt ii, vol. i [3204–I], H.C. 1863, lvi, 1, pp. 370, 430, 456; *Census Ire., 1871*, pt i, vol. ii, no. 2, p. 275; *Census Ire., 1881*, pt i, vol. ii, no. 2, p. 275; *Census Ire., 1891*, pt i, vol. ii, no. 2, pp. 275, 404.

the county, where practically two-thirds of the people could neither read nor write in 1841. After the schoolmaster had been abroad in the land for sixty years, only about one-fifth of the county population was still illiterate, as Table 45 demonstrates. [154]

TABLE 45   Percentages of the population who were literate and illiterate in Cork, 1841–91

year	neither read nor write		read and/or write	
	county	city	county	city
1841	65·6	35·6	34·4	64·4
1851	59·5	35·7	40·5	64·3
1861	50·7	32·1	49·3	67·9
1871	42·7	29·4	57·3	70·6
1881	30·3	21·0	69·7	79·0
1891	20·8	15·9	79·2	84·1

The influence of primary education was felt in many directions, but it would be difficult to overestimate the contribution that it made to the vocal nationalism and the turbulent agrarian agitation of the 1880s. Both the home rule and land movements largely depended upon mass support from a literate, avid newspaper-reading public. David B. King, an American college professor who visited Ireland in 1881 and 1882 and later wrote one of the best contemporary works on the early phase of the land war, saw this point clearly.

In a third class railway car in which there were probably twenty-five Irish farmers and laborers, I noticed that more than one-half of the people read the morning papers, even those who looked the least intelligent showing a great interest in the news. I discovered the man who sat opposite me, and who was a rather ragged-looking individual, read the other side of my paper with evident interest. The violent agitation has helped on the influence of the press and set the people to reading. [155]

It is often implied that the storm which broke around the land question in late 1879 and 1880 acquired almost its entire force from the agricultural crisis which immediately preceded it. Such a view tends to overlook the fundamental material and psychological changes in rural life since 1850, some of which had subtle but important implications for the future. Late, arranged marriages, for instance, left many farmers' sons acutely dissatisfied with a system which required that they often remain 'boys', subservient to their

[154] *Census Ire., 1841*, pp. 168–9; *Census Ire., 1851*, pt iv, pp. 68–9, 72–3, 76–7; *Census Ire., 1891*, pt i, vol. ii, no. 2, p. 394.
[155] King, *Irish question*, p. 293.

fathers, until they reached their mid-thirties. Their sense of social inadequacy (some might say sexual frustration) may well account for their prominence among the 'moonlighting' bands of the land war. The influence of emigrants through their letters, newspapers, and visits or returns may be seen not only in the desire to end landlordism and secure real self-government but also in the desire to maintain and increase the material wealth gained since 1850. Material progress can help to undermine the established order of things, especially if it is threatened with temporary check or reversal, as it was in the late 1870s. Little enough progress had been achieved when the agricultural crisis of the early 1860s—which was every bit as serious as the one of 1877–9—reversed the upward movement of the farming classes. By the late 1870s, however, progress and prosperity had given the rural community much more to defend against mutilation or erosion. In a very real sense, the land war was a product not merely of agricultural crisis, but also of a revolution of rising expectations.

VI

THE LAND WAR:
FIRST PHASE, 1879–84

~~~~~~

THE ROOTS OF THE COMING CONFLICT

THE RELATIONS BETWEEN landlords and tenants in County Cork
at the beginning of 1877 appeared so calm that the violent land war
which erupted within less than three years could only have been
foreseen by a great leap of the imagination. With excellent prices for
both livestock and butter as well as generally good harvests (potatoes
excepted) between 1870 and 1876, farmers had good reason to be
content, even to the point of complacency about the need for further
land reform. Of course, the recent increases of rent were detested, but
only a minority were affected by them; and the same might be said
of the notorious leases foisted upon tenants since 1870 by landowners
anxious to preserve their full property rights. While the 1870 land
act had indeed resulted in a restriction of free sale on some estates,
there were so few tenants who wanted or needed to sell during the
prosperous seasons before 1877 that this restriction was not felt as a
practical grievance. The political domination of the landlords was
resented, and the extremely limited distribution of landownership
did arouse discontent in special instances, but neither of these issues
seemed of central importance to most tenants. The causes of home
rule and national independence were also far from the thoughts of
the overwhelming majority of farmers. In a sense, they were too busy
enjoying the significant gains in farm income, housing, and diet made
during the previous quarter of a century to be concerned with such
constitutional questions.

The agricultural crisis of the late 1870s, however, transformed the whole situation. An extended period of general economic improvement was now abruptly broken by a peculiar combination of bad weather, poor harvests, and falling prices. When hard times suddenly replace an era of prosperity, enormous tensions and frustrations can easily build up within a society, especially one marked by glaring inequalities of wealth. History affords numerous examples of the dissolution of traditional political and social fabrics under the intense strains produced when economic adversity threatens to erode or obliterate the material gains of a preceding period of substantial economic advance.[1] In its origins if not in its results, the great agrarian agitation that began in Ireland in 1879 partly conforms to this recognized pattern of social upheaval. The small farmers and cottiers who had shared marginally if at all in the agricultural prosperity of the preceding generation were no doubt drawn to the Land League by the fear or the threat of destitution and eviction. But the larger farmers, those with upwards of fifteen acres of good land (holdings of fifteen acres or more accounted for 56 per cent of the total in Ireland in 1881),[2] joined the agrarian agitation in an attempt to preserve their accumulated gains at a time when their incomes were reduced and when landlords were slow to make adjustments in their rents. Townsmen whose livelihood was intimately bound up with the welfare of the farming classes, especially shopkeepers and publicans, also supported the Land League and provided much of the local leadership and organization as well.[3] Along with the larger farmers, these townsmen had experienced a revolution of rising expectations since 1850 and were unwilling to abandon their conviction that economic progress could and must be perpetuated. It was by welding together these differently motivated social groups—townsmen and large farmers, cottiers and small farmers—that the agricultural crisis of the late 1870s gave rise to an almost irresistible agrarian movement.

The entire agrarian economy suffered serious damage in the late 1870s, but the tillage sector was particularly hard hit. 'The oat & barley crops are bad this year as well as the potatoe, owing to the cold & wet summer', wrote the Cork land agent Richard Doherty, sen., in October 1877.[4] This was the first of three successive seasons of unusually wet and cold weather that afflicted Irish farmers.

[1] J. C. Davies, 'Toward a theory of revolution' in *American Sociological Review*, xxvii, no. 1 (Feb. 1962), pp. 5–19.

[2] Schrier, *American emigration*, p. 163.

[3] S. Clark, 'The social composition of the Land League' in *I.H.S.*, xvii, no. 68 (Sept. 1971), pp. 447–69.

[4] Doherty papers, Letter book, 1876–8: R. W. Doherty, sen., to J. J. Oswald, 13 Oct. 1877, p. 361.

Compared with the abundant harvest of 1876, the production of oats in Cork declined by more than one-quarter, of barley by almost one-fifth, and of potatoes by as much as one-half.[5] On the other hand, the pastures were 'not better within the memory of the oldest inhabitant', and as a result the make of butter—Cork's principal export—was unusually large.[6] True, butter prices fell by almost 20 per cent during the year, but this was a decline from the nineteenth-century peak recorded in 1876. Store cattle also declined in price, but only slightly, and the demand for both sheep and pigs remained strong.[7] Had good crops returned, and had the fall in butter prices been halted in 1878, little irreparable damage would have been done to the economic well-being of the farming classes. Instead, the situation deteriorated. The rains ceased long enough during July to permit the saving of the greatest hay crop on record in Cork, but this was the only bright spot in an otherwise dismal season.[8] The storms and floods of August and September helped to spread the potato blight, injured the crops of oats and barley, and added substantially to the cost of saving the prostrated and tangled grain, which in some places was not considered worth saving at all. Not only did butter prices continue to fall, but there were also loud complaints of low cattle prices at the local fairs during the second half of the year.[9]

Almost everything went wrong with agriculture in the bitter year of 1879. Livestock suffered greatly from the severity and duration of the winter, the coldest within memory.[10] In the spring liver-fluke disease broke out as the ground began to thaw. 'The sheep in all parts of the country are dying in numbers, some in many cases losing their entire flock', Richard Doherty, sen., gloomily reported in April.[11] The prices of certain key farm products fell well below the levels of 1876. According to Barrington's index of agricultural prices, butter in 1879 was down 27 per cent since 1876; mutton, 14 per cent; and store cattle, 12 per cent.[12] In the case of store cattle, the price fall was in fact greater than Barrington's index shows, for the index was based on reports from country fairs held in May and June only, before the downward slide fully manifested

[5] *Irish agricultural statistics for 1881*, p. 39.
[6] *C.C.*, 28 Sept. 1877.
[7] Barrington, 'Agricultural prices', p. 252.
[8] *Irish agricultural statistics for 1881*, p. 39.
[9] *C.E.*, 20 July, 1, 23, 30, 31 Aug., 4, 25, 26 Sept., 2 Oct. 1878.
[10] Doherty papers, Letter book, 1876–9: R. W. Doherty, sen., to S. H. Clerke, 6 Jan. 1879, p. 201; Doherty to J. J. Oswald, 20 May 1879, p. 508.
[11] Ibid.: Doherty to F. A. Wheeler, 4 Apr. 1879, p. 417.
[12] Barrington, 'Agricultural prices', p. 252.

itself. After June farmers found it extremely difficult to dispose of their young stock except at a great sacrifice and drove their beasts to one fair after another in the vain hope of a stir in prices. [13] At the September fair in Kinsale, prime lots of young cattle reportedly realized 25 per cent less than they would have six months earlier, and sheep were said to have fallen in price to the same extent. [14] Both pastures and livestock deteriorated in condition as a result of the excessive rainfall and the unseasonably cold weather. Adding to the jeremiad, the crops were poor for the third year in a row. The yield of hay was average, and that of oats was only slightly below normal, but those of barley, wheat, turnips, and above all potatoes were sadly deficient. Table 46, which shows the percentage differences between expected and actual crop production in Cork from 1877 to 1879, summarizes the crop damage of the wet years. [15]

TABLE 46 Percentage differences between expected and actual crop production in Cork, 1877–9

year	oats	barley	wheat	potatoes	turnips	hay
1877	−22·4	−14·1	+ 7·7	−36·7	−17·0	+22·1
1878	−16·4	−10·4	− 2·7	−50·0	+ 8·5	+28·0
1879	− 7·5	−30·8	−24·4	−46·7	−30·8	0·0

Inclement seasons, bad crops, and low butter and cattle prices were plunging the county and indeed the country into a major agrarian crisis. There was a steep rise in the number of bankrupt farmers in the first half of 1879. These failures naturally occurred most frequently among the smaller tenants, whose credit with banks, shopkeepers, meal merchants, and local moneylenders was exhausted. Agricultural credit was reported to have exceeded prudent limits in the 1870s, partly as a result of the enhanced security of tenure afforded by the 1870 land act, and partly because of the series of prosperous seasons up to 1876. [16] The great contraction of credit during 1879 aggravated an already critical situation. 'The number[s] of eject[ment]s & processes at the sessions court are very great,

[13] Doherty papers: W. Forde to R. W. Doherty, sen., 29 July 1879.

[14] *C.C.*, 19 Sept. 1879. See also ibid., 3 Sept. 1879.

[15] *Irish agricultural statistics for 1871*, p. lii; *Irish agricultural statistics for 1881*, p. 39. Expected production from 1877 to 1879 has been taken as the average yield of each of the above crops between 1871 and 1876.

[16] *Preliminary report from her majesty's commissioners on agriculture* [C 2778], H.C. 1881, xv, 1, p. 7.

which speaks badly of the times', Richard Doherty, sen., told Amelia Moorehead in early January.[17] To the trustees of the Fitzpatrick estate, located near Ballyvourney, Doherty declared in mid-June: 'I am about 25 years managing this property with several others & never had the same diff[icult]y; the small farmers in . . . this part of the country are in a most distressed condition; no end to sheriff's sales'.[18]

Requests for reductions on the first gale of rent payable in 1879 nevertheless received an unsympathetic hearing from landlords and agents. Typical was the reply of William B. Leslie, who managed the Falkiner estates as well as those of the earl of Shannon, to one such request in March 1879. Leslie told the Falkiner tenants at Kilbarry near Mallow that while 'individual & isolated' farmers suffering special hardship might be relieved, no uniform abatement applicable to all occupiers would be granted. 'I have made enquiry generally,' Leslie asserted, '& I have not heard of any case where landowners dependent on their land property have made any allowance.'[19]

The case for abatements on the second gale of rent payable in 1879 was undeniable. About forty Cork landowners whose allowances were reported in the local newspapers between August and December reduced their rents on the average by approximately 25 per cent.[20] But on many properties, including some of the largest, there was continued procrastination, in spite of the fact that all the signs pointed to a winter of acute distress for the smallholders. On the estates of the earl of Kenmare and the dowager countess of Kingston, no concessions were made to the tenants.[21] When the Dublin land agent J. R. Stewart, who collected the rents on the Ponsonby estate near Youghal, inquired about abatements on the other properties in the same locality, James Penrose Fitzgerald replied in mid-November:

I am not making any reduction in the rents on my brother's or Lord Midleton's estate that are payable this autumn, but look forward to the necessity of doing so next spring; on the high lands to the north of this, the farmers are rather worse off than they are about here [i.e., Midleton]. The landlord of Clonmult [Augustus Smith] is making reductions in individual cases where the rents are up to the full value; each case should stand by

[17] Doherty papers, Letter book, 1876–9: R. W. Doherty, sen., to Mrs A. Moorehead, 11 Jan. 1879, p. 219.
[18] Ibid.: Doherty to Messrs Park, Nelson, Morgan and Co., 16 June 1879, p. 569.
[19] Falkiner papers: W. B. Leslie to D. Desmond, 29 Mar. 1879.
[20] *C.E.*, Aug.–Dec. 1879; *W.C.E.*, Aug.–Dec. 1879.
[21] Kenmare papers, Letter book, 1879–80: S. M. Hussey to H. Townsend, 10 Oct. 1879, p. 584; *C.E.*, 3 Dec. 1879.

itself. [Mountifort] Longfield and [Arthur Hugh] Smith-Barry are not giving reductions on their autumn rents. The crops except oats are very inferior. [22]

When tenants fell heavily into arrears or went bankrupt, landowners and agents did not hesitate to take the customary legal steps. They obtained almost 1,100 civil-bill decrees and writs for the recovery of rent or possession at Cork quarter sessions and from the superior courts during the year. The great majority of those against whom proceedings had been taken somehow managed to satisfy or postpone the landlord's demand for rent and retained possession of their holdings. But nearly 150 Cork tenants, together with their families, were permanently evicted. [23]

By enforcing the payment of the customary rents in spite of the depressed state of agriculture, landlords and agents unwittingly assisted the birth and growth of agrarian agitation in 1879. The immediate occasion for the agitation was provided by the ill-considered attempt of a catholic clergyman, the Rev. Geoffrey Canon Burke, to squeeze arrears of rent from the impoverished tenants of a small estate near Irishtown in south Mayo for which he was acting as executor. [24] No part of Ireland suffered more from the agricultural crisis of the late 1870s than Connaught, and Canon Burke's threat to evict those tenants who could not pay their arrears showed extreme harshness. This case of abusive landlordism came to the attention of Michael Davitt in March 1879 while he was visiting Claremorris during a tour of the west. [25] In the months since his release in December 1877 from over seven years of imprisonment for his activities as a Fenian organizer and arms agent in Britain, Davitt had given serious thought to the abolition of landlordism in Ireland and to the establishment in its place of peasant ownership of the soil. [26] As a native Mayoman whose father had been evicted from

[22] P.R.O.I., ref. no. 978, Midleton papers, Letter book, 1873–80: J. P. Fitzgerald to J. R. Stewart, 18 Nov. 1879, p. 401.

[23] *Returns showing, for the counties of Clare, Cork, Kerry, Galway, and Mayo respectively, the number of civil bills in ejectment, on title, for non-payment of rent, or for overholding, entered at quarter sessions for each of the years from 1879 to 1888 inclusive . . .: and, of the number of writs issued in actions for recovery of rent or possession in each of the counties of Clare, Cork, Kerry, Galway, and Mayo in the queen's bench, exchequer, and common pleas divisions of the high court of justice for each of the years from 1879 to 1888 inclusive . . .*, H.C. 1889 (211), lxi, 417, pp. 3–7 (hereafter cited as *Return of civil bills in ejectment and superior-court writs, 1879–88*).

[24] Davitt, *Fall of feudalism*, pp. 146–7.

[25] Ibid., p. 146.

[26] T. W. Moody, 'The new departure in Irish politics, 1878–9' in *Essays in British and Irish history in honour of James Eadie Todd*, ed H. A. Cronne,

his holding in 1852, Davitt's sympathies were immediately engaged by the plight of Canon Burke's tenants. Aided by a small group of like-minded local men, Davitt organized a great and precedent-setting demonstration attended by perhaps 10,000 persons at Irishtown on 20 April. [27] The tremendous success of the Irishtown meeting not only induced Canon Burke to lower his rents substantially but also served to ignite the fires of revolt against landlordism in other parts of Mayo as well as in neighbouring Galway and Roscommon. [28] As the area of agitation widened, the need for central direction and for a clearly defined programme of action became more pressing. In mid-August Davitt established the National Land League of Mayo, an organization pledged by its founder to 'the abolition of the present land laws of Ireland' and to the elimination of rack rents, evictions, and land grabbing. [29]

When the autumn of 1879 brought a disastrous harvest and low cattle prices on top of the summer's dismal butter sales, the land movement spilled over the borders of Connaught into Munster and parts of Leinster. [30] At Mallow on 14 September, a throng estimated at 20,000 persons cheered resolutions calling for substantial reductions in rent and for public works to alleviate the widespread distress anticipated during the coming winter. [31] As many as 25,000 to 30,000 people gathered in Cork city on 5 October to hear Charles Stewart Parnell, M.P. for County Meath, who had first identified himself with the agrarian agitation at Westport in the previous June. The huge crowd in Cork city gave an enthusiastic reception to the main resolution demanding that landlords accept a fair share of the losses suffered by tenants. The resolution declared that

in consequence of three successive bad and inclement seasons, which have rendered the land unproductive, concurrently with low prices for corn, butter, and cattle, and with losses by disease in cattle and sheep, it is utterly impossible for farmers to pay the present rent. [32]

The greatly expanded agitation was firmly consolidated by the founding of the Irish National Land League in Dublin on 21 October.

[27] Davitt, *Fall of feudalism*, pp. 147–51; Palmer, *Land League crisis*, pp. 132–4.
[28] Davitt, *Fall of feudalism*, p. 151; Palmer, *Land League crisis*, p. 137; Moody, 'New departure', pp. 327–8.
[29] Davitt, *Fall of feudalism*, pp. 160–3.
[30] Palmer, *Land League crisis*, pp. 137–9.
[31] *C.C.*, 15 Sept. 1879.   [32] *W.C.E.*, 11 Oct. 1879.

T. W. Moody, and D. B. Quinn (London, 1949), pp. 316–17; Brown, *Ir.-Amer. nationalism*, pp. 89–90; T. W. Moody, 'Irish-American nationalism' in *I.H.S.*, xv, no. 60 (Sept. 1967), p. 443.

Into this new organization were merged not only Davitt's Mayo league but also the more moderate tenants' defence associations that had sprung up in certain parts of the country during the 1870s. [33] The objectives of the Irish National Land League were essentially the same as those of the Mayo league: the 'reduction of rackrents', the defence of 'those who may be threatened with eviction for refusing to pay unjust rents', and 'the ownership of the soil by the occupiers'. Compulsory land purchase was not specified as the appropriate means for the achievement of peasant proprietorship, but the idea of compelling landlords to sell was implicit in the stipulation that every Irish tenant was 'to become the owner of his holding by paying a fair rent for a limited number of years'. With Davitt's hearty approval, Parnell was elected president of the league. [34]

Parnell's assumption of formal leadership of the agrarian agitation was the most important Irish political development of 1879. Parnell was already the recognized head of the small but aggressive band of advanced Irish nationalist M.P.s at Westminster. Their obstructionist parliamentary tactics were a standing rebuke to the moderate home rule M.P.s led by Isaac Butt until his death in May 1879 and then until April 1880 by William Shaw. Shaw's days as leader of the constitutional nationalists were clearly numbered, and Parnell was just as clearly the heir apparent to Shaw's position. By assuming the presidency of the Land League, Parnell wedded the forces of advanced constitutional nationalism to the rapidly growing land movement. He was also bidding for the support of revolutionary nationalists, but on his own terms. There was never any formal alliance between Parnell and the Fenian leaders in Ireland and America, and the Land League under Parnell's brilliant generalship was not the product of an acknowledged combination of constitutional and revolutionary nationalists. To the famous 'new departure' proposals made in October 1878 and subsequently developed by Davitt and by John Devoy, a powerful figure in the United Brotherhood (Clan na Gael) in America, Parnell had given no response. Those proposals, endorsed by Clan na Gael, had envisaged a combined political and agrarian movement in which revolutionary and constitutional nationalists would work together, openly, and on specific terms towards the goals of national independence and peasant proprietorship, but with the political objective receiving the primary emphasis. Despite its attractiveness, the new departure was not implemented for a number of reasons. Parnell refused to commit

[33] Davitt, *Fall of feudalism*, p. 170.
[34] *Freeman's Journal*, 22 Oct. 1879.

himself to it, the Irish Republican Brotherhood formally rejected it, and Davitt lost interest in its political side as he increasingly concentrated all of his energies on promoting the agrarian agitation.[35]

Thus the Land League of October 1879 was really the product of the deepening agricultural crisis and not of the new departure as properly understood. The league over which Parnell presided eschewed the constitutional question in favour of an exclusively agrarian programme. Yet there were significant links between the league and the new departure of 1878. Though the I.R.B. as a body officially held aloof from the agrarian agitation, it did not forbid participation by its members as individuals. Permitted this freedom of action, many Fenians joined local branches of the Land League. Extreme nationalists also constituted a majority of the elected officers of the central league at its foundation: of the seven officers, four were Fenians or ex-Fenians. And from Clan na Gael and other American supporters of Irish political and economic aspirations came badly needed financial support for the agrarian movement.[36] The economic crisis of the winter of 1879–80 underscored the importance of this support.

THE CRISIS OF 1879–80

Land League agitation continued during the winter of 1879–80, but much of the league's energies and resources were devoted to the relief of distress in the west of Ireland. While the agricultural crisis of the late 1870s seriously reduced the income of farmers in Cork, its impact there was much less severe than in Connaught and Donegal, where the majority of the inhabitants were the prisoners of a primitive economy which had changed little since 1850.[37] Because of the minute subdivision of holdings, the heavy dependence on the potato crop for food, and the loss of the opportunity for harvest work in Britain, destitution was acute and widespread in the western counties in late 1879 and early 1880.[38] Suffering and sickness were increased by the lack of turf, which had been only partly saved because of the heavy rains.[39] Yet conditions in the most

---

[35] Moody, 'New departure', pp. 317–33. See also Brown, *Ir.-Amer. nationalism*, pp. 85–98.

[36] Moody, 'New departure', pp. 327, 332; idem, 'Irish-American nationalism', pp. 444–5; R. B. O'Brien, *Parnell* (London and New York, 1910), p. 155.

[37] Solow, *Land question*, pp. 111–17.

[38] Palmer, *Land League crisis*, pp. 67–71.

[39] *Correspondence relative to measures for the relief of distress in Ireland, 1879–80* [C 2483], H.C. 1880, lxii, 157, pp. 3–4.

stricken counties of Ireland did not approach a general state of famine resembling that of the winter of 1846–7.

In County Cork it was a time of some privation for middle-class and well-to-do farmers, and of severe hardship for smallholders and labourers. For several months many of those in distress were reduced to only two meals a day, and a few to only one, but no deaths were reported in Cork from starvation. Sickness and disease arising from malnutrition and leading to death did occur. An epidemic of fever and measles on the island of Cape Clear afflicted about 100 persons, of whom eighteen had died by November 1879. [40] The death rate for the county rose from an average of about 16 per thousand in the early 1870s to 18·7 in 1878, 19·0 in 1879, and 18·7 in 1880. [41] The distress also produced a sharp rise in the number of persons receiving poor-law relief. Almost 16,400 persons were being assisted under the poor laws on the first Saturday in March 1880, as compared with only 10,800 on the corresponding day in 1878. [42]

Several factors, however, helped to contain the suffering. Indian meal had become a staple article of diet for the poorer classes in the years since the famine. During the 1870s it was regularly imported in large quantities; an average of almost 63,000 tons a year arrived at the port of Cork between 1871 and 1876. In happy contrast to the fatal delay in the arrival of foreign supplies of food after the disastrous potato failure of 1846, there was an immediate response to the blight of 1877. Cork imports of Indian corn climbed to more than 118,000 tons, and between 1877 and 1880 they averaged over 109,000 tons a year. [43] A normal sowing of potatoes in early 1880 was assured by the distribution at cost price or less of disease-resistant 'champion' seed potatoes under the seed supply act. [44] Nearly £50,000 was advanced for this purpose in County Cork, and almost £600,000 in Ireland as a whole. [45]

[40] *C.E.*, 1 Nov. 1879; *W.C.E.*, 1, 15 Nov. 1879.

[41] *Fourteenth detailed annual report of the registrar-general of marriages, births, and deaths in Ireland, 1877* [C 2301], H.C. 1878–9, xix, 523, p. 92; *Fifteenth . . . report . . . , 1878* [C 2388], H.C. 1878–9, xvi, 429, p. 92; *Sixteenth . . . report . . . , 1879* [C 2688], H.C. 1880, xvi, 429, p. 92; *Seventeenth . . . report . . . , 1880* [C 3046], H.C. 1881, xxvii, 897, p. 92.

[42] *Return of numbers in receipt of relief in the several unions in Ireland on the 1st day of January, the 1st day of March, and the 1st day of June in 1878, 1879, and 1880*, H.C. 1880 (420–sess. 2), lxii, 289, pp. 6–7, 14–15, 22–3.

[43] Harbour Commissioners, Cork: Yearly abstracts of receipts, expenditures, etc., of the Cork harbour commissioners, 1871–80.

[44] 43 Vict., c. 1.

[45] *Annual report of the local government board for Ireland, being the ninth report under the Local Government Board (Ireland) Act, 35 & 36 Vic., c. 69* [C 2926], H.C. 1881, xlvii, 269, pp. 126–9.

While the government relied exclusively upon the poor-law system and upon private relief organizations to supply direct food relief, it recognized the need to provide employment for the labourers and cottiers left idle by the heavy retrenchment forced upon the farming classes. In January 1880 the treasury authorized the expenditure of £500,000, to be advanced on generous terms to Irish landowners and sanitary authorities for projects normally carried out under the land-improvement acts and public-health legislation. [46] So attractive were the terms of these loans that there was a mad rush to obtain the money. By the end of February applications for almost £1,330,000 had been received from all over Ireland, and Cork landowners and sanitary authorities alone had requested more than £180,000. [47] Disraeli's ministry responded halfheartedly to the obvious need for additional funds. Its relief of distress act made available from the Irish church surplus fund only £250,000 beyond the £500,000 already authorized, to be used mainly for loans to landowners and sanitary authorities. [48] Amending legislation enacted under Gladstone in early August, however, added £750,000 to previous appropriations. [49] The government also promoted local public works, which were chiefly executed under the supervision of extraordinary baronial presentment sessions. [50] Exclusive of the sums advanced under the seed supply act, total government-initiated expenditure for the relief of distress in Ireland amounted to more than £1,020,000 up to the end of March 1881. [51]

Government expenditures, however, were not made quickly enough in the most critical months between November 1879 and June 1880, and during this period the enormous work undertaken by private relief organizations was considerably more important than government activity in relieving distress. Private charity accomplished wonders in the first half of 1880 in alleviating the most pressing wants for food, fuel, and clothing in distressed districts.

[46] *Correspondence relative to measures for the relief of distress in Ireland, 1879–80,* pp. 11–15, 26, 29–30.

[47] *Return of all applications from landed proprietors and sanitary authorities in scheduled unions for loans under the notices of the commissioners of public works in Ireland, dated the 22nd day of November 1879 and the 12th day of January 1880 respectively; with result of applications to the 20th day of March 1880, arranged by baronies,* H.C. 1880 (154), lxii, 209, pp. 1–7.

[48] 43 Vict., c. 4, s. 17.

[49] 43 & 44 Vict., c. 14, s. 2.

[50] *Return showing the amount allowed for relief works in Ireland, the amount authorized to be expended, and the amount expended up to the present date,* H.C. 1881 (274), lvii, 705, p. 1.

[51] S.P.O., C.S.O., Registered papers, 1891, no. 17944: 'Expenditure on relief of distress, 1879 and 1890', 13 July 1891.

Money from America and Australia flowed into the hands of the Duchess of Marlborough's Committee and the Dublin Mansion House Relief Committee, and contributions came from many other sources and through many other channels.[52] The Mansion House Committee estimated that no less than £830,000 in private charitable donations had been spent throughout Ireland by early October 1880.[53] Some of this money reached those in need through the medium of the Land League, helping further to raise the prestige of that organization in the eyes of the farming classes and among the catholic clergy. New branches of the league were often established for the purpose of distributing relief funds, with the result that 'the work of combination kept pace with the relief operations among the people'.[54] The sharp rise which took place in the volume of emigrant remittances, however, contributed as much as either government or private undertakings, and perhaps more, towards the alleviation of want. The amount of remittances sent from North America alone to the United Kingdom (at least 90 per cent of which went to Ireland) increased from £4,280,000 in 1879 to £7,020,000 in 1880. Even if half of the increase in remittances to Ireland was 'passage money', this would still leave more than £1,200,000 in extraordinary funds for the improvement of the welfare of the emigrants' families in Ireland.[55]

In the long run, however, the most effective remedy for privation was the decided improvement in agricultural prices and the return of fair weather. As early as March 1880, Richard Doherty, sen., claimed that distress in the Bandon district was 'not so great as represented'. 'The rents will be somewhat later than usual,' he predicted, 'but I expect all will be paid. I trust this year will prove better than last; there is a very good price for butter, which greatly assists the farmers.'[56] The recovery in butter prices was indeed remarkable. The May-to-November average price of first-quality Cork butter rose from 101s. per cwt in 1879 to 124s. per cwt in 1880; with the exception of 1874–6, Cork butter prices had never

[52] Palmer, *Land League crisis*, pp. 83–105.

[53] Dublin Mansion House Relief Committee, *The Irish crisis of 1879–80: proceedings of the Dublin Mansion House Relief Committee, 1880* (Dublin, 1881), p. 73.

[54] Davitt, *Fall of feudalism*, p. 211.

[55] Schrier believes that one-twelfth is a reasonable estimate of the remittances of British emigrants, and that 'only about 40 per cent of all remittances were used to pay for emigration' from Ireland to North America (*American emigration*, pp. 106, 110, 167).

[56] Doherty papers, Letter book, 1880–6: R. W. Doherty, sen., to J. J. Oswald, 24 Mar. 1880, p. 68.

been higher. [57] Store-cattle prices were also buoyant in 1880, especially at the autumn fairs. Indeed, younger stores one to two years old were sold at an average price which exceeded that of all previous years since 1840, with the sole exception of 1876. [58] Farmers profited fully from the increased demand for cattle. In contrast to what had occurred during the crisis of the early 1860s, the wet years of the late 1870s saw no significant diminution in cattle numbers in Cork. While the number of cows slightly declined, dry cattle rose from 175,000 in 1877 to 206,000 in 1880. [59] The encouraging reports on the state of the crops in August were more than vindicated by the results: a bountiful harvest consolidated the other gains. [60] The importation of 'champion' seed potatoes resulted in abundant yields. In the Blackwater valley near Fermoy, potatoes 'did not prove so good since 1842, the champions being particularly fine in quantity and quality'. [61] All the crops in County Cork were excellent, as illustrated by Table 47, which gives the percentage differences between expected and actual production. [62]

TABLE 47 Percentage differences between expected and actual crop production in Cork, 1880

crop	% difference	crop	% difference
oats	+19·4	potatoes	+63·5
barley	+20·5	turnips	+22·3
wheat	+18·6	hay	+ 5·4

When rents again became payable in March and May 1880, the improvement in economic conditions had not yet become apparent, and abatements of about 20 per cent were common, although by no means universal. [63] After returning from his collection at Bantry, Samuel Hussey told Lord Kenmare at the beginning of May: 'I got about half the rents. The tenants promise to pay the balance on the 9th of June & I think they will. . . . *I made no abatement.*' [64] Whether

[57] T. J. Clanchy and Co., *Half-a-century's butter prices*, 1 p.

[58] Barrington, 'Agricultural prices', p. 252.

[59] *Irish agricultural statistics for 1877* [C 1938], H.C. 1878, lxxvii, 511, p. 57; *Irish agricultural statistics for 1880*, p. 57.

[60] *C.E.*, 16, 20, 25, 26 Aug. 1880.   [61] Ibid., 29 Sept. 1880.

[62] *Irish agricultural statistics for 1881*, p. 39. Expected production in 1880 has been taken as the average yield of each of the various crops between 1871 and 1876.

[63] *C.E.*, Jan.–May 1880.

[64] Kenmare papers, Letter book, Jan.–Oct. 1880: S. M. Hussey to earl of Kenmare, 1 May 1880, pp. 421–2. See also Doherty papers, Letter book, 1880–6: R. W. Doherty, sen., to C. Gillman, 18 June 1880, p. 118.

reductions were made or not, it was no easy matter screwing rents from tenants seriously weakened by three poor seasons when prices were only beginning to recover. 'It is well to get in the rents without loss, as very few landlords are able to do so', Richard Doherty, sen., congratulated James Oswald in mid-June.

There are very large arrears due on the d[uke] of D[evonshire's] estates. I am doing very well on Lord Bandon's, but much labour to induce the tenants to pay. Parnell & Co. are doing vast mischief setting the tenants against the landlord. [65]

THE GREAT ANTI-LANDLORD ASSAULT

With the general election of April 1880 and the National Land Conference held in Dublin at the end of the same month, the agrarian agitation entered upon a new and more formidable phase. The general election which returned Gladstone to power in Britain brought a considerable accession of strength to Parnell's parliamentary following, and the squire of Avondale was chosen to be chairman of the rejuvenated Irish parliamentary party. The agrarian and the parliamentary wings of the national land movement were now firmly tied together under Parnell's leadership. [66] The National Land Conference of 29 April advanced a radical programme for legislative action. In response to the current emergency, the convention called for the enactment of a bill suspending for a period of two years both the eviction of any tenant whose holding was valued for poor rates at £10 or less, and the power of recovering from any tenant a rent higher than the poor-law valuation of his land. The convention also sought to translate the league's slogan of 'the land for the people' into a practical proposal for permanent reform by outlining a comprehensive measure of land purchase under which landlords could be forced to sell on terms very advantageous to the tenants. [67] While these proposals made no headway in parliament during 1880, they powerfully shaped the character of a great extra-parliamentary assault against Irish landlordism.

The assault developed slowly at first in County Cork. Local Land League bodies were not at all numerous before the spring of 1880. A branch was not established in Cork city until mid-April, when dissensions came to a head between moderates and radicals within the Cork Farmers' Club. When the moderates refused to accept the

---

[65] Doherty papers, Letter book, 1880–6: Doherty to J. J. Oswald, 19 June 1880, p. 115.

[66] C. C. O'Brien, *Parnell and his party*, pp. 11–35.

[67] Davitt, *Fall of feudalism*, pp. 240–4.

full Land League programme, the radical faction seceded and set up its own organization. [68] Local branches of the league were soon multiplying rapidly, however, with the one in Cork city serving as a central branch for the county and for parts of Kerry as well. [69] In the country as a whole, the agrarian agitation gathered increasing momentum from the late summer of 1880. Land League meetings averaged as many as ninety-one a month between August and December, as compared with only fourteen a month between April and July. [70] The greatly increased tempo of the land movement was partly the result of political factors, especially the rejection of the compensation for disturbance bill by the house of lords in early August and the return of Parnellite M.P.s to speaking platforms in Ireland after the parliamentary session closed in early September. [71] But the increasing strength and activity of Land League organizations during the latter part of 1880 were also in large measure the outcome of the steady economic improvement taking place in almost all parts of the country, and conspicuously in Cork and the other Munster counties. [72]

While the economic improvement gave momentum to the agitation, it came too late to save many small farmers from bankruptcy and the loss of their holdings. Civil-bill decrees and superior-court writs were about as numerous in Cork in 1880 as they had been during the previous year, and evictions progressed at a somewhat greater rate. [73] Landlords and agents apparently intended to do business as usual. In earlier years they had been encouraged to evict defaulting tenants in the certain knowledge that the lands would not be left untenanted. Land grabbing, or taking a farm from which the previous tenant had been evicted for non-payment of rent, or which he was forced to surrender because he could no longer pay the rent, had always carried a measure of public disapproval and had occasionally resulted in private vengeance. Nevertheless, all the execution sales, evictions, and land grabbing of

[68] *C.E.*, 19 Apr. 1880.

[69] Ibid., 20 Sept. 1880.

[70] J. L. Hammond, *Gladstone and the Irish nation* (London and New York, 1938), pp. 191–2.

[71] O'Brien, *Parnell and his party*, pp. 49–55.

[72] This point is completely missed by Palmer, who claims that at the beginning of June 'thousands of the Irish people were threatened with actual starvation and the agitation was increasing daily in violence and strength' (*Land League crisis*, p. 153). To the extent that economic conditions played a role in the increasing momentum of the land movement during the summer of 1880, the recession of privation rather than the threat of starvation was the cause.

[73] *Return of civil bills in ejectment and superior-court writs, 1879–88*, pp. 3–5.

1879 took place with surprisingly little disturbance. Ten Cork landlords received threatening letters for refusing to reduce their rents, or because of past or pending evictions on their estates, but none of these threats was executed. In the entire county in 1879, there were only six cases of incendiarism, four of them meant to discourage land grabbing. [74]

The course of events was far different in 1880. While the league vigorously combated evictions and rack rents, great emphasis was also placed upon the elimination of land grabbing. During a meeting of the Cloyne branch in July, the chairman observed that nothing had yet been said of harsh landlords. This caused him no concern, he asserted, because 'the real enemies of the people were the farmers themselves'. Fix the blame where it belonged: 'The man who gave a high rent over his neighbour and robbed himself, his family, and his neighbour was the person that should be denounced'. [75] Only when the landlords learned by repeated demonstration that people would have nothing to do with evicted farms, would they cease their evictions. By a further step of reasoning, it seemed probable that since few landlords possessed either the will or the resources to stock evicted holdings, the financial sacrifice of derelict land would eventually compel them to reinstate the evicted tenants. Success depended upon the proper organization and deployment of public opinion. The technique most frequently used by the league was brutally simple. Any evicted tenant who was the victim of a land grabber was welcome to present his case to the members of the nearest league branch, who then considered it and decided upon appropriate action. A vocal demonstration of the public's indignation was usually held on the grabber's own land or nearby, and this was often all that was needed to bring him to a belated recognition of his failings. [76]

Grabbers who defied the league were easy targets for reprisals. The single most important motive behind the agrarian outrages in Cork between February and September 1880 was the desire to punish or thwart land grabbers. As many as twenty-four out of the forty agrarian outrages reported in the east riding of Cork during these

[74] The most serious outrage occurred in April, when a bailiff was shot after attempting to carry out an eviction, but it was the only case of this kind, and no other shootings were reported in Cork during the year (*Return of all agrarian outrages which have been reported by the Royal Irish Constabulary between the 1st day of January 1879 and the 31st day of January 1880, giving particulars of crime, arrests, and results of proceedings*, H.C. 1880 (131), lx, 199, pp. 25–8).

[75] *W.C.E.*, 10 July 1880.

[76] *C.E.*, 13, 21 Sept. 1880.

months fell into this category. Of these twenty-four cases, only five involved letters warning tenants to surrender or to shun evicted farms; in fourteen cases, hayricks, out-offices, or dwelling houses were burned. On the estate of Peter Penn-Gaskell near Shanagarry, three unoccupied dwelling houses located on evicted farms were destroyed by fire on 30 March and 6 and 27 May. A determined grabber named William Prendergast was also struck more than once. A dwelling house and three outbuildings belonging to him were burned on 14 April and 3 July.[77] Anyone who purchased the interest in an evicted farm at an execution sale became a prime candidate for an attack. Sir George St John Colthurst observed to the other county grand jurors in July that

the worst thing he saw in this class of crime [i.e., malicious injury] was that 40 out of the 60 were cases in which tenants who had purchased farms in the open market had the vengeance of the previous occupiers wrecked upon them immediately that they took possession.[78]

Taking literally Parnell's advice that they keep a firm grip on their homesteads and their lands, tenants often resisted eviction and, even more often, forcibly retook possession after they had been evicted. Widespread sympathy developed in Cork during 1880 for this method of challenging the property rights of landlords. Richard Doherty, sen., encountered fierce resistance to an eviction on Charles Gillman's estate. As Doherty explained to James Oswald on 19 June:

I had to get the sheriff out from Cork to Dunmanway yesterday to take possession of a farm about 2 miles from that town where there were 2 years' rent due last March, & [where the tenants] got as much time as could be possibly given. They resisted the sheriff tho' he had 30 of the constab[ular]y with loaded guns. The fellows had the houses barricaded & over 100 men armed with pitchforks.[79]

When Daniel Conner evicted Patrick Crowley from his farm at Aultagh near Dunmanway in mid-August, Crowley and his cohorts poured scalding water on the sheriff's bailiffs and stoned four of the thirty policemen assisting in the eviction.[80] Two months later, with the aid of a party of armed men, the Crowleys forcibly retook possession and barricaded themselves inside. Arriving in a rage with

[77] *Return (in continuation of the return ordered on the 15th March 1880) of all agrarian outrages . . . between the 1st day of February 1880 and the 31st day of October 1880 . . .*, H.C. 1881 (6), lxxvii, 273, pp. 38–47 (hereafter cited as *Return of agrarian outrages, 1 Feb.–31 Oct. 1880*). [78] *C.E.*, 19 July 1880.

[79] The sheriff eventually succeeded in taking possession; the tenants owed £234 (Doherty papers, Letter book, 1880–6: R. W. Doherty, sen., to J. J. Oswald, 19 June 1880, p. 115).

[80] *Return of agrarian outrages, 1 Feb.–31 Oct. 1880*, pp. 44–5.

an escort of police and a revolver in his hand, Conner entered by a window when he found the door blocked by stones and physically ejected Mrs Crowley and her two daughters. [81] Almost twenty cases of the forcible retaking of possession were reported in Cork between August and December, and in most of these cases parties of armed men assisted in restoring the evicted tenants. [82]

While the Land League and peasant terrorism were thus disciplining land grabbers and challenging landlords, the cry was raised in the autumn of 1880 that no more than the government valuation of any farm should be paid as rent. This new direction in the agrarian agitation stemmed from the National Land Conference proposal of the previous spring for a law which, in effect, would have fixed the valuation of every holding in the country as the rent of that holding for the next two years. It was scarcely surprising that Gladstone's government showed no interest in this proposal, for the valuation, conducted under an act of 1852 but over a long span of years ending in 1865, was not uniform throughout the country. [83] Moreover, the valuation was largely based on the average agricultural prices of 1849–51, when the demand for Irish farm produce had been at a very low level indeed. Given the great rise in farm prices since 1851, the valuation was generally a low standard by which to determine the real letting value of Irish land. The leaders of the Land League could hardly have been ignorant of this fact. [84]

The clamour for the government valuation caused consternation especially among the landlords and agents of Cork and the other southern counties, because rents there were much higher in relation to the valuation than in the rest of the country. Whereas only about 30 per cent of the area of Ireland was let at more than 20 per cent above the valuation, over 60 per cent of the land in Munster was rented at this rate. [85] When landowners contrasted the official scale

---

[81] *C.E.*, 21 Oct. 1880; *W.C.E.*, 23 Oct. 1880.

[82] *Return of agrarian outrages, 1 Feb.–31 Oct. 1880*, pp. 40–2, 44–7; *Return of all agrarian outrages . . . between the 1st day of November 1880 and the 30th day of November 1880 . . .*, H.C. 1881 (6–I), lxxvii, 409, pp. 19–26; *Return of all agrarian outrages . . . between the 1st day of December 1880 and the 31st day of December 1880 . . .*, H.C. 1881 (6–II), lxxvii, 487, pp. 26–37. See also *C.E.*, 10 Sept., 21 Oct., 15 Nov. 1880.

[83] Since the valuation was carried out under the supervision of Richard Griffith, the noted geologist and civil engineer, it was frequently referred to as Griffith's valuation (*Report from the select committee on general valuation, &c. (Ireland); together with the proceedings of the committee, minutes of evidence, and appendix*, H.C. 1868–9 (362), ix, 1, pp. 6–7, 21, 54).

[84] Ibid., pp. 14, 173; Solow, *Land question*, pp. 59–68, 74.

[85] These percentages are derived from the Irish Land Committee's table of the proportional amount of land in the four provinces of Ireland let

of prices upon which the valuation was based with recent prices, and even with those of 1879, they must have been amazed by the striking differences. Table 48 sets out both the prices specified in the valuation act of 1852 and the agricultural prices of 1876–80 in index numbers. [86] The excellent harvest of 1880 provided landlords with yet another reason for hardening their attitude.

There never within the memory of the oldest man [was] so splendid a harvest [declared Richard Doherty, sen., to James Oswald in mid-October]; the potato crop [is] the most abundant; but instead of returning thanks to the Almighty, there is nothing but murder & outrage & league meet[in]gs trying to prevent payment of rents. [87]

TABLE 48   Index numbers of Irish agricultural prices in the valuation act of 1852 and of prices prevailing between 1876 and 1880

(base 1840 = 100)

	butter	beef	mutton	pork	oats	barley	wheat
1852 act	77	74	88	82	77	80	61
average, 1876–80	129	147	176	138	128	121	81
1879	113	135	160	132	137	118	90
1880	129	135	160	146	120	114	76

Equal treatment for all tenants on the same principle and enforced by collective bargaining now became the goal of the agrarian agitation. Through the medium of the local branch of the league, the tenants of each landlord in every district were asked to agree to tender the valuation in discharge of all rent due, and if this were not accepted from all of them, to withdraw in a body without paying anything. This was obviously an attractive programme calculated to have an almost universal appeal, and its salutary lessons thundered forth from league platforms Sunday after Sunday during the autumn and winter of 1880. An aroused and increasingly

[86] *Irish Farmers' Gazette*, 1 Nov. 1879; Barrington, 'Agricultural prices', p. 252.
[87] Doherty papers, Letter book, 1880–6: R. W. Doherty, sen., to J. J. Oswald, 13 Oct. 1880, p. 178.

---

under, at, and over the government valuation. The committee's figures were based on a very good sample in which about 25 per cent of the land in Munster and 30 per cent of the total area of Ireland were represented (Irish Land Committee, *The land question, Ireland*, no. 3: *Facts and figures*, Table 2).

defiant populace thronged to enthusiastic demonstrations addressed by the leading Parnellite M.P.s. Bands played national tunes, and banners boldly proclaimed the intentions and aspirations of the demonstrators: 'Hold the crops', 'Griffith's valuation', 'The people's voice is the highest law—landlordism must go', 'National Line—the shortest passage from New York to Ireland, the Irish exiles will yet return', and 'Remember Kilclooney wood' (a reference to Peter O'Neill Crowley's abortive Fenian raid in 1867). [88] Parnell himself addressed an estimated 30,000 people in Cork city on Sunday, 3 October, just two weeks after he had elaborated at Ennis the famous policy of 'moral Coventry' for land grabbers—a policy soon extended to other enemies of the league under the name 'boycotting' and used with great effect against the Cork landlord William Bence Jones. [89] A huge parade of farmers, tradesmen, and labourers two miles long marched from Blarney into Cork for Parnell's speech. [90] In the opinion of Conor Cruise O'Brien, this enormous demonstration for Parnell 'probably marked the climax both of the land agitation and of his own popularity as a semi-revolutionary leader'. [91]

Tim Healy, Parnell's political secretary and a native of Bantry who was soon to begin a great parliamentary career, delivered blistering attacks on certain West Cork landlords and agents at Castletown-Berehaven and Kealkill on 24 and 31 October. At Castletown-Berehaven the youthful Healy expressed scant remorse over the recent attempted murder of Samuel N. Hutchins, [92] a prominent landowner and agent in the Bantry district, and urged united resistance to the financial exactions of Lord Charles Pelham-Clinton. Clinton's offence was that, after purchasing Bere Island from the debt-ridden earl of Bantry in the early 1850s, he had withdrawn the large abatement granted by Bantry during the famine. Roared Healy:

Were the men of Bere Island fools? Were they going to continue paying that rent? They should now tell Lord Clinton that he would not get a penny more than the government valuation, and if they did that, they might depend on it that Lord Clinton would knuckle down. [93]

[88] *W.C.E.*, 25 Sept. 1880; *C.E.*, 10, 13 Dec. 1880.

[89] For Parnell's Ennis speech, see *Freeman's Journal*, 20 Sept. 1880.

[90] *C.E.*, 4 Oct. 1880; Palmer, *Land League crisis*, pp. 162–3.

[91] O'Brien, *Parnell and his party*, p. 54.

[92] The attack took place near Drimoleague on 16 October while Hutchins was receiving rent for himself, his son, and his two sisters. The driver of his wagon was killed, perhaps because the lone assassin mistook him for Hutchins (*C.E.*, 18, 19, 20 Oct. 1880; *W.C.E.*, 23 Oct. 1880).

[93] *C.E.*, 26 Oct. 1880.

Another of Healy's targets was the earl of Kenmare, who had just finished building a £100,000 mansion at Killarney and who was also refusing to reduce his rents.

From their brows [Healy reminded the tenants] was wrung the sweat that was spent in the baronial halls of Lord Kenmare. Every furrow their ploughs went through, every movement they gave to their spades or their picks was not for themselves or for their wives or children, but for Lord Kenmare! [94]

The enforcement of the league's programme by acts of terrorism was considered to be as necessary to the achievement of its aims as were the legal activities of the organization. All over the county during the autumn and winter of 1880, notices threatening the direst consequences to tenants who paid more than the government valuation were prominently posted in public places, on the doors of catholic chapels, and on the tenants' own houses and farm buildings. Many Cork landowners were threatened with 'an ounce of lead in the belly' if they dared to defy the league and demanded the usual rent. In some places, notably between Bantry and Kenmare and along the whole Berehaven peninsula, all payment of rent was apparently interdicted. Almost forty cases involving the posting of threatening notices or the sending of threatening letters, all directly connected with the league's demand for the acceptance of the valuation by landlords, were reported by the constabulary in November and December alone. In several instances, armed parties of men with blackened faces attacked the houses of tenants suspected of wavering in their allegiance to the cause. The open or secret payment of the usual rent, however, was not widespread; at least there were no reports of outrages committed for this reason in which violence was done to either persons or property. Thus far, the mere threat of retribution had achieved its end. [95]

Under the initial shock of the agrarian agitation, Cork landlords were temporarily rendered powerless to collect rents. 'I hope soon that the Sept[ember] rents of 1879 will be paid,' Richard Doherty, sen., apologized to the trustees of the Fitzpatrick estate in early November 1880, 'but it is next to impossible to get rents; if the people were let alone, they would pay willingly, but those Land Leagues are destroying the country.' 'I sent my bailiff lately to Macroom', reported Doherty, 'to request the tenants to pay their rent, & the answer several made was that they would only pay [the]

[94] Ibid., 1 Nov. 1880. See also *W.C.E.*, 6 Nov. 1880.
[95] *Return of agrarian outrages, 1–30 Nov. 1880*, pp. 19–26; *Return of agrarian outrages, 1–31 Dec. 1880*, pp. 26–37; *C.E.*, 30 Sept. 1880.

gov[ernmen]t valuation.'[96] 'The . . . [Cripple] Hill tenants have all refused to pay unless getting a large reduction', Doherty informed their landlord James F. Sweeney in the same month. 'The country is in a most lawless state; in fact, it is next to impossible to collect rent, and where it is to end I know not.'[97] To Amelia Moorehead, whose tenants also refused to pay more than the valuation, and whose rents were 'very far over' it, Doherty patiently explained that a reduction of 5 or even 10 per cent would hardly satisfy them. 'I cannot get my own rents tho' they have . . . [their lands] scarcely anything over the government valuation', he told her at the beginning of December.[98]

The propertied classes all over Ireland were horrified in October and November 1880 by the persecution of Captain Charles Boycott, the agent of Earl Erne's estate at Lough Mask in Mayo, after Boycott had refused to allow Erne's tenants in effect to fix their own rents.[99] In December a similar campaign was initiated against William Bence Jones in County Cork. Jones was not a typical Cork landlord. Educated at Harrow and at Balliol College, Oxford, he had practised for several years as a lawyer on the home circuit before coming to Ireland to reside permanently on the family estate at Lisselan near Clonakilty just prior to the great famine.[100] Except for holidays spent in London, Jones lived all year round at Lisselan and had devoted himself wholeheartedly to practical agricultural improvement for almost forty years.[101] He belonged to the doctrinaire *laissez-faire* tradition of socio-economic thought, as shown by his spirited defence of the rights of property and by his rigid insistence upon freedom of contract in his book, *The life's work in Ireland of a landlord who tried to do his duty*, published in 1880. At a time when nationalism was fostering a new and heightened sense of pride and self-identity in the Irish people, Jones's jejune comments on the deficiencies in character of Irish tenants were certain to arouse indignation.

[96] Doherty papers, Letter book, 1880–6: R. W. Doherty, sen., to Messrs Park, Nelson, Morgan, and Co., 2 Nov. 1880, p. 184.

[97] Ibid.: Doherty to J. F. Sweeney, 12 Nov. 1880, p. 191.

[98] Ibid.: Doherty to Mrs A. Moorehead, 1 Dec. 1880, p. 198.

[99] T. H. Corfe, 'The troubles of Captain Boycott, part I: the Land League' in *History Today*, xiv, no. 11 (Nov. 1964), pp. 758–64; idem, 'The troubles of Captain Boycott, part II: the campaign', ibid., no. 12 (Dec. 1964), pp. 854–62; Palmer, *Land League crisis*, pp. 197–210.

[100] Rev. John O'Leary, 'Mr Bence Jones' story of his experiences in Ireland' in *Contemporary Review*, xl (June 1881), reprinted in full in *W.C.E.*, 9 July 1881.

[101] W. B. Jones, *Life's work*, pp. 1–21.

There has been no difficulty in the way of any man in Ireland that ordinary industry and energy could not get over [he wrote]. The true hindrances have been his own faults. Drink, indolence, debt, and scheming, with ignorance and want of self-reliance as consequences.[102]

As an intensely business-oriented landlord, Jones was easily made the supreme embodiment and symbol of the worst features of Irish landlordism, its history, and its myths. He had purchased part of his 3,800-acre estate in the landed estates court during the 1860s. Popular opinion tarred almost all such purchasers with the same black brush: he belonged to

the class of landlords, admittedly the bane of the country, *novi homines*, who buy land solely as a commercial speculation, and caring nothing for the sentiment which attaches to landed property, and discarding the relations which it entails, look only for usurious returns.[103]

Jones undoubtedly appeared bigoted when in 1861 he brought over a tenant from England for a large farm of about 250 acres, because he believed that it would be impossible to find a tenant in Ireland with sufficient capital and skill.[104] He was also a middleman, holding the townland of Cloheen from the earl of Shannon at a few shillings an acre and charging the undertenants almost £3 an acre. Merely by being a middleman, he made himself odious.[105]

The 1,000-acre demesne which Jones farmed so successfully had been formed by consolidating the holdings of small tenants crushed during the great famine. Whether these tenants were evicted, as his enemies charged, or 'went away of themselves', as Jones claimed, was unimportant. What mattered was that the demesne once contained 'the homesteads of many a happy family who are now scattered to the ends of the earth'.[106] The sharp reduction in the number of tenants on some parts of his estate and the frequent changes of tenancy on others labelled him as a great exterminator. Worst of all, his rents were said to be higher than those of any other landowner in the south of Ireland. Because the farms on the neighbouring estates of the earls of Bandon and Shannon were generally let at 25 or 30 per cent above the valuation, Jones's rents seemed all the more exorbitant. The combined rents of thirty-three of his forty-odd tenants amounted to over £1,850 per annum, while the government valuation of their lands was less than £1,000.[107] On

[102] Ibid., pp. 86–7.
[103] Rev. John O'Leary, quoted in *W.C.E.*, 9 July 1881.
[104] *C.C.*, 6 Feb. 1882.
[105] *W.C.E.*, 9 July 1881.
[106] *C.E.*, 4 Dec. 1880.
[107] *W.C.E.*, 9 July 1881.

such an estate as his, where so much capital had been invested in permanent improvements, Jones could never admit that the rents should in any way be related to the valuation. In fact, said Jones, Sam Kingston, a tenant of his who paid £112 a year for a farm valued at only £51, 'has often laughed with me at the silly talk of Griffith's valuation and compared it with the rent he pays'.[108]

A small incident in which Jones attempted to raise the rent of one farm from 14s. 3d. to £1 an acre finally sparked the campaign against him.[109] Within the space of a few days in the first week of December 1880, his tenants received threatening letters, a symbolic grave was dug before his hall door, the Rev. John O'Leary, chairman of the local branch of the league, denounced him as a harsh, exterminating rack-renter, and his tenants, after tendering the valuation, which he refused, withheld the £1,300 that they owed him. On Saturday, 11 December, his demesne labourers received notices proclaiming: 'Strike on Monday. Bence Jones is boycotted. God save Ireland.' Shopkeepers were warned to stop selling him provisions, and tradesmen were cautioned to cease giving him their services. Only a few servants stayed with him.[110] Deprived of his rents and his labourers, Jones also encountered difficulty in disposing of some of his livestock, which comprised about 400 sheep and sixty head of cattle.[111] Pressure from the cattle dealers forced the Cork city shipping companies to refuse on 14 December to carry his stock over to Bristol. The drovers abandoned them, and for several hours they wandered loose and untended through the streets of Cork before being rounded up by the police and sent by rail to Dublin.[112] They were temporarily boycotted by Dublin dealers and shippers and were without food, but on 17 December they were finally taken aboard Liverpool-bound vessels and sold after some further difficulty outside that English city.[113]

Jones's plight aroused widespread anger in England. London society was reportedly 'seething with indignation'.[114] Twenty Oxford undergraduates offered to come over to work or fight.[115] An English customer warned a Cork butter exporter, 'The English can

[108] W. B. Jones, 'My answer to opponents' in *Contemporary Review*, xl (Sept. 1881), reprinted in full in *W.C.E.*, 17 Sept. 1881.

[109] Becker, *Disturbed Ire.*, pp. 268–70.

[110] *C.E.*, 4, 13, 14, 17 Dec. 1880; *The Times*, 8, 15 Dec. 1880. Jones claimed that he had received £100 out of the £1,300 due (*Life's work*, p. x).

[111] *C.E.*, 17 Dec. 1880.

[112] *The Times*, 15 Dec. 1880.

[113] Ibid., 16, 18 Dec. 1880; Davitt, *Fall of feudalism*, p. 313.

[114] *C.E.*, 23 Dec. 1880.

[115] *The Times*, 24 Dec. 1880.

boycott Irish butter and all kinds of provisions if necessary, and can do without them'.[116] Gladstone himself sent Jones a message of sympathy, and Forster, the chief secretary, offered him additional military and police protection.[117] The beleaguered landlord fought back gamely. He was apparently able to obtain provisions by subterfuge, although one of his servants, recognized while shopping for supplies in Skibbereen, was roughly treated.[118] In order to harvest his turnip and potato crops, Jones enlisted the aid of the Property Defence Association. By the second week of January 1881, he had twenty-two new labourers working in small groups, each under the protection of a rifleman. Most of them had been found in the town of 'Orange' Bandon, but Norris Goddard, an organizer of the expedition to relieve Captain Boycott, shepherded six stalwart Orangemen from County Cavan to Lisselan.[119] After failing to entice his own workmen to desert the league, Jones brought proceedings against all of them in February and March for over-holding their cottages. Several then defected, but about twenty-five of those evicted were provided with houses and employment by the league.[120] Although Jones carried the farms of three of his principal tenants to execution sales at the end of May, a fairly united resistance to the payment of rent without a reduction was maintained until well after the passage of the 1881 land act, when the tenants entered the land courts.[121]

THE COUNTERATTACK OF THE LANDLORDS AND THE BATTLE FOR RENTS

With the assistance of Gladstone's government, the landlords recovered in early 1881 from the temporary paralysis induced by the first shock of agrarian agitation. Michael Davitt was arrested in early February, and Parnell and thirty-five other members of his party were suspended and ejected from the house of commons for

---

[116] Quoted in *C.E.*, 21 Dec. 1880.
[117] *The Times*, 23 Dec. 1880.
[118] *C.E.*, 1 Jan. 1881.
[119] *The Times*, 6 Jan. 1881; *C.E.*, 6, 13 Jan. 1881.
[120] *C.E.*, 8 Feb., 1, 12 Mar. 1881.
[121] The league executive assumed the costs of the execution sales, and Fr O'Leary and two other priests active in the boycotting campaign reclaimed the farms for the tenants at the auction by paying their rents and costs (ibid., 19, 23, 30 May 1881; *W.C.E.*, 28 May 1881). The rents came in slowly and secretly, if at all; in November civil-bill decrees were obtained against nine of the tenants who owed at least two, and in some cases three, gales of rent (*C.E.*, 5 Aug., 21 Sept. 1881; *W.C.E.*, 26 Nov. 1881).

protesting his imprisonment too vociferously. The coercion bill, suspending *habeas corpus*, and the arms bill passed the commons on 28 February and 11 March respectively, after the ordinary rules of the house had been waived in order to shorten debate and to overcome the dogged obstructionism of the Parnellites. The permanent secession of the Irish party from parliament, to be followed by a no-rent campaign in Ireland, was considered, but Parnell adhered to his constitutional course, and the party returned to the fight with the aim of making the promised land bill as radical as possible. [122]

Although the landlords could hardly be pleased by the prospect of conciliatory land legislation that would reduce their incomes, they welcomed the coercion measures in the largely mistaken belief that these would suppress agrarian terrorism and conflicts over rent. [123] Moreover, in attempting to frustrate the aims of the league, landlords could now obtain valuable assistance from the Emergency Committee of the Orange Lodge of Ireland and from the Property Defence Association, both established in the previous December. [124] The officials and employees of these organizations, contemptuously labelled 'emergency men', attended execution sales, where they bid for farms and other property seized for rent by the landlords and thus prevented the sales from being rendered abortive. Caretakers were supplied for evicted holdings in order to prevent the whole neighbourhood from sending its cattle to graze on the vacant land, and also to prosecute the inevitable trespassers. Labourers were procured, usually from Ulster, and equipped to carry out harvest and other farming operations for boycotted Cork landlords, such as Thomas Sanders, Samuel Hutchins, Richard Notter, and John Harnett, whose ordinary workers had deserted them.[125] The Property Defence Association, generally better organized and financed than the Emergency Committee, was especially active in Cork; its offices were located on Tuckey Street in Cork city, where Major Barry Broadley, a professional land agent, handled the many urgent appeals for assistance. [126]

Disturbance and argumentation over rent marked 1881 on perhaps a majority of Cork estates. Although the number of evictions

[122] O'Brien, *Parnell and his party*, pp. 57–65.

[123] See the letter from Gurnett, Mahony, and Co., the Dublin land-agency firm, to R. Walsh, a tenant in County Cork, 9 Mar. 1881, quoted in *C.E.*, 28 Mar. 1881.

[124] Palmer, *Land League crisis*, pp. 225, 228.

[125] *C.E.*, 30 July, 3, 18 Aug. 1881; Palmer, *Land League crisis*, pp. 227–9.

[126] *C.E.*, 1, 9 Apr., 23 May 1881; P.R.O.I., ref. no. 978, Midleton papers, Letter book, 1882–5: J. P. Fitzgerald to Maj. B. Broadley, 24 May 1882, p. 18.

in the county declined from 182 to 104, civil-bill decrees and writs increased enormously from 1,030 in 1880 to 2,723 during the following year, giving unassailable testimony to the difficulties of rent collection. Over 85 per cent of the decrees against Cork tenants in 1881 were obtained from the superior courts in an effort to increase the tenants' legal costs and in that way to overawe further resistance. [127] The valuation continued to be the only rent that was offered on some estates, such as those of Sir Joseph McKenna, Peter Penn-Gaskell, Viscount Midleton, and Lord Charles Pelham Clinton. [128] Although some of them accepted it because they badly needed the money in order to meet pressing engagements, most landlords resisted the offer but showed a willingness to compromise by proposing temporary abatements. Tenants on many estates seemed prepared to listen to these overtures if really substantial reductions of 20 per cent or more were offered. In fact, they were encouraged to do so by the chairman of the Cork city branch of the league, who denied in late March that the government valuation was 'the religion of the Land League'; if the landlords 'were disposed to give a fair and just settlement, the tenants should settle with them, for there was no use at all in making rows over the matter'. [129]

This weakening of the original demand was a necessary truce with reality. Of the 800 to 900 tenants on the duke of Devonshire's estates in Cork and Waterford, only ten reportedly attended in mid-March a meeting of those who refused on principle to give more than the valuation; the rest had already paid their September or November 1880 rents after receiving a 20 per cent reduction. [130] But concessions of this magnitude were commonly won only after a hard fight, for the landlords naturally sought to retreat as little as possible. When Robert Cole Bowen adamantly refused either to accept the valuation or to give a 20 per cent reduction, his tenants took unprecedented action. In a step that clearly foreshadowed the 'Plan of Campaign' of 1886, they retired in a body to the Land League office in Kildorrery, entrusted their rents, less 20 per cent, to the local curate, the Rev. J. Collins, and decided to fight their landlord in the courts. [131] Richard Doherty, sen., reluctantly advised the trustees of the Fitzpatrick property in June to offer the tenants an abatement of at least 20 per cent (the tenants were demanding 25 per cent), since no process server would venture any

---

[127] *Return of civil bills in ejectment and superior-court writs, 1879–88*, pp. 3–5.
[128] *C.E.*, 12 Feb., 19, 21, 28 Mar. 1881.
[129] Ibid., 28 Mar. 1881.
[130] Ibid., 8 Jan., 18 Mar. 1881.
[131] *C.E.*, 6 May 1881.

longer into the wild and remote Ballyvourney district. A farmer on an estate near the Fitzpatrick property had recently had an ear cut off because he had paid his rent behind the backs of the other tenants. 'In fact,' declared Doherty, 'this country is in a state next to rebellion; but for the number of troops & constabulary in this part of the country, no one would be safe who had any connection with land.'[132] 'The Land League[s] are destroying the country', cried Doherty in September, '& a lot of protestants have joined them': the earl of Bandon's protestant tenants at Durrus 'would pay no rent unless allowed 25 per c[en]t off. More like savages than human beings.'[133] These conflicts lasted until the landlords either capitulated or conceded most of what was demanded, or until numerous tenants on the embattled estates were served with civil-bill decrees or superior-court writs and had their farms carried to execution sales.[134] The agitation achieved a substantial measure of success. 'Without boasting,' exulted the secretary of the Charleville Land League in June, 'they could now say that they had compelled every landlord in this district, from the noble earl down to the meanest squireen, to lower his flag before them.'[135] Between March and September 1881 almost fifty Cork landowners were reported to have given abatements acceptable to their tenants that averaged about 20 per cent.[136]

One extraordinary episode in 1881 helped immeasurably to bolster the fighting spirit of tenants throughout the south of Ireland, while it also persuaded landlords to assume a more reasonable attitude. This was the spectacle of the use of an army for the collection of rent on the Kingston estate. Landlord-tenant relations on this 25,000-acre dairy estate near Mitchelstown had previously been harmonious. Evictions were almost unknown and rents were in general very moderate—from 15 to 20 per cent over the government valuation. Most of the tenants possessed long leases, and all enjoyed the right of free sale. The fall in butter prices between 1877 and 1879 and again in 1881 was disturbing, but nearly the same rents had been paid before without complaint when prices were as low or lower still.[137] In mid-December 1880, however, over 1,600 tenants

---

[132] Doherty papers, Letter book, 1880–6: R. W. Doherty, sen., to Messrs Park, Nelson, Morgan, and Co., 28 June 1881, p. 336.

[133] Ibid.: Doherty to Capt. P. B. Bernard, 22 Sept. 1881, p. 383.

[134] The agents of both the earl of Bantry and the earl of Kenmare scattered writs among the striking tenants, and Bantry's agent even resorted to a few evictions, said to be 'the first . . . since the famine years' (Kenmare papers, Letter book, 1880–2: S. M. Hussey to J. A. Godley, 6 June 1881, pp. 450–5; *W.C.E.*, 25 June, 30 July 1881).

[135] *C.E.*, 16 June 1881.

[136] Ibid., Mar.–Sept. 1881.   [137] Ibid., 9 June 1881.

from the two estates of the dowager countess of Kingston and William Tankerville Webber [138] paraded through the main streets of the town to Mitchelstown Castle, where a deputation tendered the valuation in lieu of the September gale of rent then payable. When it was refused, the tenants put their money back in their pockets and 'went directly for the shops, where they paid for the provisions that sustained their families the past summer'. [139] The withholding of the rents was acutely embarrassing to the dowager countess and her husband William Downes Webber. Because of a ruinously expensive family resettlement in 1869, the Kingston estate was already in grievous financial trouble. [140] In 1875 the Representative Church Body—the governing body of the recently disendowed Church of Ireland—had taken a mortgage of £236,000 on the property; the interest payments on this enormous charge alone reduced the gross income from nearly £18,000 to about £8,000 a year. [141] The pressure of this huge debt prompted the refusal to accept the valuation or even to grant a small abatement.

Almost none of the September 1880 rents had been paid when a second gale became due in March 1881. The dowager countess and her husband refrained from taking legal proceedings but again refused to reduce the rents. The impasse could not be allowed to continue much longer. The tenants were raising a legal-defence fund and were stiffened by the fact that Henry L. Young, the owner of a large estate in the same district, had recently accepted the mediation of the Mitchelstown Land League and reduced his rents by 22½ per cent. [142] Another great demonstration of tenants from the Kingston and Webber estates was held on Sunday, 27 March: 'All the streets of the town and the avenue to the Mitchelstown Castle entrance were paraded by a torchlight procession, the local band playing national airs throughout'. [143] The dowager countess of Kingston finally took up the challenge and obtained civil-bill decrees against

---

[138] William Downes Webber, the husband of the dowager countess of Kingston, managed the neighbouring estate of his relative William Tankerville Webber.

[139] *C.E.*, 18 Dec. 1880.

[140] Moore, Keily, and Lloyd, Kingston papers: Heads of the proposed resettlement of the Mitchelstown estate, 24 May 1869. This document provided for the creation of a charge of £120,000 at 5 per cent per annum in favour of the honourable Robert E. King, and for the raising of money at a reduced rate of interest in order to redeem the existing charges of £104,000.

[141] Ibid.: Mortgage of the Representative Church Body on the dowager countess of Kingston's estate, 5 Feb. 1875. The stipulated rate of interest was 5½ per cent per annum, reducible to 4½ per cent upon prompt payment.

[142] *C.E.*, 22 Mar. 1881.

[143] Ibid., 28 Mar. 1881.

a large number of tenants at the Midleton quarter sessions in April. When served with ejectment warrants, some of these tenants either paid their rents in full or agreed to pay in instalments, after their legal costs had been waived.[144] Others who had also been served, however, began organizing resistance to the imminent evictions, gathering parties of men to defend their houses and tearing up access roads.

When the first evictions involving five families occurred on 27 May, they provoked a serious riot between the excited people and the constabulary in Mitchelstown. Several policemen were severely stoned, and the constabulary almost fired on the crowd; many were injured by the charging horses of the dragoons or by the flats of swords and rifles, but no lives were lost.[145] For taking part in the eviction riot, James Mannix, a prosperous farmer, and his son Maurice, the secretary of the Mitchelstown Land League, were arrested under the coercion act.[146] The arrests and the dismissal of her labourers by the countess of Kingston only goaded the people to further resistance.[147] The evictions had to be abandoned temporarily because the small constabulary force assisting the sheriff was unable to contend with the large and unruly crowds gathered from the surrounding countryside by couriers and the pealing of chapel bells.[148]

By the end of June, however, a small army consisting of about 700 soldiers and 300 police had taken up quarters in an improvised military camp on the grounds around Mitchelstown Castle, with the object of enabling the sheriff to resume the evictions. All were under the command of General Thomas Steele.[149] In early June fourteen tenants were evicted only to be reinstated when they paid their rents and the full costs of the ejectment warrants. There was then a pause in order to determine whether the tenants would abandon the struggle. But the campaign was just beginning, for it soon became clear that the people remained defiant, and that rents could be collected only if there were massive evictions. Accordingly, nearly 200 writs were served on the tenants in the second half of July.[150] Morale could hardly have been better. Over 200 mowers and about 400 assistants gathered on Sunday, 25 July, in order to save the hay

144 Ibid., 26 Apr. 1881.
145 *W.C.E.*, 28 May 1881; *C.E.*, 30 May 1881.
146 *C.E.*, 6 June 1881.
147 Ibid., 7 June 1881.
148 Ibid., 2 June 1881.
149 Ibid., 30 June, 1 July 1881.
150 Ibid., 23 July 1881.

on two farms belonging to James Mannix, who was imprisoned in Limerick gaol. Once this work was finished,

a procession was formed, headed by children carrying green boughs and singing 'God save Ireland'. After them came the pipers band, followed by the stalwart mowers to the number of 205. Each man carried his scythe, the handle of which was decorated with green branches, and the men marched in military order four deep. The procession passed through the town, cheers being repeatedly given for the Land League, Parnell, the 'suspects', etc., and groans were as freely given for the landlord of the Kingston estate.[151]

By 10 August the army had completed its preparations and stood ready to support the sheriff in proceeding with the evictions. For their part, the tenants were not unprovided The league executive in Dublin had promised the Rev. Timothy O'Connell, chairman of the local branch of the league, that it would defray the tenants' legal costs, amounting in each case to about £7.[152] The tenants prepared for the arrival of the 'crowbar brigade' by blocking all the entrances to their dwellings with boulders, furze, and thorn bushes, with the object of protracting the struggle and of embarrassing the government and the military authorities. Baton charges had to be employed to suppress stone throwing by the angry crowds that collected at the evictions.[153] Immense satisfaction was drawn from the fact that the government had become the willing instrument of 'landlord extortion'. After the ritual of 'tearing down the porches, smashing in the doors, throwing out the thorns, and placing a few articles [of furniture] outside in the yards' had taken place, the tenants invariably paid their rents and were reinstated.[154] In early September the league executive gave Fr O'Connell nearly £1,000 for the discharge of the costs of the decrees executed up to that time, in unfeigned admiration for the 'extraordinary courage and union of the passive resistance applied to the exercise of legal tyranny' on the Kingston estate.[155]

The final series of evictions, affecting about 100 tenants, in this strange rent-collection drama opened in mid-September. Less ingenious obstruction was offered to the sheriff and his bailiffs than in previous months, since the farmers were now immersed in the saving of another good harvest, and the dreary work was concluded

---

[151] Ibid., 26 July 1881.

[152] Ibid., 10, 11 Aug. 1881.

[153] Ibid., 15 Aug. 1881.

[154] Ibid., 19 Aug. 1881. See also ibid., 22 Aug. 1881.

[155] T. Sexton to Rev. T. O'Connell, 2 Sept. 1881, quoted ibid., 8 Sept. 1881. See also ibid., 6 Sept. 1881.

in little more than a week.[156] Although nearly 200 evictions had occurred since the end of May, only about twenty tenants were not reinstated on the day of their eviction, and of these, at least three-quarters subsequently paid their rents and recovered possession.[157] On no other estate in Ireland during the days of the Land League was there such an impressive demonstration of unity by so numerous a body of tenants. The Kingston tenantry had achieved a great moral victory that inspired the tenants of other estates to resist their landlords.

THE CAMPAIGN OF VIOLENCE

Although the Kingston tenants had conducted a generally non-violent campaign of civil disobedience, the great rent strikes of 1881 in Cork were marked by an unprecedented amount of violence which powerfully contributed to the success which they achieved. The number of reported agrarian outrages increased from 289 between February and December 1880 to 651 during the following twelve months. Threatening letters and notices accounted for most of the increase, but there was a startling rise in the number of outrages against persons and property, including aggravated assault, firing into dwelling houses, incendiarism, and cattle maiming. Such cases increased in number from seventy-eight between February and December 1880 to 134 during 1881—far more than in any other year of this troubled decade.[158] Some of the violence was directed against landlords and agents. In late March a twelve-acre plantation at Ballyknockane near Mallow belonging to Samuel Hutchins, whose life had been attempted in the previous October, was set ablaze.[159] The office of the Clonakilty land agents T. R. Wright and Sons was blown up with dynamite in June.[160] A West Cork landlord, Robert Swanton, nearly eighty years old and deaf, was ambushed at Crooked Bridge near Ballydehob in early August and died of his wounds; his son had been fired upon in the same area recently.[161]

[156] Ibid., 15, 19 Sept. 1881.

[157] Ibid., 23 Sept. 1881.

[158] *Return by provinces, of agrarian offences throughout Ireland reported to the inspector general of the Royal Irish Constabulary between the 1st day of January 1881 and the 31st day of December 1881, showing the number of cases in which offenders were convicted; the number of cases in which persons were made amenable but not convicted; the number of cases in which accused are awaiting trial; and the number of cases in which offenders were neither convicted nor made amenable*, H.C. 1882 (72), lv, 17, pp. 2–3 (hereafter cited as *Return of agrarian offences, 1881*).

[159] *C.E.*, 29 Mar. 1881.

[160] *W.C.E.*, 18 June 1881.

[161] Ibid., 6 Aug. 1881.

Much more often, however, the violence was directed at those who co-operated with the landlord system. The caretakers of evicted farms, land grabbers, and 'grazing grabbers' (persons who hired grazing land on evicted farms) were commonly the objects of terrorist attacks.[162] Bailiffs, rent warners, and process servers performed their duties in great and well-warranted fear of bodily harm. One unfortunate process server was attacked near Bandon in early June and hurled into a cesspool; another, near Mallow, was stripped naked, beaten with furze, and tarred [163] Three of the earl of Bantry's writ servers were stoned in the district of Castletown-Berehaven; four persons were arrested for this offence and fined £5 each and costs, which were immediately raised in the town. [164] These incidents became so numerous that landlords and agents in several parts of Cork either found it impossible to obtain anyone to serve their legal papers or else had to pay enormously for these dangerous missions. [165] In many cases it became necessary to obtain decrees from the superior courts that made it possible to dispense with personal service entirely and to substitute service by post. Even her majesty's mails, however, were not immune from attack, and in mid-June, not far from Mallow, a large crowd stopped the mail coach, opened the mailbags, removed the writs, and burned them on the spot. [166]

Since unity was the main guarantee of success in the rent struggles that marked the year, it is scarcely surprising that farmers who paid rent behind the backs of the other tenants or without a substantial abatement were frequently and severely punished. At the end of May, moonlighters destroyed the houses of six farmers and two labourers at Lahadane near Bantry, because all of these men had paid their rents to Samuel Hutchins. [167] Two of the earl of Bantry's tenants in the district of Castletown-Berehaven who had paid rent after eviction were severely beaten in August, because other tenants had accepted eviction rather than pay more than the valuation. [168] Four tenants on the earl of Kenmare's estate at Rathmore Station near Millstreet were shot in the legs by moonlighters in early

---

[162] *C.E.*, 28 Mar., 29 Apr. 1881; 9 Jan. 1882; *W.C.E.*, 25 June, 26 Nov. 1881.

[163] *W.C.E.*, 4 June 1881.

[164] Ibid., 25 June 1881.

[165] Falkiner papers: J. D. Docasley to W. B. Leslie, 10 Mar. 1881; Doherty papers, Letter book, 1880–6: R. W. Doherty, sen., to Messrs Park, Nelson, Morgan, and Co., 28 June 1881, p. 336.

[166] *C.E.*, 16 June 1881.

[167] Ibid., 30 May 1881.

[168] *W.C.E.*, 27 Aug. 1881.

December for having paid their rents. [169] The most chilling outrages occurred on the Ballyvourney estate of Sir George St John Colthurst. In late June, after a few tenants had paid rent at the reduction of 15 per cent offered by the landlord while the rest persisted in their demand for a larger allowance, one of the renegades had an ear scissored off *pour encourager les autres*. [170] But Colthurst largely destroyed the combination by bringing the farms of seventeen ringleaders to execution sales in August, when the tenants reclaimed their holdings by paying two gales of rent and heavy costs. [171] This led to a vicious outrage on Sunday, 29 August. A large group of Colthurst's tenants, comprising about 100 men, women, and children, were gathered that evening in a field, singing, dancing, and drinking porter in celebration of their landlord's marriage earlier that day in Cork city. Suddenly, they were encircled by about fifty disguised moonlighters. Upon the leader's command, shots rang out, felling some, and then the attackers moved in on the dazed remainder, beating them with wooden clubs. Ten persons were wounded, two of them seriously. [172]

The Rathmore Station and Ballyvourney outrages may both have been the work of a single agrarian secret society that apparently took definite shape during the summer of 1881 in the Millstreet area, where turmoil was hardly new. The Millstreet district had previously been brought to a high pitch of excitement by the boycotting of Jeremiah Hegarty, a prosperous Millstreet shopowner. Hegarty had used the profits of his business to acquire the interest in no less than twelve separate holdings on the Wallis estate.[173] He was also the sub-agent of the Wallis estate and another property in the same locality, and during the recent hard times had lent his money or pledged his credit for the sake of several impecunious farmers. [174] To the Millstreet Land League, he appeared triply odious as a land grabber, landlord's 'bum', and gombeen man. When Hegarty pressed for the repayment of debts following the abundant harvest of 1880, he was formally declared boycotted, and his many customers, labourers, and friends were warned to shun him.[175]

---

[169] Ibid., 3 Dec. 1881.   [170] Ibid., 25 June 1881.

[171] Kenmare papers, Letter book, 1880–1: S. M. Hussey to editor of *The Times*, 10 Sept. 1881, pp. 704–6.

[172] *C.E.*, 30 Aug. 1881.

[173] Hegarty paid rents of almost £600 a year for 800 acres of land valued at only £240. He invested a large amount of money in reclamation and other improvements, employed about sixty labourers, and paid more than £1,000 a year in wages (*The Times*, 4 Jan. 1881).

[174] *C.E.*, 28 Dec. 1880; 9, 28 Sept. 1881.

[175] Ibid., 4 Jan., 1 Feb. 1881.

Popular feeling hardened against Hegarty after the Cork assizes in March 1881, when he successfully prosecuted two prominent members of the Millstreet Land League for having injured his business.[176] Hegarty managed, however, to retain some of his customers and some of his friends. This helped to polarize the town and district into rival factions, a process that was magnified by the open hostility of the local parish priest, the Rev. Canon Griffin, towards the land movement in general and towards the boycott of Hegarty in particular.[177] To these sources of discontent must be added the rent struggles taking place on several estates in the neighbourhood.

Canon Griffin soon saw fit to lecture his parishioners sternly on the immorality of membership in agrarian secret societies, and he had good reason to be alarmed. According to one local resident magistrate, armed and disguised bands of moonlighters attacked no less than thirty houses in the Millstreet district during the last three weeks of August and demanded weapons and money from the frightened occupants. In a raid in early September, one of the moonlighters, the son of a small farmer, was killed in a police ambush, and two others, both young servant boys, were captured.[178] In early October a farmer named Patrick O'Leary was shot near Kishkeam for having paid rent, and died as a result of his wound.[179] For nearly five months, from August through December, a wide district of northwest Cork was kept in a thoroughly terrorized state by these sudden nocturnal attacks. Even though the identities of at least some of the raiders were said to be known, a resentful, sullen silence was maintained during the investigations made by the authorities.[180]

Then, on 29 December, the Macroom police, acting upon secret information, captured a discharged soldier named Connell in a farmer's house at Mushera, midway between Macroom and Millstreet.[181] Connell, as it happened, was the 'captain' of at least the main band of Millstreet moonlighters. These moonlighters were all sworn members of a body calling itself the 'Royal Irish Republic'. Some of them wore military-style uniforms and carried military ranks; most participated in drilling exercises organized by Connell

---

[176] Ibid., 28, 29 Mar. 1881.

[177] Ibid., 30 Aug. 1881.

[178] Ibid., 3 Sept. 1881.

[179] Ibid., 6, 7 Oct. 1881; E. Cant-Wall, *Ireland under the land act: letters contributed to the 'Standard' newspaper; with an appendix of leading cases under the act, giving the evidence in full, judicial dicta, &c.* (London, 1882), p. 252 (hereafter cited as *Land act*).

[180] *C.E.*, 10 Sept. 1881, 22 Mar. 1882; *W.C.E.*, 3, 31 Dec. 1881.

[181] *W.C.E.*, 31 Dec. 1881.

at Coolykeerane near Millstreet.[182] Documents discovered in Connell's possession at the time of his capture showed that he and his followers had been acting as jury, judge, and executioner whenever their unwritten agrarian code was violated.[183] Soon after he was taken into custody, Connell became an informer and supplied the police with the names of the members of his band. Thus enlightened, the police arrested and charged with treason-felony as many as forty-six persons by the end of March 1882; ten further arrests of alleged conspirators occurred in late April.[184] Not surprisingly, the moonlighters were recruited mainly from the ranks of the sons of farmers, and from among the small farmers themselves, with a sprinkling of labourers, some tradesmen, and one assistant national-school teacher. Of the twenty-eight persons arrested up to the end of March whose social status was indicated in newspaper accounts, fifteen were described as sons of farmers and seven as farmers. The ten men arrested in April were 'principally the sons of farmers'.[185] The 'Royal Irish Republic' was not the only agrarian secret society operating in northwest Cork at this time, for similar organized violence continued there in the months following the break-up of Connell's band.[186]

THE LAND ACT OF 1881 AND THE SUPPRESSION OF THE LAND LEAGUE

While a British army was collecting rent on the Kingston estate, and while the Millstreet moonlighters were raiding the surrounding countryside, the land act finally received the royal assent on 22 August 1881. The celebrated 'three Fs'—fair rents, fixity of tenure, and free sale—were recognized by statute at last, but it had required a great national movement and an unprecedented wave of agrarian violence in order to bring this to pass. In the English context, such legislation would have been unthinkable, and even in the Irish context, Gladstone's measure was revolutionary. Under this act, subcommissioners were appointed and empowered to determine the 'fair rent' of all yearly tenancies; once determined, such rents were to be valid for a period of fifteen years. Either the tenant or the landlord, if dissatisfied with the subcommissioners' decision, could lodge an appeal with the chief land commissioners.

[182] *C.E.*, 14 Feb., 19 Apr. 1882; *W.C.E.*, 22 Apr. 1882.
[183] *C.E.*, 7 Jan. 1882.
[184] Ibid., 28 Mar., 19 Apr. 1882.
[185] Ibid., 2, 4, 11, 16, 28 Jan., 1 Feb., 19 Apr. 1882.
[186] Ibid., 29, 30 Mar., 1 Apr., 6 June 1882; *W.C.E.*, 1 July 1882.

Fair rents could also be fixed outside the courts, either by amicable agreement between the parties or by arbitration, and then registered with the land commission, when they would also become valid for fifteen years. Subject to a number of reasonable conditions, a yearly tenant was given fixity of tenure. So long as he paid his rent, did not sublet or subdivide or erect buildings without the consent of the landlord, and did not commit persistent waste, his landlord could not evict him. Every yearly tenant was given the right to sell the interest in his holding to the highest bidder, provided that he complied with certain conditions, particularly that of advising his landlord of both the purchaser and the purchase price. The landlord retained the right, however, of refusing on reasonable grounds to approve the sale, and he could always pre-empt the prospective purchaser and buy the holding himself at a price determined by the subcommissioners. Lastly, the act contained a modest provision for land purchase. Whereas the land act of 1870 had authorized the board of works to advance up to two-thirds of the purchase money to the tenant, that of 1881 empowered the land commission to lend up to three-fourths of the money, repayable in annuities over a period of thirty-five years at 5 per cent interest.[187]

It was the fond hope of Gladstone and his colleagues that, once Irish tenants occupied their holdings at rents set fairly by the new land courts and enjoyed full liberty to sell their improvements as well as the opportunity to become owners of their farms, they would quickly be weaned from agitation and terrorism. All the government asked was a free and fair trial for its bold experiment in conciliation. But it was not bold enough. It offered no redress to the 125,000 tenants who had taken leases before the passage of the 1870 land act, and who were excluded by this fact from entering the courts in order to have a judicial rent fixed.[188] And less than 150 of the thousands of leases taken since 1870 would qualify for nullification under section twenty-one of the 1881 land act.[189] Moreover, there were almost 200,000 holdings in Ireland whose valuations were between £4 and £10.[190] The new act could not give the occupiers of these subsistence holdings a decent living, even if they were to obtain enormous reductions from the courts. For the yearly tenants who

[187] 44 & 45 Vict., c. 49.

[188] Some 135,000 holdings, or about 20 per cent of the total number, were held under lease in 1870 (*Returns showing the number of agricultural holdings in Ireland and the tenure by which they are held by the occupiers*, p. 1).

[189] See below, pp. 302–3.

[190] *Return of agricultural holdings in Ireland, compiled by the local government board in Ireland from returns furnished by the clerks of the poor law unions in Ireland in January 1881* [C 2934], H.C. 1881, xciii, 793, p. 13.

were largely free of debt and arrears of rent, much would obviously depend on the size of the reductions made by the courts within the next year or so. Meanwhile, the landlords would probably demand two or more gales of the usual rent. Only continued combination and resistance would bring about substantial reductions until the tenants could go into court.

There was some feeling that the three Fs no longer satisfied the real demands of Irish farmers. Certainly, the ideology of undiluted anti-landlordism, the ultimate object of which was to drive the landlords bag and baggage from Irish soil, had been firmly implanted in the national consciousness, even within the short space of two years. Witness the outburst of an obscure countryman named James Donovan barely a week after the land act had reached the statute book:

The land for the people—that's the right bill. Millions of acres lying waste in want of reclaiming, and [not] giving employment to the poor people that are starving, and millions of acres also in the hands of those big lords and earls feeding their bullocks, and the unfortunate peasantry flying to other lands for a living. Talk of the three Fs as long as you like, but the right F is the land for the people.[191]

Yet, even if one grants that the purchase clauses of the land act, and even more the selling terms of the landlords, were not very tempting, it seems clear that in general tenants did not have a strong desire to become proprietors.

It is rather remarkable [observed the *Cork Examiner* in September 1882] that in the vast majority of cases the purchase of their holdings, so far from being a spontaneous idea or even an ardent wish of the mass of the tenants, seems to be hardly ever mentioned by a farmer.[192]

But Michael Davitt and other leaders of the Land League, as well as Clan na Gael, remained firmly committed to the revolutionary doctrine of 'the land for the people' and were disgusted with piecemeal reform.

The great Land League conference that opened in Dublin on 15 September 1881, although at first about evenly split between acceptance and rejection of the land act, unanimously adopted Parnell's astute compromise formula aimed at testing its provisions.[193] The conference resolved that the league should select,

---

[191] *C.E.*, 31 Aug. 1881. Donovan was a member of the Kilmeen Land League, but rarely did league farmers express themselves so strongly on this demand, although they may have paid lip service to the general idea.

[192] Ibid., 26 Sept. 1882. See also ibid., 24 Aug. 1883.

[193] Palmer, *Land League crisis*, pp. 283–6; O'Brien, *Parnell and his party*, p. 70.

adopt, and prosecute a large number of cases involving not clearly rack-rented tenants, but rather 'tenants whose rents hitherto have not been considered cruel or exorbitant', and that the league should restrain farmers from rushing indiscriminately into court until these test cases had been decided. [194] This policy, besides appealing to the tenants' innate cautiousness, could be defended on several grounds: it was convenient for both the litigants and the courts and saved costs on each side; agreements could perhaps be reached out of court once the basic principles and standards were established; and it was unnecessary for the league to prosecute the cases of rack-rented tenants in which any impartial court would have to order a large reduction. [195]

There were, however, certain signs which made it appear to the government that the test cases were only a façade for strenuous efforts to destroy its hopes for peace. The league executive in Dublin and the Cork city branch were no longer advising that farmers who considered their rents to be exorbitant should passively resist only up to the point of eviction; rather, they were urging them to let their holdings go to the landlords' emergency men. [196] 'The present plan of paying [rent] when the sheriff comes will not do', Anna Parnell told the Kingston tenants at the conclusion of their campaign in late September. 'I must impress [upon you]', she declared, 'the absolute necessity of making a stand against the payment of rent.' [197] Also alarming to the government in late September was a report that the league executive had issued a call asking two tenants in each district throughout the country to determine for every holding a fair rent that would enable the occupiers to obtain 'a more improved mode of living, better food, better clothing, and better houses'. [198] Once the amount of the league's fair rent was registered by the local branch, no higher rent was to be paid. The faithful execution of the plan, warned the Irish correspondent of the *Standard*, would give 'every tenant in Ireland the certainty of a special private grievance. . . . He will come to regard the league-registered rent as the "fair" one, and to compare it constantly with the inevitably higher sum fixed by the sub-commissions.' [199] Nor did the government receive any indication of a decline in the number of combinations against rent when payment became due as of 29 September.

[194] Quoted in Cant-Wall, *Land act*, p. 12.
[195] Ibid., pp. 10, 33.
[196] *C.E.*, 8 Aug., 1 Sept. 1881.
[197] Ibid., 22 Sept. 1881.
[198] Quoted in Cant-Wall, *Land act*, pp. 14–15.
[199] Ibid., p. 15.

The final provocation was given by Parnell himself in a series of speeches in late September and early October. Attempting to placate the disgruntled left wing of the land movement in both Ireland and America, Parnell strongly emphasized the 'hollowness' of the land act and closely linked any final settlement of the land question to the achievement of legislative independence for Ireland.[200] As many as 50,000 to 60,000 people assembled for a wildly enthusiastic demonstration in Parnell's honour in Cork city on Sunday, 2 October.[201] The government, which considered its legislation as already a final solution to the land question, and the political demand as a separate problem, was angered by Parnell's ominous statements and gravely concerned that the league was sabotaging the land act. The Irish leader was arrested in Dublin on 13 October and imprisoned in Kilmainham, where he was soon joined by John Dillon, William O'Brien, and others who had organized indignation meetings around the country following his arrest.[202]

By imprisoning the leaders of the agrarian agitation, the government made it impossible for them to carry out the policy of testing the land act in the manner upon which they had resolved, namely, through calculated intimidation of the courts.[203] The loss of their liberty had the effect of driving them to the extreme measure of a call for a general strike against rent. Perhaps because he foresaw that the radical course he now approved would by its very failure strengthen the forces of moderation, Parnell agreed to sign the famous 'No Rent Manifesto' drafted by William O'Brien. It appeared in the *Freeman's Journal* on 19 October; the very next day, Gladstone's government took steps to suppress the Land League.[204]

The No Rent Manifesto was as coldly received in County Cork as it was nationwide. In the judgment of the *West Cork Eagle*, it was an 'inopportune and ill considered document', a 'rash and suicidal declaration of war, which put an extinguisher upon an organization of unprecedented solidity of combination'.[205] The manifesto generally failed to command the allegiance of Cork tenants, many of whom joined the rush into the land courts in late 1881.[206]

---

[200] O'Brien, *Parnell and his party*, p. 71.

[201] Cant-Wall, *Land act*, pp. 25–6.

[202] O'Brien, *Parnell and his party*, p. 72.

[203] *United Ireland*, the organ of the Land League, had declared on 17 September: 'The spirit which cowed the tyrants in their rent offices must be the spirit in which the land commission courts are to be approached' (quoted in R. B. O'Brien, *Parnell*, p. 234).

[204] *Freeman's Journal*, 19, 21 Oct. 1881; O'Brien, *Parnell and his party*, pp. 73–4; F. S. L. Lyons, *Dillon*, pp. 55–60.

[205] *W.C.E.*, 19 Nov. 1881.   [206] Ibid., 26 Nov. 1881.

Though rent strikes continued on numerous estates, it became steadily clearer in late 1881 and early 1882 that the tenants, deprived of national leadership and benefiting from the improvement in economic conditions, no longer possessed the will to engage in protracted struggles against their landlords. Many Cork proprietors quickly overcame combinations among their tenants by offering small abatements of about 10 per cent. [207] Typical of such successful efforts was that made on the still embattled Kingston estate. By late April 1882, the Rev. David Burdon, a local curate, had persuaded more than half of the almost 400 tenants who had been served with writs to accept token reductions of 5 per cent or less. [208] On other properties where no abatements were made, and where the tenants at first resisted the payment of the usual rent, landlords and agents usually found that once civil-bill decrees or writs were served or even only threatened, the combinations were shattered and the rents were paid soon afterwards. [209] Merely for the sake of putting landlords to trouble and expense, it hardly seemed sensible for tenants to allow their farms to be carried to execution sales now that the legal costs of up to £20 in each case would not be defrayed by the Land League. [210] Consequently, the number of execution sales noticeably declined.

Nevertheless, the continued imprisonment of the Irish leaders, the necessity of legal proceedings before current rents could be obtained on many estates, and the attempts to collect large arrears of rent on some others all helped to keep the county and indeed the country very unsettled. Although peasant terrorism gradually declined in County Cork during 1882, there was scarcely room for complacency when the number of reported agrarian outrages remained as high as 328 (compared with 651 in 1881), including seventy-eight violent crimes against persons and property (compared with 134 in 1881). [211] The government's strong desire to reduce the level of agrarian violence in Ireland, combined with Parnell's

---

[207] *C.E.*, 2, 11, 12 Jan., 4 Feb., 11 Mar., 11 May 1882; Kenmare papers, Letter book, 1881–2: M. Leonard to H. H. Townsend, 26 Jan. 1882, p. 123.

[208] *C.E.*, 22, 26, 27 Apr. 1882.

[209] Ibid., 12, 16, 18, 21, 23 Jan., 7 Feb., 13, 22 Mar. 1882. Between 1881 and 1882 the number of ejectment decrees and writs declined slightly from 2,723 to 2,566, but the number of evictions rose from 104 to 140 in Cork (*Return of civil bills in ejectment and superior-court writs, 1879–88*, pp. 3–5).

[210] *C.E.*, 10 Feb. 1882.

[211] *Return by provinces, of agrarian offences . . . between the 1st day of January 1882 and the 31st day of December 1882 . . .*, H.C. 1883 (12), lvi, 1, pp. 8–9 (hereafter cited as *Return of agrarian offences, 1882*).

growing eagerness to regain his liberty, paved the way for the famous 'Kilmainham treaty' which Parnell concluded with Gladstone in April. The Irish leader promised to abandon the land agitation and to throw all his influence against agrarian violence and intimidation if the government would provide tenants in arrears with grants enabling them to satisfy the claims of their landlords, thereby making these tenants eligible to enter the land courts. Parnell also indicated his belief that if the 1881 land act were amended by the admission of leaseholders to its benefits and by the 'full extension' of its land-purchase provisions, the result would be accepted in Ireland as 'a practical settlement of the land question'. [212] Hoping that its action would lead to the quelling of agrarian turmoil, the government released Parnell, John Dillon, and J. J. O'Kelly on 2 May. [213] This 'pact' was not destroyed, as it might well have been, by the fiendish murders of Lord Frederick Cavendish, the new chief secretary, and T. H. Burke, the under-secretary, with surgical knives in Phoenix Park only four days after Parnell's release.

The question of arrears of rent was not so momentous in County Cork as it was in the west of Ireland in mid-1882. Nevertheless, arrears were very large on some estates, and ironically, they suddenly became a considerable problem on many others once tenants learned that the arrears bill would cancel a large part of their debts. [214] In general, heavy arrears were confined to properties in the extreme southwestern part of the county—notorious for its small holdings and high population density. Many of the earl of Bandon's tenants, principally those at Durrus near Bantry, had paid no rent since 1880, according to the agent's son. 'Their arrears', he wrote in July 1882, 'amount to over £10,000; this we are taking every step to collect in but cannot; until the arrears bill is passed, the tenants will not pay, although several have been evicted.' [215] The tenants on the property of Thomas McCarthy Collins, located between Skibbereen and Skull, reportedly owed as much as two and one-half years' rent in September. [216] The roll of the fifteen Cork landlords who received more than £500 under the arrears act which became law in August is almost exclusively composed of owners of large estates in the

---

[212] C. S. Parnell to Capt. W. H. O'Shea, 28 Apr. 1882, quoted in King, *Irish question*, pp. 189–90. See also Hammond, *Gladstone*, pp. 263–82.

[213] O'Brien, *Parnell and his party*, p. 77.

[214] Doherty papers, Letter book, 1880–6: R. W. Doherty, sen., to St L. R. M. Tighe, 28 July 1882, p. 563.

[215] Ibid., Letter book, 1881–4: R. W. Doherty, jun., to J. H. Franks, 22 July 1882, p. 398.

[216] *C.E.*, 15 Sept. 1882.

districts of Bantry, Skibbereen, and Castletown-Berehaven.[217] In County Cork as a whole, almost 4,800 tenants, or slightly above 10 per cent of all occupiers of over one acre, had arrears amounting to £141,000 erased under the act. The landlords received about £44,000, and the remaining arrears of rent of almost £97,000 were cancelled. [218]

After the release of the Irish leaders from Kilmainham in May, economic conditions, which had been favourable from about the middle of 1880 and continued so down to the summer of 1884, contributed significantly to the reduction of agrarian conflict. The gradual shift within pasture farming from dairying to the rearing of store cattle accelerated, and the earlier sheep losses arising from disease as well as the previous decline in the number of pigs as a result of the potato failures were both being replenished, as Table 49 illustrates. [219]

TABLE 49 Number of cattle, sheep, and pigs in Cork, 1877 to 1881–4

year	dry cattle	cows	sheep	pigs
1877	175,126	186,674	330,260	195,172
1881	207,921	178,284	264,165	144,856
1882	205,663	177,621	257,897	171,636
1883	214,597	175,800	282,864	176,440
1884	226,583	170,516	303,040	156,407*

* A temporary reversal of the improving trend began in 1884, when the long summer drought reduced milk yields and forced farmers to curtail pig breeding with dairy by-products.

Crop yields were either above average or better than average as compared with those of 1871–6, as Table 50 shows. [220]

With the major exception of butter, the prices of the principal agricultural exports were satisfactory in comparison with those of

[217] *Return of payments made to landlords by the Irish land commission, pursuant to the 1st and 16th sections of the [arrears of rent] act; and also a return of rent charges cancelled pursuant to the 15th section of the act* [C 4059], H.C. 1884, lxiv, 97, pp. 178–93.

[218] In Ireland as a whole, arrears amounting to some £2,632,000 were erased; the landlords received almost £815,000, and the remaining arrears of about £1,817,000 were cancelled (ibid., pp. iv, 224).

[219] *Irish agricultural statistics for 1877*, p. 57; *Irish agricultural statistics for 1881*, p. 44; *Irish agricultural statistics for 1882* [C 3677], H.C. 1883, lxxvi, 825, p. 44; *Irish agricultural statistics for 1883* [C 4069], H.C. 1884, lxxxv, 313, p. 46; *Irish agricultural statistics for 1884* [C 4489], H.C. 1884–5, lxxxv, 1, p. 50.

[220] *Irish agricultural statistics for 1871*, p. lii; *Irish agricultural statistics for 1881*, p. 39; *Irish agricultural statistics for 1891*, pp. 52, 57.

TABLE 50   Crop yields per acre in Cork, 1871–6 and 1881–4

year	oats (cwt)	barley (cwt)	wheat (cwt)	potatoes (tons)	turnips (tons)	hay (tons)
average, 1871–6	13·4	15·6	13·8	3·0	11·7	1·8
1881	14·9	15·0	14·4	3·9	11·8	1·8
1882	15·0	15·4	13·6	2·9	12·3	2·0
1883	15·2	16·0	13·5	4·7	12·9	2·0
1884	14·0	16·6	14·7	4·1	10·2	1·7

the early 1870s. In late 1881 and during 1882, a temporary decline in American shipments of beef and bacon to Liverpool enabled Irish farmers to realize highly remunerative prices for their store cattle and pigs. [221] The reports of sales at local fairs were exuberant. At the Bandon fair in early February 1882, 'the demand for anything with meat on it was the briskest since the fair was established'. [222] The excellent livestock prices had a tonic effect on farmers. After the Clonakilty fair in February, when 'everything was in great demand', they were observed 'in groups at the street corners and in the public houses, busily engaged [in] matchmaking'. [223] Tenants pleading for more time to pay their rents were given none. Richard Doherty, sen., bluntly informed one such tenant in June that it was 'quite idle for [you to] tell me that you could not sell your cattle at Ballygurteen fair, as there never was for years such prices for *every description of cattle*'. [224]

This exceedingly favourable trend continued in 1883. Cattle prices might have soared even higher had it not been for the damaging effect of outbreaks of foot-and-mouth disease in March and again in the autumn. [225] A hard, dry spring also produced a temporary reluctance among graziers to purchase young cattle for fattening, but by July some of them were sorely complaining of the luxuriant pastures and the great difficulty of keeping them down because of 'the enormous prices at present for all kinds of stock'. [226] Greatly encouraged by this trend, dairy farmers were rearing all their calves at almost any inconvenience; few calves were being slaughtered, and there was little veal in the butchers' shops. [227] To

[221] *C.E.*, 3 Jan., 5 June 1882.
[222] Ibid., 3 Feb. 1882.   [223] Ibid., 8 Feb. 1882.
[224] Doherty papers, Letter book, 1880–6: R. W. Doherty, sen., to D. Connell, 29 June 1882, p. 552.
[225] *C.E.*, 8, 9, 16 Mar., 6, 15, 18, 19 Sept., 9 Oct., 17 Nov. 1883.
[226] Ibid., 10 July 1883. See also ibid., 28 Mar., 8 May 1883; *C.C.*, 4, 6, 18 Apr. 1883.
[227] *C.E.*, 5 June, 29 Aug. 1883; *C.C.*, 21 June 1883.

some extent, the increase in the number of his young cattle together with the high prices he obtained for them compensated the dairy farmer for the lower butter production and the disheartening butter prices of the early 1880s.

The suppression of the Land League, the improvement in economic conditions, and the operation of the land act—probably in that order—all contributed to the pacification of County Cork between late 1881 and mid-1884. The level of agrarian violence and intimidation gradually subsided, as Table 51 illustrates. [228]

TABLE 51   Number of agrarian outrages reported in Cork, 1881–4

	offences against			
year	persons	property	public peace	total
1881	52	82	517	651
1882	14	62	252	328
1883	5	22	71	98
1884	2	38	68	108

The settlement of land-grabbing or eviction disputes often helped to restore peace to once disturbed districts. Landlords sometimes permitted former tenants long out of possession to sell their interests, and land grabbers were only too happy to pay a price to escape continued persecution. [229] Because it remained next to impossible for landlords and agents to find new tenants for costly evicted farms, they were occasionally prepared to forego large arrears if a settlement could be reached with some other member of an evicted tenant's family. [230] Many police protection posts, such as those at Carrigane and Sandyhill in the Midleton district for the safety of caretakers of evicted farms, were disbanded. [231] Although there were sporadic incidents of violence in northwest Cork and northeast Kerry, the nightly patrols by about 140 soldiers and police to suppress

---

[228] *Return of agrarian offences, 1881,* pp. 2–3; *Return of agrarian offences, 1882,* pp. 8–9; *Return by provinces, of agrarian offences ... between the 1st day of January 1883 and the 31st day of December 1883 ...* [C 3950], H.C. 1884, lxiv, 1, pp. 8–9; *Return by provinces, of agrarian offences ... between the 1st day of January 1884 and the 31st day of December 1884 ...* [C 4500], H.C. 1884–5, lxv, 1, pp. 8–9.

[229] *C.E.,* 24, 29 Jan. 1883, 17 Jan. 1884; *C.C.,* 9 Apr. 1883.

[230] Kenmare papers, Letter book, 1882–3: S. M. Hussey to Messrs Benbow, Saltwell, and Tryon, 26 Mar. 1883, pp. 771–2; Hussey to Messrs Benbow, Saltwell, and Tryon, 30 Apr. 1883, pp. 863–4.

[231] *C.E.,* 24 Jan., 13 Aug. 1883.

moonlighting gradually became superfluous. [232] The special police tax previously imposed upon the inhabitants of the notoriously disturbed Castleisland district of Kerry was abolished in early 1884. [233] Meetings of the Irish National League, held to denounce the glaring shortcomings of the land act, were sometimes dispersed by the authorities, but this was usually an unnecessary precaution because these meetings signally failed to generate much interest or excitement. [234]

THE WORKING OF THE LAND ACT

In defusing the agrarian agitation, the land act was undoubtedly a potent factor. Slightly more than 6,100 tenants in County Cork, or about one-fifth of all occupiers of holdings of over five acres, derived benefit from the rent provisions of this act up to the end of August 1885. Rents were determined not only by the subcommissioners, and in a small number of cases by the county-court judges in the civil-bill courts, but also by specially appointed valuers of the land commission and by agreement between landlord and tenant. Table 52 summarizes the results in County Cork of all the methods used in the fixing of fair rents up to 22 August 1885. [235]

TABLE 52   Disposition of cases concerning fair rents in Cork under the 1881 land act, Aug. 1881–Aug. 1885

method	no. of cases	old rent	judicial rent	% reduction
subcommissioners	3,656	119,857	100,384	16·2
civil-bill courts and valuers	274	7,559	6,349	16·1
agreements and arbitration	2,177	60,703	50,619	16·6
total	6,107	188,119	157,352	16·4

[232] Ibid., 26 Apr., 17 May 1883; 9, 28 Apr., 18 Aug. 1884.
[233] Ibid., 29 Mar. 1884.
[234] Ibid., 4 Feb., 24 Apr. 1884.
[235] *Report of the Irish land commissioners for the period from 22nd August 1881 to 22nd August 1882* [C 3413], H.C. 1882, xx, 265, pp. 8–19; *Report of the Irish land commissioners for the period from 22nd August 1882 to 22nd August 1883* . . . [C 3897], H.C. 1884, lxiv, 41, pp. 7–20; *Report of the Irish land commissioners for the period from 22nd August 1883 to 22nd August 1884* . . . [C 4231], H.C. 1884–5, lxv, 53, pp. 7–36; *Report of the Irish land commissioners for the period from 22nd August 1884 to 22nd August 1885* . . . [C 4625], H.C. 1886, xix, 467, pp. 7–36.

The subcommissioners were conciliators and arbitrators with large discretionary powers rather than land judges strictly bound to assign a rental value to farms in accordance with current agricultural prices. [236] Thus it is not surprising that they were influenced by the varying intensity of the agrarian agitation to a much greater extent than by price fluctuations. In spite of the brighter prospects for farmers and the suppression of the Land League, the county was still, as has already been shown, very much disturbed by rent struggles and violence in late 1881 and throughout 1882. Relative quiet was restored during the next two years. Although economic conditions took a decided turn for the worse beginning in the summer of 1884, Cork was not stirred by a new agitation until late 1885. These developments were impressively reflected in the annual average rent reductions made by the subcommissioners, although not in those made by mutual agreement between 1881 and 1886 (see Table 53). [237]

TABLE 53   Average annual rent reductions made in Cork by the subcommissioners and by fair-rent agreements, 1881–6

years (Aug.–Aug.)	subcommissioners (%)	agreements (%)
1881–2	18·7	20·1
1882–3	17·3	16·0
1883–4	12·4	14·5
1884–5	14·9	13·9
1885–6	23·7	15·8

The influence of the agitation in prompting special efforts towards conciliation during the first two years of court operations can be seen in the judicial decisions affecting several Cork estates. The subcommissioners were satisfied that rents on the Gillman estate near Skibbereen had not been raised since 1850, and that Gillman had granted generous allowances for his tenants' improvements. But they still concluded that even on 'this liberally managed estate', the tenants were 'paying too much', and therefore reduced the combined rent of eighteen tenants by 25 per cent. [238] 'The rents have

[236] Cant-Wall, *Land act*, p. 10.

[237] In addition to the sources cited for Table 52, see *Report of the Irish land commissioners for the period from 22nd August 1885 to 22nd August 1886* [C 4899], H.C. 1886, xix, 503, pp. 7–36.

[238] *W.C.E.*, 3 June 1882; Financial Reform Association, Liverpool, *The financial reform almanack for 1885* (Liverpool, 1885), p. 102. In the discussion that follows, the references to average rent reductions have all been taken from the selective list that appeared in the almanac.

not been increased for many years', said the subcommissioners of Lord Charles Pelham-Clinton's estate near Castletown-Berehaven. But it appeared to them that Clinton had given little assistance towards his tenants' improvements. The aggregate rent of 168 tenants was therefore reduced by as much as 26·7 per cent. [239] Similarly, rents had not been increased on the earl of Bantry's properties 'for 30 or 40 years', but the subcommissioners doubted whether 'the noble proprietor has done much to assist his tenantry in the way of improvement—the buildings, the fences, and the drains, such as they are, having been made by the peasantry with very little assistance from the landlord'. As a result, they reduced the rents of seventy tenants by an average of 19·5 per cent. [240] Henry L. Puxley's rents were also found excessive, not because they had been recently or frequently raised, but because it appeared to the subcommissioners that the tenants had formerly paid them partly out of wages they earned in the Berehaven copper mines. 'This was not a sound state of things at any time,' the subcommissioners tersely remarked, 'but now, when the prosperity of the mines has so much declined, it certainly demands rectification.' The combined rent of forty-six tenants was therefore slashed by 29 per cent. [241] Thus there was probably some justification for the bitter complaints of many landlords and agents, who often referred dejectedly to 'the inevitable 20 per cent' and seriously doubted 'whether evidence has any effect in the land court'. [242] On the other hand, where landlords had themselves made extensive permanent improvements, the subcommissioners were apparently inclined to deal leniently with them. On the Cork estates of three notably improving landlords—the earl of Kenmare, Sir George St John Colthurst, and Viscount Midleton— the judicial reductions were far less than average. The combined rent of fifteen tenants on Kenmare's Bantry property was reduced by only 5·6 per cent; that of thirty tenants on Colthurst's estates, by 11 per cent; and that of thirty tenants on Midleton's property, by 13 per cent.

In the southwestern part of the county, amicable settlements of the rent question, including both fair-rent agreements and permanent reductions that were not registered with the land commission, seemed advantageous to both landlords and tenants. They were attractive to landlords because the average reductions made by the subcommissioners in that part of Cork were apparently larger than

[239] *C.C.*, 18 Aug. 1882.
[240] Ibid.   [241] Ibid.
[242] P.R.O.I., ref. no. 978, Midleton papers, Letter book, 1882–5: J. P. Fitzgerald to R. K. McBride, 1 Dec. 1882, pp. 305–6.

elsewhere.[243] The tenants, most of whom paid very small amounts of rent, might well have preferred to seek judicial relief, but the legal expenses of about £3 in each case would have largely destroyed the value of any reduction. As the solicitor for a number of such small-holders on the McCarthy minor estate near Skibbereen said in December 1885, 'In the case of a man paying £5 or £6 a year, the reduction he would get would not pay the costs'.[244] Under these circumstances, many southwestern landlords made substantial permanent abatements that were acceptable to their tenants during 1882.[245] In granting these reductions, landlords sought to escape action by the courts with as little financial sacrifice as possible; if their tenants had been able to obtain judicial relief less expensively, larger concessions would generally have been necessary to satisfy them.

Elsewhere in Cork, landowners who feared that the courts would slash their rentals commonly undertook new valuations of their estates. On the basis of these valuations, they then proposed to make either permanent or temporary abatements or to conclude fair-rent agreements. As a rule, however, tenants regarded landlord-initiated settlements with extreme scepticism, if not outright disdain; rarely did they accept the outcome of a new valuation without question. On the Moorehead estate, where the former rents greatly exceeded the government valuation, permanent reductions of about 15 per cent were offered.[246] But Richard Doherty, jun., regretfully informed the landlord in March 1882: 'Tim Donovan . . . [did] not accept your offer to settle. I think none of them will, for Daniel McCarthy, Denis, & Burke have now served notices for fixing their rent, so that all the tenants I may say are now in court, & we will have to fight every case. . . .'[247] Similarly, in December 1882 James Penrose Fitzgerald sent H. G. Warren copies of the reports of a valuer named Hunt. 'You will see', said Fitzgerald, 'that he leaves Doyle, Twomey, Pyne, and one of Riordan's [holdings] as they were, & reduces Barry & the other of Riordan's.' Fitzgerald advised Warren to make 'temporary abatements in accordance with Hunt's reports in the two cases named' and to enforce the customary rents 'in the other cases, as they are evidently fair'.[248] Not surprisingly, the

[243] Financial Reform Association, Liverpool, *Almanack*, p. 102.

[244] *C.E.*, 15 Dec. 1885.

[245] *W.C.E.*, 8 July 1882; *C.E.*, 25 Sept., 12 Dec. 1882.

[246] Doherty papers, Letter book, 1881–4: R. W. Doherty, jun., to J. H. Bryan, 4 Feb. 1882, p. 109.

[247] Ibid.: Doherty to Dr Moorehead, 2 Mar. 1882, p. 159.

[248] P.R.O.I., ref. no. 978, Midleton papers, Letter book, 1882–5: J. P. Fitzgerald to H. G. Warren, 2 Dec. 1882, p. 307.

tenants were intensely dissatisfied with this outcome, and all of them entered the land court. Apparently, they fared poorly. 'I had no doubt that Hunt has done substantial justice', Fitzgerald boasted in October 1883. 'Barry was the only one whose rent was at all a high one, & he has had a substantial reduction. It is quite too much to expect that they will be satisfied nowadays with anything you do for them.' [249] From the landlord's point of view, these new valuations were worth their cost because they sometimes helped to dissuade tenants from going to court. After Viscount Lismore revalued his vast estates in the counties of Cork, Limerick, and Tipperary and reportedly reduced his rental by 25 per cent, only sixty-four tenants from his Cork and Limerick properties had their rents fixed judicially; they obtained reductions averaging 21 per cent. [250]

When landowners firmly believed that the subcommissioners would deal leniently with their rents, they often did not bother with revaluations. Instead, they waited for some of their tenants to enter the courts and then endeavoured to settle with the remainder on the basis of these judicially decided cases. Richard Doherty, jun., declared in November 1881:

Lord Bandon is going to save no expense in his cases, as his are regarded as test cases in this part of the country, the rents on his property being looked upon as lower than that [*sic*] of the surrounding landlords, and I am now engaged in taking extracts from the old ledgers which show that both the rents have been reduced and also sundry allowances from time to time made to them. [251]

About sixty of Bandon's tenants had applied to have judicial rents fixed by early January 1882, and the earl wished to 'finish those in court & see how matters stand'. [252] When the subcommissioners reduced the rents of thirty-six of Bandon's tenants by an average of only 8·5 per cent, the rest withdrew their cases in disgust, and some tenants who had considered seeking judicial relief instead concluded fair-rent agreements with the earl. [253] For the same reason, this discreet policy was also pursued by Samuel Hussey on the earl of Kenmare's estates in 1883. [254] Although the expense of contesting a substantial number of cases in court was considerable, Hussey was soon placed in an excellent bargaining position for concluding

[249] Ibid., Letter book, 1883–4: Fitzgerald to Warren, 25 Oct. 1883, p. 13.
[250] *C.E.*, 28 Sept. 1885. See also *C.C.*, 2 Mar. 1882; *W.C.E.*, 9 Dec. 1882.
[251] Doherty papers, Letter book, 1880–1: R. W. Doherty, jun., to S. Bushe, 10 Nov. 1881, p. 948.
[252] Ibid., Letter book, 1881–4: Doherty to W. Hooper, 7 Jan. 1882, p. 53.
[253] Ibid.: Doherty to [illegible], 25 Apr. 1883, p. 699.
[254] Kenmare papers, Letter book, 1882–3: S. M. Hussey to Messrs Benbow, Saltwell, and Tryon, 11 May 1883, pp. 893–4.

agreements, since the subcommissioners reduced the rents of forty-two tenants on Kenmare's Kerry estate by 12·5 per cent, and those of fifteen tenants on his Cork estate by only 5·6 per cent. [255]

Several factors help to explain why only about one-third of the yearly tenants with holdings of over five acres in County Cork directly benefited from the rent provisions of the land act. [256] To begin with, the small reductions given to the first few tenants from many large estates who entered the courts discouraged the remainder from following the same treacherous path. Because the landlords' terms in offering fair-rent agreements following court decisions naturally tended to be no better than the terms obtained by the tenants in court, the number of agreements on such estates usually was also small. These circumstances largely account for the relative scarcity of both judicial rents and fair-rent agreements on such estates as those of the earls of Bandon and Kenmare, the dowager countess of Kingston, Sir George St John Colthurst, and Mountifort Longfield. [257] Moreover, tenants eligible to seek judicial relief were discouraged by the substantial decline in the size of reductions made by the subcommissioners between August 1883 and August 1885. The MacDevitt subcommission's decisions in particular clearly disgusted many of them. In October 1884 the earl of Egmont's tenants sent to the honourable John O'Hagan, the judicial commissioner, a memorial in which they bitterly complained that when the MacDevitt subcommission succeeded the Reeves subcommission in the Kanturk and Mallow districts, 'a different procedure was soon apparent, the reductions became beautifully less, and to our minds and in the opinion of the public, partiality reigned supreme'. Those tenants whose cases were listed for hearing grew extremely apprehensive: 'Many more of us whose rents are too high, in truth, rack rents, have waited all the time without seeking relief, afraid to go into court because of the late commission'. [258]

[255] 'Have you seen the judicial rents fixed by the subcommission in Bandon; certainly the estate [of Lord Kenmare near Bantry] got off beautifully' (ibid., Letter book, 1883–4: M. Leonard to J. E. Barrett, 29 June 1883, p. 69).

[256] *Returns showing the number of agricultural holdings in Ireland and the tenure by which they are held by the occupiers*, pp. 6–17.

[257] The number of court cases and the average rent reductions on these five estates were as follows: Bandon, thirty-six and 8·5 per cent; Kenmare (Cork estate), fifteen and 5·6 per cent; Kingston, seventeen and 9 per cent; Colthurst, thirty and 11 per cent; and Longfield, sixteen and 11·4 per cent. The combined acreage of these five estates was almost 134,000 in 1876 (Financial Reform Association, Liverpool, *Almanack*, p. 102).

[258] Memorial to Hon. J. O'Hagan from E. Dunlea and other tenants on Lord Egmont's estate, 20 Oct. 1884, quoted in *C.E.*, 13 Jan. 1885.

Another, though less important, factor in curtailing the resort to the land courts was that landlords and agents occasionally punished tenants who used them by requiring payment of judicial rents earlier than they demanded payment of non-judicial rents. On the Kenmare estates, where a 'hanging gale' of six months had formerly been allowed for payment of the rents after they became due, those tenants bold enough to have sought judicial relief were made to suffer. 'Go to all the tenants who got their judicial rent fixed,' the sub-agent peremptorily instructed the bailiff of Kenmare's Bantry property in early April 1884, 'and notice them that I will require them to pay me the 12 months' rent at Carriganass on Tuesday the 15th inst.'[259] These judicial tenants were apparently being pressed for the hanging gale. Viscount Midleton's agent always permitted three months for the payment of non-judicial rents after they became due, but he demanded that the tenants who had gone into court pay within one month.[260] As has already been noted, the smallholders, especially in the southwestern part of the county, were restrained by the legal fees of a few pounds from having their rents fixed judicially. Finally, tenants on such liberally managed estates as those of the duke of Devonshire often relied upon their landlords to grant substantial temporary abatements when economically justified, and they were inclined to remain out of court while cattle prices were still high.[261]

To Cork landlords, it may well have seemed like a pleasant dawn after a dread, dark night when in early 1882 the chief land commissioners made it quite plain that they would narrowly restrict the exercise of their power to break 'unreasonable or unfair' leases that tenants had been compelled to accept since 1870 'by threat of eviction or undue influence'.[262] Although some 1,500 leaseholders in Ireland applied to have their leases declared void within six months after the passage of the new act, the commissioners broke only 138 leases. As many as half of the leases declared void were held by tenants in County Cork, where 382 applications were submitted.[263] While the commissioners expressed sympathy for those who had

[259] Kenmare papers, Letter book, 1883–4: M. Leonard to E. Godfrey, 3 Apr. 1884, p. 906.
[260] P.R.O.I., ref. no. 978, Midleton papers, Letter book, 1882–5: J. P. Fitzgerald to T. J. Kelleher, 3 Oct. 1882, p. 206.
[261] Only four tenants on Devonshire's Cork estates of almost 33,000 acres went into court, even though these four obtained an average reduction of 15 per cent (Financial Reform Association, Liverpool, *Almanack*, p. 102).
[262] 44 & 45 Vict., c. 49, s. 21.
[263] *Report of the Irish land commissioners for the period from 22nd August 1884 to 22nd August 1885*, p. 31. The number of applications is not an indication of the number of leases taken since 1870.

accepted leases debarring them from claiming compensation for improvements under the 1870 land act, they did little else for such tenants.[264] The commissioners did invalidate some of those preposterous compound leases that sought to deprive tenants of whatever benefits might be conferred by post-1870 legislation on the Irish land question.[265] Nor did they hesitate to nullify the notorious leases of William Bence Jones after his tenants had regaled the court with graphic descriptions of the landlord's threats and fits of temper, and after their solicitor had read aloud the many objectionable covenants.[266] The commissioners generously interpreted the meaning of 'unreasonable or unfair terms' to include, for example, reservation to the landlord of all rights of turbary, vexatious preservation of game, disallowance of testamentary disposition, and prohibition of assignment or the assumption of debts or mortgages upon the land.

But what they gave with one hand the commissioners took away with the other. Although leaseholders wished to have their contracts invalidated in order to enable them to qualify for a judicial rent, the commissioners often merely suggested that 'unreasonable' covenants be struck out of the leases and refused to break them if this were done.[267] The exaction of an exorbitant rent was held in a few cases to be 'a term of the lease which might be unfair and unreasonable to the tenant', but this opinion was not widely adopted.[268] The commissioners declined to break the lease of one farmer on Sir James W. Mackey's estate near Kanturk even though Mackey had raised his rent from £16 to £30 in 1870 and had allegedly threatened him with eviction if he failed to perfect an agreement for a lease. In court opinions handed down in two important cases, neither the serving of a notice to quit nor the use of threatening language in order to force a tenant to accept a lease was considered sufficient reason of itself to warrant the voiding of a lease.[269]

Because leaseholders were excluded from its benefits, and because only a fraction of the yearly tenants entitled to take advantage of its rent provisions actually did so, the 1881 land act failed to make a major impact on the incomes of Cork landowners before 1885. The act probably affected less than 10 per cent of the gross annual rental of landed property in the whole county. The former rents of those

[264] *C.C.*, 2 Feb. 1882.   [265] Ibid., 1 Mar. 1882.
[266] Ibid., 23, 28 Feb. 1882.
[267] Ibid., 4, 20, 27 Feb. 1882.
[268] Quoted in Cant-Wall, *Land act*, p. 251. See also *C.C.*, 22 Feb. 1882.
[269] It had also to be shown that the tenant had protested against unreasonable covenants or an exorbitant increase of rent (*C.C.*, 22, 25 Feb. 1882).

Cork tenants who did take advantage of this legislation amounted to only £188,000 by August 1885, while the total rent paid by all Cork tenants was perhaps £2,250,000 in 1880.[270] By far the greater portion of landlord incomes would still have been left untouched even if three or four times the rental affected by this act had been affected by private settlements of similar scope. For incumbered landlords, this outcome was indeed most fortunate. Most land-owners in the south of Ireland had burdened their estates with fairly heavy charges. Samuel Hussey, whose wide experience made him a competent judge, calculated in June 1883 that the in-cumbrances on estates in Munster generally amounted to six or seven times their gross annual rental. This was a conservative estimate; it purposely excluded the jointures, annuities, head rents, and charges under the land-improvement acts that existed on most estates, because 'as these vary so much, no average can be correctly made'. Taking the case of a landlord with property worth £1,000 per annum, and with estate charges of £6,000, Hussey demonstrated that once poor rates, expenses of management, normal losses, tithe rent-charge, and interest were deducted, the net rental came to only £520. This led Hussey to conclude that 'the commissioners, in taking off 20 per cent on the gross, are taking off about 40 per cent on the nett'.[271] Eventually, the land act would ruin some owners of incumbered estates, but, as yet, landlords whose net income had so drastically diminished were quite exceptional.

Even though the land act did not have a major impact on the current incomes of most landowners, the agrarian agitation that produced the land act had extremely damaging effects on other aspects of their financial position. Almost overnight, their sources of credit largely evaporated. The mere prospect of legislation con-cerning Irish land in 1880 had placed mortgagees of Irish estates on their guard. While the Gladstone government's compensation for disturbance bill was before the house of commons in early July,[272]

[270] The figure of £2,250,000 is an estimate based on the assumption that Cork landlords collected about 25 per cent more in rent in 1880 than they are estimated to have received on the eve of the great famine (Crotty, *Irish agricultural production*, p. 305).

[271] Kenmare papers, Letter book, 1883–4: S. M. Hussey to W. Erck, 29 June 1883, pp. 66–7.

[272] The compensation for disturbance bill would have required landlords to pay compensation to tenants dispossessed for non-payment of rent, if their holdings were valued for poor rates at £30 or less, and if their inability to pay rent arose from the effects of the bad seasons of 1877–9. Passed by the house of commons, the bill was rejected overwhelmingly by the house of lords. Though a moderate measure, it was correctly regarded as an entering wedge for more radical reform (O'Brien, *Parnell*, pp. 181–3).

Samuel Hussey vehemently protested to the duke of Argyll that it was 'a land confiscation bill, as no rent will be paid for the next two years, no money will be lent, no credit given to landlords, & mortgages will be enforced with merciless severity'. Hussey continued:

Already the insurance offices, the greatest mortgagees in Ireland, have declined to lend any more money, & all negotiations for loans have been broken off. . . . I have bought £3,000 per annum worth of land, & no one will now lend £5,000 on it. This is as cruel a case of confiscation as could be perpetrated. In order to show you that I am not exaggerating, I enclose you [a] copy of a letter I rec[eive]d from the manager of the Standard Ass[uran]ce Co. in Dublin, who has lent more money than any [other] man in Ireland. [273]

The compensation for disturbance bill was thrown out by the house of lords, but the land act of the following year severely tightened the mortgage market. 'No capitalist will now lend on Irish estates,' complained Hussey in a letter to *The Times* in February 1882, 'as they naturally argue, if the government forcibly reduce rents 25 per cent in an exceptionally good year, what in a bad year.' [274] A deputation of Irish landowners conveyed this same message to Gladstone in a letter and later met with him to discuss the subject in July 1883. The prime minister was told: 'There are few (if any) sources for borrowing money on land in Ireland now open, and . . . trustees, assurance societies, and private lenders are steadily refusing to advance upon mortgages on Irish estates'. [275]

All landowners were also affected after 1879 by the drastic reduction in the capital value of their estates, and those pressed by creditors to raise money through land sales could not sell except at an enormous sacrifice. Cork property purchased in the landed estates court between 1871 and 1878 realized on the average almost twenty years' purchase. [276] But the agrarian agitation had an immediately depressing effect on the land market. In November 1880 one land judge remarked that applications for the postponement of sales of incumbered properties had multiplied to such an extent that the court 'in almost all cases had to appoint a receiver to get the rents in if they were able, and had almost abandoned its proper function of the sale of estates'. [277] In 1881 and 1882 the judges

[273] Kenmare papers, Letter book, Jan.–Oct. 1880: S. M. Hussey to duke of Argyll, 2 July 1880, pp. 589–96.
[274] Hussey to editor of *The Times*, 9 Feb. 1882, quoted in *C.C.*, 20 Feb. 1882.
[275] Quoted in *C.E.*, 1 Aug. 1883.
[276] *Cairns committee evidence*, appendix L, pp. 460–2.
[277] *C.E.*, 5 Nov. 1880.

themselves often considered the bids made as totally inadequate and refused to allow public sales to proceed. [278] Only about eight years' purchase was bid for Lord Fermoy's 19,350-acre estate when it was pushed into the market in June 1881 by the principal mortgagee, the Norwich Insurance Company, and the sale had to be abandoned. [279] Less than twelve years' purchase was offered for the small Roberts property at Shanballymore when it was put up for public sale in 1884, although it was later bought privately for about fourteen years' purchase. [280] Indeed, by 1884 the land market had reached a state of complete deadlock, comparable in some ways to the one of 1849 that had been broken by the incumbered estates act.

The land-purchase provisions of the 1881 act could not even begin to relieve the deadlock. Sales to tenants were practically out of the question, so far apart were the estimates held by landlord and tenant of their respective interests in the land. Although the 'Bright clauses' of the 1870 land act had generally proved a disappointing failure in Cork and elsewhere in Ireland, they had encouraged and assisted tenants to pay their landlords as much as twenty-seven or twenty-eight years' purchase in order to become the owners of their own holdings. Had it not been for the Bright clauses, these holdings 'would have been considered well sold at 20 years' purchase'. [281] If landlords had ever expected to realize such prices by sales to their tenants under the 1818 act, they were quickly freed from this strange deception. J. R. Heffernan, addressing a meeting of the Mallow Land League in September 1881, cynically advised his listeners that 'the landlords cannot last; the mortgagees will close upon them, and the question is how much will you give them for their lands'. 'As little as you can', Heffernan answered. 'He would not give them their twelve years' purchase.' [282] Speeches such as this prompted Samuel Hussey to say in October 1881, 'Until the tenants are disabused of the idea that they will get the land for nothing, I cannot swear that one tenant in all Ireland will buy'. [283] Richard Doherty, jun., informed the trustees of the Fitzpatrick estate in March 1882, when sales to the tenants were being discussed, that they might begin negotiations by asking twenty-three years' purchase and should not sell unless they obtained twenty. But Doherty warned that the

---

[278] Ibid., 21 July 1883; *C.C.*, 1 Aug. 1883.

[279] *C.E.*, 22 July 1884.

[280] Ibid., 18 Aug. 1884.

[281] B. Verlin to secretary of Duhallow Farmers' Club, quoted in *C.E.*, 8 July 1878.

[282] *C.C.*, 8 Sept. 1881.

[283] Kenmare papers, Letter book, 1880–1: S. M. Hussey to W. Hickes, 10 Oct. 1881, pp. 760–1.

Fitzpatrick tenants were 'so excited and misled at present that they would not do anything rational or that would benefit them, being told they will have the land yet for nothing'. [284] Few would now have disagreed with the view that Samuel Hussey had expressed in March 1878: 'I do not think any man of common understanding can avoid coming to the conclusion that landed property in Ireland cannot resist the repeated attacks made upon it unless the number of proprietors be increased.' [285] But Hussey's solution to the mutual standoff, which was to force tenants to buy under legislative constraint whenever they were offered their holdings at twenty years' purchase of the judicial rent, was really no solution at all. [286] It merely served to illustrate how far apart in their thinking were landlord and tenant at the inconclusive end of the first phase of the land war.

[284] Doherty papers, Letter book, 1881–4: R. W. Doherty, jun., to Messrs Park, Nelson, Morgan, and Co., 2 Mar. 1882, pp. 161–2.

[285] Kenmare papers, Letter book, Jan.–Aug. 1878: S. M. Hussey to Lord de Vere, 21 Mar. 1878, pp. 413–14.

[286] Ibid., Letter book, 1883–4: Hussey to W. Erck, 17 Mar. 1884, pp. 871–2.

VII

THE LAND WAR:
SECOND PHASE, 1884–92

~~~~~~

ECONOMIC MALAISE

THE SECOND PHASE of the land war in Cork, like the first, was rooted in economic difficulties. Just as the multiple adversities of 1877–9 had originally ignited the agrarian agitation, so too another series of severe setbacks beginning in the summer of 1884 quickly rekindled it. Hard, dry weather in April and May 1884 was followed by a major drought during the summer months, with the result that cattle-feeding costs rose steeply and yields of milk and butter fell sharply. This pattern repeated itself with even greater force in 1887, the worst year for dairy farmers since the great famine and perhaps the driest year of the entire nineteenth century.[1]

It was not the effects of bad weather alone that disheartened farmers. They were even more disturbed by the sharp downturn in the prices of the principal Irish agricultural exports, especially cattle exports. The high price of store stock had largely offset the low price of butter between 1880 and 1883, but the prices of both plunged downward at once in 1884. Most Cork farmers, but graziers above all, suffered from the fall in the price of cattle, which began in earnest in June.[2] Those who had purchased stock in the previous spring were forced to sell without profit and often at a loss late in the following autumn and winter.[3] One cattle buyer at the Bandon fair in December happily remarked that he 'could easily obtain at £6 what

[1] See above, Chapter III, pp. 151–3.
[2] *C.E.*, 5, 19, 23 June 1884.
[3] Ibid., 8 Oct., 13 Nov. 1884.

he would readily have paid £10 for in May'. [4] Prospects remained gloomy throughout most of 1885 and 1886. Those farmers who were unable to rear young stock of superior quality often could not find buyers at any price. After visiting several fairs in West Cork, the land agent and valuer H. R. Marmion reported in August 1885 that 'good cattle sold at 40 per cent under prices obtainable [at] this time two years [ago]. Rubbish [was] unsaleable.'[5] And it was noted of cattle sold at the Kinsale fair in October that 'in each case the price quoted was admitted to be £4 a head under their value at the corresponding period last year. . . . With regard to calves and inferior cattle, no one seemed to care to ask the price.'[6] The trough of the decline was reached in the middle of 1886,[7] but the rise during the rest of that year was slow and slight.[8]

The evidence with respect to the course of cattle prices in 1887 is conflicting. On the one hand, Barrington's index numbers show that while the price of two-to-three-year-old cattle continued to decline, that of one-to-two-year-old cattle soared by more than 50 per cent between 1886 and 1887, when the price was supposedly higher than in any other year since the great famine.[9] On the other hand, the dejected comments of landlords and agents as well as the consistently despairing reports from local fairs cast considerable doubt on an increase of this magnitude, which could hardly have gone unnoticed if it had in fact taken place. While cattle prices may have improved temporarily in early 1887, they were abnormally low from June through the end of the year. The earl of Kenmare explained to one of the trustees of his estates in July that although the tenants were not paying their March and May rents, 'certainly it was not their fault, for there was no demand whatever for any description of stock, owing to the dreadful dry weather we have had for some weeks'.[10] Viscount Midleton's agent heard in the same month that although the cattle fair in Midleton was very well stocked, scarcely any business was transacted: 'Buyers are afraid of a regular famine this year in grass and hay, and so, it is said, are afraid to buy'.[11] The Clonakilty fair in October was equally depressing.[12] And with the sole exception of

[4] Ibid., 4 Dec. 1884.
[5] Ibid., 14 Aug. 1885.
[6] *C.C.*, 22 Oct. 1885.
[7] Ibid., 22, 27 July 1885.
[8] Ibid., 9, 31 Aug., 3, 22 Sept., 18 Nov. 1886.
[9] Barrington, 'Agricultural prices', p. 252.
[10] Kenmare papers, Letter book, 1885–93: earl of Kenmare to W. Bentham, 4 July 1887, pp. 610–11.
[11] P.R.O.I., ref. no. 978, Midleton papers, Letter book, 1886–8: J. J. Sullivan to J. P. Fitzgerald, 11 July 1887, p. 501.
[12] *C.E.*, 11 Oct. 1887. See also *C.C.*, 7 Oct. 1887.

weanling calves, there were few sales at the important Dromcolliher fair in November: 'Prices of other descriptions of stock were such as to send farmers home for a sleepless night. Yearlings and two-year-olds were sold only at ruinous sacrifices.'[13] Dismal reports continued to be received from the local markets during the first four or five months of 1888.[14] In view of the universal lamentation, it may be concluded that despite Barrington's evidence, all branches of the cattle trade were affected by the depression in 1887.

No Irish agricultural export commodity was more affected by the downward plunge of prices after 1883 than butter, and butter was the mainstay of agriculture in Cork. This bewildered dairy farmers and filled them with dread, partly because of their mistaken belief that the bottom of the market had already been reached. 'The almost unparalleled decline in the prices of butter in our local market', it was reported from Mitchelstown in May 1885, 'has given rise to the gravest anxiety among the producers.'[15] It was pointed out with alarm in early November that the expected seasonal price rise, which had occurred in every October since the great famine almost without exception, had failed to materialize in 1885. The average price of first-quality Cork butter was then only 98s. per cwt, as compared with 149s. and 150s. in October 1874 and 1876 respectively.[16] The Kanturk land agent Henry Harte Barry told one Cork landowner in May 1886, when the Cork quotation dipped to 83s., that 'the price of butter, having fallen very much & going down almost daily, is one of the causes which in this district at any rate helps very much to make the farmers either unable or [un]willing to pay rents'.[17] This situation produced a widespread attitude among the tenants of 'let the landlord be damned'. Throughout the summer of 1886, butter had in fact to be sold at prices which 'could scarcely pay for its production', and at prices lower than 'we have seen for considerably over a quarter of a century'.[18] As if the farmer's cup of sorrow were not already filled to overflowing, there followed the disastrous drought of 1887, with no price rise compensating for the ensuing scarcity.

The immediate causes of the depression of agricultural prices were something of a mystery to contemporaries. In the case of cattle, they

---

[13] *C.C.*, 9 Nov. 1887. See also ibid., 15 Nov. 1887.
[14] Ibid., 28 Feb., 10, 18, 19 Apr. 1888; *C.E.*, 1 May 1888.
[15] *C.E.*, 22 May 1885.
[16] *C.C.*, 4 Nov. 1885.
[17] Barry papers, Letter book, Feb.–Nov. 1886: H. H. Barry to Mrs Duncan, 19 May 1886.
[18] *C.C.*, 6 Jan. 1887.

attributed great significance to the unfavourable weather conditions which frightened away prospective purchasers of livestock that had to be fattened and finished in Ireland or in England. The profit margins of the graziers and dealers were lowered by the increase in feeding costs resulting from major summer droughts in 1884 and 1887, from the winterfeed shortages of 1884–5 and 1887–8, and from cold, dry spring weather in 1884, 1885, 1887, and 1888. Contemporaries attached even greater importance to the continuance of British free trade in the face of growing foreign competition. It was obvious to almost all intelligent observers that, as William J. Lane told the select committee on Irish industries in 1885, 'while British free-trade legislation continues, it would be simply impossible for Ireland to compete as a grain-producing country with the ever increasing wheat areas of Canada, United States, Russia, India, Egypt, and Australia'. [19] Irish agricultural prosperity hinged upon the prosperity of the country's dairy and cattle industries, both now depressed. It was equally obvious that foreign competition, especially from France, Holland, and the Scandinavian countries, was undermining the traditional supremacy and good reputation which Irish butter had formerly enjoyed in the British market. The continued decline of Irish butter prices after 1883 was widely felt to be related directly to vastly increased British imports of foreign butter. It therefore seemed only logical that the growing foreign competition was also exerting severe downward pressure on cattle prices. [20] In July 1886 the earl of Kenmare's agent Maurice Leonard reported the widespread failure of the earl's tenants to pay rent and claimed that this was 'solely due to their not being able to dispose of their cattle, as there has been no demand for anything for several months'. [21] Leonard was perfectly convinced that unless Britain retreated from its cherished adherence to complete free trade and imposed duties on cattle imports from abroad, the agricultural depression in Ireland would only deepen. [22]

In retrospect, the emphasis placed by contemporaries on unfavourable climatic conditions and on foreign competition as causes of the Irish agricultural depression from mid-1884 to early 1888 seems exaggerated. Although both factors undoubtedly exerted some influence over prices, they were not of primary importance in driving them to such low levels. In the first place, the increase in feeding costs and the fall in graziers' profit margins associated with drought conditions and scarcity of winterfeed in earlier years (1864,

[19] *Industries committee evidence*, p. 727.   [20] Ibid.
[21] Kenmare papers, Letter book, 1885–93: M. Leonard to Colonel Dease, 11 July 1886, pp. 456–7.   [22] Ibid.

1868, 1874, and 1876) did not affect Irish cattle prices adversely, at least not in any marked degree. [23] And in the second place, the close correlation that might have been expected to exist between Irish agricultural prices on the one hand and British imports of livestock, meat, and butter on the other was largely absent. This is made clear by a comparison of the movement of Irish prices with that of British imports between 1883 and 1891 (see Tables 54 and 55). [24]

TABLE 54   Index numbers of Irish agricultural prices, 1883–91

(base 1840 = 100, except store cattle, base 1845 = 100)

years	store cattle		beef	mutton	pork	butter
	1–2 yrs	2–3 yrs				
1883	240	240	140	173	133	110
average, 1884–7	204	199	115	143	117	95
average, 1888–91	239	243	115	144	111	99

TABLE 55   British imports of non-Irish livestock, meat, and butter, 1883–91 (in thousands)

years	cattle (no.)	beef (cwt)	sheep (no.)	mutton (cwt)	bacon & hams (cwt)	butter (cwt)
1883	475	805	1,116	236	3,696	2,334
average, 1884–7	354	811	927	628	3,940	2,524
average, 1888–91	521	1,500	584	1,383	4,448	3,115

Two facts emerge clearly from this comparison of Irish prices and British imports. From 1884 to 1887 store-cattle prices fell sharply, even though the reverse might have been expected to result from the combination of declining imports of live cattle and stagnating carcass-beef imports. Then between 1888 and 1891 store-cattle prices returned to the high level of 1883, and other agricultural prices tended to remain stabilized at a low level, even though an altogether different outcome might have been predicted on the basis of the enormous rise in beef and mutton imports, and of the more moderate increase in pig-meat and butter imports. Especially when considered together, these facts strongly point to the conclusion that the basic cause of the depression in Irish agricultural prices between

[23] Barrington, 'Agricultural prices', pp. 251–2.
[24] Ibid., p. 252; *Agricultural returns of Great Britain . . . 1892*, pp. 102–3.

1884 and 1887 was not the increase in foreign competition under British free trade.

The principal cause of the distressed condition of Irish agriculture during these years was the slackening of British manufacturing and investment activity. This unfavourable turn of the British trade cycle—one of the most severe of the century—created large-scale unemployment, particularly among workers in heavy industry, and led in turn to a significant contraction of the British demand for meat and dairy products. The downturn coincided with the end of the American railway boom of 1880–3 as well as with the completion of a great surge in British shipbuilding and reached a trough in 1886.[25] In that year the unemployment figure among members of certain important trade unions rose slightly above 10 per cent, and it has been suggested that general unemployment was about 9·5 per cent.[26] By 1887 a recovery began, and in the non-metal trades, unemployment dropped to only 3·9 per cent, but it nevertheless remained as high as 10·4 per cent in the engineering, shipbuilding, and metal trades.[27] One of the most prominent features of this brief period of British industrial inactivity was the sudden reversal of the earlier trend of fairly continuous growth in British imports of livestock and meat from abroad. The total value of such imports declined from almost £28,239,000 in 1883 to only £20,493,000 in 1887. The pressure exerted on British working-class budgets by the industrial depression caused an acceleration in the shift away from more expensive livestock towards cheaper dead meat. This replacement effect may be inferred from the fall in the value of livestock imports alone from £11,984,000 to just £6,149,000 between 1884 and 1887.[28] The Irish farmers' difficulties, then, were for the most part the inevitable outcome of the almost total dependence of Irish agriculture upon conditions in the British market.

RESURGENCE OF THE AGRARIAN AGITATION

A resurgence of agrarian agitation was a distinct possibility by the end of 1884. Samuel Hussey could not ignore the bad weather and the falling prices of August, when he made his customary half-yearly report to the trustees of the earl of Kenmare's estates; he saw a troubled winter looming ahead, since the tenants were beginning to fall into arrears again.[29] There were a few other signs of a

[25] Clapham, *Modern Britain*, iii, 6.
[26] Ibid., ii, 454; iii, 29.   [27] Ibid., iii, 6–7.
[28] *Agricultural returns of Great Britain . . . 1892*, pp. 104–5.
[29] Kenmare papers: S. M. Hussey's report, Aug. 1884, Rental and account of the earl of Kenmare's estates, Jan.–June 1884.

gathering storm. At the end of November, a dynamite explosion partly demolished Edenburn House, Hussey's residence at Gortatlea in Kerry. Constitutional nationalists loudly condemned this and all similar violent outrages as providing a convenient excuse for the continuation of the crimes act, which was soon to expire.[30] On the duke of Devonshire's estates, the tenants organized in order to press their claims for a reduction in rent, but their activity was not widely imitated.[31] On the whole, the winter of 1884–5 was undisturbed either by violence or by a concerted refusal to pay rent.

As the depression deepened in the first half of 1885, however, the storm clouds became more ominous. It was reported in January that 'the dead walls of all the towns in the northern part of the county are covered with auction bills of the sales of farms, and only in a few instances are the sales effected'.[32] Perhaps the report exaggerated, but there was a larger measure of truth to the claim made in late March that almost all the farmers of north Cork who had paid rent in the previous year 'had to draw on capital or add to their load of debt to satisfy the landlord'.[33] The rent question was again moving into the forefront. 'I am sorry to say rents are coming in very slow indeed,' Samuel Hussey lamented in the middle of May, '& I am afraid we will have a very hard fight for them this year.'[34] The land act of 1881 had been unsatisfactory to begin with, and it was woefully inadequate in preventing new discontent from accumulating. As the *Cork Examiner* reasoned in early June, less than

a third of the tenantry of Ireland have had judicial rents settled. A hundred thousand, or one-sixth of the whole number, are, by the fact of their being leaseholders, outside the benefit of the land act. Even those who have obtained judicial rents are by . . . [no] means all satisfied, especially seeing how [the] values of farm produce have tumbled since many of these rents were settled.[35]

It could not easily be denied that, as the agent James Penrose Fitzgerald told one Cork landowner in May, 'the way things are at present, the judicial rents are quite high enough'.[36]

Yet, when tenants sought remissions of rent, landlords generally

[30] *C.E.*, 1 Dec. 1884.
[31] Ibid., 25, 27 Nov., 3 Dec. 1884; 1 Jan. 1885.
[32] Ibid., 22 Jan. 1885.
[33] Ibid., 1 Apr. 1885.
[34] Kenmare papers, Letter book, 1884–5: S. M. Hussey to Messrs Benbow, Saltwell, and Tryon, 15 May 1885, pp. 733–4.
[35] *C.E.*, 4 June 1885.
[36] P.R.O.I., ref. no. 978, Midleton papers, Letter book, 1884–6: J. P. Fitzgerald to J. A. Smith, 19 May 1885, p. 215.

turned a deaf ear. The duke of Devonshire and a few other land-owners granted abatements of up to 20 per cent, but they were exceptions. [37] A very prevalent landlord attitude was that expressed in July by the agent of the Kingston estate. In rejecting the tenants' request for 20 per cent off the rents due in March, he told the parish priest that

the tenants have had the full benefit of the high prices of the last few years, & it does not seem fair or reasonable to expect a reduction when prices have merely reverted to the level at which the present rents were fixed.[38]

Significantly, it was reported in June that the announcement of the abatement on the Devonshire estates had been received 'with the greatest disfavour by a number of landlords, who were secretly granting insignificant reductions', particularly because '20 per cent on the duke's 32,000 acres in the county of Cork' was 'equivalent to 50 per cent on the great majority of lettings throughout the county'. [39] Devonshire's liberality was a shocking embarrassment to a solid phalanx of less wealthy or less considerate landowners.

The deepening depression, the growing difficulty in the payment of rent, and the landlords' insistence upon the full measure of their income were placing tenant farmers in an increasingly defiant mood. Both locally and nationally, this mood was assuming organized form. The tenants of two townlands on the Fitzpatrick estate near Bally-vourney, for example, would not be denied some remission of rent. They sent a deputation to the agent Richard Doherty, jun., who relayed their determined message to the estate trustees in early June:

They stated their grievances boldly as to the price of cattle & butter (which no doubt are very low) & that they could not pay their rents without a reduction; & that if they got a fair reduction, they would pay up within a month, & if not, they said 'that to a man the two townlands would refuse to pay their rents & let you take what steps you wished, & there would be a troublesome job with them'. [40]

Even more pregnant for the future was the sudden emergence of a strong national organization from relative obscurity. For about two years the Irish National League, which had been established in October 1882 primarily in order to advance the cause of 'national self-government' and only secondarily to promote 'land-law

[37] *C.E.*, 6 Feb., 30 May, 8 July 1885.
[38] P.R.O.I., ref. no. 978, Midleton papers, Letter book, 1884–6: J. P. Fitzgerald to Rev. D. Burdon, 6 July 1885, p. 276.
[39] *C.E.*, 5 June 1885.
[40] Doherty papers, Letter book, 1880–6: R. W. Doherty, jun., to Messrs Park, Nelson, Morgan, and Co., 2 June 1885, pp. 771–2.

reform', attracted little attention and achieved little worthy of mention. [41] But in the first half of 1885, the National League grew remarkably in the number and in the membership of its local branches. By early July there were throughout the country somewhat more than 800 branches, almost as many as the now outlawed Land League had had at the very height of its power. [42]

As National League branches proliferated, the size and scope of the tenants' demands increased. From the fall of 1885 through the summer of 1886, Cork landlords and agents were asked to give up a larger proportion of the usual rent than ever before, with the possible exception of the disastrous winter of 1879–80. Tenants regularly sought abatements of 25 or 30 per cent, and often even larger ones. [43] The widening difference of opinion as to what constituted a reasonable adjustment of conflicting claims was well illustrated by the duke of Devonshire's estate. In this instance the tenants, who were proffered in December 1885 the same reduction of 20 per cent that they had been given in the previous summer, responded by presenting a memorial in which they pointedly asked: 'Does your Grace believe, from your own knowledge and experience, that 20 per cent at all approaches the loss we have sustained by the great fall in the prices of butter, cattle, and other agricultural produce?' The tenants did not believe they were 'overstepping the bounds of a moderation which depressing times makes with us a necessity' by requesting the duke to double his allowance. [44]

As if the size of the abatements demanded were not threatening enough to the landlords, that minority of the tenants whose rents had been newly fixed by the land courts or by agreement now generally repudiated these recent reductions as totally inadequate and attempted to range themselves alongside the non-judicial tenants with respect to the new demands. In early September 1885 the Churchtown branch of the National League loudly applauded William O'Brien for exposing in parliament what they considered the egregious error of the land courts 'in the fixing of rents which are now impossible to pay in consequence of the great depression in the value of all farm produce caused by foreign competition'. [45] The spread of such an attitude among the tenants deeply angered the propertied classes. Shortly after the Churchtown branch of the league had taken its stand, one Cork land agent called attention to the existence of what he termed 'a widespread conspiracy through the

---

[41] O'Brien, *Parnell and his party*, p. 127.
[42] Ibid., p. 133.
[43] *C.E.*, Sept.–Dec. 1885; Jan.–July 1886.
[44] Quoted in *C.C.*, 18 Dec. 1885.   [45] *C.E.*, 2 Sept. 1885.

country against the payment of even judicial rents unless at an abatement of from 25 to 30 per cent'. He castigated this as nothing less than 'an organized attempt to rob all owners of property of their just rights' and strongly urged landlords 'not to give one shilling abatement off judicial rents, or rents which have been fixed outside the court since 1880, and if tenants refused to pay them, to fight them to the bitter end'. [46] The tenants and their leaders were quick to realize that the establishment of the landlord doctrine of distinction between judicial and non-judicial rents could dangerously weaken their organization and seriously jeopardize their objectives. They therefore fought strenuously to ensure that this distinction did not gain currency. Addressing a meeting of tenants from the estates of Viscount Doneraile and the earl of Egmont in early January 1886, the Rev. C. Buckley, C.C., Buttevant, persuasively argued:

Everybody knows that a judicial lease is of very little value in such a season as this—in fact, it is rather a misfortune to have taken out one at all—and the paltry reduction made a few years ago to certain farmers who had been paying exorbitant rents for many a long day, could not meet the universal depression which has fallen upon every commodity land yields. There should then be no distinction between judicial and non-judicial tenants, both being pressed upon with equal severity. And there should be no distinction between them for another reason—namely, that it is in their united power and their combined stand that the secret of success lies. [47]

Unity and combination were essential to any movement, but financial resources were just as vitally necessary if success were to be achieved. The landlords were almost certain to take legal action, to threaten eviction, and in extreme cases to carry it out, in order to 'bring the tenants to their senses', unless some means were devised to discourage them. The recognition of this reality led to the proliferation of special funds, called variously 'defence', or 'indemnity', or 'sustentation' funds, for use in the fight against the legal manoeuvres of the landlords. This tactic enjoyed the blessing of some members of the Irish parliamentary party, which as a whole was very reluctant at this stage to encourage the growing agrarian agitation. In late December 1885, however, William J. Lane, M.P., offered the following advice to the tenants of Sir Joseph N. McKenna; despite his membership in the Parnellite party, McKenna had refused to reduce the rents on his estate near Youghal and was busily serving writs in order to destroy a combination among his tenants:

If the members of every branch of the National League contributed even a few pence each per week, which none would miss, the evicted tenants of the

[46] *C.C.*, 14 Sept. 1885.   [47] *C.E.*, 9 Jan. 1886.

country could be easily and comfortably maintained, and landlords would very quickly drop the writ serving. This would of course require organization, but it would be no sacrifice compared with the gigantic evil it would crush out of existence. . . . The above collections could be made at the chapel doors on Sundays. [48]

Well before Lane recommended them to his friends at Youghal, defence funds had appeared in several parts of Cork, for example, on the estates of Colonel Grant, F. Barry, and Colonel Stuart in the Millstreet district, where the tenants had been denied abatements of 30 per cent in September. [49] The tenants of Major Nash, who had also been refused an allowance of 30 per cent, resolved in the same month 'to establish a fund for their own special defence, independently of the National League. One shilling to the pound on the rent was agreed on to start with.' [50] Spurning his 'perfectly laughable' offer of a 10 per cent reduction, the earl of Bandon's Carbery tenants decided in November to pay no rent unless the allowance were increased, and promised to raise a fund to aid anyone evicted during the struggle. [51] In actuality, however, defence funds were of limited usefulness and held little terror for the landlords. Just as in the case of trade unions, combinations of tenants needed much time in order to build up their financial resources as well as to perfect their central organization and control.

Probably with these considerations in mind, Tim Healy, one of the three secretaries of the Irish National League in Dublin, proposed a different course of action. Speaking at a well attended meeting in Killarney on 29 August 1885, Healy reportedly told his listeners:

If they entered into a combination, his advice to them would be this . . . , namely, to bank the rents in the names of two or three trustees at a reduced figure. Then let them demand a reduction which they would all stand by, and if there was some sleveen [i.e., a backslider] amongst them, they need not be afraid, for the rent was in the bank, and there were very few rich enough to pay two rents. When the landlord saw such combination and determination upon the part of the tenants, he would give in and give a reduction, but if he did not, they would have funds—hundreds, or perhaps thousands, of pounds to fight him with, to help the evicted to keep back the bailiff, and by that means the landlord, having no resources to fall back upon, would be compelled to do justice. [52]

[48] W. J. Lane to J. H. Ronayne, 21 Dec. 1885, quoted in *C.E.*, 6 Jan. 1886.
[49] *C.C.*, 16 Sept. 1885; *C.E.*, 17 Sept. 1885.
[50] *C.C.*, 17 Sept. 1885.
[51] Ibid., 6 Nov. 1885.
[52] Ibid., 31 Aug. 1885.

If properly implemented, Healy's scheme offered an immediate solution to the problem of inadequate financial resources. It had other merits. It encouraged the formulation of reasonable demands, discouraged backsliding once the issue had been joined, and generally strengthened the bonds of combination at the local level. On the other hand, it made one untested assumption of crucial importance, namely, that where landowners had money to fight, tenants in large numbers would allow themselves to be evicted rather than accept something less than what they had originally demanded. And it left open the question of a remedy for the landlord's seizure of the tenant's stock, crops, or other effects in satisfaction of unpaid rent.

Healy's proposal at first received little national attention. In October 1885, however, the *Nation* briefly reported a similar speech that he had made in County Monaghan, under the headline, 'A Plan of Campaign'. Soon John Dillon and *United Ireland* were strongly urging tenants to take it up.[53] The scheme was put into practice on at least a dozen estates in County Cork between October 1885 and February 1886. Originally, no remissions of rent whatsoever had been offered on most of these properties, such as those of the earl of Kenmare near Bantry, Norman Uniacke near Youghal, the earl of Egmont at Churchtown and Buttevant, and the dowager countess of Kingston at Mitchelstown.[54] Very insignificant allowances of 10 per cent or less were offered on a few of these estates.[55] The tenants usually insisted upon general reductions applicable to all alike, regardless of the terms of their tenures. The size of the allowances demanded ranged from as little as 15 per cent on Lord Carbery's estate to as much as 35 per cent on the earl of Kenmare's Bantry property.

The success achieved under Healy's scheme was hardly unqualified. In some instances a compromise beneficial to the tenants was eventually reached. In accordance with a resolution of the Cloyne branch of the National League, J. C. Longfield's tenants demanded a general abatement of 25 per cent in early November 1885, but Longfield was only willing to give 15 per cent in most cases. About 120 dissatisfied tenants then deposited over £1,500 in the Midleton National Bank in the names of two local clergymen. In late December, however, Longfield increased his offer to 20 per cent to all tenants, and they agreed to accept it.[56] Norman Uniacke escaped more lightly than Longfield. He had tried to collect the full

[53] Lyons, *Dillon*, pp. 74–5.
[54] *C.E.*, 20, 21 Oct. 1885; 7 Jan. 1886; *C.C.*, 9 Nov. 1885.
[55] *C.C.*, 6 Nov. 1885; *C.E.*, 8, 11, 14 Jan. 1886.
[56] *C.C.*, 23 Dec. 1885.

rent and had failed. In late October his tenants lodged their rents, less the 20 per cent reduction sought, in the bank in the name of the Rev. J. Savage, C.C., Inch. But when Uniacke conceded 10 per cent in early January 1886, the tenants abandoned their original demand. [57] The best fight, with probably the best results, was made by the earl of Egmont's tenants. In September 1885 they sought an all-round reduction of 30 per cent, but the earl absolutely refused. [58] Vigorously led by two local clergymen, the tenants placed their rents in the bank and maintained a united resistance for over four months. Most grudgingly, Egmont finally offered a 20 per cent reduction, but only to the non-judicial tenants. Rather than run the risk of treachery after they had made such a determined stand, Fr Buckley and Fr Williams persuaded all the tenants to agree to Egmont's terms; the abatement was shared with the judicial tenants. [59]

On other estates, however, little or nothing was achieved by the adoption of Healy's scheme. Viscount Midleton's tenants sought a general allowance of 30 per cent and lodged their rents, less the reduction, in the hands of trustees in early January. [60] The Midleton branch of the National League enthusiastically supported their demand as one which 'no one but a high handed landlord or agent could refuse, seeing the low prices of stock & farm produce, coupled with the fact that those tenants rec[eive]d no abatement off the March [1885] rents'. [61] On the point of a general allowance, however, Lord Midleton was immovable. He flatly stated that he did not believe that 'an all round reduction could be at any time fair or equitable', nor did he think it proper for judicial tenants 'to ask for a further reduction'. He pointed out that he had 'offered, unasked, such an abatement, both to leaseholders and yearly tenants, as I thought would meet the case' of an unfavourable season, and that he had authorized his agent 'to consider any individual case which might present special features'. 'Beyond this I cannot go', Midleton concluded. [62] Within a matter of days, the tenants were served with writs, and their combination rapidly disintegrated. [63] Similarly,

[57] *C.E.*, 21 Oct. 1885, 9 Jan. 1886.
[58] Ibid., 28 Sept. 1885.
[59] Ibid., 28, 29 Jan. 1886.
[60] Minute book, Midleton branch of the Irish National League, 1885–9, 6 Jan. 1886 (in the possession of Mr Michael Powell, Solicitor, Grand Parade, Cork).   [61] Ibid., 4 Jan. 1886.
[62] Viscount Midleton to R. Parker, 6 Feb. 1886, quoted in *C.E.*, 15 Feb. 1886.
[63] Minute book, Midleton branch of the Irish National League, 1885–9, 14 Feb. 1886.

Lord Carbery's tenants, offered the paltry allowance of $7\frac{1}{2}$ per cent, made a brief show of resistance but then caved in as soon as the landlord's Dublin agents—Messrs Stewart and Kincaid—had a large number of writs issued against them. [64] The dowager countess of Kingston's tenants also fared poorly. In January some of them apparently banked their rents, minus the 20 per cent reduction that they were seeking. [65] William Downes Webber, the husband of the dowager countess, agreed, perhaps ingenuously, to concede the tenants' demand, provided that the mortgagee of the estate—the Representative Church Body—would reduce its annual interest charge by an equivalent amount. [66] When the Representative Church Body refused to accept less than its full due, Webber skilfully scattered some token abatements among the tenants, and a campaign that had never really gathered momentum collapsed completely. [67]

Unrealistic hopes of victory and exaggerated claims of success frequently marked the meetings and demonstrations of the National League. Addressing a meeting in Killarney at the end of December 1885, the Parnellite M.P. Thomas Sheehan told tenants from the Kenmare and Herbert estates that since the landlords had refused to accept 70 per cent of the rent due in the previous March, they should 'offer only 50 [per cent] next time, and nothing at all in March [1886], as by then the new Irish parliament would allot the land free to the present holders without any compensation to the exterminating landlords'. [68] At a large demonstration held at Kilworth in late January 1886 in order to protest the Rev. Maurice Collis's refusal to reduce rents, it was claimed that most landlords in that district had made allowances of from 20 to 40 per cent. [69] And at another demonstration held near Killeagh in late March in order to denounce the niggardly Sir Joseph N. McKenna, all the other neighbouring landowners were said to have lowered their rents by 15 to 25 per cent. [70] Even if these specific claims were strictly true, which is doubtful, they did not represent the effect of the movement in general.

Measured against the tenants' objectives and against the depression in prices, the struggles waged by the local branches of the

[64] *C.E.*, 14 Jan. 1886.
[65] Ibid., 7 Jan. 1886.
[66] Ibid., 30 Jan. 1886.
[67] Ibid., 9 Feb. 1886.
[68] *C.C.*, 28 Dec. 1885. Sheehan's comment was obviously inspired by the recent public intimation of Gladstone's 'conversion' to home rule, the so-called Hawarden kite.
[69] *C.E.*, 1 Feb. 1886.   [70] Ibid., 29 Mar. 1886.

National League between the autumn of 1885 and the summer of 1886 were on the whole failures. Most landlords lowered their rents by only about 15 per cent and normally excluded their judicial tenants from the benefits. The reported allowances made by slightly more than fifty Cork landowners during this period averaged about 18 per cent, but this figure leaves out of consideration the reported instances in which no abatements whatever were made. [71] Without the enthusiasm and self-sacrifice generated by a truly national land movement, the achievement of the tenants' full or nearly full demands was impossible on a wide scale. While Gladstone's home rule bill was before parliament and the country in the spring and early summer of 1886, the conviction was widespread in Ireland that a final solution of the land question on terms generous to the tenants was imminent. The tenants believed that they would soon enjoy their farms free of rent, that they would shortly have the land for nothing, or so the landlords claimed. [72] This psychology hardly encouraged boldness and pertinacity in pursuit of demands or willingness on the part of a substantial number of tenants to face eviction in order to obtain their objectives. As long as this willingness to risk eviction was absent, tenants were more or less compelled to accept their landlords' definition of what constituted a reasonable allowance. And the landlords and their agents quickly perceived that tenant resistance had its limits, and that they still had the whip hand when a conflict arose. [73]

VIOLENCE AND NON-VIOLENCE

It is somewhat surprising that the revival of the agrarian agitation in 1885 and 1886, made manifest by the rent conflicts on so many estates, was not accompanied by a substantial increase in the resort to violence. This is not to say that violence was conspicuously lacking. While the rest of the county was relatively peaceful, moonlighters were active sporadically in both the Millstreet and Kanturk districts. There were several reports during November and December 1885 of arms raids as well as of firing into dwellings in order to punish tenants for paying rent or for associating with boycotted farmers. [74]

---

[71] Ibid., Aug. 1885–July 1886; *C.C.*, Aug. 1885–July 1886.

[72] Doherty papers, Letter book, 1882–7: Doherty and Jones to Messrs Park, Nelson, Morgan, and Co., 25 May 1886, pp. 638–9; Kenmare papers, Letter book, 1885–93: M. Leonard to earl of Kenmare, 27 Mar. 1886, pp. 366–7; Leonard to Colonel Dease, 18 May 1886, pp. 433–4.

[73] Doherty papers, Letter book, 1882–7: Doherty and Jones to Messrs Park, Nelson, Morgan, and Co., 25 May 1886, pp. 638–9.

[74] *C.C.*, 13 Nov., 3 Dec. 1885.

Moonlighting was again rife during the summer and autumn of 1886. In May a party of armed and disguised men visited a well-to-do farmer named Horgan at Drominagh and forced him to 'go on his knees and swear that he would give an abatement to his dairyman'. [75] Midnight raiders also attacked the houses of Patrick Cronin of Keale near Millstreet, who was engaged in a dispute with one of his labourers over an acre of land on which to build a house, and of Timothy O'Mahony of Flintfield, who was suspected of having paid his rent. [76] During another attack, on the house of a dairyman named Herlihy at Kishkeam in June, the moonlighters, reportedly searching for arms, seriously wounded three members of Herlihy's family. [77]

The arms raiders were desperate, determined young men, and their activities earned them little sympathy among the people of the districts in which they operated. There was a loud outcry when two daughters of a large farmer and popular National League member named David Jones were wounded, one of them fatally, after they had refused to admit a party of moonlighters searching for arms near Kingwilliamstown in early October. [78] Resistance to these apparently wanton attacks was becoming more common, and there was much greater willingness than in the past to give information to the authorities. After another farmer was wounded near Rockchapel in the same month while attempting to drive off a party of moonlighters, the police were able to arrest four suspects. [79] The quarryman on the earl of Cork's estate, severely beaten by about fifteen disguised moonlighters for refusing to give up his blasting powder or his gun, chose to identify at least four of his assailants to the police. [80] It was reported in mid-October that the police had succeeded in capturing at Boherboy the alleged leader of the moonlighters of Cork, Limerick, and Clare. An ex-soldier named John O'Keefe, he was said to have been identified by two Limerick farmers whose houses he had attacked in search of arms. [81] It is extremely doubtful that O'Keefe was in fact the 'Captain Moonlight' of three counties, but after his arrest, there was a temporary lull in agrarian violence in northwest Cork until early 1887. [82]

In other parts of the county, two classes of persons were regular

[75] Ibid., 13 May 1886.
[76] Ibid., 17, 21 May 1886.
[77] Ibid., 18 June 1886.
[78] Ibid., 5, 6 Oct. 1886.
[79] Ibid., 9 Oct. 1886.
[80] Ibid., 11 Oct. 1886.
[81] Ibid., 12, 13 Oct. 1886.
[82] *C.E.*, 8, 9, 11 Feb. 1887.

targets of violence because of the particularly odious nature of their occupations—writ-serving bailiffs and caretakers of evicted farms. The popular resentment against caretakers, who often refused to be easily intimidated into laying down their charge, was unusually strong. In August 1885 one caretaker of an evicted farm, then held by a Clonakilty shopkeeper and notorious gombeen man named W. S. Bateman, was shot in the legs just outside his own door. [83] In January 1886, after the local branch of the National League had warned the labourer-caretakers of an evicted farm near Ballydehob to leave their employment, the only one to neglect the warning was also shot in the legs. [84] A caretaker on the Ponsonby estate was more fortunate; he was merely stoned as he left Gortroe chapel, located between Killeagh and Youghal. [85] Four total strangers approached another caretaker of an evicted farm near Mallow in May, and with a heavy stick, administered a severe blow to the face, leaving him with an ugly wound. [86] Yet another caretaker was found drowned in a well near Charleville in the same month. [87]

With the exceptions of the violence against caretakers and process servers, and of the desperate raids of moonlighters in northwest Cork, the revival of the agrarian agitation did not bring about a new wave of violence. In fact, the number of reported agrarian outrages in the county climbed only slightly above the low level of 1884 during the next two years. There were 120 outrages reported by the constabulary in 1885, and 117 in 1886, as compared with 108 in 1884. [88] Although it would be rash to deny that outrages and evictions were often connected, with evictions frequently leading to outrages, it is difficult to establish any close correlation between the two during these years. Both evictions and threats of eviction increased substantially in 1886 without any apparent effect on the rate of agrarian crime. [89]

One of the most important factors in curtailing the resort to violence at this time was the courts of the National League. The

[83] Ibid., 10, 11 Aug. 1885.
[84] *C.C.*, 6 Jan. 1886.
[85] Ibid., 26 Jan. 1886.
[86] Ibid., 4 May 1886.
[87] Ibid., 26 May 1886. For attacks on bailiffs, see ibid., 8 Jan., 23 Feb., 9 Sept. 1886.
[88] *Return by provinces, of agrarian offences throughout Ireland reported to the inspector general of the Royal Irish Constabulary between the first day of January 1885 and the 31st day of December 1885* ... [C 4701], H.C. 1886, liv, 1, pp. 8–9; *Return by provinces, of agrarian offences* ... *between the 1st day of January 1886 and the 31st day of December 1886* ... [C 5024], H.C. 1887, lxviii, 1, pp. 8–9.
[89] *Return of civil bills in ejectment and superior-court writs, 1879–88*, pp. 3–5.

landlords protested vehemently against the operations of these extralegal tribunals. In a published letter to the lord lieutenant in January 1886, Arthur H. Smith-Barry, the chairman of the Cork Defence Union, a landlord organization recently formed to contend with the growing incidence of boycotting, complained bitterly of the situation. It was virtually impossible, declared Smith-Barry, for a private association like the C.D.U. effectively to 'neutralize the influence of a movement which sets the law of the land at defiance, holding its own courts and issuing orders and decrees which are generally even more dreaded than those of her majesty the queen'. [90] In late July the earl of Kenmare's new agent Maurice Leonard vented his indignation to the secretary of the Irish land commission:

The National League have established no less than 8 branches on Lord Kenmare's estate, at whose weekly courts his lordship's relations with his tenantry are discussed & investigated, & the tenants are practically debarred from paying their rents, unless on the conditions there laid down. [91]

The tenants and their leaders, on the other hand, denied that they were doing anything illegal or unprecedentedly novel. Timothy Harrington, one of the secretaries of the central branch of the league, contradicted in January 1886 charges that local branches held courts, inflicted fines, and possessed a judicial procedure of their own. He admitted that 'discussions' of agrarian disputes took place at National League meetings, comparable to those at meetings of the old tenant-right associations in Ireland, of the English Farmers' Alliance, or of the British trade unions. It was common knowledge that parish priests were regularly elected chairmen of local branches of the league, and Harrington concluded by pointing out that agrarian disputes had usually been referred for settlement to the catholic clergy by their parishioners, and that this traditional practice had been found 'most useful in the preservation of social order in Ireland'. [92] While the catholic clergy may have been the customary arbiters of agrarian disputes in the past, the ethical frame of reference in which both they and their parishioners viewed these disputes had changed substantially in recent years. Widely acceptable solutions now could only be more radical ones, and the priests exercised their unquestioned authority to bring about settlements in an entirely new and different context.

[90] A. H. Smith-Barry to earl of Carnarvon, 16 Jan. 1886, quoted in *C.E.*, 19 Jan. 1886.

[91] Kenmare papers, Letter book, Jan.–Dec. 1886: M. Leonard to J. H. Franks, 23 July 1886, pp. 392–3.

[92] T. Harrington to editor of *The Times*, 26 Feb. 1886, quoted in *C.E.*, 1 Mar. 1886.

Without question, local branches of the league in effect convened courts, summoned offenders, rendered decisions sometimes conflicting with those of ordinary courts of law, and had dissatisfied litigants submit their claims to the central branch in Dublin, just as if the central branch possessed appellate jurisdiction. The minute book of the Midleton branch provides a good illustration of the usual procedure. It was recorded of a meeting in early August 1885:

The case of taking the grass of the farm of an evicted tenant in Bilberry having been brought before us, we again express our horror & de[te]station of such conduct, & we call on the members of our branch & the several adjoining branches to have no dealings whatever with this grass grabber. . . . [93]

There was close co-operation in the enforcement of decisions. For example, farmers from the Saleen branch attended a meeting at Aghada in May 1886 in order to protest that 'a gentleman from Castlemartyr had the audacity to take grazing land in their neighbourhood, thereby doing them an injury'. The Aghada branch decided unanimously to extend the boycott to its own locality, since 'the gentleman referred to had by no means a "good record" in his own district, having given serious offence to Mogeela and Shanagarry N. L. branches'.[94]

While local branches of the league did not exactly impose fines on those who violated their code, they sometimes required the offenders to compensate the ousted tenants in proven cases of land grabbing. A tenant named Henry O'Connor was summoned before the Ballyhay branch of the National League in August 1885 on the charge of having grabbed the farm of another tenant named David Walsh in 1879. After hearing both sides, the Ballyhay branch convicted O'Connor and ordered him either to pay Walsh £600 or to surrender the farm. For some time O'Connor refused to comply with the order, but in late October the chairman of the branch, the Rev. T. Rice, happily announced that O'Connor had given Walsh £600 and even praised O'Connor for displaying 'a manly spirit in fulfilling the obligation imposed upon him'.[95] A very similar case took place on C. P. Coote's estate in 1886.[96]

It has been argued above that the judicial activities of the league's local branches substantially curtailed the resort to agrarian violence.

[93] Minute book, Midleton branch of the Irish National League, 1885–9, 2 Aug. 1885.

[94] *C.C.*, 19 May 1886. See also *W.C.E.*, 16 Jan. 1886.

[95] *C.E.*, 28 Oct. 1885, 8 Feb. 1886; *C.C.*, 8 Mar. 1886.

[96] Cork Defence Union, *Boycotting in the county of Cork* (Cork, 1886), p. 24; *C.C.*, 15 Mar. 1886.

But it is also true that in several instance~~~~ ~~~~nctions imposed by these extralegal tribunals were e~~~~ ~~~~ ~~~~nt fashion by moonlighters, to whom the la~~~~ ~~~~an~~~~ ~~~~conservative press often referred disparaging]~~~~ ~~~~ ~~~~al League police'. The still closely boycotte~~~~ ~~~~ ~~~~mer-shopkeeper, Jeremiah Hegarty, was the targ~~~~ ~~~~ar ~~~~cessful assassin in mid-September 1885. Moonlighters visi~~~~ ~~~~umber of boycotted tenants who had taken evicted farms and h~~~~ed into their dwellings. Another boycotted farmer suffered by having his cattle shed set on fire. A grabber of grazing land on the estate of Thomas M. Beamish near Drimoleague and the caretakers of evicted farms near Clonakilty and Midleton were all shot (one fatally wounded) in December 1885. [97]

The principal sanction applied by National League branches, however, was the boycott. So effectively could this essentially moral sanction be used that the need for violent measures largely disappeared. Especially after the expiration of the crimes act in August 1885, boycotting increased enormously in County Cork and in Ireland as a whole. [98] Persons declared boycotted became unable to obtain food, drink, or other supplies and could not sell their crops or livestock at local markets; blacksmiths often refused to shoe their horses, and carpenters to build or mend their carts. Old friends passed them by on the opposite side of the road, making the sign of the cross in order to emphasize their isolation from the fold, their outcaste status. Membership in the league developed in many places into a kind of loyalty test and was a source of economic protection for shopkeepers and tradesmen as well as farmers. The Midleton branch learned in August 1885 that a number of local blacksmiths who did not belong to the league had performed work for 'obnoxious persons'. Its members were pointedly asked whether they would 'continue to support men who show such indifference to the national cause, when their brethren throughout the country are foremost in their determination to advance . . . [it] & put down land grabbing'. [99] The Kinsale branch passed a resolution in August 1886 prohibiting those members who owned threshing machines from hiring them to farmers who had not joined the league. [100]

In a country where Sunday Mass was a focal point of communal activity, it was natural that demonstrations of disapproval frequently took place there. After a Millstreet cattle dealer named Cornelius

[97] Cork Defence Union, *Boycotting*, pp. 11–12, 14–15, 17–19.

[98] The number of reported cases of boycotting in Ireland rose from 227 in June to 741 by October 1885 (Curtis, *Coercion & conciliation*, p. 56, n. 40).

[99] Minute book, Midleton branch of the Irish National League, 1885–9, 30 Aug. 1885.

[100] *C.C.*, 9 Aug. 1886.

Conner had been declared boycotted for taking an evicted farm, he could not attend Mass without having the entire congregation leave the church.[101] When another land grabber named J. McCarthy of Barrahaurin tried to attend Mass at Christmas in 1885, he was left with one side of the chapel all to himself. While being escorted home afterwards by four policemen, McCarthy was pursued by a jeering, mud-slinging crowd.[102] A tenant named Michael O'Keefe of Lisnaboy, boycotted for having not only paid his rent but also taken an evicted farm, was forced to stop attending Mass because the congregation always left whenever he or members of his family entered the church. On one occasion O'Keefe and his family had even been pelted with stones outside the church.[103] But this was not uncommon. It was reported in August 1886 that several families censured by the league in Donaghmore were unable to attend Mass because they had frequently been assaulted when they attempted to do so. Even a strong letter of protest from the bishop of the diocese was apparently ignored.[104]

Although the weapon of the boycott was ultimately aimed at the destruction of the abuses of landlordism, its immediate targets in most instances were not landlords or their agents. A detailed list of 101 cases of boycotting in Cork compiled in 1886 amply demonstrated that farmers were by far the most frequently censured group. In as many as forty-five out of 101 cases, those boycotted were tenants who had incurred disapproval by grabbing either farms or grazing land, by paying their rents or being suspected of doing so, or simply by refusing to join the league. Tradesmen were shunned in twelve cases and labourers in nine, almost always because they had dared to perform work for persons known to have aroused the ire of the League. The businesses of shopkeepers were boycotted in seven cases, either for the reason that they did not belong to the league or because they had forced one or more farmers into bankruptcy by pressing them for debts and then had taken possession of their holdings. In only fourteen cases were either landlords or agents the targets of boycotting that arose from the failure to lower rents, the serving of writs, or the eviction of tenants.[105]

[101] Conner, who was also unable to purchase stock at local fairs, had paid the National Bank £1,000 for the interest in this farm, but he eventually surrendered the land and forfeited his money (Cork Defence Union, *Boycotting*, p. 18).

[102] Ibid., p. 11. See also *C.C.*, 23 Sept. 1885.

[103] Cork Defence Union, *Boycotting*, p. 9.   [104] *C.C.*, 9 Aug. 1886.

[105] There were also fourteen miscellaneous cases of boycotting which do not fall into any of the above-mentioned categories (Cork Defence Union, *Boycotting, passim*).

Boycotting did not so much threaten the persons as it did the economic interests of the propertied classes. Landowners in other parts of Ireland seemed almost incapable of uniting to defend their interests, but such was not the case in County Cork, where a small group of landlords and agents, led by Arthur H. Smith-Barry and Pasco Savage French, conceived the idea of forming an allegedly non-sectarian and non-political association that would assist all those who came under attack from the league. The meeting which led to the establishment of the Cork Defence Union was held in September 1885, and soon afterwards the C.D.U. became a legally constituted body with authority vested in five trustees (Smith-Barry, French, James Penrose Fitzgerald, D. P. Sarsfield, and John H. Bainbridge). [106] In October another body calling itself the Irish Defence Union was organized in London under the aegis of yet another Cork landlord, the earl of Bandon, in order to solicit funds and distribute them in Cork and other counties where defence unions were supposedly 'in active operation'.[107] In reality, however, the C.D.U. was and continued to be the only active and effective association of its kind in Ireland.

From the beginning, the C.D.U. refused to interfere in rent collections or in execution sales and similar legal activities. This organization initially confined its attention to the provision of relief in the form of provisions, employment, portable forges, or threshing machines to the swelling number of boycotted persons. It did lease an evicted grazing farm at Carrigrohane near Cork city, where the otherwise unsaleable livestock of boycotted tenants and demesne-farming landlords could be brought to prime condition before the C.D.U. had them shipped to England.[108] But the South of Ireland Cattle Dealers' Association, in co-operation with the Cork city branch of the National League, almost succeeded in frustrating the sales function of the C.D.U. shortly after it had begun operations. The dealers demanded in early October 1885 that the City of Cork Steam Packet Company stop shipping cattle supplied by the C.D.U. from the herds of boycotted persons. When the company refused because they were legally obliged as common carriers to convey all livestock consigned to them, the dealers, given financial help by farmers at the fairs, started a rival line of steamers.[109]

[106] *C.C.*, 25 Oct. 1886.
[107] It was claimed that defence unions were already functioning in north and south Tipperary, Wexford, Waterford, Kilkenny, Cavan, and Queen's County, as well as in Cork, and that one was about to be started in Kerry (ibid., 24 Nov. 1885). See also Curtis, *Coercion & conciliation*, pp. 56–7, n. 42.
[108] *C.C.*, 25 Oct. 1886.   [109] Ibid., 14 Nov. 1885.

The C.D.U. responded by entering into business as a cattle dealer in support of the Steam Packet Company and collected its own staff of buyers and drovers. Although its buyers consistently overbid in an effort to break down the reluctance of sellers to have anything to do with emergency men, the attempt was not especially successful.[110] The police failed to provide the C.D.U.'s buyers with the protection they needed: an angry mob drove away the cattle purchased by one buyer at the Charleville fair in November, and another buyer was severely beaten and left for dead on a public road after he had attended the Millstreet fair in December.[111] By then the C.D.U. was reportedly able to supply only some sixty head of cattle per week to the company, which was losing money at the rate of £4,000 per month.[112] By comparison, the Cattle Dealers' Association, with its specially chartered and fully loaded steamers, appeared to be doing a thriving business, but it was also losing heavily. When the Steam Packet Company generously offered to convey the dealers' cattle without charge for two months and at half of normal rates for two months longer, the dealers abandoned their original demand.[113]

For the C.D.U., this episode represented something of a victory. It had succeeded in keeping the port of Cork open to the export of livestock belonging to boycotted persons. Its efforts in other directions also enabled those under attack from the league to maintain their stubborn resistance in spite of great obstacles. Its pressure on the government actively to combat the activities of the league, which it regarded as illegal, was partly responsible for a court decision in early 1886 that the publication of a resolution to boycott was a punishable offence under the old Whiteboy acts. In practice, however, this unfavourable decision made almost no difference to the operation of the local branches of the league. As the Cork landlord and agent Thomas Sanders of Charleville told the C.D.U. in late February 1886,

the resolution to 'boycott' me was put to the meeting of the league, and upon the majority of the votes being in favour of it, the chairman said significantly, 'You know what to do', and this was communicated verbally to the people.[114]

THE GENESIS OF THE PLAN OF CAMPAIGN

Events in the political sphere between June 1885 and June 1886 did

[110] Ibid., 18 Nov. 1885.
[111] Cork Defence Union, *Boycotting*, pp. 10, 12.
[112] *C.C.*, 7 Dec. 1885.
[113] Ibid., 30 Dec. 1885; Cork Defence Union, *Boycotting*, p. 13.
[114] Quoted in *C.C.*, 1 Mar. 1886.

little to relieve the bitterness of agrarian tension in Ireland. Expectations were aroused concerning home rule, an independent Irish parliament, and a conclusive settlement of agrarian grievances only to be dashed again. The conservatives assumed office under the leadership of the marquis of Salisbury in June 1885, after Gladstone's liberal ministry had resigned when unexpectedly defeated on the spirits clauses of its budget. Because they were in a minority in the house of commons, the conservatives could continue in office only by maintaining an alliance with the Parnellites and by following a policy of conciliation in Ireland, at least until new elections could be held in the winter. Accordingly, they allowed the coercion act passed at the time of the Phoenix Park murders in 1882 to expire in August 1885.[115] They also passed what proved to be the first successful land-purchase act but received no thanks for it from either the Parnellites or the tenants of Ireland.[116] As a sop to the nationalists and in a move to restore calm, the conservatives sent to Dublin as lord lieutenant an imperial federationist, the earl of Carnarvon. Even if he had been of a mind to curb the excesses of the mounting agrarian agitation, Carnarvon would have been handcuffed from the start, since coercion measures were politically out of the question. From Ireland Carnarvon submitted reports that obscured the seriousness of the situation there, and within the cabinet he attempted to promote the idea of an Irish parliament with powers sufficient to meet the demands of moderate Irish nationalists.[117] Although he in fact won no friends for his proposals, Carnarvon gave Parnell an entirely different impression of the government's intentions, and Salisbury's public speeches led Gladstone and many other liberals to believe that the conservatives might bring forward a home rule measure of their own if they won the election called for November.[118]

Pursuing a chimera, the Irish party threw its support to the conservatives. When the dust settled after the election, the results showed that the Parnellites were the only real victors, for they now held the balance of power in the house of commons with eighty-six seats, as against 250 for the conservatives and 334 for the liberals.[119] Since they were now even more at the mercy of the Parnellites than before, the conservatives decided to stand pat and do nothing to conciliate the Irish nationalists. They realized that this decision would force a break with the Parnellites and were scarcely surprised

---

[115] Curtis, *Coercion & conciliation*, p. 39.
[116] Ibid., pp. 44–5.
[117] Ibid., p. 56.
[118] Ibid., pp. 58–60.
[119] O'Brien, *Parnell and his party*, p. 159.

when the latter joined with the liberals to defeat them in late January 1886. But they were reconciled to leaving office by the conviction that their return would be only a matter of time. For they fully anticipated that Gladstone, by working with Parnell and by bringing in a home rule measure, as he did in early April, would wreck the liberal party, many members of which could not stomach either the Parnellites or their goals.[120] Unfortunately for Irish aspirations, events confirmed all the conservatives' expectations. Gladstone fractured his party. In the early hours of 8 June, a coalition of liberal unionists and conservatives defeated home rule by thirty votes.[121] Gladstone then plunged the country into another general election and lost badly. The English electorate decisively rejected home rule, and the unionists received a majority of 118 over the Gladstonian home rulers. By 20 July Salisbury and his conservatives were back in office with the support of seventy-eight seceding liberals.[122] The defeat of home rule was doubly repugnant to Ireland, for Gladstone's measure had coupled the setting up of a largely autonomous parliament in Dublin with an unexpectedly generous series of proposals to appease Irish farmers and to banish the land question from politics.

When the conservatives decided soon after assuming control to postpone any measures dealing with Irish land or government reform until February 1887, they committed a serious error, for they gave the Irish party an excuse and an opportunity to throw its prestige and resources onto the side of the National League and the tenants. At a meeting of the central branch of the league in late August 1886, Timothy Harrington announced that 'the time had come when all the branches of the National League in the country should reorganize themselves and be ready to fight the battle of the tenants'.[123] Harrington was really proclaiming the beginning of a new stage in the history of the Irish land war. The conservatives missed another opportunity to head off the coming storm by allowing the tenants' relief bill introduced by Parnell in late September to die. In a thinly veiled threat, Parnell had solemnly warned them that if his relief measure failed to become law, he would find it impossible to prevent the farmers of Ireland from banding together for their protection. But the conservatives refused to listen while the special commission under the chairmanship of Earl Cowper was still studying the question.[124] At the end of September, Parnell therefore appealed to

[120] Curtis, *Coercion & conciliation*, pp. 69–77.   [121] Ibid., pp. 105–6.
[122] O'Brien, *Parnell and his party*, p. 194.
[123] *Irish Times*, 24 Aug. 1886, quoted ibid., p. 200, n. 3.
[124] Curtis, *Coercion & conciliation*, pp. 143–4.

the Irish National League of America to support an anti-eviction campaign, and a similar appeal for subscriptions was launched in Ireland, with Timothy Harrington promising that the money collected 'would be devoted to the evicted tenants in those localities where the tenants made the best fight'.[125]

It is worthwhile to examine at this point whether a disgruntled Irish parliamentary party intended to create a new wave of agrarian protest, or whether the danger of widespread evictions arising from inability or refusal to pay rent already existed and therefore made agitation imminent. Even without a nationally organized campaign, it is highly probable that rent conflicts in late 1886 and early 1887 would have been more numerous than during the previous twelve months. It is true that the price of store cattle suddenly swung upward at the fairs in Cork during the autumn of 1886,[126] but this swing was merely temporary, and the ground that needed to be recovered in this sector of the economy was great. Moreover, the price of butter remained at practically a record low, and then the grain harvest, which had originally promised to be abundant, was badly damaged in many places by unusually heavy rains.[127] This was especially true of the barley crop in all the coastal districts. The money to pay rent consequently dwindled. The Killeagh and Inch branch of the National League passed a resolution in late September 1886 stating bluntly that 'in consequence of the present low prices and bad harvest weather, half the rent is more than the tenants can pay this year, as the corn crop is everywhere black and rotten'.[128] Although the agricultural returns do not support so bald a contention, land agents who experienced difficulty in collecting the September rents attributed the fact to the same cause. The firm of Doherty and Jones, which managed the earl of Bandon's estates, explained its difficulties to one of the earl's creditors in early October:

We have tried evictions, & the holdings of the tenants so evicted are lying idle, as no one will take them; nearly every week we [have] had 5 or 6 seizures of cattle, but owing to the terrible system of boycotting so prevalent, [the tenants are?] afraid to purchase at the sales; we have another great difficulty to contend with; the harvest in this county is nearly all destroyed

---

[125] *Irish Times*, 29 Sept. 1886, quoted in O'Brien, *Parnell and his party*, p. 201.

[126] *C.C.*, 19, 31 Aug., 3, 22 Sept., 18 Nov. 1886.

[127] 'Cattle have again gone back, & butter is selling in the markets at $4\frac{1}{2}d.$ to $5d.$ per lb.; unless some change sets in, there will be great trouble in getting in the next rents' (Doherty papers, Letter book, 1882–7: Doherty and Jones to W. P. Moorehead, 7 July 1886, p. 670).

[128] *C.C.*, 1 Oct. 1886.

by the continual wet weather, & the prospect before us this winter is very gloomy.[129]

There was thus wide scope for the new direction which the land war was about to assume under the tutelage of national leaders.

The formal announcement of this new direction came with the publication of an article entitled 'A Plan of Campaign' in *United Ireland* on 23 October. It set forth a course of action recommended more than a year earlier by Tim Healy, M.P., in Killarney, and very recently by John Dillon, M.P., on the marquis of Clanricarde's estate near Woodford in County Galway. Although the article was anonymous, it is known to have been written by Timothy Harrington. The tenants of the country were advised to decide by resolution on each estate what reduction they would demand, and if that were refused, to transfer the rents, less the abatement sought, to a few trustees in whom they possessed confidence; the money was to be used to support any tenants evicted by the obdurate landlord. The National League promised to guarantee the estate funds against misappropriation and, if necessary, to continue supporting evicted tenants after these local funds had been exhausted. A long campaign was therefore anticipated.[130]

Once the Plan had been made public, John Dillon and William O'Brien, who soon emerged as the most active leaders, fanned out along with several other Parnellite M.P.s over the south and west of the country in order to explain it to the tenants and to assist them in carrying it into operation. Professor F. S. L. Lyons has stated that Dillon and O'Brien gave 'the first demonstration of the new tactics' on the Clanricarde estates in Galway during the third week of November.[131] But the distinction of being the first estate in Ireland on which the Plan of Campaign was adopted may well belong to C. W. T. Ponsonby's property, located between Killeagh and Youghal in Cork. Ponsonby's tenants felt acutely both the damage done to their barley crops by the heavy rains and the low price of butter. On 22 October a deputation visited Ponsonby's agent and boldly declared that the tenants could not pay their rents unless he was authorized to make large allowances—35 per cent to the non-judicial tenants, who were by far the majority, and 25 per cent to those whose rents had been fixed judicially. The delegation flatly rejected the agent's offer of 20 and 10 per cent reductions.[132] Then

[129] Doherty papers, Letter book, 1882–7: Doherty and Jones to Lady Bernard, 6 Oct. 1886, p. 756.
[130] Lyons, *Dillon*, pp. 83–4; O'Brien, *Parnell and his party*, pp. 201–2.
[131] Lyons, *Dillon*, p. 84.
[132] *C.C.*, 23 Oct. 1886.

at a decisive National League meeting in Youghal on Sunday, 7 November, Ponsonby's tenants as well as those of the neighbouring landowner, Sir Joseph N. McKenna, were roused to action by William J. Lane, M.P.

> He advised them all [to] follow the programme laid down in *United Ireland*— to band together and make a fund out of the rents which they were able to pay, and support out of that any tenants who were evicted. As soon as the landlords found that they themselves were supporting the evicted tenants, they would give in. They should follow the example of the British government, who laid down that the man who deserted in face of the enemy should be shot. The farmer who deserted his brothers in the present life and death struggle should be shot. [133]

On Tuesday, 16 November, the town hall in Youghal was converted into a rent office, and there a large number of Ponsonby's tenants entrusted their self-reduced rents to Lane and four local clergymen, who were to choose someone with whom secretly to lodge the money. [134] Thus began an epic struggle that was to last for more than five years. Less than two weeks later, McKenna's tenants imitated their bolder neighbours on the Ponsonby estate. [135]

The second great estate in Cork on which the Plan of Campaign was put into operation belonged to the dowager countess of Kingston. It will be recalled that this property had already been the scene of a momentous struggle during the days of the Land League in 1881. A tremendous mortgage burdened the proprietress and her husband, and rock-bottom butter prices crippled the tenant farmers in this dairying district around Mitchelstown. Of the 750 agricultural tenants, all but 120 were leaseholders ineligible to enter the land courts, and of the 120 yearly tenants eligible to have their rents determined judicially, only about forty had gone into court, where the reductions made had been small indeed. Although offered abatements of from 10 to 25 per cent in proportion to the valuation of their holdings, the Kingston tenantry insisted upon an all-round reduction of 20 per cent in November 1886. When this was denied them, they cheerfully consigned their rents to William O'Brien and two other Parnellite M.P.s during a series of collection meetings beginning late in the following month in different parts of the estate. [136]

The Plan spread rapidly to other estates in County Cork during the winter of 1886–7, under the guidance of members of the Irish

[133] Ibid., 8 Nov. 1886.
[134] Ibid., 17 Nov. 1886.
[135] Ibid., 29 Nov. 1886.
[136] Ibid., 8 Aug. 1887.

parliamentary party. Shortly after John Dillon had addressed William N. Leader's tenants in late December 1886, it was put into force on Leader's estate at Curraghs near Kanturk.[137] The tenants turned aside the request of Leader's agent, the Kanturk solicitor Henry Harte Barry, that the judicial tenants (who formed the majority) pay their rents less an abatement of 10 per cent, and the non-judicial, less one of 20 or 25 per cent. Instead, they countered with a demand for reductions of 25 and 37½ per cent respectively, and when this was rejected, deposited their self-reduced rents with a safe trustee.[138] Barry was unfortunate enough to have the management of another, smaller property where the tenants were at serious odds with their landlord Sir James W. Mackey, a successful importer of seeds and agricultural implements and a former lord mayor of Dublin. The tenants of this estate, located in the mountainous Knocknagree district near Kingwilliamstown, suffered grievously from the downward plunge of butter prices. As Barry had reminded Mackey in the previous August,

> you have a miserable lot [of tenants] to deal with, & located too in the very worst part of the County Cork, & about half of them hopelessly insolvent, so that it is by no means an easy task to get rent out of them.[139]

At a well-attended demonstration held at Knocknagree in early January 1887, J. C. Flynn, M.P., caustically observed that when the estate was purchased from the crown in the incumbered estates court in 1854, the rental stood at only £205. By serving a large number of notices to quit, Mackey had forced the tenants since 1870 to agree to large increases of rent, so that his annual income from the property now stood, according to Flynn, at about £500.[140] Mackey's tenants at first sought to return to the old crown rents of 1854; but they later shifted their position and demanded a reduction of only 30 per cent for the judicial tenants, but still one of 50 per cent for the non-judicial.[141] Although they adopted the Plan when Mackey refused to hear of such enormous concessions, the tenants were in such poor circumstances that they could only entrust their rents to Flynn by instalments.[142]

[137] Ibid., 10 Aug. 1887.
[138] *C.E.*, 1, 14 Jan. 1887; 21 June 1888.
[139] Barry papers, Letter book, Feb.–Nov. 1886: H. H. Barry to Sir J. W. Mackey, 26 Aug. 1886, pp. 759–60.
[140] Mackey's rental in 1887, having been reduced since 1881 by the land courts from £510 to £446, was no longer as high as Flynn claimed, but otherwise Flynn's statements were accurate enough (*C.E.*, 4 Jan. 1887).
[141] Ibid., 15 Jan. 1887.
[142] Ibid., 4 June 1887.

A few Cork landlords quickly capitulated to their campaigning tenants. In early February 1887 Sir Henry de Capel Brooke reportedly 'yielded to his Killeagh tenants by accepting the rent less [a] 35 per cent reduction which they had lodged' with trustees. [143] Another victory was claimed for the Plan when Sir Joseph McKenna accepted the rents of his tenants less an abatement of 20 per cent and remitted the costs of legal proceedings that he had taken for recovery, 'making the reduction over 40 per cent all round'. [144] On the other hand, the Plan was speedily overthrown on the Crofton minors estate, part of which was situated near Macroom, and part near Donaghmore. The tenants of this property, managed by a receiver specially appointed by the court of chancery, adopted the Plan at a public meeting in February, when they resolved not to pay rent without an allowance of 30 per cent. The chancery judge responded by instructing the receiver John Hingston to seize the livestock and effects of the eight ringleaders, but to extend an allowance of 20 per cent to the other tenants if they paid at once. This strategy shattered the tenants' earlier unity, and the campaign collapsed when the leaders paid their full rents plus the law costs, and the others at the reduced figure. [145]

Generally, however, there was a more or less protracted and almost always bitter confrontation of wills on Plan estates, regardless of the final outcome. On few properties were the campaigning tenants so careless or foolhardy as to leave the landlords an opening to drive a wedge by the seizure of stock and other effects. Within less than two weeks of the adoption of the Plan on the Ponsonby estate, those tenants against whom writs had been issued were disposing of their cattle in order to avoid seizures. [146] In January 1887 the Mitchelstown branch of the National League organized a special fair that allowed the Kingston tenantry to clear their farms of cattle which might otherwise have been distrained for non-payment of rent. More than 1,000 head of cattle were reportedly sold during the fair, and over £9,000 was realized by their owners. [147] At a great auction held in Kanturk in the same month, the Curraghs tenants of W. N. Leader sold 300 head of cattle and shortly afterwards disposed of an additional 200 head at the fair in Mallow. [148] The strong action taken by the Ponsonby, Kingston, and Leader tenants served as an instructive model in the new warfare and scarcely passed unnoticed.

[143] Ibid., 11 Feb. 1887.
[144] Ibid., 3 Mar. 1887.
[145] Ibid., 15 Mar. 1887.
[146] *C.C.*, 30 Nov. 1886.
[147] Ibid., 18, 20 Jan. 1887.
[148] *C.E.*, 1, 5 Jan. 1887.

The spectacle of tenants even on relatively few estates entrusting rents that they had fixed themselves to chosen trustees, and then making every preparation to stand firm, had the salutary effect of persuading many landlords and agents to be more conciliatory than in the past, if only because they hoped to avoid costly conflicts by timely and somewhat less costly compromises. Even before the Plan of Campaign was well launched, it had produced a noticeable impact on the attitudes of land agents especially. The trustees of the earl of Kenmare's estates were slow to authorize the request made in mid-October 1886 by the agent Maurice Leonard for an all-round reduction of 25 per cent to both judicial and non-judicial tenants who would pay the current gale before 1 December.[149] 'All the landlords in this county [i.e., Kerry]', Leonard informed Viscount Castlerosse, one of the trustees, at the beginning of November, 'are giving abatements from 20 to 35 per cent, & judicial rents are treated everywhere as if they were yearly lettings'; if 'Messrs Dillon and Co.' held a meeting on the estate and encouraged the tenants to demand large concessions before the trustees acted upon his request, the consequences, warned Leonard, would be most damaging to the estate.[150] After the trustees had authorized a reduction of 20 per cent to the non-judicial tenants only, Leonard hesitated to take vigorous action that would force the judicial tenants to pay in full. As he pointed out to another trustee in December, 'the tenants would adopt the Plan of Campaign, which would be a most unfortunate thing to happen'.[151] Doherty and Jones, who had never before been conspicuous in urging their employers to appease dissatisfied tenants, also moved towards a policy of large concessions. In November 1886 they advised the trustees of the Fitzpatrick property to allow them to abate by 25 per cent not only the current gale but also the outstanding arrears—a significant addition. 'We have made careful inquiries', they stated, '& find that landlords having property adjoining the Fitzpatrick estate are making reductions varying from 35 to 40 per cent; but we think that the allowance we recommend would be ample. . . .'[152]

Practically all landlords in County Cork offered to make at least some reduction in their rents during late 1886 and early 1887. Of the forty landlords with property in the two large parishes of

---

[149] Kenmare papers, Letter book, 1885–93: M. Leonard to Messrs Benbow, Saltwell, and Tryon, 16 Oct. 1886, pp. 492–3.

[150] Ibid.: Leonard to Viscount Castlerosse, 1 Nov. 1886, pp. 501–2.

[151] Ibid.: Leonard to Colonel Dease, 12 Dec. 1886, pp. 508–9.

[152] Doherty papers, Letter book, 1882–7: Doherty and Jones to Messrs Park, Nelson, Morgan, and Co., 19 Nov. 1886, pp. 809–10.

Drimoleague and Caheragh, where the Plan had been adopted on the Hutchins estate, as many as thirty-seven reportedly granted abatements, in some instances of 30 or 35 per cent.[153] The local newspapers carried notices of the allowances offered by about thirty Cork landowners between October 1886 and March 1887, and these averaged about 25 per cent.[154] Although some landlords, like the earl of Bandon, still refused to alter rents that had been fixed judicially,[155] the number of such cases seems to have declined very substantially, and on Viscount Lismore's vast domains, the numerous judicial tenants participated along with the non-judicial majority in an allowance of 30 per cent.[156] Even in its earliest stage, the Plan of Campaign thus had a widespread impact extending far beyond the relatively few estates where the tenants had formally adopted it.

Even though under heavy pressure from Irish landlords, the conservative government was unable to deal effectively with the challenge presented by the Plan of Campaign during the first half of 1887. A rent-collection meeting on a Plan estate at Loughrea in County Galway was successfully raided by the constabulary, and at the same time, the Plan was declared 'an unlawful and criminal conspiracy' by a decree of the lord lieutenant.[157] To the delight of Irish nationalists, however, the jury acquitted of the conspiracy charges those Plan agents arrested at Loughrea, and the collections were now made under clandestine circumstances.[158] On the Mackey estate in early June, for example, the tenants reportedly 'resorted to stratagem, and though all the roads leading to Knocknagree were guarded by vigilant constables, they succeeded in meeting their member [of parliament, J. C. Flynn], and under his supervision securely paid in whatever money they could raise'.[159] The conservative government was indeed unable to mount any real counter-offensive because of a series of heavy blows to its prestige. The Cowper commission largely vindicated Parnell's tenants' relief bill of the previous September by recommending the quinquennial revision of judicial rents and the admission of leaseholders to the land courts.[160] In a sudden explosion, Lord Randolph Churchill

[153] *C.E.*, 12 Jan. 1887.
[154] Ibid., Oct. 1886–Mar. 1887; *C.C.*, Oct. 1886–Mar. 1887.
[155] *C.E.*, 10 Mar. 1887.
[156] *C.C.*, 12 Oct. 1886.
[157] Curtis, *Coercion & conciliation*, pp. 159–60.
[158] Ibid., pp. 164–5.
[159] *C.E.*, 4 June 1887.
[160] *Report of the royal commission on the Land Law (Ireland) Act, 1881, and the Purchase of Land (Ireland) Act, 1885; with evidence, appendices, and index* [C 4969], H.C. 1887, xxvi, 1, pp. 12–15.

resigned from the cabinet, and his departure was followed shortly by the physical collapse and retirement of the Irish chief secretary Michael Hicks Beach, whose tenure of office had been characterized by a vacillatory policy on the land question. [161]

The replacement of Hicks Beach by Arthur Balfour, who proved to be 'one of the ablest and toughest chief secretaries Ireland had ever had', [162] was a turning point. Balfour was as good as his word when he promised to be 'as relentless as Cromwell in enforcing obedience to the law, but at the same time . . . as radical as any reformer in redressing grievances, and especially in removing every cause of complaint in regard to the land'. [163] Balfour introduced a severe crimes bill in the house of commons at the end of March, but despite the repeated use of the 'guillotine' in order to shorten debate, the measure did not become law until 19 July. [164] A few days after the crimes bill had gone before the commons, a land bill was introduced in the house of lords; it sparked heated and prolonged debate in both houses and was not enacted until 23 August. [165] The crimes act immensely strengthened the hands of the government in grappling with the agrarian agitation. Resident magistrates drawn almost exclusively from the landed classes were empowered summarily to punish with up to six months' imprisonment persons found guilty of boycotting, conspiracies against the payment of rent, intimidation, resistance to eviction, and the incitement of others to commit such acts. In order to guarantee the impartiality of jury trials and to prevent a repetition of the Loughrea fiasco, the crimes act allowed the authorities to order a change of venue. It authorized the lord lieutenant to declare by proclamation that these provisions would be enforced in disturbed parts of the country, and that a local branch of the National League engaging in illegal activities was 'dangerous', thus making all its members liable to prosecution. [166] The land act, although it deferred the weighty question of land purchase to the following year, incorporated one long-overdue reform plus a number of stopgap provisions. The land courts were at last given jurisdiction to fix the rents of leaseholders. They were also permitted to revise in accord with the decline in agricultural prices those judicial rents fixed between 1881 and 1885, but only for a period of three years. County-court judges could now stay evictions

[161] Curtis, *Coercion & conciliation*, pp. 161–4, 169–73.
[162] Lyons, *Dillon*, p. 87.
[163] Quoted in Curtis, *Coercion & conciliation*, p. 179.
[164] Ibid., pp. 181, 183.
[165] Ibid., pp. 339–42.
[166] 50 & 51 Vict., c. 20, ss. 2–7, 11; Curtis, *Coercion & conciliation*, pp. 180–1.

for cause and could spread the repayment of arrears over a reasonable length of time. And landlords were obliged to dispense with the formal eviction that had previously occurred prior to the six-month redemption period, and to substitute instead what were contemptuously termed 'eviction-made-easy notices'.[167]

THE KINGSTON ESTATE EPISODE

The coming clash between the British government, now armed with a punitive crimes act and a promising land act, and its rebellious Irish subjects, massed under the banner of the Plan of Campaign, was powerfully shaped by the explosive events that shook the Kingston estate in the second half of 1887. It was on the Kingston estate that the effectiveness of the crimes act and the willingness of the tenants to accept the new land legislation were first put to the test. Since the summer of 1881, when an army had been needed to collect the rents, the controlling factors in the history of the Kingston estate had remained basically unchanged. The landlords were still trapped by their indebtedness to the Representative Church Body. Since interest payments consumed almost £9,500 of the annual rental of about £17,000,[168] the concession of the demand for a 20 per cent abatement would have left only a very small margin for the discharge of all the other expenses. With a normal amount of default in rent payments because of the depression, the gross income would almost certainly have been insufficient to meet the estate's outgoings, let alone furnish a scant living to the dowager countess of Kingston and her husband. Of course, the tenants could not be expected to be sympathetic towards the plight of the estate's owners. For if the landlords went bankrupt, the tenants would in all probability become proprietors of their farms at sacrifice prices.

The tenants responded enthusiastically to the exhortations of the Plan's leaders, such as Arthur O'Connor, M.P., who had told them in January 1887: 'To-day you are at war for your homes and your

---

[167] 50 & 51 Vict., c. 33, ss. 1, 6–7, 29; Curtis, *Coercion & conciliation*, pp. 337–43.

[168] According to the correspondent of *The Times*, the Representative Church Body's mortgage on the Kingston estate stood at £200,300 in December 1887 (*C.C.*, 30 Dec. 1887). The original charge had been £236,000. The English lawyer George Pellew, who visited the estate in 1887, stated that the annual interest on the mortgage amounted to 'a little less than £9,500' (*Castle and cabin*, p. 90). The gross rental of slightly more than £17,000 included about £700 derived from ground rents in Mitchelstown. The rental of the agricultural property was actually less in 1887 than it had been in 1845—£16,523 as compared with £16,704 (*C.E.*, 17 Dec. 1887).

children. Then steel your hearts and go to war, in the name of God and with the blessing of the church.'[169] Other speakers evoked the proud memories of the 1881 struggle and delighted in pointing out that if the tenants again chose physically to obstruct and resist evictions, it would be months, if not years, before the landlords and government could clear the estate of all 800 tenants.[170] When the ritual of writ serving recommenced in early February 1887,[171] the affected tenants completely disposed of their stock and effects in order to thwart seizures.[172] Six Mitchelstown shopkeepers, who also held farms on the Kingston estate, disposed of their shop goods and closed their doors.[173] Support for those tenants who had made these heavy sacrifices came from adjacent branches of the National League, which sent contingents that performed spring sowing operations. In late February hundreds of farmers and labourers—bringing butts, pitchforks, spades, harrows, and ploughs—gathered to prepare and sow about 150 acres on twenty different farms in the Ballygiblin and Killarney districts of the estate.[174] Vigilance committees were formed in order to check the movements of the estate agent Henry Frend and other 'outposts of the castle'.[175] So well had they done their work that by late April no less than 290 persons, exclusive of policemen, were unable to obtain any kind of accommodation. Boycotting was brought into play on a prodigious scale.[176]

Despite the adoption of forceful measures by the castle authorities, the Kingston tenants remained firm. When the agent ordered his bailiffs to make midnight seizures in April, the tenants reportedly repelled this 'latest assault of the castle by disposing of their effects and forestalling the decrees of the law agent'.[177] Neighbouring landlords made it difficult for Henry Frend and bolstered the tenants' cause by granting sizeable abatements. Henry L. Young reduced the rents on his estate near Mitchelstown by $22\frac{1}{2}$ per cent, in addition to a permanent abatement of 20 per cent granted earlier.[178] The tenants on the Robertson estate near Glanworth, who

[169] *C.C.*, 15 Jan. 1887.
[170] Ibid., 18 Jan. 1887.
[171] Ibid., 5 Feb. 1887.
[172] *C.E.*, 4 Feb. 1888.
[173] Ibid., 19 Feb. 1887.
[174] *C.C.*, 22, 25 Feb. 1887; *C.E.*, 22 Feb. 1887.
[175] Pellew, *Castle and cabin*, pp. 90–1.
[176] *C.C.*, 28 Apr. 1887. The Property Defence Association opened a special store in Mitchelstown in late February in order to supply all boycotted persons with provisions (ibid., 25 Feb. 1887).
[177] *C.E.*, 27 Apr. 1887.
[178] Ibid., 29 Apr. 1887.

had been allowed 32½ per cent on the November 1886 gale, received a drastic concession of 50 per cent in May. 'This reduction is almost equal to an entire remission of rent on other properties', noted an envious report from Mitchelstown. [179] Frend scattered yet another shower of civil-bill decrees over the estate in June. About seventy other tenants had received superior-court writs, and innumerable civil-bill decrees were still awaiting service in the hands of the hated catholic law agent Standish O'Grady. Yet, to the knowledge of the National League, only five tenants had paid their rents since the beginning of the struggle. [180]

Heralding the 'collapse of the Plan of Campaign' on the Kingston estate in early August, the *Cork Constitution* gleefully noted that one of the principal tenants had just paid rent and costs, and claimed that the others were by now 'heartily sick and disgusted with the life they have been living for the last nine months'. [181] This obituary was premature, for the tenants had been urged to barricade their houses in expectation of the threatened evictions. [182] Apparently, they needed little encouragement:

Many houses have been converted into standing fortifications. Huge trunks of timber and immense ledges of limestone have been removed into many houses. The brunt of the fight apparently is to be carried out in the streets of Mitchelstown, where the business establishment of Mr [Maurice] O'Sullivan has many tons of timber placed in the windows and projected against the walls. [183]

With the passage of the land act in mid-August and the final admission of such dissatisfied leaseholders as the Kingston tenants to the courts, there developed doubts as to whether there would be any evictions at all. But for a variety of reasons, the Plan's leaders saw no excuse abruptly to change course. The agents of the castle were untrustworthy and unpredictable, tenants under notice of eviction were ineligible to have 'fair rents' fixed, and the land commissioners had earlier shown themselves to be susceptible to the pressures of agrarian agitation. On 11 August, John Mandeville, a farmer who was later designated the 'director of the Plan of Campaign in the Mitchelstown district', and William O'Brien, M.P., one of its national leaders, cautioned the tenants. Said Mandeville:

Now, I ask every man who has a house to defend to get his house in order, at all events not to be caught by those false prophets who say that evictions

[179] Ibid., 10 May 1887.
[180] Ibid., 16 June 1887.
[181] *C.C.*, 6 Aug. 1887.
[182] Ibid., 30 June 1887.
[183] Ibid., 11 Aug. 1887.

will not take place. Remember what I tell you, that evictions will take place if they see that there is a way for evictions to be carried on, and the only way to prevent them is for you to be prepared to defend your houses whenever these people get it into their heads. [184]

O'Brien also anticipated evictions by the dowager countess of Kingston's order before the land legislation could benefit the tenants, and he explained his reasons:

Because she knew that in a couple of months that new land bill would brand her as a rackrenter. They knew well [that] if this bill was to be administered with anything like honesty, . . . her income will be pulled down double what the Plan of Campaign proposed, and therefore it was that she and Mr O'Grady and all the rest of the troop of attorneys and bum-bailiffs . . . would play upon your industry. That was why they were so anxious to drag whatever plunder they could drag within the next few weeks that remained to them. . . . [185]

Incitement to resist eviction was a punishable offence under the new crimes act, and the government could hardly have asked for a clearer case. Accordingly, both O'Brien and Mandeville were summoned to appear before a crimes act court in Mitchelstown on 9 September. [186] Large crowds of country people assembled on that day in Mitchelstown to see the crimes act tested by a famous Parnellite and by a local hero, but neither of them appeared for trial. Instead, a great protest meeting attended by John Dillon and several English radical M.P.s including Henry Labouchere, was held in the market square. The Rev. B. MacCarthy had just been moved to the chair in order to address a gathering of several thousands when about twenty police tried to open a passage to the speakers' platform for the government's customary note taker. Observing this, Thomas Condon, M.P., reportedly stood up and shouted: 'Stand together, boys; don't let one of them through; they're near enough'. Cheering, the crowd turned and confronted the police, who were hopelessly outnumbered and had to retreat under a barrage of blackthorns and stones. A reinforcement group of forty police charging up the square on foot was halted by men on horseback at the edge of the crowd and then repulsed when they attempted to make a baton charge. Condon succeeded temporarily in restoring order and Dillon spoke, but halfway through his speech the police made a second baton charge. They were again driven back by an angry portion of the crowd that kept up a barrage of rock

[184] Ibid., 12 Aug. 1887.
[185] Ibid., 26 Sept. 1887.
[186] Ibid., 25, 29 Aug. 1887.

throwing. From the barracks that overlooked the square, the frustrated and provoked police fired two volleys into the ranks of their tormentors below, killing two, and seriously wounding twenty persons.[187] Following this 'massacre', O'Brien and Mandeville were apprehended, and on 24 September they were convicted of having incited the Kingston tenants to resist eviction in the previous month. Mandeville was sentenced to two, and O'Brien to three months in prison.[188] The government was opening its arsenal. Shortly before, the orders under the crimes act had been signed to suppress the branches of the National League in the districts of Mitchelstown, Kanturk, and Millstreet, although it was widely expected that meetings would continue in secret.[189]

The so-called Mitchelstown massacre had serious and significant repercussions. It badly embarrassed the conservative government (Arthur Balfour was thereafter known in Ireland as 'bloody Balfour'), it shocked English public opinion, and it drove Gladstonian liberals and Parnellites closer together.[190] One thing it definitely did not do, however; it did not destroy the Plan on the Kingston estate. If anything, it helped to polarize the feelings of the belligerents and to postpone the possibility of a settlement for several months. In early October the agent made a feeble, halfhearted effort at compromise. Three gales of rent had by then accumulated, and if the tenants would pay two of them in full at once, he offered to reduce the third gale by the amount of the court's future abatement, if any.[191] Even though a future court reduction could not legally affect rent already due, this was a meagre concession, and the tenants' reaction was predictable. At a meeting over which Thomas Condon and Ambrose Mandeville presided, they flatly rejected Frend's gambit and decided to wait to see if the land courts would give them justice.[192] Ambrose Mandeville and Maurice Healy, brother of Tim and a prominent catholic solicitor in Cork city, had filed 540 applications to have 'fair rents' fixed on behalf of as many leaseholding tenants on the Kingston estate.[193]

[187] Killed were Maurice Murphy and John Shinnick; a third man, John Casey, later died of gunshot wounds. In addition to the twenty persons seriously wounded, twenty others received wounds and bruises of a less serious nature (ibid., 10, 12 Sept. 1887). Cf. Lyons, *Dillon*, pp. 88–9; Curtis, *Coercion & conciliation*, pp. 197–8.
[188] Curtis, *Coercion & conciliation*, p. 223.
[189] Ibid., pp. 435–8; *C.C.*, 22 Sept. 1887.
[190] Lyons, *Dillon*, p. 89.
[191] *C.C.*, 4 Oct. 1887.
[192] Ibid., 7 Oct. 1887.
[193] *C.E.*, 29 Sept. 1887.

The first decisions in the Kingston estate cases, affecting about 100 tenants, were rendered in late December.[194] Suspiciously, the average reduction amounted to 20·5 per cent, almost exactly the original demand of the campaigners, but in individual cases the abatements varied from zero to about 30 per cent.[195] The campaigners were committed to a general allowance of at least 20 per cent, and since William O'Brien had told the tenants in the previous August that a reduction twice as large would be fair, it seemed as if the conflict would continue. On New Year's Day, 1888, the tenants gathered in the National League hall in Mitchelstown and heard Thomas Condon say that 'these were anything at all but adequate reductions'. Condon also strongly reaffirmed the commitment of the Plan's leaders to the full reinstatement of every tenant who had been evicted or disturbed during the campaign. The meeting therefore resolved unanimously that the judicial reductions were inadequate.[196]

Not surprisingly, however, many tenants were content to accept the verdict of the land court as it applied to their own rent, and cracks soon began to appear in the formerly united front of the Plan. In exasperation, the Representative Church Body moved to place the Kingston estate under the administration of the court of chancery but agreed to the appointment of the dowager countess of Kingston's husband William Downes Webber as receiver.[197] Then some 120 leaseholders whose cases had been decided were served with civil-bill decrees for a year's rent. The castle strategists prudently avoided angering these tenants with expensive superior-court writs and only called for payment of two-thirds of the rent due. Pressure mounted for a negotiated settlement, especially because there had been a few prominent defectors from the ranks. Condon admitted as much at a meeting in mid-January; after encouraging the tenants to maintain their unity, he made the significant declaration that they were 'never averse to a reasonable settlement, and they now were as prepared to make a reasonable settlement as they were at any time; but that must be a settlement that will embrace every tenant on the property'.[198]

Events moved rapidly towards a successful conclusion. Within ten days of Condon's declaration, negotiations were opened with Webber, and through him, with the Representative Church Body, which was also anxious for a settlement of its outstanding claims

[194] *C.C.*, 27 Dec. 1887.
[195] Ibid., 22 Feb. 1888.
[196] Ibid., 3 Jan. 1888.
[197] Ibid., 22 Feb. 1888.   [198] Ibid., 17 Jan. 1888.

against the estate. An agreement vindicating the Plan's objectives was reached in early February, after only about a week of discussions.[199] Webber conceded the original demand for a general abatement of 20 per cent, and this reduction was to apply to two of the three gales of rent currently due. For their part, the tenants promised to pay one year's rent by 25 March 1888, but those suffering special hardship were to be granted further indulgence. All tenants evicted or disturbed since the Plan had come into operation in December 1886 were to be fully reinstated without incurring any liability for law costs. Although Webber would not remit old arrears of rent, he expressed his willingness to deal leniently in regard to them. Even the thirty to forty tenants evicted before the Plan began were to be given an opportunity to purchase their former holdings under the Ashbourne land act of 1885.[200] Understandably, the Kingston tenants were jubilant over what they considered a decisive victory.[201]

THE PROGRESS OF THE AGITATION

While the struggle proceeded on the Kingston estate in 1887, the collection of rent became desperately difficult almost everywhere in County Cork. Doherty and Jones reported in September that 'the tenants on all the properties which we manage are doing their utmost to evade payment, & this is not the complaint alone of us, but likewise of nearly every other landlord & agent in the county'.[202] Adding to the landlords' difficulties was the fact that the land courts were slashing rents in late 1887. Judicial abatements ranging from 15 to 20 per cent had been more or less expected under the new land act passed in August. But the subcommissioners in Clare worked with a vengeance and gave reductions averaging 45 to 50 per cent; their decisions were 'rec[eive]d with dismay by all the landlords in this county', especially because they affected estates that had previously been regarded as 'very moderately let'.[203] After William O'Brien and John Mandeville were sent to Tullamore gaol for violating the crimes act, tenants frequently refused to pay rent until they were released, and the government's coercion policies abandoned.[204]

---

[199] Ibid., 3, 4 Feb. 1888; *C.E.*, 4 Feb. 1888.

[200] *C.E.*, 13, 22 Feb. 1888; *C.C.*, 22 Feb. 1888.

[201] *C.E.*, 10 Feb. 1888.

[202] Doherty papers, Letter book, 1882–7: Doherty and Jones to Rev. J. N. Hicks, 28 Sept. 1887, p. 976.

[203] Ibid.: Doherty and Jones to Col. J. F. Sweeney, 29 Sept. 1887, pp. 981–2.

[204] *C.E.*, 16, 19, 29 Nov., 1 Dec. 1887.

These developments threw the propertied classes into the gravest alarm. The earl of Shannon's agent William B. Leslie seriously wondered how many landowners would be fortunate enough to escape the poorhouse. The only parallel to these disturbing events, suggested Leslie, was the plagues of Egypt. [205]

Landlord prospects remained gloomy throughout 1888. Most landowners were practically compelled by the agitation to reduce rents substantially, and even when they did so, most tenants paid anything but promptly. Abatements of 20 to 30 per cent were very common, and allowances tended to be larger and more numerous than in the previous three years. [206] Whenever reductions of less than 20 per cent were offered, as for example on the Bandon, Townsend, and Carbery estates in West Cork, [207] little rent could be collected without legal proceedings. Mounting arrears were a grave concern to a growing number of landlords and agents. 'Since I undertook the agency of Lord Castletown's estates here, I have not got one 6*d*. from the Dromdeer tenants & shall have to take immediate proceedings ag[ains]t them', declared Matthew H. Franks in February 1888. 'All of them owe a large arrear of rent. . . .' [208] After Sir J. N. McKenna had capitulated to his tenants in early 1887, his rents had nevertheless been poorly paid, for the arrears amounted on the average to three years' rent in August 1888. [209] Doherty and Jones justified their failure to collect the rents on the Fitzpatrick estate by pointing out in January 1889 that the agents of two neighbouring landlords, Sir George Colthurst and the earl of Kenmare, were 'getting no rent from their properties at Ballyvourney'. [210] Doherty and Jones had done little better on the earl of Bandon's estates, where arrears of £16,000—almost one year's income—had accumulated by March 1889, and 'not as much as one penny' was currently being paid. [211] On the small property of the Rev. J. N. Hicks near Skull, as much as three to four years' rent was outstanding in early 1889. [212] Default seems to have been nearly universal in northwest Cork. 'I am sorry to say that there are a great many people

[205] *C.C.*, 18 Nov. 1887.

[206] *C.E.*, Nov. 1887–Dec. 1888.

[207] Ibid., 6 Dec. 1887; 23 Jan., 25 Feb. 1888.

[208] Doneraile papers, Letter book, 1888–9: M. H. Franks to G. L. Taylor, 24 Feb. 1888, pp. 26–7.

[209] *C.E.*, 19 Nov. 1889.

[210] Doherty papers, Letter book, 1889–90: Doherty and Jones to Messrs Park, Nelson, Morgan, and Co., 16 Jan. 1889, p. 15.

[211] Ibid.: Doherty and Jones to V. and P. Evard, 1 Mar. 1889, p. 58; Doherty and Jones to Rev. Forrest, 28 Sept. 1889, p. 158.

[212] *C.E.*, 4 Jan. 1889.

in this district and the part of Kerry adjoining it, not getting their rents', Henry Harte Barry observed in May 1889.[213]

In general, Cork landowners could have considered themselves fortunate if they did not lose more than one year's rental income in the late 1880s, for the owners of the estates on which the Plan had taken root went without their rents altogether. While the Plan of Campaign was fully functioning between late 1886 and early 1891, less than twenty Cork properties were directly affected by it, and the exact number seems to have been closer to fifteen than to twenty. Most of these properties were small. William N. Leader's estates near Kanturk were occupied by less than fifty tenants,[214] and Herbert B. O'Sullivan's property near Macroom, by only thirty-five or forty.[215] Arthur Langford's estate near Newmarket had less than twenty-five tenants,[216] Thomas R. Marmion's island properties in Roaring Water Bay off Skull, only eleven,[217] and Arthur Blenner-hassett's estate near Macroom, just five tenants.[218] Besides the Kingston property, there were in fact only two great estates in Cork on which the tenants adopted the Plan—the 10,600-acre Ponsonby estate with nearly 240 tenants,[219] and the 13,400-acre Massy estate with 500 to 600 tenants.[220]

The National League appears to have selected its targets carefully, for the owners of these Plan estates were generally too poor to resist for a long period without external assistance. Sir Joseph N. McKenna, for example, defaulted on the interest payments on a £7,000 incumbrance and filed a petition for the sale of his Cork estate as early as June 1885.[221] Arthur Langford also had no reserves and faced the loss of his property within only a few months of the adoption of the Plan. Appearing before the court of land judges in November 1888 in order to oppose the demand made by some of his tenants for an allowance of 30 per cent, Langford complained bitterly that he had been 'reduced to such a pitch of poverty by these people boycotting his turbary and refusing to pay him rent that he was unable to fee counsel'.[222] H. B. O'Sullivan's estate had

---

[213] Barry papers, Letter book, 1888–9: H. H. Barry to Sir J. W. Mackey, 16 May 1889, pp. 683–4.

[214] *C.E.*, 23 Aug. 1887; *C.C.*, 8 June 1889.

[215] *C.E.*, 24 Mar. 1890, 20 June 1891.

[216] Ibid., 29 Nov. 1887.

[217] Ibid., 12 Aug. 1890.

[218] Ibid., 8 Mar. 1890.

[219] *C.C.*, 31 Jan. 1890.

[220] *C.E.*, 14 Jan. 1889.

[221] Ibid., 26 Jan. 1888, 19 Nov. 1889.

[222] *C.C.*, 13 Nov. 1888. See also *C.E.*, 30 Apr., 2 July 1889.

been hopelessly insolvent long before the Plan was put in force early in 1888. The total incumbrances on this property, which was only worth some £750 a year, amounted to no less than £31,000 by 1891.[223]

The Plan was often instituted on estates where the landlord was in a weak bargaining position because of the accumulation of arrears. At the time that the Plan was adopted on the Leader property at Curraghs, all the tenants owed at least one year's rent.[224] On the Gollock estate near Macroom, the tenants owed in September 1888 'on an average about three years' rent, which they were unable to pay in the past bad years'.[225] The non-remission of heavy arrears was at the root of the dispute on the Massy estate. After the request of nearly eighty Massy tenants for the pardon of these arrears had been rejected in late 1888, dissatisfaction mounted until all the tenants joined the Plan in early 1889.[226] A generous settlement of their debts had been offered to the tenants of the Tuohill estate, who embraced the Plan in 1888, but without result. As the agent reported in April 1889,

No settlement has been made with the tenants. Ejectment decrees have been obtained against almost all of them, there being in every case 5 & 6 years' rent due. One year's rent less 25 per cent would be taken in each case in full of all arrears & still they will not settle.[227]

On the Marmion properties, at least two years' rent had accumulated before these island tenants joined the Plan in July 1890.[228]

If the Plan estates in Cork were generally small and loaded with debt, they were also heavily concentrated in the northwestern part of the county, where the low prices of butter and calves were perhaps most severely felt. Of the fifteen estates where the Plan is known to have been adopted, as many as ten were situated in this region. By the middle of 1888, four estates in the Kingwilliamstown district near the Kerry border were involved in the turmoil, including those of Sir James W. Mackey, Nicholas Dunscombe,[229] Mrs Richard Tuohill, and Captain T. A. Townsend.[230] These four properties, as well as those of William N. Leader and Arthur Langford, all lay

[223] *C.E.*, 5 Jan. 1889, 20 June 1891; *C.C.*, 12 Dec. 1891.
[224] *C.C.*, 6 Sept. 1888.
[225] *C.E.*, 25 Sept. 1888.
[226] Ibid., 14 Jan., 8 June, 2 Nov. 1889.
[227] Barry papers, Letter book, 1888–9: H. H. Barry to surveyor income tax, 23 Apr. 1889, p. 570.
[228] *C.E.*, 8 July 1890.
[229] *C.C.*, 25 Feb. 1888.
[230] *C.E.*, 23 May 1889.

within the barony of Duhallow. The other main centre of strife was
located south of Duhallow in the Macroom district, where four more
estates were entwined in the Plan, including those of H. B.
O'Sullivan, James Gollock, [231] Arthur Blennerhassett, [232] and
Mrs Elizabeth Massy. There was unquestionably some contagion
as the organized conflict took hold in these two areas of northwest
Cork, and the Leader tenants provided most of the inspiration for the
spread of the Plan here.

Leader's property was divided into two sections, one to the
northeast of Kanturk at Curraghs, the other to the northwest above
Newmarket at Meelin. The Curraghs tenants first adopted the Plan in
late December 1886, after Leader had rejected their demand for
abatements of 37½ per cent to the non-judicial and 25 per cent to the
judicial tenants. [233] When Leader's agent Henry Harte Barry
pressed the Meelin tenants for their rents in May 1887 without
offering the desired reductions, they joined the Curraghs tenants in
revolt. [234] Leader responded slowly and cautiously, waiting until
August before evicting only three of the Curraghs tenants. [235] The
local reaction to these evictions, however, was intense and spirited.
Moonlighting and incendiarism broke out. [236] A wildly jeering
crowd, headed by several priests, intimidated the harvest labourers
from working on Leader's demesne at Dromina, [237] and Leader
himself was severely boycotted. He retaliated by calling upon the
Cork Defence Union for help in the gathering of his crops and by
prosecuting several Kanturk shopkeepers, three of whom were
convicted under the crimes act in January 1888. [238] The government
assisted him by arresting in March the fiery leader of the tenants, the
Rev. M. B. Kennedy, C.C., Meelin, along with nine farmers, for
holding a proclaimed meeting. They received sentences of two
months in gaol in late June. [239] Nine more evictions were carried out
at Curraghs in September, and several of the tenants were sent to gaol
for violently resisting the sheriff and his bailiffs, just as the first three
evicted tenants had done. [240] These prosecutions, however, did not
uproot the Plan on the Leader estates but only succeeded in
spreading it to others in northwest Cork. [241]

[231] Ibid., 25 Sept. 1888.   [232] Ibid., 31 Jan. 1889.
[233] Ibid., 1, 5, 14 Jan. 1887.   [234] Ibid., 10 May 1887.
[235] *C.C.*, 10 Aug. 1887; *C.E.*, 16 Sept. 1887.
[236] *C.C.*, 12 Aug. 1887.
[237] Ibid., 25 Aug. 1887.
[238] Ibid., 4, 5 Jan. 1888.
[239] Ibid., 24 Feb., 30 June 1888; *C.E.*, 21 June 1888.
[240] *C.C.*, 6 Sept. 1888.
[241] *C.E.*, 15 Oct. 1888.

COUNTER OFFENSIVE

Lacking the resources and the cohesiveness needed if they were to combat the agrarian agitation effectively, Irish unionist landowners leaned heavily upon government initiative and support. Most of them believed that only strong rule was required in order to suppress the disturbances and the unrest. As Lord Castletown told Balfour in July 1887:

The Irish populace will lean to whichever side proves itself strongest. They are sick and tired of Land League tyranny, but they will not cut themselves away from it until they are convinced that the government is stronger and more certain in its action than the league. [242]

The government's resolute counteroffensive began in the following month with the suppression of the most troublesome National League branches in Kerry and Clare. [243] In September Balfour seized the opportunity offered by the 'Mitchelstown massacre' and ordered the suppression of no less than 200 branches of the league, mostly in the disturbed southwestern part of the country, and including all the branches in the districts of Kanturk, Millstreet, and Mitchelstown in Cork. [244] He also rewrote the instructions of the Royal Irish Constabulary, whose mishandling of the admittedly explosive situation at Mitchelstown had led to the fatal collision between police and demonstrators. Under these new instructions, crowds that defied police orders to disperse faced serious consequences. As Balfour explained to his uncle Lord Salisbury on 21 September, the police should not club their rifles and act as baton men,

but they should either fire or charge with fixed bayonets, as the exigencies of the particular case may seem to require. This is the general disposition of a police force in the face of a hostile mob which both humanity and efficiency seem to require; and on this point Buller and the three resident magistrates (all soldiers) who were present agreed. [245]

Besides reinstructing the police and suppressing the most radical branches of the league, the government pressed its counteroffensive in several other ways, most dramatically by prosecuting the leading spirits of the agitation—radical Irish M.P.s and 'revolutionary priests'. When in March 1887 the Rev. Canon Keller, the parish

[242] Lord Castletown to A. Balfour, 17 July 1887, quoted in Curtis, *Coercion & conciliation*, p. 185.
[243] Ibid., pp. 184–5.
[244] Ibid., pp. 217–18.
[245] Quoted ibid., p. 437.

priest of Youghal and the leader of the campaigning Ponsonby tenants, refused to appear in a Dublin court and there identify the trustees of the tenants' 'war chest', he was arrested and imprisoned in Kilmainham. [246] As noted earlier, the Rev. M. B. Kennedy, who helped to organize the Plan on the Leader estates, was prosecuted for addressing a proclaimed meeting in December 1887 and was sentenced to two months in prison in June 1888. [247] Although twenty-three priests were tried for crimes act offences in different parts of the country between 1887 and 1890, only a minority actually went to prison. [248] While the government was extremely cautious in restraining 'revolutionary priests', it showed much less leniency in dealing with radical Irish M.P.s. Shortly after William O'Brien had finished serving his sentence for having incited the Kingston tenants to resist eviction, both he and John Dillon were arrested and in May 1888 were ordered to gaol for six months. No less than twenty-one members of Parnell's party had faced prosecution up to August 1888, and they were joined by eleven more before the end of the year. [249] Nor did the lesser agitators escape the net of the crimes act, although public attention was focused upon the trials of the leaders of the agitation. The barony of Duhallow saw the act enforced in all its rigour, with ordinary law practically superseded altogether. There were more than 200 prosecutions of rank-and-file National League members in Duhallow between 1887 and 1891, and more men were probably sent to prison from the Meelin branch of the league than from any other branch in the entire country. [250]

The government's stern law enforcement greatly buoyed the sagging spirits of Irish landlords and prompted the Cork Defence Union to intensify its efforts against the league. The C.D.U. expanded its aid to farmers and landowners who were unable to obtain labourers to milk their cows or to cut their crops. By October 1890 the C.D.U. employed over 100 men in farm work at fifty-eight different stations throughout the county, at a cost of almost £3,000 during the previous year. [251] The boycotting of livestock also received greater attention. It was an uphill fight at least until 1890, because

[246] To the consternation of unionists, Canon Keller's removal to Dublin was one great triumphal progress: in Cork city he received a laudatory address from the corporation; at Cashel the archbishop and the clergy turned out to greet him; and in Dublin there was yet another enthusiastic demonstration in his honour (*C.E.*, 19, 21 Mar. 1887).

[247] *C.C.*, 24 Feb., 30 June 1888; *C.E.*, 21 June 1888.

[248] Curtis, *Coercion & conciliation*, p. 236.

[249] Ibid., pp. 203–4.

[250] *C.E.*, 5 May 1891.

[251] *C.C.*, 27 Oct. 1890.

the vigilance committees and special agents of the league made it extremely difficult for persons considered obnoxious to buy or sell at the local fairs. Partly by borrowing the tactic of 'shadowing' used by the league itself, and partly by disguising themselves as cattle dealers in order to obtain evidence of conspiracy against league agents, the police and the C.D.U.'s employees succeeded in breaking up several boycotting rings. [252] While the boycotting of 'obnoxious' persons and their livestock constituted a serious problem, it was the boycotting of evicted farms (or the inability to evict lest boycotting follow automatically) that gave landowners their worst headache, as it tightly pinched their financial nerves. In order to relieve the pain, the C.D.U. set up in March 1887 a special farm committee that assumed the management of derelict holdings. [253] This committee, headed by the land agent Pasco Savage French, helped landowners to stock and work their vacant farms by advancing them one-third of the necessary capital; the C.D.U. provided all the capital in a notable number of cases where the landlord was too poor to make it a joint enterprise. [254] Handsome profits of 53 per cent were claimed for these farms in March 1889, [255] and the C.D.U. used its share of the proceeds to finance the extension of the scheme. The province of the farm committee reached its widest extent during 1890. By October of that year, twenty-nine holdings, encompassing nearly 5,000 acres, had been rescued from their derelict condition and stocked by the C.D.U. with about 900 cattle and 500 sheep. [256] These figures are not particularly striking, but it would be a mistake to assess the impact of the C.D.U.'s farm scheme upon the problem of boycotted land by them alone, since the scheme must have inclined many defaulting tenants to accept reasonable settlement terms rather than allow themselves to be evicted, and thus must have limited the magnitude of the problem.

What the C.D.U. and the government desired above all was the resounding defeat of the Plan of Campaign. The realization of this objective seemed to hinge largely upon the outcome of the struggles in progress on a small number of great estates. Because these conflicts consistently received lavish attention in the press, they were considered capable, whether rightly or wrongly, of exercising a profound influence over the whole course of the land war, and both

[252] Curtis, *Coercion & conciliation*, pp. 220–1; *C.C.*, 14 Oct. 1889.
[253] *C.C.*, 14 Mar. 1887.
[254] Ibid., 14 Oct. 1889.
[255] Profits were so large because no rent was paid; if it had been necessary to pay rent, profits would have been only 12 per cent (*C.E.*, 18 Mar. 1889).
[256] *C.C.*, 27 Oct. 1890.

sides were therefore prepared to commit a large part of their energies and resources to a few strategic localities. The government realized that it could not fight the Plan effectively everywhere, and Balfour decided to concentrate upon winning the contests on a half-dozen 'test estates' in different parts of the country.

The premier test estate in Ireland and the only one in Cork belonged to Charles William Talbot Ponsonby, a retired English naval officer who had inherited it in 1868. His 10,600-acre property stretched for fourteen miles along the southeastern coast from the mountainous moors bordering the Blackwater to the marshes at the western side of Youghal Bay; the quality of this narrow strip of land, devoted to dairying and barley growing, was very uneven. [257] The relations between Ponsonby, a resident landlord for at least half of the year, and his 240 tenants had not been cordial before late 1886, [258] when the tenants were in a particularly foul mood. Because of the drastic fall in the price of both butter and young stock, especially since 1884, the tenants stood £5,000 in arrears. [259] Moreover, they were said to owe over £10,000 to the shopkeepers and traders of Youghal. [260] Heavy rains in the autumn of 1886 had ruined most of the tenants' malting barley, and their attempts to dispose of it even at an enormous sacrifice had proved largely futile. [261] In contrast with neighbouring landlords, half a dozen of

---

[257] *C.E.*, 21 Aug. 1889.

[258] There had been a handful of evictions during the 1870s, and some slight increases in the annual rental, which stood at nearly £7,500 in December 1886 (*C.C.*, 4 Oct. 1887). Far more importantly, however, the tenants had derived virtually no benefit from the 1881 land act, even though as many as 90 per cent of them were yearly tenants rather than leaseholders. Several of the yearly tenants were sufficiently convinced that they were paying grossly exorbitant rents to spurn Ponsonby's offer of a 10 per cent reduction in 1882 and to begin proceedings in the land courts. But the courts dealt so cavalierly with their grievances that some of those who had entered their cases for a hearing later withdrew them in disgust. The twenty-seven tenants who went as far as a decision received reductions averaging only 11 per cent (ibid., 27, 31 Jan. 1890). In November 1885 the disgruntled tenants pooled their rents in order to fight Ponsonby when he refused to give more than a 20 per cent allowance to the 210 non-judicial tenants and offered no abatement whatsoever to the judicial tenants. After only three weeks, however, Ponsonby yielded reductions of 20 and 10 per cent to the non-judicial and judicial tenants respectively, and these were accepted (Rev. D. Keller, *The struggle for life on the Ponsonby estate* (Dublin, 1887), reprinted in *C.E.*, 30 Sept. 1887).

[259] Ponsonby offered to cancel these arrears, provided the tenants accepted his terms concerning abatements, but they would not hear of it (*C.C.*, 4 Oct. 1887).

[260] *C.E.*, 4 July 1887.

[261] Ibid., 30 Sept. 1887.

whom made abatements ranging from 30 to 50 per cent,[262] Ponsonby seemed a grinding tyrant when he offered one of only 20 per cent in November 1886. It was thus hardly surprising that his tenants became the earliest public adherents of the Plan of Campaign in Ireland in the following month.

Ponsonby was not completely unconciliatory, although he did evict nine tenants in May 1887 because they had joined the Plan.[263] The first of many settlement proposals and counterproposals was made in the following month, when Ponsonby offered to cancel arrears of over £8,000 and to allow the tenants to buy their holdings at twenty years' purchase of their current rents.[264] The tenants' solicitor Matthew J. Horgan rejected these terms as 'preposterous' but substituted others almost as outlandish: sales at fourteen years' purchase of reduced rents, the remission of all arrears, and the reinstatement of the evicted tenants.[265] Of course, Ponsonby had no intention of surrendering so easily, and he would have carried out more evictions in order to impress the tenants with his resolve but for the interference of the 1887 land act.[266] The failure of another settlement proposal at the end of October, when the tenants spurned substantial concessions by the landlord, marked a turning point in the history of the Plan on this estate. Ponsonby now proposed to accept one and one-half years' rent, less 20 and 35 per cent on the judicial and non-judicial rents respectively, in lieu of all arrears, and to sell at seventeen and one-half years' purchase. But the tenants were only willing to give a year's rent, less 35 per cent, and to buy at thirteen or fourteen years' purchase, and said that otherwise Ponsonby could proceed with the evictions.[267] These terms represented the ultimate points to which each side was prepared to move for many months thereafter, and the gap between them proved impossible to bridge. Ponsonby carried out three more evictions in February 1888 with the help of a battering ram made essential by the strongly fortified state of the tenants' houses.[268] He also frustrated the desire of many tenants to let the dispute be settled through the land courts when he served a substantial number of them with 'eviction-made-easy notices' that disqualified them from seeking judicial relief.[269] With

[262] Ibid., 16, 22 Feb., 30 Sept. 1887.

[263] Ibid., 26, 27, 28 May 1887.

[264] Messrs O'Keefe and Lynch to M. J. Horgan, 27 June 1887, quoted ibid., 4 July 1887.

[265] M. J. Horgan to Messrs O'Keefe and Lynch, 29 June 1887, quoted ibid.

[266] *C.C.*, 28, 29 Sept. 1887.

[267] *C.E.*, 31 Oct. 1887; *C.C.*, 31 Oct. 1887.

[268] *C.C.*, 24 Feb. 1888.   [269] Ibid., 25 Feb., 10, 26 Mar. 1888.

but one exception, the tenants' cases to have their rents fixed were adjourned by the land courts. [270]

Unlike many other landlords attacked by the Plan, Ponsonby was not saddled at the outset with heavy estate charges. Yet, if the struggle were to be prolonged, with no rent coming in, he would obviously require outside help in order to pay even his modest charges and food bills, and to fee counsel in the legal manoeuvres against his litigious tenants. Local and national landlord associations provided some limited assistance. The C.D.U. declared early its readiness to supply Ponsonby 'with the necessary number of labourers, horses, and all farm machinery requisite to labour and crop any land[s] thrown on his hands which are under tillage'. [271] The Land Corporation was later engaged to manage the property and to work the twelve evicted farms, after Ponsonby had dismissed his land agent in July 1888. [272] The Cork Landowners' Association launched a drive to raise funds in England in March 1887; this body sought to 'defray the necessary expenses in the contest which has been forced upon us by the enemies of England and Ireland'. [273] The drive appears to have been a failure, but it was widely rumoured that A. H. Smith-Barry, the richest landlord belonging to the C.D.U. and its chairman, was privately replenishing Ponsonby's empty coffers. [274]

By the winter of 1888–9, however, Ponsonby had reached the end of his tether. He had lost almost £25,000 in rent and owed some £4,000 or £5,000 to his solicitors, Messrs O'Keefe and Lynch of Cork city. [275] The worried yet ever-resourceful Balfour informed Lord Salisbury in January 1889:

Ponsonby is completely '*broke*' and has lost all nerve. He has no money to pay his charges and none to provide himself with bread and butter. I must try and get him some by hook or by crook: on condition he fights on. [276]

What Balfour interpreted as a loss of nerve was Ponsonby's willingness to reopen talks with the tenants through his former agent J. E. Brunker, who held a series of meetings with Canon Keller between late December 1888 and mid-January 1889. [277] The gap

[270] Ibid., 5 Apr., 5 May 1888.
[271] Ibid., 7 Feb. 1887. See also ibid., 18 Feb., 1 Mar. 1887.
[272] Ibid., 15 July 1889.
[273] Ibid., 7 Mar. 1887.
[274] *C.E.*, 29 Sept. 1887.
[275] Ibid., 14 Mar. 1889.
[276] A. Balfour to Lord Salisbury, 18 Jan. 1889, quoted in Curtis, *Coercion & conciliation*, p. 248.
[277] *C.C.*, 4 Jan., 19 Feb. 1889.

between the parties was somewhat narrowed, [278] but the negotiations ended abruptly on 22 February, when Ponsonby's trustee telegraphed Brunker: 'Having fully considered offer made by Canon Keller, and the sum being so far below price named by Mr Ponsonby, trustee cannot advise him to accept'. [279]

On the very next day after Canon Keller's offer had been declared unacceptable, the *Cork Constitution* announced the sale of Ponsonby's estate to a glittering group of English capitalists. [280] Naturally, this report caused consternation among nationalists, who saw in the formation of this syndicate a dark conspiracy to save the bankrupt Ponsonby, to smash the Plan on his estate, and to snatch victory out of the jaws of defeat. [281] During the previous month, Balfour and Smith-Barry had worked diligently to prevent the sale of the estate to the tenants on terms that would have been unfavourable to Ponsonby personally, and that could have greatly depreciated land values in the south of Ireland and given the whole agitation a renewed impetus. About a dozen of the wealthiest landowners in England and Ireland were persuaded to subscribe £10,000 each, Smith-Barry was named as one of the three directors chosen to supervise the management of the estate, and Ponsonby was left as merely the nominal owner. [282] Smith-Barry cajoled the reluctant H. H. Townsend into becoming agent for the syndicate in place of the Land Corporation and promised him £10,000 for use in stocking the lands as well as additional funds for the creation of a large central farm, with no obligation to show any profit for at least four years. [283] If the tenants persisted in clinging to the Plan, the syndicate was prepared to evict them all and to turn the entire estate into one vast cattle and sheep ranch.

---

[278] The degree to which the gap had been narrowed was bitterly disputed. Landlord partisans claimed that Brunker was authorized to accept £110,000 for the whole estate, but only on the condition that the tenants would agree to redeem the government charges (tithe rent-charges, board of works' loans, crown and quit rents). The addition of these charges brought the total selling price to £127,000, or seventeen years' purchase of the rents. Canon Keller's final offer of slightly more than £106,000, or fourteen years' purchase, left the charges to be redeemed by the landlord, and he claimed to have understood Brunker's mention of £110,000 in precisely this sense. Brunker was dismayed by the break-off of talks and was convinced that if they had been allowed to continue, he and Canon Keller would have reached a satisfactory compromise (*C.E.*, 22 Aug. 1889).

[279] Quoted in *C.C.*, 31 Jan. 1890.
[280] Ibid., 23 Feb. 1889.
[281] Ibid., 7 Mar. 1889.
[282] Curtis, *Coercion & conciliation*, p. 250.
[283] *C.E.*, 14, 15 Mar. 1889.

Before embarking on this extreme course, however, the syndicate proposed in April a settlement on terms substantially the same as Brunker's; it offered to remit all arrears up to 25 March 1889, or almost three and one-half years' rent, if the tenants would buy their farms at seventeen years' purchase under the Ashbourne act. Had they accepted this offer, the tenants would in effect have reduced their judicial rents by 24 per cent and their non-judicial rents by as much as 32 per cent, or scarcely less than the abatements demanded originally. [284] But Canon Keller believed that these terms were less generous than those he had already wrung from Brunker and therefore threw his great weight into the scale against them. At the crucial meeting of the Youghal branch of the National League on 12 April, the syndicate's proposals were unanimously rejected as 'insulting and ridiculous'. [285] Keller was unshakably convinced that seventeen years' purchase of their rents was far too high a price for the tenants to pay, for in his opinion, their rents were considerably in excess of those on neighbouring estates where sales had been concluded at lower rates. [286] This was not a purely partisan view, but one that received embarrassing confirmation in an extraordinary letter written in mid-June by H. H. Townsend to the Land Corporation and published several weeks later by the *Cork Examiner* after falling into the wrong hands:

From what I have seen of the Ponsonby estate, I am sorry to say that I believe the land commission, if it ever goes before it, will reduce the rents on it very heavily. . . . It is quite good enough for fighting, the tenants having required an equal all-round reduction and then gone to the Plan of Campaign, but I consider that the late agent should have given larger allowances than 20 per cent on a good deal of the lands, and have [had] all revalued at the commencement of the row before the Plan of Campaign was adopted. . . . I advise Mr Smith-Barry and the other members of the syndicate to make public as soon as possible that they are only fighting the way in which the tenants want to get the rents down. Of course, they have put this forward in their circulars, but this view has not been brought enough before the public, who are led to believe that the purchasers' object is to recover the rents, which are too high. [287]

Having failed to induce the Ponsonby tenants to settle, the syndicate proceeded to clear the estate in three major eviction

[284] If they did not wish to purchase their farms, the tenants could have settled by paying one year's rent, less 20 per cent, and annual interest of 3 per cent on the arrears outstanding (*C.C.*, 11, 12 Apr. 1889).

[285] Ibid., 13 Apr. 1889. See also ibid., 26, 27 Apr. 1889.

[286] *C.E.*, 29 Apr. 1889.

[287] H. H. Townsend to W. Gyles, 17 June 1889, quoted ibid., 27 July 1889.

campaigns. Although twenty-six more tenants were quietly dispossessed in June 1889,[288] almost another year passed before the dreary work could be resumed. After the National League had exhausted the possibilities of legal defence and delay at a cost of some £4,500,[289] a sweeping clearance of 150 tenants was made during the second half of April 1890.[290] When the final eviction campaign involving thirty-one tenants was concluded in the last week of October, the estate stood virtually denuded of its former occupants.[291] Only two tenants refused to the bitter end to join the Plan and retained their holdings.[292] Sympathetic farmers on adjoining estates gave shelter to about 100 of the evicted tenants in converted out-offices, but the majority had to be content with dingy, three-room timber huts in four villages at Ardagh, Ballinvarrig, Clonard, and Dysart, which were scarcely made more habitable by being renamed after John Dillon, William O'Brien, and Canon Keller.[293] These villages badly lacked proper drainage and sanitary facilities, and soon there was an outbreak of typhoid fever at Ardagh.[294] The evicted tenants received a subsistence allowance of £2 or £3 per month from the league treasury, but even this paltry sum seems to have been reduced occasionally.[295] The elaborate system of boycotting devised in November 1889 by the Cork city branch of the National League with the Ponsonby estate in mind had failed to prevent the syndicate from placing over £10,000 worth of livestock on the evicted farms by mid-June 1890.[296] Feelings of despair and desperation began to take hold as the tenants saw the syndicate's cattle graze their former holdings, and there were a number of outrages, including one in which an evicted campaigner apparently burned down his own house.[297] If the syndicate had not yet smashed the Plan on the Ponsonby estate by the autumn of 1890, it had already scored a high measure of success. Although the Plan did not collapse here until February 1892, already the syndicate had not only rescued Ponsonby from certain defeat but also completely reversed the power relationship.

[288] *C.C.*, 18, 19, 20, 24 June 1889.
[289] Ibid., 19 Mar., 2 Apr. 1890.
[290] Ibid., 16 Apr., 1 May 1890. Some fifteen tenants who had been left undisturbed in April on account of illness were dispossessed in September (ibid., 19, 23 Sept. 1890).
[291] Ibid., 24, 25, 27 Oct. 1890.
[292] Ibid., 28 Oct. 1890.
[293] Ibid., 20 Feb., 10 Mar. 1890.
[294] Ibid., 9, 16 Dec. 1890.
[295] Ibid., 30 July 1890.
[296] Ibid., 1 Feb., 17 June 1890.
[297] Ibid., 7, 12, 26 June 1890.

THE WINDING DOWN OF THE LAND WAR

Even before the disastrous split in the Irish parliamentary party in late December 1890, there were many signs that the land war was winding down. Settlements were reached on a majority of the Plan estates where disputes had still been unresolved at the beginning of 1889, and in most cases the tenants of these estates realized their original demands. [298] Agrarian outrages were on the decline; their number was cut in half throughout Ireland between 1886 and 1889. [299] In Cork they fell more slowly, mostly because northwest Cork remained highly disturbed. Arms raids, firing into dwellings, cattle maiming, and rick burning continued almost unabated in that district at least until 1892. [300] In the county as a whole, however, the constabulary returns showed that the number of disturbances was progressively declining, from 117 in 1886 and ninety in 1887 to eighty-two in 1889 and seventy-four in 1890. While offences against property remained fairly stable over this period, those against the public peace (including threatening notices) fell from eighty in 1886 to only forty-seven by 1890, and those against persons, from fourteen in 1887 to just five by 1890. [301] The courts of the National League almost ceased to function, with only a few clandestine meetings reported in the local press after late 1888. [302] Boycotting also relaxed in intensity. By October 1890 the C.D.U. took pride in the fact that boycotting in general had 'enormously decreased'. [303]

The most revealing sign of the weakening of the agrarian agitation, however, was the increasing ability from early 1890 of landlords and agents to relet evicted farms. Even in 1889 some farmers had been

[298] *C.E.*, 28 Mar. 1889 (James Gollock); ibid., 23 May 1889 (Capt. T. A. Townsend); ibid., 9 Oct. 1889 (Sir J. W. Mackey); ibid., 14 Jan. 1890 (Mrs Richard Tuohill); ibid., 8 Feb., 24 Mar. 1890 (H. B. O'Sullivan); ibid., 14 Oct. 1890 (Arthur Blennerhassett); Barry papers, Letter book, 1890–1: H. H. Barry to C. Dunscombe, 9 Dec. 1890, p. 956.

[299] Curtis, *Coercion & conciliation*, pp. 264–5.

[300] *C.C.*, 17 Aug., 14 Sept. 1889; 13 May, 13, 29 Sept. 1890; 8, 16 Mar., 4, 20, 25 Apr., 11 Nov. 1892.

[301] *Return by provinces, of agrarian offences . . . between the 1st day of January 1886 and the 31st day of December 1886* . . . [C 5024], H.C. 1887, lxxviii, 1, pp. 8–9; *Return by provinces, of agrarian offences . . . between the 1st day of January 1887 and the 31st day of December 1887* . . . [C 5345], H.C. 1888, lxxxiii, 399, pp. 8–9; *Return by provinces, of agrarian offences . . . between the 1st day of January 1889 and the 31st day of December 1889* . . . [C 6008], H.C. 1890, lix, 795, pp. 8–9; *Return by provinces, of agrarian offences . . . between the 1st day of January 1890 and the 31st day of December 1890* . . . [C 6327], H.C. 1890–1, lxiv, 805, pp. 8–9.

[302] *C.E.*, 4 Sept. 1888; *C.C.*, 11 Jan. 1889, 18 May 1892.

[303] *C.C.*, 27 Oct. 1890.

bold enough to hire evicted land on a temporary basis for grazing purposes, but few of them dared to risk the consequences of becoming permanent tenants. During 1890 and the following years, many farmers threw aside their earlier hesitation and brazenly defied the weight of public opinion. 'I am happy to inform you', Maurice Leonard boasted to one of the trustees of the Kenmare estates in February 1890, 'I have let 2 farms to good, substantial tenants which were waste since 1882 and 1885.'[304] Two glaring cases of land grabbing, the first in the Macroom district since the start of the agitation, were reported from the Plan estate of Mrs Elizabeth Massy in May 1890.[305] These instances could easily be multiplied.[306] Land grabbers did not always escape the retribution that their acts had often inspired in the past,[307] but after 1890 they could realistically feel more secure from this danger, and their transgressions increased greatly. As many as ten of the twenty-nine evicted holdings under the management of the C.D.U.'s farm committee in October 1890 were successfully relet during the following year, and new occupiers had been found for thirteen more by October 1892.[308]

Unionist landlords began to rejoice over these unmistakable signs of a faltering agitation as early as February 1889, and whenever they saw evicted farms being relet or broken tenants selling the interest in their holdings, they invariably attributed the fact to the relentless enforcement of the crimes act by Balfour and his lieutenants.[309] Professor Curtis has expressed scepticism concerning the decisiveness of the government's repressive measures in bringing the land war under control by 1889, yet he leans to the view that although the land legislation and an economic recovery played their parts, coercion was by far the most important factor.[310] It seems much more reasonable, however, to give primacy to the economic improvement, even though it did not pervade the entire agricultural economy or endure beyond 1890. As James Penrose Fitzgerald told one Cork landowner in May 1888:

[304] Kenmare papers, Letter book, 1887–91: M. Leonard to S. J. Robinson, 27 Feb. 1890, pp. 329–30.

[305] *C.E.*, 27 May 1890.

[306] See, e.g., *C.C.*, 28 May, 30 Aug., 7 Nov. 1890.

[307] Kenmare papers, Letter book, 1887–91: M. Leonard to S. J. Robinson, 22 May 1890, p. 345; *C.C.*, 20 June, 5, 9 Aug., 28 Oct. 1890; 20 Apr., 6 June 1891.

[308] *C.C.*, 24 Oct. 1892.

[309] See A. H. Smith-Barry's address to a great unionist gathering at the Imperial Hotel in Cork city in mid-February (*C.C.*, 15 Feb. 1889).

[310] Curtis, *Coercion & conciliation*, pp. 263–4.

The rent collection is not very satisfactory, & things are not improving at this time; every half year tenants seem less willing to pay, & every change in the law makes it more difficult to compel them: *a rise in prices would do us more good than anything else* [my italics]. [311]

Ever since the summer of 1884, the depression in prices had fuelled agrarian discontent. Fitzgerald's hope began to become a reality, however, in July 1888, when livestock prices made strong advances at the local fairs. [312] The heavy summer rainfall caused an abundant growth of grass as well as a large make of butter and was a delightful contrast to the disastrous drought of the previous year. [313] Unfortunately, rain blighted the early promise of a good harvest. 'We have had dreadful weather for the past four weeks', Maurice Leonard reported at the end of August; 'the oats & hay through the country are half rotten, & the potatoes are, I am sorry to say, getting black.' [314] Still, since the price of young stock had risen considerably during the summer, James Penrose Fitzgerald could truthfully say in mid-September that farmers were 'in better spirits' than they had been for three or four years. [315] Certainly, the economic improvement in 1888 was very marked in comparison with the previous year, although it resulted almost entirely from the steep rise in livestock prices after June that followed closely the upswing of the British trade cycle. [316] Graziers, having bought cheaply in the spring, reaped windfall profits by selling dearly during the autumn and winter, while stockbreeders also did well. But because of the deficient harvest and the continued low prices of butter and grain, recovery in the dairy and tillage sectors was incomplete. [317]

Throughout 1889 Cork farmers had reason to regret their failure to maintain their cattle herds when livestock prices tumbled after mid-1884. [318] Although the decline in the number of dry cattle from

[311] P.R.O.I., ref. no. 978, Midleton papers, Letter book, 1886–8: J. P. Fitzgerald to R. K. McBride, 1 May 1888, p. 1143.

[312] *C.C.*, 10 July 1888.

[313] *C.E.*, 13 Sept. 1888.

[314] Kenmare papers, Letter book, 1887–91: M. Leonard to W. Bentham, 31 Aug. 1888, p. 88. See also *C.E.*, 13, 22 Sept. 1888.

[315] P.R.O.I., ref. no. 978, Midleton papers, Letter book, 1888–90: J. P. Fitzgerald to R. K. McBride, 13 Sept. 1888, p. 75.

[316] By the end of the year, store cattle had risen in price by as much as 20 per cent, and sheep by as much as 30 per cent throughout the south of Ireland, but prices increased less sharply in Dublin (*The Times*, 2 Jan. 1889).

[317] Irish butter was 12 to 15 per cent cheaper during the peak-producing months of April to November 1888 than in the same period of 1887, although this loss was more than offset by the gain in output over the previous year of major drought (*C.C.*, 28 Jan. 1889).

[318] Ibid., 12, 21 Mar., 9 Apr. 1889; *C.E.*, 25 Apr. 1889.

227,000 in 1884 to 208,000 by 1888 was not all that serious, demand clearly outpaced supply until 1890, when the number of horned stock reached and surpassed the level of 1884.[319] Carefully hedging their bets against a rising market, farmers refrained from selling for as long as possible in 1889.[320] Livestock prices soared to such heights that James Penrose Fitzgerald declared in August, 'Agricultural prospects are better in this country at present than they have been for the last 10 years'.[321] Glowing reports of extremely satisfied farmers came from the local fairs.[322] Only the graziers and the cattle dealers saw fit to complain, and they received scant sympathy.[323] The harvest was the most bountiful of the decade and gave further cause for elation.[324] Even the price of butter inched forward. All factors considered, this was probably the best season enjoyed by Irish agriculture between the prosperous days of the early 1870s and the turn of the century, and it provided the driving force for the winding down of the land war.

Economic conditions remained bright during the first several months of 1890. Brisk sales of cattle and sheep at fancy prices were reported from local markets until September.[325] By autumn, however, the outlook was beginning to turn bleak once again. A long downward slide in livestock prices, slow at first, but remorseless and lasting almost four years, began to assert itself.[326] Early in September, Dowdall Brothers, the butter-export firm, reported what Cork dairy farmers already knew only too well:

The summer months now closing have shown a lower range in price for butter than the average of the past thirty years.... The public in this generation have been seldom supplied so abundantly and cheaply as during the past three months.[327]

Cold weather and heavy rains during July and August damaged the

---

[319] *Irish agricultural statistics for 1884* [C 4489], H.C. 1884–5, lxxxv, 1, p. 50; *Irish agricultural statistics for 1888* [C 5785], H.C. 1889, lxxxiii, 215, p. 44; *Irish agricultural statistics for 1890*, p. 60.

[320] P.R.O.I., ref. no. 978, Midleton papers, Letter book, 1888–90: J. P. Fitzgerald to P. Penn-Gaskell, 21 Mar. 1889, p. 347; *C.C.*, 16 Apr. 1889.

[321] P.R.O.I., ref. no. 978, Midleton papers, Letter book, 1888–90: J. P. Fitzgerald to R. K. McBride, 14 Aug. 1889, p. 515.

[322] *C.C.*, 16 May, 4, 11 June, 13 Aug., 16 Sept., 10 Oct. 1889.

[323] Ibid., 19 Dec. 1889.

[324] *Irish agricultural statistics for 1891*, pp. 52, 57.

[325] *C.C.*, 9, 22 Apr., 27 May, 3, 19 June, 15, 16 July 1890.

[326] Doneraile papers, Letter book, 1889–91: M. H. Franks to Lord Castletown, 16 Oct. 1890, pp. 621–4; Barrington, 'Agricultural prices', p. 252.

[327] *C.C.*, 2 Sept. 1890.

hay and grain crops,[328] but the worst feature of the harvest of 1890 was the partial failure of the potato crop. Conditions varied widely from place to place. Only a quarter of the crop was blighted in the Fermoy district, but as much as half or more was destroyed in all the coastal districts.[329] Although local nationalists warned of mass starvation in many places unless government aid were forthcoming, it seems well established that only extreme southwest Cork, from Glandore Harbour across to Bantry Bay, was threatened by famine.[330] There was great distress and semi-starvation in this region during the winter.[331] It was substantially mitigated, however, by the revival of the fishing industry in the districts of Baltimore, Unionhall, and Castletownsend as a result of the philanthropic work of Baroness Burdett-Coutts since 1879.[332] Far more importantly, during the winter the government advanced £522,000 in repayable seed loans and for urgent relief works in order to meet the most pressing needs in southwest Cork and the other congested districts along the western coast of Ireland.[333]

The partial loss of the potato crop was a relatively minor setback for the farmers in the rest of County Cork. It produced no crisis in any way comparable to the one associated with a similar failure in 1879. The reasons for this lay in two striking differences in circumstances between 1879 and 1890. In the first place, the two seasons before 1879 had been extremely unfavourable for the farming classes, whereas the two seasons before 1890 were relatively prosperous. Secondly, the crisis of 1879 had been aggravated by low livestock prices, with farmers driving their cattle to one fair after another without being able to sell them, whereas young stock remained almost as dear during the winter of 1890–1 as they had been in 1889.[334] Land agents complained that farmers greatly exaggerated their difficulties in 1890. 'A few [are] grumbling about the times,' Matthew Franks told Lord Castletown in October, 'but that is only an echo of what they read in the nationalist press; the constant wet has naturally done some harm to crops, & cattle & sheep have not

---

[328] *Irish agricultural statistics for 1891*, pp. 52, 57.

[329] *C.C.*, 3 Sept. 1890; *C.E.*, 8 Oct. 1890.

[330] For detailed reports of conditions in southwest Cork, see *C.E.*, 5, 29 July, 1, 5, 6, 9, 13 Aug. 1890.

[331] In remote Goleen and Crookhaven, there was 'absolute famine in its saddest and most hideous form' (ibid., 31 Dec. 1890). See also ibid., 10 Jan., 5 Feb. 1891.

[332] Ibid., 6 Aug. 1890.

[333] S.P.O., C.S.O., Registered papers, 1891, no. 17944: 'Expenditure on relief of distress, 1879 and 1890', 13 July 1891.

[334] *C.C.*; 22 Jan. 1891.

thriven . . . , but there is not that widespread havoc so much written about.'[335] On the whole, the season was not much below average and was certainly no worse than that of 1888.

The seasons of 1891 and 1892, however, were almost as damaging to the economic position of the farming classes as those of 1884 and 1885 which had led to a resurgence of the agrarian agitation. The pattern of a long winter followed by a hard, dry spring that had been so common a climatic phenomenon of the 1880s recurred in 1891.[336] The coldness and the intense drought from January to June, when total rainfall was less than half of normal, brought a famine in grass and compounded the feeding difficulties arising from the rain-damaged hay crop of the previous season.[337] The price of butter remained as low as ever, even though the deficiency in Cork Butter Market supplies because of the drought amounted to no less than 33,000 firkins by early September.[338] Cattle were practically unsaleable except at wretched prices throughout most of the year.[339] The only bright spot was the grain harvest, which, with the exception of hay, was more abundant than for many years. 'Your people should do well this autumn,' James Penrose Fitzgerald cheerily informed R. K. McBride in November, 'as they have had a good crop of oats & are getting a splendid price for it, the highest for many years.' As Fitzgerald himself admitted, however, store cattle and sheep were 'practically unsaleable',[340] and this factor combined with the deficiency and cheapness of butter to obliterate the real and psychological effects of a good harvest.[341]

The familiar scenario of bad weather and slack demand was repeated in 1892. The spring was again backward, with cold easterly winds, an absence of rain which retarded vegetation, and rising feeding costs until far into May.[342] Once warmer weather arrived

---

[335] Doneraile papers, Letter book, 1889–91: M. H. Franks to Lord Castletown, 16 Oct. 1890, pp. 621–4.

[336] P.R.O.I., ref. no. 978, Midleton papers, Letter book, 1890–2: J. P. Fitzgerald to R. K. McBride, 28 Apr. 1891, p. 487.

[337] Ibid.: Fitzgerald to McBride, 27 May 1891, p. 560; Kenmare papers, Letter book, 1887–91: M. Leonard to S. J. Robinson, 15 June 1891, p. 796; *C.C.*, 2 May 1891.

[338] *C.C.*, 8 Sept. 1891. See also *C.E.*, 31 Dec. 1891.

[339] Kenmare papers, Letter book, 1887–91: M. Leonard to earl of Kenmare, 23 June 1891, p. 806; *C.C.*, 7 July, 4, 11, 20 Aug., 26 Oct., 17 Nov., 15 Dec. 1891.

[340] P.R.O.I., ref. no. 978, Midleton papers, Letter book, 1890–2: J. P. Fitzgerald to R. K. McBride, 10 Nov. 1891, p. 795.

[341] *C.C.*, 14 Jan. 1892.

[342] Ibid., 22 Mar., 4 May 1892; P.R.O.I., ref. no. 978, Midleton papers, Letter book, 1890–2: J. P. Fitzgerald to T. St L. Bland, 3 May 1892, p. 1080.

and grass came up, livestock prices failed to respond. The demand at the August fair in Bandon was 'almost nil',[343] and farmers were sorely disappointed by the extremely low prices at the September fair in Clonakilty:

It may be stated without fear of contradiction that store cattle and calves fetched only half the price [they did] at this time last year. This year's calves were bought at from 30s. to 35s., and yearlings from £2 10s. to £3, and two year olds from £4 to £5.[344]

A drought in July was succeeded by the rainiest August in twenty-eight years, with more than double the average monthly rainfall.[345] Both the Blackwater and the Bride rivers overflowed their banks, and there were severe floods and heavy crop losses in all lowland districts.[346] Surprisingly, the harvest was above average, with the exception again of hay, the yield of which was extremely light.[347] But farmers hardly escaped without loss, for harvesting was very costly. 'What with this and the wretched price going for stock,' Matthew Franks was told in late September, 'it is no doubt hard for some farmers to get money to pay rents.'[348] This was to understate the difficulty. Maurice Leonard stressed the fact that on the Kenmare estates, he had to 'distrain for every penny that is got in'.[349] With landlords again frequently neglecting to give temporary abatements, because tenants 'only spend the ab[atemen]t given in the next public house',[350] a revival of agrarian unrest might well have been expected. But the disastrous split in the Parnellite party in December 1890 had shattered the national land movement, and the remedial legislation passed since 1885 had extracted much of the sting from Irish economic grievances.

Between 1885 and 1891 the conservatives groped towards a permanent solution to the exasperating Irish land question by passing three land-purchase acts, in the hope of transforming a substantial fraction of all discontented tenants and National

[343] *C.C.*, 4 Aug. 1892. See also ibid., 31 May, 16 June, 3 Aug. 1892.

[344] Ibid., 6 Sept. 1892. See also ibid., 11 Oct., 9, 15, 17 Nov., 12 Dec. 1892.

[345] Ibid., 2 Sept. 1892.

[346] Ibid., 25, 26 Aug. 1892.

[347] Ibid., 8, 26 Sept. 1892.

[348] Doneraile papers, Letter book, 1892–5: G. Levinge to M. H. Franks, 26 Sept. 1892, pp. 43–5.

[349] Kenmare papers, Letter book, 1891–3: M. Leonard to Mr Douglas, 3 Jan. 1893, pp. 415–16.

[350] Ibid.: Leonard to Viscount Castlerosse, 17 Dec. 1892, pp. 384–5. See also Doneraile papers, Letter book, 1892–5: G. Levinge to M. H. Franks, 12 Nov. 1892, pp. 118–19.

Leaguers into solid peasant proprietors and upright, law-abiding citizens. It was well known that ownership of their farms had made the French peasantry peculiarly tenacious of law and order, and it was confidently predicted that the same relationship would develop in Ireland. [351] A total of £10 million was appropriated under the Ashbourne act of 1885 and the legislation extending it in 1888. [352] This modest sum was greatly augmented by Balfour's act of 1891, which set aside an additional £33 million in guaranteed loans. [353] For the first time, it became possible in 1885 for a tenant to borrow the entire purchase price, which he was to repay in annuities at 4 per cent interest over forty-nine years; his annuity could not exceed his former rent. [354] The idea of compulsory sales was raised in connection with the land-purchase bills enacted in 1888 and 1891, but on both occasions the idea foundered upon the rocks of strenuous landlord opposition, and the legislation left the value of land to find its own level. [355] Only a very small proportion of Cork farmers took advantage of these three land-purchase acts. In slightly less than eight years between August 1885 and March 1893, only about 1,100 tenants became peasant proprietors, paying an average of fifteen years' purchase of their rents to do so and acquiring somewhat less than 68,000 acres. [356]

While there was a general scramble from the north of Ireland for the first £5 million granted under the Ashbourne act, the reaction in the south generally ranged from complete indifference to outright hostility. From the beginning, local branches of the National League often did all in their power to discourage purchases on landlord terms. When the Kingston tenants were offered an opportunity to buy their farms in September 1885, the Mitchelstown branch of the league ordered them not to pay more than twelve years' purchase. [357] Michael Davitt came from Dublin in order to dampen the ardour for sales among some of the more prosperous Kingston tenants. [358] Davitt's position on the land question was unique in that, almost alone among Irish leaders, he favoured the nationalization of the land along the lines of the American radical Henry George. 'The

---

[351] See William B. Leslie's letter in *C.C.*, 11 Dec. 1888.

[352] 48 & 49 Vict., c. 73, ss. 2, 24; 51 & 52 Vict., c. 49, s. 1.

[353] Curtis, *Coercion & conciliation*, p. 351.

[354] 48 & 49 Vict., c. 73, ss. 2, 4.

[355] *C.C.*, 20 Sept. 1888; 31 Mar., 15 May 1891; Curtis, *Coercion & conciliation*, pp. 345–6, 350.

[356] *Report of the Irish land commissioners for the period from 22nd August 1891 to 31st March 1893* [C 7056], H.C. 1893–4, xxiv, 1, p. 68.

[357] *C.E.*, 12 Sept. 1885.

[358] *C.C.*, 11 Oct. 1885.

landlord must be bought out by the state as a general economic nuisance, as an incubus no longer compatible with healthy agriculture or social progress', declared Davitt in November 1887. 'The settlement of the land question must be made between the Irish state and the Irish landlords.'[359] Davitt's colleagues at least agreed with him that home rule must precede a final solution of the land question, and that the conservatives' remedial measures were really intended to uncouple the locomotive of the land from the home rule train. As Tim Healy declared at a meeting of the central branch of the league in Dublin in September 1888,

Until a great treaty of peace had been made between England and Ireland, no Irish farmer ought to make a treaty of peace on his own account, and 'the man who purchased under Ashbourne's act was making a treaty of peace behind the backs of the nation as a whole'.[360]

Of course, many farmers could not live up to these high standards of patriotic self-denial, especially when agricultural prospects improved temporarily from mid-1888. And the influential local clergy frequently refused to draw a hard and fast line against all purchases. Indeed, the extent of clerical involvement was one of the most striking features of land purchase during this period. Fr O'Connell acted as the tenants' negotiator in the sale of the earl of Shannon's Castlemartyr estate in 1888, and Fr Lucey served in the same capacity in the purchase of Shannon's Clonakilty property.[361] The local parish priest obtained very satisfactory terms of purchase for the tenants of the Butcher estate near Banteer.[362] The parish priest of Kingwilliamstown, Fr O'Riordan, was instrumental in arranging the sale of two Plan estates in his district— Captain T. A. Townsend's in May 1889 and Clement Dunscombe's in December 1890.[363] In the protracted negotiations leading to the purchase of H. B. O'Sullivan's estate in December 1891, Fr O'Donovan played a crucial role.[364]

The tension between local clerical opinion favourable to sales and the opposition of the national leaders surfaced briefly in September 1889, when the purchase of the entire 16,600-acre estate of the earl of Egmont was announced. Egmont sold his Kanturk property at

[359] Ibid., 18 Nov. 1887.

[360] *Freeman's Journal*, 26 Sept. 1888.

[361] *C.C.*, 30 Oct. 1888; *C.E.*, 30 Oct. 1888, 3 Jan. 1889; *The Times*, 29 Jan. 1890.

[362] *C.E.*, 22 Nov. 1888, 23 Jan. 1889.

[363] *C.C.*, 23 May 1889; Barry papers, Letter book, 1890–1: H. H. Barry to C. Dunscombe, 9 Dec. 1890, p. 956; Barry to Rev. O'Riordan, 27 Dec. 1890, p. 1053.

[364] *C.C.*, 26 July 1890, 12 Dec. 1891.

the average rates of fourteen years' purchase of the non-judicial and seventeen years' purchase of the judicial rents, and his Churchtown estate at somewhat lower rates. [365] Lord Castletown's sub-agent was not alone in thinking that these rates were '*absurdly low*' and liable to spoil the chances of sales on other estates at higher ones. 'It is quite ridiculous,' commented the worried Nicholl, 'as the property is said to [be] one of the very best, if not *the* best, in all Ireland. The rents are very low and well paid, & the buildings [were] done by the landlord.' [366] Egmont's tenants obviously thought that they had concluded a shrewd bargain and did not greatly mind giving about £250,000 in order to rid themselves of the Percevals forever. Michael Davitt almost went into a rage, however, when he learned that the tenants and the Rev. Cornelius Buckley, C.C., Buttevant, had thanked Egmont for agreeing to pocket 'the wee sum of £250,000'. [367] Stung by Davitt's rebuke, Fr Buckley asked Davitt to look at the sales from the point of view of a sober-minded farmer who had often gone to the estate office with less than the full rent. He also reminded Davitt that Egmont's tenants had promised publicly that

far from sitting down under our own fig trees, we would in freedom support with pen and purse every oppressed body of tenantry on the adjoining estates if the thumb of the landlord or the agent was not taken from off their throats. [368]

Davitt remained unforgiving, however, and accused the Egmont tenants of having in effect stabbed their comrades in the back by their use of the Ashbourne act, which he roundly denounced as 'a gigantic swindle of public funds as well as an anti-home rule enterprise'. [369]

Although many Cork farmers, to Davitt's dismay, showed interest in purchase, it was an interest tempered by the search for bargains. Many landlords ready to sell on their own terms would have agreed with James Penrose Fitzgerald, who said, 'There are so many incumbered owners who are being forced by mortgagees & others to sell at ruinous rates that tenants don't understand being asked a fair price'. [370] As a result, a large number of contemplated sales

[365] *C.E.*, 2, 7, 28 Sept. 1889.
[366] Doneraile papers, Letter book, 1888–9: L. D. Nicholl to M. H. Franks, 4 Sept. 1889, pp. 964–5.
[367] M. Davitt to Rev. C. Buckley, 26 Sept. 1889, quoted in *C.C.*, 1 Oct. 1889.
[368] Rev. Buckley to Davitt, 27 Sept. 1889, quoted ibid.
[369] Davitt to Rev. Buckley, 28 Sept. 1889, quoted ibid.
[370] P.R.O.I., ref. no. 978, Midleton papers, Letter book, 1888–90: J. P. Fitzgerald to R. K. McBride, 7 Sept. 1888, p. 72.

never materialized. The earl of Bandon sought twenty-two years' purchase of the judicial rents for a portion of his property in south-west Cork, but his tenants there offered only thirteen years' purchase of the valuation. 'Ye gods, 22 years' purchase!' exclaimed one observer. 'I am informed the gross rental on the Bandon estate is about £20,000 per annum. At 22 years' purchase that would mean £440,000. Extraordinary if the tenants don't take immediate steps to put that trifle of cash in his lordship's pocket.'[371] Miss E. M. O'Leary offered to sell her property near Macroom at seventeen years' purchase of the judicial rents, but her tenants bid only thirteen, thinking that she would 'climb down further, as she always treated her tenants fairly'.[372] When Sir Augustus Warren suggested a sale at twenty years' purchase of the valuation to the tenants of his 7,700-acre estate in the same district, he was promptly turned down.[373] Doherty and Jones, attempting to sell the Fitzpatrick property at eighteen years' purchase of the current rents, found that the tenants

evinced, whether real or assumed, a total indifference to becoming peasant proprietors, some even preferring not to buy; for the best land in or near the town of Macroom, the highest offer was 16 years, whilst for the Bantry & Ballyvourney portion[s] none exceeded 13.[374]

Viscount Castlerosse wished to sell his Limerick estate and was willing to remit the one year's rent in arrears and another year's rent pending the collection of the first instalment of the purchase money.[375] Maurice Leonard told him that the property was well worth twenty years' purchase, and that 'it would be simply throwing it away for nothing if you were to part with it for any sum less'.[376] At that price, said the tenants, Lord Castlerosse could keep it.[377]

The interest of neither landlords nor tenants in land purchase was increased by Balfour's act of 1891. The new legislation provided for the reimbursement of the landlords in government stock bearing interest at only $2\frac{3}{4}$ per cent.[378] This provision alone was a serious barrier to sales during the 1890s, because of the fear of depreciation

[371] *C.E.*, 2 Feb. 1889. See also ibid., 30 Jan. 1889.

[372] Ibid., 11 Jan. 1889.

[373] Ibid., 16 Jan. 1889.

[374] Doherty papers, Letter book, 1889–90: Doherty and Jones to H. P. Fitzpatrick, 3 Apr. 1889, pp. 75–6.

[375] Kenmare papers, Letter book, 1888–9: M. Leonard to Very Rev. Canon Scully, 16 Feb. 1889, pp. 196–7.

[376] Ibid.: Leonard to Viscount Castlerosse, 31 Jan. 1889, pp. 186–9.

[377] Ibid., Letter book, 1887–91: Leonard to Very Rev. Canon Scully, 23 Nov. 1889, p. 299.

[378] 54 & 55 Vict., c. 48, s. 1.

and the poor performance of the government's stock between 1891 and 1896.[379] James Penrose Fitzgerald doubted in February 1892 whether R. K. McBride would still consider sales now that the funds under the Ashbourne act were exhausted: 'The new act does not give the landlord such good terms, as he is not paid in cash but in land stock which will stand below par'.[380] With the approach of a general election in 1892, and the prospect of a Gladstonian victory and home rule, tenants showed even less interest than usual in land purchase. On the Warren estate near Midleton, where the landlord offered to sell at from seventeen to eighteen years' purchase of the judicial rents, one of the many tenants who refrained from bidding stated in October 1891 that 'it would be better to have the tenants wait until after the general election, when they could secure better terms'.[381]

Also curtailing the interest in land purchase between 1885 and 1892 was the availability of alternative relief in the form of judicial rent reductions, coupled with the deadening effect of unfavourable economic conditions during more than two-thirds of this period. Before 1886 the bitter experience of tenants in Cork and throughout most of the country had gradually diminished the business of the land courts. The courts had first overreacted to the improvement in economic conditions beginning in 1881 and then underreacted to their deterioration beginning in the summer of 1884. Judicial reductions came to reflect the deepening depression more adequately in 1886. By early 1887 abatements of nearly 40 per cent for the judicial term of fifteen years had become typical, the backlog of unheard cases was enormous, and the landed classes were beginning to cry out in horror at the thought of losing so much income.[382] The Cork land agent H. H. Townsend had by then come to advocate the shortening of the judicial term to five years or less and the fixing of rents on the basis of a sliding scale of prices. Townsend warned in late April 1887 that unless

an elastic system of the kind be introduced, a remedy will not be found against a recurrence of the present state of things, and against tenants fixing rates they consider they are entitled to themselves, making unreasonable demands, resisted by landlords and supported by boycotting, outrages, and the Plan of Campaign.[383]

[379] Curtis, *Coercion & conciliation*, p. 355.
[380] P.R.O.I., ref. no. 978, Midleton papers, Letter book, 1890-2: J. P. Fitzgerald to Rev. D. Lynch, 16 Feb. 1892, p. 913.
[381] *C.E.*, 23 Oct. 1891. See also *C.C.*, 12 May 1892.
[382] *C.E.*, 27 Jan., 26 Mar. 1887.
[383] *C.C.*, 28 Apr. 1887.

Such a system of produce rents had been recommended by the Cowper commission earlier in the year only to be rejected by Balfour and the other members of the cabinet, who merely accepted with reluctance the commission's recommendation to admit leaseholders to the courts. [384] Since judicial reductions in rents, however, averaged no less than 38 per cent during the first four months of 1887, as compared with only about 20 per cent between August 1881 and August 1886, a compelling case could be made for the revision of judicial rents fixed before 1887. [385] Even Archbishop William J. Walsh of Dublin joined the chorus of dissent against the government's opposition to the revision of such rents. [386] Although the landowners of Cork and many other counties protested vehemently, [387] the government was ultimately forced to empower the land commissioners in the land act of 1887 to revise the judicial rents of 1881–5 in accord with prevailing local prices, but only for a period of three years. [388] The average reductions in Ireland as a whole under this controversial provision fell from 11·5 per cent in 1887 to only 5 per cent in 1889, when prices recovered temporarily. [389]

Cork leaseholders, long denied relief from the depression, benefited most from the 1887 land act. Some 4,150 of them entered the local land courts between August 1887 and March 1893 and received reductions averaging 25·5 per cent. [390] Yearly tenants fared almost as well. Over the same period, about 3,020 of them obtained abatements averaging 23·9 per cent. [391] Probably because of the general bitterness of landlord-tenant relations during this period, fair-rent agreements were no longer as popular as in the early 1880s. Only 1,365 tenants reached amicable settlements with their landlords in this way, as compared with 2,337 between August 1881 and August 1887, even though the average reduction of 24·1 per cent was fully equivalent to what was obtained in court. [392] There is little doubt that the 1887 land act was a potent force in the winding down of the land war in Cork. By March 1893 the number of judicial rents fixed under all methods had reached nearly 10,500, bringing the total since 1881 to more than 15,000. About 40 per cent of the tenants

[384] Curtis, *Coercion & conciliation*, p. 336.
[385] *Cowper comm. report*, p. 6; *C.E.*, 19 July 1887.
[386] *C.E.*, 19 July 1887.
[387] *C.C.*, 17 Aug. 1887.
[388] 50 & 51 Vict., c. 33, s. 29.
[389] *C.C.*, 8 Jan. 1890.
[390] *Report of the Irish land commissioners for the period from 22nd August 1891 to 31st March 1893*, pp. 26, 33.
[391] Ibid., pp. 22, 31.
[392] Ibid., pp. 35, 37.

of the county and roughly the same proportion of its total acreage had by then been affected by the legislation concerning rents, which had been reduced since 1881 by an average of 21·8 per cent. [393]

The notorious O'Shea divorce case and its disastrous repercussions administered the finishing stroke to the Plan of Campaign and to the second phase of the land war in Ireland. In November 1890 Captain W. H. O'Shea's case for divorce on the grounds of his wife's adultery with Parnell finally went to trial. By the time it ended in a decree *nisi*, with the charges declared proven, the public revelations of the squalid alleged details of Parnell's long, illicit affair with Mrs O'Shea had largely destroyed his leadership position and political career. [394] If the verdict rescued the conservative government from certain humiliation at Westminster during the winter of 1890–1, [395] it also probably spared them yet another round of agrarian agitation in Ireland, as the economic situation there was rapidly deteriorating once again. Parnell's adultery scandalized and outraged the English nonconformist conscience, an electoral cornerstone of the liberal party, and thereby threatened to rupture the alliance of Gladstone's liberals with the Irish party. [396] Gladstone's famous letter calling upon Parnell to retire from the leadership appeared in *The Times* on 26 November 1890, and within a few days Archbishops Croke and Walsh, as well as Dillon and O'Brien, openly declared against Parnell, who refused to retire voluntarily. [397] These developments led to the bitter meetings in Committee Room Fifteen of the house of commons that ended on 6 December with the fateful split in Irish party ranks. While some twenty-six members remained behind to support Parnell, forty-five others withdrew from the room and elected Justin McCarthy as their chairman. [398] Anticipating a move that undoubtedly would otherwise have come from the Parnellites, the anti-Parnellites took steps to freeze the party funds, amounting to £50,000, in a Paris bank. [399] When Dillon and O'Brien tried desperately but failed to bring about a reconciliation with Parnell at Boulogne in January and February 1891, the freezing of the Paris fund became a crippling blow to the agrarian agitation. [400]

Once the Boulogne negotiations had failed, the agrarian agitation progressively disintegrated. As the Parnellite and anti-Parnellite

[393] Ibid., p. 51.
[394] Lyons, *Fall of Parnell*, pp. 38–9.
[395] Curtis, *Coercion & conciliation*, p. 308.
[396] J. F. Glaser, 'Parnell's fall and the nonconformist conscience' in *I.H.S.*, xii, no. 45 (Mar. 1960), pp. 119–38.
[397] Lyons, *Fall of Parnell*, pp. 93–4, 113–17.
[398] Ibid., pp. 148–50.   [399] Ibid., pp. 152–4.
[400] Ibid., p. 244, and Chapters VIII and IX.

factions of the party quarrelled bitterly and in public over finances and the freezing of the Paris fund (public opinion in the south of Ireland, and especially the clerical segment of it, was strongly anti-Parnellite in sympathy), [401] the tenants on the few remaining Plan estates rapidly lost whatever enthusiasm remained for the continuation of the struggle. [402] Their loss of confidence deepened when the Parnellite John Redmond declared in late April 1891 that the Plan of Campaign could no longer be sustained. The split, said Redmond, made it impossible to obtain money sufficient to support the evicted tenants, and the anti-Parnellites' publication of the accounts enabled the landlords to 'calculate with mathematical precision when the tenants would be at their mercy'. [403] As early as February, the split had precipitated the complete collapse of resistance on A. H. Smith-Barry's Cashel estate, [404] where the tenants had originally adopted the Plan at William O'Brien's urging in order to show their solidarity with the Ponsonby tenants soon after the formation of the notorious syndicate almost two years before. [405] Smith-Barry's tenants in and around the town of Tipperary, where an unusually bitter fight had raged for several months, held out until May, but then they too began to settle on the landlord's none-too-generous terms. [406] The surrendering tenants pointed out that 'since the division among the Irish parliamentary party, a strong feeling has grown up in the minds of the tenants here that the struggle with their landlord had become hopeless, and that instead of ruining him, they were ruining themselves'. [407] The once-celebrated town and mart of 'New Tipperary', William O'Brien's proud achievement, built at a cost of nearly £40,000 for the accommodation of shopkeepers and other tenants evicted from premises in the 'old town', lay totally deserted by October. [408]

In Cork as well, the last embers of the agrarian agitation were dying. The Plan on the Massy estate had evidently fallen apart by

[401] *C.E.*, 9, 17 Mar., 4 May 1891.

[402] Of the eighteen Irish estates still involved in the Plan of Campaign in May 1891, four were located in County Cork: Arthur Langford's, W. N. Leader's, T. R. Marmion's, and C. W. T. Ponsonby's (S.P.O., Crime Branch special, secret/13408: 'List of estates on which the Plan of Campaign was originally established and on which settlements have not as yet been completed', 19 May 1891).

[403] *C.E.*, 22 Apr. 1891.   [404] *C.C.*, 10, 19 Feb. 1891.

[405] Ibid., 25 June 1889.

[406] Ibid., 13 May, 6, 19 June 1891; *C.E.*, 29 May 1891.

[407] *C.E.*, 1 June 1891.

[408] The master of the rolls, at the suit of Smith-Barry, ordered the removal of the 'William O'Brien arcade' (*C.C.*, 2 Oct. 1891). On party finances, see *C.E.*, 18, 25 June 1891.

late April, as the tenants threatened with eviction were making separate arrangements with the agent.[409] About the same time, William N. Leader's tenants at both Curraghs and Meelin finally came to an agreement that, under the altered circumstances, could not be regarded as unfavourable to them.[410] Yet the tenants complained in June that the terms 'would have been better only for the unfortunate split in the national ranks . . . brought about by the misconduct and treachery of him who should be our defender and protector, Mr Parnell'.[411] On the Ponsonby estate, the landlord syndicate succeeded in breaking and overthrowing the Plan. While their leaders held out hopes of the release of the Paris fund and gave no encouragement to renewed attempts to reach a settlement,[412] a sizeable fraction of the Ponsonby tenants asked Smith-Barry in mid-October to send a duly accredited agent to Youghal for negotiations concerning purchase under clause thirteen of the 1891 land act.[413] The syndicate's terms were very stiff, and the tenants tried with little success to have them softened.[414] Canon Keller deplored the exorbitant terms in January 1892; he declared that if the tenants yielded to landlord dictation under the pressure of need, they would 'no more be free agents than the man who sees the highwayman's blunderbuss levelled at his head'.[415] The division came in late January and early February, when 103 of the 240-odd tenants signed agreements to buy their holdings at Smith-Barry's price.[416] The non-signing campaigners shared their bitterness and dis-illusionment with the rest of the betrayed evicted tenants of Ireland. Where, many of them asked reproachfully, 'are now the members of parliament and others who induced them to give up their farms, under promises which have not been redeemed, and who now leave them to their fate'?[417]

---

[409] *C.E.*, 30 Apr. 1891.

[410] The terms were as follows: the Meelin tenants were to pay one and one-half years' rent in lieu of all arrears up to 29 September 1890, and to apply jointly to the recorder's court in order to have judicial rents fixed; the Curraghs tenants were to pay two years' rent in lieu of arrears and to buy their farms at fourteen years' purchase (ibid., 5 May 1891).

[411] Ibid., 17 June 1891. [412] *C.C.*, 14 Oct. 1891.

[413] Ibid., 16, 20 Oct. 1891.

[414] The syndicate insisted upon the payment of one and one-quarter to one and one-half years' rent in lieu of arrears, and upon sales at seventeen and nineteen years' purchase of the non-judicial and judicial rents respectively (*C.E.*, 4, 18 Nov., 22 Dec. 1891; *C.C.*, 17 Nov., 3, 17 Dec. 1891).

[415] Rev. Canon Keller to Cork Evicted Tenants' Association, 20 Jan. 1892, quoted in *C.C.*, 22 Jan. 1892.

[416] Ibid., 28 Jan., 5 Feb., 1 Mar., 28 Sept. 1892.

[417] Ibid., 10 Feb. 1892.

CONCLUSION

~~~~~~

EVEN THOUGH THE land war produced no final solution to the land question, it greatly hastened the eventual disintegration of Irish landlordism. Inclement seasons, poor crops, and low cattle and butter prices between 1877 and 1879 reversed temporarily the economic progress of the farming classes. Farm profits quickly evaporated. Many small and some large tenants went bankrupt after exhausting their credit with local banks and other lenders of money. Deposits in Irish joint-stock banks, a sensitive indicator of agricultural conditions, declined from a peak of £32,815,000 in 1876 to a low of £28,289,000 in 1881, or by 14 per cent. It was not until 1889 that deposits again reached and surpassed the level of 1876.[1] Under these unfavourable circumstances, the payment of the customary rent became an unacceptable burden. Most Cork farmers no doubt could have shouldered such a burden, but only if they had been willing to surrender to their landlords a substantial portion of the material gains made since 1851. Many tenants would have been compelled to make this sacrifice had not the Land League arisen to direct a national campaign of resistance, for landlords were extremely reluctant to make meaningful concessions.

Agrarian agitation originated in the western counties under conditions of severe hardship in 1879 but gathered real momentum in Cork only after economic prospects had brightened considerably during the summer and autumn of 1880. What followed was a militant assault upon the traditional order which blended elements of 'agrarian trade unionism', civil disobedience, and violence into a great social upheaval. Farmers heartily joined in public denunciations of such rack-renting, evicting landlords as William Bence Jones and such land grabbers as Jeremiah Hegarty, both of whom were subjected to rigorous boycotts. Determined resistance was offered to eviction parties, and evicted tenants forcibly retook possession of their holdings. Urged by the league to pay no more

[1] 'Irish joint stock banks, 1800–1901' in Coyne, *Ire.*, p. 127.

377

rent than the government valuation of their farms, tenants organized massive rent strikes, of which the one on the Kingston estate in 1881 was the most prominent. Landlords responded with writs and ejectment decrees and sought to frustrate the leagye's designs through the operations of the Emergency Committee and the Property Defence Association. But the concerted action of their tenants generally forced them to capitulate or compromise. What made the league such a formidable foe was the enforcement of its programme through a reign of terror directed primarily against those who co-operated with the landlord system—land grabbers, caretakers of evicted farms, bailiffs, process servers, and farmers who secretly paid rent. Most of this agrarian terrorism lacked permanent organization, but at least one large and well-drilled secret society was very active in northwest Cork during 1881.

Without this unprecedented wave of agrarian violence, it is extremely doubtful that Gladstone's conciliatory land act of 1881, with its drastic curtailment of property rights, would have been approved by the British parliament. For all its limitations, this gesture of appeasement drove the first heavy nail into the coffin of Irish landlordism. The force of law was given to the three Fs, thus creating a situation of co-ownership—a kind of halfway house between contractual landlord-tenant relations and peasant proprietorship. The most serious weaknesses of this legislation from the tenants' point of view—the omission of leaseholders, the unattractive purchase clauses, and the absence of special provision for smallholders—were not exploited immediately for a combination of political and economic reasons. Gravely alarmed that the league, under the façade of testing the land act, really intended to destroy all possibility of agrarian peace, the government jailed Parnell and other nationalist leaders in October 1881. When they responded by issuing the ill-fated No Rent Manifesto, the government at once suppressed the Land League. Although rent strikes and terrorism persisted for several months, the agitation, deprived of national leadership and central organization, rapidly lost its militancy. Since Parnell agreed to abandon the agrarian struggle in April 1882, its continuation would have been extremely difficult under any circumstances. Fair weather, good crops, exceedingly favourable cattle prices, and to a much lesser extent, the benefits of the recent land act assured a pause in the bitter conflict.

As for their rental incomes, landowners absorbed the land act with only slight loss, for less than 10 per cent of the total rent paid by Cork tenants was judicially fixed under its provisions. The rents of leaseholders, who formed the majority of tenants in the county, tended to remain at their old levels. Nevertheless, landlords painfully realized that an irremediable breach had been made in their legal position. They angrily scorned all assurances that the ultimate limits of concession had been reached and fully expected tenants' appetites to increase. Agitation and state intervention dried up their sources of credit, and landowners were faced with ominous threats of foreclosure or, alternatively, insistent demands for higher interest rates from skittish mortgagees. The market value of their estates declined enormously. Few capitalists were willing to invest any longer in the purchase of land in Ireland, and those who were, invariably expected great bargains. Sales to tenants were practically out of the question at this stage, since farmers correctly anticipated that better terms would soon be forthcoming. This depression in the land market inclined many landlords to view peasant proprietorship, at least on a limited scale, much more favourably than they had a few years earlier. Samuel Hussey went so far as to call the conservatives' land purchase bill of 1885 'our last chance of safety in Ireland'. [2]

Subversion of the traditional order expanded during the second phase of the land war. The deterioration in economic conditions between 1884 and 1888, compounded of hard, dry spring weather, two severe summer droughts, and the downward plunge of butter and cattle prices, provided fertile ground for the radicalization of tenants' demands. Although the Irish parliamentary party held aloof from the growing agitation for some time, National League branches rapidly extended throughout the country. Between the autumn of 1885 and the summer of 1886, Cork landowners were presented with demands for larger abatements than ever before. Fear and anger consumed the propertied classes when judicial tenants sought to repudiate as inadequate rent agreements supposedly binding for fifteen years. But these early rent strikes usually fell far short of their objectives. The landlords' definition of what constituted a fair reduction, backed up by large-scale service of writs and by seizures of livestock, generally carried the day. While the home rule bill, accompanied by a comprehensive land-purchase measure, remained alive at Westminster, the firmness of farmers in pursuit of demands and their readiness to undergo eviction in order to obtain them understandably flagged. Tenants, it was declared, not only believed that the bill would pass but were also convinced that when it did, 'they will have no rents to pay'. [3]

[2] Kenmare papers, Letter book, 1884–5: S. M. Hussey to R. Blenner-hassett, 10 Aug. 1885, p. 907.

[3] Ibid., Letter book, 1885–93: M. Leonard to Colonel Dease, 18 May 1886, pp. 433–4.

Yet, even before the Plan of Campaign was instituted in October 1886, signs of militancy were conspicuous. It is true that in marked contrast to 1880 and 1881, there was much less resort to violence, with the major exception of northwest Cork, where desperate arms raids were quite frequent. But militancy assumed other forms. Local branches of the National League convened courts that audaciously presumed to regulate landlord-tenant relations and rendered decisions which occasionally conflicted with the opinions handed down by properly constituted tribunals. The ability of these irregular, unauthorized courts to mobilize public opinion and to coerce offenders into a recognition of their authority to adjudicate agrarian disputes made them an effective force for greater order in the countryside. Just as the league's courts curbed violence, so too did boycotting, which was used on a vastly extended scale after the expiration of the crimes act in August 1885. So effective did this essentially moral weapon become, especially against land grabbers, that landlords hesitated to evict defaulting tenants because their holdings invariably lay derelict.

The defeat of home rule, the conservatives' refusal to act upon Parnell's tenants' relief bill, and a rain-damaged harvest coupled with continued low prices put farmers in such a defiant mood in the autumn of 1886 that they responded readily to the announcement of the Plan of Campaign. Essentially the same scheme had been employed earlier with very limited success, but two new factors were now brought into play. First, the Plan was supported by the financial resources and the immense prestige of the Irish parliamentary party; and second, the exasperated tenants, assured of this support, were prepared to face large-scale evictions in order to drive home their demands. Less than twenty Cork estates, and only three great ones, became directly involved in the Plan up to 1890. But the tenants' unilateral determination of what rent should be paid on these estates, together with the disposal of livestock in order to avoid seizures, had a profound and widespread impact upon landlords and agents, who were generally compelled to make expensive concessions in which even judicial tenants were included. Rent strikes, boycotting, and the unauthorized courts collectively delivered an ominous message to the landlords and the government: tenant farmers were indeed seeking to carry out a social revolution and to impose from below a new economic and legal order.

The change in command at Dublin Castle in early 1887 was a turning point. Arthur Balfour's effective combination of coercion and conciliation gradually shored up the traditional order. Summary justice was meted out to agrarian offenders, while the land courts were empowered to fix the rents of the long-denied leaseholders as well as to revise the rents of judicial tenants for three years. These measures, however, did not yield immediate results. Angered by the 'Mitchelstown massacre' in September 1887, and by the subsequent imprisonment of William O'Brien and John Mandeville, Cork farmers intensified their struggle. Even when landlords agreed to reduce rents substantially, tenants very often continued to withhold payment. Arrears steadily mounted, particularly in northwest Cork, where the Plan was most deeply entrenched. The loss of one year's rental income was common during the late 1880s, and in many instances arrears amounted to between two and four years' rent.

Fortunately for the landlords, agrarian warfare gradually subsided from about mid-1888. The government's prior suppression of the most obstreperous branches of the league and its rigorous prosecution of those who had violated the new crimes act began to show results. Outrages declined, the league's courts ceased to function, and boycotting became less widespread and less intense. From early 1890 new tenants were increasingly found for long-vacant evicted farms—the most significant indication of the wane in militancy. The relieved landlords were convinced that Balfour's coercion policies were primarily responsible for the faltering of the agitation. But economic improvement, above all the rise in cattle prices, probably contributed more to this end than anything else, despite the fact that it did not affect the whole agricultural economy or endure after 1890. The 1887 land act was also a very significant factor in the calming of the unrest. More than twice as many judicial rents were fixed between 1887 and 1893 than during the previous six years, and by March 1893 about two-fifths of all Cork tenants had received reductions averaging 22 per cent. After the disastrous split in the Parnellite party in December 1890 as a result of the O'Shea divorce case, the remaining agrarian struggles rapidly collapsed. It would be interesting to speculate on what might have happened if the split had somehow been avoided, for the seasons of 1891 and 1892 were nearly as damaging to the farmers' economic position as those of 1884 and 1885, which had witnessed renewed agitation.

Even though the Plan of Campaign ended ignominiously, the landlords had been dealt a series of crippling blows. Within little more than a decade, they lost most of their local political power. One observer remarked favourably in September 1889 on the change in the districts of East and West Carbery:

The so-called gentry have been driven from their time-honoured strongholds in the public boards, the representation of which is now in the hands of the representatives of the people. Nationalists at the present abound in the poor-law and town commission bodies, and have even invaded the sanctity of the very bench itself. . . . Bandon is no longer the citadel of that ignorant, blustering Orangeism that used to vow eternal damnation to everybody who dealt in brass money or who wore wooden shoes [i.e., all catholics]. Bullies like Bence Jones no longer rule the roost in the courthouse at Clonakilty. [4]

The finishing touches were placed upon this transfer of power by the local government act of 1898. Under this highly important legislation, county councils and rural and urban district councils assumed the fiscal and administrative, though not judicial, responsibilities of the landlord-dominated grand juries. As Curtis has well said, 'the election to these councils of small farmers, shopkeepers, and publicans, however inexperienced in public affairs, was a giant stride toward democracy in Ireland. . . '. [5]

Besides forfeiting political authority, landowners were also deprived of much of their economic power. The 1887 land act, by restraining the rents of leaseholders, curbing the power of eviction, and extending the time for payment of arrears, interfered with property rights even more drastically than the legislation of 1881. The resulting loss of income was gradual and varied widely, but the land agents Doherty and Jones spoke in April 1897 of 'many estates in this county not being within 30 per cent of their rental even of 10 years ago'. [6] From the late 1880s, then, landlords faced an exceedingly dismal future of severe financial retrenchment in a state of political impotence.

Moreover, they were now generally despised as a class and regarded as unwelcome intruders in the local communities over which they had once ruled with such ease and some esteem. One of the earl of Kenmare's tenants frankly admitted in August 1887 that Kenmare was a considerate landlord, but hastened to add that 'in the eyes of the peasants . . . , the best landlord is good for nothing. They want the land, and they will have it.' [7] For some landlords, life in Ireland became unbearable. Count Moore, who owned large estates on the Tipperary side of the Galtees and resided for half the year at his magnificent country seat of Mooresfort near Limerick Junction, decided in 1888 to live permanently in London as a result of a bitter feud with his tenants. Having been publicly denounced 'from the very altar erected by his late revered father', Count Moore

[4] From *The Nation*, quoted in *C.E.*, 28 Sept. 1889.
[5] Curtis, *Coercion & conciliation*, p. 417.
[6] Doherty papers: Doherty and Jones to Messrs Maunsell and Darley, 24 Apr. 1897.
[7] *C.C.*, 24 Aug. 1887.

naturally came to consider himself an alien.[8] This feeling of alienation increased among the Anglo-Irish gentry as the new nationalism
assumed linguistic and cultural overtones represented by the Gaelic
League, the literary revival, and the Gaelic Athletic Association, all
launched between 1884 and 1893.[9]

Under these circumstances, landlords became increasingly willing
to sell their estates, and the only available purchasers were their own
tenants. Although the desire for ownership grew steadily among
farmers during the 1880s, it was strongly discouraged by all leading
nationalists. They vehemently denounced the conservatives' land-
purchase acts as insidious attempts to undermine the political
demand for home rule, which, they adamantly insisted, must be
answered in advance of a settlement of the land question. It is doubtful, however, whether this opposition exerted much influence over
the fact that only about 1,100 Cork tenants bought their holdings
between August 1885 and March 1893. Local opinion, especially that
of the clergy, was decidedly favourable towards land purchase,
provided that generous terms could be obtained from the landlords.
But this was precisely the overriding obstacle to the establishment of
peasant proprietorship. For while the rewards of landlordism had
seriously diminished, landlords were naturally unwilling to part with
their property at what they considered too great a sacrifice. In
most instances, in their view, the offenders of their bargain-hunting
tenants fell into this category. Generally unfavourable economic
conditions before 1895, the availability of alternative relief from the
land courts, and the hope of better terms from a liberal government
all helped to make tenants wary of buying at the landlord's price.

This stressful impasse was finally broken by the great land act of
1903, which was largely a concession to yet another agrarian
agitation. William O'Brien's United Irish League, founded in Mayo
early in 1898, was at first confined to the western counties, where its
local programme of expropriating wealthy graziers appealed strongly
to multitudes of poor smallholders.[10] After becoming identified with
a national programme of compulsory land purchase in 1900,
however, the league spread rapidly throughout the country, and
by June 1901 it possessed almost 1,000 branches with nearly 100,000
members.[11] Although still adamantly opposed to compulsion, most
landlords by now favoured a final solution based on compromise,
and the offer to negotiate actually came from their camp. With the
conservative government's blessing and the support of moderates on

[8] *C.E.*, 20 Oct. 1888.
[9] O. MacDonagh, *Ireland*, pp. 63–6; Cullen, *Life in Ire.*, p. 154.
[10] Lyons, *Dillon*, pp. 181, 201–2, 210–11.   [11] Ibid., pp. 222–3.

both sides, a conference of landlords' and tenants' representatives met in Dublin in December 1902 and quickly produced a unanimous report urging state-aided land purchase on a monumental scale.[12] Closely following the recommendations of this report, the land act that passed in August 1903 rang the death knell of Irish landlordism and heralded the arrival of peasant ownership. By encouraging the sale of entire estates, extending the period for the repayment of loans to sixty-eight and one-half years, lowering the interest rate to $3\frac{1}{4}$ per cent, and above all by providing a cash bonus of 12 per cent on the purchase price to selling landlords, this legislation decisively broke the long stalemate.[13] Under this act and amending legislation of 1909, the British government advanced £83 million up to the end of March 1920 for purchases already completed, and a further sum of £14 million was authorized for pending sales. By the early 1920s tenants had become the owners of over 326,000 holdings under the acts of 1903 and 1909, whereas only about 74,000 holdings had been purchased under the provisions of all the legislation passed between 1870 and 1896. Altogether, nearly two-thirds of Ireland's total area had ceased to be the property of the landlords by the early 1920s.[14]

The achievement of owner-occupancy, although contributing to improved rural living standards after 1900, failed to remove the demand for home rule, as the conservatives had fervently hoped. On the other hand, peasant proprietorship did not bring about a prosperous new era in agriculture. Though the years before the first world war were indeed prosperous ones for Irish farmers, this was largely the result of the recovery of farm prices.[15] Production tended to stagnate after reaching a peak in about 1910 only slightly higher than that of 1876.[16] But if in the cool judgment of a recent historian, 'owner-occupancy was an economic irrelevance by the time it was achieved',[17] this would scarcely have mattered to Irish farmers had they been able to realize it. For them, the overarching fact was that after a generation of continued and bitter struggle, their agitation was eminently vindicated. The landlords were finally being driven from Irish soil.

[12] Ibid., pp. 227–8.

[13] 3 Edw. VII, c. 37.

[14] *Report of the estates commissioners for the year from 1st April 1919 to 31st March 1920, and for the period from 1st November 1903 to 31st March 1920, with appendix* [Cmd 1150], H.C. 1921, xiv, 661, pp. iv–v.

[15] Barrington, 'Agricultural prices', p. 253.

[16] Solow, *Land question*, pp. 200–1; Crotty, *Irish agricultural production*, p. 84.

[17] J. Lee, 'Irish agriculture' in *Agricultural History Review*, xvii, pt i (1969), p. 71.

BIBLIOGRAPHY

〰〰〰〰〰〰〰〰〰〰〰〰〰

SYNOPSIS

NOTE ON MANUSCRIPT MATERIAL

MOST OF THE manuscript material consulted for this study of nineteenth-century Cork consists of estate records. Though increasingly recognized as an especially rich source of data, such records have been surprisingly little used for studies concerned with the agrarian economy and the land question. Yet they can yield a wealth of precise and detailed information across a wide spectrum of topics, including patterns of land holding and land use, terms of tenure, the movement of rents and land values generally, levels of agricultural investment, and fluctuations in both market conditions and farm profits.

By no means all estate papers are highly significant, however, and in the bibliography only the most important items in each collection are noted. Some of the material of this type—garden accounts, labourers' accounts, day ledgers—may be of relevance only for highly specialized economic or social inquiry, and other documents included in the collections—old charters, patents, and deeds—may be of mainly antiquarian interest. Considerably more important are estate maps and leases for what they reveal about agricultural practices. Rentals are of course extremely valuable, especially when extant in semi-annual or annual series, with rents due and paid, arrears, and disbursements set out for the whole estate. Most illuminating of all are annual reports, periodic surveys or valuations, and agents' letter books containing copies of outgoing correspondence, particularly that conducted with landowners. These administrative records not only elucidate the framework of economic activity but often contain penetrating commentary on general economic trends.

Locating estate papers consumed a great portion of the eighteen months I spent in Ireland and England between 1967 and 1969 doing research for this book. Altogether, I was able to locate and use thirty-one sets of estate records relating to my chosen period and area of inquiry. Only nine of these collections were in public depositories, partly because the frequent bulkiness of such material can impose unacceptable burdens on relatively scarce library space; the remaining twenty-two were all in private keeping, though some have since been transferred to public archives. The periodic reports of the Irish Manuscripts Commission and the National Library of Ireland on manuscripts in private hands led me to half of these twenty-two; the other half I discovered myself by contacting descendants of nineteenth-century Cork landowners, by writing letters to or visiting solicitors and land agents, as well as by other methods not easily described.

My own experience and that of others indicates that Irish estate records have had an extremely poor survival rate, even for a period as recent as the second half of the nineteenth century. Partly this stems from the country's turbulent history, especially between 1919 and 1923. Many landlord residences, often record depositories, were burnt to the ground by the I.R.A. during the war for independence or by the anti-treaty forces during the civil war. The land commission has added to the destruction of residences, razing them before selling demesne land to neighbouring farmers and making few if any provisions for the preservation of documents they may have contained. In recent times the pressure of heavy rates has furthered the work of demolition. Wastepaper campaigns have also wrecked havoc upon estate records, both the patriotic campaigns during the acute paper shortage of the second world war (as many Cork solicitors sorrowfully told me) and the charitable ones since then. One church-sponsored paper drive in Cork city in the late 1950s claimed an enormous collection of documents from the South Mall firm of Hussey and Townsend, probably the largest land-agency concern in all of Ireland during the 1880s, with some ninety estates under its management. Fortunately, impressive efforts have been made in Ireland within the last few years to locate private archival material and to transfer it into public depositories. In County Cork this important work is now performed by the Cork Archives Council.

Of the privately held estate papers consulted for this study, the most valuable collections in both quantity and quality were the Kenmare papers, which contain numerous letter books concerned with estate administration. Three smaller collections also proved highly useful: the Barry papers, for information about the earl of Egmont's properties and for the letters of the land agent Henry Harte Barry; the Jephson-Norreys papers; and the Ormathwaite papers, for the rich and revealing journals of Sir John Benn-Walsh. While the other private collections contain important documents relevant to the present work, they are fragmentary in varying degrees and were of considerably less usefulness. Of the estate records in public depositories, four extensive collections were highly important: the Doherty papers, which relate to a land-agency firm widely active in West Cork and are in the custody of the Cork Archives Council; the Donevaile papers, which are housed in the National Library of Ireland; that part of the Middleton papers which is deposited in the Public Record Office, Dublin; and the Lismore papers, which pertain to the estates of the dukes of Devonshire and are housed in the National Library of Ireland. No other known collection of nineteenth-century Irish estate papers approaches the Lismore MSS in bulk. Although they provide a complete picture of the financial aspects of the Devonshire estates for the greater part of the nineteenth century, their usefulness for this study was considerably diminished by the absence of most of the agents' correspondence, which is still at Lismore Castle. Unfortunately, permission could not be obtained to consult this material. Nor could three other private collections be inspected. J. R. Stewart and Sons, Land Agents, 47 Upper Mount Street, Dublin, denied a request to consult the Carbery papers; John G. Ronan, Cuskinny, Cobh, Co. Cork, the French papers; and the honourable Mrs Bertram Bell, Fota Island, Carrigtohill, Co. Cork, the Smith-Barry papers. These refusals were particularly regrettable in view of the relatively small quantity of estate records that has survived.

I SOURCES

(A) MANUSCRIPT MATERIAL

I IN PRIVATE POSSESSION

Bandon papers: In the possession of Rev. Thomas A. O'Regan, C.C., Kilbrittain, Co. Cork.

    Rental of the earl of Bandon's estates, 1857–61.

Bantry papers: In the possession of Mrs C. E. M. Shelswell-White, Bantry House, Bantry, Co. Cork.

    Rentals of the earl of Bantry's estates, 1856–7, 1864–5, 1881–2.

    Petition to the incumbered estates court, 1851.

    Trustees' report concerning the Bantry estates, May 1899.

Barry papers: In the possession of Charles M. Barry and Son, Solicitors, Cashel, Co. Tipperary.

Printed copy of documents of respondents presented to the English court of chancery, *Egmont v. Darell* (1861).

Printed copy of affidavits filed by petitioner in the English court of chancery, *Egmont v. Darell* (1861).

Letter books of Henry Harte Barry, Feb.–Nov. 1886, Dec. 1888–July 1889, June 1890–Feb. 1891, 3 vols.

Beamish papers: In the possession of Mr R. P. Beamish, Ghleanncarn, Castlelyons, Co. Cork.

Letter books of Richard Pigott Beamish, Dec. 1853–Oct. 1859, Mar. 1860–Nov. 1866, 2 vols.

Colthurst papers: In the possession of Sir Richard La Touche Colthurst, Turret Farm, Blarney, Co. Cork.

Abstract rentals of the Colthurst estates, 1845–51.

Rentals and accounts, 1886, 1906.

Statement of incumbrances and the funds available for their discharge, 1859.

Copy of exchequer court pleadings of defendant, *Hussey v. Colthurst* (1887).

Conner papers: In the possession of the executors of the late Henry L. Conner, Manch House, Ballineen, Co. Cork.

Rentals of the Conner estates, 1853–4, 1857–60, 1883–4.

Documents relating to the sale of property in the incumbered estates court, 1851–2.

Letters from Mountifort Longfield to Daniel Conner, jun., Aug. 1851–July 1853.

Ballineen petty-sessions complaint book, 1825–40.

Conolly papers: In the possession of Mr John Francis Conolly, Quarry, Leades, Aghinagh, Co. Cork.

Report concerning Francis Woodley's estate, 1820.

Falkiner papers: In the possession of P. W. Bass and Company, Solicitors, 9 South Mall, Cork.

Rentals of the Falkiner estates, 1835–6, 1881–2.

Letters to Valentine Barry and Matthew Leslie from Dr John O'Neill *et al.*, Apr. 1847–Mar. 1851.

Correspondence between William B. Leslie and Thomas Barry, July 1863–June 1876.

Gollock papers: In the possession of Mr Thomas H. M. Gollock, Monkstown, Co. Cork.

Demesne accounts, 1824–6, 1838–43, 1846–67, 3 vols.

Hodder papers: In the possession of Miss Phyllis Hodder, Fountainstown House, Fountainstown, Co. Cork.

Draft settlement of the Hodder family estates, 1822.

Holroyd-Smyth papers: In the possession of Mr H. H. D. Holroyd-Smyth, Ballynatray, Youghal, Co. Cork.

Printed copy of documents presented to the house of lords, on appeal from her majesty's court of appeal (Ireland), *Mountcashel v. Helen Stirling More-Smyth* (1894).

Jephson-Norreys papers: In the possession of Commander M. C. M. Jephson, Mallow Castle, Mallow, Co. Cork.

Rentals of the Jephson-Norreys estate, 1841–67, 4 vols.

Workmen's accounts, 1840–9, 1869–77, 2 vols.

Letter books of Sir Denham Jephson-Norreys, June 1839–June 1870, 2 vols.

Letter book of D. W. Jephson-Norreys, June 1863–Feb. 1870.

Kenmare papers: In the possession of Mrs Beatrice Grosvenor, Killarney, Co. Kerry.

Rentals of the earl of Kenmare's estates, 1830–50, 1865, 3 vols.

Semi-annual rentals and accounts, 1874–85, 20 vols (3 vols missing).

Letter books of Samuel M. Hussey and Maurice Leonard, Apr. 1877–Nov. 1893, 10 vols.

Letter books of Maurice Leonard, Jan. 1886–Mar. 1893, 7 vols.

Kingston papers: In the possession of Moore, Keily, and Lloyd, Solicitors, 31 Molesworth Street, Dublin.

Heads of the proposed resettlement of the Mitchelstown estate, 24 May 1869.

Mortgage of the Representative Church Body on the dowager countess of Kingston's estate, 5 Feb. 1875.

Kingston papers: In the possession of W. E. O'Brien and Company, Solicitors, Mitchelstown, Co. Cork.

Landed estates court title book for the dowager countess of Kingston's estate, 1875.

Midleton papers: In the possession of Warrens, Solicitors, 5 Bedford Square, London.

Receipts and disbursements of Viscount Midleton's estates, 1836–8.

Account of rents received, 1838–48.

Newenham papers: In the possession of Mr W. P. Worth Newenham, Coolmore, Carrigaline, Co. Cork.

Rental and account of W. H. W. Newenham's estate, 1817–33.

Copy of rolls court pleadings, *Mountcashel v. Newenham* (1857).

The O'Donovan papers: In the possession of The O'Donovan, Hollybrook House, Skibbereen, Co. Cork.

Rental of The O'Donovan's estate, Carbery only, 1839–69.

Journal of The O'Donovan, Sept. 1839–Dec. 1846.

Lissard house journal, kept by The O'Donovan, Apr. 1853–July 1872.

Ormathwaite papers: In the possession of Lord Ormathwaite, Penybont Hall, Llandrindod Wells, Radnorshire, Wales.

Journals of Sir John Benn-Walsh, Apr. 1823–Aug. 1864.

Account of the property and income of Sir John Benn-Walsh, 1829–66.

Powell papers: In the possession of Mr Michael Powell, Solicitor, Grand Parade, Cork.

Minute book, Midleton branch of the Irish National League, Feb. 1885–Apr. 1889.

2 IN PUBLIC DEPOSITORIES: IRELAND

CORK

Archives Council

Minute books, boards of guardians, consulted for the following poor-law unions:

    Bantry: Aug. 1846–Aug. 1847, Jan. 1848–June 1851, 6 vols.
    Bandon: Mar. 1839–June 1851, 8 vols.
    Castletown: Nov. 1849–Jan. 1851, 2 vols.
    Cork: Nov. 1845–July 1847, Mar. 1849–Apr. 1851, 5 vols.
    Dunmanway: Apr. 1845–Apr. 1851, 8 vols.
    Fermoy: Feb. 1847–Jan. 1848.
    Kinsale: Apr. 1844–Mar. 1846, Aug. 1849–Jan. 1851, 3 vols.
    Mallow: Oct. 1844–Apr. 1851, 5 vols.
    Midleton: Dec. 1845–Nov. 1850, 6 vols.
    Youghal: June 1850–Jan. 1851.

Doherty papers:

    Rent roll of the earl of Bandon's estates, Nov. 1821.
    Rentals, 1826–48, 1882–5.
    Schedule of leases, 1864.
    Letter books of Richard Wheeler Doherty, sen., Aug. 1871–Jan. 1880, 6 vols.
    Letter books of Richard Wheeler Doherty, jun., Jan. 1880–Dec. 1884, 2 vols.
    Letter books of R. W. Doherty and Son, and Doherty and Jones, Jan. 1880–Mar. 1890, 2 vols.

Harbour Commissioners

Yearly abstracts of receipts, expenditures, etc., of the Cork harbour commissioners, 1871–1900.

Public Museum

Minute book, Cove famine relief committee, Apr. 1846–Mar. 1847.
Cork Butter Market MSS:

    Minutes of the committee of merchants, 1829–57, 2 vols.
    Correspondence of the committee of merchants, 1827–48.
    Minutes of the subcommittee of merchants, 1851–61, 1868–84, 4 vols.
    Minutes of the market trustees, 1884–7.
    Butter-quality ledgers, 1825–53, 1862–92, 6 vols.
    Newspaper cuttings.

Bibliography

DUBLIN

Irish Folklore Commission

MSS 107, 172, 437, 462, 577, 591, 1068, 1071, 1363, 1365, 1417, 1459.

National Library of Ireland

Ainsworth reports on MSS in private keeping.
Earl of Bantry papers: MS 8599.
Bowen papers: Box 30, iv.
Doneraile papers:
  Rentals of Viscount Doneraile's estates, 1819–38, 1847–87, 10 vols.
  Workmen's accounts, 1837–71, 7 vols.
  Demesne accounts, 1849–73.
  Letter book of Lewis D. Nicholl, Jan. 1888–Oct. 1889.
  Letter book of Lewis D. Nicholl and R. A. Anderson, Oct. 1889–Jan. 1891.
  Letter book of R. A. Anderson and Godfrey Levinge, Jan. 1891–July 1892.
  Letter book of Godfrey Levinge, Aug. 1892–May 1895.
Harrington papers: MS 8582.
Harrison papers: D. 6982–7073.
Earl of Kingston papers: MS 3276.
Lismore papers: MSS 6799-817, 6929, 7116-29, 7182-93.

Public Record Office

Distress papers, 1846–7.
Incumbered estates court index to conveyances, Apr. 1850–Oct. 1858, 7 vols.
Landed estates court index to conveyances, Dec. 1858–July 1877, 6 vols.
Land judges index to conveyances, Feb. 1878–Aug. 1881.
O'Brien rentals, 1850–81.
Cork district probate registry will books, 1858–60, 1869–71, 2 vols.
Midleton papers:
  Rentals of Viscount Midleton's estates, 1847, 1854–86, 6 vols.
  Valuation of the Midleton estates, 1840, with Charles Bailey's report, 6 Apr. 1840.
  Letter books of James Penrose Fitzgerald, Oct. 1867–Nov. 1872, May 1873–Feb. 1880, May 1882–Sept. 1892, 10 vols.

State Paper Office

Crime Branch special, secret/13408: 'List of estates on which the Plan of Campaign was originally established and on which settlements have not as yet been completed', 19 May 1891.
Chief Secretary's Office, Registered papers, 1891, no. 17944: 'Expenditure on relief of distress, 1879 and 1890', 13 July 1891.

Bibliography

KINSALE

Regional Museum

Kilbrittain Castle account books, 1864–6, 2 vols.

THURLES

Tipperary County Library

Rentals of Robert Cole Bowen's estates in the counties of Cork and Tipperary, 1847–83, 5 vols.

3   IN PUBLIC DEPOSITORIES: ENGLAND

CHICHESTER

West Sussex County Record Office
Cowdray archives: MS 1914.

GUILDFORD

Muniment Room, Castle Arch

Midleton papers:
 Rent roll of Viscount Midleton's estates, with schedule of tenancies, 1828.
 Extracts from the correspondence between Thomas Foley and Henry Marshall, Oct. 1839–Apr. 1845 (copies).
 Correspondence from Thomas Foley to Joseph Tatham and Reginald Bray, Jan.–Feb. 1852 (copies).

LONDON

House of Lords Record Office

House of lords committee on the Cork & Waterford railway bill, vol. iv of 1846.
House of lords committee on the Cork, Blackrock & Passage railway bill, vol. v of 1846.
House of lords committee on the Cork & Limerick direct-railway bill, vol. iii of 1860.
Viscount Midleton estate act, 1850, no. 601.

Public Record Office

Customs 5. Ledgers of imports, England:
 Corn exported from Ireland to Great Britain, 1830–49, nos 19–35, 37, 39, 41.
 Corn imported into Ireland from outside Great Britain, 1840–69, nos 29–36, 38–66 (even nos), 70, 71, 78, 84, 90, 95, 99.

(B) PRINTED MATERIAL

I   PARLIAMENTARY PAPERS

(a) *Returns of agricultural produce in Ireland* (in chronological order)

Returns of agricultural produce in Ireland in the year 1847, pt i: *Crops* (923), H.C. 1847–8, lvii, 1.

Returns of agricultural produce in Ireland in the year 1847, pt ii: *Stock* [1000], H.C. 1847–8, lvii, 109.

Returns of agricultural produce in Ireland in the year 1848 [1116], H.C. 1849, xlix, 1.

Returns of agricultural produce . . . 1849 [1245], H.C. 1850, li, 39.

Returns of agricultural produce . . . 1850 [1404], H.C. 1851, l, 1.

The census of Ireland for the year 1851, pt ii: *Returns of agricultural produce in 1851* [1589], H.C. 1852–3, xciii, 1.

Returns of agricultural produce . . . 1852 [1714], H.C. 1854, lvii, 1.

Returns of agricultural produce . . . 1853 [1865], H.C. 1854–5, xlvii, 1.

Returns of agricultural produce . . . 1854 [2017], H.C. 1856, liii, 1.

Returns of agricultural produce . . . 1855 [2174], H.C. 1857 (sess. 1), xv, 81.

Returns of agricultural produce . . . 1856 [2289], H.C. 1857–8, lvi, 1.

(b) *The agricultural statistics of Ireland* (in chronological order)

The agricultural statistics of Ireland for the year 1857 [2461], H.C. 1859 (sess. 2), xxvi, 57.

The agricultural statistics . . . 1858 [2599], H.C. 1860, lxvi, 55.

The agricultural statistics . . . 1859 [2763], H.C. 1861, lxii, 73.

The agricultural statistics . . . 1860 [2997], H.C. 1862, lx, 137.

The agricultural statistics . . . 1861 [3156], H.C. 1863, lxix, 547.

The agricultural statistics . . . 1862 [3286], H.C. 1864, lix, 327.

The agricultural statistics . . . 1863 [3456], H.C. 1865, lv, 125.

The agricultural statistics . . . 1864 [3766], H.C. 1867, lxxi, 201.

The agricultural statistics . . . 1865 [3929], H.C. 1867, lxxi, 491.

The agricultural statistics . . . 1866 [3958–II], H.C. 1867–8, lxx, 255.

The agricultural statistics . . . 1867 [4113–II], H.C. 1868–9, lxii, 645.

The agricultural statistics . . . 1868 [C 3], H.C. 1870, lxviii, 439.

The agricultural statistics . . . 1869 [C 239], H.C. 1871, lxix, 347.

The agricultural statistics . . . 1870 [C 463], H.C. 1872, lxiii, 299.

The agricultural statistics . . . 1871 [C 762], H.C. 1873, lxix, 375.

The agricultural statistics . . . 1872 [C 880], H.C. 1874, lxix, 199.

The agricultural statistics . . . 1873 [C 1125], H.C. 1875, lxxix, 131.

The agricultural statistics . . . 1874 [C 1380], H.C. 1876, lxxviii, 131.

The agricultural statistics . . . 1875 [C 1568], H.C. 1876, lxxviii, 413.

The agricultural statistics . . . 1876 [C 1749], H.C. 1877, lxxxv, 529.

The agricultural statistics . . . 1877 [C 1938], H.C. 1878, lxxvii, 511.

The agricultural statistics . . . 1878 [C 2347], H.C. 1878–9, lxxv, 587.
The agricultural statistics . . . 1879 [C 2534], H.C. 1880, lxxvi, 815.
The agricultural statistics . . . 1880 [C 2932], H.C. 1881, xciii, 685.
The agricultural statistics . . . 1881 [C 3332], H.C. 1882, lxxiv, 93.
The agricultural statistics . . . 1882 [C 3677], H.C. 1883, lxxvi, 825.
The agricultural statistics . . . 1883 [C 4069], H.C. 1884, lxxxv, 313.
The agricultural statistics . . . 1884 [C 4489], H.C. 1884–5, lxxxv, 1.
The agricultural statistics . . . 1885 [C 4802], H.C. 1886, lxxi, 1.
The agricultural statistics . . . 1886 [C 5084], H.C. 1887, lxxxix, 1.
The agricultural statistics . . . 1887 [C 5477], H.C. 1888, cvi, 415.
The agricultural statistics . . . 1888 [C 5785], H.C. 1889, lxxxiii, 215.
The agricultural statistics . . . 1889 [C 6099], H.C. 1890, lxxix, 371.
The agricultural statistics . . . 1890 [C 6518], H.C. 1890–1, xci, 277.
The agricultural statistics . . . 1891 [C 6777], H.C. 1892, lxxxviii, 285.
*Agricultural statistics of Ireland, with detailed report on agriculture, for the year
    1892* [C 7187], H.C. 1893–4, ci, 285.

(c) *Returns by provinces, of agrarian offences throughout Ireland* (in chronological
    order)

*Return of all agrarian outrages which have been reported by the Royal Irish Con-
    stabulary between the 1st day of January 1879 and the 31st day of January 1880,
    giving particulars of crime, arrests, and results of proceedings,* H.C. 1880 (131),
    lx, 199.

*Return (in continuation of the return ordered on the 15th March 1880) of all
    agrarian outrages . . . between the 1st day of February 1880 and the 31st day of
    October 1880 . . . ,* H.C. 1881 (6), lxxvii, 273.

*Return of all agrarian outrages . . . between the 1st day of November 1880 and the
    30th day of November 1880 . . . ,* H.C. 1881 (6–I), lxxvii, 409.

*Return of all agrarian outrages . . . between the 1st day of December 1880 and the
    31st day of December 1880 . . . ,* H.C. 1881 (6–II), lxxvii, 487.

*Return by provinces, of agrarian offences throughout Ireland reported to the inspector
    general of the Royal Irish Constabulary between the 1st day of January 1881 and
    the 31st day of December 1881, showing the number of cases in which offenders
    were convicted; the number of cases in which persons were made amenable but not
    convicted; the number of cases in which accused are awaiting trial; and the number
    of cases in which offenders were neither convicted nor made amenable,* H.C. 1882
    (72), lv, 17.

*Return by provinces, of agrarian offences . . . between the 1st day of January 1882
    and the 31st day of December 1882 . . . ,* H.C. 1883 (12), lvi, 1.

*Return by provinces, of agrarian offences . . . between the 1st day of January 1883
    and the 31st day of December 1883 . . .* [C 3950], H.C. 1884, lxiv, 1.

*Return by provinces, of agrarian offences . . . between the 1st day of January 1884
    and the 31st day of December 1884 . . .* [C 4500], H.C. 1884–5, lxv, 1.

*Return by provinces, of agrarian offences . . . between the 1st day of January 1885
    and the 31st day of December 1885 . . .* [C 4701], H.C. 1886, liv, 1.

*Return by provinces, of agrarian offences . . . between the 1st day of January 1886
    and the 31st day of December 1886 . . .* [C 5024], H.C. 1887, lxviii, 1.

Return by provinces, of agrarian offences . . . between the 1st day of January 1887 and the 31st day of December 1887 . . . [C 5345], H.C. 1888, lxxxiii, 399.

Return by provinces, of agrarian offences . . . between the 1st day of January 1888 and the 31st day of December 1888 . . . [C 5691], H.C. 1889, lxi, 521.

Return by provinces, of agrarian offences . . . between the 1st day of January 1889 and the 31st day of December 1889 . . . [C 6008], H.C. 1890, lix, 795.

Return by provinces, of agrarian offences . . . between the 1st day of January 1890 and the 31st day of December 1890 . . . [C 6327], H.C. 1890–1, lxiv, 805.

Return by provinces, of agrarian offences . . . between the 1st day of January 1891 and the 31st day of December 1891 . . . [C 6649], H.C. 1892, lxv, 449.

(d) *Reports of the Irish land commissioners* (in chronological order)

Report of the Irish land commissioners for the period from 22nd August 1881 to 22nd August 1882 [C 3413], H.C. 1882, xx, 265.

Report of the Irish land commissioners for the period from 22nd August 1882 to 22nd August 1883, and as to proceedings under the Arrears of Rent (Ireland) Act, 1882, to the 27th October 1883 [C 3897], H.C. 1884, lxiv, 41.

Report of the Irish land commissioners for the period from 22nd August 1883 to 22nd August 1884, and as to proceedings under the Arrears of Rent (Ireland) Act, 1882, from the 27th October 1883, to the 22nd August 1884 [C 4231], H.C. 1884–5, lxv, 53.

Report of the Irish land commissioners for the period from 22nd August 1884 to 22nd August 1885, and as to proceedings under the Arrears of Rent (Ireland) Act, 1882, from the 27th October 1884 to the 22nd August 1885 [C 4625], H.C. 1886, xix, 467.

Report of the Irish land commissioners for the period from 22nd August 1885 to 22nd August 1886 [C 4899], H.C. 1886, xix, 503.

Report of the Irish land commissioners for the period from 22nd August 1886 to 22nd August 1887 [C 5223], H.C. 1887, xxv, 185.

Report of the Irish land commissioners for the period from 22nd August 1887 to 22nd August 1888 [C 5586], H.C. 1888, xxxiii, 239.

Report of the Irish land commissioners for the period from 22nd August 1888 to 22nd August 1889 [C 5876], H.C. 1889, xxvii, 409.

Report of the Irish land commissioners for the period from 22nd August 1889 to 22nd August 1890 [C 6233], H.C. 1890–1, xxv, 305.

Report of the Irish land commissioners for the period from 22nd August 1890 to 22nd August 1891 [C 6510], H.C. 1890–1, xxv, 381.

Report of the Irish land commissioners for the period from 22nd August 1891 to 31st March 1893 [C 7056], H.C. 1893–4, xxiv, 1.

(e) *Other parliamentary papers* (in chronological order)

Papers presented by his majesty's command, relative to the disturbed state of Ireland, H.C. 1822 (2), xiv, 741.

Report from the select committee on the butter trade of Ireland, H.C. 1826 (406), v, 135.

Copies of papers relating to proposed experimental improvements on a tract of mountain land, called the lands of Pobble-ô-Keefe, in the barony of Duhallow, in the county of Cork, belonging to the crown, H.C. 1831–2 (355), xlv, 207.

Return of the population of the several counties in Ireland, as enumerated in 1831, H.C. 1833 (254), xxxix, 1.

Copies of papers relating to experimental improvements in progress on the crown lands at King William's Town, in the barony of Duhallow, in the county of Cork; and to the new lines of public road in course of construction through the district in which the said lands are situated, in the counties of Cork and Kerry; for the purpose of encouraging the employment of the labouring poor in similar improvements on other estates in Ireland, H.C. 1834 (173), li, 69.

First report from his majesty's commissioners for inquiring into the condition of the poorer classes in Ireland, with appendix (A) and supplement, H.C. 1835 (369), xxxii, pt i, 1.

Third report of the commissioners for inquiring into the condition of the poorer classes in Ireland [43], H.C. 1836, xxx, 1.

Poor inquiry (Ireland): Appendix (C), pt i: Reports on the state of the poor, and on the charitable institutions in some of the principal towns, with supplement containing answers to queries; pt ii: Report on the city of Dublin, and supplement containing answers to queries, with addenda to appendix (A) and communications [35], H.C. 1836, xxx, 35.

——: *Appendix (D) containing baronial examinations relative to earnings of labourers, cottier tenants, employment of women and children, expenditure; and supplement containing answers to questions 1 to 12 circulated by the commissioners* [36], H.C. 1836, xxxi, 1.

——: *Appendix (E) containing baronial examinations relative to food, cottages and cabins, clothing and furniture, pawnbroking and savings banks, drinking; and supplement containing answers to questions 13 to 22 circulated by the commissioners* [37], H.C. 1836, xxxii, 1.

——: *Appendix (F) containing baronial examinations relative to con-acre, quarter or score ground, small tenantry, consolidation of farms and dislodged tenantry, emigration, landlord and tenant, nature and state of agriculture, taxation, roads, observations on the nature and state of agriculture; and supplement* [38], H.C. 1836, xxxiii, 1.

Second report of the commissioners for inquiring into the condition of the poorer classes in Ireland [68], H.C. 1837, xxxi, 587.

Second report of the commissioners appointed to consider and recommend a general system of railways for Ireland [145], H.C. 1837–8, xxxv, 449.

Further report of Richard Griffith, Esq., dated 15th July 1839, to the commissioners of her majesty's woods, &c., on the progress of the roads and land improvements on the crown estate of King William's Town, county of Cork, 1839, H.C. 1839 (515), xlvii, 553.

Copy of a further report of Richard Griffith, Esq., to the commissioners of her majesty's woods, &c., on the progress of the roads and land improvements on the crown estate of King William's Town in the county of Cork, dated 13th August 1841, H.C. 1841 (8–sess. 2), ii, 395.

Report from select committee on the spirit trade (Ireland), with the minutes of evidence, H.C. 1842 (338), xiv, 423.

Report of the commissioners appointed to take the census of Ireland for the year 1841 [504], H.C. 1843, xxiv, 1.

A copy of the report on the experimental improvements on the crown estate of King William's Town in the county of Cork, submitted to her majesty's commissioners of woods and forests by Richard Griffith, Esq., dated 24 July 1844, in continuation of his last report presented to parliament and ordered to be printed on 6 September 1841, H.C. 1844 (612), xliii, 43.

Returns of parliamentary electors; also, of tenements valued under the act 1 & 2 Vic., cap. 56, for relief of the poor in Ireland, 1842–3, H.C. 1844 (533), xliii, 323.

Report from her majesty's commissioners of inquiry into the state of the law and practice in respect to the occupation of land in Ireland [605], H.C. 1845, xix, 1.

Evidence taken before her majesty's commissioners of inquiry into the state of the law and practice in respect to the occupation of land in Ireland, pt i [606], H.C. 1845, xix, 57.

Evidence taken before her majesty's commissioners of inquiry into the state of the law and practice in respect to the occupation of land in Ireland, pt ii [616], H.C. 1845, xx, 1.

Evidence taken before her majesty's commissioners of inquiry into the state of the law and practice in respect to the occupation of land in Ireland, pt iii [657], H.C. 1845, xxi, 1.

Appendix to minutes of evidence taken before her majesty's commissioners of inquiry into the state of the law and practice in respect to the occupation of land in Ireland, pt iv [672], H.C. 1845, xxii, 1.

A return from the poor law commissioners, showing the name of each union in Ireland; the name of the county in which situated; the name of each electoral division in each union; the total numbers of occupiers in each electoral division on whom the rate is made; the total estimated extent of statute acres in each electoral division, the rate for which is made on the occupier; the total number of hereditaments not exceeding £4 in each electoral division, for which the rate is made on the immediate lessor; the total estimated extent, statute acres, in each electoral division, the rate for which is made on the immediate lessor; the total estimated extent of bog or waste not rated, in each electoral division, H.C. 1846 (262), xxxvi, 469.

Correspondence explanatory of the measures adopted by her majesty's government for the relief of distress arising from the failure of the potato crop in Ireland [735] H.C. 1846, xxxvii, 41.

Correspondence from July 1846 to January 1847, relating to the measures adopted for the relief of the distress in Ireland, board of works series [764], H.C. 1847, l, 1.

Correspondence from July 1846 to January 1847, relating to the measures adopted for the relief of distress in Ireland and Scotland, commissariat series [761], H.C. 1847, li, 1.

Correspondence from January to March 1847, relating to the measures adopted for the relief of the distress in Ireland, board of works series, pt ii [797], H.C. 1847, lii, 1.

Correspondence from January to March 1847, relating to the measures adopted for the relief of the distress in Ireland, commissariat series, pt ii [796], H.C 1847, lii, 333.

A return of the valuation of each electoral division in Ireland, with population in 1841, H.C. 1847 (159), lvi, 379.

First annual report of the commissioners for administering the laws for relief of the poor in Ireland, with appendices [963], H.C. 1847–8, xxxiii, 377.

A return . . . of the valuation of each electoral division in Ireland, with its population in 1841, and the total poundage directed to be raised by any rate or rates made upon every such electoral division during the year ending the 31st day of December 1847, H.C. 1847–8 (311), lvii, 183.

Return from the registrar's office of the court of chancery in Ireland, of the number of causes, description of property, rental of estates, arrears of rent, when receiver was appointed, and when receiver last accounted; also, the profession and residence of receiver; gross amount of costs paid by receiver since his appointment, as allowed in his account, in each county in Ireland, during the years 1844, 1845, and 1846, and up to the 1st day of December 1847; together with a statement of the amount expended on improvements during the same years; also, copy of all general rules or instructions given since 1843 for the guidance of receivers in reference to allowances for improvements, or the management of estates, or the letting of lands, by the lord chancellor or master; similar return from the chief remembrancer's office in reference to estates under the court of exchequer in Ireland, H.C. 1847–8 (226), lvii, 213.

First report of the commissioners for inquiring into the number and boundaries of poor-law unions and electoral divisions in Ireland [1015, 1015–II], H.C. 1849, xxiii, 369.

Second annual report of the commissioners for administering the laws for relief of the poor in Ireland [1118], H.C. 1849, xxv, 87.

Returns from the courts of queen's bench, common pleas, and exchequer in Ireland, of the number of ejectments brought in those courts respectively for the last three years, beginning with Hilary term 1846 and ending with Hilary term 1849, both included; specifying the number in each term and year, and the counties in which they have been brought, and the number of persons served in each ejectment, according to the affidavits of service, distinguishing the number brought for non-payment of rent and the number brought for overholding: and, from the assistant barrister's court of each county in Ireland, of the number of civil bill ejectments entered in each of such courts for a similar period, together with the number of the defendants in each civil bill ejectment, and distinguishing the number sued for non-payment of rent, and the number for overholding, and the number for desertion, H.C. 1849 (315), xlix, 235.

A return, in continuation of parliamentary paper no. 311 of session 1848, and in the same tabular form, of the valuation of each electoral division in Ireland, with its population in 1841, and the total poundage directed to be raised by any rate or rates made upon every such electoral division during the year ending the 31st day of December 1848; distinguishing the unions in which out-door relief has been administered for the able-bodied poor, made under the order of the poor law commissioners; and specifying the date of such order, H.C. 1849 (198), xlix, 243.

Bibliography

Third annual report of the commissioners for administering the laws for relief of the poor in Ireland [1243], H.C. 1850, xxvii, 449.

A return, in continuation of parliamentary paper no. 198 of session 1849, and in the same tabular form, of the valuation of each electoral division in Ireland, with its population in 1841, and the total poundage directed to be raised by any rate or rates made upon every such electoral division during the year ending the 31st day of December 1849; distinguishing the unions in which out-door relief has been administered for the able-bodied poor, made under the order of the poor law commissioners, and specifying the date of such order, H.C. 1850 (254), li, 425.

Fourth annual report of the commissioners for administering the laws for relief of the poor in Ireland: with appendices [1381], H.C. 1851, xxvi, 547.

A copy of any reports on the experimental improvements on the crown estate of King William's Town in the county of Cork, submitted to her majesty's commissioners of woods and forests since the 8th day of August 1844 (in continuation of parliamentary paper no. 612 of session 1844), H.C. 1851 (637), l, 437.

Return of the rates which have been made on each of the several electoral divisions in Ireland for the year 1850, distinguishing the dates on which such rates have been made, H.C. 1851 (382), l, 631.

A return of the number of licensed distillers in Ireland in each year from the year 1835 to 1850 inclusive, specifying the different places where their distilleries were situated, H.C. 1851 (369), l, 659.

An account of the quantity of spirits distilled in Ireland, the quantity of spirits on which duty was paid for home consumption in Ireland, and the quantity of spirits imported from Ireland into England, on which duty was paid, in each year from 1841 to 1850 inclusive, H.C. 1851 (368), liii, 455.

Twelfth general report of the colonial land and emigration commissioners, 1852 [1499], H.C. 1852, xviii, 161.

A return, in continuation of parliamentary paper no. 254 of session 1850, and in the same tabular form, of the valuation of each electoral division in Ireland, with its population in 1851; and the total poundage directed to be raised by any rate or rates made upon every such electoral division during the year ending the 31st day of December 1851; distinguishing the unions in which out-door relief has been administered for the able-bodied poor, if any, and specifying the date when the order authorizing such out-door relief was given by the poor law commissioners, H.C. 1852 (323), xlvii, 341.

Report of the commissioners appointed to inquire into the state of the fairs and markets in Ireland [1674], H.C. 1852–3, xli, 79.

The census of Ireland for the year 1851, pt i: showing the area, population, and number of houses by townlands and electoral divisions, vol. ii, province of Munster, county of Cork [1550, 1551], H.C. 1852–3, xci, 429, 499.

Return of the total number of gallons of spirits distilled and charged with duty in Ireland in each year from 1800 to 1852, both inclusive; the total amount of duty received in each year and the rate of duty per gallon, distinguishing the number of gallons charged with duty for consumption, H.C. 1852–3 (547), xcix, 549.

Report of the commissioners appointed to inquire into the state of the fairs and markets in Ireland, pt ii: Minutes of evidence [1910], H.C. 1854–5, xix, 1.

Twenty-fourth report from the board of public works, Ireland: with appendices, 1855 [2140], H.C. 1856, xix, 357.

The census of Ireland for the year 1851, pt iv: *Report on ages and education* [2053], H.C. 1856, xxix, 1.

——, pt v: *Tables of deaths*, vol. i, *containing the report, tables of pestilences, and analysis of the tables of deaths* [2087–I], H.C. 1856, xxix, 261.

——, pt v: *Tables of deaths*, vol. ii, *containing the tables and index* [2087–II], H.C. 1856, xxx, 1.

——, pt vi: *General report* [2134], H.C. 1856, xxxi, 1.

The census of Ireland for the year 1861, pt i: *showing the area, population, and number of houses by townlands and electoral divisions*, vol. i [3204], H.C. 1863, liv, 1.

——, pt ii: *Report and tables on ages and education*, vol. i [3204–I], H.C. 1863, lvi, 1.

——, pt ii: *Report and tables on ages and education*, vol. ii [3204–I], H.C. 1863, lvii, 1.

——, pt iii: *Vital statistics*, vol. i: *Report and tables relating to the status of disease* [3204–II], H.C. 1863, lviii, 1.

——, pt iii: *Vital statistics*, vol. ii: *Report and tables relating to deaths* [3204–II], H.C. 1863, lviii, 169.

——, pt iv: *Reports and tables relating to the religious professions, education, and occupations of the people*, vol. i [3204–III], H.C. 1863, lix, 1.

——, pt iv: *Reports and tables relating to the religious professions, education, and occupations of the people*, vol. ii [3204–III], H.C. 1863, lx, 1.

——, pt v: *General report* [3204–IV], H.C. 1863, lxi, 1.

Report from the select committee on Tenure and Improvement of Land (Ireland) Act; together with the proceedings of the committee, minutes of evidence, appendix, and index, H.C. 1865 (402), xi, 341.

Report from the select committee on general valuation, &c. (Ireland); together with the proceedings of the committee, minutes of evidence, and appendix, H.C. 1868–9 (362), ix, 1.

Two reports for the Irish government on the history of the landlord and tenant question in Ireland, with suggestions for legislation. First report made in 1859; second in 1866. By W. Neilson Hancock, LL.D. [4204], H.C. 1868–9, xxvi, 1.

Reports from poor law inspectors on the wages of agricultural labourers in Ireland [C 35], H.C. 1870, xiv, 1.

Reports from poor law inspectors in Ireland as to the existing relations between landlord and tenant in respect of improvements on farms, drainage, reclamation of land, fencing, planting, &c.; also, as to the existence (and to what extent) of Ulster tenant-right in their respective districts, &c., &c., &c. [C 31], H.C. 1870, xiv, 37.

Returns showing the number of agricultural holdings in Ireland and the tenure by which they are held by the occupiers [C 32], H.C. 1870, lvi, 737.

Report from the select committee of the house of lords on the Landlord and Tenant (Ireland) Act, 1870; together with the proceedings of the committee, minutes of evidence, appendix, and index, H.C. 1872 (403), xi, 1.

Census of Ireland, 1871, pt i: *Area, houses, and population: also the ages, civil condition, occupations, birthplaces, religion, and education of the people,* vol. ii, *province of Munster,* no. 2, *county and city of Cork* [C 873–II], H.C. 1873, lxxii, pt i, 119.

——, pt ii: *Vital statistics,* vol. i: *Report and tables relating to the status of disease* [C 876], H.C. 1873, lxxii, pt ii, 477.

——, pt ii: *Vital statistics,* vol. ii: *Report and tables relating to deaths* [C 1000], H.C. 1874, lxxiv, pt iii, 1.

Eighth annual report of the registrar-general of marriages, births, and deaths in Ireland, 1871 [C 968], H.C. 1874, xiv, 357.

Summary of the returns of owners of land in Ireland, showing, with respect to each county, the number of owners below an acre, and in classes up to 100,000 acres and upwards, with the aggregate acreage and valuation of each class, H.C. 1876 (422), lxxx, 35.

Copy of a return of the names of proprietors and the area and valuation of all properties in the several counties in Ireland, held in fee or perpetuity, or on long leases at chief rents, prepared for the use of her majesty's government and printed by Alexander Thom, 87 and 88, Abbey-street, Dublin, by the direction of the Irish government and at the expense of the treasury, H.C. 1876 (412), lxxx, 395.

Report from the select committee on Irish land act, 1870; together with the proceedings of the committee, minutes of evidence, and appendix, H.C. 1877 (328), xii, 1.

Report from the select committee on Irish land act, 1870; together with the proceedings of the committee, minutes of evidence, and appendix, H.C. 1878 (249), xv, 1.

Annual report of the local government board for Ireland, being the sixth report under the Local Government Board (Ireland) Act, 35 & 36 Vic., c. 69; with appendices [C 2116], H.C. 1878, xxxviii, 1.

Fourteenth detailed annual report of the registrar-general of marriages, births, and deaths in Ireland, 1877 [C 2301], H.C. 1878–9, xix, 523.

Fifteenth detailed annual report of the registrar-general of marriages, births, and deaths in Ireland, 1878 [C 2388], H.C. 1878–9, xix, 657.

Annual report of the local government board for Ireland, being the seventh report under the Local Government Board (Ireland) Act, 35 & 36 Vic., c. 69; with appendices [C 2363], H.C. 1878–9, xxx, 1.

Sixteenth detailed annual report of the registrar-general of marriages, births, and deaths in Ireland, 1879 [C 2688], H.C. 1880, xvi, 429.

Annual report of the local government board for Ireland, being the eighth report under the Local Government Board (Ireland) Act, 35 & 36 Vic., c. 69 [C 2603], H.C. 1880, xxviii, 1.

Correspondence relative to measures for the relief of distress in Ireland, 1879–80 [C 2483], H.C. 1880, lxii, 157.

Further correspondence relative to measures for the relief of distress in Ireland, 1879–80 [C 2506], H.C. 1880, lxii, 187.

Return of all applications from landed proprietors and sanitary authorities in scheduled unions for loans under the notices of the commissioners of public works in Ireland, dated the 22nd day of November 1879 and the 12th day of January 1880 respectively; with result of applications to the 20th day of March 1880, arranged by baronies, H.C. 1880 (154), lxii, 209.

Return of the loans applied for and granted in each of the various unions in Ireland scheduled as distressed, . . . up to 7th February 1880; Return (in continuation of return ordered on the 10th day of February) of the loans applied for and granted in the various unions in Ireland since they were scheduled as distressed, up to the 29th day of February, H.C. 1880 (158), lxii, 283.

Return of numbers in receipt of relief in the several unions in Ireland on the 1st day of January, the 1st day of March, and the 1st day of June in 1878, 1879, and 1880, H.C. 1880 (420–sess. 2), lxii, 289.

Return showing the unions and electoral divisions scheduled by the local government board for Ireland under the Seed Supply (Ireland) Act, 1880, H.C. 1880 (299–sess. 2), lxii, 339.

Preliminary report from her majesty's commissioners on agriculture [C 2778], H.C. 1881, xv, 1.

Minutes of evidence taken before her majesty's commissioners on agriculture, vol. i [C 2778–I], H.C. 1881, xv, 25.

Minutes of evidence taken before her majesty's commissioners on agriculture, vol. ii [C 3096], H.C. 1881, xvii, 1.

Report of her majesty's commissioners of inquiry into the working of the Landlord and Tenant (Ireland) Act, 1870, and the acts amending the same [C 2779], H.C. 1881, xviii, 1.

——, vol. ii: *Digest of evidence; minutes of evidence,* pt i [C 2779–I], H.C. 1881, xviii, 73.

——, vol. iii: *Minutes of evidence,* pt ii; *appendices* [C 2779–II], H.C. 1881, xix, 1.

Seventeenth detailed annual report of the registrar-general of marriages, births, and deaths in Ireland, 1880 [C 3046], H.C. 1881, xxvii, 897.

Annual report of the local government board for Ireland, being the ninth report under the Local Government Board (Ireland) Act, 35 & 36 Vic., c. 69 [C 2926], H.C. 1881, xlvii, 269.

Return of the names of landowners and sanitary authorities who have obtained loans under the provisions of the relief of distress (Ireland) acts, 1880, distinguishing those obtained at the reduced rate of interest, showing the dates of application and of sanction, the amount of the loans, the description of works, together with the dates of first advances and gross amounts of money issued on account of such loans, to the 31st day of December 1880 inclusive, arranged by counties and baronies, H.C. 1881 (99), lvii, 653.

Return showing the amount allowed for relief works in Ireland, the amount authorized to be expended, and the amount expended up to the present date, H.C. 1881 (274), lvii, 705.

Return by provinces and counties (compiled from returns made to the inspector general, Royal Irish Constabulary), of cases of evictions which have come to the knowledge of the constabulary in each of the years from 1849 to 1880 inclusive, H.C. 1881 (185), lxxvii, 725.

Return of agricultural holdings in Ireland, compiled by the local government board in Ireland from returns furnished by the clerks of the poor law unions in Ireland in January 1881 [C 2934], H.C. 1881, xciii, 793.

First report from the select committee of the house of lords on land law (Ireland);

together with the proceedings of the committee, minutes of evidence, and appendix,
H.C. 1882 (249), xi, 1.

*Second report from the select committee of the house of lords on land law (Ireland);
together with the proceedings of the committee, minutes of evidence, and appendix,*
H.C. 1882 (379), xi, 547.

Report from her majesty's commissioners on agriculture [C 3309], H.C. 1882,
xiv, 1.

Minutes of evidence taken before her majesty's commissioners on agriculture,
vol. iii [C 3309–I], H.C. 1882, xiv, 45.

*Eighteenth detailed annual report of the registrar-general of marriages, births, and
deaths in Ireland, 1881* [C 3368], H.C. 1882, xix, 891.

*Annual report of the local government board for Ireland, being the tenth report under
the Local Government Board (Ireland) Act, 35 & 36 Vic., c. 69; with
appendices* [C 3311], H.C. 1882, xxxi, 1.

Census of Ireland, 1881, pt i: *Area, houses, and population: also the ages, civil or
conjugal condition, occupations, birthplaces, religion, and education of the people,*
vol. ii, *province of Munster,* no. 2, *county and city of Cork* [3148–II], H.C.
1882, lxxvii, 119.

——, pt ii: *General report, with illustrative maps and diagrams, tables, and
appendix* [C 3365], H.C. 1882, lxxvi, 385.

*Return of payments made to landlords by the Irish land commission, pursuant to the
1st and 16th sections of the [arrears of rent] act; and also a return of rent
charges cancelled pursuant to the 15th section of the act* [C 4059], H.C. 1884,
lxiv, 97.

*Report from the select committee on industries (Ireland); together with the proceed-
ings of the committee, minutes of evidence, and appendix,* H.C. 1884–5 (288),
ix, 1.

*Report of the royal commission on the Land Law (Ireland) Act, 1881, and the
Purchase of Land (Ireland) Act, 1885* [C 4969], H.C. 1887, xxvi, 1.

——: *Minutes of evidence and appendices* [C 4969–I], H.C. 1887, xxvi, 25.

*Returns showing, for the counties of Clare, Cork, Kerry, Galway, and Mayo
respectively, the number of civil bills in ejectment, on title, for non-payment of
rent, or for overholding, entered at quarter sessions for each of the years from 1879
to 1888 inclusive, according to form return no. 1: and, of the numbers of writs
issued in actions for recovery of rent or possession in each of the counties of Clare,
Cork, Kerry, Galway, and Mayo in the queen's bench, exchequer, and common
pleas divisions of the high court of justice for each of the years from 1879 to
1888 inclusive, according to the form return no. 2,* H.C. 1889 (211), lxi, 417.

*Twenty-eighth detailed annual report of the registrar-general (Ireland); containing a
general abstract of the numbers of marriages, births, and deaths registered in
Ireland during the year 1891, transmitted pursuant to the provisions of the 7 & 8
Vic., cap. 81, s. 56; 26 Vic., cap. 11; and 26 & 27 Vic., cap. 90* [C 6787],
H.C. 1892, xxiv, 313.

*Agricultural returns of Great Britain, with abstract returns for the United Kingdom,
British possessions, and foreign countries, 1892* [C 6743], H.C. 1892,
lxxxviii, 1.

Census of Ireland, 1891, pt i: *Area, houses, and population: also the ages, civil or conjugal condition, occupations, birthplaces, religion, and education of the people,* vol. ii, *province of Munster, no. 2, county and city of Cork* [C 6567–I], H.C. 1892, xci, 123.

——, pt ii: *General report, with illustrative maps and diagrams, tables, and appendix* [C 6780], H.C. 1892, xc, 1.

Census of Ireland, 1901, pt i: *Area, houses, and population: also the ages, civil or conjugal condition, occupations, birthplaces, religion, and education of the people,* vol. ii, *province of Munster, no. 2, county and city of Cork* [Cd 1058–I], H.C. 1902, cxxiv, 179.

——, pt ii: *General report, with illustrative maps and diagrams, tables, and appendix* [Cd 1190], H.C. 1902, cxxix, 1.

Census of Ireland, 1911: Area, houses, and population: also the ages, civil or conjugal condition, occupations, birthplaces, religion, and education of the people, province of Munster, county and city of Cork [Cd 6050–I], H.C. 1912–13, cxv, 153.

Report of the estates commissioners for the year from 1st April 1919 to 31st March 1920, and for the period from 1st November 1903 to 31st March 1920, with appendix [Cmd 1150], H.C. 1921, xiv, 661.

2   TRADE AND NAVIGATION RETURNS
(Custom House Library, London)

Annual statements of the trade and navigation of the United Kingdom with foreign countries and British possessions, 1853–92, London, 1854–93. These returns are also printed in the sessional papers of the house of commons.

3   CONTEMPORARY NEWSPAPERS AND PERIODICALS

Constitution; or Cork Advertiser, 1846–73; *Cork Constitution,* 1874–92.
Cork Examiner, 1841–92.
Grocer, 1862–77.
Irish Farmers' Gazette, Jan. 1850–Feb. 1882; *Farmers' Gazette,* Mar. 1882–Dec. 1885.
Munster Farmers' Magazine, 1813–17.
Southern Reporter and Cork Daily Commercial Courier, 1846, 1848–9.
The Times, 1879–81.
West Cork Eagle and County Advertiser, 1877–83.

4   MEMOIRS, DIARIES, LETTERS, TRAVELLERS' ACCOUNTS, AND DOCUMENTARY MATERIAL

Anketell, W. R., *Landlord and tenant, Ireland: letters by a land agent on I, agricultural leases; II, tenants' improvements; III, tenant right; IV, fixity of tenure; V, tenants' claims; VI, covenants; VII, capricious evictions; VIII, valuation rents; corn rents; IX, peasant proprietorship; X, settled estates—Montgomery's act; XI, Scotch land tenure; XII, the Irish land—Mr Campbell's proposals; XIII, landlord and tenant—an agent's proposal; appendix: a model case of Ulster tenant-right,* Belfast, 1869.

Barry, J., 'The duke of Devonshire's Irish estates, 1794–1797: Reports by Henry Bowman, agent, with a brief description of the Lismore Castle MSS in the National Library' in *Analecta Hibernica*, no. 22 (1960), pp. 269–327.

Becker, B. H., *Disturbed Ireland, being the letters written during the winter of 1880–81*, London, 1881.

Burritt, E., *A journal of a visit of three days to Skibbereen and its neighbourhood*, London, 1847.

Cant-Wall, E., *Ireland under the land act: letters contributed to the 'Standard' newspaper; with an appendix of leading cases under the act giving the evidence in full, judicial dicta, &c.*, London, 1882.

Carleton, W., *The autobiography of William Carleton*, with a preface by Patrick Kavanagh, rev. ed., London, 1968, original edition 1896.

Central Tenants' Defence Association, *Full and revised report of the eight days' trial in the court of queen's bench on a criminal information against John Sarsfield Casey at the prosecution of Patten Smith Bridge from November 27th to December 5th, 1877*, Dublin, 1877.

'Charity souphouse at Skibbereen, 1846' in *Journal of the Cork Historical and Archaeological Society*, ser. 2, li, no. 174 (July–Dec. 1946), pp. 189–90.

Congested Districts Board, *Base-line reports to the congested districts board, 1892–8*. 'Confidential' printed reports collected in one volume, deposited in Trinity College Library, Dublin.

Cork Corporation, *Report of the law and finance committee of the Cork corporation on the Cork butter market*, Cork, 1884.

County of Cork Agricultural Society, *Discussion and correspondence on the abuses of the Cork butter market between the editor of the 'Cork Examiner' . . . and certain members of the County of Cork Agricultural Society*, Cork, 1866.

Daunt, W. J. O'N., *A life spent for Ireland, being selections from the journals of the late W. J. O'Neill Daunt*, edited by his daughter, London, 1896.

Davitt, M., *The fall of feudalism in Ireland, or the story of the Land League revolution*, London and New York, 1904.

de Tocqueville, A., *Journeys to England and Ireland*, ed. J. P. Mayer, trans. G. Lawrence and K. P. Mayer, New Haven and London, 1958.

Dublin Mansion House Relief Committee, *The Irish crisis of 1879–80: proceedings of the Dublin Mansion House Relief Committee, 1880*, Dublin, 1881.

Dufferin and Ava, marquis of, and Boyle, G. F., *Narrative of a journey from Oxford to Skibbereen during the year of the Irish famine*, 2nd ed., Oxford, 1847.

Dun, F., *Landlords and tenants in Ireland*, London, 1881.

Ellis, E., 'State-aided emigration schemes from crown estates in Ireland c. 1850' in *Analecta Hibernica*, no. 22 (1960), pp. 329–94.

Foster, T. C., *Letters on the condition of the people of Ireland*, 2nd ed., London, 1847.

Gregory, Sir W., *Sir William Gregory, K.C.M.G., formerly member of parliament and sometime governor of Ceylon: an autobiography*, ed Lady Augusta Gregory, 2nd ed., London, 1894.

Hall, S. C. and A. M., *Ireland: its scenery, character, &c.*, 3 vols, London, 1841–3.

Hamilton, J., *Sixty years' experience as an Irish landlord: memoirs of John Hamilton, D.L., of St Ernan's, Donegal*, ed H. C. White, London, 1894.

Hurlbert, W. H., *Ireland under coercion: the diary of an American*, 2 vols, 2nd ed., Edinburgh, 1888.

Hussey, S. M., *The reminiscences of an Irish land agent, being those of S. M. Hussey*, compiled by Home Gordon, London, 1904.

Inglis, H. D., *Ireland in 1834: a journey throughout Ireland during the spring, summer, and autumn of 1834*, 4th ed., London, 1836.

Jones, W. B., *The life's work in Ireland of a landlord who tried to do his duty*, London, 1880.

Kegan, J., *A young Irishman's diary (1836–1847), being extracts from the early journal of John Kegan of Moate*, edited with preface and notes by Rev. Wallace Clare, n.p., 1928.

Kennedy, J. P., *Digest of evidence taken before her majesty's commissioners of inquiry into the state of the law and practice in respect to the occupation of land in Ireland*, 2 pts, Dublin, 1847.

Kerry, knight of, *Irish landlords and tenants: recent letters to 'The Times' and further correspondence on the above subject*, Dublin, 1876.

Kohl, J. G., *Ireland: Dublin, the Shannon, Limerick, Cork, and the Kilkenny races, the round towers, the lakes of Killarney, the county of Wicklow, O'Connell and the Repeal Association, Belfast, and the Giant's Causeway*, London and New York, 1844.

Lyons, F. S. L., 'Vicissitudes of a middleman in County Leitrim, 1810–27' in *Irish Historical Studies*, ix, no. 35 (Mar. 1955), pp. 300–18.

MacLagan, P., *Land culture and land tenure in Ireland: the result of observations during a recent tour of Ireland*, Edinburgh, 1869.

MacLysaght, E., ed., *The Kenmare manuscripts*, Dublin, 1942.

Morris, W. O'C., *Letters on the land question of Ireland*, London, 1870.

O'Brien, W., *Christmas on the Galtees: an inquiry into the condition of the tenantry of Mr Nathaniel Buckley by the special correspondent of the 'Freeman's Journal'*, Dublin, 1878.

O'Brien, W., *Recollections*, London, 1905.

O'Brien, W., *Evening memories, being a continuation of 'Recollections' by the same author*, Dublin, 1920.

O'Leary, P., *My story*, trans. C. T. Ó Céirín, Cork, 1970; original edition 1915.

Pellew, G., *In castle and cabin, or talks in Ireland in 1887*, New York and London, 1888.

Report of the select committee appointed to inquire into the statistics of distress in the parishes of Mallow and Rahan, Mallow, 1846.

Rosse, earl of, *Letters on the state of Ireland by a landed proprietor*, London, 1847.

Shea, T., 'The minute book of the Ballineen Agricultural Society, 1845–47: a famine document' in *Journal of the Cork Historical and Archaeological Society*, ser. 2, li, no. 173 (Jan.–June 1946), pp. 52–60.

Society of Friends, *Transactions of the central relief committee of the Society of Friends during the famine in Ireland in 1846 and 1847*, Dublin, 1852.

Trench, W. S., *Realities of Irish life*, Boston, 1880, originally published 1868.

Tuke, J. H., *Irish distress and its remedies; the land question: a visit to Donegal and Connaught in the spring of 1880*, London, 1880.

Young, A., *Arthur Young's tour in Ireland (1776–1779)*, ed A. W. Hutton, 2 vols, London and New York, 1892; original edition 1780.

5   OTHER CONTEMPORARY WORKS

Blacker, W., *Prize essay, addressed to the agricultural committee of the Royal Dublin Society, on the management of landed property in Ireland; the consolidation of small farms, employment of the poor, etc., etc., for which the gold medal was awarded*, Dublin, 1834.

Carleton, W., *Valentine McClutchy, the Irish agent, or chronicles of the Castle Cumber property*, 3 vols, London, 1845.

Carleton, W., *Traits and stories of the Irish peasantry*, 2 vols, 5th ed., London, 1864.

Clanchy, T. J., *Guide to the buying of Irish butter*, Cork, 1870.

T. J. Clanchy and Co., *Half-a-century's butter prices, showing the fluctuations and the cheapest and dearest months of each year for 50 years, as a guide to buyers and sellers of butter*, Cork, 1892.

Cork Defence Union, *Boycotting in the county of Cork*, Cork, 1886.

de Beaumont, G., *Ireland: social, political, and religious*, ed W. C. Taylor, 2 vols, London, 1839.

Financial Reform Association, Liverpool, *The financial reform almanack for 1885*, Liverpool, 1885.

Fisher, J., *The history of land-holding in Ireland*, London, 1877.

Fitzgerald, P. H., *The story of the incumbered estates court*, London, 1862.

Hancock, W. N., *On the causes of distress at Skull and Skibbereen during the famine in Ireland: a paper read before the statistical section of the British Association, at Edinburgh, August 2nd, 1850*, Dublin, 1850.

Healy, T. M., *A word for Ireland*, Dublin, 1886.

Hill, Lord G., *Facts from Gweedore, compiled from notes by Lord George Hill, M.R.I.A.*, 2nd ed., Dublin, 1846.

Irish Land Committee, *The land question, Ireland*, no. 3: *Facts and figures*, Dublin, 1880.

Irish Land Committee, *The land question, Ireland*, no. 5: *Arrested progress, January 1881*, Dublin, 1881.

Irish Loyal and Patriotic Union, *Mad Tipperary: a history of the National League agitation on the Smith-Barry estate, with illustrations and appendices*, Dublin, 1890.

Keller, D., *The struggle for life on the Ponsonby estate*, Dublin, 1887.

King, D. B., *The Irish question*, New York and London, 1882.

Lavelle, P., *The Irish landlord since the revolution, with notices of ancient and modern land tenures in various countries*, Dublin, 1870.

Leslie, T. E. C., *Land systems and industrial economy of Ireland, England, and continental countries*, London, 1870.

Lewis, G. C., *On local disturbances in Ireland, and on the Irish church question*, London, 1836.

Lewis, S., *A topographical dictionary of Ireland; with an appendix describing the electoral boundaries of the several boroughs, as defined by the Act of the 2d. & 3d. of William IV*, 2 vols, London, 1837.

Locke, J., *Ireland: observations on the people, the land, and the law in 1851; with especial reference to the policy, practice, and results of the incumbered estates court*, 3rd ed., Dublin, 1852.

Mahony, R. J., *A short statement concerning the confiscation of improvements in Ireland, addressed to the right hon. W. E. Forster, M.P., chief secretary to the lord lieutenant of Ireland, by a working landowner*, Dublin, 1880.

Marmion, A., *The ancient and modern history of the maritime ports of Ireland*, 3rd ed., London, 1858.

Montgomery, W. E., *The history of land tenure in Ireland, being the Yorke prize essay of the University of Cambridge for . . . 1888*, Cambridge, 1889.

Morris, W. O'C., *The Irish land act, 33 & 34 Vict., cap. 46, with a full commentary and notes*, Dublin, 1870.

Nicholls, Sir G., *A history of the Irish poor law in connexion with the condition of the people*, London, 1856.

O'Brien, R. B., *The parliamentary history of the Irish land question from 1829 to 1869; and the origin and results of the Ulster custom*, London, 1880.

O'Brien, R. B., *Fifty years of concessions to Ireland, 1831–1881*, 2 vols, London, 1883–5.

O'Rourke, J., *The history of the great Irish famine of 1847, with notices of earlier Irish famines*, Dublin, 1875.

Pim, J., *Observations on the evils resulting to Ireland from the insecurity of title and the existing laws of real property; with some suggestions towards a remedy*, Dublin, 1847.

Porter, G. R., *The progress of the nation in its various social and economical relations from the beginning of the nineteenth century*, rev. ed., London, 1851.

Prendergast, J. P., *Letter to the earl of Bantry, or a warning to English purchasers of the perils of the Irish incumbered estates court, exemplified in the purchase by Lord Charles Pelham Clinton, M.P., of two estates in the barony of Bere, county of Cork*, 2nd ed., Dublin, 1854.

Richey, A. G., *The Irish land laws*, London, 1880.

Sheldon, J. P., *Dairy farming, being the theory, practice, and methods of dairying*, London, 1888, originally published 1879.

Spillar, W. A., *A short topographical and statistical account of the Bandon union, with some observations on the trade, agriculture, manufactures, and tideways of the district*, Bandon, 1844.

Stokes, W. L., 'Irish creameries' in *Co-operative Wholesale Society Annual for 1897* (Manchester, 1897), pp. 419–49.

Stuart, H. V., *Prices of farm products in Ireland from year to year for thirty-six years, illustrated by diagrams, with observations on the prospects of Irish agriculture, including the substance of letters addressed to the rt. hon. W. E. Gladstone, M.P., in February and March of this year*, Dublin, 1886.

Sullivan, A. M., *New Ireland*, 2 vols, 3rd ed., London, 1877.

Townsend, H., *Statistical survey of the county of Cork, with observations on the means of improvement; drawn up for the consideration and by the direction of the Dublin Society*, Dublin, 1810.

Townsend, W. R., *Directions on practical agriculture for the working farmers in Ireland, originally published in the 'Cork Southern Reporter' under the signature of 'Agricola'*, 2nd ed., Dublin, 1843.

Trench, G. F., *The land question: are the landlords worth preserving? Or forty years' management of an Irish estate*, Dublin, 1881.

Trevelyan, C. E., *The Irish crisis*, London, 1848.

Trimmer, J. K., *A brief inquiry into the present state of agriculture in the southern part of Ireland, and its influence on the manners and conditions of the lower classes of the people, with some considerations upon the ecclesiastical establishment of that country*, London, 1809.

Youatt, W., *Cattle: their breeds, management, and diseases*, London, 1834.

Youatt, W., *Sheep: their breeds, management, and diseases; to which is added 'The mountain shepherd's manual'*, London, 1837.

Youatt, W., *The pig: a treatise on the breeds, management, feeding, and medical treatment of swine; with directions for salting pork and curing bacon and hams*, London, 1847.

II LATER WORKS

(A) GENERAL

Beckett, J. C., *The making of modern Ireland, 1603–1923*, London and New York, 1966.

Chart, D. A., *An economic history of Ireland*, Dublin, 1920.

Court, W. H. B., *A concise economic history of Britain from 1750 to recent times*, Cambridge, 1964, originally published 1954.

Cullen, L. M., *Life in Ireland*, London and New York, 1968.

Cullen, L. M., *An economic history of Ireland since 1660*, London, 1972.

Curtis, E., *A history of Ireland*, 6th ed., London, 1950.

Edwards, O. D., ed., *Conor Cruise O'Brien introduces Ireland*, London, 1969.

Locker-Lampson, G. L. T., *A consideration of the state of Ireland in the nineteenth century*, London, 1907.

Lyons, F. S. L., *Ireland since the famine*, London and New York, 1971.

MacDonagh, O., *Ireland*, Englewood Cliffs, New Jersey, 1968.

Mansergh, N., *The Irish question, 1840–1921: a commentary on Anglo-Irish relations and on social and political forces in Ireland in the age of reform and revolution*, rev. ed., London, 1965.

Moody, T. W., and Martin, F. X., ed., *The course of Irish history*, Cork, 1967.

Paul-Dubois, L., *Contemporary Ireland*, with an introduction by T. M. Kettle, Dublin, 1911; original English translation, 1908.

Strauss, E., *Irish nationalism and British democracy*, New York and London, 1951.

Bibliography

(B) SPECIAL

Adams, W. F., *Ireland and Irish emigration to the new world from 1815 to the famine*, New Haven and London, 1932.

Akenson, D. H., *The Irish education experiment: the national system of education in the nineteenth century*, London and Toronto, 1970.

Arensberg, C. M., *The Irish countryman: an anthropological study*, Gloucester, Mass., 1959, originally published 1937.

Ashworth, W., *An economic history of England, 1870–1939*, London and New York, 1960.

Barrington, T., 'A review of Irish agricultural prices' in *Journal of the Statistical and Social Inquiry Society of Ireland*, pt ci, xv (1927), pp. 249–80.

Black, R. D. C., *Economic thought and the Irish question, 1817–1870*, London, 1960.

Bourke, P. M. A., 'The extent of the potato crop in Ireland at the time of the famine' in *Journal of the Statistical and Social Inquiry Society of Ireland*, xx, pt iii (1959), pp. 1–35.

Bourke, P. M. A., 'The scientific investigation of the potato crop in 1845–6' in *Irish Historical Studies*, xiii, no. 49 (Mar. 1962), pp. 26–32.

Bourke, P. M. A., 'Notes on some agricultural units of measurement in use in pre-famine Ireland' in *Irish Historical Studies*, xiv, no. 55 (Mar. 1965), pp. 236–45.

Bourke, P. M. A., 'The agricultural statistics of the 1841 census of Ireland: a critical review' in *Economic History Review*, ser. 2, xviii, no. 2 (Aug. 1965), pp. 376–91.

Bourke, P. M. A., 'The use of the potato crop in pre-famine Ireland' in *Journal of the Statistical and Social Inquiry Society of Ireland*, xxi, pt vi (1968), pp. 72–96.

Bowen, E., *Bowen's Court*, 2nd ed., London and New York, 1964.

Broeker, G., *Rural disorder and police reform in Ireland, 1812–36*, London and Toronto, 1970.

Brookfield, H. C., 'A microcosm of pre-famine Ireland: the Mallow district, 1775–1846' in *Journal of the Cork Historical and Archaeological Society*, ser. 2, lvii, no. 185 (Jan.–June 1952), pp. 7–10.

Brown, T. N., 'Nationalism and the Irish peasant, 1800–1848' in *Review of Politics*, xv, no. 4 (Oct. 1953), pp. 403–45.

Brown, T. N., *Irish-American nationalism, 1870–1890*, Philadelphia, 1966.

Buckley, K., 'The fixing of rents by agreement in Co. Galway, 1881–5' in *Irish Historical Studies*, vii, no. 27 (Mar. 1951), pp. 149–79.

Buckley, K., 'The records of the Irish land commission as a source of historical evidence' in *Irish Historical Studies*, viii, no. 29 (Mar. 1952), pp. 28–36.

Burn, W. L., 'Free trade in land: an aspect of the Irish question' in *Transactions of the Royal Historical Society*, ser. 4, xxxi (1949), pp. 61–74.

Burnett, J., *Plenty and want: a social history of diet in England from 1815 to the present day*, Harmondsworth, Middlesex, 1968, originally published 1966.

Chambers, J. D., and Mingay, G. E., *The agricultural revolution, 1750–1880*, London, 1966.

Clapham, J. H., *An economic history of modern Britain*, 3 vols, Cambridge, 1926–38; vol. i revised, 1930.

Clark, S., 'The social composition of the Land League' in *Irish Historical Studies*, xvii, no. 68 (Sept. 1971), pp. 447–69.

Connell, K. H., *The population of Ireland, 1750–1845*, Oxford, 1950.

Connell, K. H., 'Land and population in Ireland, 1750–1845' in *Economic History Review*, ser. 2, ii, no. 3 (1950), pp. 278–89.

Connell, K. H., 'The colonization of waste land in Ireland, 1780–1845' in *Economic History Review*, ser. 2, iii, no. 1 (1950), pp. 44–71.

Connell, K. H., 'The history of the potato' in *Economic History Review*, ser. 2, iii, no. 3 (1951), pp. 388–95.

Connell, K. H., 'Peasant marriage in Ireland after the great famine' in *Past and Present*, no. 12 (Nov. 1957), pp. 76–91.

Connell, K. H., 'The land legislation and Irish social life' in *Economic History Review*, ser. 2, xi, no. 1 (Aug. 1958), pp. 1–7.

Connell, K. H., 'Peasant marriage in Ireland: its structure and development since the famine' in *Economic History Review*, ser. 2, xiv, no. 3 (Apr. 1962), pp. 502–23.

Connell, K. H., 'The potato in Ireland' in *Past and Present*, no. 23 (Nov. 1962), pp. 57–71.

Connell, K. H., *Irish peasant society: four historical essays*, Oxford, 1968.

Conroy, J. C., *A history of railways in Ireland*, London, 1928.

Corfe, T. H., 'The troubles of Captain Boycott, part I: the Land League' in *History Today*, xiv, no. 11 (Nov. 1964), pp. 758–64.

Corfe, T. H., 'The troubles of Captain Boycott, part II: the campaign' in *History Today*, xiv, no. 12 (Dec. 1964), pp. 854–62.

Cousens, S. H., 'The regional pattern of emigration during the great famine, 1846–1851' in *Transactions and Papers of the Institute of British Geographers*, no. 28 (1960), pp. 119–34.

Cousens, S. H., 'Regional death rates in Ireland during the great famine, from 1846 to 1851' in *Population Studies*, xiv, no. 1 (July 1960), pp. 55–74.

Cousens, S. H., 'Emigration and demographic change in Ireland, 1851–1861' in *Economic History Review*, ser. 2, xiv, no. 2 (Dec. 1961), pp. 275–88.

Cousens, S. H., 'The regional variations in population changes in Ireland, 1861–1881' in *Economic History Review*, ser. 2, xvii, no. 2 (Dec. 1964), pp. 301–21.

Coyne, W. P., ed., *Ireland, industrial and agricultural*, Dublin, 1902.

Crawford, W. H., *Domestic industry in Ireland: the experience of the linen industry*, Dublin, 1972.

Crotty, R. D., *Irish agricultural production: its volume and structure*, Cork, 1966.

Cullen, L. M., *Anglo-Irish trade, 1660–1800*, Manchester, 1968.

Cullen, L. M., 'Irish history without the potato' in *Past and Present*, no. 40 (July 1968), pp. 72–83.

Cullen, L. M., ed., *The formation of the Irish economy*, Cork, 1969.

Cullen, L. M., *Merchants, ships, and trade, 1660–1830*, Dublin, 1971.

Curtis, L. P., Jr, *Coercion and conciliation in Ireland, 1880–1892: a study in conservative unionism*, Princeton and London, 1963.

Danaher, K., *In Ireland long ago*, Cork, 1962.

Danaher, K., *Gentle places and simple things*, Cork, 1964.

Danaher, K., *Irish country people*, Cork, 1966.

Danaher, K., *The pleasant land of Ireland*, Cork, 1970.

Davidson, W. D., 'The history of the potato and its progress in Ireland' in *Saorstát Éireann, Department of Agriculture, Journal*, xxxiv (1937), pp. 286–307.

Davies, J. C., 'Toward a theory of revolution' in *American Sociological Review*, xxvii, no. 1 (Feb. 1962), pp. 5–19.

Donnelly, J. S., Jr, 'Cork market: its role in the nineteenth century Irish butter trade' in *Studia Hibernica*, no. 11 (1971), pp. 130–63.

Donnelly, J. S., Jr, 'County Cork: two research experiences. 2. The nineteenth century' in *Irish Archives Bulletin*, ii, no. 1 (May 1972), pp. 61–6.

Donnelly, J. S., Jr, *Landlord and tenant in nineteenth-century Ireland*, Dublin, 1973.

Dowling, P. J., *The hedge schools of Ireland*, rev. ed., Cork, 1968.

Drake, M., 'Marriage and population growth in Ireland, 1750–1845' in *Economic History Review*, ser. 2, xvi, no. 2 (Dec. 1963), pp. 301–13.

Edwards, R. D., and Williams, T. D., eds, *The great famine: studies in Irish history, 1845–52*, New York, 1957, originally published 1956.

Ernle, Lord, *English farming, past and present*, with introductions by G. E. Fussell and O. R. McGregor, 6th ed., London and Chicago, 1961.

Evans, E. E., *Irish folk ways*, London, 1957.

Freeman, T. W., *Pre-famine Ireland: a study in historical geography*, Manchester, 1957.

Gill, C., *The rise of the Irish linen industry*, Oxford, 1925.

Glaser, J. F., 'Parnell's fall and the nonconformist conscience' in *Irish Historical Studies*, xii, no. 45 (Mar. 1960), pp. 119–38.

Green, E. R. R., *The Lagan Valley, 1800–50: a local history of the industrial revolution*, London, 1949.

Griffiths, A. R. G., 'The Irish board of works in the famine years' in *Historical Journal*, xiii, no. 4 (Dec. 1970), pp. 634–52.

Hammond, J. L., *Gladstone and the Irish nation*, London and New York, 1938.

Hawkins, R., 'Gladstone, Forster, and the release of Parnell' in *Irish Historical Studies*, xvi, no. 64 (Sept. 1969), pp. 417–45.

Hooker, E. R., *Readjustments of agricultural tenure in Ireland*, Chapel Hill, North Carolina, 1938.

Horn, P. L. R., 'The National Agricultural Labourers' Union in Ireland, 1873–9' in *Irish Historical Studies*, xvii, no. 67 (Mar. 1971), pp. 340–52.

Hurst, M., *Parnell and Irish nationalism*, London, 1968.

Hurst, M., *Maria Edgeworth and the public scene: intellect, fine feeling, and landlordism in the age of reform*, London, 1969.

Jephson, M. D., *An Anglo-Irish miscellany: some records of the Jephsons of Mallow*, Dublin, 1964.

Johnson, J. H., 'The population of Londonderry during the great Irish famine' in *Economic History Review*, ser. 2, x, no. 2 (Dec. 1957), pp. 273–85.

Johnson, J. H., 'Marriage and fertility in nineteenth century Londonderry' in *Journal of the Statistical and Social Inquiry Society of Ireland*, xx, pt i (1958), pp. 99–117.

Johnson, J. H., 'Agriculture in Co. Derry at the beginning of the nineteenth century' in *Studia Hibernica*, no. 4 (1964), pp. 95–103.

Jones, E. L., *The development of English agriculture, 1815–1873*, London, 1968.

Keep, G. R. C., 'The Irish migration to North America in the second half of the nineteenth century', Ph.D. thesis, University of Dublin, 1951.

Kerr, B. M., 'Irish seasonal migration to Great Britain, 1800–38' in *Irish Historical Studies*, iii, no. 11 (Mar. 1943), pp. 365–80.

Lansdowne, marquis of, *Glanerought and the Petty-Fitzmaurices*, London and New York, 1937.

Larkin, E., 'Economic growth, capital investment, and the Roman catholic church in nineteenth-century Ireland' in *American Historical Review*, lxxii, no. 3 (Apr. 1967), pp. 852–84.

Larkin, E., 'The devotional revolution in Ireland, 1850–75' in *American Historical Review*, lxxvii, no. 3 (June 1972), pp. 625–52.

Lee, J., 'Money and beer in Ireland, 1790–1875, I' in *Economic History Review*, ser. 2, xix, no. 1 (Apr. 1966), pp. 183–90.

Lee, J., 'The construction costs of Irish railways, 1830–1853' in *Business History*, ix, no. 2 (July 1967), pp. 95–109.

Lee, J., 'The provision of capital for early Irish railways, 1830–53' in *Irish Historical Studies*, xvi, no. 61 (Mar. 1968), pp. 33–63.

Lee, J., 'Marriage and population in pre-famine Ireland' in *Economic History Review*, ser. 2, xxi, no. 2 (Aug. 1968), pp. 283–95.

Lee, J., 'Irish agriculture' in *Agricultural History Review*, xvii, pt i (1969), pp. 64–76.

Lee, J., 'The dual economy in Ireland, 1800–50' in *Historical Studies*, viii, ed T. D. Williams (London, 1971), pp. 191–201.

Lynch, P., and Vaizey, J., *Guinness's brewery in the Irish economy, 1759–1876*, Cambridge, 1960.

Lynch, P., and Vaizey, J., 'Money and beer in Ireland, 1790–1875, II' in *Economic History Review*, ser. 2, xix, no. 1 (Apr. 1966), pp. 190–4.

Lyons, F. S. L., *The Irish parliamentary party, 1890–1910*, London, 1951.

Lyons, F. S. L., 'The economic ideas of Parnell' in *Historical Studies*, ii, ed M. Roberts (London, 1959), pp. 60–78.

Lyons, F. S. L., *The fall of Parnell, 1890–91*, London, 1960.

Lyons, F. S. L., *Parnell*, Dundalk, 1965, originally published 1963.

Lyons, F. S. L., 'John Dillon and the Plan of Campaign, 1886–90' in *Irish Historical Studies*, xiv, no. 56 (Sept. 1965), pp. 313–47.

Lyons, F. S. L., *John Dillon: a biography*, London, 1968.

Lyons, J., 'The history of our dairying industry' in *Agricultural Ireland*, xvi, no. 7 (July 1959), pp. 90–3.

McCaffrey, L., *Irish federalism in the 1870s: a study in conservative nationalism*, Philadelphia, 1962.

MacCarthaigh, D., 'Marriage and birth rates for Knockainy parish, 1822–1941' in *Journal of the Cork Historical and Archaeological Society*, ser. 2, xlvii, no. 165 (Jan.–June 1942), pp. 4–8.

McCourt, D., 'Infield and outfield in Ireland' in *Economic History Review*, ser. 2, vii, no. 3 (Apr. 1955), pp. 369–76.

McDowell, R. B., *Public opinion and government policy in Ireland, 1801–1846*, London, 1952.

McDowell, R. B., ed., *Social life in Ireland, 1800–45*, Dublin, 1963, originally published 1957.

McDowell, R. B., *The Irish administration, 1801–1914*, London and Toronto, 1964.

Macintyre, A., *The liberator: Daniel O'Connell and the Irish party, 1830–1847*, London, 1965.

McNeill, W. H., 'The introduction of the potato into Ireland' in *Journal of Modern History*, xxi, no. 3 (Sept. 1949), pp. 218–22.

Maxwell, C., *Country and town in Ireland under the Georges*, rev. ed., Dundalk, 1949.

Moody, T. W., 'The new departure in Irish politics, 1878–9' in *Essays in British and Irish history in honour of James Eadie Todd*, ed H. A. Cronne, T. W. Moody, and D. B. Quinn (London, 1949), pp. 303–33.

Moody, T. W., 'Irish-American nationalism' in *Irish Historical Studies*, xv, no. 60 (Sept. 1967), pp. 438–45.

Moody, T. W., 'A new history of Ireland' in *Irish Historical Studies*, xvi, no. 63 (Mar. 1969), pp. 241–57.

Moody, T. W., and Beckett, J. C., eds, *Ulster since 1800: a political and economic survey*, London, 1955; corrected impression, 1957.

Moody, T. W., and Beckett, J. C., eds, *Ulster since 1800: a social survey*, London, 1957; corrected impression, 1958.

Murphy, J. A., 'The support of the catholic clergy in Ireland, 1750–1850' in *Historical Studies*, v, ed J. L. McCracken (London, 1965), pp. 103–21.

Nolan, P., 'Records of the Cork butter market and a note on the great famine' in *Journal of the Cork Historical and Archaeological Society*, ser. 2, lxvi, no. 204 (July–Dec. 1961), pp. 117–25.

Norman, E. R., *The catholic church and Ireland in the age of rebellion, 1859–1873*, London, 1965.

Nowlan, K. B., 'Agrarian unrest in Ireland, 1800–1845' in *University Review*, ii, no. 6 (1959), pp. 7–16.

Nowlan, K. B., *The politics of repeal: a study in the relations between Great Britain and Ireland, 1841–50*, London and Toronto, 1965.

O'Brien, C. C., *Parnell and his party, 1880–90*, Oxford, 1957; corrected impression, 1964.

Bibliography

O'Brien, G., *The economic history of Ireland from the union to the famine*, London, 1921.

O'Brien, R. B., *Dublin Castle and the Irish people*, London, 1909.

O'Brien, R. B., *The life of Charles Stewart Parnell*, London and New York, 1910, originally published 1898.

O'Donovan, J., *The economic history of live stock in Ireland*, Cork, 1940.

O'Mahony, D., 'The Cork butter market' in *Blarney Magazine*, xii (summer 1957), pp. 49-53.

O'Neill, B., *The war for the land in Ireland*, London, 1933.

O'Neill, T. P., 'The scientific investigation of the failure of the potato crop in Ireland, 1845-6' in *Irish Historical Studies*, v, no. 18 (Sept. 1946), pp. 123-38.

O'Neill, T. P., 'The Society of Friends and the great famine' in *Studies*, xxxiv, no. 154 (June 1950), pp. 203-13.

O'Neill, T. P., 'Food problems during the great Irish famine' in *Journal of the Royal Society of Antiquaries of Ireland*, lxxxii (1952), pp. 99-108.

O'Neill, T. P., 'The Irish land question, 1830-1850' in *Studies*, xliv (autumn 1955), pp. 325-36.

O'Neill, T. P., 'From famine to near famine, 1845-1879' in *Studia Hibernica*, no. 1 (1961), pp. 161-71.

Orwin, C. S., and Whetham, E. H., *History of British agriculture, 1846-1914*, London, 1964.

Ó Súilleabháin, S., *Irish folk custom and belief*, Dublin, 1967.

O'Sullivan, W., *The economic history of Cork city from the earliest times to the act of union*, Cork, 1937.

Palmer, N. D., *The Irish Land League crisis*, New Haven and London, 1940.

Palmer, N. D., 'Irish absenteeism in the eighteen-seventies' in *Journal of Modern History*, xii, no. 3 (Sept. 1940), pp. 357-66.

Pomfret, J. E., *The struggle for land in Ireland, 1800-1923*, Princeton, 1930.

Razzell, P. E., 'Population growth and economic change in eighteenth and early nineteenth-century England and Ireland' in *Land, labour, and population in the industrial revolution*, ed E. L. Jones and G. E. Mingay (London, 1967), pp. 260-81.

Robinson, O., 'The London companies as progressive landlords in nineteenth-century Ireland' in *Economic History Review*, ser. 2, xv, no. 1 (Aug. 1962), pp. 103-18.

Rogers, P., *Father Theobald Mathew: apostle of temperance*, Dublin, 1943.

Salaman, R. N., *The influence of the potato on the course of Irish history*, Dublin, 1944.

Salaman, R. N., *The history and social influence of the potato*, Cambridge, 1949.

Schrier, A., *Ireland and the American emigration, 1850-1900*, Minneapolis and London, 1958.

Shearman, H., 'State-aided land purchase under the disestablishment act of 1869' in *Irish Historical Studies*, iv, no. 13 (Mar. 1944), pp. 58-80.

Solow, B. L., *The land question and the Irish economy, 1870-1903*, Cambridge, Mass., and London, 1971.

Spring, D., *The English landed estate in the nineteenth century: its administration*, Baltimore and London, 1963.

Staehle, H., 'Statistical notes on the economic history of Irish agriculture, 1847–1913' in *Journal of the Statistical and Social Inquiry Society of Ireland*, xvii (1951), pp. 444–71.

Steele, E. D., 'Ireland and the empire in the 1860s. Imperial precedents for Gladstone's first Irish land act' in *Historical Journal*, xi, no. 1 (1968), pp. 64–83.

Steele, E. D., 'Gladstone and Ireland' in *Irish Historical Studies*, xvii, no. 65 (Mar. 1970), pp. 58–88.

Thompson, F. M. L., *English landed society in the nineteenth century*, London and Toronto, 1963.

Thornley, D., *Isaac Butt and home rule*, London, 1964.

Wall, M., 'The rise of a catholic middle class in eighteenth-century Ireland' in *Irish Historical Studies*, xi, no. 42 (Sept. 1958), pp. 91–115.

Walsh, B. M., 'A perspective on Irish population patterns' in *Eire-Ireland*, iv, no. 3 (autumn 1969), pp. 3–21.

Whyte, J. H., *The independent Irish party, 1850–9*, London, 1958.

Woodham-Smith, C., *The great hunger: Ireland, 1845–1849*, New York, 1964, originally published 1962.

III   WORKS OF REFERENCE

(A) CONTEMPORARY

Burke, J. and Sir J. B., *A genealogical and heraldic dictionary of the landed gentry of Great Britain and Ireland*, 3 vols, London, 1843–9.

Burke, J. and Sir J. B., *A genealogical and heraldic dictionary of the landed gentry of Great Britain and Ireland*, 2 vols, 9th ed., London, 1898.

de Burgh, U. H. H., *The landowners of Ireland: an alphabetical list of owners of estates of 500 acres or £500 valuation and upwards in Ireland, with the acreage and valuation in each county; and also containing a brief notice of the education and official appointments of each person, to which are added his town and country addresses and clubs*, Dublin, 1878.

de Moleyns, T., *The landowner's and agent's practical guide*, ed A. W. Quill and F. P. Hamilton, 8th ed., Dublin, 1899.

Guy's city and county Cork almanac and directory for 1892, Cork, 1892.

Guy's county and city of Cork directory for the years 1875–1876, Cork, 1875.

Henry and Coghlan's general directory of Cork for 1867, with which is incorporated Wynner & Co.'s business directory of the principal towns in the province of Munster, Cork, 1867.

Hodges, R. J., *Cork and County Cork in the twentieth century*, Brighton, 1911.

Joyce's atlas and geography of Ireland, with thirty-three coloured maps by John Bartholomew, London, 189[?].

Lewis's atlas, comprising the counties of Ireland and a general map of the kingdom, London, 1837.

Thom's Irish almanac and official directory, Dublin, 1844–.

Bibliography

(B) LATER

Analecta Hibernica, 1944–. Consulted for surveys of documents in private keeping.

Black, R. D. C., *A catalogue of pamphlets on economic subjects published between 1750 and 1900 and now housed in Irish libraries*, Belfast and New York, 1969.

Carty, J., *Bibliography of Irish history, 1870–1911*, Dublin, 1940.

Hayes, R. J., ed., *Manuscript sources for the history of Irish civilization*, 11 vols, Boston, 1965.

MacLysaght, E., *Irish families: their names, arms, and origins*, Dublin, 1957.

Mulvey, H. F., 'Thirty years' work in Irish history (III). Nineteenth-century Ireland, 1801–1914' in *Irish Historical Studies*, xvii, no. 65 (Mar. 1970), pp. 1–31.

O'Neill, T. P., *Sources of Irish local history*, Dublin, 1958.

Prendeville, P. L., 'A select bibliography of Irish economic history Part three: the nineteenth century' in *Economic History Review*, ser. 1 iv, no. 1 (Oct. 1932), pp. 81–90.

INDEX

~~~~~~

Index